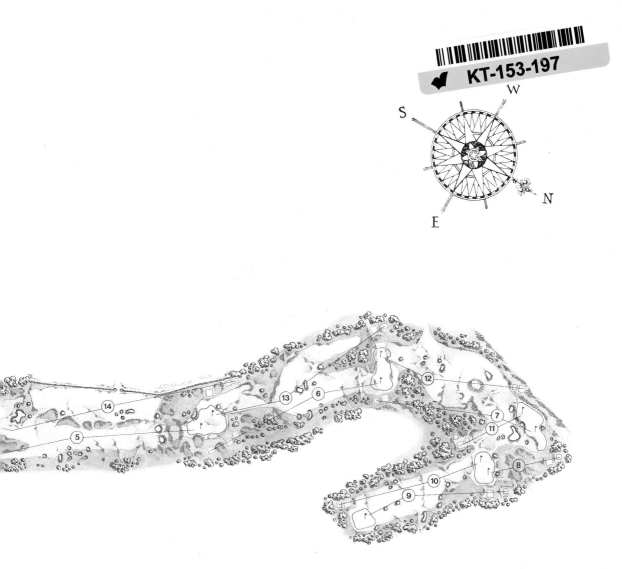

THE OPEN

The British Open Golf Championship
since the War

By the Same Authors

Peter Alliss

Alliss Through the Looking-Glass
(with Bob Ferrier)

Easier Golf
(with Paul Trevillian)

Play Golf with Alliss

An Autobiography
(with Bob Ferrier)

The Shell Book of Golf
(with Michael Hobbs)

Bedside Golf

More Bedside Golf

The Peter Alliss Golfer's Log Book

The Duke

The Who's Who of Golf

Golf: The Game for a Lifetime
(with Michael Hobbs)

Michael Hobbs

Sudan Today

Kampala, City of the Seven Hills

The Aborigines

Great Opens

Golf to Remember
(with Peter Alliss)

Golf for the Connoisseur

In Celebration of Golf

A Day in World War II

The Medieval Village

Fifty Masters of Golf

THE OPEN

The British Open Golf Championship
since the War

Peter Alliss

with
Michael Hobbs

COLLINS
8 Grafton Street, London W1

1984

Alliss, Peter
The open.
1. Golf – Great Britain – Tournaments
I Title   II Hobbs, Michael, 1934–
    796.352'73'0941   GV970

ISBN 0 00 217175 9

William Collins Sons and Co. Ltd
London · Glasgow · Sydney · Auckland
Toronto · Johannesburg

Set in 12/13pt Linotron Bembo by
Rowland Phototypesetting Ltd, Bury St Edmunds, Suffolk

Designed by Caroline Hill

Made and printed in Great Britain by
W. S. Cowell Limited, Ipswich, Suffolk

Contents

Maps

All statistics shown have been
compiled from recent sources

Illustrations

Introduction

The Open Championship story began in 1860 at Prestwick in Scotland with just eight competitors. It was not truly 'open', for the club which started this momentous event considered that the game was then almost entirely Scottish. But Royal Blackheath Golf Club specially requested that one of its members, George Brown, be allowed to play, and this was granted.

The two great players of the day, Willie Park and Old Tom Morris, came out on top, Park winning by two strokes over three rounds of the twelve-hole Prestwick course in the single day's play. He was awarded the champion's belt, the original trophy, probably symbolic of victory in a knights' tournament.

Perhaps the first really great player to come on the scene was Young Tom Morris, who made the belt his own by winning three in a row in the years 1868 to 1870, playing golf of a calibre never seen before. There is little doubt that he was by far the greatest player until the Great Triumvirate of Vardon, Taylor and Braid began to make their mark during the 1890s.

In 1871 came the first break not caused by war. Young Tom had won the belt outright. What should be done next? The Royal and Ancient, Prestwick and the Honourable Company of Edinburgh Golfers, then playing at Musselburgh, clubbed together to provide a new trophy, the claret jug still competed for to this day. In 1872, Young Tom was the first of the golfing giants to have his name inscribed on it.

The Open Championship story can largely be told in terms of the great players, and what a roll call there is: Morris, Taylor, Vardon, Braid, Hagen, Jones, Sarazen, Cotton, Snead, Locke, Hogan, Thomson, Player, Palmer, Nicklaus, Trevino and Watson. This is what I have chosen to do, beginning from 1946, the year the golfers of the world reassembled at St Andrews after World War II.

For some years, the championship was not held in particularly high regard by the great golfers of America, though the rest of the world always saw it as the premier event of the year. In 1960, however, Arnold Palmer made his first entry and nearly won. His continuing participation and that of Jack Nicklaus did much to raise the status of the event. With increasingly strong American entries and the continuing support of the rest of the world, the Open Championship once again became a kind of world championship of golf during the 1960s. All the great players came, and only a player of the very highest class could win it – something that cannot quite be said of any of the other major championships.

The Open Championship is among the greatest of annual sporting events. What follows is its history since World War II, told in terms of many of the key personalities – but not forgetting those who enjoyed a memorable hour upon the stage, perhaps never again to share the limelight.

Peter Alliss
Michael Hobbs
October 1983

·1·
The Autumn of Henry Cotton

St Andrews, 1946

When the first post-war championship began on 3 July 1946, the title had been held by Dick Burton through the seven long years of war. He had won in 1939 at St Andrews, completing his final round with a drive daringly close to the out of bounds along the right, then lofted in a high pitch to the middle of the green and holed the putt to beat Johnny Bulla, the man from Chicago, by a couple of strokes. Bulla continued to make headlines after World War II, particularly in the Open. Dick Burton, however, was a childhood hero of mine and features in one of my earliest golf memories. I remember seeing a picture of him tossing his putter confidently to his caddie, the ball still a couple of yards short of, but obviously on its way to the hole. 'What bravado!' I thought, mightily impressed.

I was later, as a fifteen-year-old, to watch Burton play at Ferndown quite frequently with the Bradford professional, Jimmy Wade. My father had been professional there since a little before the war so it was there I learned to love the game and the little I know of how it ought to be played. Young Alliss felt that Burton, despite a flailing swing reminiscent of someone whipping a top, struck the ball beautifully and played my home course in fine style. I felt he could well be champion again.

Not so. Burton, perhaps regretting the money and fame he might have had from being champion (he made virtually nothing because the commerce of golf was at a standstill during the war), began the defence of his title ingloriously indeed, paired with Alf Perry, who had himself won the championship – at Muirfield in 1935. They were faced with surely one of golf's easiest driving holes, the 1st at St Andrews. Alf almost achieved the impossible of knocking his ball sharp left out of bounds. Burton went the other way, cutting his drive onto the beach, and eventually took 6 on this relatively easy par-4. A seven-year wait to hit your next shot in golf's greatest major championship is a long time indeed. And then to slice it out of bounds. . . . Yet Burton pulled himself together after this highly unpromising start and when he had completed four rounds was quite well up the field.

The first post-war champion was a man who hadn't wanted to come at all, Samuel Jackson Snead. There are various accounts of how it happened that the man heralded as the greatest golfer in the world was persuaded to make the trip from the relatively lucrative US tournament scene. One has it that Johnny Bulla, himself a great supporter of the championship, encouraged him to come – and was rewarded by finishing in joint second place! Another related that a certain L. B. Icely, at that time president of the Wilson Sporting Goods Company, felt that it would do sales in the British Isles no harm at all if Sam Snead, one of their contracted players, should win the title. He also suggested that the vast St Andrews greens might improve his touch on long putts.

I prefer yet another version of why Snead came. At the time, Fred Corcoran was both Snead's manager and the supremo of the US Tour. He found Snead, at the Inverness Fourball event in the USA, declaring that his putting was too hopeless for it to be worth his going to Scotland. Corcoran arranged a lesson with the great Walter Hagen, who directed Snead to strike his putts just above the equator of the ball. Sam immediately improved. Hagen's judgement: 'OK, you've got it now. Go ahead over there to St Andrews and win it.'

Unfortunately a local journalist was present. His piece appeared under the headline: 'SNEAD TO PLAY IN BRITISH OPEN – TAKES PUTTING LESSON FROM WALTER HAGEN'. No harm there, you may well say, but it appeared very close indeed to Snead's syndicated column. That week it was headed 'HOW TO PUTT by Sam Snead'!

Whatever the truth of these stories, it is undeniable that Sam was none too keen to play in the Open, in which he had made only one appearance before, after the 1937 US Ryder Cup victory. With the rest of the team he had gone to Carnoustie and performed creditably enough but finished in 11th place, ten strokes behind Henry Cotton. His first sight of St Andrews elicited the comment that it looked 'an old abandoned sort of a place'. And this despite the fact that German prisoners of war had done their best to tidy up the course. Indeed, so soon after the war, St Andrews may well have been chosen as the best conditioned course available but it was also, of course, the most historic.

Sam Snead, however, was not the favourite. The Americans Walter Hagen and Bobby Jones had dominated during the 1920s but none had won since Densmore Shute in 1933. Although eleven Americans were entered, there was not at all the feeling that one of them *must* win, as is usually the case today. Lawson Little, US Open Champion in 1940 and legendary for his play in the 1934 and 1935 Amateur Championships was probably highly regarded because of his achievements on British soil. Bobby Locke (about four stone heavier than in his last appearance in 1939) was the thinking man's choice as a result of his tournament performances on the sparse 1946 British tour. But popular sentiment plumped for Henry Cotton to add a third title to his wins at Royal St George's in 1934 and Carnoustie in 1937.

First there came the 36 qualifying holes, which were still to persist for almost two decades. The better players were expected to come through but there was a certain fascination in awaiting the failure of one of the great names, as in the case of Gene Sarazen after an 85 in high winds at Troon in 1923.

The test itself was none too severe. One hundred qualified out of 264 entries and a total of just one under a pair of 80s was good enough to proceed to the championship proper. After these two rounds, Norman von Nida had impressed more than anybody, particularly because of his bold approaches to the flag. With 73, 72 he was leading qualifier, followed by Arthur Lees and a new name, Fred Daly, in joint second place, followed by Jack McLean, who had come so close to winning the 1936 US Amateur, Snead, Harry Bradshaw, Bill Branch, Syd Scott and Henry Cotton.

On the first day of the championship proper, Cotton was out first and, though observers felt that – as usual – he looked uncomfortable on the greens and had a tendency to stand broody and immobile over the ball, he was round in a finely played 70, as was Norman von Nida. At the end of the first day, their score was bettered only by Bobby Locke with a 69. This was a standard not to be maintained as both conditions and pressure worsened. Only one other player was to break 70 in the championship. My father Percy, then nearly 50,

My father Percy (left) before the final of the 1937 Matchplay Championship.
Next to him are Ted Ray and James Braid, both Open Champions, and his opponent, Jimmy Adams.

13

went round in 74, but the hard luck story of the day concerned Johnny Bulla. After 16 holes, he was four under level 4s (approximately the same as being six under par today) and then faced the challenge of the much-feared Road Hole, at the time a par-5. Much later, Norman von Nida was to write that on this hole Bulla averaged 'about 7½ a round'. Though this was an exaggeration, Bulla certainly foundered on the 17th throughout the championship. In this first round, a 67 or 68 within his grasp, he sent his second shot onto the road (in those days flint-strewn and not the neatly surfaced path it now is); his chip from there failed to climb the slope and returned to his feet. He then played his fourth shot only onto the footpath just short of the green. From there, he very nearly ran his ball across the slope into the Road Bunker, which cuts into the left of the green, but eventually holed out in 7. Sam Snead, meanwhile, had been demonstrating his power game. He had not once taken a wood from the fairway; the longest club he had used for a second shot was a 3-iron. He was on 71, along with Bulla, Joe Kirkwood, Bill Hancock and Reg Whitcombe (1938 Champion). Dick Burton, after his disastrous start, had finished with a very desirable pair of 3s for a 74.

Throughout the first round St Andrews had been benign. There was a light wind and the course was damp. On the second day, conditions were similar and at the end of it Henry Cotton stood supreme, having added a second 70. Snead was a stroke behind, and Dai Rees had followed his opening round of 75 with a 67. This set a new record for St Andrews, beating the target of 68 first set by Bobby Jones in the first round of his 1927 victory. It had been equalled in 1933 by Craig Wood, Abe Mitchell and Walter Hagen. However, as a result of course changes, St Andrews was reckoned to be about 1½ strokes harder than in 1927.

Dai's card was an interesting one. He went to the turn in 33 but was bunkered on both the 12th and 13th, dropping a shot at the latter for his only 5 of the round. He regained the shot on the very next hole and was still three under after 15 holes. He then holed from some 3 yards for a birdie on the 16th, pitched to 6 feet at the dreaded Road Hole for what was then a birdie 4, and on the last stuffed in a 5-yarder for his seventh birdie of the round. His 67 was against a par of 73.

Snead was equally effective over the first nine. After a 4, 3, 3 start he reached the turn in 33 but slipped just a little coming home. Cotton was at the turn in 35 but dropped the occasional shot thereafter before a fine finish of 3, 5, 3, which included the satisfaction of knocking in a putt of about a dozen yards on the last.

In close pursuit on 143 were Johnny Bulla and Bobby Locke. Locke had not single-putted seven greens as in the first round and had taken 74. Next came my father Percy on 146. He was a quick and mercurial player with tremendous strength in the forearms, which were of Popeye proportions. He used a three-quarter swing and had the air of a man swishing daisies with a stick. He had come close to winning an Open on more than one occasion and this was his last real run at the championship. He came back in 34 for a 72. The next day, alas, he was gone, having soared to an 82 in tougher conditions.

What made conditions tougher on the last day, during which 36 holes were played, was the stiff wind. The greens had quickened during the championship and putting had become progressively more difficult (the great Belgian Flory van Donck, on one occasion faced with a 20-foot downhill putt, chose to send his ball *up*hill away from the hole and even then it drifted 10 feet past, taken on and on by the slope and the weight of the ball). Cotton began shakily, only one under level 5s for the first six holes, but, though unsure on the greens for the rest of the event, pulled himself together well enough to finish in 76. The best scores of the morning, 72s, came from Lawson Little, who was already out of it, and Johnny Bulla, still a real contender. He must have been encouraged by a putt on the 1st hit much too hard which thumped against the back of the hole, leaped in the air and plunged from view.

With a round to go it was still very much all to play for:

215 Snead (71, 70, 74), Bulla (71, 72, 72), Rees (75, 67, 73);   216 Cotton (70, 70, 76);   218 Locke (69, 74, 75);   219 Ward (73, 73, 73); 220 von Nida (70, 76, 74)

In the afternoon, the wind blew up even more and scoring was generally higher, particularly by those who were in contention. In such conditions Cotton was a narrow favourite, but he started badly, putting his second shot in the Swilken Burn which fronts the 1st green and then taking three putts on the 2nd. It was perhaps Dai Rees's best chance to win an Open in his whole career. His start was truly disastrous. His drive at the 1st hit both the out-of-bounds rails and a spectator and he was lucky to be still in play by a couple of feet. A little later, however, he too found the burn and eventually ran up a 7. That sickening start was just about enough to finish the Welshman off but he then continued by taking three putts at both the 2nd and 3rd. Thereafter, all hope gone, he played as well as anyone but still took 42 to the turn. The best of his round came at the end, with a 3, 4 finish.

The first half was playing by far the more difficult and Cotton could manage no better than 40. On the inward nine he was steady rather than inspired and finished by three-putting the last, including a miss from just a couple of feet.

Bobby Locke was the first to set a target. He began with a birdie on the 1st but faltered at the finish, missing a short putt on the 17th and taking three to get down at the last for a 76 and a 294 total. The first challenger was the tall, handsome figure of Johnny Bulla, as likely to putt left as right-handed, whose scoring over the first three rounds had been the steadiest of anyone. With two holes to play he needed only a 5, 4 par finish to beat Locke by two strokes. The Road Hole once more did for him. He played cautiously short this time, no doubt with his previous encounters with the road in mind, but then chipped very poorly and three putts followed. On the last, he had the shortest of putts to beat Bobby Locke and failed: two holes, an extravagant six putts.

With all his rivals falling apart, Sam Snead was finding the going no easier. He, too, was no better than 40 to the turn with one temper tantrum behind him. On the par-4 6th, he was twice bunkered and once in a whin bush and relieved his feelings by hurling a club at a post. In the end, his 6 must have been something of a lucky escape. Thereafter, of the real contenders only Snead benefited from the easier conditions on the second half. He had the championship won with several holes left to play. The only moment of doubt came on the 16th. Snead had an uphill putt which returned to his feet at the first attempt but he made up for this by single-putting the 17th and cruised in by an emphatic four-stroke margin.

Cotton found what today seems an odd explanation for the American's success. He felt that Snead's fitness had been too much for 'our underfed players'. The dietary notions of the time were very different from those of today. It was widely thought that the meagre meat ration was the cause of any British failure in any sport. Cotton found his own answer by making his second visit to America both to compete on the growing tournament circuit but also to regain fitness and eat red meat. Locke made his own point by inviting Snead to play an exhibition series against him in South Africa, which took the gloss off Snead's Open success: he lost by 12 matches to 2 and was so unsettled by Locke's wizardry on the South African greens that he developed a putting twitch – or so Snead was later to claim. He earned less than $10,000 in both of the following US seasons before a new putter brought back confidence and he was once more number one.

I don't know how Snead sees his achievement today. Perhaps his view of that far-off Open has mellowed, particularly as he never went on to win the US Open. At the time, Snead had a distaste for the course in general and thought the double greens absurd. He was not overfond of his caddie either, especially when the man begged the champion's ball, declaring he would treasure it all his days – and then immediately sold it! The glory of the Open Championship he dismissed as 'just another tournament'. He did not play in it again until 1962, then long past his best though still a formidable player. He will long be remembered not only for the unique combination of power and elegance in his swing, but also for his gift of turning a phrase with painful candour. One oft-quoted example was his reply on being asked if he had enjoyed Scotland: 'Whenever you leave the USA, boy, you're just camping out.'

HOW THEY FINISHED

S. J. Snead *USA*	**71**	**70**	**74**	**75**	**290**	G. Knight	77	75	82	76	310
						E. E. Whitcombe	75	79	77	79	
A. D. Locke *South Africa*	69	74	75	76	294						
J. G. Bulla *USA*	71	72	72	79		Mr R. K. Bell	81	73	81	77	312
						J. A. Jacobs	76	77	80	79	
N. G. von Nida *Australia*	70	76	74	75	295						
C. H. Ward	73	73	73	76		Mr J. C. Wilson	78	76	81	78	313
T. H. Cotton	70	70	76	79		A. Perry	78	77	78	80	
D. J. Rees	75	67	73	80							
						F. van Donck *Belgium*	76	78	83	78	315
F. Daly	77	71	76	74	298	A. M. Robertson	79	75	80	81	
J. Kirkwood *USA*	71	75	78	74		Mr A. Dowie	81	71	80	83	
L. Little *USA*	78	75	72	74	299	Mr R. J. White	76	79	84	77	316
						T. B. Haliburton	78	76	81	81	
H. Bradshaw	76	75	76	73	300	A. H. Padgham	79	74	76	87	
R. Burton	74	76	76	76	302	N. Sutton	76	77	80	84	317
W. Shankland	76	76	77	75	304	F. Bullock	80	75	87	76	318
						W. H. Green	76	76	83	83	
W. Anderson	76	76	78	75	305						
R. A. Whitcombe	71	76	82	76		A. J. Isherwood	77	78	83	81	319
L. B. Ayton	77	74	80	75	306	Mr J. M. Urry	79	75	87	85	326
Percy Alliss	74	72	82	79	307						
F. Jowle	78	74	76	80	308						
A. Compston	77	74	77	80							
A. Lees	77	71	78	82							

NB All players are from the British Isles unless another country of origin is given. 'Mr' denotes an amateur golfer, as does a military rank.

Hoylake, 1947

The Open Championship had made a good re-start in 1946, for the field had been a good one. In 1947, there was of course no Snead, while Bobby Locke was busying himself with the most successful season ever achieved by an overseas player in the USA: he won four out of five consecutive events and seven in all, to finish just behind the leading money-winner Jimmy Demaret, having played a much shorter season.

There was an overseas entry of moderate strength, however. The Australian von Nida was at Hoylake for the championship and in the process of setting a record which still stands of seven first places during the competitive season in Britain. He began as favourite. Vic Ghezzi, who had tied for the US Open and lost the play-off the previous year, was entered, as was Johnny Bulla and the great American amateur Frank Stranahan. The latter caused some stir by arriving with his full weight-lifting kit and asking for, nay, *demanding* changes at the Adelphi Hotel in Liverpool to accommodate both himself and his gear satisfactorily. There were tales of doors removed, floors strengthened and extra rooms hired. All this caused sniggers among British golfers, though many were impressed in spite of themselves when they saw the American's impressive build. This side of the Atlantic, golf had never been considered a game in which supreme fitness was of any importance at all. With the rest, I had grown up believing that one needed to be able to walk round without the legs becoming tired but that real strength was needed only in the hands, as Henry Cotton had preached. Small wonder then that the very young Peter Alliss, just sixteen and making his first appearance at an Open Championship, for years afterwards remembered Frank as a muscular giant of at least 6 feet 2 inches. So much for impressionable youth; Frank Stranahan is about 5 feet 8 inches tall, as I noted when I met him again a few years ago!

Stranahan's golf had already made some impression in Britain for he had reached the last sixteen in the 1946 Amateur Championship at Birkdale, accounting among others for the great Ronnie White before Gerald Micklem beat him comfortably in the 6th round. He reached the 5th round at Carnoustie the following year before his fellow-countryman Willie Turnesa dispatched him and went on to be champion.

In contrast to Snead's low opinion of St Andrews, I recall that I regarded the Royal Liverpool Golf Club's home at Hoylake with awe. Never had I seen greens of such quality (few courses at the time had recovered from wartime neglect). I can still hear the precise click, click, click of the hand-mowers that many of us think produced far better putting surfaces than the vehicles upon which greenkeepers ride today. It was said that 'The man who can't putt at Hoylake, can't putt anywhere.' I found the surfaces unnervingly fast but utterly true. They were also relatively flat, which helps confidence a great deal.

The rest of the course was less helpful. The rough was very severe, and to be in it usually meant taking a lofted iron and the shortest route back to the fairway. Carries from the tee were also testing, often 180 yards or more: no problem in still weather but many found they could not reach some of the fairways when the wind got up. The course was a little under 7000 yards long.

There was good weather for the two qualifying rounds, in which my father Percy Alliss began with a 74 but, alas, then faded away. Von Nida was again the favourite and justified this by leading the qualifiers with 139, which included a new Hoylake record of 69. Arthur Lees was a couple of strokes behind, followed on 142 by Johnny Bulla, who had nine holes in 30 strokes at one of the qualifying courses, Arrowe Park. Bert Gadd, a name from the 1930s, had a 66 at Arrowe Park, but when the championship proper began, collapsed to an 86. I did not qualify this time: an 86, followed by a round in the high 70s.

Of course, the sole aim in these rounds was to qualify but it was nevertheless encouraging to score well. Again and again we shall see that a man in form at this point often featured strongly in the championship proper.

Von Nida, however, was initially an exception. On the 1st hole, where an out of bounds is marked by a low turf bank known as 'the Cops', threatening both the drive and, even more, the second shot where it lies hard alongside the green, he sent his approach shot out. The old-time champion, Jamie Anderson, would have sympathized. He once dismissed five balls in succession and said: 'My God, it's like playing up a spout.'

The first day belonged to the maestro, Henry Cotton, as always the British flag-bearer. Although cutting his iron shots, he was trying an erect putting stance that worked very well. He went to the turn in 33 and came home in par for a 69. This score was equalled by Laurie Ayton, of the famous St Andrews family. Little more, however, was expected from him and indeed he declined to an 80 in the second round. Frank Stranahan followed up with 71 while on 73 were Flory van Donck, John Burton, brother of the 1939 champion, Jimmy Adams and Fred Daly, making a fairly rare excursion from Northern Ireland. Two who seemed to have already put themselves out of it were Dai Rees with a 77, and Johnny Bulla, even worse, with an 80. He had begun with three 5s and later had two balls out of bounds to reach the turn in 44. The out of bounds were indeed a terrifying feature of the Hoylake of that time. I used to reckon that it was possible to manage it on seventeen of the eighteen holes. The course is a little more kindly arranged these days so that, for example, where you were once inevitably on the Stanley Road at the 17th if you hit a running cut shot, you may now well get a bounce back from the fencing. Then there is also the Dowie, a 'short' hole of 200 yards with the out of bounds a step or two left of the green. Try playing that with your natural draw and the wind howling in from the right!

The second day was mainly a story of changed fortunes. In general, those who had begun well, such as Henry Cotton, fell away, in Henry's case to a 78, assisted by once being out of bounds through a green when not far beyond the flag. He was not pleased. Johnny Bulla, on the other hand, was back in business after a 72. His fellow American, Frank 'Muscles' Stranahan, had a 79. These scores in the 1980s may appear rather contemptible but note that Hoylake that year was one of the fiercest tests presented to an Open field. I also believe that in all sports the performers are mentally very much influenced by what is required to win in their own day. No one could manage to run a mile in under four minutes until Roger Bannister did it and then hosts immediately followed: the barrier was down and it had been shown that the feat was physically possible. In the Open Championship, there was always the feeling that one bad round was allowed the frail human being who could still become champion.

Golf history now shows us that this 1947 Open was the last time that a man won with worse than a 75 among his four rounds. So it was that at dusk on 4 July 1947, a year in which Denis Compton hit the record number of centuries, with Bill Edrich not far behind, in the best weather the middle-aged among us can recall, the strong winds of the final day were faced by:

143 Daly, Cotton, Lees, von Nida;   222 Stranahan;   223 Perry, Horne;   224 Rees;   225 Shankland

Bill Shankland produced the best last round in terms of figures and, many said, 'should' have won. With five holes to play, he was six under level 4s but then closed with a salvo of 5s and a 6, alleviated by a 3 for a round of 70. With Perry's earlier round it was the best of the day and set the first target at 295. In due course, Reg Horne, one of the neatest players and sweetest strikers I have ever seen but usually lacking in flair for the great occasions of golf, beat it. He needed to finish with three 4s for a 69 but had to be content with a 71 and a 294 total. His long putt on the last for a 3 was in – and out again.

In his final round, Fred Daly went to the turn in 38 and changed up a gear by beginning his return 3, 3, 4, 3. The last 3 was significant. Fred had hit a poor tee shot to the par-3, half-shanked his next but then holed out from some 15 yards. After the 16th, he was one under 4s but then three-putted the 17th for a 6. At the last, he knew he needed a 4 to tie Reg Horne's total. Instead he holed a putt of a dozen yards to become the leader in the clubhouse with hours of play remaining. So far, Daly had impressed with the quality of his long irons ('a prince among long-iron players' the not over-generous Snead had judged him) and excellent putting on fast greens. How well his old hickory-shafted putter with rusty blade had worked for him.

So, many years before the custom of grouping leaders at the end of the field began, there was the classic situation of a target having been set by an early finisher. The gauntlet was thrown down by Daly; the pursuers were Cotton, von Nida, Jimmy Adams and Frank Stranahan.

Cotton reached the turn in 36 and needed to be home in 36 to tie but began with a 6 and never threatened again. Von Nida was out in 39 and he too finished in 76 to be four behind Daly. Jimmy Adams needed a 69 to tie and, for a while, this seemed more than possible, with a score of several under level 4s, but it all drifted away from him.

The news began to go out that Fred Daly was Open Champion. Still out on the course was Frank Stranahan. He reached the turn and found himself needing an unlikely 33 back to tie with Daly. With three holes to go, the target was more defined. He needed a 4, 4, 3 finish. On the 16th, he was bunkered to the right of the green but got down in two. On the next, he went boldly from 15 yards for the 3, ran a yard past – and missed the return. Apparently it was all over, barring a miracle. On the last, Stranahan did produce the exceptional. From some 150 yards off the green he was within inches of holing out his second shot, still one of the most exciting single shots played in an Open. Nevertheless, the ball stayed out and Fred Daly was the surprise champion. His performances in the next few years were to show that he was worthy of the title – talk that he had won only because the wind had risen once he was safely home did him much less than justice. Ulsterman Fred Daly won the championship fair and square over what Bernard Darwin called 'the toughest course I have ever seen'.

HOW THEY FINISHED

F. Daly	**73**	**70**	**78**	**72**	**293**

R. W. Horne	77	74	72	71	294
Mr F. R. Stranahan *USA*	71	79	72	72	

W. Shankland	76	74	75	70	295

R. Burton	77	71	77	71	296

J. G. Bulla *USA*	80	72	74	71	297
C. H. Ward	76	73	76	72	
S. L. King	75	72	77	73	
A. Lees	75	74	72	76	
N. G. von Nida *Australia*	74	76	71	76	
T. H. Cotton	69	78	74	76	

J. Adams	73	80	71	75	299

A. H. Padgham	75	75	74	76	300
R. A. Whitcombe	75	77	71	77	

F. Bullock	74	78	78	72	302
L. B. Ayton	69	80	74	79	

N. Sutton	77	76	73	77	303

E. E. Whitcombe	77	76	74	77	304
V. Ghezzi *USA*	75	78	72	79	
A. Perry	76	77	70	81	

F. van Donck *Belgium*	73	76	81	75	305
D. J. Rees	77	74	73	81	

A. Waters	75	78	76	77	306

J. Burton	73	79	76	81	309

J. A. Jacobs	75	80	76	79	310
J. H. Busson	80	76	71	83	

A. Havers	80	76	79	76	311
B. Shepard	78	78	77	78	
K. Bousfield	78	76	79	78	
N. Quigley	79	77	76	79	

T. E. Odams	80	76	79	77	312

W. Anderson	74	81	80	79	314
F. Jowle	75	80	80	79	
M. Faulkner	78	76	81	79	

W. B. Thomson	78	76	78	83	315

J. D. Henderson	78	78	81	79	316

T. Gardner	77	76	77	89	319

B. Hodson	79	77	84	84	324

D. McEwan	77	79	87	84	327

Muirfield, 1948

Undeterred by the international tensions of the Berlin Airlift and the slaughter in India and Pakistan, an excellent field gathered at Muirfield for the 1948 Open. This time there was a potentially very strong American contingent, which included the man who had three months before equalled the four-round Augusta record in winning the Masters – Claude Harmon, he of the strange backswing and shut face. Lawson Little was back again and so was Frank Stranahan, refreshed by having taken the Amateur Championship at Royal St George's without being extended in any round. So also were two Americans of Scottish birth: Bobby Cruickshank, who had lost a play-off for the 1923 US Open, thus giving Bobby Jones his first major championship; and Jimmy Thomson, one of the most prodigious hitters of all time. He played round with Fred Daly, no mean hitter himself, in the qualifying rounds and usually outdrove Daly by 50 yards and more, yet failed to qualify.

Henry Cotton was particularly keen this year to add a third title to his record, for his time was running out. He decided that the main threat came from the South Americans. He played a lot with them in practice, feeling that if he could beat them he could beat anyone. The two principals were the charming, stick-like Mario Gonzalez, then an amateur but now professional at Gavea, Rio de Janeiro (with a son Jaimé on the US Tour) and, making his first entry, Roberto de Vicenzo, who was to feature centrally in the championship for many years. Observers quickly noted the beauty and power of his hitting and Bernard Darwin thought he 'gave more aesthetic pleasure than any other

Still the maestro: Henry Cotton.

man in the field'. Some accolade indeed from a man whose judgement over a fifty-year career in golf writing can seldom be faulted.

The betting at every Open tends to favour men who have been in good form in Europe. Norman von Nida was a 6–1 choice, with a considerable gap between him and Frank Stranahan at 11–1. Thereafter, the most money was on Little and Harmon. But it was Cotton who caught the eye during the pre-qualifying, his pair of 69s approached only by Daly's 69, 71, and Roberto's 72, 68. The first-round leaders, however, were Charlie Ward, Sam King and Flory van Donck, all on 69. They were followed by Roberto de Vicenzo and Frank Jowle on 70, while Cotton, von Nida and Reg Horne were handily placed a stroke further away.

The next day, with King George VI, a keen golfer and tennis player, in his gallery, Henry Cotton went out and won the Open. The Muirfield record of 67 had stood since 1929 and was Walter Hagen's 67, equalled by Alf Perry in 1935. This was Cotton's card:

$$3, 4, 5, 3, 4, 4, 3, 4, 3 \ (33); \quad 4, 4, 4, 3, 4, 3, 3, 4, 4 \ (33)$$

He began with a long putt for a birdie and had his only flaw on the 382-yard 3rd, perhaps the simplest hole on the course, when he three-putted. On the 14th, he was dead with a putt from some 30 yards and on the next celebrated with a birdie putt of near cricket-pitch length. On the last his putt for a 65 lipped out. I always felt that Henry was a far better putter than either the public or the player himself believed. The problem was that he *looked* uncomfortable on the greens and changed his stance or putter frequently. There was, too, the contrast with the ease, efficiency and accuracy of his play through the green. Above all, he had good nerve and no one ever accused Henry of giving up.

With this round, Henry had opened up a four-stroke gap on 137, followed by Ward and King (141), Arthur Lees and van Donck (142) and then at 143 Alf Padgham, who had set an early target, von Nida, Daly and Roberto de Vicenzo.

On the final day, all went well for Henry over the opening holes, as he parred the first four. Suddenly, he began dropping shots, one at each of the next five holes to the turn and on the second half added two more bogeys. In a matter of minutes, Sam King, still three strokes behind after Henry's shakey outward 39, caught him with 3, 4 to Cotton's pair of 5s. Then the pendulum swung the other way as Cotton birdied the 12th and 13th with 12-foot and 6-foot putts to King's par and bogey. The lead of three was back and was maintained to the end of the round.

There had also been a challenge from Alf Padgham, 1936 Open Champion. Starting six strokes behind, he played the first nine in 34 and made for home in 4, 4, 4, 2, another two under par. However, he failed to hold a superb round together, dropping shots on four of the last five holes and had the sour taste in

MUIRFIELD
The Championship Course

1	449 yards par 4	10	475 yards par 4
2	349 yards par 4	11	386 yards par 4
3	379 yards par 4	12	381 yards par 4
4	181 yards par 3	13	153 yards par 3
5	558 yards par 5	14	447 yards par 4
6	471 yards par 4	15	396 yards par 4
7	185 yards par 3	16	188 yards par 3
8	444 yards par 4	17	524 yards par 5
9	495 yards par 5	18	447 yards par 4

Out 3,511 yards par 36   In 3,415 yards par 35
Total 6,926 yards par 71

Scale 50 yds 100 yds   200 yds   300 yds

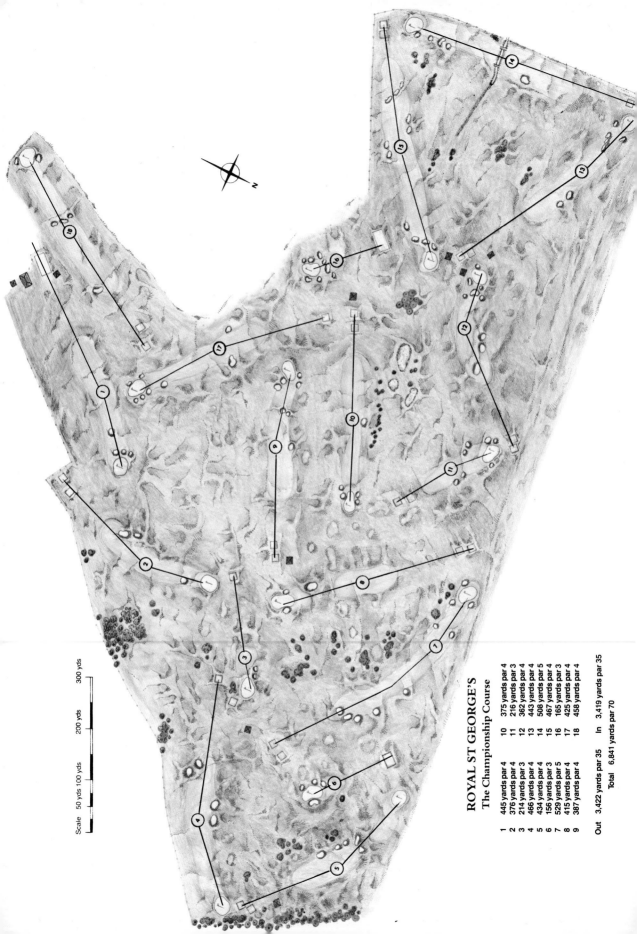

ROYAL ST GEORGE'S
The Championship Course

1	445 yards par 4		10	375 yards par 4
2	376 yards par 4		11	216 yards par 3
3	214 yards par 3		12	362 yards par 4
4	466 yards par 4		13	443 yards par 4
5	434 yards par 5		14	508 yards par 5
6	156 yards par 3		15	467 yards par 4
7	529 yards par 5		16	165 yards par 3
8	415 yards par 4		17	425 yards par 4
9	387 yards par 4		18	458 yards par 4

Out 3,422 yards par 35   In 3,419 yards par 35

Total 6,841 yards par 70

Scale 50 yds 100 yds   200 yds   300 yds

the mouth of missing a tiny putt on the last. Nevertheless, it was still a fine 71 and he was just two shots behind the maestro, Cotton.

As the players went out for the second time that day, the position after three rounds was:

212 Cotton;   214 Padgham;   215 King, Lees, van Donck, de Vicenzo;   216 Ward (with a hole in one on the 13th)

Cotton and King were out early, which put them in the enviable position of being able to set a target. King played the first nine in 36 to Cotton's 37 but Henry was back to level 4s after the 13th and, Sam King by now fallen away, faced the last hole needing a 4 for a 71 and a certain victory. His second shot found sand by the green and, before a packed gallery, Henry shanked his bunker shot and the ball came off the face and back into sand. A 73 was now in prospect. He got the ball out this time, to 9 feet, and then holed the putt, his face thunderous as he snatched his ball from the hole. Quickly overcoming his rage, however, he left the last green hand in hand with his wife Toots.

Yet play was far from over. Alf Padgham needed a 70 to catch Henry. His 77, however, left him well out of the hunt in 7th place. A 70 was in fact the best score that day, so it had been possible for Alf to prevent what was not only a popular but an historic win. In 1937, Henry had become the first British player since the Great Triumvirate of Vardon, Taylor and Braid to win the Open more than once, a record that still stands. I believe that this third victory, despite Tony Jacklin's wins in both US and British Opens, means that Henry Cotton must still be considered the greatest British player at least since those early great ones. My own opinion is that he is the greatest British golfer ever.

With this final laurel on his brow, Henry withdrew from the Open Championship for several years, not returning until he could hardly be expected to win. He played a restricted programme of tournament golf after this win, not even appearing in the following year's Ryder Cup, where his presence at Ganton could well have tipped the balance of the USA's 7–5 winning margin in our favour. Yet even today, in his mid-70s, he keeps his enthusiasm for golf, still experimenting with new designs of clubhead and shaft. And, of course, putters, a great array of them.

There is a simple illustration of this. The most prized possession in the boardroom of the PGA at the Belfry near Birmingham is the set of clubs with which Henry won the 1948 Open. Attached is a tag in Henry's own handwriting remarking that he used his driver 56 times during the championship and hit the fairway 52 of those times. 'But where', I once asked, 'is the putter?' 'Ah,' came the reply, from PGA secretary Colin Snape, 'Henry visited us a couple of years or so ago and his wife Toots mentioned that he had putted particularly well with that one. Henry gave his wife a mischievous smile, winked at me and tucked it under his arm.'

25

HOW THEY FINISHED

T. H. Cotton	**71**	**66**	**75**	**72**	**284**	J. Fallon	73	74	74	75	296
						K. Bousfield	76	71	73	76	
F. J. Daly	72	71	73	73	289						
						A. Perry	77	71	76	73	297
N. G. von Nida *Australia*	71	72	76	71	290	Mr F. R. Stranahan *USA*	77	71	75	74	
J. Hargreaves	76	68	73	73		T. B. Haliburton	73	74	76	74	
C. H. Ward	69	72	75	74		N. Sutton	72	73	77	75	
R. de Vicenzo *Argentina*	70	73	72	75							
						C. Harmon *USA*	75	73	78	72	298
J. G. Bulla *USA*	74	72	73	72	291						
F. van Donck *Belgium*	69	73	73	76		O. Hayes *South Africa*	74	73	75	78	300
S. L. King	69	72	74	76		R. W. Horne	71	77	73	79	
A. H. Padgham	73	70	71	77							
						H. Gould	75	73	78	75	301
Capt. E. C. Kingsley *USA*	77	69	77	70	293	A. E. Clark *USA*	74	71	75	81	
Mr Mario Gonzales *Brazil*	76	72	70	75							
A. Waters	75	71	70	77		R. A. Cruickshank *USA*	74	74	77	77	302
A. Lees	73	69	73	78		L. Little *USA*	72	76	76	78	
						W. S. Collins	77	69	77	79	
E. E. Whitcombe	74	73	73	74	294	C. A. Whitcombe	74	72	75	81	
M. Faulkner	75	71	74	74							
D. J. Rees	73	71	76	74		W. B. Lyle	72	75	80	80	307
F. Jowle	70	78	74	73	295						
R. A. Whitcombe	77	67	77	74							
R. Burton	74	70	74	77							

·2·
The Stately Progress of Bobby Locke

Royal St George's, 1949

There was no Cotton at Royal St George's for the 1949 Open, neither was there that gritty competitor, Norman von Nida. To compensate, Bobby Locke, at the time rivalled only by Ben Hogan in world golf, was there and a firm favourite to win. One professional, asked who would win, replied: 'Anyone at all – if he can beat Bobby Locke.'

Otherwise, the overseas challenge was almost non-existent, at least in terms of numbers. Johnny Bulla and Frank Stranahan were unfailingly loyal (I sometimes feel that the R and A might consider giving them honorary membership as the only Americans who always competed in those early years after World War II), Stranahan having strolled through the Amateur Championship at Portmarnock until rudely dismissed 4 and 3 by Max McCready in the last eight. Otherwise there was Roberto de Vicenzo, no doubt encouraged by his third-place finish at Muirfield, and a name from the past, Willie Hunter, who had walloped Allan Graham, conqueror of Bobby Jones in an earlier round, by no fewer than 12 and 11 in the final of the 1921 Amateur Championship. He had gone on to reach the semi-final of the US Amateur the same year, becoming in the process one of the select few ever to beat Jones. He had later turned professional and only travelled to Sandwich from his home in California to see old friends on his native soil.

Once again, the qualifying rounds were a fair indication of what was to follow in the championship proper. On the first day, Locke and Bulla led at Royal Cinque Ports, Deal, with 69s, while at Sandwich Harry Bradshaw had a 67, his nearest pursuer the elegant Ken Bousfield with a 69. After the field had played both courses, Harry was top of the heap with a 139 total, Locke was at 140, Bulla at 141 and Reg Horne 142. My father was comfortably in at 146 and there was also a certain P. A. Alliss Junior, whose 76, 78 was just good enough to qualify. This was my brother Alec, then professional at Weston-super-Mare. Peter Alliss, alas, was not there. On 16 June 1949, three weeks before this Open, I started my National Service in the RAF Regiment.

Before I looked again at this Open I had felt that this last Royal St George's Open until 1981 was rather dull, enlivened only by that old story about Harry Bradshaw and the beer bottle (of which more later) and that otherwise Bobby Locke had been expected to win and did. This is not a scenario of high drama. Yet drama in plenty there was.

Jimmy Adams, then professional at Wentworth and twice second in the championship before the war, was the first-round leader – a 67 after needing a par for a 66 – followed by Bradshaw and de Vicenzo a stroke behind, with several on 69, the most significant of whom, by far, was Bobby Locke.

All eyes had been on Locke and he had given spectators their money's worth. We tend today to think of Bobby as a golfing oddity, the only man in golf's history who aimed so far right of the target. He swung the club around his right leg with a looping swing, the ball swinging in from right to left. This was unusual, but only in recent years has the received wisdom of golf been that, in Lee Trevino's famous words: 'You can talk to a fade but a hook won't listen.' Locke is also thought of as a superlative putter with a rather gentle long game but this is not at all how his contemporaries and close observers saw him. It was noted at the time that 'he hits the ball very hard indeed', yet still with a 'lovely rhythmic almost drowsy grace'. He had also learned the American mastery of the low-flying wedge shot played from the back foot, even from only a few feet short of the green. This was the shot that used to amaze British golf followers, more accustomed to the pitch and run or, alternatively, a lofted shot towards the flag. Locke's wedges at the time followed the American pattern of biting on the second bounce and braking to a halt very rapidly indeed. With universal watering of greens and far more dense growth of grass, this shot has now gone out of favour, being replaced by shots of higher trajectory. His sole weakness, I felt, was that like Palmer and Nicklaus in later years his bunker play was not outstanding.

Locke, 'with gorgeous pin-splitting iron play' started off by three-putting the 1st, but then went 3, 2 against a par of 4, 3, and despite again three-putting at the 8th, reached the turn in 32. On the 4th, the Maiden, he nearly hit the flag but missed his putt from 6 feet. After the turn he began home in 4, 4, 3, 3 to be six under level 4s but then sliced his drive out of bounds on the 14th, the Canal. He took a 7 here before completing his round without further problems.

On the second day, the winds were stiff and from the north-west. Royal St George's had been partly tamed because 1949 was one of those rare long, hot summers. Rough was wispy rather than clinging, with a good run on the fairways, and the new watering of greens meant that approach shots held comfortably. Because of the wind, however, only Sam King broke 70, and he was the leader at the end of the day on 140, followed by Max Faulkner and Bill Shankland on 142, with Dick Burton and Roberto de Vicenzo on 143. Jimmy Adams had followed his 67 with a less appealing 77 to be next in line, while on 145 there were Locke (76) and Bradshaw (77).

Bobby Locke at Royal St George's, 1949.
Note the perfect balance.

The genial Harry Bradshaw, 1949.

In that round, Bradshaw had hit what is still one of the most famous shots ever played in an Open Championship. He is usually thought to have risked life and limb by crashing his sand wedge into a broken beer bottle, when he ought to have waited for an official to arrive with the Tablets from the Mount, which would have decreed a free drop for him. I cannot imagine a player in 1984 at St Andrews shrugging his shoulders and giving both glass and ball a whack. However, that is roughly what Harry did. When he spoke at the 1981 Open at Royal St George's, he said that at the 5th hole he had found his ball not in a beer bottle but resting against broken glass. With a sand wedge he moved the ball some 20 yards and eventually holed out in 6 instead of 4 or 5. A piece of glass struck his eye but did no harm.

Legend has it that this mischance cost Harry Bradshaw the Open Championship. Perhaps it did, though I doubt it. It certainly cost him one shot and he may have been unsettled by the incident. After his start of four 4s he was shaky on the remaining holes of the first half, which he completed in 39. His 38 on the inward nine kept him in contention, however.

Bradshaw seemed to retrieve it all at the beginning of the final day. He began 3, 4, 3 and was out in 32 to Bobby Locke's 33. Both finished in 68, to lead on 213 with Max Faulkner, who had three consecutive 71s. Sam King and Charlie Ward were a shot further behind. For the last round, Bradshaw had the advantage of beginning some 40 minutes before Bobby Locke and went to the turn in 33 before starting home 4, 4. He later had 5s on both the 14th and 15th but finished with two 4s for a 70.

Locke went to the turn in only 32 but was less convincing over the homeward half. He dropped a shot on the 10th but had a 3 on the 12th to be level. On the 14th and 15th, like Bradshaw, he had 5s, alternately slicing and hooking his second shots. He had now to par the last three holes in 3, 4, 4 to tie Harry. On the 16th, a hole of some 150 yards, he put his tee-shot about 8 or 9 yards from the hole but dragged his first putt to be still about 6 feet away, an exceptionally poor effort for Locke – and missed that one. The 17th, a hole then of 423 yards, he birdied with a 10-foot putt, and then he had to par the last, no easy task, to tie. With his long approach, Bobby was nearly 20 yards short with a swinging putt to come. He got it to about 4 feet and holed out.

So that 1949 Open was, as the Duke of Wellington might have put it, 'a damn close-run thing'.

Happenings the following day obscured this fact. The play-off was over 36 holes, the first since Craig Wood and Densmore Shute confronted each other over the same distance at St Andrews in 1933. (My own view is that 36 holes is an excessive distance, just as a sudden-death play-off is ludicrously short and 18 holes strikes just the right balance. For more than 20 years the latter has been the distance set by the R and A.) Locke was almost entirely dominant in the play-off. He was round in the morning without a 5 on his card in 67 to the Irishman's 74. For Harry, worse was to come. He re-started 6, 5 to Locke's pair of 4s. By the 5th, he was no fewer than 11 strokes behind. In matchplay terms, when Harry birdied the 9th in his second round, it was the first hole he had 'won'. Thereafter, Harry had to bow to the inevitable and the result became a matter of statistics, one of which was that Locke had his first play-off 5 on the 33rd hole, but then was one under par on the last three holes. He finished 12 strokes better than Harry in 135 to 147. Locke had played his last four rounds in a total of 273, superbly consistent scoring.

The confrontation, on a Royal St George's playing fairly easily, had been between two superb putters who were equally unorthodox in the long game. Locke's idiosyncrasies are well-known but Harry had one of the most unusual grips I have ever seen. Instead of the conventional Vardon grip, in which the little finger of the right hand overlaps, he only allowed one finger of his right hand, the forefinger, to touch the shaft. He had what was often described as a scythe-like swing (very flat) but was a master at keeping the ball in play. He also watched the clubhead strike the ball and kept his eyes on the point of impact for, it seemed to watchers, a matter of seconds, a habit that could never do anyone any harm at all. This was particularly noticeable when Harry was putting. He hit the putt and was content to *listen* to what the result was.

But Bobby Locke was champion. Having largely abandoned the US circuit after a ban in 1949 for non-attendance at a routine US event, he continued to be the major figure playing in British and European golf.

HOW THEY FINISHED

A. D. Locke *South Africa*	**69**	**76**	**68**	**70**	**283**	W. Lees	74	72	69	78	293
H. Bradshaw	68	77	68	70							
						A. Waters	70	76	75	73	294
Play-off: Locke	67	68	135								
Bradshaw	74	73	147			N. Sutton	69	78	75	73	295
R. de Vicenzo *Argentina*	68	75	73	69	285	G. W. McIntosh	70	77	76	73	296
						W. A. McMinn	70	75	78	73	
C. H. Ward	73	71	70	72	286	R. W. Horne	73	74	75	74	
S. L. King	71	69	74	72		E. A. Southerden	69	76	74	77	
						A. J. Lacey	72	73	73	78	
A. Lees	74	70	72	71	287						
M. Faulkner	71	71	71	74		J. Wade	71	74	77	75	297
W. D. Smithers	72	75	70	71	288	H. E. Osborne	73	74	75	76	298
J. Fallon	69	75	72	72							
J. Adams	67	77	72	72		J. G. Bulla *USA*	71	73	76	79	299
K. Bousfield	69	77	76	67	289	U. Grappasonni *Italy*	70	76	77	77	300
W. Shankland	69	73	74	73							
						E. W. H. Kenyon	72	75	77	77	301
Mr F. R. Stranahan *USA*	71	73	74	72	290						
						G. M. White	74	71	80	78	303
W. J. Branch	71	75	74	71	291						
J. Knipe	76	71	72	72		Mr F. Francis	72	74	82	79	307
R. Burton	73	70	74	74							

Royal Troon, 1950

Troon and the 1950 Open saw Bobby Locke once again the clear favourite, his reputation by this time on a high plateau. Most of the attributes of his play were by this time fully recognized: superb long putting and good holing out; consistent driving, often with a 2- or 3-wood; excellent short irons and chipping; outstanding judgement of distance without benefit of yardage charts or pacing each hole out. I believe, even today, that Bobby was the best I have seen for estimating and executing the exact weight of shot. If he missed a green with his approach, he was very seldom yards short and never long, but erred to either side, usually being pin-high.

This year the overseas entry was lacking in Americans, though the faithful Bulla was here once more, as was Frank Stranahan, who had six weeks before demolished another formidable American, Dick Chapman, by 8 and 6 in the final of the Amateur Championship at St Andrews. Von Nida was hopeful again and there was the rare appearance in Europe of his compatriot, Ossie Pickworth. The latter had won the Australian Open a record three times in a row in 1946–8 and was third in the Order of Merit in Britain in 1950, winning the Irish Open and tying for another tournament. From Argentina, there was a new name, Antonio (Tony) Cerda, while Roberto de Vicenzo was highly favoured, having been third the previous two years.

From the championship tees, the Troon of today can be stretched to more than 7000 yards but in 1950 it was 6583 yards. The rough was thick and intimidating enough for de Vicenzo often to sacrifice length by taking irons from the tee, a practice far less common than it has since become. (Remember Cotton using his driver throughout at Muirfield in 1948?) The condition of the fairways left a lot to be desired. They were unevenly cut in places and there were bare patches in plenty. The greens, on the other hand, were magnificent, von Nida describing them as being 'like velvet'. Unusually for the time, they were watered nightly. Some said this was unfairly to Locke's advantage. He replied: 'They couldn't have done it for a nicer fellow.'

All was set up therefore to favour accurate hitters and good putters. As a result of Bradshaw's trouble with a bottle the year before, there was a rule change that would allow players to lift and drop. The championship was also to cause another new decision from the R and A, but of that more later.

After the first qualifying round, the talk was mostly of two men. Playing on the championship course, Flory van Donck had gone round in 65 with no bogeys and no 5s on his card, coming home in 31. The other was a German amateur, Herman Tissies, who had won the German Closed Amateur in 1949, the first year it was re-started after the war. Tissies came spectacularly to grief on the famous 126-yard Postage Stamp 8th hole, which seems to have been good for a tale in nearly every Troon Open. He missed the green with his tee-shot and then spent several minutes scurrying his ball backwards and forwards across the green from bunker to bunker, by no means always getting out at the first attempt. In the end he single-putted for a 15!

At the end of the second day, the qualifiers were led by the American Johnny Bulla with two 70s, followed by von Nida, a 6–1 bet for the title, on 141, with Locke, van Donck and Wally Smithers a further stroke behind.

On the first day of the championship proper, conditions favoured good scoring in just a light easterly breeze. Few fancied players knocked themselves out of contention, though Frank Stranahan had his problems. He began with a couple of 3s on the opening par-4s but then hooked his second shot into a bunker and took two to get out. Back to level par. He then had 5s at the 4th and 5th (one a par-3 hole) and ran up a 7 on the long 6th. In the end, he was an unsightly 43 to the turn. But Frank was a gutsy competitor and put his troubles firmly behind him to come home in 34. Dai Rees made an encouraging beginning with 33 to the turn but could finish in no better than 71, a good chance lost. At the end of the first round the leader was Arthur Lees, at that time and for so many years afterwards the professional at Sunningdale. Following him were Eddie Whitcombe, son of Ernest, one of the famous Whitcombe brothers, and Locke on 69. Then came Sam King (a name much to the fore in Opens at this time, though a nervy short putter) with a 70, and several on 71.

The weather the second day was very similar but once again a few were able to break 70. One who did was Rees, whose 68 gave him a lead of one at 36 holes over Bill Branch, with Bobby Locke one stroke further back. During his 72, Locke had given a fine demonstration of his ability to survive disaster. On the long par-3 5th hole he hooked his tee-shot into long grass but was only about 20 yards from the flag. He then pitched into a bunker beneath his nose, took two to get out and there was a 6 to go down on his card. There was trouble brewing again on the 7th when he looked up on his second shot and topped into a bunker, but he recovered to hole out for his par from 3 yards. On the next hole, the Postage Stamp, he hooked his short iron into a bunker, hit out into another but survived with no worse than a 4, holing from 7 feet.

For the final 36 holes on the Friday, there was no wind at all. Low scoring was again expected. Fred Daly put in a fine finish and hauled himself many places up the field with 69, 66, but after his 75, 72 start was never really in contention. In the last round, Frank Stranahan was eleven strokes better than his first round for a 66, still the best score over Troon by any amateur, though, with later course lengthening, no longer recognized as the record.

But these were rounds from men not in real contention – unless the leaders met with disaster. After Rees had got to the turn in 33 more was expected of him than his eventual 72, which included two 6s, but he was still in the lead, joined on 211 by Bobby Locke, also to the turn in 33, and Roberto de Vicenzo. The Argentine declared he was playing 'badly' but still managed a 68, employing no more than a 3-iron for many of his tee-shots.

Dai Rees, Troon, 1950.
Plenty of attack into the ball here.

It was Roberto who set the first target and a good one it was, 281, a new Open record total, beating the 283 of Locke in 1949, Perry in 1935, Cotton in 1934 and Sarazen in 1932. He reached the turn in a 33 which included one historic incident. On the Postage Stamp 8th he found his ball plugged in a bunker, declared it unplayable, and with his second ball needed only two strokes for his par 3. The powers that be decided later that the rules were too lenient and a change soon followed. No blame attached to Roberto, however, who had used the rules sensibly and to his advantage.

His second half was a mixture of good and bad. He had birdies on the 11th, 16th and 17th and played the last three holes in two under par, a fine finish to his championship. But there had been some faltering as well. He dropped one shot at the 10th, two on the 12th and had two other bogeys in his round of 70. Playing behind him, Locke also was out in 33 but held his round together with far more consistency, though missing a couple of short putts. His 279 became the target and replaced Vicenzo's new Open record.

It was now up to Dai Rees, needing a 68 to tie. For the third time, he reached the turn in 33 but then immediately dropped two shots at the 10th. That was virtually that. Locke was home and dry by three strokes, the first man to win consecutive Opens since Walter Hagen in 1928–9 and Bobby Jones in 1926–7.

HOW THEY FINISHED

Name	R1	R2	R3	R4	Total
A. D. Locke *South Africa*	**69**	**72**	**70**	**68**	**279**
R. de Vicenzo *Argentina*	72	71	68	70	281
F. Daly	75	72	69	66	282
D. J. Rees	71	68	72	71	
E. Moore *South Africa*	74	68	73	68	283
M. Faulkner	72	70	70	71	
F. Bullock	71	71	71	71	284
A. Lees	68	76	68	72	
Mr F. R. Stranahan *USA*	77	70	73	66	286
F. van Donck *Belgium*	73	71	72	70	
S. L. King	70	75	68	73	
J. Adams	73	75	69	70	287
W. D. Smithers	74	70	73	70	
H. Thomson	71	72	73	72	288
J. G. Bulla *USA*	73	70	71	74	
H. Bradshaw	73	71	75	70	289
Mr J. B. McHale *USA*	73	73	74	70	290
R. W. Horne	73	75	71	71	
E. E. Whitcombe	69	76	72	73	
A. H. Padgham	77	71	74	69	291
N. G. von Nida *Australia*	74	72	76	69	
J. Panton	76	69	70	76	
E. C. Brown	73	73	73	73	292
G. M. White	74	74	73	72	293
N. Sutton	71	75	74	73	
W. J. Branch	71	69	78	75	
S. S. Field	73	71	73	76	
T. W. Allen	77	70	75	71	
F. G. Allott	72	71	77	74	294
H. Hassanein *Egypt*	73	72	77	73	295
Maj. D. A. Blair	72	72	77	74	
S. S. Scott	75	71	75	75	296
A. Perry	73	74	76	75	298
J. Carroll	73	72	74	79	
Mr J. C. Wilson	72	76	79	72	299

Royal Portrush, 1951

In 1951, the Open went to Northern Ireland, the only time the event has not been held either in Scotland or England. The Amateur Championship, on the other hand, has even been in Eire, at Portmarnock in 1949. On that occasion, I believe competitors had to get themselves passports!

For me, this was a very important year for I had just completed my National Service with the RAF Regiment and was barely back into full practice but eager to do well. I was interested to hear recently that I had attracted the attention of the great Bernard Darwin. I am not trying to kid you that I read *The Times* in those far-off days but this was what Darwin had to say about me:

> First of all came Peter Alliss, the son of a distinguished father, having only lately completed his National Service and got back into full practice. Many people have predicted a great future for him and yesterday confirmed their prophecies. He is a beautiful golfer and plays beautiful golf, with no abnormal luck to help him and with the minimum of mistakes. He has a style free, elegant and upstanding, with the gift, so hard to describe but so easy to recognise, of keeping his weight well back and seeming to push the ball away from him. He was out in 33 and went on without the least appearance of being frightened of his own score till he had holed 15 holes in 5 under an average of 4s.

I remember dropping a couple of shots after that but was more than delighted to come in with a 69. Together with a 76, I qualified very comfortably for the championship proper but did not quite keep it up, failing to qualify for the final day's play. Nevertheless, it was an experience I greatly enjoyed, and I still have the odd memento. One is a hotel bill for the double room I shared with my brother Alec, there to act as chaperone for me. I see that it cost us 17 shillings and 6 pence a night plus two baths for 2 shillings. We were there four days or so and it seems I didn't wash as often in those days! I assure you things are much changed, and for the better.

There was an even more significant first appearance, that of the 21-year-old Australian Peter Thomson. Not fancied to win, it was noted, however, that he had a fine, simple style, great composure and self-confidence. Even less fancied was a player who had begun to feature in previous Opens, Max Faulkner. During the practice rounds, his fellow professionals had refused to play him for money, so afflicted was Max with a horrendous slice. Bobby Locke was also in relatively poor form but had to a very high degree the ability to keep going. He could continue to turn three shots into two near the green or recover after a bad start. I remember once partnering him in a tournament at Went-worth when he began with a 6 at the 1st, 5 on the 2nd and 7 on the 3rd. He went

A very slimline Alliss.

Tony Cerda has gone well down the grip for more control. 1951.

quietly on and had managed to come back to par by the end of his round of 73.

At the end of the qualifying rounds, Tony Cerda, who had failed to cross this hurdle the previous year, had come out on top with a pair of 69s. He was followed on 139 by the out-of-form Locke, Tom Haliburton, a steady under-powered player who was an excellent putter, and Norman von Nida, still fancied by many to win a championship. Then came the brutally powerful Harry Weetman, just beginning to make his name and always a big draw because of his savage – although sometimes wild – hitting.

Jimmy Adams had a brilliant beginning when the championship proper opened, taking only 19 strokes to play the first six holes, five under par. He was out in 31 and held his score together to finish in 68. So also did Norman von Nida. The latter then faded to 77, 80 and had no return in the last round, all mainly the result of illness, migraine I believe. Norman looked a highly probable Open winner in several of those early post-war years, but at the end of his career was still one of the best players not to win the championship. Dai Rees and Peter Thomson followed on 70 and a stroke further away were Locke and Faulkner with van Donck on 73. Tony Cerda showed his mettle by recovering from 40 to the turn to be round in 74. Young Peter Alliss was somewhat less mettlesome, having a 79.

After the second day Max Faulkner had taken the lead. The wild slice was gone but he was playing with little authority through the green, tentative and waiting for the slice to reappear. Once he got there, however, Max had a new toy. This was an ultra-lightweight putter, only about 8 ounces, with a bladed

Max Faulkner: a fine impact position.

aluminium head and a pencil-slim shaft and grip. Max never used a normal sensible set of clubs in his career and his choice of putters was usually even more bizarre. He was fond of making his own, and one that attracted attention for a while featured a billiard cue for a shaft and a wooden head that Max had sculpted from a piece of driftwood from Selsey beach. As well as changing his putters, Max was also an experimenter with putting style and indeed the full swing. As a result of all this, he was one of the greatest manipulators of a golf ball that I have seen, particularly remarkable for his ability to bend shots with even the most lofted clubs. The pencil-slim device worked well that second day and he single-putted no fewer than ten greens.

Max was highly delighted and brimmed over with confidence. Although at this stage he had only a two-stroke lead over Norman Sutton, a doughty competitor and ex-Tranmere Rovers centre forward, with such other players as Locke, von Nida, Cerda and Daly well within range, Max began to sign the autograph books and the odd scraps of paper that get thrust into one's hands:

'Max Faulkner. Open Champion 1951.' I don't believe I'd ever have done that even with a twenty-stroke lead and just one round to play!

However, on the final day that confidence did not seem at all misplaced after Max's third round. He went round in 70, this time with his long game working well and less inspiration needed from the putter. Now he really was beginning to pull away from the field, having a six-stroke lead on Tony Cerda and Norman Sutton. Peter Thomson was one stroke further away, in a most promising first Open, and then came Harry Weetman and Bobby Locke, who had struggled round to a 71, despite a poor long game.

Confidence fully maintained, Max went to the turn in his final round in 34, increasing his lead on most of those still remotely in contention. The victory became even more certain when he began home with a couple of pars, followed by two birdies. He dropped a stroke, however, on the 14th before parring the next to be four under level 4s with only three holes to play. From the 16th tee he then hooked almost out of bounds towards a fence on this 440-yard hole, leaving himself with a much restricted backswing. He managed to move the ball along some 170 yards with a choppy wood shot, however, but then played a weak third shot, followed by none too good a chip. Two putts followed so that was a 6 on the card and easily the worst hole Max had yet played in the championship. Still there was no threat to him but Max then created one by finishing nervously with two 5s. A 6, 5, 5 finish, not good at all.

This gave Tony Cerda a chance. So far, he had scored lower each round with his low, almost half-thinned iron shots, coming from a swing with much lateral movement, proving increasingly effective. Tony got himself first within reach of Max and then, when the latter faltered, he had a chance to tie if he produced three 4s to finish. Unfortunately, Cerda handled that par-4 16th as badly as Max had done, taking 6, and though he had his 4s on the last two holes that meant only a comfortable second place, three ahead of Charlie Ward but two strokes worse than Max Faulkner.

As an indication of how times have changed, prize money in this 1951 Open had by now risen to a *total* of £1700 and Max's share was £325. This was at least showing some improvement on the days when Walter Hagen could happily accept the trophy but give the cheque straight to his caddie! The scores too, though not as low as in the 1950 Open, were beginning to achieve the consistency of those of the modern era. In retrospect, my 69 in qualifying looks increasingly good, for Royal Portrush had largely won the battle with the golfers: only Jimmy Adams, Charlie Ward and von Nida broke 70 in the championship proper.

The Portrush Open marked the end of quite a long era. From Henry Cotton's 1934 Open victory to 1951, British golfers had won nine of the twelve events, the others going to Snead and Locke. The barren years were to follow, with only Tony Jacklin once breaking the long sequence of overseas victories that has lasted with that one interruption for more than thirty years.

HOW THEY FINISHED

M. Faulkner	**71**	**70**	**70**	**74**	**285**	P. Traviani *Italy*	74	79	73	74	300
						E. E. Whitcombe	74	74	76	76	
A. Cerda *Argentina*	74	72	71	70	287	F. van Donck *Belgium*	72	76	76	76	
						Mr J. B. Carr	75	76	73	76	
C. H. Ward	75	73	74	68	290						
						A. Poulton	77	77	73	75	302
J. Adams	68	77	75	72	292	J. McKenna	74	76	76	76	
F. Daly	74	70	75	73		W. D. Smithers	75	73	76	78	
W. Shankland	73	76	72	72	293	G. N. Roffe	78	76	78	71	303
A. D. Locke *South Africa*	71	74	74	74		C. Rotan *USA*	76	76	76	75	
H. Weetman	73	71	75	74		Wing Cdr C. H. Beamish	76	78	73	76	
P. W. Thomson *Australia*	70	75	73	75		A. Lees	75	74	76	78	
N. Sutton	73	70	74	76							
						S. L. King	78	76	77	73	304
J. Panton	73	72	74	75	294	W. C. A. Hancock	78	74	72	80	
D. J. Rees	70	77	76	72	295	J. Fallon	78	73	80	74	305
R. Burton	74	77	71	73		J. A. Jacobs	76	77	77	75	
Mr F. R. Stranahan *USA*	75	75	72	73		F. G. Allott	74	79	77	75	
H. Bradshaw	80	71	74	71	296	E. C. Brown	74	77	83	72	306
						R. Halsall	80	74	77	75	
E. Cremin *Australia*	73	75	75	74	297	A. J. Lacey	75	76	79	76	
						G. W. McIntosh	76	71	80	79	
A. Waters	74	75	78	71	298						
Mr K. E. Enderby	76	74	75	73		H. Hassanein *Egypt*	79	73	74	81	307
Australia											
						C. Kane	75	76	81	77	309
W. J. Henderson	77	73	76	73	299						
C. O'Connor	79	74	72	74							
K. D. G. Nagle *Australia*	76	76	72	75							
U. Grappasonni *Italy*	73	73	77	76							
J. Hargreaves	73	78	79	69							

Bobby Locke and trusty putter.

Royal Lytham and St Anne's, 1952

By the time the 1952 Open arrived at Royal Lytham and St Anne's, the magic of the pencil-slim putter had departed for Max Faulkner. This time he was equipped with another eccentric item, a long-shafted implement which looked rather like an antique cleek. I really think he would have been a far greater player if he had settled down to make the best use of conventional clubs rather than, for instance, turning up with his bag containing three drivers, one shallow-faced with a whippy shaft, one extra, extra stiff and 3 inches longer than normal, and some other dubious magic in the third. On the other hand, most of us have experimented with a variety of putters and putting styles, though the players most effective on the greens have tended to stay loyal to a single club and method.

Bobby Locke, for example, as a teenager had already acquired the hickory-shafted putter with its rusty iron blade to which he remained loyal all his career. It is said that he went to bed with it while on his travels to ensure against theft – almost certainly a tall story. I remember his letting me try it out once. I don't know whether it would have cured my own putting problems but I recall how beautifully balanced it was. The putter seemed to want to swing truly and almost have a will of its own. Bobby also remained consistent in his method on the greens. He positioned the ball further forward than normal, almost outside the left toe and, rather unusually, drew his right foot well back, giving the impression of aiming well to his right. All this was to help him strike his putts with an inside to out swing (the Americans used to say 'This guy from the bush duck-hooks every shot, including his putts'). Locke felt that the worst fault in a putting action was to cut across the ball. Instead, he wanted topspin. Of course, this is impossible to achieve but it was important to Bobby that he felt he did. Certainly with a Locke putt the ball almost always looked as if it would pull up short of the hole, but no, it ran gently on and on. You could always hear the ring of the putter head, indicative of his trueness of strike. Locke's method was also distinctive in its mental aspect. First he would slowly parade the

41

green, surveying the line of putt, yet surprisingly seldom bothering to remove debris. Although the purpose was to note the lie of the grain and the important minute undulations and slopes close to the hole, he was really trying to get the feel of the strength required into his fingertips. Finally, he peered into the hole to see which way the grass had been cut. The survey completed, Locke went into the second stage of his drill. Two long practice swings and then away the ball went. However important the putt, to win a championship or to finish 40th rather than 41st, Locke never varied this drill, which greatly helped him avoid tension: everything at this stage was automatic.

Bobby was indeed always true to his routine. This even extended to air travel. A wartime Liberator bomber pilot in the Mediterranean theatre, with more than a hundred missions to his credit, he kept habits that came from these experiences. I remember flying with him when Constellations were the Rolls-Royces of air travel. Most of us merely sat down and fitted the buckle of our seat belts together. Not Locke, he always adjusted the straps meticulously so that he was clamped firmly into his seat. He would not risk injury if the plane hit a pocket or bounced on landing. He kept the belt fastened right through the flight and chose seat number 7 – near an exit should things go wrong!

Then again, there were his procedures before playing. Everything was done slowly to avoid the dreaded tension that haste can so easily bring on. Usually he breakfasted in bed and dressed very slowly. He then allowed an excessive amount of time to get himself to the course. If I, for instance, was playing with him that day, as I often did in exhibitions, young Alliss had to be the driver. Once we reached the locker room to change, his clothing was always the same. The shoes were always white (because, he said, white matches everything and you don't travel with suitcases full of shoes) as were the socks, knitted for him by one of his many admirers. He always wore a loose-fitting freshly laundered white shirt with a South African Air Force or club tie and very baggy navy-blue plus-fours. Topping the lot, there was a white cap. All this attire was donned slowly, with many a pause for a spurt of conversation or the telling of a story. A little later came the feature of his play which caused the most controversy: he walked in slow and stately manner between shots.

At this Lytham Open in 1952, there was, in fact, a formal complaint from Norman von Nida that Locke was holding up play. Locke blamed inadequate crowd control but nevertheless lost three holes on the grouping ahead during the third round and took over 3½ hours (which does not sound long today!) as compared with Gene Sarazen's and my time of about 2¼ hours. Privately, however, Bobby admitted to me that he had learned to play slowly in America where, by that time, US Open and Masters Champion Dr Cary Middlecoff was widely famed as the slowest player golf had yet seen.

Sarazen, our Open Champion of 1932 and a frequent visitor in the 1920s and 1930s, was making his first appearance in the Open since 1937 (when he had failed to qualify for the last day), at the age of fifty. At both Lytham and Fairhaven, the other qualifying course, over which Sarazen had won his first British competition many years before, he had 69s, despite once taking 8 on the 1st! The leading qualifier, however, on 34 was the Scot John Panton of the slow speech and elegant iron play followed by Harry Bradshaw with a 136 total that included a 65 at Fairhaven, a course that used to boast a bunker for every day of the year. Faulkner, despite the putting cleek, was in good form with 69, 68, and Harry Weetman was on the same mark. Sarazen, Tony Cerda, Peter Thomson and Locke were all placed well up the qualifying list. It was also to be a significant year for the 21-year-old Peter Alliss: my 76, 71 was well within the 152 qualifying mark. Just behind me there was Henry Cotton, making his first entry since his 1948 championship win and declaring this was to be his last appearance, as he was to continue to say for some years ahead!

For the first round proper, the feature pairing was the established champion, Bobby Locke, and 22-year-old Peter Thomson, New Zealand Open Champion in 1950 and 1951 and Australian title-holder in 1951 for the first time. There was an indication of the shape of things to come. Locke was round in 69 but trailed Thomson by a stroke. The leader, however, was Fred Daly, striking the ball superbly, with 67. The defending champion, Max Faulkner, was well placed on 72, as was I. Young Alliss, however, was in some distress. During several months' courtship of a very fair maid, Pamela Mackrell, at the time a skater at the Bournemouth Summer Ice Show, I had just spent a day on the beach at Barton-on-Sea. My legs had never before seen so much sun and I went to Lytham quite badly sunburned and bandaged from thigh to heel, not the ideal condition in which to try to win the Open.

I was paired with Gene Sarazen and found it difficult to concentrate when playing with him. He played his shots with such speed that he gave me the feeling he was not really interested. This was particularly noticeable on the putting green, where he seemed not even to glance at the line before he putted. It has since occurred to me that Gene might have had the yips and that this was his solution: walk up to the ball and send it at the hole without giving himself the time for tension to get into the hands and arms.

Daly continued well the following day. His long game became unreliable (he topped two shots) during the second nine but his short game rose to the occasion: he single-putted the last five greens. His eventual 69 put him four clear of Locke, with Thomson a further stroke behind. Locke and Thomson were again paired and this time the championship committee had taken the precaution of leaving a 40-minute gap before the next pair were due to tee-off!

On the final day the west wind blew firmly and the scores rose. A 70 was the best round of the day and there were only three 71s. I believe I was in the lead at about the nine-hole mark after my two 72s but thereafter nerves and my sunburn intruded and I fell away well down the field. After the third round, this was the position:

Daly's lead had just about gone. He had begun with some luck on the 1st, where his tee-shot skipped over a bunker onto the green, and he continued to play well enough for seven holes. However, on the 8th his wild second shot hit the out-of-bounds fence and he was in the end lucky to drop no more than two strokes. One of these he immediately retrieved on the short 9th. Although his tee-shot was through the green, he holed out with his next. He then followed with a 7 on the par-5 11th and dropped a shot on each of the next two holes. He then played more steadily but could only finish in 77. However, Thomson's challenge had been somewhat defused, also by a 77, with a shot out of bounds on the railway at the 2nd.

For the afternoon, Locke was instructed to play faster but probably paid the powers that be little attention. His morning 74 had been steady enough and in the afternoon, when a quarter of the field failed to break 80, he reached the turn in 34. He came to the last two holes needing two 4s for a 71 but, the championship in his grasp, lapsed to a pair of 5s instead.

This gave Daly a chance. He had begun badly, using up 26 shots on the first six holes against a par of 23. He completed the half without further alarms in 37 and birdied the next two holes. Playing the 15th, he was back in contention but, suddenly, out again as a 6 went down on his card. He birdied the next and parred the 17th which left him with the statistical chance of tying Locke if he could hole out his second shot to the last – shades of Stranahan at Hoylake in 1947. Of course, it was not to be and although Fred nearly holed his putt for a 3, he finished two behind Bobby.

That left only the young Australian Peter Thomson in with a chance. He had begun his last round four behind Locke. Thomson now proceeded to play the best round of the day. He reached the turn in 36 and followed with bogey, birdie, birdie and five straight pars before a birdie 3 on the last. His total was 70 but Locke was champion by a stroke.

Meanwhile Henry Cotton was still declaring this would be his last appearance. Perhaps his mind was changed by his finish of birdie 3s on the last two holes for a 71 and 4th place in the championship. His final day's total of 145 was the lowest but he had begun that morning nine strokes behind Locke and no fewer than thirteen behind Fred Daly. The wind had brought out the best in him and allowed him to demonstrate his control over the flight of a golf ball.

For Locke, this meant three wins in four years, which had been achieved before only by James Braid (1905–8), Harry Vardon (1896–9) and early figures in Open Championship history such as Young Tom Morris, Old Tom Morris, Jamie Anderson and Bob Ferguson, when total fields were below fifty (and sometimes as few as eight). It was a great achievement for the stately South African, but by no means the crowning glory of his career – the hickory-shafted putter still had some magic left in it!

HOW THEY FINISHED

Player					Total
A. D. Locke *South Africa*	**69**	**71**	**74**	**73**	**287**
P. W. Thomson *Australia*	68	73	77	70	288
F. Daly	67	69	77	76	289
T. H. Cotton	75	74	74	71	294
A. Cerda *Argentina*	73	73	76	73	295
S. L. King	71	74	74	76	
F. van Donck *Belgium*	74	75	71	76	296
F. Bullock	76	72	72	77	297
A. Lees	76	72	76	74	298
N. G. von Nida *Australia*	77	70	74	77	
E. C. Brown	71	72	78	77	
W. Goggin *USA*	71	74	75	78	
S. S. Scott	75	69	76	78	
H. Bradshaw	70	74	75	79	
H. Weetman	74	77	71	77	299
J. Panton	72	72	78	77	
M. Faulkner	72	76	79	73	300
G. Sarazen *USA*	74	73	77	76	
W. D. Smithers	73	74	76	77	
N. Sutton	72	74	79	76	301
E. Noke	72	78	76	76	302
J. Hine *USA*	73	78	74	77	
F. G. Allott	77	71	76	78	
K. Bousfield	72	73	79	78	
J. A. Jacobs	74	72	81	76	303
A. Poulton	71	74	76	82	
J. Hargreaves	75	75	79	75	304
D. J. Rees	76	74	77	77	
J. R. M. Jacobs	72	76	79	77	
Mr J. W. Jones	73	70	78	83	
R. W. Horne	77	74	80	74	305
Peter Alliss	72	72	80	81	
Mr D. Rawlinson	74	73	79	80	306
Mr A. T. Kyle	71	75	80	81	307
R. Halsall	74	75	78	81	308
Mr H. de Lamaze *France*	73	72	80	83	
T. B. Haliburton	75	76	80	78	309
H. Thomson	73	77	80	79	
J. H. Hawkins	76	72	82	79	
Mr F. R. Stranahan *USA*	75	76	78	80	
G. Johnson	73	75	78	83	
H. A. J. Young	70	77	77	85	
G. Knight	74	75	80	82	311
R. G. French	72	78	79	83	312
Mr F. Morrell	75	74	86	79	314
B. J. Hunt	75	75	82	83	315

•3•

The Iceman Cometh

Carnoustie, 1953

Up to 1953 and from 1954 onwards the Open Championship story is dominated by great figures in golf's history who played a major role for several – sometimes many – years. But in 1953 there arrived at Carnoustie a man who came, saw and conquered: Ben Hogan. His record is therefore perfect, if limited: played one, won one.

Like Sam Snead, he had to be persuaded to enter, but by men with a sense of golf history, Gene Sarazen included. They pointed out that, though US golf was at that time completely centred on American events, no golfer with aspirations to greatness could consider his major championship record wholly convincing without an Open title. The argument was specially convincing in 1953, for Hogan had already won the US Masters and the US Open. If he competed at Carnoustie, he would not be able to play in the US PGA, then a matchplay event, for the dates clashed. Hogan, after the serious injuries which had brought him close to death in a car accident in 1949, did not anyway intend to enter. He did not have the stamina to withstand a whole week of matchplay at a rate of 36 holes a day. Before his accident, Hogan had planned to be a champion until he was at least fifty; afterwards, he knew this was no longer possible. Having been one of the most successful players ever on the US Tour he almost completely abandoned it, concentrating on appearances in major championships. For a few years, he felt he could build up a formidable record if he was tunnel-visioned in pursuit of them alone. Hogan wanted to be considered the greatest golfer of all time and knew that championship victories do not fade in the memory with the passing of the years. It is intriguing that Hogan realized this so early, for the concept of 'the four major championships' did not become established until the 1960s.

He came to Carnoustie early to accustom himself to the smaller 1.62-inch British ball but much more to learn how to deal with what many had told him were the different demands of links golf. There would be the need to learn the pitch and run; to play off highly uneven stances; to hit from hard ground; and

Carnoustie, 1953. Ben Hogan getting into practice.

perhaps to accept that perfectly struck shots are frequently punished by unlucky bounces into rough or forwards and on through a green into trouble.

Observers of Hogan, as he played the course alone except for his caddie, Timms (an elegant man who wore Cashmere before I learned to), were specially impressed by his efforts to learn Carnoustie, so bleak and gaunt, quite possibly the most difficult course in the world in a rising wind.

Hogan had been told of the natural contouring and keenness of links greens but what he found dismayed him. They were slow and not cut short to championship length. He even offered to send back to Texas for a lawn-mower, a remark not appreciated in high places. However, when the 36 qualifying holes were to be played, Hogan was fully prepared, pleased at the extra distance he was hitting the small ball and had made a major adjustment to his iron play so that he had the clubhead skimming the turf, instead of taking his normal deep divot.

Although attention was concentrated on Hogan, the overseas field was of good quality. Lloyd Mangrum had won the 1946 US Open and reached a play-off for that title in 1950, losing to Hogan. He was also a dominant force on the US Tour (with a career total of 34 victories, which still ranks him in 8th place on the all-time winners' list). In 1953 he was Vardon Trophy winner for the season's lowest stroke average and captained the US Ryder Cup team later in the year at Wentworth, my own first year of Ryder Cup play. There were also the more familiar faces of Peter Thomson, Ossie Pickworth, Tony Cerda, Roberto de Vicenzo, Frank Stranahan and Bobby Locke, as formidable as ever.

Locke quickly showed he would not surrender his title easily, leading the qualifiers by five strokes with 136. He was followed by John Panton and Christy O'Connor, then a new name. Peter Thomson gave himself a fright. He began with an 80 and made the 154 qualifying mark with not a stroke to spare. Mangrum also had his alarms, beginning with a 78, but a 67 then showed his worth. Hogan did not extend himself and was on 145.

I was paying my first visit to Scotland since I had played in the Boys' Championship at Bruntsfield in 1946 and was also comfortably into the championship proper. Like so many others, I was a little overawed by the presence of the great man. I wanted to see Hogan but tended to keep in the background.

After the first day of the Championship proper, the leader was Frank Stranahan, whose 70 had equalled the Carnoustie record set during the 1937 Open. He was followed by Eric Brown, setting Scottish hopes alight. Brown had gone out in 38 but then came storming home in 33 for a total of 71 despite going out of bounds on the last – Eric's tendency to hook with his very strong left-hand grip remained throughout his career, despite using off-set woods.

On 72, there were Locke, Thomson, Rees and de Vicenzo. Despite inaccurate iron play, Bobby had rescued a bad round with resolute chipping and used only 28 putts. Hogan, with the ever-present tendency to cramp in the legs after his accident, could not have enjoyed the weather, though it was what he might have expected: cold, windy, with occasional hail. He was round in 73 but had allowed a position of one under par to slip away over the testing finishing holes of 243, 458 and 525 yards with 4, 5, 5. Observers had been impressed with his length from the tee and he was reckoned to be hitting the ball as far as the more obviously muscular de Vicenzo. Indeed, because of Carnoustie's length, Hogan had decided long wooden club play was essential and had concentrated much of his practice on this. Perhaps more significant, however, had been the

ROYAL TROON
The Championship Course

1	362 yards par 4		10	437 yards par 4
2	391 yards par 4		11	481 yards par 5
3	381 yards par 4		12	432 yards par 4
4	556 yards par 5		13	468 yards par 4
5	210 yards par 3		14	180 yards par 3
6	577 yards par 5		15	457 yards par 4
7	400 yards par 4		16	542 yards par 5
8	126 yards par 3		17	223 yards par 3
9	419 yards par 4		18	425 yards par 4

Out 3,422 yards par 36   In 3,645 yards par 36

Total 7,067 yards par 72

Scale   50 yds 100 yds   200 yds   300 yds

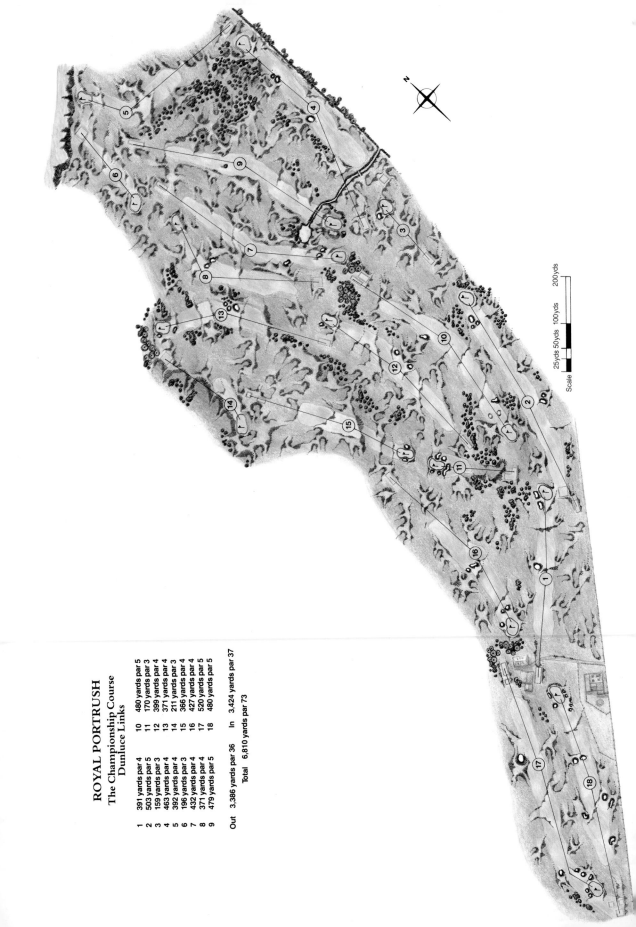

ROYAL PORTRUSH
The Championship Course
Dunluce Links

1	391 yards par 4		10	480 yards par 5
2	503 yards par 5		11	170 yards par 3
3	159 yards par 3		12	399 yards par 4
4	463 yards par 4		13	371 yards par 4
5	392 yards par 4		14	211 yards par 3
6	196 yards par 3		15	366 yards par 4
7	432 yards par 4		16	427 yards par 4
8	371 yards par 4		17	520 yards par 5
9	479 yards par 5		18	480 yards par 5

Out 3,386 yards par 36   In 3,424 yards par 37

Total 6,810 yards par 73

Scale

25yds 50yds 100yds   200yds

placement of those tee-shots. Hogan had decided on the ideal positioning of the drive for each hole and proved able to carry out his strategy. At St Andrews, although the 'safe' drive is left, the second shots are generally much easier if you place your tee-shots to the extreme right of the fairways; at Carnoustie, there is no hard-and-fast rule, but there is a specific correct placement on almost every hole.

As in practice, Hogan continued to find putting a problem. First he had declared the greens to be 'like putty' and, even cut to championship shortness, he still found them slow. When a birdie chance came along, he was usually short, but his putting total of 32 was respectable enough. As regards putting, there continued to be interest in what strange device Max Faulkner would turn up with. This year, he had decided on one with a croquet mallet grip and damaged shaft. It must have worked well enough, for he was round in 74.

On the second day, Hogan, having caught a cold, once again faced the daunting course, which in 1953 looked like this:

Hole	Yards	Par	Hole	Yards	Par
1st	406	4	10th	446	4
2nd	468	4	11th	370	4
3rd	343	4	12th	473	4
4th	429	4	13th	168	3
5th	389	4	14th	485	5
6th	565	5	15th	460	4
7th	386	4	16th	243	3
8th	163	3	17th	458	4
9th	475	4	18th	525	5
	3624	36		3628	36
				3624	36
				7252	72

The links had seen golfers at least since 1560, while the first great Scottish professional, Allan Robertson, had laid out 10 holes in the middle of the nineteenth century, with Old Tom Morris bringing the total to 18 in 1867. James Braid 'modernized' the course in 1926 and James Wright made further changes after Carnoustie's first Open in 1931 in time for the 1937 event. In recent times, the only significant change has been to make the last hole a very testing long par-4.

With the final day's 36 holes to play, this was the position:

142 Rees, Brown; 143 de Vicenzo; 144 Hogan, Stranahan, Thomson; 145 Locke

Rees had equalled the course record with his 70, a round made by his brilliant 3, 3 finish – a birdie followed by an eagle at two of the most daunting holes in golf. Eric Brown continued to carry Scottish hopes with his second 71, while many thought that Roberto de Vicenzo was long overdue for an Open victory. Hogan had played steadily for his 71. Unsmiling, intense, gaunt and clad in sombre greys; he had moved up the field. I was pleased with my 147 total, while the 17-year-old Geoff Hunt (younger brother of Bernard) was delighted to qualify for the last day, well within the final qualifying aggregate of 154. Equally well outside that target was the Vicomte de St Sauveur, who had followed an opening 93 with a slightly improved 87!

On the final morning, Dai Rees again performed well, having 4s on the first twelve holes (one shot dropped on the par-3, with birdies at the par-5s to compensate. He then had his first 3 but his finish of 4, 5, 4 meant that he had fallen away to a 73. Tony Cerda set a new course record with his 69, while Hogan had looked likely to return the same score. He began with three pars before dropping shots on both 4th and 5th but then had birdies on the par-5 6th and a 3 on the 7th. More birdies followed and, after he had passed the test of holding the domed green of the 243-yard 16th, he was four under par. Hogan then hit the first bad shot of the round and perhaps his worst in the championship through the green. He half-thinned his 4-wood second shot to the 17th into a bunker, came out well short of the hole and three-putted for a 6. A birdie 4 at the last improved matters, so he was round in 70.

Hogan was followed by a horde of thousands who wanted to seize the chance of watching the great American, and Locke by a smaller and more reverent congregation. Perhaps it was the crowds that produced the highly unusual sight of the slow progress of Bobby Locke being held up by Hogan's match.

At the end of the third round, Hogan had moved into the joint lead and this is how they stood:

214 Hogan, de Vicenzo; 215 Thomson, Cerda, Rees; 217 Stranahan, Brown; 218 Faulkner, Fairbairn; 219 Daly, King, Locke

De Vicenzo, in fact, was no longer a real threat. Years later he told how he had convinced himself in the break between rounds that he had no real chance – his putting was bound to break down under the stress of a tight finish. Though the most prolific tournament-winner in all golf history, Roberto lacked inner arrogance and was always prey to doubts.

Frank Stranahan was the first to set a target. His outward half in 37 was no threat but he finished very strongly, single-putting the last six greens, including the last from 14 yards, for an eagle 3 and a total of 286. This was also achieved by Dai Rees, whose 71 was marred by shots dropped on the 15th and 16th, only partly redeemed by a birdie on the final hole.

Hogan began with four pars and at the 389-yard 5th found his drive in a poor fairway lie. He put his second shot at the edge of a bunker in a horrid sandy lie with a poor stance. From there he chipped in. For the first time he was the outright leader. Encouraged, perhaps, he hit two huge woods to the par-5 6th and two-putted for another birdie. He went on to reach the turn in 34 and it was now becoming apparent that all he needed to win was par golf.

Ahead of him, Thomson was playing well but was unlikely to set a target much lower than the 286 of Stranahan and Rees. Further back in the field, only Tony Cerda posed any kind of threat. Hogan set out for home with three pars and then had a 2 on the short 13th. Soon there was only the barrier of the formidable 'long' short 16th, the menace of the Barry Burn on the 17th and the out of bounds on the last hole. Hogan passed through with pars and completed his round with a birdie on the 18th and a round of 68, a new record. Some of the field had still to complete but Hogan had won the championship in classic style with four good rounds, each one better than the one before.

In the history of the Open, no golfer except Arnold Palmer in 1960 has made so great an impact on press and public at a first appearance. Here are some comments made about Hogan at the time.

'His game has that stamp of inevitability which is only to be found among a handful of players.'
'In the one class Hogan and in the other class all the other golfers.'
'That small colossus bestrode and dominated the tournament.'
'Everyone with any knowledge of golf came back overawed and abashed by the splendour of his game.'

Of his technique, many noted one striking difference between him and other players. The right hand and arm thrust through the ball and kept the clubhead low along the ground far beyond the time when others would have begun to lift up and away. 'The long right arm through the ball' had arrived in Britain.

His victory raised Hogan's total of major championship victories to nine and gave him the distinction he still retains of being the only man to win three of the four professional titles in a single year. This still is the only achievement to equal (some might say surpass) Bobby Jones's slam of the Open and Amateur titles both sides of the Atlantic in one year, 1930.

On 10 July 1953 he seemed unbeatable and, despite his forty years, destined for many more great achievements. However, 'the Wee Ice Mon', as the Scots had named him, approached victory in a major championship many times in the next few years but was not destined to win another. In his victory speech at Carnoustie he promised 'I'll be back,' but this was his only entry and the first time a golfer had won at his first attempt (since achieved by Tony Lema and Tom Watson).

Ben Hogan played just once again in Britain when he paired with Sam Snead at Wentworth to win the Canada Cup for the United States. Inevitably, it seemed, Hogan took the individual title.

HOW THEY FINISHED

B. W. Hogan *USA*	**73**	**71**	**70**	**68**	**282**
Mr F. R. Stranahan *USA*	70	74	73	69	286
A. Cerda *Argentina*	75	71	69	71	
P. W. Thomson *Australia*	72	72	71	71	
D. J. Rees	72	70	73	71	
R. de Vicenzo *Argentina*	72	71	71	73	287
S. L. King	74	73	72	71	290
A. D. Locke *South Africa*	72	73	74	72	291
Peter Alliss	75	72	74	71	292
E. C. Brown	71	71	75	75	
F. Daly	73	75	71	75	294
M. Faulkner	74	71	73	77	295
A. Lees	76	76	72	72	296
H. Weetman	80	73	72	72	297
J. R. M. Jacobs	79	74	71	73	
T. H. T. Fairbairn	74	71	73	79	
E. Lester	83	70	72	73	298
C. H. Ward	78	71	76	73	
H. Hassanein *Egypt*	78	71	73	76	
F. van Donck *Belgium*	77	71	78	73	299
R. W. Horne	76	74	75	74	
S. S. Scott	74	74	78	74	300
H. Thomson	76	74	74	76	
R. A. Knight	74	79	74	74	301
C. O'Connor	77	77	72	75	
L. Mangrum *USA*	75	76	74	76	

J. Panton	79	74	76	73	302
U. Grappasonni *Italy*	77	75	72	78	
A. Poulton	75	77	75	76	303
T. B. Haliburton	75	76	76	76	
R. Ferguson	77	75	74	77	
N. Sutton	76	72	76	79	
J. Hargreaves	81	73	76	74	304
K. Bousfield	78	76	79	72	305
J. H. Ballingall	80	74	77	74	
B. J. Hunt	79	74	77	75	
E. E. Whitcombe	76	78	73	78	
R. G. French	79	71	77	79	306
R. P. Mills	80	73	72	81	
J. B. Ado *France*	75	77	75	81	308
W. Shankland	78	76	78	79	311
G. Knight	75	78	81	78	312
L. Topping	77	73	81	81	
J. R. Moses	81	73	76	82	
W. J. Henderson	78	74	80	81	313
G. M. Hunt	74	74	79	86	
R. Burton	80	74	80	80	314
G. W. McIntosh	78	75	80	81	
J. Burton	75	77	87	78	317

·4·

Thomson Dominates

Royal Birkdale, 1954

In his first three championship entries, the young Australian Peter Thomson had much impressed by the composure of his play. His results had been highly impressive: 6th, 2nd, 2nd. Now, however, he was to move to centre stage and remain there for a period unparalleled in the international years of the Open Championship, until the advent of Tom Watson.

In 1954, the Open came to Royal Birkdale for the first time. Though it had been scheduled there for 1940, Adolf Hitler's personal plans had disrupted the arrangements. The qualifying rounds were held on the championship course and neighbouring Hillside, scene of the 1982 PGA Championship. British golfers who believed with Henry Cotton that plenty of good red meat in the diet was essential to sporting success could have no excuse now for failure. It was off the ration.

The favourite, however, was again Bobby Locke, and the American challenge featured Jimmy Demaret and Jim Turnesa. The latter had blighted my life the previous year by beating me in a Ryder Cup singles that I ought to have won, in a competition which the USA should have lost. Stranahan was again in attendance, perhaps by now a little past his best, though he had reached the last sixteen in the Amateur Championship at Muirfield. So also was a great name from the past, Al Watrous, who had so narrowly lost to Bobby Jones at Royal Lytham in 1926. Gene Sarazen had come again and had just before beaten my father to be the first World Senior Champion at Southport and Ainsdale. Asked why he had entered the Open, he replied tersely: 'To play golf, I guess.' The name of Peter Alliss was also in the listings, and I was particularly hopeful that year, with two sound performances behind me in the championship.

Again, Norman von Nida shone in the qualifying stages. His 70 at Birkdale equalled the record and he followed up with a 67 at Hillside. His 137 led those who had qualified at 151 or better by four from Frank Stranahan, Gene Sarazen and Peter Mills. Tony Harman had a 69 to beat the course record but faded out when the championship proper began.

That new record was equalled by the first-day leaders, Bill Spence, a beautiful striker who did not fulfil his potential, and Sam King, who, though well into his forties, still continued to make an impact almost every year. Norman Sutton followed on 70, John Jacobs, George Howard and Tony Cerda followed with 71s and there was a group on 72, which included Thomson, Turnesa, Rees and Peter Alliss, described as 'growing daily more powerful in appearance'. Perhaps it was all that red meat I was stuffing down.

The next day, Bill Spence, who had played no competitive golf for some time and was truly a club professional, still clung to the lead, but it was Syd Scott who stole more headlines. Underpowered, he was an excellent pitcher and putter and, having single-putted seven greens, broke the course record and played comfortably the lowest round of the championship, a 67. After an opening 76, this pulled him into third place with Thomson, Rees and King, one behind Tony Cerda's 142. At this point the Alliss threat lurked five behind the lead after some troubles on the 10th from which I escaped without hurt. I hooked my tee-shot well off-line into the willow scrub famous at Royal Birkdale, sent my second into a bush by the green and my third into a bunker. Full of woe, I then whacked it out – and into the hole. 'That', I thought, 'is how championships are won.'

A sad note to the day was that Henry Cotton, troubled by a sprained side, failed to make the qualifying mark of 151 for the final 36 holes. The American challenge still held up, with both Demaret and Turnesa on 144, and Locke, after 74 and 71, was still well in the hunt for his fourth championship.

On the final day Syd Scott, like Spence not a tournament regular, was out early and, having reached the turn in 33, finished with a 69 to set the target of 212. He was later joined by Dai Rees, who had now had the descending rounds of 72, 71, 69, as had Peter Thomson. Was one of them about to emulate Hogan with an even better fourth round? The Australian's scoring was being made by excellence through the green rather than putting. At the time, Thomson's putting was not highly rated, its main merit being that he was seldom short of the hole. In his third-round 69 he holed nothing longer than 7 foot – not normally the way to win a championship. Thomson did not use a driver throughout, preferring a 3-wood to keep the ball in play. This was in keeping with his simple philosophy of golf: hit it from tee to fairway, then to the green in the right number and never three-putt. Much easier said than done.

Bobby Locke was still in the hunt, also with a 69, which put him two strokes behind the leaders. His shot to the last green had particularly impressed the spectators, a high, curling right-to-lefter to a couple of feet. Spence and Turnesa followed a stroke behind with Tony Cerda, prominent for several years in the early 1950s. I felt that I was still in with a chance on 217, with Harry Bradshaw and Sam King but I knew I needed a strong last round with a few more putts dropping.

Syd Scott, an occasional competitor at that time, held together over the final

18 holes. His 72 set a good target at 284 and could easily have been a couple of strokes better. On the 13th, from no great distance, his first putt was at least 3 yards too strong and he missed the return. On the 17th he hit the hole from the same distance and it spun out.

Readers may remember Dai Rees's disastrous 7 at the 1st at St Andrews in 1946. Indeed, he was often a nervous starter and in this Birkdale championship did not once play the 1st with any sort of authority. However, in his final round he did manage a par 5 and reached the turn in 36. This meant that he had to be back in 35 to beat Scott. In fact he came to the last few holes needing a 5, 3, 4 finish (the 17th was then a par 3). He managed the first two, helped by a chip dead on the 17th, and then sent his second shot at the last through the green but still not many yards from the hole. If he got down in two he had a chance of winning or at worst would set a new target at 283. He chipped about 6 feet short and missed his putt. Both Rees and Scott were in on 284.

This left Peter Thomson with 71 to win. He reached the turn in 35, as calm and sunny-faced as ever. He then had a spell of relatively poor iron shots to the

Peter Thomson's first Open Championship victory, Royal Birkdale, 1954.

green but retrieved his pars with inspired long putting and nerveless holing-out. He did, however, miss a short one at the 12th. He made up for this on the 14th with a good long putt and then, bunkered on the 16th, came out to little more than a foot. He needed to par the 17th, some 180 yards, and get a 4 on the last, some 470 yards, to win by two strokes.

Thomson got his 3 without any trouble, was bunkered by the green in two at the 18th but came out well. He missed his first putt narrowly, and then, with all the confidence in the world (foolhardy some thought him), leaned over the hole on one leg and tapped his ball in backhanded with his simple blade putter.

So the target was now 283, the championship still far from over but the money heavily on Thomson. Jim Turnesa reached the position of three under 4s with five holes to play but faltered. His eventual 71 left him three strokes adrift.

Still playing, almost last in the field and the ante-post favourite, was Bobby Locke, who did little for his chances by uncharacteristically three-putting two greens consecutively. He came to the last needing a 3 to tie, by no means impossible, for weren't there still memories of that wood to a foot or so in the morning's round? This time, Locke was some 15 yards away, and rolled his putt up. It was dead on line – but a foot short.

Peter Thomson had become the first Australian to win the Open. Only one other, Jim Ferrier, had previously won any of the four major championships when he beat Chick Harbert in the final of the 1947 US PGA Matchplay Championship.

It had been by far my best Open to date. Though finishing 'only' 8th, this was just four strokes behind the winner's total and I was pleased with my final round of 70. If only I could have produced putting to match my play through the green. . . . However, as someone wrote at the time, 'His turn will come.' Sadly it didn't.

HOW THEY FINISHED

P. W. Thomson *Australia*	**72**	**71**	**69**	**71**	**283**
A. D. Locke *South Africa*	74	71	69	70	284
S. S. Scott	76	67	69	72	
D. J. Rees	72	71	69	72	
J. Adams	73	75	69	69	286
J. Turnesa *USA*	72	72	71	71	
A. Cerda *Argentina*	71	71	73	71	
Peter Alliss	72	74	71	70	287
S. L. King	69	74	74	70	
F. van Donck *Belgium*	77	71	70	71	289
J. Demaret *USA*	73	71	74	71	
A. Angelini *Italy*	76	70	73	71	290
H. Bradshaw	72	72	73	73	
T. W. Spence	69	72	74	75	
R. Halsall	72	73	73	73	291
Mr P. Toogood *Australia*	72	75	73	71	
G. Sarazen *USA*	75	74	73	70	292
U. Grappasonni *Italy*	72	75	74	71	
C. Kane	74	72	74	72	
J. Hargreaves	77	72	77	67	293
J. R. M. Jacobs	71	73	80	69	
N. V. Drew	76	71	74	72	
L. Topping	75	76	69	73	
M. Faulkner	73	78	69	73	
E. Lester	72	75	73	73	
C. O'Connor	74	72	72	75	

E. B. Williamson *Holland*	76	73	75	70	294
N. Sutton	70	80	72	72	
B. Shelton	74	77	71	73	295
J. Hitchcock	73	72	76	74	
Mr F. R. Stranahan *USA*	73	75	71	76	
T. Travena *South Africa*	75	74	75	72	296
J. Garaialde *France*	76	73	72	75	
R. P. Mills	73	76	70	77	
N. G. von Nida *Australia*	76	74	74	73	297
W. J. Branch	73	78	71	75	
F. Daly	74	72	74	77	
J. B. Ado *France*	72	78	76	72	298
E. Bertolino *Argentina*	74	76	74	74	
A. Casera *Italy*	75	73	72	78	
W. Shankland	72	72	79	76	299
A. Watrous *USA*	76	72	74	78	300
W. J. Henderson	74	72	76	78	
C. S. Denny	74	77	79	71	301
R. G. French	75	75	77	75	302
G. Howard	71	77	74	80	
F. Jowle	80	70	79	75	304
F. Bullock	72	77	77	78	
H. Thomson	76	75	74	79	
R. M. Mandeville	74	73	78	79	

St Andrews, 1955

It is often said that during Thomson's greatest years there was no American challenge. Yet a brief glance at the records immediately shows that this is untrue. At St Andrews in 1955, there was George Fazio, good enough to have tied with Hogan and Mangrum for the 1950 US Open before losing the play-off; Ed Furgol, US Open Champion in 1954; and Byron Nelson. Some would contend that Byron is the greatest player ever. His peak was from 1944 until his partial retirement in 1946, a period in which he established the greatest winning sequence ever in US tournaments, winning a total of eighteen in 1945, including eleven consecutively. Nelson had also won the US Open, PGA and Masters and would inevitably have added to his total of four major championships had he not retired in his early thirties. He still competed when the spirit moved him, however, had won the 1951 Crosby and was to take the French Open convincingly shortly after this Open.

But it was Thomson who started favourite. No less a judge than Bernard Darwin said of him: 'It is impossible to imagine a better temperament, marked by unruffled composure, courage and commonsense.' Of me, he wrote in assessing the chances of leading players: 'If one hesitates over Alliss it is because he has not yet made his peace with the Old Course and it is an implacable enemy.'

Alas, the remarks were prophetic. I began in the qualifying round with a 67 on the New course, followed by a 79 on the championship course – but I qualified with a couple of strokes to spare. In the championship proper, I began with a 78 – not good at all – and, though I improved to a 73 at my third attempt, my two-round total was not good enough to qualify for the final day. I did eventually 'make my peace' but that is a story for later.

As at the start of the 1970 St Andrews Open, the course was unguarded by wind, this time, however, for every day of the championship. The results were evident during the qualifying rounds. Frank Jowle, for instance, an excellent Yorkshire player who deserved Ryder Cup honours but who was never selected, opened up on the New with six 3s in succession, which included driving the 1st hole, 328 yards, and eagling the 500-yard 3rd. He finished in 63, which broke that course's previous record by no fewer than six strokes. Charlie Ward was not far behind with a 65, while Irish amateur Joe Carr, Harry Weetman and I were amongst those whose 67s were below the previous record.

At the end of the second day, Jowle led those who had qualified on 135, followed by Laurie Ayton, 136, and Harry Weetman, 138. Thomson had played two very consistent rounds of 69 on the Old and 70 on the New. George Fazio had failed to meet the rather low 148 qualifying mark but those who followed Thomson most closely in the betting – Tony Cerda, Byron Nelson and Ed Furgol – were all safely through.

In the first round proper, Syd Scott, Dai Rees and Eric Brown continued their good spells in the Open and jointly led with 69s, followed on 70 by Cecil Denny, Denis Smalldon (later to die in a road accident), Bernard Hunt, Jowle, Jimmy Martin of the magical putting and . . . Henry Cotton. By then aged 48, Henry had been paired with Thomson and showed much of his old magic, getting home in one stroke fewer than the Australian, who had missed chance after chance on the greens. Furgol was among those on 71 and Byron Nelson was a stroke more, a total shared by a name to become famous at St Andrews a few years later – Kel Nagle. Nagle made few forays at this time from his native Australia and was very unsure of his abilities. Eventually it was Peter Thomson who convinced him that he was a very good player indeed. There was another oddity about Kel Nagle's career. He had come to the fore as a long, often wild, hitter who could do little right on the greens. He then apparently disappeared from the tournament scene to reappear both a better golfer and a very different one. Kel was now a fairly short hitter but almost error-free, while on the greens he was as solid as a rock, a highly unusual transformation. He never told us how he managed to do it.

On the second day, the lead was shared by Smalldon, Eric Brown and Peter Thomson. Smalldon and Thomson had moved up with 69s and Brown had held steady with a 70. The roars of the Scots echoed round as their men kept going. The round of the day, however, and what was to prove the lowest of the championship, came from an Anglo-Scot and lover of St Andrews, Johnny Fallon, with a 67, made by an inward half in 31. It pulled him up to second position on 140 and there were, in the fairly easy conditions, hosts of other players within a few shots of the leaders. The question most heard from the spectators (no giant scoreboards in those days) was 'How is Henry doing?' With a 72, 'Very nicely thank you', might have been the reply. One oddity to be observed on course was Johnny Bulla, playing his seventh Open. A right-handed golfer, Johnny was to a high degree ambidextrous and at this time was quite often choosing to putt left-handed, the first man I recall seeing do this. Indeed it is a rare sight, though one of the best current Canadians, Jim Nelford, who had a good US season in 1983, also does it. It must have worked well enough for Bulla that day, for he finished with three 3s, for once thoroughly mastering the Road Hole, which had caused him much grief in 1946.

Thomson had played with all the composure for which he was becoming famous. He smiled his way through the tensions of an Open Championship, 'unmoved', it was said, 'by the prospects of either victory or defeat'. On the surface, that is, for the writer knew that 'underneath he minds tremendously'. He had nothing much to mind about that day. He was out in 33 and after the 12th had had five 3s in six holes. His final total of 69 was perhaps mildly disappointing, especially as he had taken 31 putts, as opposed to his 35 the previous day.

Sam King putts across the road at the 17th at St Andrews, 1955.

Peter had struck up a very good partnership with his caddie, Wallace Gillespie, though there had been difficulties early in the relationship. With so many blind tee-shots on the Old course, it is more necessary than usual to have a man with local knowledge to have him point out the exact line on a tee-shot. This might be: 'On yon church spire to the right' or 'On the right-hand corner of the aircraft hangar.' For one drive, Gillespie gave Thomson a line which the champion followed with geometric precision. However, when they got to the ball, it lay only a yard or so from some bunkers. Thomson pointed out that he was using golf clubs not a rifle and couldn't keep this standard up. Gillespie's reply is difficult to fault: 'Well, after all you *are* the Open Champion!'

This 7 July was a highly important day for golf and the Open in particular, being the occasion of the first live TV transmissions. Television was a great force in the development of golf for both the US Tour and in Europe, and especially helped the Open to become an international event as coverage went out to the USA and Canada, Australia and New Zealand, and Japan.

There was another first this year, as the prize money for the winner reached the dizzy heights of £1000, but let us also remember that the money for winning, much though it may be stressed in the press and on TV, matters very little. The prestige of being Open Champion counts for far more: Henry Cotton, when the first prize was worth £100, said that he would willingly have paid £10,000 to be champion. The winner commands the highest exhibition fees, is likely to be asked to design golf courses, endorse clubs, and attend functions of all kinds. In more recent years, income from advertising products unconnected with golf has soared, and continues to do so. Looking back, commercialism was still very much in its raw stages then.

But back to the golf. After the morning round, the man who had returned a 63 over the New course in qualifying, Frank Jowle, was again prominent, as his 69 pulled him up the field to second place on 210, two clear of Eric Brown, Harry Weetman and John Jacobs (just beginning to emerge, with his slow, wide, slightly artificial swing, allied to excellent putting). Locke and Johnny Fallon were on 213, Flory van Donck on 214 and Tony Cerda, Bernard Hunt and Barbieri of Argentina on 215.

Leading them all, many thought inevitably, was Peter Thomson on 209, his reliable driving and excellent iron play arousing much admiration. In the afternoon, several of his closest pursuers mounted no sort of challenge. John Jacobs, for instance, took 76 to fall well down the field, as did Eric Brown. Jowle and Weetman had 74s. In general, as a look at our final scores will illustrate, it was those who had little chance with 18 holes to go who put in the best last rounds, rounds that could pull them up the field but from too far back to win. Fears of winning behind them, they swung more freely.

The scores alone do not, however, bring out all the drama of the final afternoon. O'Connor, for example, starting at 216, seven behind Thomson, was six under 4s at one point but fell away on the closing holes to finish in 71. Johnny Fallon was even more the man who could have won – if he had kept a superb score going. He went to the turn in 31, which included a 5-foot putt missed on the 9th, but began to falter. His troubles began on the par-3 11th, where he put his tee-shot into Strath bunker and took two to get out. (This, incidentally, was the bunker in which the only amateur to qualify for the last day, Melville Bucher of Elie, had perished in the morning. It had, it was recorded, 'detained him for half a dozen strokes or so' and a 10 was the result.) People began to recall that Fallon had taken Thomson to 38 holes before the Australian won the final of the previous year's PGA Matchplay Championship. Could Fallon take his revenge in this year's Open? But Fallon, though the weather was calm, took 39 strokes on the homeward half. His 70 was a good score, but it never looked quite good enough.

Thomson set out knowing that he needed 73 to win. Immediately he lightened his task with a birdie on the 1st and, despite a 6 on the long 5th hole, reached the turn in 35. He then picked up shots at the far end of the course and was three under 4s for his round, as he stood on the 14th tee. He then hooked

61

into the Beardies bunkers and sent his third stroke into one of the Graves bunkers short of the par-5 14th green. He had to play out sideways and took 7, the same result Ed Furgol had twice achieved on this hole. But, as champions tend to do, he repaired much of the damage by sinking a 3-yard putt for a birdie on the very next hole.

That was just about that. He completed his round with no further alarms for a 72 and a two-stroke victory. His 281 total beat the St Andrews Open record, which had stood at 285 since Bobby Jones won after spreadeagling the field with an opening 68 in 1927. With Jones, Locke, James Braid and Walter Hagen, he was one of the select few who have won consecutive Opens this century. In both of Thomson's years so far, there had been a strong international challenge and, on paper, formidable American opposition. Two overseas players I particularly remember from that year are Hassan Hassanein, from Gezira in Egypt, one of the blackest and most charming men I have ever met. He had a most beautiful swing and a hand action without equal. Tragically, he met a bizarre death later, blown up by a little cooking stove.

The other is a vignette of Ed Furgol, who the young Alliss, still slightly overawed in the famed clubhouses of British golf, heard coming in after a round at St Andrews that year, shouting 'Locker! Locker!' This was normal American practice on entering a plush country club locker room. It seemed that Ed wanted a drink and a shower. He was told by the steward that drinks were not served in the locker room at St Andrews and there were no showers: 'This is the Royal and Ancient Golf Club of St Andrews, Sir.' Ed commented that he wanted more of the new and less of the ancient, particularly as regards shower arrangements. The snub that followed was one I shall never forget: 'Their Lordships always repair to their castles when they wish to bathe, Sir.'

HOW THEY FINISHED

P. W. Thomson *Australia*	**71**	**68**	**70**	**72**	**281**	D. J. Rees	69	79	73	73	294
						H. Hassanein *Egypt*	73	72	76	73	
J. Fallon	73	67	73	70	283	N. Sutton	71	74	75	74	
F. Jowle	70	71	69	74	284	J. Martin	70	72	79	74	295
						Mr J. B. McHale *USA*	72	76	72	75	
A. D. Locke *South Africa*	74	69	70	72	285						
						B. Nelson *USA*	72	75	78	71	296
K. Bousfield	71	75	70	70	286	T. B. Haliburton	75	72	73	76	
A. Cerda *Argentina*	73	71	71	71		T. H. Cotton	70	72	78	76	
B. J. Hunt	70	71	74	71							
F. van Donck *Belgium*	71	72	71	72		J. Burton	75	73	75	74	297
H. Weetman	71	71	70	74		M. Faulkner	73	74	74	76	
C. O'Connor	71	75	70	71	287	C. C. Potente *Spain*	73	75	76	74	298
R. Barbieri *Argentina*	71	71	73	72		W. Shankland	73	74	77	74	
						B. Wilkes *South Africa*	75	73	74	76	
F. Daly	75	72	70	71	288	J. G. Bulla *USA*	75	70	73	80	
J. R. M. Jacobs	71	70	71	76							
E. C. Brown	69	70	73	76		K. Beckett	74	74	76	75	299
						U. Grappasonni *Italy*	72	72	77	78	
J. S. Anderson	71	72	77	69	289	C. Kane	73	71	76	79	
W. J. Henderson	74	71	72	72							
						G. A. Farmer *South Africa*	73	73	79	75	300
A. Sotto *Argentina*	72	73	72	73	290						
D. F. Smalldon	70	69	78	73		K. G. Geddes	74	74	77	76	301
						C. S. Denny	70	76	76	79	
E. Furgol *USA*	71	76	72	73	292						
S. S. Scott	69	77	73	73		T. H. T. Fairbairn	73	74	79	76	302
K. D. G. Nagle *Australia*	72	72	74	74							
						G. Howard	73	74	79	78	304
Lt J. W. Conrad *USA*	72	76	74	71	293						
R. W. Horne	72	75	75	71		Mr A. M. M. Bucher	72	74	85	80	311
R. Halsall	71	74	76	72							
W. J. Branch	75	72	73	73							
H. Bradshaw	72	70	73	78							

Hoylake, 1956

The Hoylake Open of 1956 saw a particularly international field assembled. Excluding Europe, there were entries from the USA, Canada, the Philippines, Japan, Argentina, Formosa, South Africa, Australia, Brazil, Mexico and Chile, mainly a result of playing the Canada Cup at Wentworth not long before.

Though Thomson was the favourite, there were doubts about him. He was not in form, and had just gone round Wentworth in 82 during the Canada Cup, won by Hogan and Snead. Nevertheless, there was no general decline in his powers and his putting had improved. The question asked by most was whether he could become the first player since Bob Ferguson in 1882 to win the championship three times in a row. It had never been done over 72 holes and the maximum field in Ferguson's years had been 46. Thomson faced 360 attempting to qualify, with around 100 likely to get into the championship proper. If he could win, it was obvious that the feat would be without parallel.

This Open was to be the first significant appearance of a certain young South African, Gary Player, who had caused great surprise by winning the Dunlop Tournament at Sunningdale earlier that season. At the time he was a crude golfer with an excessively flat swing and a bad grip. I recognized his almost agonized will to win, something I never possessed, but felt quite simply that he had no real feel for the game of golf. Desire is vital but at the time I, and most of my contemporaries, felt that he simply did not have the ability to reach the top. I remember Gary earnestly questioning another professional about his future prospects and being told, with perhaps unkind Yorkshire bluntness, to 'Go home, lad, get an honest job and play golf just for fun!'

However, Gary showed his mettle in the qualifying rounds by starting with a 68 and sharing the position of leading qualifier on 140 with the inevitable Peter Thomson, apparently recovered from his Wentworth troubles. Following on 141 was the evergreen Henry Cotton, aged 49 and in his 33rd season as a professional, declaring that he had turned up just for the fun of playing. Still, I'm sure he would not have minded a fourth title at all and the distinction of being easily the oldest man to win. Sharing the same mark were Angel Miguel from Spain, Flory van Donck and George Howard from Malden. On 142 were Bruce Crampton from Australia, the future Iron Man of the US Tour, who won his national Open title that year, Syd Scott, Christy O'Connor and John Jacobs.

The 1951 champion, Max Faulkner, failed to qualify, as did Norman von Nida and a certain Liang Huan Lu, later to occupy the centre of the stage as 'Mr Lu' so many years later in the 1971 Open. Although he had a fine 67, there was a well-nigh unbelievable 89 to go with it, 22 strokes difference in 24 hours!

In the first round proper, Denis Smalldon, as in the previous year, opened up well to lead with a 68 (despite finishing with three 5s), which equalled the Hoylake record. Enrico Bertolino from Argentina was a stroke behind and on

A very young Gary Player, Hoylake, 1956.

70 were Eric Lester, Thomson, the tall Canadian Al Balding, an impressive striker, and a new name, 21-year-old David Thomas, who had begun to prove his promise by winning the British Assistants' Championship and the Belgian Open the previous year. They were followed on 71 by Player, van Donck, de Vicenzo, who hadn't entered since 1953, Angel Miguel and Carlos Celles. (People think the rise of Spanish golf should be dated from the early 1970s. The mid-1950s is the period that saw their first impact.)

Already, Bobby Locke was virtually out of it with a 76 which included an 8 on the 3rd, when he took three to escape from a bunker. So was I, having gone round in 78, putting poorly and having one out of bounds on the 7th, that frightening par-3 of 200 yards with an out of bounds a stride or so left of the green. Cotton was on 72, full of confidence, having recently led the sectional qualifying for the US Open.

The luck of the draw was vital the second day. The weather was windy with torrential sheeting rain in the morning, some of the worst I can remember. I was paired with Bobby Locke and can vividly recall his entering the locker room, and with deadpan face upending his bag to produce several pints of water. A look at the final scores will reveal the effect of the weather, with so many rounds higher than the previous day. Both Bobby and I failed to make the 152 qualifying mark. By late afternoon, the weather was fine with just a brisk wind and Peter Thomson was one of those who benefited, cruising round in 70 for a one-stroke lead. Two Argentines were a stroke behind, de Vicenzo and Bertolino, and these three had opened up a crucial gap on Angel Miguel and Flory van Donck on 145.

De Vicenzo, however, almost immediately put himself out of contention on the final morning. On the par-4 1st, fearsome with that out of bounds along the right, he took three to reach the green and then, from no great distance at all, took three putts. Another 6 followed on the 3rd and Roberto eventually struggled in with a 79. Future events were to show that a 70 in this round would probably have seen him home by a street.

Of the contenders, only the Belgian van Donck, with a 70, seemed to pose any threat to Thomson when all had completed the third round, having pulled up to three strokes behind the Australian. This is how they stood (though it must be remembered that the players off first in the last round went out before many in the field had completed their third round):

212 Thomson; 215 van Donck; 217 Bertolino; 219 Cotton; 220 de Vicenzo, Player, Stranahan, Miguel; 221 Cerda; 222 Panton, Souchak

The last of these, Mike Souchak, a massively powerful player, was the best American in the field in 1956 and in 1955 had set the US Tour record (which still stands) of 257 for 72 holes. He had a 60 in the first round, playing the second nine in 27!

Van Donck's chance of catching Thomson did not last long. He began by cutting his second shot to the 1st hole out of bounds into the practice grounds. He managed a 6, holing a testing putt to avoid worse. He put in a fine finish in one under par over the testing last five holes (which another Hoylake champion, Bobby Jones in 1930, called the 'toughest finish in championship golf').

Thomson, with van Donck round in 74, therefore needed a 76 to win. He dropped a few shots early on and disasters from the numerous out of bounds at Hoylake are always possible, but the serenely confident Thomson, a pure straight hitter, was the least likely competitor to find them. At first, however he looked likely to reach the turn in 39. The championship might then have slipped from his hands but Peter had the rare ability to put dropped strokes out of his mind. He got to the turn in 37 and had the same score on the second half.

Thomson was the first man this century (and still, of course, the only one) to win Opens in three successive years, and one of the few to win three. Taylor, Vardon, Braid, Hagen, Jones, Cotton and Locke were the others at that time. As Flory van Donck gracefully said at the presentation: 'Peter was head and shoulders above the rest of the field.'

HOW THEY FINISHED

P. W. Thomson *Australia*	**70**	**70**	**72**	**74**	**286**	L. B. Ayton	74	78	78	72	302
						E. Moore *South Africa*	75	75	78	74	
F. van Donck *Belgium*	71	74	70	74	289	J. Adams	75	76	76	75	
R. de Vicenzo *Mexico*	71	70	79	70	290	K. W. C. Adwick	77	76	74	76	303
						S. S. Scott	78	74	74	77	
G. J. Player *South Africa*	71	76	73	71	291	D. F. Smalldon	68	79	78	78	
J. Panton	74	76	72	70	292	A. Angelini *Italy*	73	80	76	75	304
						B. J. Hunt	75	73	81	75	
T. H. Cotton	72	76	71	74	293						
E. Bertolino *Argentina*	69	72	76	76		C. P. Chen *Formosa*	78	74	77	76	305
						A. Salas *Chile*	79	72	78	76	
M. Souchak *USA*	74	74	74	72	294	M. Gonzales *Brazil*	72	81	75	77	
A. Cerda *Argentina*	72	81	68	73							
						Mr J. B. Carr	73	77	79	77	306
C. O'Connor	73	78	74	70	295	C. Greene	76	75	79	76	
H. Weetman	72	76	75	72		M. Ishii *Japan*	74	77	77	78	
						J. Martin	74	79	78	75	
F. R. Stranahan *USA*	72	76	72	76	296						
						S. Miguel *Spain*	72	78	84	73	307
B. Crampton *Australia*	76	77	72	72	297	C. Celles *Spain*	71	82	78	76	
D. J. Rees	75	74	75	73		W. Shankland	72	78	79	78	
A. Miguel *Spain*	71	74	75	77							
						F. E. Miller	72	78	78	80	308
J. R. M. Jacobs	73	77	76	72	298	H. Bradshaw	76	76	81	75	
						T. H. T. Fairbairn	80	73	81	74	
J. Hargreaves	72	80	75	73	300						
A. Balding *Canada*	70	81	76	73		T. Wilkes *South Africa*	74	78	85	75	312
C. H. Ward	73	75	78	74							
D. C. Thomas	70	78	77	75		J. M. Wilkshire	77	74	85	77	313
R. Rossi *Argentina*	75	77	72	76							
K. Bousfield	73	77	76	75	301						
G. de Wit *Holland*	76	73	74	78							
E. G. Lester	70	76	77	78							

Dr Cary Middlecoff, the main American threat at St Andrews in 1957.

St Andrews, 1957

In 1957, the Open was scheduled for Muirfield but the venue was changed to St Andrews, after a gap of only two years, because of the petrol rationing which followed the Anglo–French invasion of Egypt. Thomson was again the favourite, his game sharpened by a spell on the US Tour, and he was also fresh from having won the *Yorkshire Evening News* tournament by a mile at Sand Moor near Leeds. Locke, generally thought to be past his best, had nevertheless shown revived form by having been placed 1st, 5th and equal 1st in his last three tournaments. His putting, however, had lost some of its potency. Locke had a long backswing and little follow-through but when not at his best there was even more head and body movement.

His fellow South African Gary Player was again present, hoping to improve on his 4th place at Hoylake, though doubts were expressed as to whether he would last much longer as an effective golfer because of the continuing flatness of his backswing. Roberto de Vicenzo was not entered this year but seemed to have sent a substitute, his brother Osvaldo. During the practice days, most attention was on the main 'American threat', Cary Middlecoff, winner of the US Open in 1949 and 1956 and the Masters in 1955, who had just lost a play-off for the US Open to Dick Mayer. Because of Middlecoff's slow play, Mayer had made the gesture of taking out a camp stool to sit on while Middlecoff went about his laborious preparations. Perhaps unsettled by this ploy, Middlecoff had taken 79! Much of the slowness was caused by Middlecoff's meticulous care in aligning himself but, alas, once he had set up the machine, there were many glances at the target before he sent his ball away, a habit most noticeable in Hubert Green in recent years.

I remember Middlecoff as having an ungainly swing, made less aesthetic by a pronounced pause – even as long as a second – at the top of the backswing. However, he was a superb striker and was to hit the ball magnificently during this championship. I remember he used a mallet-type putter with a hickory shaft. He would set himself with his feet wide apart, elbows out, and hunch down over the ball. Again, he took a long time about it. This slowness was to cause complaints during the championship, though his 3 hours 20 minutes for a round does not sound excessive today.

The 36 qualifying holes were headed by Bernard Hunt and Bobby Locke on 137, followed by Dave Thomas, who had been testing himself on the US Tour, on 138, with Dai Rees, Harry Weetman and Harold Henning (how well his game, the putting stroke in particular, has lasted) a stroke further away.

The first-round leaders were Laurie Ayton and Eric Brown with 67s. For both of them, putting had been decisive. Laurie single-putted eight greens while Eric opened up with four birdie 3s, all from putts of longer than 15 yards! How the galleries loved it. After eleven holes, he had nine 3s on his card but then faltered a little before finishing 4, 3. Bruce Crampton had a 68, Norman Sutton a 69, as did Jimmy Hitchcock, Locke and Keith Macdonald.

On the second day, Eric Brown retained his lead and this was the position before the final rounds:

> 139 Brown;   140 van Donck;   141 Locke;   142 Crampton,
> Thomson, Fallon, Cerda;   143 Macdonald, Hitchcock, Panton,
> Ayton, Middlecoff, Smith

Thomson's second round had shown his resilience. After an opening 73 he began by putting his approach shot into the Swilcan Burn on the 1st (so did Locke) but had then holed a 5-yard putt on the 2nd for a birdie and followed with others on the 5th, 7th and 9th to be out in 33. His 69 re-established him as favourite.

Some indeed thought that Thomson was at the zenith of his powers. In addition to the improved putting, he was hitting with more aggression, and consequently further, while he was timing his irons perfectly to enhance his superb judgement of distance. He loved St Andrews, his favourite course, something that never does a golfer's chances any harm. Some years later he was to say: 'It will always be the greatest course, because nowhere else do you find such turf.'

Cary Middlecoff was still much fancied and, at 143, certainly not too far behind. His low-flighted driving had been much admired and through the green his play up to this point was well-nigh impeccable. Once there, his putter had gained him nothing at all.

There were two firsts on 5 July, the final day. The first TV pictures had gone out, as I have said, from the 1955 Open, and highlights had been shown the following year. Now, however, was the first time the closing stages were shown live. Perhaps to accommodate TV, the other innovation was that for the final two rounds the leaders went out last. Instead of often not knowing what one had to do because the third and fourth rounds overlapped, some leaders playing early and others late, there was now little cause for doubt. Everyone knew how the rest were doing.

Locke was the first to make a strong move. Single-putting four holes in a row (4th to 7th), he was out in 32 and came home in level par 36, despite three-putting the 13th. Thomson lost some ground with his 70: three behind.

For the afternoon the wind remained from the east, the same quarter as it had been throughout, and this was the position:

> 209 Locke; 212 Thomson, Brown; 213 A. Miguel, Haliburton;
> 214 Cerda, van Donck; 215 Smith, Cotton, Fallon, Faulkner;
> 216 Thomas, Bradshaw, Hitchcock, Drew; 217 Middlecoff,
> Lester, Panton

I was not on this reconstructed leader board but had one of the most remarkable rounds I ever played in my career in the Open – or anywhere else. I began at 218 and then birdied the 1st, with my second shot jamming against the flag but coming out. Better was to come on the 411-yard Dyke hole, where I holed my second shot for a 2 to be three under par after two holes! Obviously, if the miracles continued, I could win, even though I was nine strokes behind Locke. In the course of the round I remember ten more strokes when the ball did not drop after I had hit hole or flag with putts and approaches. I still have the club that had a charmed life that day, a Spalding Top-Flite 10-iron. I holed out with it again at the 338-yard 10th and hit the flag at the 12th. The fat bamboo poles used at the time left little room indeed for the ball to slip into the hole. However, despite the magic 10-iron, I also dropped shots fairly liberally, even missing from a yard on the last. Nevertheless, with Sebastian Miguel, I had the lowest round of the day, 68, which swept me well up the field.

Thomson set out ahead of Locke in his attempt to be the first man since Young Tom Morris in 1872 (who played against a field of only eight, or at least only eight handed in their cards) to win four successive Opens. His iron play was superb but he missed short putts on both the 1st and 3rd and took 6 on the 567-yard 5th hole, where a birdie was to be expected. He then had five 3s round the 'Loop' (the 7th to 11th holes at the far end of the course near the Eden Estuary). But his chance went when he missed from less than 5 feet on the 16th, his final 70 not likely to be good enough.

A maturing Alliss playing a little pitch and run,
in preparation for the 1957 Open. Arthur Lees is behind me.

Locke, meanwhile, had been playing with splendid composure and was just once in danger when he bunkered his third on the 560-yard Long Hole. He recovered to within a yard of the hole and that was just about that. I can still remember the gentle high hooking flight of his drive up the last, followed by a lofted iron that started well right of the green and then curved, as if on a string, towards the flag, finishing perhaps 4 feet away. Locke then marked his ball so that his playing partner could putt out. That formality completed, Locke narrowly missed and tapped in to be Open Champion once again, the first four-time winner since Walter Hagen in 1929.

For Locke, it was a late and indeed final flowering of his prodigious talent. Never again was he to feature among the leaders in an Open and his last tournament victory of any kind came in 1960.

Long after the cup and cheques had been presented, the speeches all made and the crowds had departed, came a protest. A newsreel film of the final moments showed Locke marking his ball a couple of putter heads' distance away then replacing it without going back those few inches sideways to the correct spot. The length of his putt was, of course, unaltered, but the line was.

71

Fred Bullock's moment of glory in 1957. What a traditional 'old pro' he looks.

Bobby Locke gives them a song after his 1957 victory.

The Championship Committee duly met and deliberated. They reached the very sensible decision that Locke had gained no advantage, had anyway won by a clear margin, and the result would stand. There remained the mystery of who had raised the protest. Some said Henry Cotton; others Peter Thomson, who would have become champion with Locke disqualified. Just as likely, it was a stickler for the Rules of Golf who saw himself featuring in a newspaper headline. The incident had caused a moment or so's controversy but should not be allowed to detract from Locke's great achievement.

This was virtually the end of the South African's great career. The strain of the years had begun to take its toll. There is an interesting illustration of this. Many years later, in the course of TV filming, I asked Bobby to don his familiar outfit. He took some persuading and said he had not worn those familiar baggy navy-blue plus-fours since this far-off championship. They reminded him too painfully of the strain and all the concentration he had needed to marshal in order just to keep going and win. Championship golf is not much fun.

HOW THEY FINISHED

A. D. Locke *South Africa*	**69**	**72**	**68**	**70**	**279**	R. W. Horne	76	72	72	73	293
						G. J. Player *South Africa*	71	74	75	73	
P. W. Thomson *Australia*	73	69	70	70	282	T. Wilkes *South Africa*	75	73	71	74	
						S. L. King	76	72	70	75	
E. C. Brown	67	72	73	71	283	B. J. Hunt	72	72	74	75	
A. Miguel *Spain*	72	72	69	72	285	H. R. Henning *South Africa*	75	73	71	75	294
D. C. Thomas	72	74	70	70	286						
Mr W. D. Smith	71	72	72	71		D. J. Rees	73	72	79	71	295
F. van Donck *Belgium*	72	68	74	72		P. J. Butler	77	71	74	73	
T. B. Haliburton	72	73	68	73		R. A. Knight	71	73	75	76	
						N. Sutton	69	76	73	77	
T. H. Cotton	74	72	69	72	287	L. B. Ayton	67	76	75	77	
M. Faulkner	74	70	71	72							
A. Cerda *Argentina*	71	71	72	73		K. Bousfield	74	73	75	74	296
						R. de Vicenzo *Argentina*	70	76	76	74	
Peter Alliss	72	74	74	68	288	J. Macdonald	73	71	76	76	
H. Weetman	75	71	71	71							
						R. L. Moffitt	71	75	77	74	297
C. Middlecoff *USA*	72	71	74	72	289						
						S. S. Scott	76	72	73	77	298
S. Miguel *Spain*	71	75	76	68	290	K. A. MacDonald	69	74	76	79	
E. G. Lester	71	76	70	73		B. Crampton *Australia*	68	73	78	79	
J. Panton	71	72	74	73							
N. V. Drew	70	75	71	74		Mr R. F. Galloway	70	76	79	75	300
						T. H. T. Fairbairn	73	72	77	78	
F. R. Stranahan *USA*	74	71	74	72	291						
C. O'Connor	77	69	72	73		E. B. Williamson	74	70	77	80	301
H. Bradshaw	73	74	69	75							
J. Fallon	75	67	73	76		A. Lees	75	71	77	80	303
J. Hitchcock	69	74	73	76	292	W. J. Henderson	72	75	82	76	305

Royal Lytham and Fairhaven, 1958

As the qualifying rounds for the 1958 Open began on 30 June at both Royal Lytham and Fairhaven, Peter Thomson's declaration of intent to regain his title was immediate. His score of 63 beat Fred Daly's previous Lytham record by no fewer than four strokes. Though his performance was in a sense 'wasted', it was Thomson's way of saying he was there and in form. His card is worthy of record:

$$3, 4, 4, 3, 2, 4, 5, 3, 3 \ (31); \quad 3, 4, 3, 2, 4, 4, 4, 4, 4 \ (32)$$

From the 3rd to the 11th he had seven birdies in nine holes, paused for breath with a par on the 166-yard 12th, and then eagled the 339-yard 13th! He had no bogeys during his round and just one 5 – on the 553-yard 7th, which was out of range that day in two strokes.

I ought to mention, however, that the system of par rating was not then as it is today so that some of Thomson's birdies were on holes which would no longer be rated as par-5s. Here, then, is the Royal Lytham of 1958:

Hole	Yards	Par	Hole	Yards	Par
1	208	3	10	336	4
2	424	4	11	483	5
3	456	5	12	166	3
4	393	4	13	339	4
5	188	3	14	445	4
6	466	5	15	462	5
7	553	5	15	356	4
8	394	4	17	423	5
9	164	3	18	379	4
	3246	36		3389	38
				3246	36
				6635	74

As so often, Thomson's round was made not only by straight driving but also by placement. He was never considered a long hitter and did not rate length high among his priorities. Despite a strong left-hand grip, which made hooking likely, he was unexcelled at manoeuvring his ball to the side of the fairway that gave the best approach to the green.

Lytham was indeed relatively defenceless that calm first day and others who took advantage were Bernard Hunt, 66, and the great Irish amateur Joe Carr, whose 67 beat the amateur course record by three strokes.

When the 36 qualifying holes were complete, Thomson led on 133, with Hunt on 136, while among those at 140 or better were Alfonso Angelini, Dai Rees, Harold Henning, Jimmy Hitchcock, Norman Drew, Donald Swaelens (tragically to die of cancer in his late thirties), John Panton, Henry Cotton (at the age of 51), Norman von Nida and myself. Gene Sarazen was back again and had a 68 round Lytham, a course he had won the Northern Championship on some 35 years earlier, playing with a certain Harry Vardon. He had twelve one-putt greens and might have made a 66 but for a bad slice on the 17th. The one sign of age was that he had added a very lofted wood to his armoury to substitute for decreasing ability with the long-irons.

A 'new' Gary Player also made his appearance. He had spent time with the guru Ben Hogan in Texas and emerged looking a far more orthodox golfer. His drives were some 20 yards longer, with lower flight, and the hooker's grip was no more, neither was the excessively flat backswing. One who fell by the wayside was Frank Stranahan, troubled by a bad back.

By this time, Thomson had developed a more relaxed-looking putting action with long back swing and short follow-through, copied from Locke. He was altogether more effective on the greens, which at Lytham that year were in well-nigh perfect condition. He used just eleven putts going out and his eventual score of 66 made the rest of us think that here was to be yet another easy victory for Thomson. Others who scored particularly well were Christy O'Connor, 67, and Max Faulkner, Gary Player and Henry Cotton on 68 – there were many asking if the ageing maestro could possibly do it one final time. I played steadily enough for my 72 though as usual I was criticized in the press for putting lapses. Fancied players who seemed already out of it were Locke, who ended on 76 after a salvo of 5s towards the end, von Nida with 77 and Dai Rees on the same score.

On the second day, Thomson by no means had it all his own way. His 72 must have seemed a failure to him after previous rounds of 63 and 66 and he had lost the lead, now held by Christy O'Connor. This is how the leaders stood with the final day to come:

135 O'Connor;   136 Ruiz;   138 Thomas, Thomson;
139 Faulkner, Lester

Eric Lester had moved well up the field with his 66 but the day's best score had come from Leopoldo Ruiz, known sometimes as 'the thin crust of bread'. He had reached the turn in 30, aided by having twice holed out from off the green, and finished in 65. He was a tall handsome Argentine who dropped his hands at the top of the backswing and hit the ball enormous distances with this flailing action. The name of David Thomas featuring high up was to prove significant. Although he had yet to win an important British event, he was then at the peak of his ambitions and one of the few of us to make prolonged efforts on the US Tour. He was 6 foot 2 inches, 15 stone and powerfully built, with massive shoulders. Perhaps here was a future champion.

After the third round, David was still strongly in contention, having added a 69 to his 70, 68 start. O'Connor had slipped a little with a 73 and the key figures

David Thomas at Royal Lytham.

who had moved up the field were van Donck (67), Thomson (67) and Eric Brown, with a 65 which included an amazing homeward half in 30.

The wind was beginning to rise as the higher afternoon scoring shows, and these were the lunchtime leaders:

205 Thomson;   207 Thomas, van Donck;   208 O'Connor, Brown, Ruiz;   210 Faulkner, Lester;   212 Cotton, Player, Alliss

The battle was likely to be fought out among the top six – and so it proved. Thomas began well by holing from 10 yards for a 2 on the 1st and had caught Thomson by the 4th. He was out in 33 to Thomson's 34, to be one behind the Australian. Then came disaster for the Welshman as he three-putted the 10th, 11th and 12th. Yet Thomson was to falter as well and when he took 6 on the 462-yard 15th this was in contrast to a superb 2-iron from Thomas, who put his iron shot 7 feet from the hole and birdied to lead the championship for the first time.

Yet disaster was only minutes away. David hit an immense drive down the 17th and had just a 7-iron to the green. He tells me he pulled it left into heavy rough, could only hack out and then got down in two more. The pair were level again. How Thomas wishes he could play that fatal shot again. But this was an extremely close-fought championship. In the closing stages, Brown, O'Connor and Ruiz all had their chances to tie. Brown, however, must still consider he should have won, playing ahead of all the others.

With five holes to play, he needed straight 4s for a 68 which, as events were to prove, would have been good enough for a two-stroke victory. It was his unreliable driving, always suspect in a wind, that let him down, as he missed four of the last five fairways. Nevertheless, he came to the last needing a 4 for outright victory. This, playing into the wind, menaced the drive with three fairway bunkers. Brown's drive found one of them and then, reaching the green in three, he went boldly for his first putt, was past and then missed the return. Two putts would have given him a tie and a place in the play-off. How strange that some players seize their chances while others cast them to the winds.

Next came David Thomas and Thomson. Both drove safely but Thomson's second shot was only some 10 feet from the hole with Thomas as many yards away. David only narrowly missed but his ball came to rest 2½ feet away. Thomson then missed in his turn and David bravely holed his short putt to tie. This left O'Connor and Leopoldo Ruiz with a chance to tie. Both bunkered their tee-shots at the 18th, Ruiz eventually running up a 7 on the hole.

So, for the second time since the war, there was to be a play-off, as in 1949 over 36 holes. Thomson, of course the favourite (though Thomas had almost overnight become a national figure), began strongly, his putting especially effective. He reached the turn in 31 to lead by four. Thomas then began to make up ground, primarily a result of very long straight driving. A superb long-iron on the 15th reduced the gap to two; when he holed from 4 yards at the last he could begin the afternoon with 69 to Thomson's 68.

On the 3rd, David hit a 4-iron to 1 yard to draw level. No British golfer had at the time finished ahead of Thomson in the Open since 1951! Perhaps the new man might be the one to do it. Consistently during the morning his shots to the green had finished inside the Australian's, whose putting had been a class better. The 8th hole, in retrospect, was decisive. Thomson left a long uphill putt at least 3 yards short but got it in. Thomas then missed from a shorter distance. Thomson then went further ahead on the 10th, his birdie putt going down and Thomas missing from 2 feet for a 5. At the next, both missed the green but Peter chipped dead to go four strokes ahead, a position he maintained to the end.

In David Thomas it seemed, however, that a new star had arrived. Still only 23, he would surely win the Open in due course. But sometimes chances come only once. This may also be the case for Bobby Clampett and Nick Price, who in 1982 had better chances than did David at Lytham in 1958.

For Thomson, it was a fourth victory in a five-year spell, equalled only by Young Tom Morris in 1868–72 (in his case including a year, 1871, when the event was not played). Thomson was still only 28.

HOW THEY FINISHED

P. W. Thomson *Australia*	**66**	**72**	**67**	**73**	**278**	G. de Wit *Holland*	71	75	72	73	291
D. C. Thomas	70	68	69	71		H. Bradshaw	70	73	72	76	

Play-off:	Thomson	68	71	139
	Thomas	69	74	143

E. C. Brown	73	70	65	71	279	S. Miguel *Spain*	74	71	73	74	292
C. O'Connor	67	68	73	71		A. Cerda *Argentina*	72	71	74	75	
						T. Wilkes *South Africa*	76	70	69	77	
L. Ruiz *Argentina*	71	65	72	73	281						
F. van Donck *Belgium*	70	70	67	74		A. Miguel *Spain*	71	70	75	77	293
G. J. Player *South Africa*	68	74	70	71	283	S. L. King	71	73	76	75	295
						D. Snell	72	72	72	79	
H. Weetman	73	67	73	71	284	B. J. Hunt	70	70	76	79	
T. H. Cotton	68	75	69	72							
E. G. Lester	73	66	71	74		J. M. Wilkshire	74	70	78	74	296
D. Swaelens *Belgium*	74	67	74	70	285	B. B. S. Wilkes *South Africa*	73	73	75	76	297
Peter Alliss	72	70	70	73		S. S. Scott	73	74	74	76	
						B. Crampton *Australia*	73	73	75	76	
H. R. Henning *South Africa*	70	71	72	73	286						
						Mr J. B. Carr	70	74	77	77	298
D. J. Rees	77	69	71	70	287						
J. Garaialde *France*	69	74	72	72		D. L. Melville	76	71	76	79	302
A. D. Locke *South Africa*	76	70	72	70	288	C. S. Denny	74	73	77	79	303
G. Sarazen *USA*	73	73	70	72		W. S. Large	70	72	81	80	
E. Moore *South Africa*	72	72	70	74							
M. Faulkner	68	71	71	78							
C. Greene	75	71	72	72	290						
F. Daly	71	74	72	73							
N. V. Drew	69	72	75	74							
A. B. Coop	69	71	75	75							

Muirfield, 1959

The next year, at Muirfield in 1959, Thomson continued serenely on his way. Almost by divine right, it seemed, again heading the qualifiers. It was particularly ominous that on the championship course he equalled Henry Cotton's record of 66, despite taking three putts on the 17th. At Gullane, Joe Carr had the lowest round of his career, a 64. How well he scored in many a championship. Having driven the 1st green and holed out for a 2, his score beat the professional record by three strokes and the amateur by four – all this putting with a 3-iron, a club that Joe was apt to use when all else failed.

The leading qualifiers therefore were Thomson (137); Carr, Neil Coles and Frank Jowle (138); George Low, Peter Mills, Gary Player and amateur Reid Jack (139). Bobby Locke was on 142 while Henry Cotton and I were both comfortably inside the qualifying mark of 147.

At the end of the first day, two relative unknowns led the field, Arnold Stickley (still joint professional at Ealing with his brother Owen) and Fred Bullock with 68s. They played in calm conditions while the wind got up in due course and scoring rose. They were followed by Tony Cerda (69), Sam King, Michael Bonallack and Flory van Donck (70) and a group on 71 that included Henry Cotton, now aged 52.

The next day, Fred Bullock was again fortunate with the weather and still led on 138, followed by van Donck (140), with Reg Knight, Stickley and Bonallack on 142. The amateur's total surprisingly included two shanks! Next came Tom Haliburton, Jimmy Hitchcock, Syd Scott and Tony Cerda at 143. With the qualifying total 148, many were in danger of not making the final day. Player, Cotton and Locke only got through narrowly on 146, Locke having three 3s over the last four holes to get in. Exactly on the qualifying mark were the names of Peter Alliss and, an upset to the natural order of things, Peter Thomson. He had not been driving with anything approaching his high standards and may have been affected by problems in his personal life.

After three rounds, the leaders were Bullock and Sam King (at the age of 48). These were the totals that seemed to matter most:

> 212 Bullock, King; 213 van Donck, Hitchcock; 214 Reid Jack, Bonallack (both amateurs); 215 Ruiz, Rees, Panton; 216 Knight, Cerda, Scott, Player

The last of these had saved himself from being completely out of contention by a succession of good iron shots on the second half, which he holed in 33 after being 37 to the turn.

In the afternoon, Player reached the turn in 34 and then birdied the 480-yard 10th. On the 12th he missed the green but holed a putt of half a dozen yards or more to save his par. When he birdied the 193-yard 16th, he needed to finish 4,

Flory van Donck playing a little run-up.

4 for a 66 that would set a very difficult target for those following him. He managed his 4 at the 513-yard 17th but bunkered his drive at the 427-yard final hole and then took three putts. Having thrown away his chance of winning the Open, Gary broke down in tears.

However, he had set a target and as the afternoon developed the target grew more difficult to attain. Van Donck, Cerda and Scott needed 34s home to tie. Cerda went almost immediately when he started back with two 5s. Scott lasted well until the 17th when he hooked his tee-shot into trouble and took 6, while Bullock fell away in the final stretch. Eventually, there was Flory van Donck, needing an unlikely 3 on the last to tie, but taking 5. His second-place finishes in 1956 and 1959 were the best performances by a continental golfer since the Frenchman Arnaud Massy's victory in 1907 and were not to be eclipsed until the advent of Severiano Ballesteros many years later.

It had also been a good year for the amateurs, with Reid Jack, a superb striker, finishing equal 5th, with Bonallack and Guy Wolstenholme also performing well (his last shot in the championship was a 2-iron into the hole for an eagle on the 72nd). So too did I, making a late charge up the field with the round of the day, a 67: one stroke off the course record – and I finished with a 5.

But the champion was Gary Player, seven behind the leader after one round, eight after two and still four back with 18 holes to play. At 23, he was the youngest winner since Willie Auchterlonie in 1893 and one of only four winners to have a descending score in each round. Nevertheless, I and many of my fellow British professionals, while conceding that Gary had improved, still saw his victory as rather a freak and not likely to be repeated. 'You're never', we said, 'going to be another Bobby Locke.' How wrong we all were.

For Thomson, it had been a very disappointing year, well down the list in 22nd place and never in the contest after his brisk start in the qualifying stages. None doubted, however, that he would one day return and take more championships. So it was to prove – eventually.

HOW THEY FINISHED

Name	R1	R2	R3	R4	Total
G. J. Player *South Africa*	**75**	**71**	**70**	**68**	**284**
F. van Donck *Belgium*	70	70	73	73	286
F. Bullock	68	70	74	74	
S. S. Scott	73	70	73	71	287
C. O'Connor	73	74	72	69	288
J. Panton	72	72	71	73	
Mr R. R. Jack	71	75	68	74	
S. L. King	70	74	68	76	
D. J. Rees	73	73	69	74	289
L. Ruiz *Argentina*	72	74	69	74	
B. J. Hunt	73	75	71	71	290
A. F. Stickley	68	74	77	71	
K. Bousfield	73	73	71	73	
Mr M. F. Bonallack	70	72	72	76	
J. Hitchcock	75	68	70	77	
Peter Alliss	76	72	76	67	291
Mr G. B. Wolstenholme	78	70	73	70	
H. Weetman	72	73	76	70	
H. Bradshaw	71	76	72	72	
A. Cerda *Argentina*	69	74	73	75	
J. Garaialde *France*	75	70	74	73	292
N. C. Coles	72	74	71	75	
P. W. Thomson *Australia*	74	74	72	74	294
G. M. Hunt	72	73	74	75	
R. P. Mills	75	71	72	76	
H. R. Henning *South Africa*	73	73	72	76	
J. R. Moses	72	73	73	76	
R. A. Knight	71	71	74	78	
E. E. Whitcombe	71	77	74	73	295
A. D. Locke *South Africa*	73	73	76	73	
P. J. Shanks	76	70	75	74	
J. Adams	71	74	75	75	
T. B. Haliburton	74	69	74	78	
H. Lewis	73	73	78	72	296
N. V. Drew	71	77	75	74	297
E. G. Lester	73	71	78	75	
C. H. Ward	78	70	73	76	
A. Miguel *Spain*	73	75	73	77	298
Mr J. B. Carr	72	73	74	79	
C. Kane	77	69	77	76	299
G. W. Low	75	73	78	74	300
J. Hargreaves	72	74	79	75	
T. H. Cotton	71	75	77	77	
J. Sharkey	74	74	74	78	
R. L. Moffitt	74	72	76	78	
J. J. Querelos *Brazil*	76	72	80	73	301
J. S. More	72	75	76	79	302
R. Haydon	75	72	77	79	303

•5•

Palmer Breathes New Life

St Andrews, 1960

From time to time throughout this book, I have pointed to the consistent strength of Open Championship fields from 1946 onwards. If we look at a list of US Masters Champions from 1947 to 1955, we find that each competed in the Open, as did all but three US Open Champions from 1946 to 1956. As for other nationalities, the British Open attracted a far better international field than did the US Open, Masters and PGA. During this period, therefore, the Open could well claim to be the premier world championship event, indeed the only event that was truly international.

How is it then that 1960 is such a watershed in Open Championship history? Although the top Americans did compete, except for such faithfuls as Johnny Bulla, Frank Stranahan and, to a lesser extent, Gene Sarazen, US golfers either came and conquered – as did Sam Snead and Ben Hogan – or they came once or twice, failed and did not return. Among the latter group can be numbered Claude Harmon, Cary Middlecoff, Jimmy Demaret, Ed Furgol, Lawson Little, Byron Nelson, Jim Turnesa and Lloyd Mangrum. It may be no coincidence that none of these were in contention in the championship. The Open was by no means an easy fruit, ripe for the plucking. I believe that some of these players thought they could squeeze our Open into their schedules and might as well come over and win. Unsuccessful, they were discouraged enough not to try again. It was Arnold Palmer who changed all that.

St Andrews was the obligatory choice for the Centenary Open of 1960, even though this meant making the course the venue for the third year out of the last six. The number of entries, 301, was in stark contrast to the eight golfers who had assembled in 1860, Willie Park emerging with a two-stroke margin over Old Tom Morris after three rounds in one day over Prestwick's 12 holes.

Despite the fact that this was the centenary year, the US entry was only of about average strength. There was Jock Hutchison (Scottish-born), who had been champion in 1921 after a play-off with the great English amateur Roger Wethered. At the age of 76 he was, of course, over on a sentimental journey. I expect he was quite pleased with his 82 over the Old course in the first qualifying round. Chandler Harper, a successful US Tour player whose best performance was to win the 1950 US PGA, failed by three strokes to qualify at 147; perhaps as a result, he expressed contempt for the course. In fact, only two Americans, W. Johnson and Arnold Palmer, reached the final 36 holes.

Palmer had quickly worked his way to the top of American golf. He had won the US Amateur in 1954 and had taken the US Masters in 1958 and 1960. A month before, he had added the US Open title at Cherry Hills, Denver, in most spectacular fashion. As he set out in his final round he had been seven strokes behind the leader, Mike Souchak, and five behind Ben Hogan and a promising young amateur called Jack Nicklaus. Palmer then birdied the first four holes, added more on the 6th and 7th and reached the turn in a record 30. Eventually, he won by two strokes from the young Nicklaus.

These two major championship victories meant that Arnold was one of the few players who has had the Grand Slam of all four majors remotely in his sights. As a new star, the first of real magnitude since the decline of Ben Hogan, everyone wanted to see him play.

However, on that first qualifying day, despite Palmer's convincing 67 on the New course, I managed to steal most of the headlines. Though I had previously been uneasy at St Andrews, not liking the 'natural' (and often haphazard) siting of bunkers, the vast greens or unfair bounces, this was my card:

Hole	Name	Yards	Par	Alliss	Hole	Name	Yards	Par	Alliss
1	Burn	374	4	3	10	Bobby Jones	338	4	4
2	Dyke	411	4	4	11	High	170	3	3
3	Cartgate	400	4	4	12	Heathery	360	4	4
4	Ginger Beer	439	4	4	13	Hole o' Cross	427	4	4
5	Hole o' Cross	567	5	4	14	Long	560	5	4
6	Heathery	377	4	4	15	Cartgate	413	4	3
7	High	364	4	3	16	Corner of the Dyke	380	4	4
8	Short	163	3	3	17	Road	453	4	4
9	End	359	4	4	18	Tom Morris	381	4	3
		3454	36	33			3482	36	33
							3454	36	33
							6936	72	66

It was a highly symmetrical round. There were three birdies in each half, with both halves in 33 and six 4s and the rest 3s. More important, it was a new course record, beating Dai Rees's 67 in the 1946 Open, and it was the first time the Old had been played without a 5 (or worse) on a golfer's card. I began with a putt of about 4 yards and rounded off with one of double the length on the last. Among other details I remember are that I was only once bunkered, had my iron shot dead at Cartgate coming home and, alas, three-putted the 10th, having driven the green.

There are slight regrets that this round did not come in the championship proper. Looking back on my career, I believe I might have been champion if I had once produced a blazing start and got the bit between my teeth (I was never afraid of leading), rather than a more routine level par with someone else fast out of the gate. A regret of more substance is that in the first round proper I soared to 79 and the next day failed to make the 36-hole cut!

The leading qualifiers were the defending champion, Gary Player (135); Christy O'Connor (137); Fidel de Luca, or 'filthy lucre' as we affectionately called him (139); John Jacobs, myself (140); and Thomson, Sarazen (at the age of 59) on 141. Among the distinguished names who failed to make the qualifying mark were Dave Thomas and Flory van Donck – who had both featured so strongly in recent championships – Henry Cotton, Fred Daly and Harry Bradshaw. Little had happened so far to change opinions about likely winners. The favourites remained Palmer, Player and Thomson.

However, it was Roberto de Vicenzo who opened up a two-stroke lead on the field. Out early, he went to the turn in 32, helped by a chip-in on the 4th, followed by his hitting the 567-yard 5th in two; he came home without alarms and posted a 67. That score stood all day, the closest challenges coming from Fidel de Luca, who had won the German Open in 1958, and Kel Nagle, who had won the Australian Open in 1959 and had good recent form on the US Tour, where he had finished second to Julius Boros in the Colonial Invitational. Both had played the second half in 31. De Luca had a run of five consecutive 3s, including one on the 560-yard 14th, where he had a putt of only 4 feet. A highlight of Nagle's round was a 3 on the feared Road hole, when he holed out from about 15 yards, his mind full of thoughts of three-putting this difficult green. Next, on 70, came Peter Shanks (now managing director of Petron Golf Clubs company), the amateur Major David Blair, Ken Bousfield and Arnold Palmer, who had the first of a sequence of three putts on the Road hole green.

After the second day, Roberto still headed the field. His start of 67, 67 was the best since Henry Cotton's 67, 65 at Royal St George's when he went on to win the 1934 Open. It has since been bettered only by Bobby Clampett's 67, 66 at Troon in 1982. Roberto had rounded off with a long putt on the last and had equalled my new record of having no 5s on his card (but he did 'spoil' it with a 2!). But the little-fancied Kel Nagle was still close behind, having had a 67 of his own to add to his first round 69. His play, however, attracted little attention, perhaps because he was so unspectacular and very much followed the Thomson strategy which I mentioned earlier: hit it on the fairway, get to the green in the right number of strokes and then don't three-putt. But Kel did rather better than that, using only 29 putts in his round.

The pair had opened up quite a formidable gap on the rest of the field, who were, indeed, in danger of being out of touch. After Nagle, there was a five-stroke gap before the names of Palmer, Thomson and Sebastian Miguel appeared, the American having again had three putts on the 17th. Christy

O'Connor had an unusual pair of scores. He had begun with an 80, leaving him little chance of making the 36-hole cut, which came after 149, but then his 67 saw him safely through.

At this time Roberto de Vicenzo had left Buenos Aires and taken a club job in Mexico. He appeared under that flag in 1956 and 1960 before reverting to his homeland. With his best chance so far in his thirteen-year span in the Open (he did not by any means always compete, however) Roberto began badly by missing a tiny putt at the 1st and on the 5th hit a 4-iron to less than 5 feet but missed his eagle. On the 10th, his immense effortless power sent his drive through the back of the green. He followed by chipping weakly and then taking three putts. His worst moments, however, came on the 560-yard 14th, where his tee-shot bounced on the out-of-bounds wall and he took 7.

However, after his 67, 67 start, a 75 was by no means bad enough to put him out of the hunt. He was, however, no longer the leader and one man looking pleased at the change was Peter Thomson, who had placed a bet on Kel Nagle and helped give him the confidence in his game to compete outside Australia. Nagle had followed his 69, 67 with a 71 and this gave him a two-stroke lead on Vicenzo, with Syd Scott and Arnold Palmer a further two strokes away. There were high hopes that Palmer might produce one of his famed charges in the final round. There was also, for once, an outside chance of an amateur victory. Joe Carr, having started 72, 73, had broken the amateur record for the Old course with a 67, like other long hitters aided by driving the 10th. He stood at 212, followed by Harold Henning, a consistent Open performer and one of the best South Africans of all time (as he is still proving). Next, at 214, was amateur David Blair. Among those on 215 was the defending champion, Gary Player, really too many strokes behind, as was Peter Thomson on 216.

Palmer might well have been closer, for he had come to the last two holes needing two 4s for a 68. Again the Road Hole was his downfall, as it has been for so many others in the history of Opens at St Andrews. He had his by now regular three putts there (Nagle had a 3) and then took 5 at the last, perhaps the easiest finishing hole in championship golf.

Player, after his adequate start of 72, 71, had also made a move in the third round, but after reaching the turn in 33 had managed no better than 39 on the journey homewards.

As the final round began, the question was whether or not the 35–1 outsider Nagle would keep his nerve. Also, of course, whether a more fancied pursuer could produce one of the low rounds that were not infrequent at St Andrews that year. Nagle had an advantage that few were aware of. He is one of the few professionals who actually enjoy competition. Of course, all of us enjoy winning but you can count on the fingers the number that relish the strain of keeping the ball in play, controlling the nerve-ends when faced with a delicate long putt or steeling themselves for the apparently simple task of hitting a little putt straight at the middle of a hole. For most of us, with the wear and tear of the passing years and the memory of missed putts engrained, there comes a time when the nervous system will no longer tolerate it. For me, this came several years later. I then found that when facing a short putt I could not shut out the feeling that I was going to hit the ball ludicrously hard. Instead of a gentle tap, a convulsion was about to occur in the putting action and away the ball might career, yards past. As a result I too often putted weakly, with the ball dribbling away to the right.

Joe Carr made a good start to his pursuit when he birdied the 1st. Then came the rains. In a short time, water, I remember, was streaming down the clubhouse steps and the greens then became unplayable. Play was first postponed and shortly abandoned for the day, the first time this had happened for about fifty years. All would begin their final rounds on the Saturday.

There were by now eyes in plenty on Kel Nagle but some could not see how so undramatic a golfer (especially in comparison with Palmer) should come to be leading the Open. This, too, at an age, 39, when he must surely be far past his best. In his swing there was neither power nor elegance and it seemed eccentric that he took his address with the clubhead well inside the ball. There followed a pronounced dip at the start of the backswing and the ball was certainly not propelled with rifle-shot velocity, as was the case with Palmer. But it did almost invariably finish on the fairway.

Nagle, playing immediately behind Palmer, reached the turn in 34 (with birdies on the 7th and 8th) as did Palmer, who had pitched dead at both the 1st and 2nd. Roberto de Vicenzo was contending strongly, though at this time there were always doubts about his competitiveness. He seemed to accept inevitable failure once he had missed a putt or two. Nevertheless, he also reached the turn in 34, though fading away on the homeward nine. It soon became clear the battle was between Palmer and Nagle.

At the 13th, Palmer holed from some 3 yards for a birdie to reduce the gap and this remained at three as Nagle played the 15th. Here he came up short with his second shot, dragged his first putt to be short by 3 yards or more and missed the next. Ahead, Palmer forced in a 6-foot putt on the 16th for his par so the gap was now two strokes.

On the Road hole, the drive should be as far right as the player dares, in order to give a moderately straightforward shot into this narrow green, less threatened by the small but deep bunker that eats into the left side or by the road immediately on the right. Palmer drove too far left, played for the front of the green, and finished rather short of it. From there, he got to about 2 feet from the hole and got his 4, the first time he had emerged unscathed at this hole during the championship. At the last, his drive finished on Granny Clark's Wynd, which crosses the fairway in the driving area, but from there pitched to 5 feet and holed for his birdie to a tumult of applause.

The roar that greeted this came to Kel Nagle as he was faced with a putt of 7 or more feet for his 4. If he missed, he too would have to birdie the last to win.

The Centenary Open at St Andrews in 1960, Kel Nagle.
To mark the centenary, this winner was given a replica of the trophy.

The vital putt went down; 'only' a par was needed for victory, the same task that faced Doug Sanders years later.

It was never in doubt. Nagle drove safely, had his second shot close and rolled his putt to the hole side. He was champion, probably the most unexpected of all during the years covered by this book. Yet it was the loser, Arnold Palmer, who had made this championship the most memorable since Hogan came to Carnoustie in 1953.

HOW THEY FINISHED

K. D. G. Nagle *Australia*	**69**	**67**	**71**	**71**	**278**	W. Johnson *USA*	75	74	71	71	291
						S. Miguel *Spain*	73	68	74	76	
A. Palmer *USA*	70	71	70	68	279						
						F. S. Boobyer	74	74	73	71	292
B. J. Hunt	72	73	71	66	282	G. M. Hunt	76	69	72	75	
H. R. Henning	72	72	69	69		L. B. Ayton	73	69	75	75	
South Africa						J. Martin	72	72	72	76	
R. de Vicenzo *Mexico*	67	67	75	73							
						L. Ruiz *Argentina*	72	77	73	71	293
Mr G. B. Wolstenholme	74	70	71	68	283	T. B. Haliburton	77	70	74	72	
						J. R. M. Jacobs	74	71	75	73	
G. J. Player *South Africa*	72	71	72	69	284						
						P. J. Butler	76	72	75	71	294
Mr J. B. Carr	72	73	67	73	285						
						C. O'Connor	80	67	76	72	295
D. J. Rees	73	71	73	69	286	D. Miller	75	73	74	73	
P. W. Thomson *Australia*	72	69	75	70		P. J. Shanks	70	73	77	75	
H. Weetman	74	70	71	71		E. B. Williamson	75	70	73	77	
E. C. Brown	75	68	72	71							
Maj. D. A. Blair	70	73	71	72		Mr W. D. Smith	74	71	78	74	297
S. S. Scott	73	71	67	75		J. M. Gonzales *Brazil*	72	74	75	76	
R. Sota *Spain*	74	72	71	70	287	A. B. Coop	76	73	75	74	298
A. Miguel *Spain*	72	73	72	71	288	Mr R. D. B. M. Shade	75	74	77	73	299
I. Smith	74	70	73	71		R. Verwey *South Africa*	73	76	74	76	
F. de Luca *Argentina*	69	73	75	71							
Mr R. R. Jack	74	71	70	73		M. Sota *Spain*	73	75	76	76	300
R. P. Mills	71	74	70	74	289	Dr F. W. G. Deighton	74	70	75	83	302
Mr A. M. Deboys	76	70	73	71	290	Mr R. A. G. Munro	72	77	82	77	308
R. Moffitt	72	71	76	71							
G. W. Low	72	74	71	73							
J. A. MacDonald	76	71	69	74							
K. Bousfield	70	75	71	74							

Royal Birkdale, 1961

Palmer did not arrive at Royal Birkdale in 1961 in pursuit of the Grand Slam. He had thrown the Masters away a couple of months before. He had tied Gary Player for the lead after two rounds, fallen four behind after three but had come to the last needing a par for a one-stroke victory. His approach found the same bunker to the right of the green from which Player, minutes before, had got down in two. It took Arnold four. Nevertheless, he was in form and, between them, he and Player had totalled more than $100,000 that season. The two most successful players of the British season, myself and Bernard Hunt, had been rewarded with the equivalent of about $17,000.

The favourites this year were Gary Player, now fully accepted as a golfer of great stature, Thomson, for his past Open record, and Nagle, then one of just three Australians to have won a major championship. (Even in 1984 he had been joined only by David Graham.) Palmer was only a little less favoured because there were some who thought his style unsuited to links golf.

Birkdale has been significantly changed since that time and it is worth setting down the course as it was played in 1961:

Hole	Yards	Par	Hole	Yards	Par
1	520	5	10	390	4
2	427	5	11	368	4
3	416	4	12	452	4
4	212	3	13	202	3
5	315	4	14	517	5
6	468	5	15	381	4
7	158	3	16	510	5
8	434	4	17	186	3
9	418	4	18	470	5
	3368	37		3476	37
				3368	37
				6844	74

Some of the par-5s may today appear surprising. It must be remembered that the difficulty of a hole was then considered in deciding its par, not yardage alone as today. This is a system I think should return.

The New Zealander Bob Charles had the headlines to himself after the first qualifying round. He had been less than a year in the professional ranks, having sensibly kept his job as a bank clerk after winning the New Zealand Open in 1954, and broke the course record at Birkdale with a 66. His chipping and putting had already attracted notice. After the second day, he was leading qualifier on 136. No famous names had fallen but Dai Rees, in danger, had followed a 76 with a Hillside record of 66.

For the first round proper, the weather was variable. There was wind, rain and thunder, but good spells also, so the luck of the draw had considerable bearing on the day's play. Playing in the best of the weather, Rees, Henning and Nagle led with 68s, followed by Johnson, David Miller and Jean Garaialde, the best French golfer since World War II, on 69. There were several on 70, including Palmer, who had played patchily, and Sam King yet again. Sam's achievement was a remarkable one: he was three months past his fiftieth birthday and there were some seven greens he could no longer reach in two strokes. Player had not enhanced his chances with a 73. Among those on 75 were Peter Thomson, Frank Stranahan (a professional for several years by this time, mainly so that he could claim his golf expenses against tax), Locke and the US short-game expert Paul Runyan, still competing in senior events to this day.

The second day saw the last great blow that we have had at an Open Championship. The Luncheon Tent was blown down and one wag remarked that an aircraft from Squiresgate Airport had sighted ham and egg sandwiches at 4000 feet. Of the 48 who qualified for the last day with an aggregate of 153 or better, nine scored in the 80s and another twelve had scores of 78 or 79. With his low flight, Peter Thomson had the best round of the day, a 72, and among qualifiers there were just nine scores of 75 or better. Palmer had played one of his greatest spells of golf, even if it did not last the whole round. In the very worst of the weather, he birdied five of the first six holes, rifling iron shots under the wind in a way none who saw him will ever forget. Even he could not avoid one disaster. Bunkered near the 16th green, his ball moved as he came into the shot so that he incurred both a penalty shot and, for good measure, thinned into another bunker, eventually moving on with a 7 on his card. Nevertheless, his 73 was the second lowest round of the day, while Rees and Henning were the only others to get below 75. I recall I was well pleased with my 75 and went up to the BBC commentary box to tell the nation all about it.

At the time, the commentators were Henry Longhurst, Bill Cox and John Jacobs. Ray Lakeland, a Manchester-based producer of golf and rugby league, asked me to come up and say a few words about my own round, how the course was playing and what the prospects were. This I was to do at televised events for a couple of years without payment until it occurred to someone that Alliss was worth something. The first fee I received was £5. There is by no means the instant wealth in television that people suppose!

Among those who had failed to qualify for the last day's 36 holes were Bobby Locke, Bob Charles and Frank Stranahan, all with 84s, while Joe Carr, who had played so well the previous year, was also out with an 86. My dear friend Guy Wolstenholme, by then a professional, had just survived. His 283 at St Andrews the year before, including a final 68 for 6th place, is still the lowest aggregate by an amateur in the Open.

With the last two rounds to play, Henning and Rees led on 142, with Nagle and Palmer a stroke behind. There was then a considerable gap to the 147s of Sam King, Ramon Sota of Spain (uncle of a certain four-year-old Severiano Ballesteros), Neil Coles and Peter Thomson. But first there was a pause.

Friday's play was washed out so there was a second consecutive Saturday finish. When this began, Dai Rees had yet another of his disastrous starts that perhaps say something about his highly strung temperament. He took 7 on the 1st and in retrospect this may well have cost him the championship. Yet who can say? Perhaps Dai reacted better than most of us to adversity. He certainly did that morning, managing to finish in 71.

Neither was Palmer a stranger to adversity, but his talent for recovery was remarkable. Towards the end of his third round, he played one of his greatest shots. On the 16th he hooked his drive and was many yards short with his second. He then saw his third drift away on the wind and finish a few feet from the out of bounds in very dense rough at the foot of some willow scrub. He then opened the face of a pitching club and lashed into the ball. Almost miraculously it rose near-vertically and came to rest dead to the hole. He had his par-5 when a 7 or even 8 had seemed much more likely. Winnie Palmer, his wife, years later remembered it as the shot that had won the championship. He finished in 69 to go into the lead:

> 212 Palmer; 213 Rees; 215 O'Connor; 216 Coles; 217 Henning, Thomson; 218 Nagle; 219 Brown; 220 Alliss

This was the fifth time that Dai Rees had either led or been one behind the leader with a round to go. At the age of 48 it was surely his last chance and many of us were willing him to do it.

As the championship approached its closing stages, however, it was Palmer who had increased his lead, with no one except Rees in the race. With five holes to play, even the Welshman was four strokes behind. With all hope gone, unless Palmer faltered, he was then able to produce his best. He birdied the 15th and at the 16th got down in two from some 50 yards. Even so, he needed a 2 at the 470-yard last hole to tie and his brave 3 was not quite enough.

Rees's charge had threatened Palmer, but he had proved able to respond. The plaque beside the present 16th at Royal Birkdale commemorates one shot he played in the final round, though it was not really as spectacular as the one I described earlier. This time, Palmer pushed his tee-shot into heavy rough just off what was then the 15th fairway. Others might have reached for a wedge. He took out a 6-iron, no doubt honed to a keen edge in his Latrobe workshop, where he has always liked to tinker with his clubs. He then cut through the Birkdale scrub to reach the green some 140 yards away and safely got his par.

The keys to Palmer's victory had been threefold. Besides his brilliant start on the second day in the worst of the weather and his spectacular recovery play throughout, he had dominated the par-5s, taking five birdies and an eagle from the 1st and 14th. He deserves to be only the second man (Bobby Jones is the other) to have a feat commemorated by a plaque on a British championship course. It says simply:

However, my co-author, Michael Hobbs, tells me that the Royal Birkdale committee slipped up. There was no play of consequence on that abandoned Friday, 14 July 1961, when Palmer passed the hours at the bridge table waiting to see if the course became playable. His great play was on the early holes of his second round on the 13th or on the final 36 holes played on 15 July.

HOW THEY FINISHED

	R1	R2	R3	R4	Total
A. Palmer *USA*	**70**	**73**	**69**	**72**	**284**
D. J. Rees	68	74	71	72	285
N. C. Coles	70	77	69	72	288
C. O'Connor	71	77	67	73	
E. C. Brown	73	76	70	70	289
K. D. G. Nagle *Australia*	68	75	75	71	
P. W. Thomson *Australia*	75	72	70	73	290
K. Bousfield	71	77	75	68	291
P. Alliss	73	75	72	71	
S. S. Scott	76	75	71	71	293
H. R. Henning *South Africa*	68	74	75	76	
R. Sota *Spain*	71	76	72	76	295
A. B. Coop	71	79	73	74	297
A. Miguel *Spain*	73	79	74	72	298
R. A. Knight	71	80	73	74	
S. Miguel *Spain*	71	80	70	77	
N. Johnson	69	80	70	79	
P. Runyan *USA*	75	77	75	72	299
D. Hutchinson *South Africa*	72	80	74	73	
J. R. M. Jacobs	71	79	76	74	300
H. Bradshaw	73	75	78	74	
P. J. Butler	72	76	78	74	
D. C. Thomas	71	77	77	75	
L. Platts	70	80	71	79	
R. L. Moffitt	73	80	73	75	301
J. Garaialde *France*	69	81	76	75	
B. G. C. Huggett	72	77	75	77	
E. G. Lester	71	77	75	78	
D. Miller	69	79	80	74	302
G. Will	74	75	75	78	
B. Wilkes *South Africa*	72	76	77	78	303
G. B. Wolstenholme	72	80	77	75	304
T. H. Cotton	76	77	74	77	
J. Panton	73	78	75	78	
W. McHardy	76	76	76	77	305
J. Henderson	72	78	77	78	
S. L. King	70	77	79	79	
E. Green	75	78	77	76	306
Mr R. J. White	71	79	80	76	
G. W. Low	76	76	76	78	
D. Snell	72	81	77	77	307
F. Phillips *Australia*	74	79	76	78	
T. B. Haliburton	74	79	76	78	
F. S. Boobyer	74	79	81	74	308
Mr M. J. Christmas	71	79	79	79	
W. J. Branch	77	76	78	78	309
C. Greene	77	76	78	78	

A youthful Jack Nicklaus at Troon in 1962.

Royal Troon, 1962

Palmer was by no means satisfied with his one victory and was in Scotland for the 1962 Open at Troon. Significantly, there was an increased American entry. Palmer must have convinced his fellow professionals that this British championship really was special. Entered for the first time were Gene Littler, US Open Champion in 1961 and Phil Rodgers, who was to come close in later years. Sam Snead, no longer really capable of winning at fifty but still a long hitter, was making his first entry since his 1946 win. There was also a 22-year-old, still holder of the US Amateur, who in a six months' professional career had won money in every event and less than a month before had beaten Palmer in an 18-hole play-off for the US Open, thus making himself highly unpopular with huge galleries who had eyes only for Palmer. This was Jack W. Nicklaus.

Palmer, despite this defeat, was at the height of his powers. He had won six tournaments in the year, including the US Masters for the third time. At Troon he faced two problems. One was that he was suffering lower back pain. This improved with the help of the Captain of the Royal and Ancient, Dr William Tweddell, who had won the Amateur Championship in 1927 and produced an even more remarkable performance in 1935 when he held the dominating Lawson Little to a one-hole margin in the final. (Little had won by no fewer than 14 and 13 the previous year!)

The other problem was Troon itself. After a dry summer, the course was bone-hard and dusty. I had been up there in March to do a pilot instructional strip cartoon with Bob Ferrier and Iain Reid. Eventually it was decided that my fame was not great enough on the world scene. It developed into the Gary Player series which has run for years and years and made a fortune for those involved. Iain acts as the guinea-pig, with Player providing the golfing wisdom that puts him right. Oddly though, after all those lessons, Iain's golf hasn't improved at all. He should have stuck with me and been Amateur Champion!

It was one of those perfect spring days with the larks swooping and the course in perfect order, the fairways cut tightly and looking like green Wilton and not another soul on the course, a golfer's paradise. 'What a marvellous place for the championship,' I thought. 'I can do well here.' But by July it was raddled, as if the rabbits had had the place to themselves and the greens staff had resigned en masse. Some holes, particularly the 11th, I thought unplayable. How can you hold a narrow fairway when the ball squirts away in all manner of directions?

In his final practice round, Palmer too thought it unplayable and had quite serious thoughts of simply going home. On the 15th, he had hit a superb drive which precisely split the fairway. But where was the ball? The answer was not encouraging: it had kicked at right angles into the rough and was 4 yards off the fairway in heather. Approaches to the greens were similarly unfair. The same iron shot might bite and stop quickly or bound onwards yards through the greens. Tom Watson has more recently said, however, that a golfer should not expect an Open course to be fair, that the test is of a man's nerve and composure. The Troon greens are small, which aggravated the luck of the bounce and the surfaces, and unlike 1950, when Locke won, they were not in championship condition.

Troon was, it now seems, quite probably the most unfair test presented to a championship field in all the years from the end of World War II. Many could not cope, even though its 7045 yards played short in the running conditions and the rough, after the hot, dry spell, was not severe.

In the two qualifying rounds, both Palmer and Nicklaus dealt none too satisfactorily with the first test, having 76s, but both Snead and Eric Brown were able to get round in 69. At nearby Lochgreen, the problems were fewer, and Kel Nagle broke the course record with a 65, while amateur Martin Christmas returned a 66. It was here that Palmer saved himself the following day with a comfortable 67. The leading qualifier was Eric Brown, closely followed by Nagle, Thomas, the Australian Bruce Devlin and Joe Carr.

As quite often in the Open, a relative unknown, Keith Macdonald, led with a 69. Such a man has his hour of glory and makes the headlines. Those more knowing are aware that he will soon be gone unless he has unnoticed qualities.

So it was with Keith, a 76 his lowest score in the remaining three rounds. It was much more significant that Peter Thomson lay second with a 70. Troon was a course made for Thomson's skills and composure. The Australian was always apt to be unhappy with the form of golf that demands high-flying target golf shots at the flag and very soft greens. He felt that golf should be a matter of judgement of distance (without pacing of the course and much consultation of yardage charts) and seeing what kind of shot was required to meet a particular problem. While others might be whacking an 8-iron at the flag that day and hoping it would stop, Peter would more likely choose to hit a low, gentle 6-iron that came to earth many yards short of the target and ran on and on over humps and through hollows to the heart of the green.

Palmer, despite his short and medium irons being none too accurate, was well placed with 71, as was Kel Nagle. Player had a 74 and expressed his distaste for the course. This was rather unusual for Gary. More normally he finds it psychologically helpful to his golf to convince himself that he is playing on land ideally designed by God for golf and for his golf in particular. A glance at our scores will show that few coped with the Troon problems as well as Player who, however, says he later stopped trying. Locke had a 78 and eventually failed to qualify and Littler a 79, also causing him to miss the cut in due course. Yet the story of the day concerned the young Titan, Jack Nicklaus, round in 80. He had met problems on the 11th, a hole sometimes considered the key to a Troon championship. It is a double dogleg, playing into a stiff crosswind that first day with a long stretch of rough and waist-high gorse to be carried from the tee. The carry made, the ball had to stop in a 20- to 30-yard stretch or run on into horrendous rough. Thereafter, a railway line follows along the right-hand side of the fairway to the green, where you can be out of bounds just five or six steps away. Nicklaus played it in 10 strokes and his double figures were repeated by quite a few others, Max Faulkner taking 11. It said much for his temperament that he produced a 72 the following day, which exactly made the 152 qualifying mark.

Many felt that the emergence of Nicklaus was almost a mistake and that he would not last the course as a professional. His swing had none of the balance and rhythm of a Gene Littler, Bobby Jones or Sam Snead. His physical appearance, strange as this may sound today, was also much against him. He was overweight and sported a bristly Teutonic haircut, often concealed by a jockey cap. Now frequently seen modelling the latest elegant men's fashions in upmarket American publications, at that time Nicklaus was often to be seen on the golf course in baggy khaki pants. No one was thinking of offering him a clothing endorsement contract.

That year, David Thomas and I were given the best chance amongst British players but, alas, we both opened with 77s and in danger of not qualifying. On the second day things went far better for both of us, David having a 70, while I played one of those great rounds that got away. I began birdie, par, birdie,

Arnold Palmer in his finest hour, Troon 1962.

birdie, followed by three pars, another birdie and a par to be out in 32. I then birdied the next two and followed up with two more pars to be six under and undoubtedly back in contention for the championship. On the next three holes a couple of putts slipped by and I plugged in the face of a bunker on the 16th. I finished in 69, equal best round of the day but . . . what might have been!

The other man with a 69 was Arnold Palmer, compiled in an opposite manner to my own. With problems on the greens, he reached the turn in 37 but then roared home in 32. A 64 between us which showed what could be done. This gave him a lead of two strokes over Kel Nagle, the only man in the field to have managed two steady rounds of golf. Already the rest of us were falling out of touch, 145 being the next best score to Nagle's 142. On this total were Phil Rodgers, recently 3rd in the US Open, despite an 8 on a par-3 in the last round, and Bob Charles, Ralph Moffit and Jimmy Martin. Then came myself, Macdonald and Brian Huggett on 146. Peter Thomson was almost gone after a 77. Perhaps his swing no longer had the same ease, and he was certainly far more prone to have at least one bad round in the Open.

For the final day, Nagle was paired with Palmer so a repeat of the duel at St Andrews in 1960 was in prospect. This time, however, they were playing together. Many thought Palmer, with his slashing aggressive style, would meet disaster: the steady straight-shooter Kel Nagle was the man to watch. The script was promising and the battle close – for a while.

Nagle began in the morning by having birdies on the first two holes to be level. Palmer then had his usual problems at the 545-yard 4th hole, out of range for most but not to a man equipped with the kind of 1-iron shots Palmer was playing that year. Nevertheless, in the championship proper he had two 5s and two 6s. One of the latter came in the third round and put Kel Nagle in the lead. But Palmer countered with a 2 to Nagle's 4 at the 210-yard 5th hole and then reached the 580-yard 6th hole in two to go further ahead. From the 5th to the 18th hole he was seven under 4s, at one point breaking into delighted laughter after a run of superb shots. After playing the feared 485-yard Railway hole (the 11th) in 4, 3, in previous rounds, he had another eagle in this round. After running through the green, he then holed out. It all added up to 67 and one of the greatest spells we have seen in the championship.

Nagle had done little enough wrong – he was round in the second-best score of the morning, a 70 – but at 212 to Palmer's 207 he was nearly out of touch. The rest of the field emphatically were:

> 215 Charles; 217 Rodgers; 218 Thomas; 219 Moffitt; 220 Huggett; 221 Snead, Weetman, Whitehead, Martin; 222 Alliss, Thomson

Palmer therefore went into the last round with a lead of five over Nagle with Bob Charles eight strokes away in third place, with Rodgers ten behind. The American had had an interesting finish to one round when his shot to the last green finished on the clubhouse steps – and also in a pint of beer. He managed to play his shot – and drank the beer.

Palmer was obviously unbeatable but it was still easily possible for him to beat himself as he was to do a few years later in the 1966 US Open when he handed over a greater lead to Billy Casper. Any doubts that might have remained were soon dispelled. Palmer put his approach to the 360-yard 1st hole 4 foot from the hole but missed his birdie. He was more successful at the 2nd, where he holed from 5 yards. Pars followed until he birdied the short 5th hole and again reached the 580-yard 6th in two. He was at the turn in 33 and coasted home in par for a 69, along with Tom Watson still the only champion to have three rounds under 70 in an Open Championship.

I think this was Palmer's peak performance in any major championship. Seldom in golf history has a man so dominated the rest of the field, leaving the second-place man, Nagle, who had played steadily enough to have won in most years, six behind, with the third men home thirteen strokes to the bad. At the time, Pat Ward-Thomas wrote: 'Palmer's qualities as a golfer, a competitor and as a human being are so exceptional that any measure of supremacy is within his phenomenal powers.' And so said all of us.

History was to find Palmer never again higher than 7th in a British Open and he was to win just one more major championship, the 1964 US Masters. I find it almost impossible to believe that twenty years and more have gone by since he last won the championship. The memories of his play and presence are so bright to those of us who were there during this great performance. At the time, we felt that he would go on to win again and again.

HOW THEY FINISHED

A. Palmer *USA*	**71**	**69**	**67**	**69**	**276**	A. B. Coop	76	75	75	72	298
K. D. G. Nagle *Australia*	71	71	70	70	282	D. Swaelens *Belgium*	72	79	74	74	299
B. G. C. Huggett	75	71	74	69	289	L. Platts	76	75	78	71	300
P. Rodgers *USA*	75	70	72	72		G. B. Wolstenholme	78	74	76	72	
						B. Bamford	77	73	74	76	
R. J. Charles *New Zealand*	75	70	70	75	290	H. F. Boyle	73	78	74	76	301
						K. A. MacDonald	69	77	76	79	
P. W. Thomson *Australia*	70	77	75	70	292						
S. J. Snead *USA*	76	73	72	71		G. W. Low	77	75	77	73	302
P. Alliss	77	69	74	73	293	H. Bradshaw	72	75	81	75	303
D. C. Thomas	77	70	71	75		H. R. Henning *South Africa*	74	73	79	77	
S. S. Scott	77	74	75	68	294	J. Hitchcock	78	74	72	79	
R. L. Moffitt	75	70	74	76	295	D. Beattie	72	75	79	78	304
J. Garaialde *France*	76	73	76	71	296	E. C. Brown	74	78	79	74	305
S. Miguel *Spain*	72	79	73	72		J. W. Nicklaus *USA*	80	72	74	79	
H. Weetman	75	73	73	75							
R. Whitehead	74	75	72	75		J. W. Johnson	76	74	81	76	307
J. Panton	74	73	79	71	297	Mr C. W. Green	76	75	81	76	308
C. O'Connor	74	78	73	72		D. Essig *USA*	76	72	79	81	
B. J. Hunt	74	75	75	73							
R. Foreman	77	73	72	75		D. Miller	76	74	81	78	309
J. Martin	73	72	76	76							
D. Hutchinson *South Africa*	78	73	76	70							

•6•

The Age of Nicklaus

Royal Lytham, 1963

The Lytham Open of 1963 saw changes which affect the structure of the Open Championship story. From this year, the leading players did not have to qualify. There was no longer the interest of seeing, before the championship proper began, who was in good form and who struggling, nor the occasional drama of the mighty failing to qualify – something that rarely happened to the great players, though it most certainly did to those just below them on the ladder of success. From 1914, two qualifying rounds had been introduced. In that year the leading 80 and ties went on to the championship proper, with these scores discarded. From 1963, the qualifying rounds continued, as they do today, only for those who had not earned the new exemptions.

Of course, Palmer, with the rare feat of consecutive wins immediately behind him, was a hot favourite. So great a draw was he that it was said: 'He almost *is* the championship.' Nicklaus had yet to demonstrate his powers in Britain. His performance at Troon the previous year had not impressed and he had made one other tournament appearance, in the Piccadilly at Hillside (near Royal Birkdale). He had survived that links test none too well either. There was a tendency to write off Nicklaus's abilities and the opinion was often expressed that he hadn't the touch and flair to cope with the different demands of links golf. He was too limited a player: a siege-gun-like drive into the wide blue yonder, followed by a smash with a wedge to the green. This view was not too far from the mark. Nicklaus himself has since freely admitted that this was his approach to golf. He aimed to overpower a course with a huge drive followed by a lofted iron. If his ball was in the rough, no problem. He would not be all that far from the green and had power in reserve to slash through rough, heather, gorse and whatever else nature had up her sleeve.

In America, the method had worked extremely well. First there was an amateur career that even outshone Bobby Jones's at the same age. It included two US Amateur Championships – in 1959 and 1961, the 1961 NCAA Championship and Walker Cup team membership (victorious in all of his matches at both Muirfield in 1959 and Seattle in 1961). But his amateur performance that had most aroused awe was at Merion in 1960. In winning the individual title in the World Amateur Team Championship (the Eisenhower Trophy) he had returned record scores of 66, 67, 68, 68 for 269. It was noted that his total was eighteen strokes lower than Ben Hogan's on the same course when winning the 1950 US Open. . . .

In 1963, Nicklaus had added to his three major championships (two US Amateurs and the 1962 Open) by taking his first Masters, and was later in the year to add his first PGA Championship. This was also to be the year that he first made an impact in the British Open.

The American entry was still limited: Nicklaus, Palmer (who had just lost a play-off for the US Open to Julius Boros), Phil Rodgers and Doug Sanders, who was at the peak of his powers during the first half of the 1960s on the US Tour but did not on this occasion make the 36-hole cut.

There was another young man making his first appearance in the Open: a day or two past his nineteenth birthday and only a professional since the previous year, Tony Jacklin was entered from Potters Bar, where he was under the stern tutelage of the Australian Bill Shankland.

On the first day, records fell. Both Peter Thomson and Tom Haliburton played the outward half in 29, a mark since equalled only by Tony Jacklin in 1970 and Bill Longmuir, also at Lytham, in 1979. (Denis Durnian also covered the first nine at Royal Birkdale in 28 in 1983.)

At the end of the day Thomson led on 67, together with Phil Rodgers. This short-game expert, who was many years later to coach Jack Nicklaus in this department, had used only 29 putts. Thomson had shown that he was still able to score well. Although his swing had perhaps become a shade flat and the rhythm was not quite there, he was still a jaunty figure and by this time a far more effective putter than in his early years. These scores were followed by Haliburton and Bob Charles, who had uncharacteristically missed a couple of short putts, on 68. A stroke after came Ramon Sota and Kel Nagle, who had been six under 4s after fourteen holes and at 42 was to have another admirable championship. Nicklaus did not repeat his first-round disaster as at Troon. He was round in 71 despite a 6 at the 462-yard 15th. Already well behind were Doug Sanders and Gary Player with 75s and – shock, horror – Palmer had taken a 76 after reaching the turn in a respectable 35. I had been going well but, alas, finished 6, 5 for a 74 against a par of 70.

After the second day, Rodgers had moved into the lead, with a second round under 70. This was the position:

135 Rodgers;   136 Thomson;   138 Nicklaus;   139 Nagle;   140 Charles

At the 3rd Charles had been out of bounds on the railway but had made some amends by holing a 10-yard putt. Nevertheless, he had two 6s on his card. Still in possible contention, but well back, were Gary Player (75, 70) and myself (74, 71). Young Jacklin had made a good start to his championship career with the same total from rounds of 73 and 72. Doug Sanders and Bobby Locke had failed to qualify for the final day but Jack Nicklaus had had his first really good round in Britain, his 67 equalling the course record. British golf followers eyed him with new respect. He and Thomson became those most fancied to win for, unlike many of the others, their nerve had been tested in championship golf and they had come through that fire. Bob Charles, on the other hand, had yet to establish his reputation, though he had won three times in Europe, the 1961 Bowmaker tournament and, in 1962, the Daks and the Swiss Open, while in America he had won the 1963 Houston Open. Yet the purists could not conceive of a left-hander winning.

On what was scheduled to be the final morning, Charles made his move, a 66 setting the course record. With a round to go, these were the leaders:

206 Charles;   207 Thomson;   208 Nicklaus, Rodgers

There was then a long gap to Nagle and Jean Garaialde on 213. These two and any other players in the field would need a freak last round to overhaul the leaders.

Bob Charles and Phil Rodgers were out last, behind Thomson and Nicklaus. Early on, the New Zealander was missing putts in unfamiliar style (he was already recognized as a master of the short game), while Nicklaus caused some indrawing of breath by thundering a drive up the 7th fairway and then reaching the green of this 553-yard hole with a 5-iron. Not only did he reach it but he was just 3 feet from the hole and in due course an eagle followed. I say 'in due course' because, although Jack takes his time over a putt today, during most of the 1960s he took an age. It was not particularly that he had a laborious Locke-like routine but that, preparations apparently completed, he then stood immobile over the ball before his brain would permit the device to go off. Today he is quicker but – dare I say it? – not quite as good a putter. Jack explained the reason for those long-drawn-out seconds: 'I just wait until I feel right.'

By the turn, Thomson was gone and eventually finished in 78. That did not please him one jot. At this point, Nicklaus (aided by that eagle) was level with Charles, with Phil Rodgers still there, just a stroke behind. After ten holes, Nicklaus went into the lead for the first time but, as so often at Royal Lytham, the championship was won and lost over the testing closing holes.

On the 462-yard 15th, Nicklaus struck a superb 2-iron just 5 yards past the hole but no birdie resulted. In fact he three-putted. The dropped shot was retrieved on the next, a 356-yard hole, which he birdied. But so, ominously, did both Charles and Rodgers when their turn came. Nicklaus then dropped a shot on the 17th, mainly the result of an unkind bounce, and followed by pulling his tee-shot to the last. He finished 5, 3, 5, 5, against a par of 4, 4, 4, 4 for a nevertheless highly respectable round of 70. Would it be good enough to win, we wondered?

Both Bob Charles and Phil Rodgers faced the test on the 18th which O'Connor, Leopoldo Ruiz and Eric Brown had failed in 1958 by bunkering their drives. Each had to hit it onto the fairway and then to the green and two-putt to beat Nicklaus. This they did, but though Jack Nicklaus had faltered, it was obvious that a man had arrived who was going to play a major role in the championship for many years to come.

So, on the Saturday, it was to be a play-off between a New Zealander and an American and, to be frank, the prospect did not do much to stir the blood. At the time, Bob Charles was rather uncharismatic, a sober, very professional gentleman going quietly about his job, a quiet smile the most emotion he ever expressed. Phil Rodgers was very much the reverse and caused a few raised eyebrows by what we British regarded as antics on the course. I recall how strongly BBC commentator Henry Longhurst disapproved when, on the last hole, he sank a putt to beat Nicklaus and then clowned, setting his cap over the hole. In the meantime, Bob was waiting with a 3½-footer to tie Rodgers. There might have been words said and protests made if he had missed!

A glance at the final scores for the 36-hole play-off seems to show that it was indeed a dull affair: Charles 69 and 71 to the American's 72 and 76. It all looks very reminiscent of that play-off fourteen years before between Locke and Bradshaw.

Yet this was not at all the case. Bob Charles's putter was charmed in the first round. He sank a 15-yarder on the 3rd to take the lead and in all had no fewer than eleven single-putt greens in his round. In the second round, Rodgers, when he had to make a move, proceeded to drop shots on the first two holes to make his task obviously hopeless. At this point, Bob Charles hooked his tee-shot onto the railway at the 3rd and the contest was on once again, his lead back to three. Rodgers then sank a long putt on the 4th, though Charles followed him in from closer range. On the 212-yard 5th, Bob made one of his rare putting mistakes that day, going some 3 yards past the hole and missing his return. On the next, Rodgers holed a putt of 6 or 7 yards and suddenly the gap was only one, but he followed this by dropping a shot on the 7th. The 8th was perhaps crucial. Rodgers birdied from 12 or so yards but so did Charles from a few yards nearer. That seemed to settle it. Rodgers missed each of the next six greens and fell away from contention.

Bob Charles became the only New Zealander to win a major championship and the only left-hander, a record he still holds. Oddly, the man is right-handed and only plays that way round because he started off in golf by having to borrow his father's set – which happened to be left-handed. Perhaps without that happy accident he'd still have been knocking around his local course at weekends only!

Bob Charles drives, Phil Rodgers watches, in the 1963 play-off for the Lytham Open.

HOW THEY FINISHED

R. J. Charles   **68** **72** **66** **71**   **277**
New Zealand
P. Rodgers *USA*   67   68   73   69

Play-off: Charles   69   71   140
          Rodgers   72   76   148

J. W. Nicklaus *USA*   71   67   70   70   278

K. D. G. Nagle *Australia*   69   70   73   71   283

P. W. Thomson *Australia*   67   69   71   78   285

C. O'Connor   74   68   76   68   286

G. J. Player *South Africa*   75   70   72   70   287
R. Sota *Spain*   69   73   73   72

S. Miguel *Spain*   73   69   73   73   288
J. Garaialde *France*   72   69   72   75

A. G. King   71   73   73   72   289
B. J. Hunt   72   71   73   73

S. Sewgolum   71   74   73   72   290
South Africa

H. Lewis   71   77   69   74   291
B. G. C. Huggett   73   74   70   74
B. Allen   75   71   71   74
I. D. MacDonald   71   71   74   75

P. Alliss   74   71   77   70   292
F. Phillips *Australia*   70   73   75   74

M. T. Leeder   76   73   74   70   293
J. A. MacDonald   73   75   75   70
B. Wilkes *South Africa*   70   77   74   72
N. C. Coles   73   75   72   73
M. Faulkner   77   71   71   74
H. R. Henning   76   68   71   78
South Africa

D. C. Thomas   74   74   75   71   294
J. Hitchcock   75   73   70   76
D. Sewell   75   72   73   74
A. Palmer *USA*   76   71   71   76

A. Jacklin   73   72   76   74   295
K. Bousfield   73   75   71   76
T. B. Haliburton   68   73   77   77

E. Large   78   71   76   71   296
B. Devlin *Australia*   75   70   75   76
D. Hutchinson   74   71   74   77
South Africa

W. Godfrey *New Zealand*   75   74   75   73   297
S. Davies *South Africa*   76   69   79   73
F. S. Boobyer   76   70   74   77

L. Platts   74   75   78   71   298
A. G. Grubb   77   72   74   75
G. M. Hunt   71   76   75   76

D. J. Rees   72   77   75   75   299
A. Moore   72   74   75   78

D. Swaelens *Belgium*   70   75   77   78   300

R. T. Walker   75   73   75   78   301

F. Bullock   75   74   82   74   305
H. W. Muscroft   72   77   81   75

St Andrews, 1964

By 1964, Nicklaus had the feel of the British Open. Many indeed felt that he ought to have won in 1963 yet had, in most un-Nicklaus-like fashion, faltered at the last fences. With the championship again at St Andrews, this was even more an occasion to stir his senses. He was in splendid form on the US Tour and was to finish leading money-winner for the first time, beating Palmer by a mere $82! He had already won four events, including the Whitemarsh tournament (in which Gary Player finished second), just before this championship.

This was the year when the American entry began to rise noticeably under the influence of Palmer and, I think by this time, Nicklaus also. If America's finest consistently felt it was worth entering the British Open, there must be something in it. Although Palmer himself was absent, Sanders was over again as, of course, was Phil Rodgers after his close miss at Lytham. Incidentally, when Rodgers arrived he was asked his opinion of the chances of British players and me in particular. He replied that Alliss was 'not fit to be my caddie'. Henry Longhurst earned himself one friend at least when he wrote in the *Sunday Times* that the reverse was the case. Also entered were the evergreen Johnny Bulla and Doug Ford, twice a major championship winner with his 1955 US PGA and the 1957 Masters, and the most interesting new face was Tony Lema's. After many trials and tribulations on the US Tour he had managed to become a leading player by 1962.

Yet the silly fellow was taking the British Open far too lightly. Only Ben Hogan had previously won the championship at his first attempt but he had sensibly allowed himself many days to get to know the subtleties of Carnoustie. Lema on the other hand had allowed himself no real time at all – just one hurried practice round, probably not even a full one at that.

Nicklaus in the meantime had been demonstrating his power play. It is said that in the calm conditions of one practice round he had only four times needed more than a 7-iron for his shots to the greens. On the last hole, where in 1970 he peeled off his sweater and drove the green (to awed gasps), in 1964 he was to do it as a matter of routine.

But it was by no means calm when the practice was done and play in earnest began. Winds were gusting up to 65 mph. Although the last was drivable and the long 14th just a drive and pitch, St Andrews had become a savage course to play. Let me try to look you straight in the eye and admit manfully that, yes, it took me 83 blows before I could gratefully slink into the anonymity of the locker room. And I was not alone. The South African Cobie Legrange, he of the bits-and-pieces backswing, fresh from a triumph in the Dunlop Masters, had used up 87 strokes. No doubt he counted himself fortunate in breaking 90 for he had taken 46 to reach the turn.

Many spectators know well enough that it is difficult to drive into strong wind, but this is not the half of it. A following wind presents its own difficulties. True, the drive may travel rather further than it deserves to (Craig Wood moved one 430 yards during the 1933 Open at St Andrews) but there are many perils on the shot to the green. The following wind takes backspin from the ball and it becomes very difficult to calculate where to try to land it, particularly at St Andrews with many humps and hollows to judge. To me, and many others, however, putting is affected worst of all. A competent professional should be able to vary the flight of his ball on the long shots to at least partly defeat the wind. Once on the greens, however, on fast surfaces with the wind behind it is really a matter of luck: either the putt drops or wanders on and on. There is a long – very long – one back. Putting is always a matter of delicacy and can never be helped by somehow or other having to brace one's body against the elements. One of the very best modern putters, the fine amateur Deane Beman, now US Tour commissioner, took four putts at the 10th and followed by three-putting from no more than 5 feet on the next hole!

Last year's champion, Bob Charles, in these conditions, was no better than 79, as was Thomson. Johnny Bulla, Bobby Locke, Doug Sanders and Gary Player were also already virtually out of it with 78s. But the winds had not been consistent. Lema, for instance, had played in relative calm, obeying the orders of his caddie and driving where he was told to. He, with Max Faulkner, Angel Miguel, Bernard Hunt and Hugh Boyle had 73s. On 72 were Harry Weetman and the then young Australian, Bruce Devlin, and, leading the field on 71 were the Basque Jean Garaialde and Christy O'Connor. The latter was superb in the wind and was the best player I ever saw at controlling the flight and movement of a golf ball until the arrival of Severiano Ballesteros. The Spaniard's major championship achievements mean that I must now rank him much higher in the golf Hall of Fame but Christy and the variety of both his shots and his imagination really captured my reverence in those far-off days.

Lema found St Andrews, he said: 'amusing and crotchety' which, all things considered, is a fair enough description of this quirky course. Liking it, he went into the lead on the second day. He had played superbly for his 68, a score he had produced despite missing five birdie attempts from 10 feet or less. He had driven the 9th (359 yards) and the 12th (312 yards), holing at the latter from some 12 yards for his 2. Lema stood on 141, followed by Harry Weetman with 143. A stroke further away were Bruce Devlin with Christy O'Connor and then came Jean Garaialde on 145.

At this point, there was little to be said of Jack Nicklaus. He had gone round in 76 and 74 and was therefore nine strokes behind Tony Lema. In his second round, he had used no fewer than 40 putts, unable to make himself hit the short ones firmly at the hole. But, as we shall see, he had learned his lesson.

By this time, everyone was taking far more notice of Tony Lema. They liked his posture and the easy elegance of his swing. Yet it was by no means a perfect one. He looped the club and, for the purists, had far too much lateral movement with his body. On the last day, Lema began by hitting his approach

Tony Lema entertains the press in style after the 1964 Open at St Andrews.

high over the Swilcan Burn to a foot at the 1st and later had birdies from good medium-length putts at the 4th and the 7th. As well as playing superbly through the green, Lema's putting stroke was working at its best. He again drove the 359-yard 9th, took three putts on the next and drove the 312-yard 12th. At the end of it all, Lema was in a totally dominant position so that after the third round the contenders stood as follows:

209 Lema;   216 Nicklaus (moving up the field);   217 B. Hunt, Devlin; 218 de Vicenzo, Weetman, O'Connor

Lema had opened up the biggest gap on his pursuers since Cotton's 67, 65, 72 so long before at Royal St George's in 1934. That year, Cotton had collapsed for a while in the last round but in 1964 Lema did not. Yet he faced a mounting challenge from Jack Nicklaus. First the man from Columbus, Ohio, had gone round in 66 in the third round and now he continued with the finest spell that he had had in the Open Championship up to that time.

Lema started a long time behind Nicklaus in 4, 5, 4, 5, 5, 4. Over that same stretch, Jack Nicklaus had made up no fewer than eight strokes on him. Nicklaus could hardly maintain that pace; Lema suddenly was himself again. He had a sequence of five 3s in a row, then three 4s and a finish of 3, 4, 4, 3. The final scores make it seem that Lema's triumph was easy, finishing five strokes ahead of Nicklaus, one of the few dominating victories in modern Open Championship history.

He had rounded off his championship victory in traditional style. Not for Tony Lema the by now conventional high pitch to the last hole. Instead, he played his second the way the St Andrews afficionados thought the hole should be played: first the drive, then a running shot through the Valley of Sin, that hollow in front of the green. It ran up and on, finishing little more than a yard from the hole. The crowd rose. In due course, Tony holed that putt for a 3 and a final round of 70, achieved in spite of a weak start.

Tony Lema was champion by five strokes, yet, looking back on it all from twenty years later, I can see that Nicklaus had made an emphatic declaration of intent: he had twice played St Andrews in a total of 134 strokes – 66, 68. At the time, this was the best finish produced by a competitor, champion or not, on any British course in the championship. It was the record, and was to remain the record until those momentous events at Turnberry in 1977.

So Lema was champion, a player who had won both hearts and minds. With this victory, he joined the Big Three of Palmer, Nicklaus and Player, with the South African tending to be edged into fourth place. Of Nicklaus, Pat Ward-Thomas said: 'He knew the cause was forlorn; never for an instant did he yield.' Perhaps 1965 would show that Nicklaus could triumph over the demands of British linksland golf.

HOW THEY FINISHED

A. Lema *USA*	**73**	**68**	**68**	**70**	**279**
J. W. Nicklaus *USA*	76	74	66	68	284
R. de Vicenzo *Argentina*	76	72	70	67	285
B. J. Hunt	73	74	70	70	287
B. W. Devlin *Australia*	72	72	73	73	290
C. O'Connor	71	73	74	73	291
H. Weetman	72	71	75	73	
H. R. Henning *South Africa*	78	73	71	70	292
G. J. Player *South Africa*	78	71	73	70	
A. Miguel *Spain*	73	76	72	71	
D. Sanders *USA*	78	73	74	68	293
F. Phillips *Australia*	77	75	72	70	294
D. C. Thomas	75	74	75	72	296
J. Garaialde *France*	71	74	79	72	
C. Greene	74	76	73	73	
R. L. Moffitt	76	72	74	74	
G. A. Caygill	77	74	71	75	297
R. J. Charles *New Zealand*	79	71	69	78	
P. Rodgers *USA*	74	79	74	71	298
J. A. MacDonald	78	74	74	72	
A. Murray *South Africa*	77	73	76	72	
S. S. Scott	75	74	73	76	
M. E. Gregson	78	70	74	76	

D. Ford *USA*	75	76	76	72	299
L. H. Lu *Hong Kong*	76	71	78	74	
J. Martin	74	72	79	74	
P. W. Thomson *Australia*	79	73	72	75	
A. B. Coop	75	72	76	76	
G. Will	74	79	71	76	300
P. J. Butler	78	75	74	74	301
G. M. Hunt	77	75	74	75	
R. Sota *Spain*	77	74	74	76	
S. Davies *South Africa*	74	77	71	80	302
J. Panton	78	74	77	74	303
D. Hutchinson *South Africa*	77	74	77	75	
B. Wilkes *South Africa*	77	76	74	76	
M. Murphy	76	74	76	77	
D. J. Rees	76	77	77	74	304
M. Faulkner	73	73	80	78	
S. W. T. Murray	80	73	78	74	305
N. V. Drew	76	76	79	74	
B. Allen	78	75	73	79	
L. Thomas *Australia*	76	75	82	72	
M. T. Leeder	77	76	75	80	308
K. D. G. Nagle *Australia*	77	76	80	80	313

Royal Birkdale, 1965

It had always been considered by both the United States Golf Association and the R and A that playing 36 holes on the last day was an essential test of a champion. Both bodies felt that such a marathon provided the supreme test of legs, nerve and stamina. Yet this Birkdale Open of 1965 was to be the last year that this was done. Stern principles gave away to the demands of television and the increased revenue from an extra day's play.

In practice, Nicklaus firmly established himself as favourite, and was indeed making a nonsense of some holes, if not the course as a whole. In one round he was eight under 4s after thirteen holes, finishing with a 65. He had needed just a sand wedge to the green for his second shot on the 510-yard 17th.

However, the best story of the week leading up to the championship concerned not the mighty Nicklaus but a 43-year-old American professional from Milwaukee named Walter Danecki. Off form, it seemed, in his first qualifying round at neighbouring Hillside, he took no fewer than 108 against a par of 70. The next day this was his card at Southport and Ainsdale:

7, 7, 8, 5, 5, 7, 9, 5, 5 (58 to the turn); 9, 6, 10, 4, 6, 5, 5, 4, 6 (55 back)

Obviously he was getting the hang of things by the closing stretch but, alas, Walter missed the necessary 151 qualifying total by 70 strokes.

The press was pleased to have discovered an American professional who was less than invincible. Investigation into Walter's background in golf began. Soon, it became clear that he was not a professional at all. 'Why did you lie on your entry form?' Walter replied that he had been playing golf for quite some time – seven years – and that he was no sham amateur: 'I wanted that crock of gold. My conscience made me write down "pro". Also I tried to join the US Professional Golfers' Association and I guess that also makes me a pro.'

And how had he enjoyed playing links golf?

'Well,' replied Walter, 'I guess your small British ball helped me some. If I'd had to play the big ball, I'd have been all over the place.'

There were other Americans entered, however, of more significance. Tony Lema was back again, as at St Andrews rather out of breath because of his late arrival, and so was Palmer, troubled by problems with his putting. Sam Snead, Phil Rodgers and Doug Sanders were Americans who did not do all that much better than Walter Danecki: all failed to make the qualifying aggregate of 149 for the last day's play, as did the recent champion Bob Charles.

Lema, however, began as if he was still at St Andrews, cruising to a first-round 68. His iron play had been excellent, with long putts holed at the 8th and 9th for him to be out in 33, an excellent start to a title defence. Christy O'Connor had started even more dramatically, with birdies on three of the first four holes. His eventual 69 put him in second place, with Irish amateur Joe

Carr and Arnold Palmer close behind with 70s. Two players who were attracting much attention were the 44-year-old Kel Nagle, who had just lost a play-off for the US Open to Gary Player. The middle-aged Australian had a 74, Gary a 76, including a 7 at one hole. It seemed that the South African, never backward in extolling the merits of physical fitness and his own routines, had this time gone too far and ricked his neck. Then followed a 71, and then a round of 79 on the last morning. At lunch, Gary withdrew.

At the end of the second day, British players were doing better than usual, seven being within four strokes of the leader. The winner would probably come from one of the following:

> 140 Lema, Devlin; 141 Palmer, Huggett; 142 Boyle, O'Connor, Carr, Brown, Thomson; 143 de Vicenzo; 144 Nicklaus, Will, Platts, Nagle

Lema, Palmer or Nicklaus were now favoured to win but it was also felt that the hour of the 27-year-old Australian Bruce Devlin might have arrived.

After a poor start of 74, 35-year-old Peter Thomson had moved up the field with a 68 which equalled the best score of the day. Birkdale that year suited his game: the ball was running and he could reach the five par-5s comfortably in two. His driving had been excellent, if not long. However, no one rated his chances highly. This field had too many big guns in it, they said. By this time, Thomson was virtually a figure from the past, a man from the record books. He had not finished higher than 5th since his last win in 1958. Nowadays, he was outgunned by the Young Turks. I had myself been around the championship lead that second day. After an opening 73, I had played the first nine in 32. Then, alas, came a 41 home after I took 7 at the 11th.

There had been changes to Birkdale since the previous Open. These included a new short 12th while the short 17th had been abolished. It was a long slog home with four holes of more than 500 yards in the last six:

Hole	Yards	Par	Hole	Yards	Par
1	493	4	10	393	4
2	427	4	11	412	4
3	416	4	12	190	3
4	212	3	13	517	5
5	320	4	14	202	3
6	468	4	15	536	5
7	158	3	16	401	4
8	459	4	17	510	5
9	410	4	18	513	5
	3363	34		3674	38
				3363	34
				7037	72

On the final day, there was a stiff breeze and many scores were in the high 70s and 80s. Eric Brown, for instance, who had been in contention, finished with a pair of 77s. The key pairings out last were Palmer with de Vicenzo and Lema with Thomson. After the morning round, several were no longer in contention. Nicklaus took 77, Brian Huggett 76, and Palmer, Nagle, Devlin and Lema all had 75s.

There was a new championship leader, Peter Thomson. He had begun the day two strokes behind the American but had overtaken him after 45 holes. It was a new Thomson British spectators were seeing. Gone were the smiles; he was all cold and determined, exchanging hardly a word with his playing partner, Lema.

With the afternoon to come, this was how they stood:

> 214 Thomson; 215 Lema, Devlin; 216 O'Connor, de Vicenzo, Palmer; 217 Nagle, Huggett, S. Miguel, Platts; 218 B. Hunt, Boyle

Bernard Hunt set the first target. After beginning with two 74s he played finely over the closing 36 holes for 70 and 71, the best aggregate of anyone by two clear strokes. However, his total of 289 was hardly likely to be good enough. De Vicenzo was having yet another good championship but again his putting betrayed him: he took four putts from the front of the 9th green and later dropped shots on the last two holes because of poor drives. Nevertheless, his 72 was a fine score and matched by few. His playing partner, Arnold Palmer, was soon out of it, eventually finishing with a 79, his worst round in the Open to that time.

The battle was clearly between Tony Lema and Peter Thomson. The Australian reached the turn in par and was apparently fully in control, his lead now three strokes. Then, from the 11th to the 14th, he missed putts of 5, 2, 8 and 4 feet. He was now just a stroke ahead of de Vicenzo, Huggett and Lema. Tony had, however, failed to capitalize on Thomson's errors. He had missed a tiddler of his own for his par on the short 12th and made an error of judgement on the 202-yard 14th. He failed on the sheltered tee to note the strength of the wind around the green. His ball was swept away left and he took 4.

Meanwhile, the little Welshman Brian Huggett was playing with great determination. Eventually he had the best round of the day, a 70. He holed good-length putts at both the 15th and 16th to give himself a chance of a 68 and perhaps the thought of victory was just too much for him. He approached both of the last two holes poorly. The 28-year-old Huggett was not to come as close ever again.

As Thomson and Lema stood on the 17th tee, the task was clearly defined for both of them. Thomson had to finish 4, 5 to be sure of winning, while Lema needed a pair of 4s. Though this meant a birdie, birdie finish, both of these par-5s were comfortably reachable in two strokes. If you look at the table of final scores, it is obvious that things went very wrong for the American, for there he is, down the list in 5th place. Lema, on this occasion, failed to meet the challenge, finishing with a par 5 and a 6 at the last. Nevertheless he had matched Thomson most of the day.

By contrast, Thomson finished supremely well. At each hole he drove straight and far enough and then played running long irons, pitching the ball well short of the green at both holes, which then threaded its way exactly through the gaps to the heart of the green. The approach putts were then perfectly weighted, giving him the mere formality of tap-in putts for his 4s.

It was Peter Thomson's finest hour. No longer could his achievements in the 1950s be dismissed on account of presumed rather than real poor quality of the fields. This time all the great names were there and men of a new generation at that. Thomson became the first modern to win the championship five times, his deed matched in the past only by J. H. Taylor, James Braid and bettered by Harry Vardon, with six victories. Nicklaus would have to try again. This year he finished nine strokes behind Thomson in 12th place.

HOW THEY FINISHED

Player	R1	R2	R3	R4	Total
P. W. Thomson *Australia*	**74**	**68**	**72**	**71**	**285**
B. G. C. Huggett	73	68	76	70	287
C. O'Connor	69	73	74	71	
R. de Vicenzo *Argentina*	74	69	73	72	288
B. J. Hunt	74	74	70	71	289
K. D. G. Nagle *Australia*	74	70	73	72	
A. Lema *USA*	68	72	75	74	
S. Miguel *Spain*	72	73	72	73	290
B. W. Devlin *Australia*	71	69	75	75	
J. Panton	74	74	75	70	293
M. Faulkner	74	72	74	73	
N. C. Coles	73	74	77	70	294
J. W. Nicklaus *USA*	73	71	77	73	
H. T. Boyle	73	69	76	76	
L. Platts	72	72	73	77	
A. Palmer *USA*	70	71	75	79	295
C. Legrange *South Africa*	76	73	75	72	296
T. Horton	75	73	76	72	
G. B. Wolstenholme	72	75	77	72	
E. C. Brown	72	70	77	77	
C. Greene	72	77	74	74	297
B. J. Bamford	72	76	74	75	
D. Hutchinson *South Africa*	74	72	76	75	
G. Will	75	69	74	79	
R. Sota *Spain*	75	70	78	75	298
A. Jacklin	75	73	73	77	
D. Sewell	72	75	74	77	
F. S. Boobyer	74	73	73	78	
Mr M. J. Burgess	74	73	78	74	299
H. Weetman	76	69	80	74	
A. B. Coop	78	71	78	74	301
W. Large	76	73	74	78	
Mr M. F. Bonallack	75	72	79	76	302
D. Miller	77	70	76	79	
D. Beattie	73	74	76	79	
Mr J. B. Carr	70	72	81	79	
G. W. Low	74	75	77	77	303
W. Hector	76	70	79	78	
D. C. Thomas	73	73	78	80	304
A. Gallardo *Spain*	77	71	80	77	305
T. D. Dill *USA*	75	72	79	79	
R. M. Mandeville	72	76	77	80	
D. Talbot	75	72	76	82	
G. Cunningham *Barbados*	74	75	79	78	306
J. McAllister	72	75	77	82	
R. Newdick *New Zealand*	75	72	80	80	307
B. Franklin *South Africa*	77	70	84	77	308
P. Alliss	73	73	82	80	
J. Hitchcock	75	74	85	76	310

Muirfield, 1966

After his good performances in both 1963 and 1964, the comparative failure of 1965 rankled with Nicklaus. He was more determined than ever in 1966. Two months earlier he had again won the Masters, his third success in that championship. Nicklaus was no stranger to Muirfield. He had played there in the 1959 Walker Cup and had liked what he had seen. But the Muirfield of 1966 was a very different sight. If Troon in 1962 had been unfair because of its condition, Muirfield's rough in 1966 was even more threatening.

Doug Sanders, asked about his prospects of winning, replied: 'I don't really want the 1st prize. I just want the hay concession.' I thought the rough the most fearsome sight ever. Gary Player, by contrast, said: 'This is the finest Open Championship test I have seen in a very long time.' I expect he felt outgunned by many and hoped his straight hitting would be a master card. Jack Nicklaus said that looking around from a tee was like looking at wheat whipping in the wind.

So what had the R and A done at Muirfield? Around the greens, they had let the rough grow to several inches. If a player missed a green, he would seldom be able to make clean contact between ball and clubface. The chipping skills of the modern professional would be reduced, while accurate iron play would be more highly rewarded. The R and A also imposed a special penalty on long drivers. At around 250 yards, the rough had been allowed to grow into the fairways, so that they became no more than 25 yards wide. Many would choose lofted woods or an iron in order to keep their tee-shots short of trouble. The trouble was severe indeed, the grass being maintained at nearly 2 feet high. Once off the fairway, no player would be thinking of whether it was a 3- or 4-iron to the green. He reached for a wedge and looked for the shortest way back to the fairway.

The field was perhaps the strongest ever assembled for a British Open. More and more of the very best Americans were now entering, influenced by the constant attendance of Arnold Palmer and Jack Nicklaus. This year, Julius Boros, Dave Marr and Dick Sikes were newcomers; those we had seen before included Sanders, Rodgers, Lema and of course Palmer and Nicklaus.

Entries from other parts of the world were equally strong and varied. From South Africa there was Gary Player, the Henning brothers, Barry Franklin, Bobby Cole (who had just won the Amateur Championship at the age of eighteen) and Denis Hutchinson, as good a putter as I've seen. Australia was represented by Bob Stanton, then highly promising, Bruce Devlin, Kel Nagle and the champion, Peter Thomson. It was felt that the championship would go to one of these, no British player being conceded any real chance. This was to be a woefully correct judgement – with one very honourable exception indeed.

This was the Muirfield card that year, very much as it is today. You don't need to change a Rembrandt:

Hole	Yards	Par	Hole	Yards	Par
1	429	4	10	475	4
2	363	4	11	363	4
3	385	4	12	385	4
4	187	3	13	154	3
5	516	5	14	462	4
6	473	4	15	407	4
7	187	3	16	198	3
8	451	4	17	528	5
9	495	5	18	429	4
	3486	36		3401	35
				3486	36
				6887	71

That year it looked particularly fearsome – nearly four miles of narrow alleyway, winding through that clinging rough.

It was soon apparent that many players had adopted the same 'game plan'. My great friend David Thomas was almost alone in using his driver whenever the extra length was any advantage at all – but he was probably the longest straight driver in the world at that time, even better I think than Greg Norman today. By contrast, the South African Harold Henning did not once use his driver and neither did Bruce Devlin. Palmer was more adventurous, using his at six holes, while Jack Nicklaus used his five times in the first round, the rest of the time using long-irons. Later, Jack was to be more cautious. In the championship as a whole, he used his driver just seventeen times, his 3-wood ten times and otherwise played strictly for safety and position with long-irons.

I had talked to some of the players about the problem of keeping the ball in play. There were, for instance, wise words from my close friend Guy Wolstenholme. He advised (and this is not something to be tried by handicap golfers) trying to hit the top half of the ball with the bottom half of the driver face, sweeping along and through. Roberto de Vicenzo told me he thought the only way to keep on the fairway was to tee the ball very low (apt to produce a high, faded shot) and then try to hook it. The two would cancel out and the ball fly straight. I liked the sound of this one and did hit some good ones but eventually there came a miscue and my nerve was gone.

For Nicklaus, the game plan was successful. At the end of the day, with Jimmy Hitchcock, a British professional who practised harder than perhaps any of us, he led the field with a score of 70. Those in close pursuit were:

71 Sanders, Lema, H. R. Henning; 72 Player, Nagle, Thomas;
73 Boros, Butler, Thomson, Marr, Palmer, Devlin (among others)

Immediately after came Roberto de Vicenzo, the young hopeful Tony Jacklin, yet to burst into the limelight with his victory in the 1967 Dunlop Masters, and myself.

Nicklaus had been two over par on the outward nine but had birdied the 11th, 13th and 16th. Perhaps the R and A had had Jack Nicklaus in mind when they narrowed the driving area for long hitters rather cruelly but, though often conceding his advantage in length, Nicklaus could not be deprived of his skills with the long-irons, both from the tee and into greens.

The next day, he led an Open Championship outright for the first time. He used his driver just four times and his 67 was just one above Henry Cotton's 66 on the second day of the 1948 Open, Cotton using his driver all the time.

There had been lower rounds. Peter Butler (one of the best British professionals ever), who had led the US Masters at the halfway stage two months earlier, was round in 65, a new course record, his steady faded wooden club shots almost inevitably on the fairway. British hopes rose but, alas, Peter took fifteen more strokes the following day. . . . A 66 from Phil Rodgers seemed more significant, for this was a man who had tied for the 1963 Open. He owed a lot to his putter. His driving had been rather unimpressive but he had taken just 26 strokes on the greens. The implement he had chosen to use was interesting. He had fitted a square grip and the shaft was at least 6 inches longer than standard, the idea being that he could anchor the top into the not so lean and hard flesh of his stomach and with the right hand gripped far down the shaft, use an underhand bowling action. It seemed to work well enough, for although his card had 5s in plenty (due to the unreliable driving) there were eight 3s and a 2 as well.

This is how they stood, with two rounds and two days to go, this time with a revolutionary Saturday finish:

> 137 Nicklaus; 138 Butler; 140 Rodgers, H. R. Henning, Nagle;
> 141 Sanders, Shade; 142 Devlin; 143 Caygill; 144 Boros;
> 145 Thomas, Palmer (among others)

On the Friday, Nicklaus went out with every appearance of solid assurance. By the turn, he had established a four-stroke lead on Peter Butler and was seven ahead of Rodgers, who had taken 40 for the first nine holes. Nicklaus was level par for his round after the 13th but thereafter the shots began to slip away. In the main, he failed to get down in two when finishing a touch short or just through a green. He had to sign for a 75.

Meanwhile, Phil Rodgers had been occupying himself in setting a new record for the inward half at Muirfield. He came back in 30, only the second time this had been done in the championship on any course: 4, 3, 4, 2, 4, 3, 2, 4, 4. Compare his last five holes with Jack Nicklaus's 5, 5, 4, 5, 5: twenty-four strokes for Nicklaus and seventeen for Phil Rodgers.

Small wonder that the championship leadership had changed:

210 Rodgers;   212 Nicklaus;   213 Sanders;   214 Palmer, Thomas;
215 H. R. Henning

David Thomas had played finely for his 69, while Palmer, so soon after he had dissipated that huge lead in the US Open at Olympic Country Club, San Francisco, and eventually lost a play-off to Billy Casper, had managed to come home in 32 to match it. Sanders's play had been highly consistent: 71, 70, 72. His clothing, however, had caused a stir against the subdued green background of Muirfield. He was dressed in tangerine from neck to toe. He was easy to pick out on the course for another reason. As someone remarked, 'How nice to see the hockey swing made to work effectively' – Sanders had the shortest backswing I have ever seen in a top-class golfer.

On the final day, the pairings were Thomas and Henning, Palmer and Sanders and, last of all, Nicklaus and Rodgers. In minutes, Rodgers's lead was gone as he took 5 on the 1st against Nicklaus's 8-yard putt for a birdie 3. Nicklaus continued to make the championship his own. On the 9th he had a 3-foot putt for a birdie but missed. Nevertheless, that was a very satisfactory 33 to the turn and no one was making a move against him. At the 475-yard 10th, he was home with a 1- and a 3-iron, while Rodgers ran up a 7. This meant that he was three ahead of David Thomas and four ahead of Rodgers and Doug Sanders, though the latter had the bonus of holing out from 60 yards from an eagle 3 at the 9th. Palmer was just about gone. He had driven into the rough at the 10th, taken a long-iron from a bad lie (just as he had more than once at Olympic in the US Open) and the eventual 7 was the main reason why he finished no better than 8th, with a final round of 74.

On the 11th green, Nicklaus was even more strongly placed as he lined up a putt of some 3 yards for a birdie. He missed narrowly but took his usual ponderous care over the 15-incher he had left. And missed again. Significantly, at about the same time, David Thomas was holing an enormous putt at the short 13th for a 2. The gap was suddenly down to a single stroke. On the 12th tee, Nicklaus set himself up for his normal left-to-right fade. Instead, he hooked wildly. He was, however, lucky enough to clear the worst of the rough, his ball coming to rest in the well-trampled ground beyond. He got his next onto the green and safely two-putted. One crisis over. But he dropped another shot on the 13th, being short with his tee-shot and then chipping well past the hole.

Ahead, both David Thomas and Doug Sanders were trying to set a target. Thomas, in fact, was to come almost as close to winning this Open as in 1958. At the short 16th he hit a magnificent iron shot which struck the flag and bounded some 9 or 10 feet away. He did not get his birdie. Then, on the long 17th, he sent his drive too far right, leaving him a shot to the green over the

David Thomas in the Muirfield rough of 1966.

mound that bites in on the right. His second clung in the long grass at the back of the mound. He got his 5 but it was 'only' a par, the same result as Doug Sanders's shortly after. So Thomas set the target at 283 and Sanders soon matched it.

From the 14th tee, Nicklaus pushed into the right rough and could not get home in two strokes. He now knew what he needed to tie: level par. He parred the 15th and because of the following wind, used just a 7-iron to the 198-yard 16th. Though well short of the hole, he stroked his approach putt dead.

With the wind favouring at the 528-yard 17th he could now think in terms of winning the championship rather than merely seeking to play-off with Sanders and Thomas. He took only a 3-iron from the tee, not wishing to risk reaching the rough at the angle of the dogleg. He was 240 yards from the green and followed up with a 5-iron, finishing a few yards from the hole and two-putting for his 4. He was again the championship leader but needed to par the 18th at Muirfield, one of golf's great last holes, for victory. Again, he used an iron from the tee and had a shot of about 200 yards to the green. His 3-iron whistled down the right-hand side, turning in with the wind. He putted up to about a foot and his first Open Championship title.

With his victory, Nicklaus completed the Grand Slam of having won each of the four major championships, achieved before only by Ben Hogan, Gene Sarazen and Gary Player. In the years ahead, he was to become the only man to do it twice – and then three times.

HOW THEY FINISHED

J. W. Nicklaus *USA* **70 67 75 70 282**

D. C. Thomas	72	73	69	69	283
D. Sanders *USA*	71	70	72	70	
G. J. Player *South Africa*	72	74	71	69	286
B. W. Devlin *Australia*	73	69	74	70	
K. D. G. Nagle *Australia*	72	68	76	70	
P. Rodgers *USA*	74	66	70	76	
D. Marr *USA*	73	76	69	70	288
P. W. Thomson *Australia*	73	75	69	71	
S. Miguel *Spain*	74	72	70	72	
A. Palmer *USA*	73	72	69	74	
R. H. Sikes *USA*	73	72	73	72	290
C. O'Connor	73	72	74	72	291
H. R. Henning *South Africa*	71	69	75	76	
J. Boros *USA*	73	71	76	72	292
J. Hitchcock	70	77	74	72	293
P. J. Butler	73	65	80	75	
G. A. Caygill	72	71	73	77	
Mr R. D. B. M. Shade	71	70	75	77	
P. Alliss	74	72	75	73	294
D. Sewell	76	69	74	75	
R. de Vicenzo *Argentina*	74	72	71	77	
E. C. Brown	78	72	71	74	295
Mr P. M. P. Townsend	73	75	72	75	
G. Will	74	75	73	73	
K. MacDonald	75	74	70	77	296
Mr M. F. Bonallack	73	76	75	73	297
D. Hutchinson *South Africa*	74	73	73	77	
R. J. Stanton *Australia*	73	72	73	79	
F. Boobyer	72	76	77	73	298
C. Greene	72	76	76	74	
A. Lema *USA*	71	76	76	75	
A. Jacklin	74	76	72	76	
Mr R. E. Cole *South Africa*	73	75	73	77	
A. Henning *South Africa*	73	73	74	78	

D. J. Rees	75	72	77	75	299
B. Franklin *South Africa*	77	72	79	72	300
R. J. Charles *New Zealand*	74	74	77	75	
D. Snell	73	75	76	76	
R. Bernardini *Italy*	76	73	73	78	
G. B. Wolstenholme	73	76	73	78	
C. G. Pennington	74	75	76	76	301
B. G. C. Huggett	76	73	80	73	302
H. W. Muscroft	73	75	79	75	
J. Burns	76	73	76	77	
R. T. Walker	74	72	76	80	
G. W. Low	75	72	79	77	303
M. Gregson	79	71	74	79	
E. Lester	74	76	74	79	
J. Panton	78	72	81	74	305
G. Cunningham	75	75	76	79	
F. Rennie	74	75	81	76	306
D. Miller	73	77	78	78	
C. DeFoy	76	73	79	78	
R. A. Knight	77	73	77	80	307
S. Wilson	76	74	76	81	
L. Platts	74	74	78	81	
A. B. Coop	74	76	79	79	308
A. Grubb	79	70	84	76	309
J. Carter	72	77	85	77	311
W. Hector	76	72	78	85	
L. Taylor	77	71	78	87	313
I. Clark	77	70	86	82	315

Hoylake, 1967

Nicklaus had now removed doubts about whether or not his high-flying pattern of play could succeed on British linksland in the Open Championship. When the championship returned to Hoylake (for the last time) in 1967 he was an even firmer favourite, having just won a handful of American tournaments, including the Open for the second time. At Baltusrol, he had eclipsed Arnold Palmer with his last-round 65, though Palmer too had played well.

In the first round, Nicklaus missed only one fairway and caused gasps with a drive of fully 370 yards on the 9th. However, he picked up little on the greens and had to settle for a 71.

This was another dry year, the fairways burned sepia. The ball ran on and on but, unlike many of our championship links courses, Hoylake has very flat fairways. The golfer is little in fear of those unkind bounces into the rough after a straight drive. Others on 71 were Thomson, hopeful of winning again on a course suited to his play, Sanders, again caparisoned in fine silks from the Orient, the shoes being of patent leather, and I. However, in the third round I pulled a back muscle when trying to force a ball too far from a bad lie in the rough, and had to leave the course.

Ahead of us at the time, however, were Lionel Platts on 68, and a quartet of unfamiliar names on 69: Jimmy Hulme, playing only his third professional tournament and now the pro at Gullane, David Bonthron, P. Jones and Jack Wilkshire, a fine player though not a regular in tournament golf. Close behind on 70 came Clive Clark and Gay Brewer (both of whom had played the homeward nine in 31 strokes), Roberto de Vicenzo and several others.

As if to put the popinjay Sanders to shame (small chance of that!), Nicklaus appeared on the 1st tee next day in strictly utilitarian golf attire: white shirt and grey trousers. Strange how seldom great champions appear in dazzling attire. I suspect they have an arrogance that says: 'I want you to look at my golf, not my clothes.' In due course, his 69 gave him the championship lead, shared by Bruce Devlin, a prominent name for a few years who tended to fade out in the later stages of a championship. Close behind were the gallant Hume, Fred Boobyer from Whitefield, a Manchester club, Lionel Platts, who always played with cardigan open and flapping in the breeze, and Roberto de Vicenzo, nineteen years after his first championship appearance at Muirfield, a generation before in 1948. All these were on 141. One stroke behind appears the name of Tony Jacklin, beginning his sequence of six years when his scores made news in every championship. Clive Clark and Gary Player were at 143. Among those who did not beat the cut were last year's hero, David Thomas, Bobby Locke, now mainly coming to see old friends, the 1963 champion, Bob Charles, and that very fine American player Gay Brewer, who pushed the club almost directly away from him at the beginning of the backswing before looping it around so that all was well by the time he returned it to the hitting area. He had followed his opening 70 with an 80. Brewer had played just one practice round and, they said, deserved his fate. What then of David Thomas, who had been very diligent and gone round 14 times?

The third day was very much the story of two men, de Vicenzo and Player. Both were round in 67 and their cards are worthy of record:

Hole	Yards	Par	Player	Vicenzo	Hole	Yards	Par	Player	Vicenzo
1	421	4	4	4	10	404	4	4	4
2	426	4	3	4	11	201	3	3	3
3	491	5	5	4	12	460	4	5	5
4	196	3	3	4	13	158	3	2	2
5	450	4	4	4	14	515	5	4	4
6	389	4	3	3	15	459	4	5	4
7	193	3	2	3	16	529	5	4	4
8	492	5	5	4	17	418	4	4	4
9	393	4	4	3	18	400	4	3	4
	3451	36	33	33		3544	36	34	34
						3451	36		
						6995	72		

A glance at these cards shows something of de Vicenzo's long game. He had 4s at all the long holes and dropped a shot only twice, on the 4th and 12th.

Before Roberto went to the 1st tee he had watched wistfully while Nicklaus and Deane Beman worked on their strokes on the beautiful Hoylake putting green in front of the clubhouse windows. As they finished, Roberto said: 'I wish for just two days I could putt like you do.' At the end of his round he was able to speak in different tones: 'When you find a stroke on the greens everything is OK. The weather always seems fine and the food and wine taste better.' Roberto did not have a miraculous putting streak that day but he had holed four putts of between 3 and 4 yards and had done nothing silly on the greens elsewhere. It had made all the difference.

By contrast, Nicklaus had played without serious error for his 71 but had holed nothing of any length. With a round to play, these were the leaders:

    208 de Vicenzo; 210 Player; 211 Nicklaus; 212 Devlin, Clark
    (he had birdied four of the last five holes for his 69); 213 Platts, Nagle

De Vicenzo had started the championship at odds of 33–1 and, of course, these had shortened drastically. Those who thought they were in the know, however, still said Roberto had five times finished 3rd and had twice been 2nd but his nerve, or that putting stroke in which he had so little trust, had always let him down. It always happened in the Open, said his critics, and it would happen again, despite his impressive record of some 130 victories worldwide. There were far younger lions in the field and the two with the strongest jaws, Player and Nicklaus, were close behind.

Roberto de Vicenzo had a long love affair with golf. He delighted in the lonely pleasure of the practice ground – the crack of impact and the soaring flight of a golf ball. As often as not in his homeland he would hit golf balls for four hours and then go out for his round of golf. It was not the cold pursuit of a Hogan for mastery over the flight of a golf ball. Roberto just liked to hit and watch them fly.

All those years were to pay dividends on 15 July 1967. Roberto had developed a slightly different grip to combat his tendency to hook under pressure or when concentration lapsed. It was basically the Hogan solution: set the left hand so that you can see only one knuckle. Roberto took this thought a stage further, getting his grip more out of the fingers and into the palm. For putting, he tried to reduce the hinge in the right wrist and make the stroke more of an arm and shoulder movement. Nevertheless, the battle was with himself and his nerve, not technique.

He did begin the final round with one advantage. He felt, and he was right, that 'Many peoples are with me.' Perhaps this is why he looked at Gary Player, with whom he played that day, and thought: 'You can't be afraid of this little fellow.' Roberto and Gary matched each other shot for shot over the outward nine but at the 10th that particular contest virtually ended when Roberto single-putted for a birdie, while Player took three putts from 10 feet. Earlier, Roberto had missed two greens but chipped dead to save his pars. By the 12th, Gary was well and truly gone.

Ahead were Clive Clark and Jack Nicklaus; 'I felt like a peashooter against a cannon,' said Clive later. After the 1st hole, Clive was out of contention. He cut his long-iron over the turf bank into the out of bounds. He later recovered brilliantly for a joint 3rd place with Player.

But Nicklaus was playing his typical final round of that period in his golf career. He tended to start a championship knowing that he was better than anyone else and then play cautiously, going for the safe part of a green rather than the flag, or clipping an iron off the tee, rather than letting fly a booming drive. He did not wish to surrender his superiority because of avoidable error. A different man appeared for the last round, however, if Nicklaus was behind the leaders, forced to go for everything. In my opinion, and despite Arnold Palmer's reputation for the last-round charge, Jack Nicklaus is by far the best last-round player ever born.

Nicklaus pulled a little closer to Roberto with birdies on the 7th and 8th. He had to get 4s at the long 14th and 16th to threaten Roberto. When he heard that Nicklaus had managed just a 5 on the 14th, Roberto said: 'He make his par like a good boy. I feel better.' But Nicklaus was by no means done for. He got his 4 at the 529-yard 16th and also birdied the last for a 69 and a total of 280.

Roberto by now had a clear target: level par on the last three to win. All through the championship he had been booming drives with the slightest of right to left curves down the middle. Could he produce just three more?

Roberto de Vicenzo at Hoylake, 1967.

On the 16th, he pushed his tee-shot slightly right and his line to the green lay perilously over the practice ground, which is out of bounds at Hoylake. His nerve and swing remained true. A superbly struck 3-wood shot finished in the heart of the green and he made up another stroke on Jack Nicklaus. Two more fine drives followed, each long enough to leave him needing just a 9-iron to the green. Roberto was champion. Surely there has never been a more popular one.

The Argentine was not expected to win, nor expected it himself. He explained his attitude like this: 'For years I came over trying so hard to win. This year, I simply came back to see my friends.' So he was to do for many years to come, his majestic rhythm a constant delight. His friendliness and humour I shall always cherish. So should the world of golf.

The feelings of Henry Cotton so many years before (remember he had decided that the South American was the man to beat in 1948) had been vindicated. Said Cotton in 1967: 'Roberto de Vicenzo is the best striker of a golf ball in the world.' And so said all of us.

HOW THEY FINISHED

R. de Vicenzo *Argentina*	**70**	**71**	**67**	**70**	**278**
J. W. Nicklaus *USA*	71	69	71	69	280
C. A. Clark	70	73	69	72	284
G. J. Player *South Africa*	72	71	67	74	
A. Jacklin	73	69	73	70	285
H. R. Henning *South Africa*	74	70	71	71	286
S. Miguel *Spain*	72	74	68	72	
H. F. Boyle	74	74	71	68	287
T. Horton	74	74	69	70	
P. W. Thomson *Australia*	71	74	70	72	
A. Balding *Canada*	74	71	69	73	
B. W. Devlin *Australia*	70	70	72	75	
S. Peach *Australia*	71	75	73	70	289
G. B. Wolstenholme	74	71	73	71	
M. Hoyle	74	75	69	71	
D. Beman *USA*	72	76	68	73	
L. Platts	68	73	72	76	
B. J. Coxon *Australia*	73	76	71	70	290
D. Sanders *USA*	71	73	73	73	
H. W. Muscroft	72	73	72	73	
C. O'Connor	70	74	71	76	291
R. P. Mills	72	75	73	72	292
D. Hutchinson *South Africa*	73	72	71	76	
K. D. G. Nagle *Australia*	70	74	69	79	
B. G. C. Huggett	73	75	72	73	293
B. W. Barnes	71	75	74	73	
R. R. W. Davenport	76	69	75	73	
B. Franklin *South Africa*	70	74	73	76	

F. S. Boobyer	70	71	74	79	294
J. M. Hume	69	72	73	80	
B. Allen	71	77	76	71	295
H. Weetman	76	69	79	71	
D. Sewell	71	77	74	73	
G. Cunningham	74	74	73	74	
D. Snell	77	70	73	75	
C. Pennington	77	72	74	74	297
R. Bernardini *Italy*	75	74	74	74	
H. Bannerman	74	75	74	74	
M. Leeder	72	76	75	74	
D. Melville	74	74	74	75	
N. C. Coles	74	72	76	75	
B. J. Hunt	74	73	73	77	
E. C. Brown	74	75	76	73	298
P. Rodgers *USA*	74	73	77	74	
D. Bonthron	69	75	79	75	
A. Yancey *USA*	75	73	71	79	
J. Wilkshire	69	78	79	73	299
J. Garaialde *France*	76	71	78	74	
D. Butler	75	74	75	75	
J. Panton	73	76	75	75	
R. Emery	73	75	77	75	300
M. Gregson	76	73	73	78	
S. Sewgolum *South Africa*	73	75	77	76	301
K. Bousfield	73	74	79	76	302
J. Cockin	71	78	76	78	303
J. Martin	75	73	80	80	308
W. Ferguson	74	74	80	80	

Carnoustie, 1968

In 1968, the championship returned to Carnoustie, scene of Ben Hogan's memorable triumph in 1953. This year the field featured Billy Casper, that prodigious accumulator of both money and tournaments in the USA, where he had been a winner since 1956. By 1968, he had won some 40 US events and had taken the US Open in both 1959 and 1966. The time had come to make his first attempt at the British title. His challenge was to be a strong one indeed and his quest for the British championship was to last several years. He was one of the many Keith Mackenzie recruits, then taking over as R and A secretary from Brigadier Brickman. Keith was always keen to get the strongest fields possible for the championship.

Other leading Americans entered included Bert Yancey, who had just lost the US Open to a new star in the firmament, a certain Mexican American called Lee Trevino. Most of the Americans, however, were players we had seen before: Doug Sanders, Arnold Palmer, Gay Brewer and, of course, Jack Nicklaus.

Nicklaus had a problem: he just did not like the course. He thought it wild, very badly conditioned and without subtlety. He would have liked his construction company to make changes but, to date, he has never been asked.

Indeed Carnoustie was its usual stern self and this year the longest stretch of golfing country ever presented to an Open field at 7252 yards.

Hole	Yards	Par	Hole	Yards	Par
1	406	4	10	446	4
2	468	4	11	370	4
3	343	4	12	473	4
4	429	4	13	168	3
5	389	4	14	485	5
6	565	5	15	460	4
7	386	4	16	243	3
8	163	3	17	458	4
9	475	4	18	525	5
	3624	36		3628	36
				3624	36
				7252	72

The first day was bitter chill and windy. At the end of it, there was an amateur in the lead. This was Michael Bonallack, that year's Amateur Champion, having annihilated Bill Hyndman by 8 and 7 at Newcastle, County Down, for a remarkable, and record, third consecutive victory. One of the most resolute putters and chippers I have ever seen, he had used 30 putts that first day in a round of 70. On the same total was the 1964 British Youths' Champion – but not yet a tournament-winner in Britain – Brian Barnes. Close behind, with scores of 71, were Peter Mills and Maurice Bembridge (another new British hope). At 72 was Tony Jacklin, who won some $58,000 on the US Tour that year and became the first British player to win a US event since Ted Ray took the US Open of 1920 when he was first home in the Greater Jacksonville Open. Bob Charles, Billy Casper and Irishman Paddy Skerritt had the same score. Nicklaus had started almost disastrously, with a 76, and Gary Player was not much better placed with his score of 74.

Almost out of it so early were Palmer, Thomson and Devlin with 77s and Sanders and Yancey with 78s. Bernard Hunt had totted up six 6s on his card but the disaster of the day belonged to the young John Morgan. Not only did he fail to break 90 but, to add injury to insult, he was bitten by a rat while identifying his ball in the rough!

On the second day, Billy Casper showed what a formidable golfer he was. He became only the fourth man ever to break 70 to that date in a Carnoustie Open Championship. Casper was a player who had found a 'drill' before each stroke useful. He selected his club, took two light wristy practice swings and then smoothly moved into the shot itself. If this sequence was disturbed, Casper began again from scratch – and this included putting the club back into his bag!

His 68 had opened up a four-stroke gap on the field, a very handy cushion indeed. On 144 came Bob Charles and the two young British hopefuls, Brian Barnes and Tony Jacklin. A stroke further away were Paddy Skerritt and Jack Nicklaus, who had made up much ground with his 69, which included an eagle-3 at the long 14th. One splendid sequence was broken: my friend and Ryder Cup partner Christy O'Connor failed to make the 36-hole cut for the first time since 1952. Because of the severe conditions on the first day this cut was a very high one, coming at 155.

Now the pack were after Casper and again the weather was wild. Casper retained his lead – but only just – after a 74. Bob Charles had closed up to within a stroke after his steady scoring of 72, 72 and 71. Bob could usually be counted on in foul weather. Then came Gary Player on 216, after a pair of 71s, and Jack Nicklaus on 218. He had been going well, especially after the 14th, which he birdied, but came to grief on that beast of a hole, the 'short' 16th. It has often given Jack trouble over the years. He is not alone. Once there is a crisp breeze against, the longest hitters among us have to reach for our drivers. The two young hopefuls had fallen away, Jacklin to a 75 to be five behind the leaders, and Barnes, who had concentrated on playing Jacklin rather than the course, had an 80. It was to cost him his best chance of winning in a long career. How often it is said at the time that X or Y's chance will come again. But it doesn't, except for the greatest players.

For the first time, a cut after 54 holes was initiated, reducing the final day's field from 80 to 45. The strain of leading now proved too great for Billy Casper. He slumped to a 78 when a round of just 74 would have seen him home as champion. Bob Charles also soon began to fall away and the stern duel that eventually followed for the championship was fought head to head between Gary Player and Jack Nicklaus in most testing conditions. The best round was 71 – from Brian Barnes but, alas, too late.

The first moment of crisis came on the long 6th, which Nicklaus was obviously looking to birdie. Instead, he hooked his tee-shot out of bounds. We have all come to respect Jack's impeccable behaviour in the face of triumph or disaster. This time the mask slipped. The great man gave his unoffending golf bag a very firm kick indeed!

Nicklaus now cut loose, going for extreme length from the tee, ignoring trouble round the green and firing straight at the flag. Nevertheless the necessary putts seldom dropped and Player kept his lead at three strokes. He did, however, miss the green on the short 13th and Nicklaus for a moment pulled to within two strokes.

Almost immediately, there followed one of the great shots of Open Championship history. At the 14th, Gary cracked a blind second shot over the Spectacles (a cavernous pair of bunkers) to the green. But not just 'to the green' in fact. His ball was just 2 feet from the hole: an eagle where Jack managed a birdie. On the 15th, Player's drive found the rough and he had to be content just to play back to the fairway. Nevertheless he still got down in par with a good pitch and another successful stroke from an old favourite putter he had resurrected.

That was just about that, though Nicklaus kept on trying, successfully this time getting a 3-wood to about 3 yards at the 16th and then thundering a drive over both bends of the Barry Burn on the 17th, a stupendous carry of well over 250 yards.

Player became champion for the second time, nine years after his first success. He had perhaps won by consistency, probably the only man in the field to avoid a 6 on his cards. For Nicklaus it was another starring role but, try as he might, he had not been able to prise the championship from Player's grasp.

HOW THEY FINISHED

Name	R1	R2	R3	R4	Total
G. J. Player *South Africa*	**74**	**71**	**71**	**73**	**289**
J. W. Nicklaus *USA*	76	69	73	73	291
R. J. Charles *New Zealand*	72	72	71	76	
W. J. Casper *USA*	72	68	74	78	292
M. Bembridge	71	75	73	74	293
B. Barnes	70	74	80	71	295
N. C. Coles	75	76	71	73	
G. Brewer *USA*	74	73	72	76	
A. Balding *Canada*	74	76	74	72	296
R. de Vicenzo *Argentina*	77	72	74	74	297
B. W. Devlin *Australia*	77	73	72	75	
A. Palmer *USA*	77	71	72	77	
T. Horton	77	74	73	74	298
K. D. G. Nagle *Australia*	74	75	75	74	
R. Cole *South Africa*	75	76	72	75	
P. Alliss	73	78	72	75	
B. G. C. Huggett	76	71	75	76	
E. C. Brown	76	76	74	73	299
F. Skerritt	72	73	77	77	
A. Jacklin	72	72	75	80	
D. L. Webster	77	71	78	74	300
S. Miguel *Spain*	73	75	76	76	
Mr M. F. Bonallack	70	77	74	79	
G. A. Caygill	79	76	71	75	301
P. W. Thomson *Australia*	77	71	78	75	
K. A. MacDonald	80	71	73	77	
S. Wilson	73	81	74	74	302
M. Gregson	77	75	76	74	
R. J. Shaw *Australia*	75	76	73	78	
D. C. Thomas	75	71	78	78	
J. Gallardo *Spain*	78	71	78	76	303
D. Huish	74	74	78	77	
H. Bannerman	74	73	77	79	
D. Sanders *USA*	78	76	73	77	304
M. Murphy	77	74	77	77	305
J. Martin	81	72	74	78	
G. Cunningham	80	70	75	80	
H. Habian *USA*	77	74	76	79	306
A. G. Grubb	79	74	75	79	307
M. Said Moussa *Egypt*	77	76	75	79	
C. Greene	75	77	76	79	
A. Yancey *USA*	78	75	74	84	311
B. J. Coxon *Australia*	77	72	78	84	
R. P. Mills	71	76	80	84	
H. Weetman	77	76	74	86	313

Royal Lytham and St Anne's, 1969

The championship of 1969 saw another significant rise in the quality American entry. Nicklaus's arrival was by now as predictable as dawn and dusk (he has missed no championship since his debut in 1962 and has never failed to reach the last day). Palmer, however, was absent, as on five other occasions. Other Americans were on the verge of becoming regulars, Bert Yancey, for instance, Billy Casper and Gay Brewer. There were also some new faces. Orville Moody, for example, who in one of the biggest surprises in championship history, had recently won the US Open. Over here also was a player who had bet on Moody to win, Lee Trevino. He had been equally unknown and not so much under-rated as not rated at all when he had won the US Open at Oak Hill in 1968 with four rounds under 70. Now he was making his first appearance in the British Open. So also was a man who has become more successful with the passing of the years and was 1969's US PGA Champion, Ray Floyd. To complete the field of leading Americans there was Miller Barber, the man with an enormous loop in his backswing. A prodigious money- and tournament-winner, he seldom made a strong move in major championships. Today, in his early fifties, he is still making sacksful of money on the US Senior Tour, which he dominates with Don January.

Besides the American entry, Gary Player was expected to make a strong defence of his title. There was also money on Bob Charles, who had been enjoying a good American season (with more than $50,000 banked) and was by this time far more recognized as a player of world class than he had been at the time of his championship win.

The Open Championship is apparently a money-loser for the bookies of Britain. It seems they only break even because of the 'sentimental money' on British hopefuls. Nick Faldo, for instance, attracted much attention in the days leading up to the 1983 Open because of his fine form in Europe in the weeks before, yet Nick himself declared that he was playing only well enough to make the top 20 in an American tournament. 1969's British hopeful was Tony Jacklin and that is where the sentimental money went that year. Those 'in the know' were aware that Tony had been having a poor season in America (he totalled only $33,000 for the whole year) and in the previous six weeks his fortunes had reached an all-time low, with five 36-hole cuts missed in six tournaments. However, Jacklin felt that he was playing well; Player, for his part, declared that he had never been in better form in his life (so what's new!); Nicklaus had been busy trying to cure a swing fault, but without success – as likely as not a sign that he would win.

The first day, however, and indeed much of the championship, belonged to Bob Charles. Minor revisions had been made to Royal Lytham and St Anne's and he had soon set a new course record with a 66:

Hole	Yards	Par	Charles	Hole	Yards	Par	Charles
1	208	3	2	10	344	4	4
2	439	4	3	11	540	5	4
3	458	4	4	12	200	3	4
4	393	4	5	13	339	4	3
5	212	3	3	14	445	4	4
6	490	5	4	15	462	4	5
7	553	5	4	16	356	4	3
8	394	4	4	17	462	4	4
9	164	3	2	18	389	4	4
	3311	35	31		3537	36	35
					3311	35	31
					6848	71	66

Bob Charles's good scoring came from steady driving, with only one tee-shot in the rough. His holing out had been excellent though he had one three-putt green, the 4th, but had holed one putt of as much as 20 yards and another of nearly 10 yards. Not surprisingly, he said the surfaces were magnificent.

This score gave the New Zealander a two-stroke lead over Hedley Muscroft, who faded away later, and Tony Jacklin. When he followed with a 69 on the second day, this would normally have given him a substantial lead after 36 holes but in fact he now led by just one stroke from Christy O'Connor, who had set a new record with a 65, eagling the 6th and holing out from a bunker on the 10th. His card read:

3, 4, 4, 4, 3, 3, 4, 4, 3 (32); 3, 5, 3, 3, 4, 4, 4, 3, 4 (33)

He had not dropped a shot and had one eagle and four birdies. I for one wondered if, after so many strong performances, it could at last be Christy's year.

This was how the leaders stood at the halfway point:

135 Charles; 136 O'Connor; 138 Jacklin, Caygill; 140 Casper;
141 Thomson, Moody, Wolstenholme; 142 Player, Panton;
143 Henning, Yancey, Love, Garner, Townsend; 144 Barber,
Devlin, Floyd (among others)

So many names and still no Nicklaus! He had begun with a poor first round score of 75 and after a second-round 70 was still behind some twenty other players. Of course, a bad start was apt to produce a bolder Nicklaus, so he could by no means be discounted.

Tony Jacklin's iron play had been none too good but his recovery shots and putting had been excellent. The 6th could have been disastrous for him. There, he hit a poor drive then followed by topping his 3-wood into a bunker which – Jacklin's words – 'had trees in it'. He wedged out and his 9-iron to the green

Tony Jacklin at full stretch at the 1969 Royal Lytham and St Anne's Open.

finished well away from the hole, perhaps ten or even a dozen yards. Jacklin holed the putt.

On the third day, there were two significant moves forward – or so it seemed. Jack Nicklaus had a 68 and the 46-year-old warrior, Roberto de Vicenzo, a 66. He had been encouraged by a 73 the day before, achieved despite the burden of three penalty strokes!

Even more significant, however, was the fact that there was a new championship leader and British at that. Tony Jacklin had added a second 70 to his first-round 68 and led the field by two strokes from Bob Charles. He had holed only one putt of any length but his wedge and bunker play (four times down in 2 from sand) had been excellent, saving him a stroke on several occasions. At this stage of his career, the features of his game were long and usually straight driving, excellent short-iron and bunker play and streak putting. By the latter I mean that I do not believe Tony Jacklin was ever a great putter but he was capable of inspired spells.

Asked about the reasons for his success, Jacklin gave much credit to his friend, the stylist Bert Yancey, who had been encouraging him to get away from the habit of lifting up on his toes for full shots. Instead, said Yancey, he must try to develop more hip and knee slide through the hitting area and consequently more pull and less push of the club.

Bob Charles had fallen back a little because of poor driving, while Christy O'Connor had never recovered from bunkering his first tee-shot and then taking three putts at the 2nd. With the grand climax of the final round to come, these were the contenders:

> 208 Jacklin; 210 Charles; 211 de Vicenzo, Thomson;
> 213 Huggett, Nicklaus; 214 Love, Yancey; 215 Moody,
> Brewer, Casper

The rest were out of reach of the leaders, barring miracles and disasters.

One of those well out of reach was myself, at 220. Though it was not in my mind at the time, I think 1969 was the last year I played with serious thoughts that I might win. At the time, I intended to continue tournament play for several more years, for I was still only 38. However, events moved in other directions and this was to be my last season as a full-time tournament professional.

My fourth round was highly enjoyable. I went to the turn in 30 and came home safely in 36. It was an early target for I was playing fairly well down the field. Could I win, I wondered, with my 286 total? 'Not very likely', was the sensible answer I gave myself. Nevertheless, it was by two strokes the lowest round of the day and was five strokes lower than anyone who finished higher than my 8th place. If I had averaged 71s over the first three rounds, I might have been champion. After the 66, I went off to do commentary. As the players finished, though I wished them no harm, I was not urging their putts into the hole!

The last pair out were Tony Jacklin and Bob Charles. Jacklin began with a nerve-settling pair of pars and then birdied the 3rd from about 5 yards. He then holed a much longer putt of well over a dozen yards to birdie the 4th and open up a five-stroke gap on Charles and the rest. He then dropped a stroke at the short 5th and, as usual, met trouble at the 6th. In practice, Jacklin had found that he could fly the bunkers in driving range on the left of the fairway and then had none too long a shot into this 490-yard par-5. In the championship proper, however, with the wind less favourable, Jacklin could not do it and had a sequence of 5s. This time, his second shot was played sitting astride a tree and coaxing his ball back to the fairway. However, he got a par and lost no ground to Bob Charles, who three-putted for a 5 also.

On the next hole, Charles sent his second shot into long grass but played an excellent sand wedge almost dead, while Jacklin, bunkered, recovered to a couple of yards and holed the putt. No change again. On the 9th, Charles hit a half-shank from the tee but chipped and putted well for his par. The margin still remained at four strokes, nine holes between Jacklin and the championship. Still a long way.

That gap was reduced when Bob birdied the next and Jacklin bunkered his tee-shot to the short 12th. However, he got out to 4 feet and saved par. On the 13th, the New Zealander's club grip began to unwind. Jacklin, perhaps the last top tournament player to have a solid grounding in a pro's shop, had done this job many times before. Why not lend a helping hand? They soon continued. Here, Jacklin's wedge to the green bounced unkindly from hard ground and he finished in long grass, only a hack out onto the green possible. His eventual 5 meant that he was now just two strokes ahead.

However, his lead again became more comfortable on the 14th: he parred; Charles hit a poor second shot and went three behind. Both dropped a shot on the next and hit good drives to the 17th. Charles parred while Jacklin only reached the front of the green with his second shot and then, from some 20 yards, took three putts for the first time in the championship.

With a hole to play he had a two-stroke lead. This may sound comfortable enough but plenty of doubts can intrude, such as: 'What if I bunker my drive and he birdies?' At moments such as this you find yourself remembering the anguish of the players who failed to hit the required straight drive down the 18th at Lytham in 1958.

Charles, playing first, pushed his drive but not into severe trouble. There was no real reason why he should not get to the green with his next. Tony Jacklin then had 'this drive for the championship', though I don't suppose he thought in those terms during those vital seconds. What followed was a vast drive straight down the middle of the fairway, what many thought was the longest seen all week. 'There it is. What a corker,' said Henry Longhurst. He

The simple delights of victory: Tony Jacklin holes the last putt in 1969.

had an 8- or 9-iron left but, as many of us do, chose the club he had been happiest with all week, a 7-iron. By deciding to play a half-shot, he may well have been wise. There have been many times when the adrenalin flows that a player has hit a short-iron 20 or so yards further than normal. By playing a half 7-iron, Jacklin had more feel of the strength.

It settled 5 or 6 yards from the hole and he had the luxury of knowing that unless Bob Charles holed out from much further away he was champion. Bob didn't and Tony Jacklin became the first British winner since Max Faulkner in 1951, 18 years before. To Jack Nicklaus he said: 'God, Jack, I never knew anyone could be so scared, so frightened.'

For his victory, Tony received a cheque for £4250, not much compared with the £40,000 that Tom Watson took home with him in 1983, but Jacklin's life was transformed. It is not the cheque that counts but the prestige. His fee for an exhibition game was immediately increased from around £150 to £3000. He was in demand to endorse shoes, airlines, clothes, socks, hats, whisky, golf club grips, clubs and gloves. Lucrative contracts for TV matches came his way. The money trees were all sprouting. Jacklin still makes much of his income as a result of the glory of that championship victory. For the time being, however, he bought a house at Elsham, near Brigg, in Lincolnshire, continued to play from Potters Bar Golf Club and went to the Palace to receive his OBE.

How Jacklin Did It

Hole	Par	Jacklin	Hole	Par	Jacklin
1	3	2, 3, 3, 3	10	4	4, 4, 4, 4
2	4	4, 4, 4, 4	11	5	4, 5, 5, 5
3	4	4, 3, 4, 3	12	3	3, 3, 3, 3
4	4	3, 4, 5, 3	13	4	4, 4, 3, 5
5	3	2, 3, 3, 4	14	4	5, 5, 4, 4
6	5	4, 5, 5, 5	15	4	4, 4, 5, 5
7	5	5, 5, 5, 4	16	4	4, 3, 3, 4
8	4	4, 4, 3, 4	17	4	4, 4, 5, 5
9	3	4, 3, 2, 3	18	4	4, 4, 4, 4
	35	32,34,34,33		36	36,36,36,39

It may be interesting to look at these scores in a little detail. Perhaps the most significant fact is that he did not once take 6 or worse and was never more than one stroke over par at any hole. The most difficult par-4s during the event were the 14th, 15th and 17th and Jacklin had his problems, finishing two over par for each. He did not dominate the par-5s as his long straight driving might indicate, being only three under par on these for the championship. On the par-3s, he was level, and on the 4s level also. He had fourteen birdies throughout and was ten times over par, but only once over par for any nine holes.

HOW THEY FINISHED

A. Jacklin	**68**	**70**	**70**	**72**	**280**
R. J. Charles *New Zealand*	66	69	75	72	282
R. de Vicenzo *Argentina*	72	73	66	72	283
P. W. Thomson *Australia*	71	70	70	72	
C. O'Connor	71	65	74	74	284
D. M. Love *USA*	70	73	71	71	285
J. W. Nicklaus *USA*	75	70	68	72	
P. Alliss	73	74	73	66	286
K. D. G. Nagle *Australia*	74	71	72	70	287
M. Barber *USA*	69	75	75	69	288
N. C. Coles	75	76	70	68	289
C. Legrange *South Africa*	79	70	71	69	
G. B. Wolstenholme *Australia*	70	71	76	72	
T. Horton	71	76	70	72	
G. Brewer *USA*	76	71	68	75	290
B. W. Devlin *Australia*	71	73	75	72	291
P. W. Townsend	73	70	76	72	
E. C. Brown	73	76	69	73	
H. R. Henning *South Africa*	72	71	75	73	
O. Moody *USA*	71	70	74	76	
A. Yancey *USA*	72	71	71	77	
B. G. C. Huggett	72	72	69	78	

B. J. Hunt	73	71	75	73	292
G. J. Player *South Africa*	74	68	76	74	
F. S. Boobyer	74	70	76	73	293
G. A. Caygill	71	67	79	76	
W. J. Casper *USA*	70	70	75	78	
Mr L. P. Tupling	73	71	78	72	294
H. W. Muscroft	68	77	73	76	
J. Garaialde *France*	69	77	76	73	295
D. Swaelens *Belgium*	72	73	76	74	
M. Faulkner	71	74	76	74	
M. B. Ingham	73	73	74	75	
B. J. Waites	73	75	74	74	296
V. B. Hood	75	71	74	76	
R. Floyd *USA*	74	70	76	76	
J. R. Garner	72	71	76	77	
L. Trevino *USA*	75	72	71	78	
G. Cunningham	74	72	71	79	
B. W. Barnes	73	73	76	75	297
J. Hitchcock	74	74	73	76	
A. Gallardo *Spain*	72	76	73	77	298
P. H. Wilcock	73	74	74	77	
Mr M. F. Bonallack	74	72	73	79	
J. Panton	73	69	76	82	300
H. Jackson	69	78	75	79	301

St Andrews, 1970

It was a different Jacklin who arrived at St Andrews for the 1970 Open. His Lytham victory had caused rejoicing throughout the land and it had been noted that for the first time for ten years no American golfer had finished in the top five. Welcome in the extreme though Jacklin's victory had been, few thought of him, however, as a golfer of the very highest class.

All that was to change. For the US Open at Hazeltine National the British press by no means gathered in force to report on how the young hero fared. But Jacklin led after the first and second rounds and flight bookings were hurriedly made. After the third round he was four ahead and after a stutter towards the end of the first nine suffered no alarms on the second half, finishing with a long putt for a seven-stroke victory, the first achieved by a British player since 1920 and the largest margin of the 1922–83 period.

Surely Jacklin just might be the best player in the world? Certainly there was no doubt that he had firmly established himself amongst the game's top half-dozen. Though doubts were expressed that Jacklin's hectic money-making schedule must surely limit his practice time, and drain both desire and energy, Jacklin opened up at St Andrews with a start paralleled only by one other championship contender, Peter Thomson in 1958 at Royal Lytham.

Jacklin began with a 4-yard putt for a birdie on the 1st. On the 2nd, he was just some 5 feet away and that was another birdie. After the 3rd he was three under, got his par on the next and then hit a 4-wood onto the 567-yard 5th for yet another birdie. At the 7th, he launched a 320-yard drive which finished in an extremely awkward place close to the lip of a bunker, but he managed to run it up to about a yard for another birdie. There was a par on the 8th and Jacklin did not attempt to drive the green at the 359-yard 9th, instead taking a 1-iron for safety and by now fully conscious that here was a highly spectacular round almost half achieved. His 9-iron to the green pitched on, bounced, checked twice and then ran into the hole. An eagle and, with Peter Thomson and Tom Haliburton, he had become one of the few who had played nine holes on a British Open Championship course in 29. They, however, those 12 years earlier, had faltered thereafter.

Jacklin continued on his way with no faltering of inspiration. On the 10th, only some 330 yards, he played a running approach to a couple of yards at most and holed that one for a 3. A par followed, and then came a now forgotten minor disaster.

On the 12th, a hole of little more than 300 yards, Jacklin's drive had the line and momentum to reach the green but, as the pace died away, ran into a lady marker and was checked. Instead of reaching the green, and leaving him at worst two putts for a birdie, he had now to play a short pitch. The pitch was adequate but a par 4 had to go down on his card. He also parred the next and, as a downpour began to gather intensity, with hail and thunder, drove up the

560-yard 14th. The drive was good but the 4-wood that followed was not, Jacklin later saying that he had cut his shot because he had been disturbed by a cry of 'Fore' as he began his downswing. Jacklin's ball finished in a bush. He was still considering the options as greens disappeared under water and play was suspended for the day. Early the next morning, Jacklin took a penalty drop and a 6. With other shots dropped, a likely 63 became 'just' a 67.

The first-round leader was Neil Coles, out in 31 and back in 34. He also had holed a second shot, in his case to the 7th, and had beaten the course record of 66 set by Bernard Hunt and myself in 1960 and equalled by Jack Nicklaus in Lema's 1964 Open.

St Andrews had indeed been at the mercy of golfers in good form. When the deluge stopped play on the first day, forty golfers had broken 70 and seven more were to finish off the next day under that target. This being so, it would almost fill a page to record those who finished high up after the first round!

There had been scarcely a breath of wind and the greens had been both holding and of easy pace. Trevino even tempted fate by saying, 'You can't miss from 6 feet,' while Doug Sanders had got round in 68 despite putting his first approach shot of the round into the Swilcan Burn. Sanders, who had to pre-qualify, explained his error by saying: 'I guess my game isn't built around an early morning start!'

On the second day, Trevino made his first significant move, going round in 68 for a second time and taking the lead on 136. Jacklin survived the disappointment of having completed his first round early that morning in 'only' a 67 and took 70 this time, good enough for joint second place with Jack Nicklaus.

At the time there was a question mark over Nicklaus's future. He had not won a major championship since the 1967 US Open. Many felt that after some eight years already at the top of world golf he might be 'burned out'. His putting had been off and for two years his driving had been unreliable. He had decided to slim down – successfully – yet one wondered if the quest for a new shape had cost him strength.

After these three came:

> 139 Clark, Horton, Sanders, Henning, Richardson, Coles;
> 140 Palmer, O'Connor

Scoring had gone up a little and there were only five rounds under 70.

For the third day, there was a stiff wind and only two players could break 70, the Scot Ronnie Shade and the young Peter Oosterhuis. Only twelve players were under par for the three rounds. The rape of St Andrews was over.

Trevino, a good wind player, was round in 72, which put him two strokes clear of his closest pursuers, who were Jacklin (73), Nicklaus (73) and Sanders (71), all now on 210. The latter had not three-putted until the third round but was not otherwise looking a convincing golfer. There was much shuffling of feet and adjustment of alignment, with gripping and regripping. Sometimes he gave up the whole routine and began again. His backswing had always been short but he now seemed to find it necessary to heave the ball away with his belly and finished off-balance on full shots. But despite appearances, he was playing well and showing mastery of the run-up shots. Of course, the clothes were as imaginative and colourful as ever.

A stroke further behind on 211 came Oosterhuis and Coles, then, at 212, Harold Henning. The rest of the field were probably too far behind to challenge the leaders but included Christy O'Connor and Hugh Jackson on 214. Peter Thomson, Bert Yancey and John Richardson were on 215.

For the final day, the wind blew at about 30 mph but there were gusts up to twice that speed. Fifty-seven players survived the cut after 223 (missed by Gary Player and the Americans Orville Moody and Miller Barber) and nine of these scored 80 or worse. Another 27 scored between 77 and 79. The best round all day came from the quite venerable John Panton who, at the age of nearly 54, was round in 71, which moved him up the field to 9th place. All of the real contenders would have won with that score!

Nicklaus managed to reach the turn in 35, the only one to break par on the first nine all day, but he did rather less well coming home and ended with a 73. Trevino remained in contention, despite playing to the wrong flag on one double green, and then his putting stroke deserted him over the second nine. He, together with Harold Henning, finished on 285, two behind Nicklaus's total with Jacklin a further stroke away in 5th place on 286.

It was all up to Doug Sanders. On the 17th, the Road Hole, on which he had taken 6 during his first round, his second shot finished in the Road bunker, which cuts into the left side of the green. He was faced with a terribly difficult bunker shot. Too firm and the ball would at best not be near enough for a single putt and at worst on the road; too weak and it would return to his feet, as was to happen repeatedly to the Japanese player, Tsuneyuki Nakajima, when the Open returned to St Andrews in 1978. But Sanders judged and executed his shot perfectly, his ball finishing little over a foot away from the hole. All he had to do now was par the 358-yard final hole to be Open Champion.

There are few problems on this hole. The fairway is as wide as a football field with not a bunker in sight. All in all, the easiest finishing hole in championship golf, despite that hollow, the Valley of Sin, lying in wait in front of the green.

Sanders drove safely and considered his next shot. All week he had been very successful with the pitch and run, judging the run of the ball through folds in the ground and over humps often to near-perfection. This time, however, he went back to the 'natural' American shot he was most used to, the high pitch. I am not sure if Sanders's judgement was faulty or whether he hit the ball slightly thin. No doubt about the result, however. His ball pitched at least a dozen yards past the flag and when it came to rest he had a 20-yard putt that was

first downhill, then level and finally gently uphill to get close to the hole, with the Valley of Sin in wait, just beyond.

Sanders was slightly too cautious. His first try was short, leaving him with a putt of a yard or so 'for the Open'. He shaped up for the putt but then indecision became apparent as he bent forward to remove a wisp of grass. All in all, he was trying to settle his nerves. Small chance when you're trying to hole from a yard for the championship!

The locals say that the putt Sanders had always swings rather more from left to right than the player thinks. It could be said that this is what happened though I thought myself that he struck it with little conviction. The whole attitude of his body was that of a man knowing he was going to miss. The ball dribbled away to the right.

Doug Sanders had rented a house close by for the week and was staying there with his wife Scotty and the singer and pianist Buddy Greco. Dave Thomas and I were round there often during the week and after that putt we did our best to cheer him up. Even Doug's usually irrepressible high spirits were dampered by the daunting memory of that miss. Never mind, he was still in a play-off for the Open, at the age of almost 37 the closest he had come to a major championship, though he had won the Canadian Open as an amateur.

The winds were much the same on the Sunday for the first play-off since 1963, when Bob Charles had won. This year, the players could thank the New Zealander for the fact they were playing just 18 holes. After his win against Phil Rodgers over 36 holes, Bob had mentioned that he felt 18 were really quite sufficient. The change had come about.

Nicklaus and Sanders began with two pars and Sanders then quickly fell two behind, three-putting the 3rd and driving into the rough on the 4th. On the next hole, 567 yards, they were both in trouble. Sanders drove into a bunker, made little ground with his recovery and then hit a 3-wood into thick rough. From there, he managed to get down in two more for a remarkable par. Nicklaus was also twice in trouble but eventually pitched to 4 feet and holed the putt for his 5 also. The next five holes were also halved until Sanders failed to get his par on the short 11th to fall three behind, after taking two in Strath bunker. On the 13th, Sanders hit a near-shank, dropped another shot, and was four strokes behind with five to play. Although the position appeared hopeless, he hounded Nicklaus to the end.

He birdied the long 14th from about two yards (Nicklaus missing a similar putt), and got another birdie on the next hole. At the 16th Nicklaus struck a sumptuous 4-iron to the green – but it was too strong. He ran well through and, like Simon Owen some years later, could not get down in two more. Sanders produced the counter-punch, a putt of some 6 yards for his par.

The gap was one stroke, the feared Road Hole and the 'easy' 18th to play. They had a following wind and both drove well with Sanders to play his second first. He hit a fine running 4-iron to the back of the green, some 6 or 7 yards beyond the flag. Here then was no small problem for Nicklaus, 'finished' as a great player, some were saying. (How silly that sounds today!) His response to the challenge was near-perfect, a drawn 7-iron that finished a little inside the Sanders ball. Both failed with their birdie putts.

On the last tee, Sanders was aware that Nicklaus could drive the green in the conditions and that, a stroke behind, he must try to do the same. He hurled himself into the shot and drove over 300 yards, his ball coming to rest some 30 yards short of the flag. Nicklaus deliberated a little, removed his sweater and lashed through the green and into long grass beyond. Though the shot has since become part of golf legend it actually left Sanders with the advantage. He was 50 yards away in a good lie while Nicklaus was in thick rough, only a few yards through the green with a shot to an away slope confronting him and the Valley of Sin waiting beyond.

This time, Sanders did not use the high pitch but played a 'proper' Scottish run-up to 4 feet, a very likely birdie. Nicklaus then played a good shot perhaps 3 yards short of the hole and, like Sanders the day before, had 'this putt for the Open'. For a moment it looked as if he would miss as the ball began to swing to the right but it caught the right-hand half of the hole – and was in. Nicklaus flung his putter high in the air and there was a moment of confusion as both became aware that what goes up must come down. But all was well, and the new champion shook hands with his gallant, and unlucky, challenger.

With this victory, Nicklaus became the first man to have won the Masters and US and British Opens twice and is still the only golfer with that achievement on his record. His major championship victories now totalled nine. He now entered a new era of his golfing life, with power lessened but range of strokes ever-increasing.

For Sanders, it was a last chance of a major championship. Walter Hagen had long before declared that no one remembers who finished second, yet Sanders's defeat – and the manner in which he faced that defeat – are still bright in our memories.

HOW THEY FINISHED

	R1	R2	R3	R4	Total
J. W. Nicklaus USA	**68**	**69**	**73**	**73**	**283**
D. Sanders USA	68	71	71	73	
Play-off: Nicklaus	72				
Sanders	73				
H. R. Henning *South Africa*	67	72	73	73	285
L. Trevino USA	68	68	72	77	
A. Jacklin	67	70	73	76	286
P. A. Oosterhuis	73	69	69	76	287
N. C. Coles	65	74	72	76	
H. Jackson	69	72	73	74	288
J. Panton	72	73	73	71	289
P. W. Thomson *Australia*	68	74	73	74	
T. Horton	66	73	75	75	
A. Palmer USA	68	72	76	74	290
R. J. Charles *New Zealand*	72	73	73	74	292
M. Bembridge	67	74	75	76	
A. Yancey USA	71	71	73	77	
J. C. Richardson	67	72	76	77	
R. de Vicenzo *Argentina*	71	76	71	75	293
W. J. Casper USA	71	74	73	75	
R. Bernardini *Italy*	75	69	74	75	
C. A. Clark	69	70	77	77	
C. O'Connor	72	68	74	79	
W. Godfrey *New Zealand*	71	75	74	74	294
G. B. Wolstenholme *Australia*	68	77	72	77	
T. Weiskopf USA	70	74	72	78	
G. Marsh *Australia*	75	72	74	74	295
B. W. Devlin *Australia*	72	76	72	75	
R. D. B. M. Shade	72	75	69	79	
B. G. C. Huggett	68	78	73	77	296
R. E. Cole *South Africa*	71	76	71	78	
S. D. Brown	73	73	71	79	
T. Shaw USA	73	71	73	79	
P. Alliss	69	74	78	76	297
F. Molina *Argentina*	67	75	78	77	
D. Douglass USA	75	71	73	78	
E. C. Brown	73	72	74	78	
D. Graham *Australia*	72	72	74	79	
K. D. G. Nagle *Australia*	71	74	73	79	
B. W. Barnes	69	74	75	79	
D. C. Thomas	70	72	76	79	
G. Brewer USA	69	74	74	80	
A. G. Grubb	72	77	71	78	298
G. A. Caygill	74	72	74	78	
Mr S. Melnyk USA	69	74	76	79	
D. Marr USA	71	71	74	82	
J. M. Hume	72	75	76	76	299
G. Will	69	78	74	78	
P. M. P. Townsend	72	73	74	80	
G. L. Hunt	72	70	80	78	300
J. Martin	71	74	75	80	
N. D. Wood	73	73	77	78	301
Mr W. Humphreys	73	73	76	79	
T. Aaron USA	68	74	79	80	
T. A. Lopez *Spain*	70	72	75	84	
D. Small	69	74	80	79	302
D. M. Love USA	71	74	73	85	303
D. D. S. Livingston	75	73	75	81	304
S. Walker	70	78	75	84	307

·7·

The Luck of Trevino

Royal Birkdale, 1971

With the years lost to two world wars and the pause in 1871 after Young Tom Morris had won the championship belt outright (causing some confusion as to what to do next!) the Open Championship of 1971 was the 100th, and the fourth time it had been scheduled for Royal Birkdale.

By this time it had become a much 'bigger' event, more than 80,000 having attended the previous year at St Andrews, breaking the record by some 30,000. All the great names were once again present: Palmer, Nicklaus, Casper, Trevino, Jacklin, Player, Sanders, Thomson, Nagle, Charles, Yancey, Locke and Miller Barber among them. There were also some new names to the public, making either a first appearance or a first notable one. In this category were the new Australian stars, Jack Newton and Graham Marsh, and the Americans Charles Coody, Dave Stockton, Tom Weiskopf and the 24-year-old Californian Johnny Miller.

There was also a certain Liang Huan Lu, who had played in 1956 after representing the Republic of China in the Canada Cup at Wentworth, but had bowed out after taking – you may remember – an 89 in the qualifying rounds.

Nicklaus was, almost by divine right, still the favourite, though Lee Trevino had recently beaten him by 68 to 71 in a play-off for the US Open at Merion and had gone on to win the Canadian Open. Undoubtedly, he was the form horse, just as Jacklin was the nation's emotional choice.

I believe that this was the first year in our era that the Open became an event that aspiring overseas players realized could be vital to their prestige. Before this time, it had still, at least for Americans, been the championship that Palmer, Nicklaus and a few others tried for, just as Hagen, Sarazen and Jones had done during the 1920s and 1930s. In retrospect, the entry of Johnny Miller is particularly interesting. He had yet to win an American tournament but the desire to be a great player was there – and so he came to Birkdale.

There was hazy sunshine at the beginning of play, later succeeded by brilliant sunshine. The course was essentially the Birkdale that faced competitors in 1983, but some changes were made after 1971 to transform the 1st into a long par-4 and the last into an even longer one, like the 6th. I sometimes feel that championship committees pay rather too much attention to par figures, worrying how many strokes the winner may be under par. At the end of the day, all that matters is how many strokes the winner uses, be it twenty over par or twenty under. But this was the 1971 Birkdale:

Hole	Yards	Par	Hole	Yards	Par
1	493	5	10	393	4
2	427	4	11	412	4
3	416	4	12	190	3
4	212	3	13	517	5
5	358	4	14	202	3
6	473	4	15	536	5
7	158	3	16	401	4
8	459	4	17	510	5
9	410	4	18	513	5
	3406	35		3674	38
				3406	35
				7080	73

The first-round leaders were two of the favourites, Jacklin and Trevino, accompanied by two unknowns, the Argentine Vicente Fernandez and Howie Johnson, an eccentric for whom I have a great deal of affection. He used to punish himself and his clubs for misdemeanours. On one occasion, having missed a short putt, I remember that he banged the shaft of his putter against his forehead. The toe of the club swung round and struck the back of his head. Poor Howie was unconscious for several minutes.

Close behind on 70 were Irishman John O'Leary, Tommy Horton, the Australians Nagle and Thomson (still featuring but possibly no longer capable of staying in contention throughout a championship), Billy Casper, Liang Huan Lu and 31-year-old Brian Waites, who at that time competed almost solely in the Midlands, thinking he was 'not quite good enough' to be a tournament golfer. A host followed on 71 or 72 in what looked set, if the fine weather continued, to be a low-scoring championship. It seemed that some had already come near to putting themselves out of it, for example Palmer, with a 74 (he did not qualify for the final day), Yancey, Weiskopf and Marsh at one stroke more and certainly Bob Charles with a 77. Young Nick Job and Simon Hobday both had 89s.

Jacklin's iron play had been off, despite his 69. He started with three consecutive birdies, but dropped a shot at the 4th and two more at the remaining three short holes. On the 17th, he hooked high up into the sandhills but played out sideways and reached the green with a 3-wood. Nicklaus, who had a 71, should really have led the field but had finished with a pair of 6s.

Trevino had been badly off form on his outward half. He had missed four

Liang Huan Lu as a long putt goes down at the 10th
during the third round of the Royal Birkdale Open in 1971.

fairways and both the par-3 greens but had used up just eleven putts – five of those by no means short ones. He was therefore 33 for the first nine!

Already, Liang Huan Lu had become just 'Mr Lu', as I had christened him on TV, and his polite practice of raising his hat to applause was immediately much appreciated. On the last hole, he holed a 4-foot putt and raised his hat to what can hardly have been rapturous applause no fewer than six times.

After a 70, Jacklin again led the field after the second day but had now been joined by Trevino, with Mr Lu on 140, de Vicenzo and Player at 141 with the delightful Irishman Jimmy Kinsella, Nicklaus, Casper, Malcolm Gregson and Horton at 142. The field was close-packed indeed and many other players were still within reach of the championship.

Kinsella had played the first nine in 30 strokes, only eleven of which were putts: 4, 3, 4, 2, 4, 3, 3, 3, 4. It was his only day of glory in the championship throughout his career but that day his 68 was, if only for 24 hours, the Birkdale record. The next day he took 80. *Sic transit gloria mundi.*

Trevino came back in 33, showing that facility at holing long putts typical of his early competitive years in the championship. He holed four that day. Gary Player produced a storming finish, having birdies at all but one of the last six holes, while Nicklaus was chipping without confidence – a missed green as often as not meant a stroke dropped to par.

On the third day, Trevino was outright leader for the first time, his scores now reading 69, 70, 69. It seemed quite likely that the championship would develop into a three-horse race, with Jacklin and Mr Lu just a stroke behind but a three-stroke gap before the 212 totals of Gary Player and Craig DeFoy, another golfer enjoying his best performance in the Open. The course record had fallen to Peter Oosterhuis but his 66 followed rounds of 76 and 71 and he was five behind Trevino, together with Dale Hayes and Roberto de Vicenzo, still showing his superb talents at the age of 48.

It was either ominous or encouraging that Jacklin, who had gone round in 70, should announce 'I have never played so badly and shot 70.' Looking back on those years when Tony featured so consistently in the championship shows us that he was more than a winner of the British and US Opens. He was also a man who for a while was able consistently to raise his game for the great occasion and score well when not playing well. At this time, one reason was that his putting was almost infallible in the 2½- to 4-feet range. Although this may not sound very significant, it did mean that Jacklin was able to make the best of his good bunker play, chipping and short pitch shots, and it gave him confidence if his approach putts were less than perfect.

Along with many others, however, the performance I found the most surprising was Liang Huan Lu's. He was no stranger to me. I had played with him in an exhibition series and had little difficulty in beating him. His general game was unimpressive and on the greens he had as bad a twitch as I – allied with body movement on the stroke as well. Nevertheless, as often as not he had contrived to get the ball in the hole. This he was still doing in fine style at Birkdale, but surely he couldn't hold on.

On the final day, Trevino began with one of his best putting spells ever. He was down in just one putt at seven of the first eight greens, five of the putts being of more than three yards. One 10-yarder must have been a blow to Mr Lu, with whom he was playing, for it gave Trevino a 4 against Mr Lu's 3, preventing a dramatic swing.

I dare say Trevino was pleased not to be playing with Jacklin this final day. He had become visibly angry as British cheers rang out for a Jacklin success but not for him. The smiles and banter ceased and Trevino instead muttered, glowered and – most uncharacteristically – shut up!

This inspirational spell with his putter seemed to have locked up the championship for Trevino. He played the first nine in 31, which gave him a four-stroke margin over Lu and six over anyone else and he held this margin until the par-5 17th. Here, the Trevino fade did not 'take' and his ball stuck high into the sandhills on the left. Trevino slogged his way up and found his ball half-buried. He had a full-out hack at it but it caught scrub and moved only a yard or so. With his next attempt, Trevino was content to play more directly back to the fairway. This time the ball flew out – and into the rough on the other side.

As the pair began playing this hole, the American's lead was three strokes. All of that could have disappeared on this one hole. Lu was just short of the green in two strokes but he failed to get down in two more. Trevino's 7 to Lu's 5 left him still a vital one stroke ahead as they played the last hole.

But the dramas were not yet over. Lu's pulled second shot from a bad lie hit a woman spectator in the face but he, if not the lady in question, survived the incident and got his 4. Some years later, he sent the lady involved tickets for a holiday at his expense in his Taiwan hotel. A man with a long memory.

Trevino, on the fringe in two, was faced with getting down in two from a long way. His judgement of pace was exact and his ball died away just past the hole. With Bobby Jones, Gene Sarazen and Ben Hogan, he had won both British and US Opens in the same year, a feat since achieved only by Tom Watson in 1982.

It was his victories this year that caused Trevino at last to be recognized as a great player. After his US Open victory of 1968, he had won four more events in three seasons on the US Tour. Even though he was leading money-winner in 1970 it was still felt that his swing, of which almost the politest description was that it was 'agricultural', contained far too many contradictions for his game to last. He had a hooker's left-hand grip, hands far forward, and the face of the club was fully shut at the top of the backswing. He only avoided duck-hooking every shot by leading in emphatically with the left hand and side and by standing wide open to the target. Trevino described his technique at the time very simply: 'I just stand open to the hole and shovel the ball towards it.' Later he was to think better of himself and produce a book advocating that all golfers should adopt the Trevino method.

It had been another good championship for Tony Jacklin yet in some ways an even finer performance had come from a younger player, the 24-year-old Craig DeFoy. His finish of 68 and 69 was the best achieved by anyone and brought him up the field to 4th place, only three strokes behind the champion.

HOW THEY FINISHED

Player		R1	R2	R3	R4	Total
L. Trevino	*USA*	**69**	**70**	**69**	**70**	**278**
L. H. Lu	*Formosa*	70	70	69	70	279
A. Jacklin		69	70	70	71	280
C. DeFoy		72	72	68	69	281
C. Coody	*USA*	74	71	70	68	283
J. W. Nicklaus	*USA*	71	71	72	69	
W. J. Casper	*USA*	70	72	75	67	284
G. J. Player	*South Africa*	71	70	71	72	
D. Sanders	*USA*	73	71	74	67	285
P. W. Thomson	*Australia*	70	73	73	69	
K. D. G. Nagle	*Australia*	70	75	73	69	287
D. Stockton	*USA*	74	74	68	71	
H. Bannerman		73	71	72	71	
A. Yancey	*USA*	75	70	71	71	
R. Sota	*Spain*	72	72	70	73	
R. de Vicenzo	*Argentina*	71	70	72	74	
D. Hayes	*South Africa*	71	72	70	75	288
R. J. Charles	*New Zealand*	77	71	71	70	289
P. A. Oosterhuis		76	71	66	76	
B. J. Hunt		74	73	73	70	290
H. Johnson	*USA*	69	76	72	73	
N. C. Coles		76	72	72	71	291
Mr M. F. Bonallack		71	72	75	73	
H. Jackson		71	73	72	75	
V. Fernandez	*Argentina*	69	79	73	71	292
W. Large		73	75	73	71	
D. Sewell		73	74	74	71	
B. G. C. Huggett		73	73	74	72	
J. Lister	*New Zealand*	74	71	74	73	
R. Vines	*Australia*	75	71	73	73	
P. J. Butler		73	73	73	73	
M. Gregson		71	71	73	77	
M-N. Hsieh	*Formosa*	77	70	74	72	293
G. B. Wolstenholme	*Australia*	75	72	73	73	
C. O'Connor Sr.		74	72	76	72	294
J. R. Garner		76	74	71	73	
B. Gallacher		72	76	75	72	295
T. Horton		70	72	79	74	
B. W. Devlin	*Australia*	74	71	75	75	
L. Platts		78	72	73	73	296
T. Weiskopf	*USA*	75	73	75	73	
P. M. P. Townsend		73	75	75	73	
W. Godfrey	*New Zealand*	72	79	71	74	
J. Kinsella		74	68	80	74	
J. O'Leary		70	75	75	76	
E. C. Brown		75	72	72	77	
P. Alliss		74	76	72	75	297
J. Miller	*USA*	72	76	70	79	
T. Britz	*South Africa*	73	78	73	74	298
Mr S. Melnyk	*USA*	76	74	74	74	
V. Barrios	*Spain*	72	74	77	75	
A. D. Locke	*South Africa*	75	73	74	76	
J. Wilkshire		75	71	76	76	
J. Newton	*Australia*	73	72	76	77	
D. Swaelens	*Belgium*	75	73	72	78	
J. Sharkey		73	75	72	78	
G. Marsh	*Australia*	75	73	72	79	299
D. Snell		75	75	74	76	300
B. Waites		70	79	72	79	
M. Bembridge		75	73	76	77	301
M. Barber	*USA*	71	74	77	79	
R. Manning	*South Africa*	73	72	76	80	
D. Talbot		77	72	75	78	302
B. W. Barnes		76	75	73	79	303

Muirfield, 1972

For 1972, and another championship at Muirfield, the characters were almost unchanged. The old faces returned and some of the newer ones, such as Graham Marsh, Tom Weiskopf and Johnny Miller, were becoming more familiar. Two players happy to be there were your author and American PGA Champion Dave Marr. We both had to enter the qualifying rounds and only just survived a play-off to get into the championship proper. One who had found the going easier was a young man from Tyneside, Matt Gunn. His 63 over the No. 2 course at Gullane (the hill you can see from Muirfield) equalled the record in a qualifying round for the Open.

Muirfield itself was not as daunting as it had been in Nicklaus's year, 1966. The rough was severe but this time there was a considerably wider fringe of semi-rough. However, as Doug Sanders said: 'The course is out there waiting for you!' Gary Player, with his normal taste for hyperbole, pronounced the greens 'magnificent' and 'the best in the world'. The course was well groomed, the fastidiously constructed faces of the bunkers attracting much favourable comment even if, as one player put it, 'You have to play out sideways.'

The favourite was Jack Nicklaus, one of the very few players of modern times who has had a chance of the grand slam of all four major professional championships. This year, by the time the British Open came round he had taken the Masters and followed by taking the US Open at Pebble Beach. He was also holder of the US PGA Championship from the previous year.

The first-round leader, however, was the 22-year-old Yorkshireman Peter Tupling, who had had a good year in 1969 as a Walker Cup player and leading amateur in the Open Championship.

Tony Jacklin was right up at the top once again, his 69 putting him alone in second place. One behind were Frank Beard, a prodigious money-winner on the US Tour during this period, Dave Marr, Peter Townsend, Jack Nicklaus and – another good performance – Craig DeFoy. Among those on 71 were Trevino, Doug Sanders, Peter Thomson and Gary Player, the latter with two eagles to his credit. Ominously, it was said that Tony Jacklin had three times missed putts of less than 4 feet. Nicklaus, adopting the same strategy as in 1966 of using irons from the tee most of the time, had nevertheless missed no fewer than seven fairways. A red face belonged to Michael Bonallack, now secretary of the R and A: he took 9 on the short 7th.

After the second day. Jacklin still led after a 72, now joined by Trevino with 70 so that both were on 141. Nicklaus, Player, Miller, Townsend, Tupling, Garner and Sanders were a stroke behind.

There were tales of disaster. Jacklin's round had been marred by a triple bogey 6 on the short 13th after being in two bunkers, a forgotten event that did much to cost him the championship. Nicklaus had hit the out-of-bounds wall on the long 9th and though he was fortunate to come back in bounds he still took 38 to the turn and immediately dropped another shot on the 10th before playing in manfully for his 72. Coming to the 18th, Doug Sanders was one of three players under par at that point. He drove into a bunker on the right, was in the rough with his recovery and then sent his third shot through the green. His troubles were not over. He fluffed the chip back into a bunker and took three more to hole out for a 7. He was round in 71 instead of the 68 which would have given him a two-stroke lead in the championship.

The round of the day had come from Johnny Miller, making his first impact in Britain. With minor changes to the course, his 66 was a new record. He had begun with four straight pars and then holed out his 3-wood second shot to the long 5th for an albatross 2, far rarer than a hole in one. He completed the first nine in 32 and came to no harm on the second nine.

The third day both belonged to Trevino and entrenched the legend that he was a 'lucky champion'. He reached the turn in 36, level par, and neither dropped nor gained a stroke on the first four holes of the homeward nine. Then an astonishing sequence began. At the 14th he birdied from about 6 yards, and followed on the next hole with another birdie putt of double that length. At the short 16th, he missed the green and was bunkered on the right. He found an awkward lie: his ball on a downslope and near the back of the bunker. His recovery was struck much too low, perhaps even thinned. His ball had just enough height to clear the bunker face, but it skipped across the green, bounced once, then clattered plumb into the middle of the flag – and into the hole. I have later read that Trevino today considers this the greatest shot he ever played, a strange choice indeed. Perhaps he spoke tongue in cheek. It may well, however, have been his luckiest one. Another birdie followed on the long 17th but this was a conventional one. Trevino reached the green with two blows and took two putts. On the last, he sent his approach through the green and about 10 yards past the hole on the fringe. He chipped that one in to finish with five consecutive birdies, of which at least three had been lucky and one outrageous.

Tony Jacklin had been a bemused spectator of all this, yet was playing some rousing golf of his own. He had taken just one more stroke than Trevino for a 67, the feature of his round being an eagle on the 5th. Again and again, however, his shots to the greens had been inside the American's. Never mind, Tony was a resilient young man and with a round to play was both the sentimental and realistic choice to be winner the next day. Surely Trevino had used up his share of luck? There was the Englishman still, just a stroke behind, the rest of the field lagging. Here are some of the key scores:

> 207 Trevino; 208 Jacklin; 211 Sanders; 212 Barnes;
> 213 Nicklaus; 214 G. L. Hunt, Miller

Nicklaus, you will remember, had decided to follow his cautious strategy of

1966. He felt the way to tackle Muirfield was to avoid trouble. But he was now a full six strokes behind the leader. Neither Trevino nor Jacklin were at all likely to play a poor last round. The only way they could be caught was by a round in the mid-60s.

The roars as the Nicklaus birdies mounted up came back to Trevino and Jacklin, playing about two holes behind. He reached the turn in 32 then birdied the 10th, one of Muirfield's most difficult holes, a par-4 just under the regulation distance of 475 yards which would make it a par-5. Another birdie followed on the 11th; 38 strokes for eleven holes: he was the championship leader.

The question of the championship now was whether or not Nicklaus could keep his inspiration going. On the next hole he missed from some 3 yards for another birdie and then could only par the next three holes. At the short 16th his tee-shot hit the front edge of the green and kicked into rough. He dropped his first shot of the day.

The 17th, in retrospect, was fatal to his chances. Nicklaus hooked his tee-shot to this par-5 into a lie from which he could do little more than knock his ball back to the fairway. He got his par and another at the last but despite his 66, equalling the new course record, either Jacklin or Trevino would now finish ahead of him with just steady golf.

Both were indeed playing steadily, with the highlight for both being eagles on the 9th, Jacklin from some 3 yards and Trevino from perhaps double the distance. Nevertheless, the American was not enjoying the devilish luck of the previous day. On the 16th, both missed the green, with Jacklin bunkered. Trevino chipped dead and Jacklin holed the 6-foot putt he had left after he had played a good bunker shot.

Now came the hole that Jacklin must have since replayed in his mind a thousand times. All went well for a start. His drive was a good one and his 3-wood second, though it did not reach the green, left him only a short pitch some 20 yards from the front left of the green. Trevino, meanwhile, had hooked from the tee into a bunker, played out and then hit a 3-wood well short of the green in thickish rough. His fourth went through the green up a bank, several yards from the hole. 'That's it', he said, 'I've thrown it away.'

Trevino obviously ought now to take 6 and indeed a 7 was very likely if the chip was not a good one. Surely Jacklin, who had started the hole with a one stroke-disadvantage would now draw level or even take the lead?

Jacklin's pitch was fair but was not close. He had a medium-length putt for his birdie. Meanwhile Trevino had reached his ball. He took a quick glance towards the hole and chipped. It looked as if he were hardly trying, as indeed he later confirmed to me. The ball skipped and ran towards the hole, on and on – and in. A par 5 that included at least three poor shots.

Jacklin had now to hole his putt if he were to draw level. His putt was firm and ran past the hole by about 3 feet. His next putt was similar to Sanders's on the last at St Andrews two years before. Jacklin looked uncomfortable over the

Jacklin drives on the 8th at Muirfield in 1972, with Lee Trevino watching.

ball and it never looked likely to drop. A 6 and the championship was gone.

On the final tee, Trevino did not give himself time to let the tension build. He stepped up to his ball and, though even then not a long driver, lashed it away some 300 yards. A magnificent second shot followed and Trevino was champion for a second consecutive time.

Poor Jacklin did not even have the consolation of second place. He dropped another shot on the last and finished behind Nicklaus. 'Ah well', I remember commentator Henry Longhurst saying, consoling the nation, 'his turn will come again.' But the man who contended strongly for six years in a row has not since finished better than thirteen strokes behind the champion. Not once has he begun a championship well enough to stir the hopes again: newspaper and television talk of Jacklin revivals have always been stilled after the first day's play. Yet his achievements were great, and he has left us some marvellous memories.

HOW THEY FINISHED

	R1	R2	R3	R4	Total
L. Trevino *USA*	**71**	**70**	**66**	**71**	**278**
J. W. Nicklaus *USA*	70	72	71	66	279
A. Jacklin	69	72	67	72	280
D. Sanders *USA*	71	71	69	70	281
B. W. Barnes	71	72	69	71	283
G. J. Player *South Africa*	71	71	76	67	285
D. Vaughan	74	73	70	69	286
T. Weiskopf *USA*	73	74	70	69	
A. Palmer *USA*	73	73	69	71	
G. L. Hunt	75	72	67	72	
C. Clark	72	71	73	71	287
D. Marr *USA*	70	74	71	72	
R. Bernardini *Italy*	73	71	76	68	288
P. M. P. Townsend	70	72	76	70	
P. J. Butler	72	75	73	69	289
R. J. Charles *New Zealand*	75	70	74	70	
J. Dorrestein *Holland*	74	71	72	72	
J. Miller *USA*	76	66	72	75	
H. Bannerman	77	73	73	67	290
F. Beard *USA*	70	76	74	70	
M. Bembridge	73	71	75	71	
A. Yancey *USA*	73	72	72	73	
C. O'Connor Sr	73	74	73	71	291
D. McClelland	73	74	72	72	
C. DeFoy	70	75	71	75	
B. G. C. Huggett	73	72	79	68	292
B. W. Devlin *Australia*	75	70	77	70	
P. A. Oosterhuis	75	75	73	70	293
J. Heard *USA*	75	75	71	72	
J. R. Garner	71	71	76	75	

	R1	R2	R3	R4	Total
V. Fernandez *Argentina*	78	74	73	69	294
K. D. G. Nagle *Australia*	79	72	74	69	
P. Alliss	74	74	77	69	
G. Cunningham	76	75	73	70	
B. Thomson	74	77	72	71	
M-N. Hsieh *Taiwan*	75	75	73	71	
R. A. Shearer *Australia*	77	75	68	74	
D. Stockton *USA*	72	72	76	74	
P. W. Thomson *Australia*	71	72	74	77	
V. B. Hood	76	74	72	73	295
C-H. Kuo *Taiwan*	74	72	76	73	
L. H. Lu *Taiwan*	77	73	71	74	
W. J. Casper *USA*	72	74	74	75	
J. Newton *Australia*	77	72	70	76	
T. Horton	76	72	73	74	
D. Oakley *USA*	72	75	77	72	296
E. Jones	75	74	74	73	
S. Torrance	72	74	76	74	
L. P. Tupling	68	74	73	81	
G. Marsh *Australia*	78	73	74	73	298
D. Sewell	75	74	75	74	
D. Talbot	72	76	76	74	
N. Wood	74	78	71	75	
A. Brooks	74	74	75	75	
B. Hutchinson	74	73	74	77	
J. O'Leary	75	76	74	74	299
D. Llewellyn	72	73	79	75	
R. T. Walker	74	74	74	78	300
T. Britz *South Africa*	75	77	73	76	301
A. Garrido *Spain*	71	77	77	76	
J. M. Hume	77	70	77	77	
G. Baleson *South Africa*	76	73	73	80	302
J. Fowler	76	76	71	81	304
S. D. Brown	81	70	74	80	305

·8·

Interregnum

Royal Troon, 1973

Though the king, Jack Nicklaus, was by no means dead by 1973, others had begun to share the centre of the stage. Nicklaus was to win again, and feature in the most thrilling Open of them all, but more of his championship successes were coming in America, and others were to make their mark in the Open.

In 1973, the championship went to Troon for the first time since Palmer had won on the parched course of 1962. There were few new names, though Chi Chi Rodriguez was making a first appearance, as was a new star, Lanny Wadkins, while Bruce Crampton entered once more after a gap of many years.

There were two relatively new players who commanded much attention before the championship began. One was a new US Open Champion, Johnny Miller, who a few weeks before had poured a superb sequence of iron shots at the Oakmont flags and come away – from well back in the field – with a 63 and the trophy. In Britain, Tom Weiskopf, for several years a big winner in America, was favoured after his emphatic victory over Lee Trevino the previous year in the final of the World Matchplay, at Wentworth. British spectators tend to favour the men they have seen on television. It was and is quite possible for an American, Australian or Japanese golfer with a formidable record on his home tour to play unnoticed in our championship.

Tom Weiskopf came to Troon on the crest of a wave. He had won the Colonial National Invitational, the Kemper Open and the Philadelphia Classic, and entered the US Open as favourite. With a round to go he had in fact headed Miller by five strokes and finished with a 70 – only good enough for 3rd place. More than at any other time in his career, however, I am sure Tom felt a major championship was his due. He gave himself plenty of time to prepare, playing eight practice rounds with much useful advice from his friend Tony Jacklin on how to manipulate shots with the small ball.

Weiskopf started very well. At the 1st, he missed a putt of about a yard for a birdie but responded by having birdies on three of the next four holes and went to the turn in 33. Many competitors had scored well on this nine but the return to the clubhouse was largely played into a 20 mph wind, not formidable but those going out in 34, let's say, tended to take 38 or 39 coming back. Not Weiskopf. He dropped a shot only at the last where he hooked from the tee, but to balance this was the only player to birdie the 468-yard 13th, the result of a 1-iron ruled on the flag all the way.

His 68 gave him a lead of a stroke on Jack Nicklaus and Bert Yancey, with Miller close behind with his 70. On 71 were Peter Wilcock, Bruce Crampton, Lanny Wadkins, Peter Butler and Neil Coles.

Delighted with his first-round lead, on the second round Weiskopf decided to limit his ambitions to par golf. His driving was long and he was able to hold the narrow fairways. He birdied all the par-5s, a main reason for his being round in 67. Only one other player managed a 67 in the second round, Brian Barnes, who had begun with a 76, however.

After 36 holes, this is how the leading contenders stood:

135 Weiskopf; 138 Miller, Yancey; 139 Nicklaus; 141 O'Connor; 143 Coles, Butler, Barnes

This year, the field had stretched out early and it looked already as if the winner would come from one of Weiskopf, Miller, Yancey and Nicklaus.

By the end of the third day, one who had already gone was Jack Nicklaus, his 76 leaving him well behind the contenders. Weiskopf and Miller were paired. Miller quickly caught up as Weiskopf dropped a shot here and there. Miller then produced three consecutive birdies to move ahead. The 8th, the Postage Stamp, became one of the crucial holes. Miller, with the honour, sent his tee-shot in to about 4 foot and gave Weiskopf a glance that, freely interpreted, meant, 'Match that if you can!'

The Postage Stamp had already collected its fair share of publicity that year. The 71-year-old Gene Sarazen, making a sentimental journey back to the course where he had failed to qualify for the 1923 Open because of an 85 in high winds, had punched in a little 5-iron on the first day and holed out. Some might say he did even better the second day. Bunkered, he splashed out into the hole. He had played the hole twice without using his putter. To Palmer, on the other hand, returning to the scene of his greatest triumph, it brought nothing but disaster. He played from bunker to bunker and took 7.

But back to Weiskopf's response. This was an iron shot that finished even closer to the hole than Miller's. Both got their birdies. At the next hole, Weiskopf's drive tailed off into gorse. He was perhaps lucky even to find it but what he then saw was not encouraging. It was, he decided, unplayable, and he walked back towards the tee some 100 yards before finding a suitable place to drop. He took 6 to Miller's 4. He was out in 37 to Miller's 32 and Miller was the new leader, one stroke ahead of Bert Yancey but two better than Weiskopf.

But a different Weiskopf had appeared at Troon. His father had died some

Troon, 1973. It rained a lot that year and the trophy changed hands. Tom Weiskopf is the Champion. Johnny Miller and Bert Yancy (seated, left to right) shelter from the downpour.

three months before and this had affected Tom deeply. It was as if he felt that his achievements up to that time, formidable though they were on the US Tour, had been a disappointment to his father. He had certainly failed to make the most of his great talents. He was one of the longest drivers in the world with a golf swing of coiling rhythmic grace, paralleled by a very good putting stroke indeed. A purist, he was still not an outstanding chipper, feeling that a golfer should hit the greens and perhaps deserved to drop a stroke if he failed to do so. His greatest flaw, however, had been his temper. When things went wrong, his temperature rose and he had been known to walk off a golf course or bat a ball along one-handed. His father's death, however, seems to have given Tom new steel. He now proceeded to justify his father's faith in him.

Through wind and rain, and despite being three times bunkered, Weiskopf covered the homeward nine in 34 to Miller's 37, and ended the day championship leader again. With the final day to come, this is how they stood:

206 Weiskopf; 207 Miller; 211 Yancey; 213 Coles; 215 Nicklaus

Although there seemed just two men left in real contention for the championship, there were great rounds still to come from Neil Coles and, no surprise, Jack Nicklaus. Coles overcame his general antipathy towards links courses and had a 66, while Nicklaus's 65, in which he dropped a stroke only on the 17th, set a new course record.

But the real battle was between Weiskopf and Miller. They set out in heavy rain and Weiskopf immediately increased his lead when Miller dropped a shot on the 1st hole and another on the 3rd. The position remained the same to the turn. It was not until the 12th that Miller had a chance to close the three-stroke gap as Weiskopf missed the green while Miller had a putt of some considerable length for a birdie. He missed it; Tom chipped dead. On the 13th, however, Miller did improve his position with a par to Tom's bogey. It was the 15th that virtually settled this championship. After three strokes, Weiskopf was dead. Miller had a putt of about 8 or 9 yards for his birdie. He shaved the hole and drifted only some couple of feet on, but missed the return. Barring the kinds of miracles and disasters that had happened the previous year at Muirfield, Weiskopf was champion. So it was to prove, his margin three strokes at the end, while his total of 276 equalled the championship record. Miller eventually found himself bunkered by the last and needing to get down in two to tie with Neil Coles for second place. He did. Weiskopf had won his first major championship and had done it without once three-putting. He had also won five of the last eight events he had entered.

His achievements throughout the year and a first championship seemed to have established Weiskopf comfortably among the handful at the very top of golf. Strangely enough, since that time, he has won only six more events on the US Tour. No more major championships have come his way.

HOW THEY FINISHED

T. Weiskopf *USA*	**68**	**67**	**71**	**70**	**276**
N. C. Coles	71	72	70	66	279
J. Miller *USA*	70	68	69	72	
J. W. Nicklaus *USA*	69	70	76	65	280
A. Yancey *USA*	69	69	73	70	281
P. J. Butler	71	72	74	69	286
R. J. Charles *New Zealand*	73	71	73	71	288
C. O'Connor Sr	73	68	74	73	
L. Wadkins *USA*	71	73	70	74	
L. Trevino *USA*	75	73	73	68	289
G. Brewer *USA*	76	71	72	70	
H. R. Henning *South Africa*	73	73	73	70	
B. W. Barnes	76	67	70	76	
G. J. Player *South Africa*	76	69	76	69	290
A. Jacklin	75	73	72	70	
A. Palmer *USA*	72	76	70	72	
D. McClelland	76	71	69	74	
D. Hill *USA*	75	74	74	69	292
D. J. Good	75	74	73	70	
B. W. Devlin *Australia*	72	78	71	71	
P. A. Oosterhuis	80	71	69	72	
E. Polland	74	73	73	72	
B. Crampton *Australia*	71	76	73	72	
H. Boyle	75	75	69	73	
P. M. Wilcock	71	76	72	73	
H. Baiocchi *South Africa*	75	74	69	74	
B. Gallacher	73	69	75	75	
D. Sanders *USA*	79	72	72	70	293
R. de Vicenzo *Argentina*	72	75	74	72	
J. A. Rodriguez *Puerto Rico*	72	73	73	75	
E. Murray	79	71	73	71	294
G. V. Marsh *Australia*	74	71	78	71	
P. W. Thomson *Australia*	76	75	70	73	
R. Wynn	74	71	76	73	
C. DeFoy	76	75	70	73	
T. Horton	75	70	73	76	
V. Baker *South Africa*	72	74	75	74	295
D. Vaughan	78	70	72	75	
G. B. Wolstenholme *Australia*	77	72	75	72	296
K. D. G. Nagle *Australia*	74	76	73	73	
D. Hayes *South Africa*	76	72	73	75	
P. Elson	75	75	72	74	
B. Dassu *Italy*	75	75	73	73	
D. Gammon *Rhodesia*	76	70	76	74	
Mr D. Edwards *USA*	75	75	71	75	
H. Bannerman	73	75	75	74	297
M. J. Moir	76	75	70	76	
D. K. Webster	73	76	72	76	
B. J. Hunt	76	74	74	74	298
J. Fourie *South Africa*	76	73	74	75	
D. Jagger	76	74	74	75	299
R. D. B. M. Shade	75	73	76	75	
P. Alliss	76	71	76	76	
J. McTear	76	74	71	78	
P. M. P. Townsend	79	73	71	77	300
R. Lambert	78	74	72	77	301
W. B. Murray	78	71	74	78	
D. Huish	74	73	76	78	
D. Dunk	73	74	74	82	303
G. Mueller *Sweden*	76	70	78	81	305

Royal Lytham and St Anne's, 1974

At Royal Lytham and St Anne's in 1974 the 'big ball', 1.68 inches in diameter instead of 1.62, became compulsory for all players in the Open Championship. I dare say 0.06 of an inch may seem a small enough matter but it makes a big difference. Players in America had been compelled to use the larger ball for some forty years. They were used to it but, as I have particularly pointed out in the case of Ben Hogan and Tom Weiskopf, they always changed to the smaller British version when competing in our championship. Although some claim the small ball is marginally more difficult to putt and chip with, and 'sits up' less well for all shots, it does go further. And professionals are more or less at one with club golfers on this matter: they would rather see their drives travel, say, 280 yards than 265, roughly the difference between the two sizes.

This change was to be highly important at Lytham because another feature of the big ball was very apparent: it is much more difficult to control in wind. There was a good blow that year. Many failed the test.

Before the championship, Gary Player was in good voice. To all who would listen he proclaimed the merits of his 'new swing'. It seemed that, despite amassing tournament victories worldwide and a total of seven major championships his swing had been 'all wrong for twenty years'; he had now remodelled it. Apparently to good effect, for not long before, at the age of 38, he had won his second Masters, clinching the event with one of those shots of a lifetime. With the field packed close together at the finish, Gary had hit his 9-iron approach at the 71st to a foot or so. He had then gone on to contend for the US Open. Significantly, in both events he had finished above Nicklaus. It was to continue a very good year for Player. At the end of it, he had established himself, without possible doubt, as the world's number one.

With the wind blowing briskly, there were many high scores from distinguished golfers. Bruce Crampton, for instance, who was enjoying excellent form on the US Tour, was round in 85. Of course he did not qualify for later play yet there were five players with scores of 80 or worse that first day who did, not because their second rounds were spectacularly good but because the qualifying score, 156, was high. Player began with a 2 at the short 1st hole and, with two more birdies and the rest all pars, reached the turn in 31. After more good play, he needed to finish with two par 4s for a round of 67. At the 453-yard 17th, the new swing did not deliver. Player was in the rough from the tee and eventually took 6. He hooked again from the last tee, was bunkered by the green but got out to some 3 yards and holed a good putt for a 69.

He was leading the championship, together with John Morgan of Stoneham and later Royal Liverpool. Only two players had got round in 70, Danny Edwards of the United States and Bobby Cole of South Africa, who had a good spell in the Open Championship for a few years and is now married to a pin-up girl of the US ladies' tour, Laura Baugh.

By this time, Peter Oosterhuis was perhaps more the main British hope in the championship than Tony Jacklin. He too produced a good round. Like Player beginning with the encouragement of a 2, he reached the turn in 32. He faltered a little coming home, the old fault of the drive blocked out to the right occurring at least once. Nevertheless he was round in 71, along with the American Hubert Green and Irishman John O'Leary.

Incidentally, 1974 was the last year that the name of P. Alliss appeared among the list of competitors. I had given up being a full-time tournament professional several years before, and my commitments to television were making it more difficult every year to play in the Open. Believe it or not, television commentary can be quite hard work, and rushing to the commentary box after many hours of competitive nerve-tingling golf was not improving the quality of golf or commentary!

On the second day the wind was strong from the west, making the second half far more difficult than the first. In general, scoring was slightly lower. Not expecting strong winds the first day, the championship committee had been severe in their pin placements. These were relaxed for the second day.

In these conditions, Player took the championship by the scruff of the neck, giving one of the finest performances of a long, long career. His use of the 1-iron to hold the hard fairways and keep the ball under the wind were credited by Player as the key to his round of 68. Not only was it the only round to break 70 but only one other player, Al Geiberger of the United States, even managed to score as low as 70. Player led the Open at the end of the day by five clear strokes, the largest margin since Henry Cotton had begun 67 and 65 at Royal St George's in 1934. Player's finish had been particularly good: 4, 4, 4, 3. Although this was just one under par it was into winds that meant both the 15th and 17th were out of range in two strokes. On the 17th, he had been in thick rough and could only knock it forward with an 8-iron, followed by another shot with the same club that left him little to do with his putter. He then gained his birdie at the last with a superbly flighted 4-iron through the cross wind to 6 feet.

Johnny Miller, after a first-round 72, was one of those attempting to catch Player during the day. He reached the turn in 32 but then produced the sequence 5, 6, 6. His 6 on the 12th, a par-3, was particularly disastrous. Into a strong left-to-right wind Miller hit a high shot left of the flag which began to swing and continued until it was saved from going out of bounds to the right of the green only by hitting the fence. Miller did not benefit much from this, however, as he followed with two poor pitches. Bobby Cole, after a first-round 70, played the first nine in 33 and was two under par with five holes to play but had a 6 on the very difficult 17th. This was how the leaders stood:

137 Player; 142 Oosterhuis, Cole; 143 Edwards; 144 Morgan, Liang Huan Lu, Weiskopf

On the third day, Player by no means had things all his own way. He was out with Peter Oosterhuis, who immediately attacked with a 2 on the 1st, though the South African countered with a birdie of his own on the 2nd. On the short 9th, however, Gary faltered badly, taking 5, having left a bunker shot in the sand. Meanwhile, Nicklaus had reached the turn in 32 and Cole in 34. following with a birdie on the 10th, where Player was soon to drop another shot. At about this time, then, Cole had caught Player, while Oosterhuis was two strokes behind and Nicklaus three.

But Cole failed to maintain his momentum. He drove badly at the 13th and then hooked his second shot into trees, eventually taking 6 on this rather short par-4 of some 340 yards. When he took another 6 on the 15th, he had lost five strokes to par in the space of seven holes. Nicklaus also could not fully maintain his challenge, though he faced the last four holes needing to par home for a 68. The 15th, at some 460 yards, was his undoing. After four strokes, he was still 60 yards or so from the flag but then managed to get down in two more for a 6. Oosterhuis also played that hole badly: a poor drive was followed by a poor wooden club shot and an approach that comfortably missed the green. He then fluffed his pitch shot but, like Nicklaus, showed his grittily competitive nature by getting down in two more.

The theme of the day was that Player's closest pursuers had played the easier first half better than he but that Player was much steadier on the difficult inward nine, dropping just one shot on a hole out of reach for him. With a round to go, few were within reach of Player, despite his 75:

212 Player; 215 Oosterhuis; 216 Nicklaus; 217 Green; 218 Cole, Weiskopf; 219 Liang Huan Lu, Edwards; 220 Morgan, Miller

For the final day, the wind was still fresh but the conditions were nevertheless by far the easiest during the championship. Out again with Peter Oosterhuis, Player delivered a virtual knock-out blow instantly with a birdie 2 against Oosterhuis's 4 to be five ahead of his closest challenger. The battle continued, both having birdies on the next, and Player then dropping shots on both the 4th and 5th. He followed by eagling the 6th and completed the first nine in 32 to 34s from both Oosterhuis and Nicklaus. Player was five or more ahead of the field and then gained another stroke immediately. At about this point, Nicklaus began dropping shots and no longer had a chance. His fine finish over the last few holes came when all hope had gone.

But there were still dramas to come on the last two holes. With a fistful of strokes to spare, Player pulled his approach to the 17th some 20 yards left of the green into rough that Player later described as 'The thickest I have seen so close to a green in my twenty years of championship golf.' Though many had seen where Player's ball pitched, no one could find it, including Gary, who was scurrying around as energetically as any ten men. His tall negro caddie, Rabbit

Royal Lytham and St Anne's in 1974, and another Championship for Gary Player,
here collecting the trophy with his daughter Jenifer.

Dyer, also joined in the panic. It began to seem just possible that if Oosterhuis should birdie and Player have to walk back to play another ball and then dump that one in the long grass. . . .

But no, the ball was found, and Player was able to hack it near the green before getting down in two more strokes for a 5. At the last, there was a final diversion. Player had his second shot through the green against the clubhouse wall, which left him to play a shot onto the green left-handed. He had won his third British Open by four strokes. He had taken his 8th professional major championship, a total at that time exceeded only by Jack Nicklaus, Walter Hagen and Ben Hogan, while he had gone ahead of Arnold Palmer. Only Harry Vardon and J. H. Taylor had previously won the Open in three different decades, something that Jack Nicklaus has achieved in the US Open and, who knows, may still manage in the British Open also. Gary Player, of course, still continues to try to make it four!

HOW THEY FINISHED

Player					Total
G. J. Player *South Africa*	**69**	**68**	**75**	**70**	**282**
P. A. Oosterhuis	71	71	73	71	286
J. W. Nicklaus *USA*	74	72	70	71	287
H. M. Green *USA*	71	74	72	71	288
D. Edwards *USA*	70	73	76	73	292
L. H. Lu *Taiwan*	72	72	75	73	
D. Swaelens *Belgium*	77	73	74	69	293
T. Weiskopf *USA*	72	72	74	75	
R. E. Cole *South Africa*	70	72	76	75	
J. Miller *USA*	72	75	73	74	294
J. R. Garner	75	78	73	69	295
D. Graham *Australia*	76	74	76	69	
P. M. P. Townsend	79	76	72	69	296
A. Tapie *USA*	73	77	73	73	
N. C. Coles	72	75	75	74	
A. Geiberger *USA*	76	70	76	74	
J. Morgan	69	75	76	76	
G. Littler *USA*	77	76	70	74	297
D. Weaver *USA*	73	80	70	74	
A. Jacklin	74	77	71	75	
P. Dawson	74	74	73	76	
R. D. B. M. Shade	78	75	73	72	298
L. Wadkins *USA*	78	71	75	74	
H. Irwin *USA*	76	73	79	71	299
C. O'Connor Jr	78	76	72	73	
A. Gallardo *Spain*	74	77	75	73	
B. Gallacher	76	72	76	75	
B. Crenshaw *USA*	74	80	76	70	300
D. McClelland	75	79	73	73	
D. Jagger	80	71	76	73	
A. O. Cerda *Mexico*	80	74	77	70	301
T. Horton	78	76	76	71	
P. J. Butler	75	77	77	72	
H. Jackson	78	76	73	74	
D. Chillas	72	78	77	74	
L. Trevino *USA*	79	70	78	74	
G. Brewer *USA*	78	77	74	73	302
V. Fernandez *Argentina*	78	73	78	73	
J. Cook	76	79	75	73	303
B. W. Devlin *Australia*	81	74	73	75	
G. L. Hunt	78	73	72	80	
B. J. Hunt	74	77	74	79	304
D. Small	73	75	77	79	
G. V. Marsh *Australia*	79	75	77	74	305
B. W. Barnes	74	79	78	74	
J. D. Mahaffey *USA*	78	77	75	75	
J. O'Leary	71	79	78	77	
M. Bembridge	76	77	73	79	
N. Hunt	73	73	79	80	
S. J. Levermore	77	77	76	76	306
M. Gregson	79	76	76	76	307
R. de Vicenzo *Argentina*	80	74	77	76	
B. J. Waites	78	74	74	81	
M. J. Slater	77	74	80	77	308
N. Wood	74	78	78	78	
I. E. Stanley *Australia*	77	79	75	78	309
C. O'Connor Sr	80	74	77	78	
J. Panton	77	75	77	80	
R. Shearer *Australia*	77	79	73	81	310
J. Fourie *South Africa*	79	73	77	81	

•9•
The Watson Era

Carnoustie, 1975

You may recall that Jack Nicklaus expressed some dislike of Carnoustie during the 1968 championship. This seemed to have vanished in 1975. During his practice rounds in benign weather, Nicklaus achieved dominance over what was considered the most difficult Open Championship course. It seemed that every time he went out he scored in the 60s. Indeed, it was a vintage Nicklaus year. In March, he had won both the Doral-Eastern Open and the Sea Pines Heritage Classic before moving on to Augusta. At the time, many felt that that Masters was the most exciting in the history of the event, perhaps even of all major championships, though such things do tend to be said in the euphoria of the moment. This is not the place to recall the details but it is worth remembering that Nicklaus holed a curling putt of 14 or 15 yards on the 16th to tie for the lead and went ahead as Weiskopf shortly afterwards three-putted the same hole. It was also the year that Johnny Miller, almost outdoing his 63 winning last round in the 1973 US Open, produced a 65, 66 finish in the Masters, with Tom Weiskopf finishing a stroke behind Nicklaus.

In that year's US Open, Nicklaus was a couple of strokes behind the winner, Lou Graham, and later in the year won his fourth US PGA Championship. He was to feature as strongly as ever in the Carnoustie championship.

A man who had finished behind Nicklaus in both of the season's first two major championships was Tom Watson. Paired with Jack Nicklaus in the final round of the Masters, he had dumped two iron shots in the lake which guards the 16th green and taken 7. Later, in the US Open, he began with rounds of 67 and 68, which tied the US Open 36-hole scoring record and gave him a three-stroke lead. Then he subsided to rounds of 78 and 77 to finish in 9th place. It was a familiar story. Watson had done much the same in the previous year's Open. Leader after three rounds, he had produced a final round of 79. Needless to say, he was overtaken. Watson had earned the reputation of being a 'choker', a cruel title which dated back to the 1973 Hawaiian Open. Watson had begun that one with rounds of 68, 65 and 68 for a dominating lead. Then, in ideal golfing conditions, he had a 75 and lost by three strokes.

However, by the time of the Carnoustie championship he had recorded a couple of successes. He had won the 1974 Western Open with, yes, a good last round and the Byron Nelson Classic in May 1975 with the best round of the day, a 65. Even so, his fellow competitors in major championships felt that Tom's good play in the early rounds could just be discounted for he would surely fade in the turmoil of the closing stages of this championship.

Watson, born in Kansas City, Missouri, attended Stanford University in California and had taken the opportunity to play from time to time on the Monterey peninsula, which among other things, means Pebble Beach, a course with a number of links-type holes. He had, however, never played a British links course and, when the first round began, that included a total ignorance of Carnoustie. Tony Lema had allowed himself time for only a hurried practice round in 1964 at St Andrews; Watson had played hardly a hole. Perhaps he had entered the championship to see what it was like, possibly as part of a European holiday. His caddie Alfie Fyles would have to tell him where to aim his tee-shots and hand him the right club for the shots into the greens. Altogether a disgracefully planned campaign for a major title!

When the championship began, Nicklaus appeared to have used up his best golf in practice. He pulled a putt on the 1st and on the 2nd thinned a chip shot and three-putted. On the 4th, which has a double green, it looked as if he had played for the wrong flag, having a putt of at least 20 yards. This he holed and then became himself again, eventually coming in with a superb 69.

The first-day leader was the main British hope, Peter Oosterhuis. His 68 was oddly compiled. On the 15th, he carved his tee-shot far enough right to reach the 4th fairway but dropped a shot despite this stroke of luck. Next he bounced off the 16th green but holed his chip for a 2, and then he birdied the very difficult 17th. Another push right followed at the last hole but somehow he managed a 5.

The rest of the first day belonged to Andries Oosthuizen and David Huish. The first was an unknown from South Africa, who was to return to relative obscurity after his strong performance in this championship. The other was the professional at the championship West course in North Berwick. Some people knew how to pronounce one of their names; few could manage both – but 'Oosthazen' and 'Hush' it was.

David Huish was a pre-qualifier who had birdied the last hole to earn a play-off with seven others and then birdied the first sudden-death hole after driving the green. He began the championship in similar vein, with birdies at the first three holes, one of these from only about two inches. Both Oosthuizen and Huish had 69s as also did the Australians Jack Newton and Bob Shearer. Also with a 69 was Hale Irwin who, after a relatively poor first five holes, had seven birdies in the next ten and had come very close to an albatross 2 on the

ROYAL LYTHAM AND ST ANNE'S
The Championship Course

1	206 yards par 3	10	334 yards par 4
2	420 yards par 4	11	485 yards par 5
3	458 yards par 4	12	189 yards par 3
4	393 yards par 4	13	339 yards par 4
5	188 yards par 3	14	445 yards par 4
6	486 yards par 5	15	468 yards par 4
7	551 yards par 5	16	356 yards par 4
8	394 yards par 4	17	413 yards par 4
9	162 yards par 3	18	386 yards par 4

Out 3,258 yards par 35   In   3,415 yards par 36

Total 6,673 yards par 71

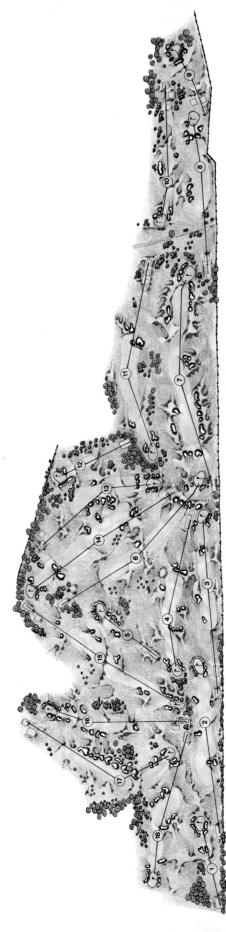

ROYAL BIRKDALE
The Championship Course

1	450 yards par 4		10	384 yards par 4
2	423 yards par 4		11	411 yards par 4
3	410 yards par 4		12	184 yards par 3
4	206 yards par 3		13	505 yards par 5
5	343 yards par 4		14	198 yards par 3
6	468 yards par 4		15	542 yards par 5
7	150 yards par 3		16	415 yards par 4
8	470 yards par 4		17	526 yards par 5
9	410 yards par 4		18	473 yards par 4

Out 3,330 yards par 34   In 3,638 yards par 37

Total 6,968 yards par 71

N

Scale 50 yds 100 yds   200 yds   300 yds

par-5 14th, when his second shot hit the flag and came to rest less than a yard away. Sadly Irwin then missed the putt! Some other leading scores were:

70 Hobday, Edwards, Leonard, Tapie; 71 Miller, de Vicenzo, Burns, Barnes, Cahill, Mahaffey (recent loser of a play-off for the US Open), Floyd, Watson

Conditions had been fairly easy, with no wind. Golfers such as Trevino, Player, Wadkins, Littler, Palmer and Charles, who had scored between 74 and 76, had already put themselves more or less out of the championship, for surely the familiar Carnoustie winds must arrive? No one who had failed to take his chance that first day would have as good an opportunity again.

But this was not so. Overnight there was heavy rain and from dawn to dusk there was again no wind. The greens were easy-paced and iron shots stopped quickly. The bounce had gone from the fairways. The course record, set by Ben Hogan in 1953 and equalled already by Peter Oosterhuis, was beaten by several. Graham Marsh, David Huish, Tom Watson and Bernard Gallacher had 67s, Bobby Cole a 66. Peter Oosterhuis, meanwhile, had thrown away what may prove to have been his best chance of winning the championship. He reached the turn in 31 and went another stroke under par with a birdie at the 11th. Thereafter he dropped stroke after stroke and completed the second nine in 39, when a round of 65 or better had been in prospect. David Huish was now two strokes in the lead. As we have already seen, although from time to time a club professional has led the championship with a freak first round, it is very rare indeed for such a man to do it after two rounds.

Yet there he was, with all of Scotland – and many more besides – hoping that he could go on to become champion. But the hard truth is that no one below the class of the 'almost great' has won the Open Championship this century. In the last twenty years or so, it has indeed come to seem impossible that a club professional could do so. David Huish had a respectable 76 on the third day and was one of four players to score 80 or worse on the final day. Still, it had been two days to remember.

The players had decided that strict par at Carnoustie was 69, for all the par-5s were reachable. Bobby Cole's 66 was, he felt, the result of a firmer position at the top of the backswing, brought about by 'shortening his left thumb'. By withdrawing it a little, he no longer swung the club past the horizontal. Bobby Cole was a former British Amateur Champion (1966) and had enjoyed a splendid season in 1974, contending in both the British Open, as we have seen, and the US PGA, winning the South African Open with a last-round 64 and being individual winner in the World Cup.

On the third day, he had another 66 and was the new leader but no longer the course record holder. That honour was freshly held by Jack Newton. He also had a new gimmick. Jack Nicklaus had suggested he try putting with the feeling of tensing the forearms in the stroke. Newton birdied the 1st from several yards and continued in fine style. The only hole he played badly was the 'short' 16th (235 yards). He pushed his tee-shot wide of the green, pitched only up to the fringe – and then holed out. He then birdied the difficult 17th and parred the last. His 65 equalled the lowest card ever returned in the championship, Henry Cotton's 65 at Royal St George's in the second round in 1934. Cotton's achievement had given him a vast lead of nine strokes; Newton's did not:

> 204 Cole; 205 Newton; 206 Miller; 207 Watson; 208 Irwin, Nicklaus, Oosthuizen, Mahaffey, Coles

Again there had been no wind, the greens remained holding and easy-paced and there was very little severe rough on the course after the dry spell. Miller was now regarded as the favourite. Of the leaders, he was the only one with a major championship to his credit (the 1973 US Open), and had come close at Troon in 1973.

Much was to change on the final day. It was as if the gods of golf could no longer tolerate the rape of the great course. At last the wind had got up. It was felt that Nicklaus, with his greater knowledge of the course and immense experience, would benefit most. The first half had now become far more testing and only Watson broke par, by just one stroke. However, almost as if by force of habit, he then proceeded to throw away the championship by taking three putts at the 10th, 11th and 12th. Everyone promptly forgot all about him.

Nicklaus also seemed to have lost the Open over the first half. His 38 to the turn surely left too much ground to make up. The best start came from Jack Newton, one under par after five holes and, though dropping a stroke here and there, only one over after nine holes. He then began to take the championship in his grasp by playing the next five holes in two under par. By this time, his target was a simple one: if he could play the last four holes in level par, there was no doubt at all that he would be champion. Others who might catch him, if he faltered, were Jack Nicklaus, Johnny Miller, Bobby Cole and Tom Watson. This is how they finished, using journalese:

Nicklaus: birdied 14th from 2 yards and holed from a little further away at the 15th for his par. On the 16th, he bunkered his shot to the green and took 4 at this short hole but followed with a par at the 17th and 18th, almost holing a chip shot on the last: 280.
Miller (playing with Nicklaus): missed green on 15th and chipped close for a par. 16th, again missed the green and chipped less close this time to drop a shot. Parred 17th and then hit a superb drive up the 18th, along the right side of the fairway so that the wind would bring it back towards the middle.

Instead, his ball caught the edge of a bunker, spun around it – and toppled in. Miller now faced a straightforward choice: needing a par to beat Nicklaus and perhaps tie with following players on 279, should he content himself with playing out or risk a straighter-faced iron and go for the green? Miller made the brave choice. It was a 6-iron. He did not clear the bunker face but, perhaps from a more favourable position, gave it another go. This time he made it to the left fringe, only a few yards from the hole, and came close to holing his chip. 280 also.

Watson: missed a birdie putt on the 15th of about 2 yards. For the fourth consecutive time failed to hit the short 16th green. On this occasion the failure was extreme. I suspect he half-shanked his long-iron and it finished in the crowd to the right and some 30 yards from the green, all in all a weekend golfer's shot – or that of a man unable to cope with the pressures of a major championship finish. He pitched well but it was no less than justice that he failed with the putt. Watson drove safely on the 17th but sliced his iron shot right of the green. He chipped well and holed the crucial putt. On the 18th, his drive was safe and he needed to be down in two strokes to beat the total set by both Miller and Nicklaus. His iron shot came to rest about 5 yards away and he holed the putt. Suddenly, he was the man to catch at 279. And highly delighted.

Cole: Missed the green with a 5-iron after a perfect drive on the 14th and was bunkered. Another dropped shot followed on the 15th when he pushed his iron shot well into the crowd. However, he played the best shot by far of any contender to the short 16th to about a couple of yards. Had he holed that putt, I believe he might well have been champion and might have gone on to be a great golfer rather than what he remained – a great talent largely unfulfilled. He mishit his drive to the 17th and from the bank of the Barry Burn had to play a wooden club shot with the ball well above the level of his feet. He dropped a shot. On the 18th, he drove well, now needing a birdie to tie Watson, and walked the whole distance to the green either to calm his nerves or get the feel of the distance on that particular day. That journey completed, he conferred with his caddie over the choice of club. All was well. Whatever they decided, Cole had his second shot some 4 yards from the hole. He missed the putt. 280.

Newton: Parred the 14th and was unlucky that his second shot to the 15th ran through the green. He then pulled his chip a little and took two putts. Like just about everyone else he did not hit the 16th green and was bunkered, came out short and took two putts. However, it was the meandering Barry Burn at the 17th that was his undoing. With the hole playing into the wind, he chose to play only a 2-iron. He cleared the first curve of the Burn but only by some 6 inches. From there, on the bank, he had no chance at all of reaching the green and took 5. On the last, he had a par to tie, a birdie to win. His approach shot was a few yards away but he had the chance that few

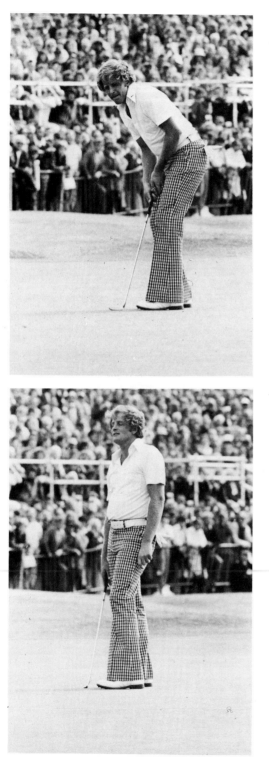

Carnoustie, 1975.
Jack Newton putts to win the Open

– and misses.

Alfie Fyles and Tom Watson, as the final putt goes down, 1975.

experience, of having 'this one for the Open'. Newton putted understandably cautiously with a play-off in mind and tapped in for his 4 and a total of 279. He was tied with Watson and possibly felt, a rising young star, that he would have little difficulty in accounting for that 'choker' on the morrow.

So Watson had tied for the championship, unnoticed by the eyes of the press or TV cameras throughout. Those who knew his name knew also that he was not of the stuff that champions are made. The next day, he won the first of his five Open championships. He parred the last and Newton did not, though it had been closely contested right through the previous 17 holes.

This had been a particularly poignant championship. Two men in the field, I am sure, Bobby Cole and Jack Newton, would have gone on to be formidable players with the glow of a championship in their systems. The same might well have applied to others who came close that year: Graham Marsh, Peter Oosterhuis, Neil Coles and perhaps even the 21-year-old Andries Oosthuizen, whose only approach to greatness this was. But, it was Tom Watson who benefited and went on to compile the best record in major championships and, in particular, the British Open in the last ten years. But more of that later.

HOW THEY FINISHED

T. Watson *USA*	**71**	**67**	**69**	**72**	**279**
J. Newton *Australia*	69	71	65	74	

Play-off:	Watson	71
	Newton	72

J. W. Nicklaus *USA*	69	71	68	72	280
J. Miller *USA*	71	69	66	74	
R. E. Cole *South Africa*	72	66	66	76	
G. V. Marsh *Australia*	72	67	71	71	281
P. A. Oosterhuis	68	70	71	73	282
N. C. Coles	72	69	67	74	
H. Irwin *USA*	69	70	69	75	283
G. Burns III *USA*	71	73	69	71	284
J. D. Mahaffey *USA*	71	68	69	76	
R. J. Charles *New Zealand*	74	73	70	69	286
P. Leonard	70	69	73	74	
A. Oosthuizen *South Africa*	69	69	70	78	
T. Weiskopf *USA*	73	72	70	72	287
M. Bembridge	75	73	67	73	288
A. Palmer *USA*	74	72	69	73	
A. Tapie *USA*	70	72	67	79	
L. Hinkle *USA*	76	72	69	72	289
S. Torrance	72	74	71	72	
T. Horton	72	71	71	75	
B. Gallacher	72	67	72	78	
M. Foster	72	74	73	71	290
R. Floyd *USA*	71	72	76	71	
B. W. Barnes	71	74	72	73	
H. Baiocchi *South Africa*	72	72	73	73	
D. Edwards *USA*	70	74	71	75	
R. de Vicenzo *Argentina*	71	74	72	74	291
G. L. Hunt	73	68	76	74	
D. Graham *Australia*	74	70	72	75	
S. F. N. Hobday *Rhodesia*	70	70	76	75	

P. Dawson	74	75	71	72	292
•G. J. Player *South Africa*	75	71	73	73	
M. Cahill *Australia*	71	73	74	74	
T. Britz *South Africa*	74	71	72	75	
D. Hayes *South Africa*	73	71	73	75	
H. M. Green *USA*	72	73	70	77	
R. Shearer *Australia*	69	72	74	77	
D. Huish	69	67	76	80	
R. Gilder *USA*	75	71	75	72	293
N. Wood	74	74	71	74	
L. Trevino *USA*	76	69	73	75	
K. D. G. Nagle *Australia*	72	73	73	75	
B. G. C. Huggett	72	71	75	75	
B. Waites	74	72	69	78	
I. Stanley *Australia*	75	71	70	78	294
B. Garrett *USA*	76	72	72	75	295
P. Wilcock	77	68	75	75	
L. Graham *USA*	73	72	74	76	
C. O'Connor Jr	72	73	73	77	
B. Brask *USA*	74	71	72	78	
E. Pearce *USA*	72	75	70	79	296
J. A. Jacobs *USA*	72	76	73	76	297
L. H. Lu *Taiwan*	76	72	72	77	
V. Fernandez *Argentina*	76	70	74	77	
D. I. Vaughan	72	71	74	80	
T. Le Brocq	72	76	72	78	298
P. M. P. Townsend	74	70	76	78	
D. J. Clark *New Zealand*	72	72	76	78	
H. Hansen *Denmark*	74	74	73	78	299
J. Dorrestein *Holland*	75	73	73	79	300
S. C. Mason	73	72	75	81	301
R. Carr	76	72	72	82	302

Royal Birkdale, 1976

In 1983, a certain Gerald Hoppy, entered as a Swiss professional, managed to return a 63 for a championship qualifying round at Pleasington. Alas, it was for nine holes, not eighteen. Michael Reece, an R and A official, suggested that Herr Hoppy might care to retire. Indeed, he may well have insisted!

In fact, this was a second triumph for Maurice Flitcroft, who appeared in the 1976 Open qualifying rounds as a crane driver from Barrow-in-Furness. He was not prevented from playing the full eighteen holes and notched up a handy 121. Although this experience (and the entry of Walter Danecki in 1965) encouraged the R and A to be more stringent in checking the credentials of 'professional' entrants it was still possible for a rabbit to slip through the net – so it was a smart move by Maurice to base himself in Switzerland.

There was another 'scandal' at Royal Birkdale in 1976, which, you may remember, was one of the hottest and driest summers of this century. The championship committee, mindful of earlier complaints from such august figures as Sam Snead and Ben Hogan about slow greens in the Open, had for many years followed a policy of encouraging the host club to provide fast putting surfaces, if not to the extremes of Augusta National and some US Open courses. At Birkdale in 1976, as the weather grew hotter and hotter, a decision had to be taken. Should the greens be watered heavily, with the risk that normal English summer downpours would then arrive to produce slow spongy and even soggy surfaces? Or should they be watered to a minimum?

As the Open began, the greens at neighbouring Hillside Golf Club could be seen an enticing emerald green away in the distance. At Birkdale, they were a dappled range of hues from burnt brown to occasional green. It was argued with some force that a good green is not one that looks like an immaculate lawn at Buckingham Palace or the White House. Traditionalists argued that there was no harm at all, especially on linksland, in turf looking a little faded. After all, it was asked, they putted well enough didn't they?

Not according to many of the players. Tom Weiskopf, renowned for a sharp temper in America but freer with sunny smiles in Britain, was outspoken about their condition in the Press Tent after his first-round 73. There had been one occasion when Tom had the good fortune to be able to watch a playing partner putt along the same line first. Weiskopf then knew, or thought he did, that he should strike the putt some 5 inches right of the hole and it would then swing left and nicely into the hole. Tom followed his policy. The pace looked exact. The ball predictably swung in towards the hole. And then twitched away!

Perhaps they did not always behave as eccentrically as this but all the players had great difficulty in judging the pace of longer putts. The ball often had to travel over both the relatively slow green patches and the much faster brown areas. Overall, I thought they putted reasonably well. Yet greenkeeping standards in Britain cannot stand comparison with the greater sophistication of America and a few other countries. It is by no means unusual to find more than a dozen varieties of grass on a British course with resultant problems for both putting and appearance. An equally severe problem was that the pins had often been set on higher parts of the green and it was these, of course, that were the most brown. Short putting was particularly difficult and time and again a ball that looked destined to find the hole twisted and turned away. Jack Nicklaus seemed to be suffering particularly badly – and what of Bobby Cole? With two good Open performances behind him, he hit his approach putt at the 1st to some 4 feet, then took four more shots to hole out. All of them, we are assured, were serious attempts!

The early starters probably had the best of it, the greens then being less fierce in pace. At 11 o'clock, just one player was under par, Christy O'Connor Junior. Having hit the first shot of the championship, he reached the turn in 30. He finished in 69 and that, oddly, included an air shot. On the 13th, his ball came to rest against a root. Christy hit a branch on his backswing and missed the ball. There are not many 69s returned in golf with an 8 on the card!

Playing in his first Open was the 24-year-old Japanese, Norio Suzuki, who rewarded Japan TV, covering the championship for the first time, with a fine performance. On the 18th tee he had been four under par but took 6 for a 69. The assembled press attempted to question him about his round but Suzuki spoke little English and an interpreter was needed.

Also in difficulty with his English was nineteen-year-old Severiano Balles-teros, the other man to have a 69, considered to have promise by close followers of European golf. He had finished 118th on the Order of Merit in 1974 and moved up to 26th in 1975. He had played moderately well in early season tournaments on the Continent, being in the top 6 of the Portuguese and Spanish Opens, but had achieved little or nothing in Britain. Altogether his money-winnings for 1976 were some £3500. Questioned about his chances for the second round, Ballesteros laughed and said he would take at least 80 if the wind got up. Modesty? Perhaps he did not yet believe how good he was.

Following these three were:

70 Barnes, Kite, Newton; 71 Marsh; 72 Player, Green, Miller;
73 Weiskopf, Jacklin, Pate; 74 Oosterhuis, Irwin, Nicklaus

An interesting threesome had been that of Johnny Miller (the favourite at about 8–1), Jack Newton (well-backed because of his tie at Carnoustie the year before) and a young hopeful, Sam Torrance, who embarrassed himself by slicing a few tee-shots high up in the sandhills and was round in 82. Miller was well there, however, and Newton's 70 was produced by a 4, 3, 5, 4 finish, which looked a lot better than Jack Nicklaus's 5, 4, 5, 6.

Although there was no real wind on the second day, Ballesteros began as

A wayward shot from Severiano Ballesteros at Royal Birkdale in 1976.

everyone expected, dropping several shots on the first nine holes. He then began holing putts and reached the 17th at four under par for the championship. There, he hit a huge drive and needed just a 3-iron to this 526-yard hole. From the right edge he nearly holed a very long putt and followed with what most thought was the longest drive of the day down the 18th. His iron was magnificently straight and left him a 3-yard putt – which he narrowly missed.

Ballesteros had a second 69 and, at 138, was outright leader. He had begun to draw the crowds during this second day and many had been delighted with the zest of his play. While Miller, for instance, was using his 1-iron for many tee-shots, Ballesteros gave everything a full right-elbow-flying lash with the driver. Sometimes he finished in unfrequented parts of the course but his power enabled him to thrash out of most bad lies.

Miller had held the lead earlier, finishing in 68 after birdies on the last two holes, for a total of 140. Other leading positions were:

142 Green, O'Connor Jr; 143 Barnes, Horton, Floyd (that year's Masters Champion); 144 Nicklaus, Marsh, Newton, Suzuki, Player, Pate, Kite (among others)

Carl Higgins, an American teaching professional, had the best round of the day, a 67. It followed a 77 but the following day Higgins took an 81. One of the best spells of golf in the championship came from David Graham. After a 77 in the first round he was headed in the same direction once more until he birdied five of the last six holes to be round in 70.

For the third round the leaders were out last, which paired Miller with young Ballesteros, who had bogeys at each of the first three holes for Miller to draw level. After the 8th Miller was two in the lead and reached the turn in 34 to the Spaniard's 38. Surely he was about to leave centre stage?

Seve then birdied the 10th but followed with a vast hook at the next hole. Not only did he need help finding his ball but also information as to the approximate direction of the green. Was this, I wonder, the real start of the Ballesteros legend? For he found his ball and was on in two. Miller, after a perfect tee-shot, took 5 and the pair were level again. After the par-3 14th Miller was one behind and hooked his drive off the 15th fairway. So did Ballesteros, but far more drastically. He found it in a reasonable lie; Miller did not and took a 6 to the Spaniard's 5. Ballesteros followed with a drive into the rough at the 526-yard 17th, an iron to the green and an eagle putt. Miller saved face on the last with a birdie and the gap was as they had started, two strokes.

Many found it scarcely credible that a nineteen-year-old was still in the lead after the third round and some contrasts were made with another young player, Jerry Pate, aged only twenty-two and already the year's US Open Champion. He reached the turn in 39, one worse than Ballesteros, and these were his figures on the homeward nine: 4, 8, 5, 4, 4, 7, 4, 5, 7. That was a grand total of 87 and obviously there was no Pate on the final day.

Just as surprisingly, there was no Tom Watson either. He had a 7 of his own on the first hole he played in the championship and never managed to pick up real momentum afterwards. With a round to come, these were the leaders:

211 Ballesteros; 213 Miller; 215 Horton; 216 Marsh, Floyd, Nicklaus; 217 Kite, O'Connor Jr

Although well behind, Jack Nicklaus was still a serious contender. Throughout, he had abandoned his frequent caution and had attacked the flag with his shots to the green. He had also putted quite well but little had dropped for him. There had even been a chip shot that appeared to drop below the rim of the hole – and then popped out again. Some also still favoured Ray Floyd, memories of his total dominance of the year's Masters being fresh in the mind. If he could produce another 67 as in the second round. . . .

But first of all, there was to be a head-to-head encounter between Miller and Ballesteros, the American by no means discounting the Spaniard's chances. He had been taken aback the day before by the stupendous recovery play, huge hitting and skill on and around the greens, and said: 'He's got a lot of courage. Maybe too much for his own good.'

The start was daunting indeed for Miller. He hit a straight tee-shot and a straight iron to the green which, however, finished through the back. Miller took three more to get down. Severiano hooked from the tee into willow scrub but was able to move it onwards, yet only into rough on the opposite side of the fairway. From there, he pitched to no closer than 10 yards – and holed the putt. Three ahead now.

Yet Miller hit back instantly with a birdie on the 2nd to the Spaniard's bogey 5. Pars followed for each on the next three holes and they reached the most difficult hole on the course, the par-4 6th, over 460 yards. It had just jolted Jack Nicklaus. The tee markers were set fully back and no one could hope to carry the cross bunkers. Nicklaus played short of them and needed a 1-iron for his shot to the green. He pushed it into dense willow scrub on the right and pride or arrogance prevented him looking for it. That was a 6 and the real end of any hope for Nicklaus.

Ballesteros, a little later, was in the same place and also took 6. For the first time Miller led the championship. He was three into the lead after the 8th, with a birdie to a bogey 5.

Miller during his peak years, 1973–6, thrived as a front-runner. He was seldom troubled by fears of pursuers but instead crowded on more sail. Indeed in this championship he used his driver for every tee-shot only once he was well in the lead. The 11th clinched the title for him. Ballesteros had just got a stroke back, with a birdie on the 10th, but then hit a huge hook into scrub once more, moved the ball scarcely at all with his first attempt, reached the green in four strokes and then three-putted for a 7 to Miller's par 4. Miller followed up with more conclusive golf: a birdie on the next and a chip-in for an eagle at the 13th. He was a mile ahead.

Confident of victory, Miller now encouraged Severiano not to give up but to try for second place, whereas 5th or 6th looked the most likely result by this time. A fine finish followed from the 14th: birdie, par, par, then for once a drive that found a fairway, the 17th, a second shot some 4 yards from the hole and an eagle putt. There remained the great arena of the 18th green and its surrounds. Severiano put his approach left of the green and had to be down in two to share second place with Jack Nicklaus, round in 69. There was little chance of stopping a high little pitch close to the hole and Ballesteros then showed all his deftness of touch, running a shot over the hump and threading between two bunkers to nestle 4 feet away. Miller putted close and generously decided to leave the centre of the stage to Seve. He tapped his little putt in for a 66, then the best last round by a champion, and Ballesteros played the last shot of the 1976 Open Championship. There had been a roar for the run-up and there was an greater one for the putt. A new favourite had arrived.

HOW THEY FINISHED

J. Miller *USA*	**72**	**68**	**73**	**66**	**279**
J. W. Nicklaus *USA*	74	70	72	69	285
S. Ballesteros *Spain*	69	69	73	74	
R. Floyd *USA*	76	67	73	70	286
M. James	76	72	74	66	288
H. M. Green *USA*	72	70	78	68	
T. Kite *USA*	70	74	73	71	
C. O'Connor Jr	69	73	75	71	
T. Horton	74	69	72	73	
V. Fernandez *Argentina*	79	71	69	70	289
P. J. Butler	74	72	73	70	
N. Suzuki *Japan*	69	75	75	70	
G. Burns III *USA*	75	69	75	70	
B. W. Barnes	70	73	75	72	290
E. Darcy	78	71	71	71	291
J. Fourie *South Africa*	71	74	75	71	
T. Weiskopf *USA*	73	72	76	71	292
J. Newton *Australia*	70	74	76	72	
G. B. Wolstenholme *Australia*	76	72	71	73	
G. V. Marsh *Australia*	71	73	72	76	
S. F. N. Hobday *Rhodesia*	79	71	75	68	293
R. A. Shearer *Australia*	76	73	75	69	
S. T. P. Ginn *Australia*	78	72	72	71	
D. Graham *Australia*	77	70	75	71	
C-S. Hsu *Taiwan*	81	69	71	72	
A. Tapie *USA*	74	72	75	72	
D. Huish	73	74	72	74	
N. Faldo	78	71	76	69	294
D. Sanders *USA*	77	73	73	71	
N. C. Coles	74	77	70	73	
G. J. Player *South Africa*	72	72	79	71	

R. de Vicenzo *Argentina*	77	71	76	72	296
P. McGuirk	76	70	77	73	
H. Irwin *USA*	74	72	77	73	
G. Littler *USA*	75	74	73	74	
G. L. Hunt	76	68	76	76	
R. E. Cole *South Africa*	75	71	72	78	
D. Jagger	78	72	74	73	297
V. Hood	76	74	73	74	
M. F. Foster	74	71	77	75	
I. Mosey	73	74	75	75	
A. Jacklin	73	77	76	72	298
P. A. Oosterhuis	74	75	77	72	
P. Dawson	80	72	73	73	
B. J. Burgess *Australia*	75	76	74	73	
M. Gregson	73	75	76	74	
W. Humphreys	73	77	73	75	
B. Garrett *USA*	74	74	78	73	299
R. Murphy *USA*	75	77	73	74	
C. I. Higgins *USA*	77	67	81	74	
D. McClelland	74	73	77	75	
P. Berry	80	72	71	76	
S. W. R. Adwick	78	71	74	76	
D. Hayes *South Africa*	77	71	74	77	
A. O'Connor	76	76	74	74	300
A. Oosthuizen *South Africa*	75	73	78	74	
J. L. Hammond	74	76	73	77	
A. Palmer *USA*	75	72	76	77	
D. Talbot	74	74	74	78	
D. Edwards *USA*	74	72	79	76	301
R. Wynn	79	70	75	77	
B. Gallacher	74	72	76	79	
W. R. Lockie	78	74	74	76	302
G. A. Caygill	80	71	75	76	
L. Higgins	77	74	75	76	
L. P. Tupling	75	71	77	79	

Turnberry, 1977

In 1977 Turnberry appeared on the Open Championship rota for the first time. This course has, in my opinion, the most potential of anywhere in the British Isles to be made into a spectacular, supreme test of golf. It is even comparable for natural beauty and seascapes with the Monterey peninsula in California which has the Pebble Beach, Cypress Point and Spyglass Hill courses.

Before this Open the firm of Alliss/Thomas (yes, David Thomas who had come so near to winning the 1958 and 1966 Opens) Golf Construction was asked by the R and A to make proposals for improvement of the design. We put forward three schemes: one for minor changes such as re-siting a few bunkers and tees, a middle plan, which went a little further, and our grand scheme. The aim of this was simple: to make Turnberry one of the world's greatest courses: a great test of golf and an even greater delight to the eye.

In the end, quite a number of alterations were made – but on a small scale. Yet the total cost of our full proposals at that time would have been £30,000 for a once-and-for-all job. How little that sounds today.

The simple intention of our ideal scheme was to create a course that would both thrill and daunt the tigers of modern golf. We felt that not enough use is made at Turnberry of the shoreline. We wanted to move the 8th green to the cliffside, create a new 9th, a short hole played across the bay, with the green set among the rocks beneath the lighthouse. The 10th we wanted as a par-5, with the fairway running hard along the beach and the green also by the sea. The

Nicklaus and Watson on the rocks at Turnberry in 1977.
Play was suspended because of thunder and lightning.

present 17th, though a par-5, is played in still conditions as a straightforward 4 by all the top players and even for club golfers is the simplest birdie opportunity on the course. We wanted to have this as a monster par-5, where nobody could get home in two, even with a following wind.

However, some of the golfing establishment were against our plans; also the finance was not forthcoming from the owners. Even so, Turnberry is still a magnificent course, perhaps, dare I say it, the best in Scotland. The setting is superb. Away in the distance is Ailsa Craig, described by John Keats as 'thou craggy ocean pyramid'. He went on:

> Thy life is but two dead eternities
> The last in air, the former in the deep;
> First with the whales, last with the eagle-skies
> Drowned wast thou till an earthquake made thee steep:
> Another cannot wake thy giant size.

If the golf becomes dull, certainly there is always the view.

But the golf was not dull in 1977. Perhaps no championship before or since has equalled this one in the appeal of having the two great players in world golf, Tom Watson and Jack Nicklaus, in a head-to-head duel that lasted through two whole days. Both played superbly, seeming to raise each other's games to fresh heights, with blow and counter blow all the way.

Over the years, Jack Nicklaus had dismissed several challenges to his supremacy. First there were Arnold Palmer and Gary Player, for a brief spell Tom Weiskopf, and Johnny Miller in the few years when he played golf of a quality no one has ever bettered. Tom Watson was the new pretender and the king was, at 37, approaching middle age, ten years older than Watson.

By the time the Turnberry Open began, Watson had added his second major championship to his record, that year's Masters. Perhaps significantly, he had outplayed Nicklaus, if only by the narrowest of margins, over the closing holes. By July, he had also won three other US events and was to finish the season as the third man to pass $300,000 in an American season. Only Nicklaus and Miller had done that before.

At the end of the first day, a man unknown to British spectators led the field, John Schroeder, son of Ted, a former US and British Open Champion – but at tennis. His 66 was seen by relatively few – he did not come off the course until 9.20 in the evening! The young Yorkshireman Martin Foster was close behind with a 67 but some more formidable names were on 68: Lee Trevino, Jack Nicklaus and Tom Watson.

Another little-known player, Roger Maltbie, headed the field after the second round. He had followed an opening 71 with a 66. Nicklaus and Watson had returned the same scores, 70. This meant that their two-round totals were the same so they were paired for the third round. The stage was set.

Nicklaus got some good blows in early on, holing several useful putts and getting to seven under par for the championship. At one hole, he had a 2 to Watson's 4. Later, however, he missed a few shortish putts, including one for an eagle on the 17th. Both provided a grandstand finish. Watson almost holed a long putt for a birdie, while Nicklaus, just through the green on the 18th, played a precisely judged little run-up shot to no more than 6 inches of the hole. Both were round in 65. Naturally they were joint championship leaders and most of the field by now had fallen out of touch. They seemed to be contesting the championship by themselves.

Interviewed in the Press Tent afterwards, Watson spoke with assurance and was keen to make the point that, though both he and Jack had 65s, his was the *better* one. He mentioned that some of Nicklaus's driving had been wayward and he had been lucky with the lies he found in the rough. Watson said he felt his own striking had been a little better.

So there the pair were, well out ahead on 203 (seven under par). Crenshaw was by this time really the only credible challenger. He had followed rounds of 71 and 69 with a 66 and was four under par at 206. There was then a considerable gap until the names of Tommy Horton (after a third-round 65), Roger Maltbie and Gaylord Burrows appeared, all at one under par. Surely none of these could make up a six-stroke deficit on either Watson or Nicklaus, let alone both! Johnny Miller and Lee Trevino were at level par, even further away.

For the final day, there was a fresh westerly breeze. Though it was by no means severe, there were many scores in the high 70s and even low 80s, which helps to put the final rounds of Watson and Nicklaus into clearer perspective.

Their only likely challenger, Ben Crenshaw, dropped five strokes in six holes in the middle part of his round and dropped away to level par for the championship, eventually coming in with a 75.

Attention was focused on Watson and Nicklaus, who was outdriven on the 1st by some 40 yards or so, but both parred the hole. First blood went to Nicklaus on the 2nd, 428 yards into the breeze. Watson's drive was straight up the middle of the fairway, while Nicklaus was in the rough and not too well-placed. He deliberated long over his choice of club and his ball then came to rest a few yards from the hole. Watson, however, ran off the left of the green and for once played a poor little pitch, several yards short of the hole. Nicklaus holed, Watson didn't and a two-stroke gap suddenly appeared. Nicklaus increased his lead on the 4th with another birdie to be nine under par but Watson then made his first real move on the 5th. He birdied to come to seven under himself and then birdied both 7th and 8th to be level with Nicklaus. Both stood at nine under par but Nicklaus again had a one-stroke advantage after the 9th, where Watson dropped a stroke.

The margin remained the same over the next few holes, both players giving themselves further chances to take the initiative. The short 15th, however, proved to be one of the holes on which the championship turned. Nicklaus was on the green with his tee-shot, Watson a little short on the left and in light rough, some 20 to 25 yards from the hole. Would Nicklaus go into a two-stroke lead? Watson took his putter – and holed out. The pair were level.

Both parred the 15th and Watson drove well down the 17th fairway (his driving had usually been superior to Nicklaus's throughout the two rounds they played together). But at this point Nicklaus launched a huge drive. He was left with just a 7-iron to this 500-yard hole. Watson then got his blow in first, a cracking iron shot over and past the flag. Nicklaus's 7-iron in response was hit a touch heavily: his ball was about 20 yards short, leaving an awkward little shot to the pin. He ran it up to about a yard and a half past. Watson putted dead. Nicklaus putted firmly but misread the line – one behind.

A 4 from Watson and a 5 to Nicklaus. For the first time Watson was in the lead with one hole to play, a par-4 of some 430 yards. Watson rasped an iron far down the middle; Nicklaus took his driver, hoping to have his ball much nearer the green for the birdie that was so desperately needed. The drive was a poor one, with 'too much belly' in it. The ball ballooned away right and Nicklaus was both lucky and relieved to see it stop only a foot or two clear of the gorse. Watson's shot to the green was impeccable, perhaps little more than 2 feet from the hole. It seemed the Open was his.

Yet Nicklaus was not quite done for. He managed to get his ball on the front of the green and then, while Watson was perhaps mentally rehearsing a few words for the presentation ceremony, holed a putt of some 15 yards. Watson now had to hole his 'for the Open'. His preparations were quick and decisive and the ball was in: 65 for Watson; 66 for Nicklaus.

Both had left previous Open Championship records far behind. Watson's 268 total had beaten the previous aggregate by eight strokes or, to put it another way, he had scored two strokes per round fewer than any previous champion. 'Oh yes,' some said, 'but the course was easy. Those fellows Alliss and Thomas didn't do much to toughen it up.' You could ask Hubert Green about that. He was the only other player to beat par for the 72 holes – by just one stroke, and finished *eleven* strokes behind Tom Watson. Or the halfway leader, Roger Maltbie who, in company with five others, took 80 or more for their last rounds. To be fair, I should perhaps put in just one piece of evidence for the other side. In the second round, the American Mark Hayes, having taken 76 the day before, decided to try out a reversed-hands putting grip and broke the Open Championship record with a 63. However, he was five over par for his remaining two rounds and four over for the championship.

Both Watson and Nicklaus had set a scoring record at 203 for the first 54 holes and Watson, with a total of 200, for the last 54 holes also. Watson's last-round 65 was the best ever by a champion. But perhaps all these records were incidental. In simple terms, what made this Open spectacular was the long, old-fashioned duel between the greatest player of modern times and the man destined to succeed him.

HOW THEY FINISHED

Player					Total
T. Watson *USA*	**68**	**70**	**65**	**65**	**268**
J. W. Nicklaus *USA*	68	70	65	66	269
H. M. Green *USA*	72	66	74	67	279
L. Trevino *USA*	68	70	72	70	280
G. Burns III *USA*	70	70	72	69	281
B. D. Crenshaw *USA*	71	69	66	75	
A. Palmer *USA*	73	73	67	69	282
R. Floyd *USA*	70	73	68	72	283
J. Schroeder *USA*	66	74	73	71	284
M. Hayes *USA*	76	63	72	73	
T. Horton	70	74	65	75	
J. Miller *USA*	69	74	67	74	
P. W. Thomson *Australia*	74	72	67	73	286
H. K. Clark	72	68	72	74	
G. L. Hunt	73	71	71	72	287
J. Pate *USA*	74	70	70	73	
R. Cole *South Africa*	72	71	71	73	
P. J. Butler	71	68	75	73	
G. V. Marsh *Australia*	73	69	71	74	
R. Shearer *Australia*	72	69	72	74	
S. Ballesteros *Spain*	69	71	73	74	
G. Player *South Africa*	71	74	74	69	288
T. Weiskopf *USA*	74	71	71	72	
P. Dawson	74	68	73	73	
J. Fourie *South Africa*	74	69	70	75	
R. Massengale *USA*	73	71	74	71	289
D. Ingram	73	74	70	72	
M. F. Foster	67	74	75	73	
J. O'Leary	74	73	68	74	
A. Gallardo *Spain*	78	65	72	74	
N. Suzuki *Japan*	74	71	69	75	
G. Burrows *USA*	69	72	68	80	
R. Maltbie *USA*	71	66	72	80	
E. Darcy	74	71	74	71	290
K. J. Brown	74	73	71	72	
M. Pinero *Spain*	74	75	71	71	291
B. Dassu *Italy*	72	74	72	73	
M-N. Hsieh *Taiwan*	72	73	73	73	
B. W. Barnes	79	69	69	74	
J. Morgan	72	71	71	77	
N. C. Coles	74	74	71	73	292
D. I. Vaughan	71	74	73	74	
J. Gonzales *USA*	78	72	71	72	293
A. Jacklin	72	70	74	77	
R. J. Charles *New Zealand*	73	72	70	78	
S. Ginn *Australia*	75	72	72	75	294
H. Irwin *USA*	70	71	73	80	
B. G. C. Huggett	72	77	72	74	295
V. Fernandez *Argentina*	75	73	73	74	
M. G. King	73	75	72	75	
R. de Vicenzo *Argentina*	76	71	70	78	
C. O'Connor Jr	75	73	71	77	296
J. C. Farmer	72	74	72	78	
B. J. Waites	78	70	69	79	
R. M. Davies *Australia*	77	70	70	79	
M. Bembridge	76	69	75	77	297
V. Tshabalala *South Africa*	71	73	72	81	
I. Mosey	75	73	73	77	298
D. Jones	73	74	73	78	
C. S. Hsu *Taiwan*	70	70	77	81	
G. D. Jacobson *USA*	74	73	70	81	
N. A. Faldo	71	76	74	78	299
S. Locatelli *Italy*	72	72	76	79	
V. Baker *South Africa*	77	70	73	79	

St Andrews, 1978

In 1978, the championship came to St Andrews for the twenty-second time, oddly enough not a record. This still belongs to Prestwick with twenty-four, though it has not been used since 1925. Despite Watson's triumph at Turnberry, Nicklaus was again the betting man's favourite at 6–1, but nearly as much money was on Watson.

On the US Tour Watson was having yet another superb season. At the end of it, with more than $360,000 won, he had beaten Johnny Miller's 1974 record. He was also acclaimed Player of the Year and took the Vardon Trophy for the season's lowest stroke average. By the beginning of May he had won three events and was one of those players who 'should' have won the Masters, finishing just a stroke behind Gary Player, who came home in 30 for a remarkable last-round 64 to snatch the title from nowhere.

It was Watson's first sight of St Andrew's but by this time he had a strong liking for links golf. He found it, he said, 'a test of the man', while American golf was 'a test of the skill alone'. This time, Watson had decided to allow ample time to learn the course. Before his victories at Carnoustie he had played no practice round and at Turnberry only two. When Bobby Jones first played the course in 1921, he had felt 'puzzled dislike'. Snead's distaste had been stronger, you may remember, despite winning the title. Watson was merely puzzled. He was surprised at how short the course played and by the slopes and swales in front of many of the greens. He felt his tactics would be to play pitch and run shots with the wind at his back but to fly the ball in high against the wind. On the practice ground, he spent much time working on high wedge and sand-iron shots.

For the last two practice days the weather had been very chill with a sea mist most of the time. The championship proper began in still clear weather.

The Japanese player Isao Aoki was the first to make a move. By about 11 o'clock, he was four under par for the ten holes he had played and managed to hold that position. His putting was attracting much attention, the wristy stroke with the toe stuck high in the air being considered highly unorthodox. So also was the rest of his game, his swing for full shots being more wristy than any other contemporary golfer I can think of, while his balance left a lot to be desired. He ended his round with putts of some 20 feet on both the 17th and 18th to finish in 68. They came to jeer and stayed to cheer.

He had become the first Japanese to lead the Open Championship outright. But a stronger challenger for the lead was not far away in the person of Tom Weiskopf. After five holes he was three under par, birdied the 6th and reached the turn in 31 (3, 4, 3, 4, 4, 3, 4, 3, 3). Lo and behold, he then birdied the 10th. This was scoring approaching Tony Jacklin's wonderful run in 1970. However, he had a couple of 5s coming back, then a 6 at the dreaded Road hole, knee-high in rough after two strokes on this par-4. In the circumstances, his 69 was disappointing and Weiskopf never regained that early momentum.

Watson was round in a steady 73, despite being out of bounds on the 14th; Nicklaus was two strokes better. Many anticipated a repeat of the 1977 duel.

At the end of the day the Japanese player (one of five in the field, as opposed to twenty-eight Americans) was still in the lead. Aoki was followed by:

69 Weiskopf, Floyd, Newton, Ballesteros; 70 Owen, Crenshaw, Hayes, Nakajima, Mason, Miller, H. Clark

After the second round, Watson had made the strongest move, his 68 being the lowest round by a contender. Nicklaus had played steadily, seldom seeming in danger of dropping a stroke, but with his birdie putts shaving the hole. The 17th for him, as for many others, produced a minor disaster. On the first day, Brian Barnes had seen his birdie putt drift away on the slope and into the Road bunker! Nicklaus played cautiously left, away from the out of bounds, and was in the rough. From there a player has no real chance of going for the green and he had to be content to knock his ball some 90 yards short of it and dropped a stroke. Ballesteros, the championship lead in sight, took a bold line down the right from the tee and went out of bounds. With temper in the shot, he then showed how the hole should be played, lashing his drive almost 350 yards and having only a 6-iron left to the green. Two players showed other ways of dealing with the problems. Crenshaw was not on in two but then holed a very long putt from the edge of the green for his 4 while Isao Aoki, from the road beyond, putted up the bank to some 6 feet and sank the putt for his par. All in all, only one-third of the field could par the hole and the number of birdies could be counted on the fingers of one hand.

Despite his problems, Ballesteros had moved up to share the lead:

139 Ballesteros, Crenshaw, Aoki; 140 Shearer, Cullen (with a 67);
141 Watson, Weiskopf, Ozaki, Nakajima, Byman, Kite;
142 Thomson, Palmer, Moody, Morgan, Oosterhuis

Three names who were to be significant on the final two days do not yet feature: Jack Nicklaus, Raymond Floyd and Simon Owen.

The best rounds of the third day were 67s from both Hubert Green, usually a good performer in the event, and Simon Owen. Green, however, had opened his campaign with a 78, so his low round (with only one 5 on his card – on the 17th) was not to move him up among the real contenders. Owen's 67 most certainly did, though most thought he would fade on the final day.

Peter Thomson, five times the champion, continued to play his favourite course well. Twenty-three years after he had won the title at St Andrews, and a month or so away from his 49th birthday, he was round in 72. At two under par for the three rounds, he found at the end of the day he was only

Peter Oosterhuis and Peter Thomson contending strongly for the 1978 Open at St Andrews.

three strokes behind the leaders. Did the hopes stir that he might do it again?

Nicklaus began very steadily, two under par for the first five holes, while Ballesteros quickly gave himself a jolt by pitching into the Swilcan Burn on the 1st. He was to continue to feature until the Road Hole eventually put paid to his chances. This time he didn't risk the out of bounds on the right but hit down the left into a bad lie in the rough. From there he found more rough, finding his ball only with difficulty, went onto the road in three and eventually took 6 to finish in 76.

Another who perished at this hole was Palmer. Late in the afternoon he was one under par for his round and three under for the championship and a very credible contender. But do you remember Johnny Bulla's deplorable record at this hole in the 1946 Open and how it probably cost Palmer the 1960 championship to Kel Nagle? Palmer had a 5 in the first round, was out of bounds and took 7 on the second day and achieved exactly the same result at the third attempt – nineteen strokes instead of the regulation twelve.

The names most prominent during the day were Aoki, Nicklaus, Oosterhuis, Watson, Nicklaus, Crenshaw, Ballesteros and Kite. When Watson birdied the 12th, there was a five-way tie at five under par, and five minutes later Watson took the lead as he birdied the next hole. Watson then joined the ranks of those who had made rather a mess of tackling the severe demands of the 17th. After two strokes to the 17th, he had the bunker between him and the flag. He then tried to cut the legs from his little pitch shot and, as so many have done before and will again when trying this shot, he shanked it. However, as shanks go it was a good – or rather a lucky – one. It hit the bank and ran up onto the green, though of course a long way from the hole. He got his 5 and at the end of the day this is how the race stood:

211 Oosterhuis, Watson; 212 Nicklaus, Owen, Crenshaw, Aoki;
213 Faldo, Schroeder, Weiskopf, Kite

One Japanese player who should still have been there, and was not, had been destroyed by the Road Hole. Rather like Brian Barnes on the first day Nakajima was on the front of the green in two strokes and, at four under par, may well have been hopeful of leading the championship. His putt had neither the borrow nor strength and curled away slowly into the bunker. The shot he next had to play had to rise steeply but with only enough forward momentum to just get out in order to be near the hole. Attempt followed attempt. In the end he got it more or less right and a 9 was his reward. At 5.37 p.m. precisely Nakajima had been putting for a birdie to go five under par. By 5.42 he was one over par for the championship. 'Bad luck', said his playing partner, Tom Weiskopf – and he really looked as if he meant it.

Nakajima's had been the only 9 for the hole that day but there had been two 7s, eleven 6s, 48 bogey 5s and only eighteen pars. No one had birdied the hole. What this adds up to is that the par-4 Road Hole is probably the most difficult hole to par on any of our championship courses, with the possible exception of the 15th at Royal Lytham. Players are unwilling to trust themselves to drive straight down the right and the second shot rapidly becomes impossible, the more the tee-shot goes left. However, too many players, after an adequate tee-shot, leaving a long approach to follow, then play the wrong kind of shot. They try to fly the ball all the way to the green when a long, low runner is needed. It should pitch perhaps 50 yards short of the green and chase along,

Tsuneyuki Nakajima in that bunker, 1978.

swinging in with the slope of the ground, before finally rolling up the bank onto the green. That is the theory, at least, but in all the rounds I played at St Andrews in my career, I can only once recall getting a 3 and only about eight 4s. It will be interesting to see how the new generation deals with it in 1984!

Overnight, there was a change in weather that was to prove of great significance. The wind shifted from east to north. Jack Nicklaus is said to have been highly delighted. He felt that his greater experience of playing the course in all the varied wind directions gave him an advantage. We heard later that he cancelled plans to fly home shortly after the close of play, in favour of remaining to celebrate his victory!

The last day had the New Zealander Simon Owen paired with the great man. Much of the story of the winning and losing of this championship was to centre on their play on just one hole, the 16th, not normally a particularly dramatic hole at St Andrews. As I have said, not very much was expected of Simon Owen and he began by justifying those predictions by dropping a shot at both the 4th and 6th. After all, his best placing in Europe that season had been 10th in the Greater Manchester Open. Otherwise, his best career performances had been a win in the 1974 German Open and the 1976 New Zealand Open. He had needed to pre-qualify to get into this championship.

Yet Owen was suddenly able to produce one of the best spells of his career, with birdies on the 9th, 10th and 12th. He then hit an excellent drive up the long 14th and was close to the green in two. He then chipped to about 6 feet and holed the putt to be six under par. On the next hole, he missed the green but then enjoyed the stroke of luck that all champions need. He chipped into the hole from 25 yards to lead the field at seven under par.

And so to the 16th. Owen drove far and straight and had just a wedge left to the green. There was very little wrong with his approach but his ball pitched on a slight down-slope and skipped through the green, finishing on a tee for the 17th hole. His return shot had to be precisely judged, with so many humps and bumps to steer the ball through. Owen's shot was good – but not good enough. His ball stopped in a hollow on the green, several yards still to go. Owen's nerve held, and the putt was an excellent one – but it didn't drop: a 5 for Simon Owen.

Nicklaus had sent his approach shot to about 8 feet and had this putt to take the championship lead. He holed it and, with a two-stroke swing on the 16th, led Owen by a stroke. The Road Hole, however, still lay ahead and, as we have seen, just about anything was possible there.

Nicklaus had had his share of 5s, though no greater disasters. Owen flew his second shot out of the left-hand rough boldly, or foolishly, for the green, and inevitably went on the road; Nicklaus played cautiously and sensibly to the front of the green. He then was able to produce a masterly putt, judging the pace and line of the shot to perfection. How well I remember his caddie, Jimmy Dickinson, urging the ball up the slope and on, on, on as he held the flag. It was

there, right by the holeside. Nicklaus had a tap-in and, with Owen taking 5, seemed to have disposed of the New Zealand threat.

Just behind, however, was the overnight joint leader, Peter Oosterhuis. He was still five under par to Nicklaus's seven. Oosterhuis too managed to coax his ball onto the front of the 17th green. He was left with a long putt which *had* to go down and then needed another birdie on the last. The putt was a good and brave one, finishing about 3 feet beyond the hole. Oosterhuis, however, missed the return and that was that. He completed his round one stroke out of the four-way tie for second place.

Nicklaus played the last with caution – and why not indeed? He used a 3-wood from the tee and played a runner with a 7-iron (perhaps remembering Sanders's poor high pitch in 1970?). His ball stopped towards the back of the green, leaving him some 20 yards from the hole. Suddenly Simon Owen was statistically back in the championship. His own approach was a far better one, only a few yards from the hole. If he should hole for a birdie and Nicklaus three-putted, the two would tie. Nicklaus coasted his putt to little more than a yard; Owen missed.

Jack Nicklaus was champion for the third time. He had also been second six times, third on three occasions and overall in seventeen attempts had only finished out of the top six in 1962 and 1965. Watson, on the other hand, had faltered on the final day to a 76 to take 14th place. Could Nicklaus re-establish his authority in major championships? Would Watson prove to be another Weiskopf or Miller, a great player who faded quickly at the height of his prowess?

J. W. Nicklaus *USA*	**71**	**72**	**69**	**69**	**281**
S. M. Owen *New Zealand*	70	75	67	71	283
R. Floyd *USA*	69	75	71	68	
B. D. Crenshaw *USA*	70	69	73	71	
T. Kite *USA*	72	69	72	70	
P. A. Oosterhuis	72	70	69	73	284
I. Aoki *Japan*	68	71	73	73	285
R. Shearer *Australia*	71	69	74	71	
J. Schroeder *USA*	74	69	70	72	
N. Faldo	71	72	70	72	
O. Moody *USA*	73	69	74	70	288
M. Cahill *Australia*	71	72	75	68	
D. Hayes *South Africa*	74	70	71	71	
M. S. Hayes *USA*	70	75	75	67	287
M. Ozaki *Japan*	72	69	75	71	
T. Watson *USA*	73	68	70	76	
R. Byman *USA*	72	69	74	73	288
T. Nakajima *Japan*	70	71	76	71	
S. Ballesteros *Spain*	69	70	76	73	
G. L. Hunt	71	73	71	73	
T. Weiskopf *USA*	69	72	72	75	
B. Gallacher	72	71	76	70	289
N. Job	73	75	68	73	
A. Garrido *Spain*	73	71	76	70	290
H. Irwin *USA*	75	71	76	68	
J. Newton *Australia*	69	76	71	74	
C. Mason	70	74	72	74	
P. W. Thomson *Australia*	72	70	72	76	
L. Trevino *USA*	75	72	73	71	291
J. Morgan	74	68	77	72	
T. Britz *South Africa*	73	74	72	72	
G. Norman *Australia*	72	73	74	72	
H. M. Green *USA*	78	70	67	76	
B. W. Barnes	71	74	75	72	292
G. J. Player *South Africa*	74	71	76	71	
G. Cullen	73	67	79	73	
K. Brown	73	72	71	76	
A. Palmer *USA*	71	71	75	75	
N. Price *South Africa*	74	73	74	72	293
M. Krantz *USA*	75	72	75	71	
Mr P. McEvoy	71	74	76	72	
G. B. Wolstenholme *Australia*	73	74	71	75	
D. Graham *Australia*	73	74	70	76	
F. Abreu *Spain*	73	73	76	72	294
H. K. Clark	70	75	73	76	
Mr M. Miller	70	74	74	76	
M. Ballesteros *Spain*	73	71	74	76	
Mr A. Brodie	73	72	75	75	295
A. Bean *USA*	72	76	72	75	
R. J. Charles *New Zealand*	73	70	79	73	
N. C. Coles	71	73	73	78	
V. Somers *Australia*	72	72	76	76	296
R. Thompson *USA*	73	73	76	74	
J. Bland *South Africa*	72	73	77	74	
S. F. N. Hobday *Rhodesia*	73	71	77	75	
W. Longmuir	75	71	75	75	
D. Good *Australia*	75	73	74	74	
R. M. Davis *Australia*	73	72	73	78	
P. J. Butler	71	74	75	77	297
Mr G. Godwin	74	73	75	76	298
R. Wynn	73	72	76	77	
P. Dawson	75	72	75	77	299
E. Murray	76	70	76	78	300

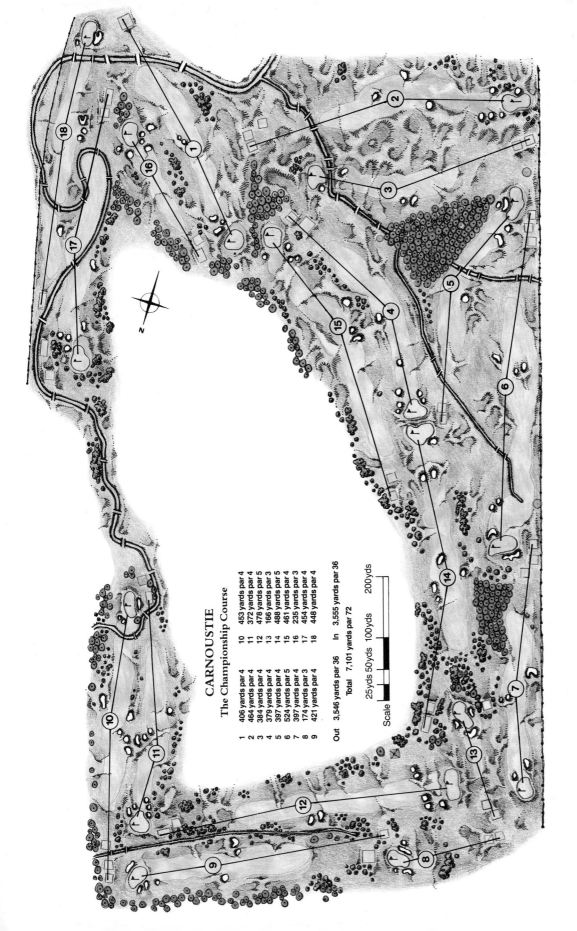

CARNOUSTIE
The Championship Course

1	406 yards par 4	10	453 yards par 4
2	464 yards par 4	11	372 yards par 4
3	384 yards par 4	12	478 yards par 5
4	379 yards par 4	13	166 yards par 3
5	397 yards par 4	14	488 yards par 5
6	524 yards par 5	15	461 yards par 4
7	397 yards par 4	16	235 yards par 3
8	174 yards par 3	17	454 yards par 4
9	421 yards par 4	18	448 yards par 4

Out 3,546 yards par 36   In 3,555 yards par 36

Total 7,101 yards par 72

Scale

25yds 50yds 100yds   200yds

TURNBERRY

The Championship Course
Ailsa

1	365 yards par 4		10	460 yards par 4
2	440 yards par 4		11	180 yards par 3
3	475 yards par 4		12	395 yards par 4
4	170 yards par 3		13	385 yards par 4
5	490 yards par 5		14	440 yards par 4
6	245 yards par 3		15	220 yards par 3
7	520 yards par 5		16	415 yards par 4
8	440 yards par 4		17	515 yards par 5
9	475 yards par 4		18	430 yards par 4

Out 3,620 yards par 36   In 3,440 yards par 35

Total 7,060 yards par 71

N

Scale   25 yds 50 yds 100 yds   200 yds

Royal Lytham and St Anne's, 1979

Before every Open Championship begins many words are expended by the nation's leading golf correspondents. There are columns to be filled for some four days leading up to the event while golf magazines seem to use well-nigh half an issue. One of the main themes, of course, is: Who is going to win?

For the first time in many, many years Jack Nicklaus was not the favourite in 1979. He had at last been displaced by Tom Watson in the betting. Watson had been again busying himself in America with four tournament victories by the end of May and had tied for the US Masters before Fuzzy Zoeller took the play-off from Watson and Ed Sneed. He was to raise the US Tour money-winning record by almost $100,000 with his eventual total of $462,636 and more, of course, won outside America.

In the betting, Severiano Ballesteros was also well favoured at 12–1, but the pundits, with almost one voice, felt he had little chance of winning. The Spaniard's fairly frequent wild drives were well known and it was thought that a claustrophobic course like Royal Lytham and St Annes would frustrate even his formidable skills in recovery play. Instead a far 'tidier' player, Hale Irwin, recent winner of the US Open, was thought particularly likely to win.

There was also the often expressed thought that no American had won at Royal Lytham. This was not true. A certain Robert Tyre Jones Junior's name can be seen on the trophy for the year of 1926 and he was, incidentally, followed past the post by Al Watrous, George von Elm and Walter Hagen, all golfers of unimpeachable American nationality. That championship was the first held at Royal Lytham and St Anne's and no American professional has ever won there.

The news story of the first day was the play of Bill Longmuir who had his lowest-ever tournament round. The Open Championship was the right time to find the inspiration. He played the first nine in 29, only the fourth time this had been done for either first or second nines in a British Open. His total of 65 equalled the lowest score for an opening round, set by Neil Coles at St Andrews in 1970 (since beaten by Craig Stadler's 64 at Royal Birkdale in 1983). Longmuir had never made the top 60 on the European Tour but he had won a couple of tournaments overseas, the 1976 Nigerian Open and the Southland Classic in New Zealand the same year. He birdied five holes in a row from the 3rd to 7th, added another at the 9th and moved smoothly into the second nine with more birdies on the 10th and 12th. Thereafter, on the more difficult run-in, he dropped two strokes.

The round gave him a three-stroke lead on the first day over Hale Irwin, who was very keen to become one of those rare birds who have won the championships of both America and Britain in the same year. Rounds under 70 were rare throughout the championship. The only others on the first day came from Irwin and his fellow American Jerry Pate.

Lee Trevino.

The second day largely belonged to Severiano Ballesteros, who notched up a 65 of his own. He reached the turn in 33 and this did not really foreshadow the score that was to come. At Royal Lytham a really good score has to be made on the first nine (three of the four 29s at that time in the Open had been recorded on this nine – by Peter Thomson, Tom Haliburton and, of course, Longmuir).

It was Ballesteros's brilliant finish that brought the 65. Because of the wind direction that day, it was reckoned that the true par for the last five holes was 4, 5, 4, 5, 4. Ballesteros finished 3, 3, 4, 3, 3 and had 32 for the inward nine.

He had played with Lee Trevino, which may well have helped his cause because the Mexican American, besides speaking his own brand of Spanish, is also a great admirer of Ballesteros's play. If Lee Trevino is not going to win himself, he likes to see Severiano take first place.

After his first-round 73, Ballesteros was now right up near the top:

136 Irwin;   138 Ballesteros;   139 Longmuir;   140 Watson;
142 Nicklaus;   144 Crenshaw;   145 Aoki

Ballesteros was later to claim that his attitude to Lytham was very different from that of so much expert opinion. The many bunkers he felt were no real problem because 'I am the best bunker player.' Probably true and even more likely to be true if the player believes it. He did not consider the rough particularly severe and later claimed that he had deliberately driven into it on his practice rounds both to test it out and to see if wide positions to right or left of some of the fairways gave better lines into the green.

Another Spanish speaker had a great influence on Ballesteros. Roberto de Vicenzo had been one of the first to recognize that Ballesteros was a major talent and did indeed recommend him to Ed Barner, the American agent/ entrepreneur, who was to manage him until Ballesteros turned to a Spanish friend and former airline-executive, Jorge Ceballos, several years later. De Vicenzo has often been seen with Ballesteros on practice days and an old master-young pupil relationship grew up between them.

De Vicenzo advised him to attack the course, pointing out that Jack Nicklaus's caution may well have cost him several British Opens, a point I have illustrated in this book. Though he felt Nicklaus was the man to beat, de Vicenzo had noticed that his strategy had been cautious on the practice rounds: taking the safest line from the tee rather than the one more likely to set up a birdie chance. He also felt that, with most severe trouble – particularly out of bounds – on the right, Ballesteros should work on the practice ground to shape his shots from right to left. Not much of a problem, as the Spaniard can fade and draw at will, right-handed or left-handed, on one leg or two or, for a lark, on his knees as well. I am sure it was this ability to manoeuvre a ball that so captured Roberto's imagination, for he had so much of the same ability – but not the putting and chipping finesse to anything like the same degree. How many times I have seen Roberto stroll the length of a par-5 bouncing a golf ball on the face of a 9-iron while discussing the merits of the scenery, the standard of food in the locality and the charms of his breakfast waitress. Try it yourself one day. Just hitting a golf ball well is difficult – but that!

Roberto gave Ballesteros one piece of general advice that I find particularly inspirational: '*Tienes las manos. Ahora juega con tu corazon.*' (You have the hands. Now play with your heart.) How about that for a great line? I think most of us would agree that Ballesteros did just that in the 1979 championship.

For the third round, Ballesteros and Hale Irwin were paired, and I dare say it was an experience that was wearing on the American's nerves. Irwin is an exemplary player, one of my favourites to watch, and in the Peter Thomson mould: hit it onto the fairway, then onto the green and don't three-putt. Here he was confronted by a man whose philosophy that year could be summed up as: 'Hit it as far as you can, find it, get it on the green and then try to one-putt. Never mind the bunkers and the rough. You're used to them.'

Both were round in 75 on a blustery day; both still led the field:

211 Irwin; 213 Ballesteros; 214 Nicklaus, James (with his second 69); 215 Crenshaw, Byman, Davis; 216 Aoki, Norman, Longmuir, Watson; 217 McEvoy, Marsh, D. J. Clark

With the gap between them only a couple of strokes, Ballesteros struck early, holing a fine putt for a 2 on the 1st to Irwin's par 3. On the 2nd, Ballesteros took the championship lead, parring the hole with a 4 while Irwin took 6 after half-hitting his tee-shot.

The Ballesteros immortalized in this championship was at his most characteristic on the 486-yard 6th hole. With a drawn tee-shot needed to this right-to-left dogleg, he hooked wildly across the 14th fairway. He reckoned he was some 90 yards off-line. From this unaccustomed position, it was no surprise that neither he nor his caddie had much idea which club to use for the second shot. Ballesteros hit about 50 yards through the green. He still got his par and reached the turn in 34.

The 10th, a relatively short par-4, had given Ballesteros trouble in each round. This time he was in rough short of the green in two. He played a weak third and was still not on the green. Rather uncharacteristically he chose to putt and ran it some 3 yards past the hole. A double-bogey threatened, but Seve holed the crucial putt that could have cost him the championship.

The 13th is another short 4 of 339 yards. De Vicenzo advised boldness as the right tactic here. Ballesteros should use his driver and attempt to carry to the green. In the first three rounds, however, he had taken an iron from the tee. On the final day he gave it every ounce. The result can be seen in a well-known photograph by Bert Neale: the momentum of the club was so extreme that there is a kind of recoil from the finish of the follow-through. But what

Ballesteros gives it everything – and a bit more – at the 13th, 1979.

Hale Irwin – the 1979 Championship had slipped away from him.

happened to the ball? It hit a mound to the right of the green and ran into a bunker. The carry was a yard or so under 300 yards. From there, the Spaniard's bunker shot was on the fringe, perhaps a dozen yards from the hole. On and on the putt went as he pointed his club, matador-like, at the hole. It dived in; a decisive moment indeed.

There remained the celebrated tee-shot to the 353-yard 16th. Conventionally, the drive should be down the left of the fairway but, because of the flag position well to the left that day, Ballesteros claims he decided to play to the right – and finished in what has often been described as a car park. This gives the impression that Ballesteros must have been about as far off-line as he had been at the 6th, or had carried the clubhouse at the 1st and put it in the road. Yet it was hardly a car park at all, just a reserved area for our BBC vehicles, little more than 30 yards from the edge of the fairway. Nevertheless, it gave certain partisan Americans the opportunity to refer to him as 'the car park champion'. From there, Ballesteros hit a sand wedge 6 or 7 yards from the hole and got the putt. He was poised for almost certain victory.

But what had been happening to the other contenders? Hale Irwin, after his poor start, seemed to lose heart and became almost invisible in contrast to the panache of the Spaniard's play. In the end he staggered in with a 78, not after all to be one of the select band who have won both American and British championships in the same year. His card showed six 5s and two 6s. Seldom can two more contrasting styles have been paired at an Open climax. The

Australian Rodger Davis, playing in elegant socks displaying his name in diamonds, was at one time championship leader, having reached the turn in 32. He went in a spell of 6, 5, 6 on the 14th to 16th holes. Crenshaw also played well that last day. When he stood on the 17th tee he was level with Ballesteros, who at that time had five holes to go. But Ben Crenshaw took a 6 – and that was that. Yet another major championship had slipped from his grasp.

Ballesteros's progress was now triumphal, for here was one of the most popular winners of modern times. The British public, of course, want a British winner but Seve was easily the next best thing. He was young, handsome, smiling, a cavalier, with an almost amateurish air about him. On the 17th he was in his last bunker and once again was down in two strokes to save his par. In the championship as a whole, he reckons he was fifteen times in greenside bunkers and just once failed to be down in two, possibly a record.

The diagonal line of bunkers on the 18th fairway has dashed the hopes of many players over the years. Ballesteros, however, was rather more worried by the gorse to the right. Naturally, then, he aimed for the left rough, to avoid both hazards, played a 5-iron to the front of the green and was down in two putts to be champion by a comfortable three-stroke margin.

Said Hale Irwin, shaking his head in disbelief, 'I cannot understand how anyone can drive as badly as that and still win an Open Championship.' There

Ben Crenshaw en route to his 6 on the 71st hole in 1979.

Ballesteros, a couple of putts away from victory in 1979.

was, indeed, justice in the American's criticism. In his final round, Ballesteros had found the fairway only once with his driver and only eight times in previous rounds. Yet his power and touch from the rough had proved wrong all the pundits who had thought that Lytham would yield only to the man who could keep the ball on the fairway.

Ballesteros had come a long way from his first championship appearance at Carnoustie in 1975. Then he had rounds of 79 and 80, probably confirming his dislike of links courses for, a little earlier, he had scored even higher at Royal St George's in the PGA Championship. Even now that course is no favourite of his, even after winning the 1983 PGA Championship there.

The 1976 Open, however, had brought him to the fore and his Lytham triumph was his 17th in world golf. The Americans who labelled him 'the car park champion' had the smiles taken from their faces by Ballesteros's dominance in the 1980 Masters. His 1983 Masters victory and fine play in the US Open that year were needed before all were prepared to concede that here was a great player.

HOW THEY FINISHED

Player	R1	R2	R3	R4	Total
S. Ballesteros *Spain*	**73**	**65**	**75**	**70**	**283**
B. D. Crenshaw *USA*	72	71	72	71	286
J. W. Nicklaus *USA*	72	69	73	72	
M. James	76	69	69	73	287
R. M. Davis *Australia*	75	70	70	73	288
H. Irwin *USA*	68	68	75	78	289
G. V. Marsh *Australia*	74	68	75	74	291
I. Aoki *Japan*	70	74	72	75	
B. Byman *USA*	73	70	72	76	
R. J. Charles *New Zealand*	78	72	70	72	292
M. Ozaki *Japan*	75	69	75	73	
G. Norman *Australia*	73	71	72	76	
S. M. Owen *New Zealand*	75	76	74	68	293
W. Armstrong *USA*	74	74	73	72	
J. O'Leary	73	73	74	73	
T. Gale *Australia*	71	74	75	73	
L. Trevino *USA*	71	73	74	76	294
Mr P. McEvoy	71	74	72	77	
N. Faldo	74	74	78	69	295
A. W. B. Lyle	74	76	75	70	
O. Moody *USA*	71	74	76	74	
G. J. Player *South Africa*	77	74	69	75	
K. Brown	72	71	75	77	
A. Jacklin	73	74	76	73	296
T. Nakamura *Japan*	77	75	67	77	
P. W. Thomson *Australia*	76	75	72	74	297
E. Sneed *USA*	76	75	70	76	
J. Pate *USA*	69	74	76	78	
T. Watson *USA*	72	68	76	81	
M. S. Hayes *USA*	75	75	77	71	298
F. R. Verwey *South Africa*	75	77	74	72	
A. E. Saavedra *Argentina*	76	76	73	73	
T. Kite *USA*	73	74	77	74	
S. F. N. Hobday *Zimbabwe-Rhodesia*	75	77	71	75	
W. Longmuir	65	74	77	82	
C. O'Connor Jr	79	73	71	76	299
P. Cowen	79	72	72	76	
L. Elder *USA*	75	72	76	76	
R. Floyd *USA*	76	73	71	79	
M. King	75	70	73	81	
M. F. Foster	77	75	74	74	300
P. Toussaint *Belgium*	76	75	74	75	
N. Ratcliffe *Australia*	79	73	72	76	
H. Baiocchi *South Africa*	72	73	78	77	
P. A. Oosterhuis	75	74	73	78	
J. Schroeder *USA*	74	75	72	79	
H. M. Green *USA*	77	71	73	79	
D. L. Watson *South Africa*	75	70	76	79	
D. J. Clark *New Zealand*	72	69	76	83	
B. W. Barnes	78	71	77	75	301
C. Mason	77	72	76	76	
D. W. Weaver *USA*	73	71	80	77	
G. Cullen	72	74	77	78	
G. L. Parslow *Australia*	75	75	76	76	302
I. Richardson	75	73	77	77	
K. Shimada *Japan*	75	74	75	78	
J. Miller *USA*	77	73	77	76	303
Y. Yamamoto *Japan*	76	74	77	76	
J. Newton *Australia*	76	73	78	76	
G. B. Wolstenholme *Australia*	77	75	71	80	
R. P. Fyfe	74	73	79	81	307

Muirfield, 1980

Like many others, I must confess that my emotions are attached to the players of my youth. I think of Charlie Ward's mastery as a chipper, the smooth putting of Bobby Locke, the long, slow backswing of Ken Bousfield for floating a pitch and the glorious long straight hitting of David Thomas. But at Muirfield in 1980 I admitted on TV that standards had risen. In my playing career, I never conceived that such a fine course could be humbled by so many low scores.

The most favoured players as the championship began were Watson, Nicklaus, Ballesteros and Trevino. Two of these, Trevino and Nicklaus, were enjoying a new lease of life. Nicklaus had had by far his worst season ever in 1979. The man who had never been out of the top four money-winners on the US Tour had plummeted to 71st. 'Of course,' they were saying, 'it had to happen, he's finished.' But Nicklaus decided that the fault lay in his short game which, putting apart, had always been his weakest area. There followed a series of lessons with Phil Rodgers and much practice behind his house. At the 1980 US Open, Nicklaus began with a 63 to tie Johnny Miller's US Open record and there was no catching him. He came in two strokes ahead of Isao Aoki for his fourth victory, equalling the records of Ben Hogan, Bobby Jones and Willie Anderson. His 272 total broke the championship record by three strokes: Jack Nicklaus was by no means finished.

Trevino is a couple of months older than Nicklaus but the health of his golf was much less often the subject of speculation. In 1980, he had won twice and by the end of the year had amassed some $385,000, a total at that time beaten only by Tom Watson in US Tour history, who set a money-winning mark of $530,808 that still stood at the end of 1983. In the season, he won six events in America and had the very rare feat of three victories in a row during the spring.

There was an immediate British Open memory for him to erase. In 1979 he had scored 81 in the final round, still his worst round in this championship. Now he began with a 68 to share the lead with Lee Trevino, one stroke ahead of Mark James, Vicente Fernandez, Jack Newton and Nick Faldo. There were a group of fancied players on 70 who included Ken Brown, Ben Crenshaw, Gil Morgan, Sandy Lyle and Mark Hayes.

The most remarkable round of the second day came from an unknown Argentine, Horacio Carbonetti. After a first round of 78, he reached the turn in 33 and began the homeward half with two birdies. He eventually came off the last green and signed for a new course record of 64. I could hardly believe it. It is one of golf's statistical oddities that he had another 78 on the third day and failed to qualify for the last day's play. Can anyone before or since have failed to qualify for anything, I wonder, with a score of 64 among their cards?

Trevino's low round of 67 was much more significant, however, and made the 36-hole position as follows:

Nicklaus won the US Open in 1980 before coming to try for the British at Muirfield.

135 Trevino; 138 Watson, Brown, Pate; 140 Crenshaw, Nicklaus, Bean, Newton, Morgan, Ballesteros; 141 Mason, Lyle, Dale Hayes, James, Cooper

Isao Aoki's card for the third round at Muirfield in 1980.

Trevino's lead was a formidable one and he was playing with brisk assurance, memories of his last British Open title in 1972, also at Muirfield, no doubt re-kindling.

A 37-year-old Japanese was the first to show what could be done on a windless third day, with holding greens and fairways. He began at six over par, having qualified with little indeed to spare, thirteen strokes behind Lee Trevino. Isao Aoki went to the turn in 32 and then had 3s on four of the next five holes to be seven under par for the round. This was the Aoki of the magic toe-in-the-air putter. He ended appropriately with a putt of some 4 yards for his par on the last. This was his card, with Muirfield pars below:

Aoki: 4, 3, 4, 3, 4, 4, 3, 3, 4 (32) 4, 3, 3, 3, 3, 4, 3, 4, 4 (31)
Par: 4, 4, 4, 3, 5, 4, 3, 4, 5 (36) 4, 4, 4, 3, 4, 4, 3, 5, 4 (35)

His 63 had broken the new Muirfield record and equalled the lowest round ever in either British or US Opens. It came from a man who, Peter Thomson told me, a few years earlier had been considered 'very nearly hopeless' by those who had seen him play in the Far East – a late developer indeed.

Yet there was another brilliant low round that day. It was played by Tom Watson. After reaching the turn in 34, he even outshone Aoki on the inward nine, using only 30 strokes, a total that has not been beaten on the second nine of an Open Championship course, though there have been four scores of 29 and one of 28 for first nines.

More important than these bare statistics, however, the 64 took Tom Watson past Trevino, who had scored steadily but had no longer looked entirely confident on the greens:

> 202 Watson; 206 Trevino, Brown; 208 Crenshaw; 210 Bean, Green (who also had a 64); 211 Nicklaus, Mason, Stadler, Aoki, Morgan, Lyle

Obviously the question of the final day was whether or not the championship was to all intents and purposes over. Alas for drama, that answer was 'Yes'. Not for an instant was Tom Watson's position threatened. Much good golf was played and there were 69s from Trevino, Crenshaw, Nicklaus, Carl Mason, Bill Rogers and Peter Oosterhuis but that score was equalled by Watson himself, who therefore came in four strokes clear of Lee Trevino.

Watson had come close to equalling his scoring in the 1977 Turnberry Open and his 271 total is the second lowest by a champion, three strokes higher than his Turnberry score. Watson's 202 after three rounds remains the record as this book goes to press and he is one of only two champions to score under 70 in three rounds (the other was Palmer in 1962).

By comparison with Jack Nicklaus, it had taken Watson six attempts to reach three victories while Jack had seventeen entries before his third success. Watson was to look even better in the years that lay ahead.

HOW THEY FINISHED

Player	R1	R2	R3	R4	Total
T. Watson *USA*	**68**	**70**	**64**	**69**	**271**
L. Trevino *USA*	68	67	71	69	275
B. Crenshaw *USA*	70	70	68	69	277
J. W. Nicklaus *USA*	73	67	71	69	280
C. Mason	72	69	70	69	
C. Stadler *USA*	72	70	69	71	282
A. Bean *USA*	71	69	70	72	
H. M. Green *USA*	77	69	64	72	
K. Brown	70	68	68	76	
J. Newton *Australia*	69	71	73	70	283
G. Morgan *USA*	70	70	71	72	
N. Faldo	69	74	71	70	284
L. Nelson *USA*	72	70	71	71	
A. W. B. Lyle	70	71	70	73	
I. Aoki *Japan*	74	74	63	73	
T. Weiskopf *USA*	72	72	71	70	285
J. Bland *South Africa*	73	70	70	72	
J. Pate *USA*	71	67	74	73	
W. Rogers *USA*	76	73	68	69	286
B. Lietzke *USA*	74	69	73	70	
N. Suzuki *Japan*	74	68	72	72	
S. Ballesteros *Spain*	72	68	72	74	
P. A. Oosterhuis	72	71	75	69	287
M. McNulty *South Africa*	71	73	72	71	
W. McColl	75	73	68	71	
G. Cullen	72	72	69	74	
T. Kite *USA*	72	72	74	70	288
N. Price *Zimbabwe*	72	71	71	74	
N. C. Coles	75	69	69	76	289
H. Baiocchi *South Africa*	76	67	69	77	
D. Graham *Australia*	73	71	68	77	
M. Hayes *USA*	70	73	76	71	290
T. Horton	76	71	71	72	
A. Jacklin	72	74	71	73	
J. D. Mahaffey *USA*	77	71	69	73	
B. Waites	75	72	69	74	
H. K. Clark	72	70	70	78	
Mr J. Sigel *USA*	72	72	74	73	291
S. Torrance	74	71	73	73	
R. Davis *Australia*	74	70	73	74	
S. Ginn *Australia*	77	70	70	74	
W. Brask *USA*	74	71	71	75	
T. Nakamura *Japan*	76	72	69	74	
D. Hayes *South Africa*	71	70	74	76	
A. North *USA*	75	72	72	73	292
W. Armstrong *USA*	77	72	70	73	
G. Marsh *Australia*	73	72	72	75	
M. James	69	72	75	76	
E. Darcy	75	68	73	76	
V. Fernandez *Argentina*	69	76	71	76	
A. Garrido *Spain*	74	71	73	75	293
R. Gilder *USA*	75	71	72	75	
B. Langer *West Germany*	73	72	72	76	
S. F. N. Hobday *Zimbabwe*	76	71	71	75	
H. R. Henning *South Africa*	77	71	69	76	
R. Shearer *Australia*	76	71	70	76	
D. Cooper	71	70	75	77	
M. Pinero *Spain*	72	72	75	75	294
B. W. Barnes	73	72	71	78	
R. J. Charles *New Zealand*	75	71	73	76	295
D. Jagger	72	77	69	77	
M. Ozaki *Japan*	73	68	73	81	
L. P. Tupling	76	70	73	77	296
S. Owen *New Zealand*	72	73	72	80	297
D. Bies *USA*	73	74	72	79	298

Royal St George's, 1981

The geographical distribution of our Open Championship course is, I suppose, distinctly odd: south-east and south-west Scotland and north-west England. After 1949 at Royal St George's the event disappeared from the south of England, such former championship courses as Deal, and nearby Prince's and Royal St George's at Sandwich being apparently ruled out for ever.

Of course, it is not only the quality of the golf course that dictates its choice as an Open Championship venue. There are other factors that must come into consideration. The north-west of England, for instance, scores well because of the wealth of accommodation available in the seaside holiday towns. This situation is not quite as good in Scotland but the Scots are great followers of golf: huge crowds can always be guaranteed.

One of the main problems for south-east Kent was a little toll bridge across the River Stour in the town of Sandwich. The queues always built up at any summer weekend and after 1949 the R and A came to feel that, with increasing crowds, access to the course was just not good enough.

The worst day of all for Nicklaus at Royal St George's in 1981; he took 83 on the first day.

By 1981, however, the toll bridge was gone and the road system in general was much improved, while the police promised (and later performed) a minor miracle in keeping traffic flowing. In the event, the main complaints concerned accommodation. There was much talk before play began of how many thousands of pounds were being charged for the rent of a house for the week and how much hotel rates had shot up for the period of the championship. Perhaps much of the talk was exaggerated. If you didn't insist on staying in Sandwich there was all sorts of seaside accommodation at Ramsgate, Margate, Broadstairs and Westgate less than ten miles away and plenty more only a little further afield. Only motel-type accommodation was rather limited.

Royal St George's is undoubtedly one of the toughest of our championship courses and rated the most difficult by Severiano Ballesteros, among others. Its 458-yard 18th is in my opinion the most severe last hole of the lot, if the wind is in the wrong direction. I remember that from our TV commentary box behind the 18th green during the 1983 PGA Championship I saw few balls on the green in two and the number of realistic birdie putts could be counted on the fingers of one hand. The 15th, 467 yards, is marginally more difficult, with a long carry to the fairway, huge bunkers in front of the green and trouble all around. All in all, a monster hole when the wind's against.

There had been quite a few course changes since the 1949 championship, mainly to bring the course up to championship standards and partly to eliminate some of the blind shots. Here was the course that faced competitors in 1981:

Hole	Yards	Par	Hole	Yards	Par
1	445	4	10	375	4
2	376	4	11	216	3
3	214	3	12	362	4
4	466	4	13	443	4
5	422	4	14	508	5
6	156	3	15	467	4
7	529	5	16	165	3
8	415	4	17	425	4
9	387	4	18	458	4
	3410	35		3419	35
				3410	35
				6829	70

As 1981 Masters Champion and with a glittering record in the Open behind him, Tom Watson was a clear-cut favourite. You could not get odds of better than 4–1 against, low indeed with such a star-studded field. He was followed by Jack Nicklaus, 6–1, Trevino, 10–1 and Ballesteros at 16–1. Others particularly highly fancied were Hale Irwin, Ben Crenshaw, Johnny Miller, enjoying much improved form, and Isao Aoki. A player who attracted little if any attention in the preliminaries was Bill Rogers. This was perhaps surprising.

After all, he had won the 1979 World Matchplay, had finished with rounds of 68 and 69 at Muirfield the previous year and had just come close to the US Open Championship, finishing tied for second place behind Australian David Graham.

However, headlines were made the first day by Jack Nicklaus. I can recall a BBC news bulletin in which his score was mentioned before the leader's. But for once, as you will no doubt remember, it was because Jack had scored extremely poorly. He had finished the second half 3, 3, 5, 4, a very brave finish in view of what had gone before. Nicklaus had reached the turn in 39 and continued 6, 5, 6, 5, 7, a run which included no fewer than four double-bogeys. He had reached a massive 11 over par after 13 holes and then hit a duck-hook up the 5-par 14th of no more than 80 yards. The fourth double-bogey came here. His eventual 83 was only achieved with a level-par finish over the remaining holes. His figures looked like the international dialling code for Tierra del Fuego. It was his worst-ever round as a professional golfer. He declined a Press interview, fearing he might say things he would later regret, sensible man, but his response the following day was loud and clear. It's corny to say it, but he let his clubs do all the talking: he scored a 66. It had seemed impossible for him to qualify for the final 36 holes; instead, he was almost back in contention. As Ian Wooldridge of the *Daily Mail* put it at the time: 'The only equivalent plunge from genius I can think of was Ernest Hemingway's tragic loss of the ability to write. Hemingway got up one morning and shot himself. Nicklaus got up next morning and shot a 66.'

Another well-fancied player had done no better than Nicklaus. Craig Stadler hit two out of bounds at the 14th, ran up a 9 and an eventual score of 83. He too came back the next day with a 68, but failed to beat the 36-hole cut by a stroke.

Perhaps we ought to get back to how the leaders were doing. Only two players equalled par, Nick Job and Vicente Fernandez. They were followed on 71 by Simon Owen, Tony Jacklin, David Graham, Johnny Miller, and Hal Sutton, who was to finish as leading amateur, though well down the field in 47th place.

Of the two leaders, Fernandez was not to reach the final day, while Nick Job held on most creditably for 14th place. His 69 in the second round might have put him in the lead but another player had made a more emphatic move. This was Bill Rogers, who had followed a neat enough opening round of 72 with a 66, to take the lead at 138. Closely following him were:

139 Crenshaw, Job; 140 Langer; 141 Torrance; 142 Watson, Jacklin, James, Graham; 143 Powell, Dunk, Townsend, Brand

The Yorkshireman Gordon Brand had followed an opening 78 with a course record 65 including a hole in one at the 16th, but was not expected to last the pace. Rogers was also not expected to continue prospering and was indeed lucky to be still playing. He had misread his starting time for the first day's round and was on the practice green when a newspaperman told him he was due to tee-off.

As the final 36 holes began, the favourite was Ben Crenshaw, so often a high finisher in major championships and with such longing to win one. Now he was ideally positioned again, with two of the big guns, Watson and Nicklaus, fairly comfortably behind him. Had his turn come at last?

The third day was sunny but with a stiff breeze from the north-east. Crenshaw had just the start he didn't want, dropping a stroke to par on the 1st hole and having a double-bogey soon afterwards. His play on the 9th was perhaps typically Crenshaw: first his driving betrayed him, as so often before. He sliced, then he pulled into the rough; then he put his third into a bunker, finally playing an exquisite bunker shot to save him from losing more than one stroke at this 387-yard hole. Nevertheless, 39 to the turn. Crenshaw dropped two more shots to par thereafter and his play on the last showed his disappointment. He pushed a short-iron, was bunkered and played quickly and carelessly, with the look of a man who knew he had cast his chances to the winds.

Rogers, meanwhile, had made the move that was to put him firmly in command of the championship. His pattern of play followed that of the previous day: he was rarely dropping a shot and one of the best putting strokes in modern golf meant that occasional birdies had to come. One of these was on the 8th, where he sank a huge putt to go four under par. At the end of the day he was one better than that.

Two players on the European Tour had by then become his only credible rivals. One was Mark James, a player who has often prospered in the championship. He likes links courses, mainly because he feels happier at playing out of rough and bunkers than when threatened by the claustrophobia of out of bounds and the luck of the draw on tree-lined courses. James had moved steadily up the field with rounds of 72, 70 and 68 to be level par for the championship.

So also was Bernhard Langer, who had already suffered so much on missed short putts in his career. However, the previous year he found a putter in Clive Clark's pro's shop at Sunningdale and for a while he was transformed. When he won the 1980 Dunlop Masters his putting was phenomenal. In 1981, his good form continued and he was undoubtedly the player of the year in Europe. Hardly anyone could hit the ball further from the tee and his iron play was particularly sharp. Once the magic of that old Acushnet Bull's Eye putter departed it has still been remarkable how well the German scores while missing so many of those short putts. He concedes several strokes a tournament to the rest of the field, yet can often make it up by his excellence through the green and on longer putts.

Yet the final day found Rogers with the widest margin over the field since Tony Lema's seven, way back in 1964 at St Andrews:

205 Rogers; 210 Langer, James; 213 Aoki, Floyd; 214 Job, Trevino, Faldo, Torrance

Watson had shown the poor form which sometimes dogs him in the Open. He had a 75, having dropped three strokes in a row on the outward nine and finishing disastrously with a double-bogey on the 17th and another dropped shot on the 18th.

Rogers felt that steady play would be good enough to bring him the championship, for only James and Langer were really within reach. Paired with Mark James, he set out at 2.15, with Langer immediately ahead. James had good chances early on. He nearly holed for a birdie on the 1st, while Rogers had a nervous first putt that sent the ball jerkily some couple of yards past, but he managed to hole the return. On the 2nd, James was well inside the American but the hole was 'halved' in par 4s. On the next, with James bunkered with his tee-shot to this long and difficult par-3, Rogers's par put him further into the lead. For him the crisis lay ahead.

It came on the long 7th, a par-5 most players were looking to birdie. Rogers pushed his tee-shot into the semi-rough on the right and then pulled his second onto a bank. He was, however, still in little danger of dropping a stroke to par. But his next was thinned well through the green and he left the return short. Rogers then played a neat little pitch to within 4 feet of the hole – and missed the putt. A very easy 7. The door had been flung open. James was back to four strokes behind the leader but Bernhard Langer was now just a stroke behind. Raymond Floyd, who had started the day eight strokes away from the leader, had also been making a very strong move of his own. Having dropped a stroke on the 1st hole, he later birdied three holes in a row, the 6th to the 8th. He stood at even par to Rogers's two under.

Interviewed after the championship, Rogers was asked when he had begun to rehearse his winner's speech. 'Early on', he replied, to laughter. The 7th, however, had made him think again: 'It got me to thinking of what the runner-up was supposed to say.'

However, Rogers told himself he was still the leader and was able to surmount a minor crisis on the 8th. Here, his approach shot was only on the front right of the green, leaving him a very long and difficult approach putt. His nerve held and Rogers got it almost dead to par the hole. The championship was no longer slipping through his fingers but there was still a long way to go.

Ahead, Raymond Floyd began to fade. He put his approach through the green at the 9th and took three more to hole out. He was then three behind, despite reaching the turn in 33. A few minutes later, Rogers played a crucial

Ray Floyd (left) and Bill Rodgers, the Champion for 1981.

stroke on the same hole. With a 7-iron from about 140 yards, he stopped his ball just 2 feet from the hole for a birdie. Another good iron shot to some 3 yards followed quickly on the 10th. The putt was holed and Rogers was back in full command, his lead stretched to four strokes. Surely he would now win the championship.

He was bunkered at the short 11th and dropped a stroke but again hit an excellent iron shot on the 12th, his third birdie in four holes, the climax of a splendid fight-back from the sudden shock of the 7 on the 7th.

Only Bernhard Langer sustained a forlorn challenge to the end. He dropped a stroke on the short 11th but birdied both the long 14th and the short 16th. Any chance he might still have had went on the 17th. Here he hit a long straight drive but his approach shot unluckily hit a sprinkler cover at the front of the green and shot his ball back off-line. He then took three more to get down.

Rogers's lead was now very comfortable indeed: a four-stroke lead playing the 18th. One last obstacle remained. As the crowds were released to flood around the players on the last hole, Rogers was stopped by a policeman who had noticed him trying to push his way through to a vantage point near the final green. 'I'm just trying to finish, pal,' said the 1981 Open Champion.

So Rogers came home at four under the par of 280. Royal St George's had also been a winner. In winds not severely testing only Rogers had broken par for the four rounds. Langer finished at level par and no one else was better than three over. From a purely practical point of view, off-course facilities and spectator comfort had been outstanding. The R and A showed its approval in the best way possible – the Open returns to Kent in 1985.

HOW THEY FINISHED

Player	R1	R2	R3	R4	Total
W. Rogers *USA*	**72**	**66**	**67**	**71**	**276**
B. Langer *West Germany*	73	67	70	70	280
M. James	72	70	68	73	283
R. Floyd *USA*	74	70	69	70	
S. Torrance	72	69	73	70	284
M. Pinero *Spain*	73	74	68	70	285
B. Lietzke *USA*	76	69	71	69	
H. K. Clark	72	76	70	68	286
B. D. Crenshaw *USA*	72	67	76	71	
B. Jones *Australia*	73	76	66	71	
L. Trevino *USA*	77	67	70	73	287
N. Faldo	77	68	69	73	
I. Aoki *Japan*	71	73	69	74	
B. W. Barnes	76	70	70	72	288
D. Graham *Australia*	71	71	74	72	
E. Darcy	79	69	70	70	
A. W. B. Lyle	73	73	71	71	
N. Job	70	69	75	74	
J. Pate *USA*	73	73	69	74	
P. M. P. Townsend	73	70	73	73	
G. Brand Sr	78	65	74	72	
G. Marsh *Australia*	75	71	72	71	
A. Jacklin	71	71	73	75	290
S. Owen *New Zealand*	71	74	70	75	
T. Watson *USA*	73	69	75	73	
A. Palmer *USA*	72	74	73	71	
J. W. Nicklaus *USA*	83	66	71	70	
H. M. Green *USA*	75	72	74	69	
M. McNulty *Zimbabwe*	74	74	74	68	
N. Price *Zimbabwe*	77	68	76	69	
T. Powell	75	68	73	75	291
D. Smyth	77	67	73	74	
G. Norman *Australia*	72	75	72	72	
J. Morgan	77	72	73	69	
R. J. Charles *New Zealand*	77	71	71	73	292
M. Ozaki *Japan*	75	72	71	74	
T. Horton	75	73	73	71	
W. Dunk *Australia*	76	67	77	72	
J. Miller *USA*	71	73	73	76	293
R. Davis *Australia*	74	71	74	74	
F. Molina *Argentina*	78	68	74	73	
S. Ballesteros *Spain*	75	72	74	72	
N. C. Coles	74	73	73	73	
T. Gale *Australia*	73	73	71	77	294
R. Streck *USA*	78	70	72	74	
K. Brown	74	72	74	74	
M. O'Meara *USA*	74	73	73	75	295
Mr H. Sutton *USA*	71	77	73	74	
J. Gonzalez *Brazil*	76	70	76	73	
B. Waites	75	69	74	78	296
D. Thorp	76	69	74	77	
D. Jones	77	71	74	74	
M. Ferguson *Australia*	75	72	71	79	297
G. Cullen	78	70	73	76	
E. Polland	75	75	72	75	
W. Humphreys	76	71	74	77	298
N. Hunt	74	73	75	76	
Mr G. Godwin	75	71	72	81	299
P. Stewart *USA*	73	75	74	77	
J. O'Leary	73	74	75	77	
D. McClean *USA*	75	73	72	83	303

Royal Troon, 1982

Winning three British Opens and a couple of Masters is all well and good but when Tom Watson came to Troon for the 1982 Open he had a special glow about him. He was hot foot from winning the championship he most desired.

A few weeks before, the long-sought US Open had become his. As he played the 17th at Pebble Beach in the final round, the championship had looked destined for Jack Nicklaus. Even more so, as Watson pulled his long-iron pin-high but just off the green in thick grass, a little downhill pitch of the utmost delicacy and accuracy facing him. He now needed to get down in two and par the last, one of the great long holes of golf, running along the Pacific, to tie with Nicklaus.

As the world knows, Watson played a superb shot, even though it might have run well past the hole. Instead, he holed out and then birdied the last for a two-stroke victory and his first US Open title. No need now to fear he might be another Sam Snead. The US Open was his sixth major championship and with it Watson reached the ranks of the great players of all time.

Of course, he began as a strong favourite at Troon but there were renewed British hopes for Tony Jacklin. At Royal St George's he had been well to the fore for the first two rounds and in 1982 had won his first event on British soil since 1973 – the PGA Championship on a fine links course, Hillside. He had selected a hickory-shafted blade putter from many spares in his Jersey garage and the putts had begun to drop. Alas, at Troon he began with a 77, as did Jack Nicklaus, and failed by a stroke to make the 36-hole cut.

Instead it was a 22-year-old member of the Mark McCormack stable, Bobby Clampett, who made all the headlines. Without a tournament win to his credit (although he had lost two play-offs on the 1981 US Tour), he began with a five-under-par round of 67. This led Nick Price of South Africa and Tom Watson by two strokes. Others had momentarily attracted attention. Ken Brown, for instance, was fast away to be four under par after only six holes, though eventually finishing in 70, slightly disappointing after so strong a start. The old warhorse, Arnold Palmer, also began well, led the championship for a spell at three under par, improved to four under, but had to settle for a 71. It must have revived memories of his great 1962 victory.

Many thought that Clampett would soon be gone from the headlines but I think this was a little unreasonable. After all, Clampett stood 20th on the US money-list at this time and had finished second in the Greater Greensboro Open at the beginning of April in a tournament played in high winds. In June he had shown he could compete under championship pressures when he featured throughout the Pebble Beach US Open, closing with a 70 for joint third place.

After the first day then, these were the leaders:

67 Clampett;   69 Watson, Price;   70 Brown, Langer, Smyth;
71 Edwards (later to soar to 81 and 86), Kuramoto, Palmer, Stadler, Ballesteros, Canizares, Miller

On the second day, Clampett made himself a 5–4 favourite to win the championship. Starting at the daunting hour of 7.40 a.m., he followed the same game plan as the previous day. From the tee, his aim was always for position and thereafter his iron play was extremely sharp. Again and again he left himself reasonable chances of birdies and by the time he reached the 15th was eleven under par and had an eight-stroke lead in the championship. He finished in 66, a new course record because of course alterations since the 1973 championship. Clampett talked happily to the press for some two hours, revelling in his great moment. His first 36 holes was the best start since Henry Cotton's 67, 65 back in 1934 at Royal St George's and the five-stroke advantage it gave him was the highest at the halfway stage since Gary Player's victory at Lytham in 1974.

Even so, a five-stroke lead with 36 holes to go can be dissipated easily enough. It was, I think, more significant that the man in second place, with a second 69, was Nick Price, a man whose golfing pedigree did not approach that of Bobby Clampett. Surely the threat to Clampett would come from further down the field? This is how they stood after Clampett's amazing performance:

133 Clampett;   138 Price;   139 Smyth, Langer;   140 Watson, Lyle;   141 Brown, Oosterhuis

Clampett's 66 was the first during the second day but not the only one. Sandy Lyle and the American Tom Purtzer also had the same scores, the American's without a bogey, but they were following opening rounds of 74 and 76. I remember talking to Clampett's adviser, Mark McCormack, that evening about the prospects of his young potential star. 'It's only a question of by how many he wins,' said Mark with a smile.

On the third day, Clampett began hitting a 3-iron from the tee too far and was bunkered 260 yards away. Soon it was evident that some of the precision of his iron play was gone. Nevertheless, he birdied both the long 4th and 5th to go to twelve under par and lead his closest pursuer, for the moment Des Smyth, by seven. Clampett was going further away from the field and his relentless putting (26 putts in each of the first two rounds) showed no sign of wavering.

On to the 6th, at 577 yards the longest hole in British championship golf. The tee-shot should be down the right half of the fairway. Clampett, who had played the hole in 5 and 4 in his first two rounds, hooked slightly from the tee and was bunkered. He moved it from there into another bunker and this time only just managed to get out. Three shots gone and still all of 280 yards from the green. After all the hours of play, a crisis point had most definitely arrived, a championship to be won or lost. A hooked wood followed into both gallery and deep rough. His forced fifth shot was again bunkered and lying very awkwardly indeed, close up against the face. A precision shot was well-nigh impossible. Clampett did well to get his ball onto the green. Loss of nerve then showed momentarily. For perhaps the first time in the championship, his first putt was tentative and pulled up perhaps 3 feet short. However, he holed it for a calamitous 8. Nick Price secured his par. For him, having begun with bogeys on the first two holes, it was a case of 'For this relief much thanks.' However, Clampett, despite the 8 on his card, should still have been in charge of the championship. He still lay nine under par to Price's four under. Clampett's choice of a 3-iron on the 1st hole had betrayed the dilemma that all who lead must suffer: to protect the lead or continue on the attack. A little earlier, Watson, with much ground to make up, had no hesitation in attacking. He took a driver on the 1st, reached the green and two-putted for a birdie.

No disaster of the magnitude of the 6th befell Bobby Clampett for the remainder of the round but he dropped four more strokes over the remaining twelve holes and had no birdies. It all added up to a 78 – and he still led by a stroke.

No one else had made a real move in the south-westerly breeze, against early on and helping coming home. Price had a 74, as did Watson, Peter Oosterhuis and Des Smyth, Lyle a 73 and Tom Purtzer a 75. Of credible contenders, the best scores came from Nick Faldo and Masahiro Kuramoto, both with 71s (also achieved by Keith Waters), the lowest rounds on one of the most puzzling days in Open Championship history. Clampett had thrown it all away; no one else had come near to seizing their unexpected chance. It was still all to play for:

211 Clampett; 212 Price; 213 Smyth, Lyle; 214 Watson;
215 Kuramoto, Oosterhuis; 217 Faldo, Watson, Zoeller,
Purtzer, Langer (who had a 78 of his own)

For the final day, there was another shift in the wind. It was from the north-west but the day was pleasantly mild and sunny. Clampett, in the highly unusual position – unprecedented in modern times in a major championship – of still leading after a 78, bravely announced that his policy was simply going to be to 'work as hard as I can'.

Nick Price, then 86th in the European money-list with bankings of £1200, was soon in the lead. With Clampett bunkered by the 1st green but nevertheless managing to salvage his par, Price drew level with a birdie. On the 2nd, Price birdied from the edge; Clampett eventually missed a tiny putt for his par to fall two behind the new leader. This three-stroke swing in just two holes was the coup de grâce for Bobby Clampett. The shooting star was utterly spent. The focus shifted to other players, Nick Price most of all.

After the final pair, Clampett and Price, had played five holes, no fewer than eight players were within three strokes of each other. Price, after a birdie on the 7th, had moved to three better than Clampett, who had been joined in second place by Watson and Des Smyth. Indeed this was very much a championship where many had their chances of winning.

Nick Price dropped shots on both the 8th and 9th, but still led by a stroke. Ahead, Tom Watson played a master stroke on the very difficult 11th, a cracking 3-iron to about a yard. Watson is seldom seen to miss from that distance. It was a welcome eagle since he had managed only one birdie up to that point.

Price responded with a charge of consecutive birdies from the 10th to the 12th, which gave him a three-stroke lead over Tom Watson. As with Clampett earlier, the championship was his to win or lose. Could this 25-year-old, who had three tournament victories to his credit, but no experience whatsoever of contending for a championship, hold on?

Price dropped a shot to par on the 13th but ahead on the 15th there was a difference of opinion between Watson and his caddie, Alfie Fyles. Watson thought his shot to the green was a 7-iron. Alfie said: 'It's a 6.' Perhaps a golfer should only trust his own judgement. Watson used the 6-iron and sent his ball through the green. He dropped his only shot of the round.

It was this same hole that caused the downfall of Nick Price. He hit his second shot into a bunker of whose existence he was unaware, gained little distance from there as he hit the bank in front of his nose. The little pitch remaining was always weak, leaving him several yards short of the flag.

His putt was a very good one indeed – but it did not drop. That 6 meant he had allowed Watson to catch him. However, Price was not done for yet and came close to a birdie on the long 16th. He had the 223-yard 17th to play next, never an easy hole. His tee-shot was well short of the green. His chip was bold, hitting the hole before running some 3 yards past. Another good putt followed, but it did not drop.

At 5.30 p.m., as Price faced his last tee-shot of the championship, there was a new leader, Tom Watson. Price had to birdie the last to force a play-off. It was not a likely prospect for only five birdies had been made on this 425-yard hole all day.

Price hooked into the crowd but was fortunate to find a good lie in the rough. From there he hit a fine iron shot to the back of the green, but many yards past the hole. His putt to gain a play-off was on line but not struck firmly enough. Watson, who had made no strong move over the last few holes, was champion for the fourth time. He had held his game together; the others hadn't.

It had been a good championship for others also, as our score lists show. There was, for instance, a man who finished tied second almost unnoticed when he holed a putt of about 2½ yards on the last for a birdie: Peter Oosterhuis. Nick Faldo also showed that he could raise his game for the great occasion, his 69 being one of the lowest rounds of the day. He finished in a tie for 4th with Smyth, Purtzer and Kuramoto of Japan.

But this was a championship lost by both Price and Clampett – and one or two others – rather than won by Tom Watson. As he said himself, and in strong contrast to his recent US Open victory: 'I didn't win this championship. I had it given to me.' But Tom knew they all count. It was his fourth title.

HOW THEY FINISHED

Player	R1	R2	R3	R4	Total
T. Watson *USA*	**69**	**71**	**74**	**70**	**284**
P. A. Oosterhuis	74	67	74	70	285
N. Price *South Africa*	69	69	74	73	
N. Faldo	73	73	71	69	286
D. Smyth	70	69	74	73	
T. Purtzer *USA*	76	66	75	69	
M. Kuramoto *Japan*	71	73	71	71	
F. Zoeller *USA*	73	71	73	70	287
A. W. B. Lyle	74	66	73	74	
J. W. Nicklaus *USA*	77	70	72	69	288
R. Clampett *USA*	67	66	78	77	
S. Torrance	73	72	73	71	289
S. Ballesteros *Spain*	71	75	73	71	290
B. Langer *West Germany*	70	69	78	73	
R. Floyd *USA*	74	73	77	67	291
C. Strange *USA*	72	73	76	70	
B. D. Crenshaw *USA*	74	75	72	70	
D. L. Watson *South Africa*	75	69	73	74	
K. Brown	70	71	79	72	292
T. Nakamura *Japan*	77	68	77	71	293
I. Aoki *Japan*	75	69	75	74	
J-M. Canizares *Spain*	71	72	79	72	294
J. Miller *USA*	71	76	75	72	
W. Rogers *USA*	73	70	76	75	
G. Marsh *Australia*	76	76	72	71	295
B. Gallacher	75	71	74	75	
J. Haas *USA*	78	72	75	71	296
G. Norman *Australia*	73	75	76	72	
A. Palmer *USA*	71	73	78	74	
L. Trevino *USA*	78	72	71	75	
D. Graham *Australia*	73	70	76	77	
M. Miller	74	72	78	73	297
L. Nelson *USA*	77	69	77	74	
M. Thomas	72	74	75	76	
E. Darcy	75	73	78	72	298
J. Ferenz *USA*	76	69	80	73	
P. Way	72	75	78	73	
C. Stadler *USA*	71	74	79	74	
B. W. Barnes	75	69	76	78	
D. J. Russell	72	72	76	78	
H. R. Henning *South Africa*	74	74	76	75	299
R. Shearer *Australia*	73	72	81	74	300
Mr M. Lewis	74	74	77	75	
G. J. Player *South Africa*	75	74	76	75	
T. Gale *Australia*	76	74	75	75	
N. C. Coles	73	73	72	82	
W. Longmuir	77	72	77	75	301
T. Britz *South Africa*	81	70	74	76	
R. Chapman	75	76	74	76	
B. Waites	75	77	73	76	
M. James	74	73	79	76	302
C. S. Hsu *Taiwan*	75	75	75	77	
M. Pinero *Spain*	75	75	74	78	
M. McNulty *South Africa*	76	74	76	77	303
P. M. P. Townsend	76	73	76	78	
M. Poxon	74	70	78	81	
K. Waters	73	78	71	81	
P. Harrison	78	74	74	78	304
M. King	73	78	74	80	305
M. Cahill *Australia*	73	76	77	80	306

Royal Birkdale, 1983

Bobby Jones once wrote that there are tournament winners and major tournament winners. Part of what he meant was that some players, even at the height of their powers, cannot withstand the fires of championship competition. There is, I believe, yet another category and a higher one. It is of players who are able to raise their games for a major championship.

Jones himself undoubtedly was a member of this élite. When he won the Grand Slam of Amateur and Open Championships of Britain and the USA in 1930 he was not at peak form, but the greater pressures of championship golf seemed to make him play better. I am sure we could make similar claims for Walter Hagen (beaten 18 and 17 by Archie Compston one week and 1928 Open Champion the next) and Ben Hogan. Of contemporary golfers, Nicklaus has more often than not just as clearly been able to bring out his best in the four major championships.

Tom Watson by 1983 had become that kind of golfer. When the Masters came round in early April his best finish on the US Tour had been a 6th place near the beginning of the season. Indeed, he was said to be more interested – and why not? – in his young family than in golf. Yet when Severiano Ballesteros began the final round of the Masters in such dazzling style, with two birdies and an eagle on the first four holes, the leaders Floyd and Stadler shrivelled to a 75 and 76, Keith Fergus and Gil Morgan to 77 and 74, while Jodie Mudd, perhaps I should whisper it, had an 86. It was not long before Tom Watson was the only player with a chance to hold the Spaniard at bay. He failed, but he made the Masters a contest for a while and produced his best placing of the season when it mattered most.

By the time the US Open came along a couple of months later, Watson had still to win a Tour event. Again he raised his game. With a round to play, he was paired in first place with Severiano, a repeat of the Masters. This time it was Watson who came out on top in their particular duel, taking control of the Spaniard with four birdies in the first six holes and reaching the turn in 31. Although he was eventually sunk by a vast putt from Larry Nelson and some imperfections of his own, his second place to Nelson was another fine major championship performance.

And so to Royal Birkdale in 1983, without a win in America since June 1982. The course was superbly prepared but many felt that it was going to be too severe a test, comparable to the Muirfield of 1966. The wet spring and early summer, followed by a heatwave, meant that the rough was long and – more important – fairly thick. Some complained that it was difficult sometimes to find a ball only a few yards off the putting surfaces. Severiano Ballesteros thought that even par would win the championship and that much of the skill had been taken from chipping – a 'mechanical' player was the most likely to win, he felt. Others, Jack Nicklaus among them, thought that golf administra-

.tors, seeking to penalize long hitters by narrowing fairways, were taking the driver out of golf.

So what happened? We had the lowest-scoring Open Championship ever (based on the scores of the top 10 finishers, as shown in the Appendix). Only three times in the history of the championship have these players averaged lower than 70 per round, and the lowest figures were returned at Royal Birkdale in 1983. Press pundits and players alike had forgotten one of the golden rules of modern golf: if the greens are holding and have true surfaces, today's tournament players will score very well indeed – and many thought these the best greens ever seen at a British championship. Tom Watson, on the other hand, felt they were much too soft and that we were making a mistake by abandoning typically British links greens.

Watson soon showed the shape of things to come, getting to four under par after the 13th. Still at four under, he faced the 542-yard 15th, the only hole which played as a true three-shotter throughout. Playing safe, he pushed his 2-iron second shot away into willow scrub, some 30 yards off-line. However, the great players are helped by having a good many folk around to look for the ball. It was found – along with a haul of a dozen or more others – Watson took a penalty stroke and walked back until he found a convenient place to drop, escaping with a 6 to be round in 67.

Ahead, the 1981 champion, Bill Rogers, played what was to remain the shot of the week. At the 17th, from 228 yards (such is the pacing of distances these days!) he holed out a full 1-iron for an albatross 2, the first in the Open since Johnny Miller's at Muirfield in 1972. Three under par on one hole is apt to do wonders for a score – and shortly afterwards Rogers too was in with a 67.

Behind was a group which included the twin stars of the European Tour that year, Nick Faldo and Severiano Ballesteros, and the new US Open Champion, Larry Nelson. Faldo had prepared earnestly for this championship, spending many days at Royal Birkdale beforehand. His start could not have been more discouraging. On the 1st he was twice in the rough and also bunkered; on the second he again put his tee-shot in the rough and then bunkered his second: two 6s and four over par in the first few minutes. Hailed as the great British hope after three successive tournament wins on the European circuit, was the strain of it all going to be too much?

Thereafter Faldo showed the courage that had many thinking he might be the first British winner since 1969. He got his first birdie at the 4th and another on the 8th to be out in a two-over-par 36. Other birdies followed on the 13th and 14th but the best came right at the end. He hit an iron to 6 or 7 yards on the 17th, holed out for an eagle and played the 18th just as well. First an excellent drive at least 300 yards down the fairway, then an iron some 5 yards short of the hole. The putt went down for a birdie and a round of 68. He had played the last sixteen holes in seven under par.

His playing partner Ballesteros, co-favourite for the championship, came to

221

the last needing a 4 for a 69. Both he and Larry Nelson carved their tee-shots well out to the right. The luck of a good lie was with Nelson, while the Spaniard found his ball buried and had to stand with the ball well below his feet. He hacked it out and then sent his third into nearly the same position from where he had played that deft run-up shot between the bunkers to end the 1976 Open. This time the shot didn't come off and Ballesteros took 6 for a round of 71. In view of the low scoring which continued throughout the championship, this 6 may well have ruined his chances, for Ballesteros was in great heart. He had won the Masters, the European PGA Championship, the Westchester Classic in America and a month before had played far and away his best US Open. But the British Open is the title Ballesteros rates the most highly of all and he was back at Birkdale, the scene of his emergence on the centre-stage of world golf in 1976.

With two holes to play, it looked as if an amateur, Philip Parkin, who shortly before had won the Amateur Championship at Turnberry, comfortably beating the fine American Jim Holtgrieve in the final, might lead the championship. However, he failed to birdie the 'easy' 17th and took 5 on the last for a round of 69.

Among British players, it was probably Sam Torrance who played the most remarkable round. Although he had four 5s and a 6 on his card he also had five birdies and an eagle from 10 feet on the 17th to be round in 68. Like so many others, he seldom used a driver but instead relied on a metal fairway 'wood'.

The hottest grouping was yet to come: Craig Stadler, Bernhard Langer and Paul Way. Stadler had decided that his strategy would be to try to reach the turn in par and attack the homeward holes. Defensive or not, he reached the turn in 31 (three under par) and then birdied the short 12th from several yards. Even more unlikely putts followed on the 14th to 16th, one going down from just off the green. At eight under par, the lowest round ever played in either British or US Open Championships was a strong possibility. He needed to birdie the 17th, which everyone could reach in two, and par the last for an unbelievable round of 62. However, at this point Stadler rejoined the mere mortals. On the 17th he hit a good safe drive but caught the mounds on the right of the green with his second, finishing some 4 yards through the green, but in a good enough lie. His chip, Stadler later said, was 'awful', and the putt that followed was apprehensive. The last hole was also nearly disastrous. He cut his drive into the rough but lashed out left of the green. From there, with the flag set well left, he attempted a high cut shot. His ball came down into an intervening bunker. From there he splashed deftly out to 2 feet for a 5. Alas, it was only a 64! In Open Championship history, there have been two lower rounds, both of course 63s and four other rounds of 64 (one yet to be played). Stadler's 64 had become the record first round in the championship.

Bernhard Langer, perhaps inspired by the American, produced fireworks of his own. He had dropped two strokes to par after four holes but had four consecutive birdies from the 12th and then hit a huge drive down the 17th and an iron to 5 yards. Langer, though so full of fears on the short putts, is still an excellent medium and long putter. Down it went. But what a contrast on the last! Another long drive and a good iron shot stopped some 10 yards from the hole. His approach putt for a 65 went some 2½ feet past. That fatal tremor reappeared and he missed, to join Watson and Rogers in second place.

These then were the main glories of the day but in every Open there are parallel disasters. What, for instance, of two of the headlined names of the 1982 championship, Bobby Clampett and Nick Price? Clampett opened up by hitting his first shot of all into the right rough, his second into the left rough and into a bush to boot. On a penalty drop his ball rolled to rest against his golf bag for a two-stroke penalty. He wound up with an 8 and did very well to complete in 74. Nick Price lasted a little longer, until he reached the 13th, a par-5 which all, with a helping wind, were expecting to birdie. Price pulled successive second shots into the bushes and was eventually on the green in 7. . . . Even worse befell Denis Watson, a fine South African golfer with some good performances in America and elsewhere to his credit. His problem came at the 10th. He drove into some very long grass, could not get out at the first attempt and reached the green in four. He missed his second putt. There followed a careless backhand flick from 8 inches, which missed. No doubt rather cross, he hit the next while the ball was still moving. A two-stroke penalty was incurred. Eight, nine and ten for Clampett, Price and Watson. The last of these withdrew with hay fever on the second day! I was hardly surprised.

After one of the more stirring and surprising days in Open Championship history, these were the front runners:

64 Stadler; 67 Watson, Rogers, Langer; 68 Faldo, Torrance, Ferguson, Sutton (soon to win the US PGA), Somers; 69 Garrido, Parkin, Irwin, Marsh, Dunk, Trevino, Darcy

The first to show on the second day was the 1971 Royal Birkdale Open champion, Lee Trevino. At the end of the first nine, he had moved to within a stroke of Craig Stadler, who was playing a few minutes behind him. Trevino reached the turn in 30 with four birdies and then birdied the next hole to be level on the course with Stadler. Thirty strokes for any half of an Open is a rare enough event and had only been bettered by 29s in earlier years by Peter Thomson, Tom Haliburton, Tony Jacklin and Bill Longmuir. That record was just about to go at the hands of Denis Durnian, who reached the turn in 28, having just missed a 10-footer for 27, which would have equalled both US and European Tour nine-hole records. This is how he did it:

Durnian	4,	3,	3,	2,	3,	4,	2,	3,	4	(28)
Par	4,	4,	4,	3,	4,	4,	3,	4,	4	(34)

It was the lowest nine holes ever played in any of the four major championships, no mean feat for a club professional rather than a permanent tournament player! He completed his round a little shakily for 'only' a 66 but was by no means done for, his 67 in the final round putting him into 8th place, worth £9000.

Trevino had changed to a baseball grip for putting. This was how his 30 on the first nine was compiled:

| **Trevino** | 4, 3, 4, 3, 3, 3, 2, 4, 4 (30) |
| **Par** | 4, 4, 4, 3, 4, 4, 3, 4, 4 (34) |

I should guess that Trevino had been feeling that his days as a major winner in championship golf were probably over. On the US Tour, he had been competing less frequently, his eye on the future. For Trevino this must surely be dominated by TV work, clinics, exhibitions and 'company days'. However, he had just won the Canadian PGA in fine style. A win is a win and ambition stirred again. This Birkdale suited Trevino, who had lost some of his length. When he couldn't carry his second shots onto the greens he could run the ball in. He finished in 66, which equalled his best round in a British Open, at Muirfield in 1972.

All day long, Stadler had been holding his own against par, on the first half dropping a couple of shots but having birdies on two holes as well. This time, he finished well. He holed none too short a putt on the 17th for his birdie and then almost holed out his little pitch shot to the last. He was round in 70 and likely to hold his narrow lead at the end of the day.

Well behind, Nick Faldo played the first two holes in five strokes better than his 6, 6 start of the first day, and went on to reach the turn in 33, despite dropping a shot on the 9th. He dropped another on the 10th. However, after a pair of 2s on the par-3s he had an excellent chance of catching Craig Stadler with three holes to play. Then it began to go wrong. He hit a poor iron to the 16th to drop a shot and then hooked his tee-shot on the 17th to scotch any real chance of a birdie. On the last he then hit a long drive but cut his iron shot into a bunker. The sheer, almost tangible desire of the crowds for a British win must have been both burden and inspiration to him. As the applause welled from the stands around the last hole he seemed close to tears. He then played a terrible bunker shot – right off the shank. He held his head in his hands, but at least the ball was on the green. Moments later he holed a crucial, brave putt for his par, a round of 68, and a total just two more than Stadler's.

Half an hour or so behind him, Watson was playing an extremely workman-like round. There was no inspirational play from him, but few errors either. He dropped a shot only once, on the 6th, and had four birdies. Unnoticed, Hale Irwin, not out until after 3 o'clock, had another good round, a 68, while Raymond Floyd pulled himself well up the field with a 66.

Craig Stadler birdies the 16th in his first-round 64 at Royal Birkdale in 1983.

Such had been the emotions flowing around the dunes and stands of Royal Birkdale that I wondered how well the Americans could withstand the support Faldo was receiving and what the effect might be on Faldo himself. Home emotions were with Nick Faldo but the hard-headed gambler's choice was Tom Watson. Of the other leaders, Stadler had cracked on the run-in when winning his 1982 Masters title, and had faded in the 1983 event at much the same stage. Trevino, at the age of 43, still had the golf game but many wondered if his nerve could survive the cauldron of the final 36 holes. Here's how they stood after two rounds:

134 Stadler;   135 Trevino, Watson;   136 Faldo;   137 Irwin;
138 Gale, Rogers, Floyd;   139 Sutton, Durnian, Langer, Marsh,
Bean;   140 Sullivan, Graham, James, Waites, Henning

Overnight, there was serious vandal damage at Royal Birkdale. Publicists for the cause of a convicted murderer, Dennis Kelly, had dug half-a-dozen or more slabs of turf out of the 6th green and covered it with slogans. One result, strangely, was that this difficult hole was made easier, R and A officials moving the tee markers forward some 40 yards.

The 36-hole cut had come at the record low score of 146. Among those who had made it with nothing at all to spare were Tony Jacklin, Bobby Clampett, Greg Norman, Tom Weiskopf and Arnold Palmer. Palmer, one of the first off on the third day, revived memories of former glories and was the only player I saw who used his driver at every opportunity. He began with two birdies and had six in all but there was a double-bogey as well. The shot of his round, perhaps, came at the 198-yard 14th. There his 3-iron came to rest just inches from the hole. He was round in 68, a score that only three players bettered all day – not bad at the age of 53. Perhaps Royal Birkdale should erect another plaque and make sure to get the date right this time!

The first credible contender to make a strong move, however, was David Graham, who had five 3s in the first six holes. Watson's beginning was nearly disastrous. Taking an iron for safety on his first tee-shot, he nevertheless hooked off the fairway and against the roots of a bush. He had to take his second penalty drop of the championship. A 6 was the result but thereafter Watson parred every hole on the first nine before his first birdie on the 10th. When Stadler holed for a birdie on the 3rd hole, he had increased his lead to three strokes. Obviously he could not expect to repeat his putting magic of the first round but he was continuing to hole vital putts. On the 8th, for example, he sent his first at least 7 feet past but got the return. Floyd, after an opening 72, had also begun to putt at his best, his second-round 66 (with a 6 on the 1st), owing much to his excellence on the greens. During the first nine on the third day, he again moved up the field and stood second on the leader boards after the 9th. This was a splendid effort from Floyd.

Of course British eyes were very much on Nick Faldo, who (as you will see from the facts and figures in the Appendix) has an excellent overall record in the few years he has played the championship. He went to the turn in level par, 34, but then dropped strokes on the next two holes. However, he birdied the par-5s coming home and was round in 71. After that 6, 6 start on the first day, he had produced one of the best sustained spells of golf ever by a British player in the Open Championship. At the end of the day, there was an entirely realistic prospect that he might be the first home winner of the championship since Tony Jacklin in 1969.

Meanwhile, Hale Irwin, who you will remember had begun with rounds of 69 and 68, was continuing on his quiet methodical way. He is just about the most unlikely man to throw away strokes carelessly. Yet he did so. On the 14th he sent his approach putt to about 3 inches from the hole, casually made to tap it in with the back of his putter and played an air shot, a stroke that some would argue lost him the championship. The following day, he was to finish just a stroke out of a tie for the Open. Perhaps the mental shock also affected his chances. Irwin dropped a shot on the next hole as well.

There were other disasters also, some which mattered and others which just illustrate the ups and downs of championship golf. Lanny Wadkins, for instance, who had been enjoying a steady but hardly newsworthy championship produced this strange scoring sequence from the 11th: 7, 3, 4, 2, 4, 3, 7. That was four consecutive birdies but a triple- and double-bogey to add unwelcome variety. A 72, Wadkins's score, is rare with a couple of 7s on the card! There was another scoring oddity: Bill Rogers followed his first-day albatross 2 on the 17th with 6s on the next two days.

Throughout the day, Craig Stadler had held on to the lead that his first-round 64 had won for him. But the 18th had already proved a problem for him and not one of his three tee-shots had found the fairway. On the third day, it cost him his championship lead as he sliced the ball wildly, only two or three paces from the out of bounds, in very deep and unfrequented rough. It needed all the power of the Stadler forearms just to lash the ball back to the fairway. His third shot was bunkered by the green and he took 6. Watson, just before, had also cut his drive into deep rough but was able to get a shot at it. He finished just through the green but got his par 4. He was one of the very few that day able to finish with a pair of 4s. The last hole had also done Trevino's cause no good. His driving accuracy left him for once. He too was in deep rough and eventually glad to escape with a 5, holing a good putt to do so. At 7.22 p.m., there was at last a new leader, the favourite Tom Watson:

205 Watson; 206 Stadler; 207 Faldo, Floyd, Graham;
208 Trevino; 209 Irwin, McNulty, Bean, Zoeller; 211 Gale,
Henning; 212 Ballesteros, Davis, Jacobsen, O'Leary, Rogers

Going down six strokes from the championship lead, this ought to include everyone with a chance. In fact there was the Australian Graham Marsh at 213 after a third round of 74. On the final day, he moved very much into the centre of the Birkdale arena.

To qualify for each stage at Royal Birkdale required the lowest totals in Open Championship history: 146 after 36 holes and 217 after 54. Even a player such as Manuel Ballesteros, with scores that read respectably enough – 73, 72, 73 – found himself on his way back to Spain after three rounds.

Graham Marsh had qualified comfortably enough but he started off on the final day only four better than the worst qualifying score and eight behind the leader, Tom Watson. Yet soon he had all the third-day leaders worried. Marsh set off about three hours before the final pairing of Watson and Stadler. At 3.12 he holed a 7-foot putt for a birdie and was momentarily the championship leader. A quarter of an hour later he had a 64 and a total of 277 on the board. It was like the pre-1957 days of the championship, before the system was changed to send the leaders out last. Time when a man could finish with hours of play still left, challenging the rest of the field to beat his target. Marsh was the first for many years to set such a target from the back of the field. His round was extremely symmetrical: out in 32 and, much better against the homeward

227

par of 37, back in 32, with seven birdies, no bogeys and not a few putts that came very close indeed to dropping. At one point, as the wind freshened, it was to seem likely indeed that Marsh could become champion.

Nevertheless, all eyes were on Faldo, who had played with splendid consistency all season. He began by finding a very unfriendly lie with his second shot to the 1st hole. A hack hardly moved the ball and he then squirted the next 8 yards or so past but holed that long putt. Yells and prolonged applause soon followed as he birdied the 2nd from long range. There were more roars at the 3rd as Faldo's iron shot stopped little more than a yard from the hole. Another birdie. At the short 4th, Faldo was 6 or 7 yards away with his tee-shot and again got the putt in. The prospects were suddenly glittering, for at 2.28 he was tied for the championship lead and the strongest feature of his game, putting, was very much on song. He faltered on the 5th, driving into the rough, and then missed the green, chipped to 3 yards or more from the hole but again got the putt. He went over par at the 6th and then was rather strong with his tee-shot to the 150-yard 7th, chipped about 4 foot past but struck his putt exactly at the middle of the hole.

At all levels of golf nerves seem most apparent when players use the driver or putter. Faldo was especially encouraging British hopes with sure judgement of line and length on the greens. As he reached the turn in 33, he was a credible winner. We had to have a home winner some time. Here looked the man who could do it. Ahead, Marsh had just set his target and was, for the moment, the man to beat. Shortly after, no fewer than thirteen players were within three strokes of each other.

The first chink in Faldo's armour showed on the 10th. Here his second shot was some 10 feet from the hole but for the first time his putt was tentative. On the 12th, he appeared highly doubtful of which club to use to this 184-yard par-3 and in the end pulled into the bank by the green and could not hole a putt of some 4 yards for his par. The 13th saw the beginning of the end. After a fine 5-iron to the green, his eagle putt was tentative, some 5 feet short, and he

Nick Faldo debates the choice of club with his caddie, 1983.

One of the putts that didn't quite drop for Graham Marsh on the last day, 1983.

missed from there. Then, on the last par-3, having hit his tee-shot some distance beyond the hole, with a downhiller to come, he must have told himself to putt aggressively. He did, hit the edge of the hole, and the ball spun some 6 feet away. The next putt, not surprisingly, did not go down. It seemed the end of his championship hopes. In the end, he was to finish sharing 8th place with Denis Durnian and Christy O'Connor Jr. Whatever the final result, Faldo, with Bill Rogers, had made a great challenge and led the European effort. Many hearts had been stirred during the four days. His future looks very bright and he soon followed this with a superb performance in the Ryder Cup in October in Florida.

The later moments of this great championship had first posed the question of whether or not Graham Marsh's target could stand up. Everyone, I think, would agree that he 'deserves' a major championship because of his achievements over a decade and more in most countries where golf is played.

It was not to be. First Hale Irwin and Andy Bean, both producing rounds of 67, slipped in a stroke ahead, having been little noticed throughout the championship. Although Bean must have been disappointed not to play-off for his first major title his money rewards were substantial. There was £23,000 courtesy of the R and A, while Bean had also thought the odds of 66–1 against him at the beginning of the championship distinctly attractive. He had wagered £200 each way on his chances.

The one-time leader, Craig Stadler, had a poor last round. Some people have said that Faldo collapsed on the last eighteen holes, which is not true. This accusation can, however, be levelled with more justification at Stadler, Raymond Floyd and David Graham, who were all two strokes worse, with 75s. The championship was equally within their grasp at various points in the third or fourth rounds.

With the advantage of knowing what actually happened, we can see that questions were asked of Tom Watson and he answered them all. He reached the turn in a two-over-par 36. His first winning move came at the 11th, when into the rising wind he hit a long-iron to about 12 feet and holed the putt. On the 12th, there was the Watson trademark of a putt past the hole and the return holed. Does anyone else in contemporary golf so often 'give the hole a chance', drift past, and then bang the return in? For my money no one since Arnold Palmer in his peak years.

Luck also ran his way. On the 13th, a wayward drive came to rest on a spectator footpath, a great deal better than being thigh deep in the rough. A 'routine' birdie followed on this par-5. At the short 14th, he was far too long with his tee-shot and his approach putt left him 6 feet short with, he later said, '3 or 4 inches of break'. It was in all the way.

Watson then parred the difficult long 15th without alarms and first had the championship in his grasp on the 16th. He hooked slightly into semi-rough and hit an 8-iron to 5 or 6 yards. The putt that followed was by no means the normal Watson rap past the hole. This time, it was of perfect dying strength – and in. He had to par the last two holes to win.

From the 17th, Watson played the kind of tee-shot that had almost cost Lee Trevino the 1971 Birkdale Open, a big hook into the sandhills. He had a poor stance for his second shot but no problem with the lie. With an 8-iron he was back on the fairway and his third even left him with an outside chance of a birdie but he two-putted for his par.

The final question to Tom Watson then was 'Can you par the longest par-4 on the course to be champion by a stroke?' The drive was exactly in the middle of the fairway. Before playing his second shot of (so he says) no more and no less than 213 yards he had to withstand the sudden pressure of having an Open gallery swarm around.

Watson had now to hit a 2-iron not too far from the hole and two-putt to win. I cannot recall a long-iron better struck at the critical moment. In it came, with a hint of draw to hold it into the wind, mathematically on line. No need to be brave. Knock it up close, tap it in and brace yourself for a speech with, if possible, a joke in it. Which is what Watson did.

For Watson, it was his fifth Open Championship title and with it he had established the greatest record of all time in any major championship. I think most of us would agree that the Open has been by far and away the most international championship of the four majors from 1970 onwards. Watson has won it those five times in nine attempts, against undeniably the strongest fields that have ever assembled year after year for this or any other championship.

Tom Watson's achievement is rivalled only in times when the competition was surely less fierce. His rivals are:

Young Tom Morris: four wins, all in the successive championships of 1868–72, with no event played in 1871.
James Braid: five wins in 1901–10.
Harry Vardon: a record six wins in 1896–1914.
J. H. Taylor: five wins in 1894–1913.
Bobby Jones: three wins in 1921–30 from four attempts.
Walter Hagen: four wins in 1922–9 but not when Jones was in the field.
Bobby Locke: four wins in fourteen attempts.
Peter Thomson: five wins in 1951–65 (fifteen attempts), but the only player in modern times to have won three championships consecutively (in 1954–6) to have won four in five years and, with Watson, to have totalled five championship victories.

Statistically, Bobby Jones has the best striking rate in Open Championship history, better surprisingly even than Young Tom Morris. Yet these were deeds accomplished back in the mists of time. Tom Watson's victories have been achieved in an era when the Open Championship had become the world championship of golf.

It will be a continuing fascination to me to see if he can surpass Harry Vardon's total of six wins. I wouldn't care to wager much against him. Onwards to St Andrews in 1984, Royal St George's in 1985, Turnberry in 1986 and Muirfield in 1987. And may the best man win!

HOW THEY FINISHED

T. Watson *USA*	**67**	**68**	**70**	**70**	**275**	A. Jacklin	71	75	71	69	286
						K. Arai *Japan*	74	67	75	70	
H. Irwin *USA*	69	68	72	67	276	R. Gilder *USA*	70	76	70	70	
A. Bean *USA*	70	69	70	67		V. Fernandez *Argentina*	70	72	72	72	
						C. Moody	74	69	70	73	
G. Marsh *Australia*	69	70	74	64	277	I. Collins	70	75	68	73	
L. Trevino *USA*	69	66	73	70	278	C. Tucker	73	71	73	70	287
						M. Kuramoto *Japan*	70	74	73	70	
S. Ballesteros *Spain*	71	71	69	68	279	M. Pinero *Spain*	74	72	71	70	
H. R. Henning	71	69	70	69		G. Burroughs	71	74	71	71	
South Africa						T. Weiskopf *USA*	73	73	69	72	
						V. Somers *Australia*	68	75	71	73	
D. Durnian	73	66	74	67	280	T. Simpson *USA*	73	69	72	73	
C. O'Connor Jr	72	69	71	68		M. McNulty *South Africa*	72	69	68	78	
W. Rogers *USA*	67	71	73	69							
N. Faldo	68	68	71	73		R. Clampett *USA*	74	72	71	71	288
						L. Nelson *USA*	70	73	73	72	
P. Jacobsen *USA*	72	69	70	70	281	S. Torrance	68	73	74	73	
C. Stadler *USA*	64	70	72	75							
						B. Langer *West Germany*	67	72	76	74	289
M. Sullivan *USA*	72	68	74	68	282	A. Palmer *USA*	72	74	68	75	
G. Koch *USA*	75	71	66	70		M. Johnson	70	72	71	76	
F. Zoeller *USA*	71	71	67	73		M. Calero *Spain*	70	75	69	76	
R. Floyd *USA*	72	66	69	75							
D. Graham *Australia*	71	69	67	75		J. O'Leary	74	68	69	79	290
G. Norman *Australia*	75	71	70	67	283	R. Rafferty	75	67	73	76	291
H. Green *USA*	69	74	72	68							
T. Britz *South Africa*	71	74	69	69		M. Ingham	71	73	70	78	292
B. Waites	70	70	73	70							
B. Gallacher	72	71	70	70		Y-S. Hsieh *Taiwan*	71	72	74	78	295
S. F. N. Hobday	70	73	70	70							
South Africa											
J. Haas *USA*	73	72	68	70							
E. Darcy	69	72	74	69	284						
H. K. Clark	71	72	69	72							
R. Davis *Australia*	70	71	70	73							
C-S. Lu *Taiwan*	71	72	74	68	285						
L. Wadkins *USA*	72	73	72	68							
J. W. Nicklaus *USA*	71	72	72	70							
T. Kite *USA*	71	72	72	70							
M. McCullough *USA*	74	69	72	70							
H. Sutton *USA*	68	71	75	71							
M. James	70	70	74	71							
T. Nakamura *Japan*	73	69	72	71							
C. Strange *USA*	74	68	70	73							
T. Gale *Australia*	72	66	72	75							

·10·
Where Do We Go From Here?

As I hope my Open Championship story has shown, the event has grown from its insignificant origins away back in 1860 to become the premier championship in world golf. Of course, my American friends might well disagree and point to the US Open or the Masters as being the pinnacle. But I would beg to disagree and not only because I am more patriotic than most!

As you will see from the figures in the Appendix, the appeal of the Open has been steadily upwards, with new attendance records set yet again in 1983, while the R and A strains, largely effectively, to see that the spectators get their money's worth by providing better stand facilities, checking on the quality of catering and pricing, improving the movement of the crowds about a championship venue and increasing the flow of information.

The championship is now very big business. Long gone are the days when an earlier secretary, Brigadier Brickman, would, it has been said – perhaps tongue-in-cheek – turn up the day before with a length of rope and his tent and check off the competitors. Today, the choice of course is set four years ahead and preliminary discussions about that choice begin even earlier.

Course preparation in recent years has been given far more intensive care, and as we have seen, many felt that Royal Birkdale in 1983 had the best greens presented to a championship field for many years. The development of our rota of Open courses is indeed a matter about which there are various opinions but we have certainly taken great steps forward since the days when the course played was just what the members had been using the week before. I have, for instance, made it very clear that I believe Turnberry could be developed into a jewel among them, though at many of the other courses I should hate to see more than minor changes. They are a part of our golfing heritage and must be preserved at all costs. One would hate to see a bulldozer at work on St Andrews.

I was, however, disturbed to see that the lowest scoring ever took place at Birkdale in 1983. It is one of the toughest links tests, as is Muirfield, yet I feel that on both these courses scoring has become indecently low. Nowadays, if you give a championship field in Britain holding greens there are just too many players in the field who will 'murder' it. Sooner or later, I fear, we are going to have champions of not quite the highest class. Jack Nicklaus, for instance, reckons that he scores roughly the same on an 'easy' course as on a truly threatening one. Tom Watson declared, in 1983, that he believed that many of our championship links had greens that were no longer truly links in character. We should take heed.

The soft, holding surfaces mean that a golfer is able to play target golf, just as he would on an inland course. Should our Open present an unaccustomed test once again? Should players be made to judge the run of a ball; when to pitch it short; how to ease the ball through the humps and hollows? Superb touch players with feel for the run of a ball like Bobby Locke and Peter Thomson at their best would, perhaps, have little chance of winning a championship today. Only the far greater demands on nerve still prevent ordinary players having a freak run for a few days and becoming champion. As we see repeatedly on both the European and US Tours, a tournament is as often as not won by a man in good form with a good spell on the greens. He wins, then backs out of the limelight, perhaps for months, perhaps indeed for ever.

Above all the Open Championship is by far and away the greatest show of the European golfing year, dwarfing any other event. It brings in an estimated £6 million outside the championship venue itself in money spent in local hotels, restaurants, shops, and elsewhere. Admission charges and broadcasting rights worldwide should have brought in well over £1½ million in 1983, the year that set a new attendance record at almost 143,000.

The Open Championship is also a very substantial employer of labour of all kinds with, for example, 5500 working at Royal Birkdale each day in 1983. Nearly half of these worked in catering, mainly local unemployed people supplied by Job Centres. At the top end of the market, 5500 lbs of fresh Tay salmon and 1600 bottles of Bollinger champagne were consumed and, at a more modest level, some 200,000 cups of tea and coffee and 150,000 sandwiches, hotdogs, cakes and the like daily.

The famous tented village is perhaps now wrongly named for it is almost a township, so much so that R and A decided that for 1983 street names were necessary as people were getting lost in the labyrinth. By a happy choice it was decided to use the names of former champions, so in 1983 we had Ballesteros Boulevard, Palmer Promenade, Miller Mile and Trevino Terrace – among others. Of course, Jack Nicklaus had to be included but that letter 'N' did cause trouble, solved by using the Scottish word 'Neuk', which means 'corner', more familiarly seen in English as 'nook'. The township now accommodates 100 companies dispensing hospitality to the extent of 7000 lunches daily.

For the golfing spectator, however, the equipment displays are of more interest. At the Open Championship, you will find nearly all of the devices known to man that ought to move a golf ball a long way or deposit it safely in the hole. There, golfers at every level of skill can wander – and dream their impossible dreams.

Finally, I should like to consult my crystal ball. We have seen throughout this book a succession of names of those who 'ought' to have won our great championship and would have done so but for a putt that didn't drop or an unlucky lie: Johnny Bulla, Reg Horne, Frank Stranahan, Harry Bradshaw, Leopoldo Ruiz, Dai Rees, David Thomas, Eric Brown, Phil Rodgers, Doug Sanders, Liang Huan Lu, Bobby Coles, Jack Newton, Peter Oosterhuis, Nick Price, Hale Irwin, and Andy Bean are all golfers who came within an inch or so of the title. Did they not succeed because of a failure of nerve or because it was just not destined that particular year and the chance never beckoned again?

Of course, some of these are still very active and successful competitors and may yet take the title. Here is my own prediction of current players I expect to see take the championship during the years after 1983 – not in order of priority.

Tom Watson: a technically complete golfer who has all the nerve required and some to spare.

Jack Nicklaus: he still has the desire to win championships.

Nick Faldo: having established himself as the most effective European golfer in 1983, I know he also has the desire to 'do it for Britain'.

Hal Sutton: with one major championship under his belt, and as one of the most successful current US golfers, I must rate him highly, despite his shut clubface at the top of the swing.

Paul Way: at twenty years of age, he has the best swing of any of the emerging golfers.

Severiano Ballesteros: of course he will win again; the only question is when and how often.

Bernhard Langer: has any golfer ever managed to perform so well with so disastrous a tremor on short putts? A winner if he can put all his iron shots 10 feet or more from the hole!

Nick Price: although he threw away the 1982 Open and chances sometimes come only once, he should feel rejuvenated by his victory in the 1983 World Series.

Craig Stadler: tends to crack towards the end of major championships – as did Watson in the past – but has power, the ability to manipulate a golf ball and is currently one of the world's best putters.

Andy Bean: a big powerful man with a fine swing and delicate touch, I wonder why he doesn't win more often.

Greg Norman: a fine striker of the ball, athletic, he must be destined to be one of the great stars of the 1980s.

Ray Floyd: he seems to win major championships (three in all) only when he starts fast. He has yet to do so in the Open Championship and has little time left.

Any Japanese: their day will surely come and if you are looking for the next left-hander likely to win that could well be Yatuka Hagawa.

Appendix: Championship Facts and Figures

Low Rounds in the Championship

Score	Player	Round	Year	Course
63	M. Hayes	2nd	1977	Turnberry
63	I. Aoki	3rd	1980	Muirfield
64	H. Carbonetti	2nd	1980	Muirfield
64	T. Watson	3rd	1980	Muirfield
64	H. Green	3rd	1980	Muirfield
64	C. Stadler	1st	1983	Royal Birkdale
64	G. Marsh	4th	1983	Royal Birkdale
65	T. H. Cotton	2nd	1934	Royal St George's
65	L. Ruiz	2nd	1958	Royal Lytham
65	E. C. Brown	3rd	1958	Royal Lytham
65	P. J. Butler	2nd	1966	Muirfield
65	C. O'Connor Sr	2nd	1969	Royal Lytham
65	N. C. Coles	1st	1970	St Andrews
65	J. W. Nicklaus	4th	1973	Troon
65	A. Gallardo	2nd	1977	Turnberry
65	T. Horton	3rd	1977	Turnberry
65	J. W. Nicklaus	3rd	1977	Turnberry
65	T. Watson	3rd	1977	Turnberry
65	T. Watson	4th	1977	Turnberry
65	W. Longmuir	1st	1979	Royal Lytham
65	S. Ballesteros	2nd	1979	Royal Lytham
65	G. Brand	2nd	1981	Royal St George's

Lowest Rounds on Other Courses used in the Championship, 1946–83

Score	Player	Round	Year	Course
67	R. de Vicenzo	3rd	1967	Hoylake
67	G. J. Player	3rd	1967	Hoylake
68	J. Adams	1st	1951	Royal Portrush
68	N. G. von Nida	1st	1951	Royal Portrush
68	C. H. Ward	4th	1951	Royal Portrush

Scores of 30 or fewer for a First or Second Nine, 1946–83

Score	Player	Nine	Year	Course
28	D. Durnian	1st	1983	Royal Birkdale
29	T. Haliburton	1st	1958	Royal Lytham
29	P. W. Thomson	1st	1958	Royal Lytham
29	A. Jacklin	1st	1970	St Andrews
29	W. Longmuir	1st	1979	Royal Lytham
30	E. C. Brown	1st	1957	St Andrews
30	E. C. Brown	2nd	1958	Royal Lytham
30	L. Ruiz	1st	1958	Royal Lytham
30	P. Rodgers	2nd	1966	Muirfield
30	P. Alliss	1st	1969	Royal Lytham
30	J. Kinsella	1st	1971	Royal Birkdale
30	H. Bannerman	1st	1972	Muirfield
30	A. Yancey	1st	1973	Troon
30	C. O'Connor Jr	1st	1976	Royal Birkdale
30	A. Palmer	2nd	1977	Turnberry
30	J. W. Nicklaus	1st	1979	Royal Lytham
30	T. Watson	2nd	1980	Muirfield
30	L. Trevino	1st	1983	Royal Birkdale

Denis Durnian's 28 is the lowest half played in any of the four major championships as at the end of the 1983 season.

Lowest 72-Hole Aggregates in the Championship, 1946–83

Aggregate	Player	Year	Course
268 (68, 70, 65, 65)	T. Watson	1977	Turnberry
269 (68, 70, 65, 66)	J. W. Nicklaus	1977	Turnberry
271 (68, 70, 64, 69)	T. Watson	1980	Muirfield
275 (68, 67, 71, 69)	L. Trevino	1980	Muirfield
275 (67, 68, 70, 70)	T. Watson	1983	Royal Birkdale
276 (71, 69, 67, 69)	A. Palmer	1962	Troon
276 (68, 67, 71, 70)	T. Weiskopf	1973	Troon
276 (72, 66, 67, 71)	W. Rogers	1981	Royal St George's
276 (70, 69, 70, 67)	A. Bean	1983	Royal Birkdale
276 (69, 68, 72, 67)	H. Irwin	1983	Royal Birkdale

Lowest Aggregates on each Championship Course, 1946–83

Course	Aggregate	Player	Year
Carnoustie	279	T. Watson	1975
		J. Newton	1975
Hoylake	278	R. de Vicenzo	1967
Muirfield	271	T. Watson	1980
Royal Birkdale	275	T. Watson	1983
Royal Lytham	277	R. J. Charles	1963
Royal Portrush	285	M. Faulkner	1951
Royal St George's	276	W. Rogers	1981
St Andrews	278	K. D. G. Nagle	1960
Troon	276	A. Palmer	1962
		T. Weiskopf	1973
Turnberry	268	T. Watson	1977

Championship Prize Money, 1946–83, for Selected Years

Year	Total prize fund	Winner's share
1946	£1000	£150
1949	£1700	£300
1951	£1700	£325
1953	£2450	£500
1954	£3500	£750
1955	£3750	£1000
1960	£7000	£1250
1961	£8500	£1400
1965	£10,000	£1750
1966	£15,000	£2100
1969	£30,000	£4250
1970	£40,000	£5250
1975	£76,000	£7500
1977	£102,000	£10,000
1979	£155,000	£15,000
1980	£207,000	£25,000
1982	£250,000	£32,000
1983	£310,000	£40,000
1984	£410,000	£50,000

In 1984 the man finishing in 60th place earned £1,000, the same as the total prize fund in 1946.

Championship Attendances, 1962–83, for Selected Years

Attendance	Year
37,098	1962
35,954	1964
40,182	1966
29,880	1967
51,819	1968
81,583	1970
84,746	1972
92,796	1974
125,271	1978
134,571	1979
142,894	1983

Most, but obviously not all, of the above years saw new record attendances. A record attendance for a single day was set at Royal Lytham in 1979 when 32,072 came to the third day's play. It was broken in 1983 with 34,200 on the second day. The above figures include attendance on practice days, if an entry fee is charged.

Playing Highlights, 1946–83

1947 Fred Daly's winning aggregate of 293 is the highest since World War II.

1948 Henry Cotton recorded his third victory. No other British player has won more than once since World War I.

1950 Frank Stranahan's 66 in the fourth round is the best by an amateur.

1952 Bobby Locke recorded his third win in four years.

1953 Ben Hogan won and never entered again.

1954 Peter Thomson became the first Australian to win the championship.

1956 Peter Thomson became the first modern to win three years consecutively. No one else has done so since the event has been played over 72 holes.

1959 Gary Player became the youngest modern to win the championship until Severiano Ballesteros in 1979.

1960 Guy Wolstenholme's aggregate of 283 is still the amateur record. The year also saw Arnold Palmer's first entry.

1962 Arnold Palmer broke the record aggregate with 276. He was the first champion to have three rounds under 70.

1963 Bob Charles became the first New Zealander to win and remains the only left-hander to have done so.

1964 Tony Lema's seven-stroke lead on the field after three rounds is the highest in 1946–83 and the best since Henry Cotton's margin of ten strokes in 1934.

1965 Peter Thomson won for the fifth time, the first man to do so since World War I, a feat duplicated by Tom Watson in 1983.

1966 Jack Nicklaus became the fourth man to win each of the four major championships.

1967 Roberto de Vicenzo won, nineteen years after his first entry. He was the oldest player (at 44 years and 93 days) to do so since Old Tom Morris (46 years 99 days) in 1867.

1969 Tony Jacklin became the first British player to win since 1951. For the first time in ten years, no American finished in the top five. Eleven months later Jacklin won the US Open.

1970 Tony Jacklin's first half of 29 is the most under par, seven strokes, recorded on either half in the championship.

1971 Liang Huan Lu's second-place finish is the best ever by an Asian.

1977 Tom Watson's 268 was – and remains – the record aggregate. Mark Hayes set the record for a single round at 63.

1979 Severiano Ballesteros, at 22, became the youngest champion since 1893, Willie Auchterlonie's year. Jack Nicklaus became the first man to finish 2nd seven times.

1980 Tom Watson's 64 in the third round is the lowest by a champion. He also set the lowest aggregate record for the first 54 holes at 202. It broke the record of 203 he and Jack Nicklaus had set at Turnberry in 1977. Isao Aoki's 63 in the third round equalled the championship record.

1982 Masahiro Kuramoto's 4th-place finish is the best by a Japanese golfer.

1983 Tom Watson achieved his third win in four years and his fifth in all. Only Harry Vardon, with six, has won more Open Championships. Craig Stadler's 64 was the lowest first round in this championship. Denis Durnian's 28 for the first nine holes is the lowest in any major championship.

Changes in the Organization of the Championship, 1946–83

1955 The first live TV transmissions went out.

1957 The leaders went out last after the first 36 holes.

1962 Poor crowd control led to greater restriction of spectator freedom.

1963 Exemptions for leading players from pre-qualifying were introduced. For the first time, the championship course was not used for qualifying rounds.

1964 It was decided that any future play-off should be over 18 holes, rather than 36.

1966 The final day was moved from Friday to Saturday with play being over four rather than three days.

1968 A 54-hole cut was introduced and remains in force.

1970 The number of qualifying courses was raised to three.

1972 The number of qualifying courses was raised to four.

1974 The 1.68-inch ball became obligatory rather than optional.

1976 Five qualifying courses became necessary.

1977 Regional pre-qualifying was introduced.

1980 The championship was re-scheduled to end on a Sunday.

Qualifying Scores in the Championship, 1946–83

Year	To play first 36 holes	To proceed to third round	To proceed to final round
1946	159	155	
1947	155	156	
1948	152	148	
1949	154	147	
1950	153	148	
1951	155	154	
1952	152	152	
1953	154	154	
1954	151	151	
1955	148	148	
1956	152	153	
1957	149	148	
1958	148	147	
1959	147	148	
1960	147	149	
1961	148	153	
1962	154	152	
1963		149	
1964		153	
1965		149	
1966		150	
1967		149	
1968		154	228
1969		148	222
1970		149	223
1971		151	224
1972		152	225
1973		152	224
1974		156	231
1975		149	221
1976		152	226
1977		150	221
1978		148	222
1979		152	227
1980		149	219
1981		150	222
1982		152	226
1983		146	217

The system of exemptions for leading players was introduced from the 1963 championship onwards, while a cut after 54 holes was brought in for the 1968 championship. The record low cuts for both third and fourth rounds both came in 1983.

Courses used in the Championship, 1946–83

St Andrews 7, Royal Lytham 6, Royal Birkdale 6, Muirfield 5, Troon 4,
Carnoustie 3, Hoylake 3, Royal St George's 2, Royal Portrush 1, Turnberry 1

Average Scores per round in the Championship, 1946–83

Year	Top 10 finishers, excluding winner	Winner	Winner's margin over others in top 10	Lowest round by any player
1946	73.83	72.50	1.33	67
1947	74.00	73.25	0.75	69
1948	72.58	71.00	1.58	66
1949	71.61	70.75	0.86	67
1950	70.86	69.75	1.11	66
1951	72.94	71.25	1.69	68
1952	73.61	71.75	1.86	67
1953	72.11	70.50	1.61	68
1954	71.47	70.75	0.72	67
1955	71.36	70.25	1.11	67
1956	73.08	71.50	1.58	68
1957	71.33	69.75	1.58	67
1958	70.36	69.50	0.86	65
1959	71.91	71.00	0.91	67
1960	70.80	69.50	1.30	66
1961	72.33	71.00	1.33	67
1962	72.61	69.00	3.61	67
1963	71.08	69.25	1.83	66
1964	72.33	69.75	2.54	66
1965	72.27	71.25	1.02	68
1966	71.50	70.50	1.00	65
1967	71.27	69.50	1.77	67
1968	73.47	72.25	1.22	68
1969	71.19	70.00	1.19	65
1970	71.63	70.75	0.88	65
1971	70.66	69.50	1.16	67
1972	70.88	69.50	1.38	66
1973	71.05	69.00	2.05	65
1974	72.72	70.50	2.22	68
1975	70.30	69.75	0.55	65
1976	71.81	69.75	2.06	66
1977	70.08	67.00	3.08	63
1978	70.86	70.25	0.61	67
1979	72.25	70.75	1.50	65
1980	70.08	67.75	2.33	63
1981	71.06	69.00	2.06	65
1982	71.77	71.00	0.77	66
1983	69.58	68.75	0.83	64

It is apparent that the most dominant champion was Arnold Palmer in 1962, while the margins in 1964 and 1977 are also impressive. The most closely contested championship was that of 1975.

OPEN CHAMPIONSHIP PERFORMANCES BY SELECTED PLAYERS, 1927–83

	Career stroke average	Best aggregate	Worst aggregate	Sub-70 rounds	75s and over	64s	65s	66s	67s	68s	69s	Worst round	Wins	2nd or 3rd	Rounds played
Peter Alliss 1952–74	73.025	285	308	6	30	0	0	1	1	1	3	83	0	0	81
Severiano Ballesteros 1975–83	72.059	279	293	8	6	0	0	0	0	2	5	80	1	1	34
Bob Charles 1961–82	73.228	277	300	7	25	0	0	2	0	1	4	84	1	2	79
Henry Cotton 1927–61	73.947	283	314	8	40	0	1	1	1	2	3	83	3	2	94
Ben Crenshaw 1974–83	71.766	277	300	6	6	0	0	1	1	1	3	80	0	3	30
Fred Daly 1946–58	73.370	282	298	4	16	0	0	1	1	0	2	81	1	3	46
Nick Faldo 1976–83	72.187	280	299	8	6	0	0	0	0	3	5	78	0	0	32
Ray Floyd 1975–83	71.643	282	299	7	6	0	0	1	1	2	3	79	0	2	28
Tony Jacklin 1963–83	72.819	280	298	7	20	0	0	0	2	1	4	80	1	2	72
Tony Lema 1964–6	72.166	279	298	3	4	0	0	0	0	3	0	76	1	0	12
Bobby Locke 1937–59	75.034	279	305	12	14	0	0	0	1	4	7	81	4	2	58

Ballesteros failed to complete all four rounds only in his first entry, 1975

Bob Charles competed in every championship between 1961 and 1982

Cotton never failed to complete all four rounds in 1927–48, at which point he did not compete for three years

Faldo never failed to complete all four rounds in 1976–83

In Jacklin's peak years, 1969–72, his stroke average was 70.375

	Career stroke average	Best aggregate	Worst aggregate	Sub-70 rounds	75s and over	64s	65s	66s	67s	68s	69s	Worst round	Wins	2nd or 3rd	Rounds played
Johnny Miller 1971–82	72.488	279	303	9	13	0	0	3	1	2	3	79	1	2	45
Jack Nicklaus 1962–83	71.09	269	305	27	10	0	2	4	3	5	13	83	3	10	89
Greg Norman 1978–83	72.913	283	296	1	6	0	0	0	1	0	0	76	0	0	23
Peter Oosterhuis 1970–83	72.449	282	300	8	13	0	0	1	1	1	5	80	0	2	49
Arnold Palmer 1960–83	72.371	276	300	12	16	0	0	0	2	3	7	79	2	1	70
Gary Player 1956–83	72.667	282	300	14	28	0	0	0	2	5	7	81	3	1	102
Dai Rees 1935–61	73.207	282	307	8	28	0	0	0	1	2	5	83	0	3	82
Peter Thomson 1951–79	72.425	278	301	15	26	0	0	1	3	5	6	81	5	4	113
Lee Trevino 1969–83	71.786	275	301	14	13	0	0	0	2	5	5	79	2	2	56
Roberto de Vicenzo 1948–79	72.663	278	307	9	20	0	0	1	4	2	2	82	1	7	80
Tom Watson 1975–83	70.805	268	297	14	6	1	2	0	2	5	4	81	5	0	36
Tom Weiskopf 1970–83	72.551	276	296	5	10	0	0	0	1	1	3	79	1	0	49

Nicklaus never failed to complete all four rounds in 1962–83

Rees never failed to complete all four rounds in 1935–61, except in 1949

Thomson never failed to complete all four rounds in 1951–73

Trevino never failed to complete all four rounds in 1969–83, if he was entered

Weiskopf failed to complete all four rounds only in 1979 but did not enter in 1981

NOTES

1 The scores used are those issued to the press of the day by the Royal and Ancient.

2 Performances at the ends of careers and, less often, the beginnings have been omitted when it was felt that these would distort a fair picture as, for example, in the case of Fred Daly and Bobby Locke late in their careers.

3 Such players as Locke, Palmer and de Vicenzo did not enter every year.

4 The lowest championship stroke average is Tom Watson's 70.805. He is followed by Nicklaus, Floyd, Crenshaw and Trevino in that order. These are the only players, of those selected, to average under 72 per round.

5 The scores include two- and three-round totals when players did not qualify for the next stage.

Acknowledgements

Although this book is written largely from personal experience, too many books to name individually have been consulted, each yielding a fact or insight here and there. Contemporary accounts in *The Times*, the *Daily Telegraph*, the *Guardian*, the *Field*, the *Illustrated London News*, and *Country Life* have also very frequently been useful.

For quick reference, *Royal and Ancient Championship Records, 1860–1980* and various annual editions of *The Golfer's Handbook* have been particularly valuable, as have the media guides published by the US and European PGAs and the United States Golf Association. Above all, the Royal and Ancient Golf Club of St Andrews has been most helpful in answering any and every query put to it. Gratitude is equally due to golfers both great and not so great who have contributed their own recollections.

A word of thanks is due to several people in the making of this book: to Dave Oswald for his superb maps; to Caroline Hill, the designer; and to Robin Baird-Smith and Gill Gibbins at Collins.

Most of all, I should like to thank all those golfers whose achievements have made this a tale well worth telling.

Index

Note: names in the finishing scores tables have not been indexed; page numbers in *italics* under courses refer to finishing scores.

The
OLD COURSE, ST. ANDREWS

1	370 yards par 4	10	342 yards par 4
2	411 yards par 4	11	172 yards par 3
3	398 yards par 4	12	316 yards par 4
4	463 yards par 4	13	425 yards par 4
5	564 yards par 5	14	567 yards par 5
6	416 yards par 4	15	413 yards par 4
7	372 yards par 4	16	382 yards par 4
8	178 yards par 3	17	461 yards par 4
9	356 yards par 4	18	354 yards par 4

Out 3,528 yards par 36   In 3,432 yards par 36

Total 6,960 yards par 72

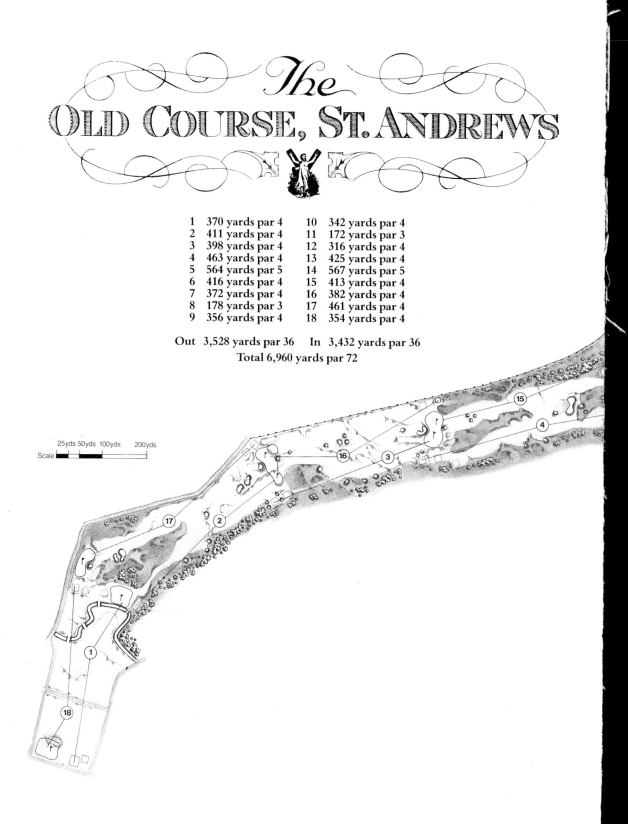

Periglacial processes and landforms in Britain and Ireland

EDITED BY

JOHN BOARDMAN

Department of Humanities and Countryside Research Unit, Brighton Polytechnic

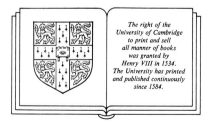

The right of the
University of Cambridge
to print and sell
all manner of books
was granted by
Henry VIII in 1534.
The University has printed
and published continuously
since 1584.

CAMBRIDGE UNIVERSITY PRESS

CAMBRIDGE

NEW YORK   NEW ROCHELLE   MELBOURNE   SYDNEY

Published by the Press Syndicate of the University of Cambridge
The Pitt Building, Trumpington Street, Cambridge CB2 1RP
32 East 57th Street, New York, NY 10022, USA
10 Stamford Road, Oakleigh, Melbourne 3166, Australia
© Cambridge University Press 1987

First published 1987

Printed in Great Britain at the University Press, Cambridge

British Library cataloguing in publication data
Periglacial processes and landforms in
   Britain and Ireland.
   1. Glacial landforms—Great Britain
   I. Boardman, John   II. Quaternary Research
   Association   III. International
   Geographical Union. *Commission on the*
   Significance of Periglacial Phenomena
   551.3'8'0941   QE576

Library of Congress cataloging in publication data
Periglacial processes and landforms in Britain and
   Ireland.

   Papers presented at a symposium held Sept. 21–24,
1985 in Manchester, Eng.
   1. Glacial landforms—Great Britain—Congresses.
2. Glacial landforms—Ireland—Congresses.   I. Boardman,
John.   II. Quaternary Research Association (Great
Britain)   III. International Geographical Union.
Commission on the Significance of Periglacial Phenomena.
GB588.43.P47   1987   551.3'15'0941   86–31059
ISBN 0 521 33250 8

Contents

Contributors

J. Åkerman	Department of Physical Geography, University of Lund, Solvegatan 13, S-223 62, Lund, Sweden
C.K. Ballantyne	Department of Geography, University of St. Andrews, St. Andrews, Fife KY16 9AL, UK
J. Boardman	Department of Humanities and Countryside Research Unit, Brighton Polytechnic, Falmer, Brighton BN1 9PH, UK
R.H. Bryant	Department of Geography, Polytechnic of North London, 383 Holloway Road, London N7 6PN, UK
R.G.O. Burton	Soil Survey of England and Wales, Government Buildings, Block B, Brooklands Avenue, Cambridge CB2 2DR, UK
C.P. Carpenter	Department of Geography, Polytechnic of North London, 383 Holloway Road, London N7 6PN, UK
J.A. Catt	Soils and Plant Nutrition Department, Rothamsted Experimental Station, Harpenden, Herts AL5 2JQ, UK
E.R. Connell	Marathon Oil Ltd., Anderson Drive, Aberdeen AB2 4AZ, UK
P. Coxon	Department of Geography, Trinity College, Dublin, Ireland
A.G. Dawson	Department of Geography, Coventry Polytechnic, Priory Street, Coventry CV1 5FB, UK
M. Dawson	Department of Geography, University College of Wales, Aberystwyth SY23 3DB, UK
T.D. Douglas	Department of Geography and Environmental Studies, Newcastle upon Tyne Polytechnic, Newcastle upon Tyne NE1 8ST, UK
E.A. FitzPatrick	Department of Soil Science, University of Aberdeen, Meston Walk, Aberdeen AB9 2UE, UK
H.M. French	Departments of Geography and Geology, University of Ottawa, Ottawa K1N 6N5, Canada
A.M. Hall	Fettes College, Carrington Road, Edinburgh EH4 1QX, UK
C. Harris	Geography Section, Department of Geology, University College Cardiff, P.O. Box 78, Cardiff CF1 1XL, UK
S. Harrison	Department of Geography and Environmental Studies, Newcastle upon Tyne Polytechnic, Newcastle upon Tyne NE1 8ST, UK
D.W. Hight	Geotechnical Consulting Group, 1A Queensberry Place, London SW7 2DL, UK
J.N. Hutchinson	Department of Civil Engineering, Imperial College, London SW7 2BU, UK
L.C. Jerwood	The Geography Laboratory, University of Sussex, Falmer, Brighton BN1 9QN, UK
J. Karte	Deutsche Forschungsgemeinschaft, Kennedyallee 40, D–5300 Bonn 2, West Germany
D.H. Keen	Department of Geography, Coventry Polytechnic, Priory Street, Coventry CV1 5PB, UK
D.S. Loewenherz	Department of Geography, University of Illinois, 220 Davenport Hall, 607 South Mathews, Urbana, IL 61801, USA
J.A. Matthews	Geography Section, Department of Geology, University College Cardiff, P.O. Box 78, Cardiff CF1 1XL, UK
P. O'Callaghan	202, Glasnevin Avenue, Dublin 11, Ireland
A. Pissart	Laboratoire de Géomorphologie et de Géologie du Quaternaire, Place du 20-aout, 7, B 4000 Liège, Belgium

I.M. Quinn — 37, Laurleen, Stillorgan, County Dublin, Ireland

D.A. Robinson — The Geography Laboratory, University of Sussex, Falmer, Brighton BN1 9QN, UK

J.D. Scourse — Department of Physical Oceanography, Marine Science Laboratories, University College of North Wales, Menai Bridge, Gwynedd LL59 5EY, UK

M. Seppälä — Department of Geography, University of Helsinki, Hallituskatu 11–13, SK–00100, Helsinki 10, Finland

R.A. Shakesby — Department of Geography, University College of Swansea, Singleton Park, Swansea SA2 8PP, UK

C.E. Thorn — Department of Geography, University of Illinois, 220 Davenport Hall, 607 South Mathews, Urbana, IL 61801, USA

J. Warburton — Department of Geography, University of Southampton, Southampton S09 5NH, UK

W.P. Warren — Geological Survey of Ireland, Beggars Bush, Haddington Road, Dublin 4, Ireland

R.G. West — Botany School, University of Cambridge, Downing Street, Cambridge CB2 3EA, UK

R.B.G. Williams — The Geography Laboratory, University of Sussex, Falmer, Brighton BN1 9QN, UK

P. Worsley — Department of Geography, University of Nottingham NG7 2RD, UK

Preface

The landscapes of the British Isles reflect not only the operation of present day geomorphic processes but also the impact of the fluctuating climates of the Quaternary Period. On several occasions during the last two million years ice sheets covered much of northern Britain and Ireland. Those areas to the south of the glacial limits experienced climatic conditions characterised by intense frost action, deep seasonal frost penetration and/or the formation of perennially frozen ground (permafrost). As the ice sheets withdrew, areas previously glaciated were subject to cold non-glacial conditions for a period of time. Today, frost action processes are important to landscape evolution only in the highlands of Scotland, and certain uplands of northern England and permafrost is no longer present.

The intimate link between periglacial geomorphology and Quaternary studies is well illustrated in the British Isles. As a consequence, both the Quaternary Research Association of the United Kingdom and the International Geographical Union Commission on the Significance of Periglacial Phenomena welcomed the opportunity of sponsoring a Symposium dealing specifically with the periglacial processes and landforms of Britain and Ireland. This took place between September 21–24, 1985 in association with, and immediately following, the First International Conference on Geomorphology, at Manchester, England. We wish to acknowledge with pleasure not only the organisers of the First International Conference on Geomorphology for their co-operation, but also Dr. John Boardman, of Brighton Polytechnic, who organised the Symposium and edited the present volume, which arises from that Symposium. We believe this volume is a most useful contribution to our understanding of the Pleistocene environments of Britain and Ireland.

HUGH M. FRENCH
Chairman, IGU Commission of the Significance of Periglacial Phenomena
Ottawa, Canada

JOHN HUTCHINSON
President, Quaternary Research Association,
United Kingdom
London, UK
March, 1986

Introduction

J. BOARDMAN

The analogue approach

The theme of the first part of the book is the search for appropriate analogues for the British periglacial landscape and traditionally this has meant climatic analogues. The problem of searching the current high latitude periglacial zone for conditions analogous to those of mid-latitude Britain in the Pleistocene is now fully appreciated. It is probable that no close analogues exist. An alternative approach, still within the analogue theme, is to use the study of present-day processes in an attempt to understand those of the past. This approach recognises that processes such as ice-wedge formation are not simply governed by mean annual regional temperature but by a host of inter-related lithological, hydrological, vegetational and microclimatic controls. For example, French points out that many relict features will be understood by an appreciation of the dynamics of permafrost aggradation and degradation. A point illustrated in the British context by Burton and Hutchinson and Hight.

We operate, however, within certain severe constraints. Active periglacial landforms are not perfectly understood. The relationship, for example, between the various ground ice features of the pingo/palsa family is still confused (Seppälä) and thus interpretation of relict forms is hazardous. There is probably a terminological problem as well as insufficient direct observational evidence. Local hydrological conditions appear to be critical – rather than regional climate. Unfortunately slope hydrology may be even more difficult to reconstruct than mean annual temperature.

Thorn and Loewenherz emphasise that the rate of adjustment of periglacial features to climatic change varies and the use of analogues will have to take this into account. The role of climatic change in influencing the rate of operation of periglacial processes has rarely been investigated. Rock glaciers in the Colorado Front Range seem to have been more active at certain times in the Holocene than now but there is a danger of circular argument – climatic change being inferred on the basis of enhanced geomorphic activity. In Europe, the response to climatic deterioration of rock-slope weathering processes was rapid (Grove, 1972) whereas that of stream channel systems was far more complex (Rose *et al.*, 1980), perhaps because of the vegetation control on overland flow. The whole topic of the influence on the British landscape of the Little Ice Age has been little studied (Sugden, 1971; Rapson, 1985).

One influential model of landscape change implies a period of rapid adjustment as glaciation ceases – the paraglacial phase (Ryder, 1971). In the British context this is an intriguing idea. Can we detect a paraglacial phase at the end of the Dimlington Stadial (Rose, 1985) or was it delayed, perhaps due to relative aridity, until the Loch Lomond Stadial?

Reviews of the evidence for periglacial conditions in mainland Europe (Pissart and Karte) underline the many similarities with Britain and Ireland and emphasise two important points. (1) The Low Countries are notable in that they have a well developed stratigraphy based on soils developed in loess. Pissart may complain that there is a degree of uncertainty in the details but, for the last glacial stage, the story is far clearer than in Britain. Due to the frequency of periglacial features climatic reconstruction of this period is well advanced. (2) The inferred climatic record emphasises the dominance of stadial conditions and the brevity of interstadial conditions during the Weischelian: periglacial conditions were the norm for the last 70,000 years in ice-free western Europe.

Application of the analogue approach requires an adequate dataset both with regard to the modern features and the relict population. This is a genuine problem with regard to the mapped distribution of ice-wedge casts and pingos in Britain. Both appear to reflect the distribution of research effort. The distributions certainly show local lithological and hydrological controls but it is difficult to argue for climatological controls with incomplete maps. The pingo distribution with clusters in west Wales and East Anglia is probably particularly misleading although new discoveries are filling in the gaps (Bryant and Carpenter). Maps may also contain features of different age: as Rose *et al.* (1985) admit, it is difficult to separate ice-wedge casts of Dimlington Stadial and Loch Lomond Stadial age in many parts of the country.

There is also the possibility that features that were formerly regarded as similar have been incorrectly grouped. West shows that small hollows in Norfolk may have a variety of origins both periglacial and non-periglacial and detailed stratigraphic examination is necessary to establish their true origin (cf. Sparks *et al.*, 1972). Despite these many problems the analogue approach to relict periglacial phenomena is widely used and has to be regarded as one of the conclusive checks on the validity of our explanations. Though we may not find simple geographical analogues in the present periglacial zone we are likely to find processes similar, but perhaps operating at different rates, to those of Pleistocene Britain and Ireland.

Periglacial processes in Britain and Ireland
Review articles by Worsley and Warren refer to the difficulty of placing evidence for periglacial conditions within unsatisfactory stratigraphic frameworks. Both authors prefer to modify the conventionally accepted stratigraphy in the light of recent findings. Although there is general unease with regard to the recommended stratigraphy of Mitchell *et al.* (1973), and revision is likely in the future, there is as yet no widely accepted alternative for terrestrial deposits in Britain and Ireland. This is an unsatisfactory situation but not one unknown to Quaternary studies in other parts of the world. The alternative approach of attempting to fit the field evidence into the schema of Mitchell *et al.* (1973) is used by Connell and Hall. Stratigraphic problems mainly relate to the terminology of pre-Devensian deposits rather than those of the last glacial stage.

Evidence for permafrost is critical in the discussion of the periglacial history of Britain and Ireland, and ice-wedge casts, because of their widespread distribution, are still the major element of this evidence. Here the analogue approach is vital and we require clear criteria for the recognition of former wedges based on the study of currently active forms. The criteria should be applicable in the field by both expert and the less experienced. The doubts expressed about features formerly regarded as evidence of thermal contraction (Black, 1976) have led to some confusion. The danger is that we proceed by the *ad hoc* acceptance or rejection of forms based on personal whim.

Problems of definition of the term 'periglacial' have not inhibited contributors to this book. Some prefer to deal with unequivocal evidence for past permafrost. Others accept that there is a range of cold-climate processes now no longer operative in Britain which may be loosely termed 'periglacial'. The problem of the origin of head looms large in such discussion (Harris). Landforms which were once regarded as good evidence of permafrost are now regarded with some suspicion: ramparted ground ice depressions fall into this category, at least while problems remain over their classification. Thus, what had once seemed an unnecessarily cautious reference to 'presumed ground ice depressions' (Sparks *et al.*, 1972) rather than pingos, now seems well justified. Currently active processes in the British uplands are regarded by Ballantyne as 'periglacial' because of the role of frost in their formation.

One of the major achievements of British Quaternary geomorphology has been the recognition of the widespread effects of the Loch Lomond Stadial on the British landscape (Sissons, 1979). The limits of Loch Lomond Stadial glacier ice have been mapped in detail and thus the periglacial zone has been delineated. It is still debatable as to whether the area beyond the ice margin was affected by permafrost. On the basis of the occurrence of ice-wedge casts, rock glaciers and pingos it has been assumed that discontinuous permafrost existed in most of the country with the exception of the south west Peninsula (e.g. Mitchell, 1977; Watson, 1977; Sissons, 1979); however, neither Ballantyne (1984) nor Worsley regard the evidence as conclusive.

Loch Lomond Stadial glacial events are well documented but the periglacial landscape has to some extent been neglected. This is unfortunate because the landforms of the stadial represent the last phase of periglaciation to affect the British landscape; they are often dramatic and they are often datable. The classic study of the Devil's Kneadingtrough in Kent illustrates this point (Kerney *et al.*, 1964). The fact that at some sites relatively precise dates are available between which sediments can be shown to have accumulated provides an opportunity for assessment of rates of operation of periglacial processes; this is particularly the case with fluvial and alluvial fan sediments e.g. Kerney *et al.*, 1964; Rose *et al.*, 1980. Transportation of gravels at a site in the northern Lake District appears to be at a rate about an order of magnitude higher under Loch Lomond Stadial periglacial conditions than under present day conditions in the same area (Boardman, in press).

Until recently periglacial effects on soils have, with notable exceptions (FitzPatrick, 1956), been neglected. Catt shows that materials resulting directly from periglacial processes, or affected by such processes, are widespread in eastern England. It is now appreciated that the effects of frost on soils can be studied using micromorphological techniques (e.g. Van Vliet-Lanoe, 1985; Kemp, 1985). Cold climate soils formed during periods of relative ground surface stability and under the influence of weathering processes may be used as stratigraphic markers (Rose *et al.*, 1985) as well as contributing to the reconstruction of former periglacial climates. There remains the problem, referred to by Catt, of a relative paucity of periglacial features which have been recognised in British soils compared to those of the continent. Is it that they have gone unrecognised or that they were not formed? A further possibility may be widespread profile truncation due to Holocene erosion especially in southern England.

The climate of periglacial Britain is still insufficiently understood. Mean annual temperature has been inferred from ice-wedge casts but these indicate *maximum* values. July temperatures have been derived from the presence of Coleopteran species. However a range of possible winter temperatures exists: Ballantyne (1984), for example, suggests a value between -15 and $-27\,°C$ for sea level Scotland during the Loch Lomond Stadial. The aridity of Devensian periglacial climates has been noted: this is based on the presence of halophytic plants and is probably due to 'widespread permafrost and the great evaporation caused by a strongly continental climate' (Godwin, 1977). The deposition of loess across southern England during the Dimlington Stadial (Catt, 1978; Wintle, 1980), emphasises the aridity of the climate and the presence of bare, unvegetated ground (Catt, 1977).

Identification of large-scale thermokarst depressions is a relatively new development in British periglacial studies (Burton). The outline of these features is established from detailed soil mapping and aerial photographs and their origin is compared to analogous depressions in Siberia. Depressions which, it is suggested, were produced by the melting of icings have also been described in Britain and are referred to by West. However, their low preservation potential makes the establishment of an icing origin very difficult (Worsley, 1986). Degradation of permafrost at the end of the Dimlington Stadial was also responsible for large

scale landsliding on slopes in the far south of England (Hutchinson and Hight). In the light of these findings, geotechnical re-examination of the camber and valley bulge structures (Hollingworth *et al.*, 1944) of southern England and the Midlands, which have been generally assumed to be the result of the aggradation and degradation of permafrost, would be welcome.

Periglacial slope deposits have a long history of investigation in Britain (de la Beche, 1839; Reid, 1887; Dines *et al.*, 1940) and periglacial processes as agents of mass wasting involving removal of previously weathered regolith are also well documented (Linton, 1955; Waters, 1964). However, the precise process by which the frost-shattered mantle is produced is not understood and laboratory experiments have failed to reproduce similar debris (Williams). Investigation of head deposits shows that at least those of a clay-rich character have moved as a series of shallow slides rather than by gelifluction (Harris). The loessic component of many heads requires further study as does the problem of the identification of breaks in deposition within head sequences. Are we to believe that the thick head sequences of south Devon or some of the chalk dry valley infills (cf. Black Rock, Brighton) are wholly Devensian in age? Must we await the satisfactory dating of raised beach deposits beneath the heads before progress can be made? If, as seems likely, at least some of the beaches are of oxygen isotope stage 7 (Andrews *et al.*, 1979; Davies, 1983) then the story is more complex than has yet been demonstrated. In the Isles of Scilly, as yet unpublished dates on organic material within the head deposits yield ages of 21–34 ka (Scourse). The overlying loess is contemporaneous with the glacial expansion of the Dimlington Stadial and thus an intriguing change of process occurred sometime around 21 ka. In the Cheviots, Douglas and Harrison report large scale solifluction probably during the Loch Lomond Stadial. The solifluction of growan in an area that was glaciated during the Dimlington Stadial raises the question as to when, and by what process, the granite was weathered and why slopes were stable during the earlier part of the Devensian but unstable in the Loch Lomond Stadial? Perhaps the greater availability of moisture in the latter period resulted in widespread mass wasting; the evidence from river systems would support such a suggestion (Rose and Boardman, 1983).

Problems of dating periglacial depositional sequences are referred to by Worsley and Pissart and the value of molluscs is reviewed by Keen. Molluscs have been widely used in Britain for both dating and climatic reconstruction. They have been especially important in periglacial deposits which frequently lack pollen and other fossil material. Two problems are apparent: the similarity of many cold-climate mollusc assemblages, a problem in common with other fossil groups – see Godwin (1977); Coope (1977); Stuart (1977); and the fact that faunal assemblages reflect micro-climatic rather than regional conditions.

In conclusion, this volume is an indication of the state of health of British and Irish periglacial studies. It is not comprehensive and certain topics are poorly represented: for example, the 1960's and 1970's interest in patterned ground seems to have waned (Williams, 1964; Ball and Goodier, 1970; Evans, 1979). However, the number and variety of contributions is encouraging. One characteristic of the British contributors is that few would regard themselves as periglacial specialists – most possess strong interests in other branches of geomorphology, soil science, geology and engineering. This situation is not without advantage since cross-disciplinary links have clearly produced a useful stimulus – to take two examples, the pedological and the geotechnical inputs to several of these papers are notable. Other aspects of periglacial studies have been slow to take off. Worsley (1977) noted the lack of interest in fluvial systems in the periglacial landscape; alluvial fans remain a potential source of information (Boardman, 1985) and snow-bed features appear to be widespread in the uplands but have been studied either as isolated examples (Colhoun, 1981; Vincent and Lee, 1982; Ballantyne, 1985), or as aspects of the Loch Lomond Stadial glacial landscape (Sissons, 1980; Gray, 1982); detailed geomorphological mapping suggests that they demand consideration in their own right (Oxford, 1985).

The comparative lack of interest in the rate of operation of periglacial processes has already been noted. Without such information the overall contribution of periglaciation to landscape development is difficult to evaluate. There are clear and necessary links in this area of study with the analogue approach. Most assessments of the impact of periglaciation have been qualitative rather than quantitative and no recent review along the lines of Williams (1968) has been attempted.

The relationship of periglacial studies with Quaternary geomorphology is obviously well established and productive; that with process geomorphology is less developed and perhaps the bill of health in this area should read 'could do better'.

Acknowledgements

I would like to acknowledge the help and encouragement of Professor H.M. French in both the organisation of the Symposium and the editing of this book. Several members of the Q.R.A. gave valuable support at the Symposium. I thank Dr R.B.G. Williams for comments on this introduction.

References (additional to contributions to this volume)

Andrews, J.T., Bowen, D.Q. and Kidson, C. (1979). Amino acid ratios and the correlation of raised beach deposits in south-west England and Wales. *Nature* **281**, 556–8.

Ball, D.F. and Goodier, R. (1970). Morphology and distribution of features resulting from frost-action in Snowdonia. *Field Studies* **3**, 193–218.

Ballantyne, C.K. (1984). The Late Devensian periglaciation of upland Scotland. *Quat. Sci. Revs.* **3**, 311–43.

Ballantyne, C.K. (1985). Nivation landforms and snowpatch erosion on two massifs in the northern Highlands of Scotland. *Scott. Geogr. Mag.*, **101**, 40–8.

de la Beche, H.T. (1839). *Report on the Geology of Cornwall, Devon and West Somerset*. Mem. Geol. Surv. United Kingdom.

Black, R.F. (1976). Periglacial features indicative of permafrost: ice and soil wedges. *Quat. Res.*, **6**, 3–26.

Boardman, J. (1985). The northeastern Lake District: periglacial slope deposits. In, *Field Guide to the Periglacial Landforms of Northern England* (Ed. J. Boardman), pp. 23–37, Quaternary Research Association, Cambridge.

Boardman, J. (in press). Glacial and Periglacial geomorphology around Keswick. *Proc. Cumbs. Geol. Soc.*

Catt, J.A. (1977). Loess and coversands. In, *British Quaternary Studies, Recent Advances* (Ed. F.W. Shotton), pp. 221–30, Clarendon Press, Oxford.

Catt, J.A. (1978). The contribution of loess to soils in lowland Britain. *Counc. Brit. Arch. Res. Rep.*, **21**, 12–20.

Colhoun, E.A. (1981). A protalus rampart from the western Mourne Mountains, Northern Ireland. *Irish Geog.*, **14**, 85–90.

Coope, G.R. (1977). Quaternary Coleoptera as aids in the interpretation of environmental history. In, *British Quaternary Studies, Recent Advances* (Ed. F.W. Shotton), pp. 55–68, Clarendon Press, Oxford.

Davies, K.H. (1983). Amino acid analysis of Pleistocene marine molluscs from the Gower Peninsula. *Nature* **302**, 137–9.

Dines, H.G., Hollingworth, S.E., Edwards, W., Buchan, S., and Welsh, F.B.A. (1940). The mapping of head deposits. *Geol. Mag.*, **77**, 198–226.

Evans, R. (1979). Observations on a stripe pattern. *Biul. Perygl.*, **25**, 9–22.

FitzPatrick, E.A. (1956). An indurated soil horizon formed by permafrost. *Jour. Soil Sci.*, **7**, 248–54.

Godwin, H. (1977). Quaternary history of the British flora. In, *British Quaternary Studies, Recent Advances* (Ed. F.W. Shotton), pp. 107–18, Clarendon Press, Oxford.

Gray, J.M. (1982). The last glaciers (Loch Lomond Advance) in Snowdonia, N. Wales. *Geol. Jour.*, **17**, 111–33.

Grove, J.M. (1972). The incidence of landslides, avalanches and floods in western Norway during the Little Ice Age. *Arc. Alp. Res.*, **4**, 131–8.

Hollingworth, S.E., Taylor, J.H., and Kellaway, G.A. (1944). Large scale superficial structures in the Northamptonshire Ironstone field. *Quart. Jour. Geol. Soc. Lond.*, **100**, 1–44.

Kemp, R.A. (1985). *Soil Micromorphology and the Quaternary*. Quaternary Research Association Technical Guide No. 2, Cambridge.

Kerney, M.P., Brown, E.H., and Chandler, T.J. (1964). The late glacial and post glacial history of the Chalk escarpment near Brook, Kent. *Phil. Trans. Roy. Soc. Lond. B*, **248**, 135–204.

Linton, D.L. (1955). The problem of tors. *Geog. Jour.*, **121**, 470–87.

Mitchell, G.F. (1977). Periglacial Ireland. *Phil Trans. Roy. Soc. Lond. B*, **280**, 199–208.

Mitchell, G.F., Penny, L.F., Shotton, F.W., and West, R.G. (1973). A correlation of Quaternary deposits in the British Isles. *Geol. Soc. Lond. Spec. Rep.*, 4.

Oxford, S.P. (1985). Protalus ramparts, protalus rock glaciers and soliflucted till in the northwest part of the English Lake District. In, *Field Guide to the Periglacial Landforms of Northern England* (Ed. J. Boardman), pp. 38–46, Quaternary Research Association, Cambridge.

Rapson, S.C. (1985). Minimum age of corrie moraine ridges in the Cairngorm Mountains, Scotland. *Boreas* **14**, 155–9.

Reid, C. (1887). On the origin of dry valleys and of coombe rock. *Quart. Jour. Geol. Soc. Lond.*, **43**, 364–73.

Rose, J. (1985). The Dimlington Stadial/Dimlington Chronozone: a proposal for naming the main glacial episode of the Late Devensian in Britain. *Boreas* **14**, 225–30.

Rose, J., and Boardman, J. (1983). River activity in relation to short-term climatic deterioration *Quat. Studies in Poland* **4**, 189–98.

Rose, J., Turner, C., Coope, G.R., and Bryan, M.D. (1980). Channel changes in a lowland river catchment over the last 13,000 years. In, *Timescales in Geomorphology* (Eds. R.A. Cullingford. D.A. Davidson and J. Lewin), pp. 159–75, John Wiley, Chichester.

Rose, J., Boardman, J., Kemp, R.A., and Whiteman, C.A. (1985). Palaeosols and the interpretation of the British Quaternary stratigraphy. In, *Geomorphology and Soils* (Eds. K.S. Richards, R.R. Arnett and S. Ellis), pp. 348–75, Allen and Unwin, London.

Ryder, J.M. (1971). The stratigraphy and morphology of paraglacial alluvial fans in south-central British Columbia. *Can. Jour. Earth Sci.*, **8**, 279–98.

Sissons, J.B. (1979). The Loch Lomond Stadial in the British Isles. *Nature* **280**, 199–203.

Sissons, J.B. (1980). The Loch Lomond Advance in the Lake District, northern England. *Trans. Roy. Soc. Edin. Earth Sci.*, **71**, 13–27.

Sparks, B.W., Williams, R.B.G., and Bell, F.G. (1972). Presumed ground ice depressions in East Anglia. *Proc. Roy. Soc. Lond. A* **327**, 329–43.

Stuart, A.J. (1977). British Quaternary vertebrates. In, *British Quaternary Studies, Recent Advances* (Ed. F.W. Shotton), pp. 69–82. Clarendon Press, Oxford.

Sugden, D.E. (1971). Did glaciers form in the Cairngorms in the 17–19th Centuries? *Cairn. Club Jour.*, **97**, 189–201.

Van Vliet-Lanoe, B. (1985). Frost effects in soils. In, *Soils and Quaternary Landscape Evolution* (Ed. J. Boardman), pp. 117–58, Wiley, Chichester.

Vincent, P.J., and Lee, M.P. (1982). Snow patches on Farleton Fell, south-east Cumbria. *Geog. Jour.* **148**, 337–42.

Waters, R.S. (1964). The Pleistocene legacy to the geomorphology of Dartmoor. In, *Dartmoor Essays* (Ed. I.G. Simmons), pp. 73–96, The Devonshire Association.

Watson, E. (1977). The periglacial environment of Great Britain during the Devensian. *Phil. Trans. Roy. Soc. Lond. B*, **280**, 183–97.

Williams, R.B.G. (1964). Fossil patterned ground in eastern England. *Biul. Perygl.*, 337–49.

Williams, R.B.G. (1968). Some estimates of periglacial erosion in southern and eastern England. *Biul. Perygl.*, **17**, 311–35.

Wintle, A.G. (1980). Thermoluminescence dating of late Devensian loesses in southern England. *Nature* **289**, 479–80.

Worsley, P. (1977). Periglaciation. In, *British Quaternary Studies, Recent Advances* (Ed. F.W. Shotton), pp. 205–20, Clarendon Press, Oxford.

Worsley, P. (1986). Periglacial environment. *Prog. Phy. Geog.*, **10**, 265–74.

PART I

The search for analogues

1 · Periglacial forms of Svalbard: a review

JONAS ÅKERMAN

Abstract

Svalbard has, in spite of its high latitude, climatic conditions which are probably very close to those which prevailed within the west and southwest parts of the periglacial zone of the last European glaciation. There is a diversity of active periglacial processes and forms and in some cases they appear to be at an optimum, or at least, extremely well developed. Compared with many other northern areas its periglacial forms and processes are fairly well known and there is abundant climatological and geological background data. However, the lack of quantitative process data is still a problem. This paper reviews the characteristics and the distribution of some major groups of periglacial processes and forms in Svalbard seen in relation to some important environmental factors.

Introduction

Svalbard is an archipelago some 800 km north of Scandinavia bounded by the Norwegian and the Barnets Seas. It covers an area of 62,400 km² between 74° and 81° N and 10° and 35° E. Svalbard with its largest island, Spitsbergen (39,000 km²), occupies a historic and strategic location for the study of glacial and periglacial phenomena (Figure 1.1).

Environmental reconstruction using evidence of relic and fossil periglacial features is necessarily based upon the characteristics and distribution of comparable active features and their climatological environments. In this respect the most useful features are those indicative of permafrost as they contain more specific climatological information than many other cold climate features. The strongest indicators of permafrost are pingos and ice wedges. Pingo remnants are proof of former permafrost and hence of mean annual ground temperatures well below 0 °C. Although different types of frost cracks may develop at mean annual air temperatures above 0 °C, ice-wedge casts indicate former permafrost. However, these two examples are among many indicators of past climate.

It has been suggested that the majority of periglacial landforms are delicate forms not likely to be fossilized. This may only be partly true. In present periglacial regions a broad spectra of cryogenic landforms and processes within the active layer may occur within small areas or regions. An example of this is on the strandflats of western Spitsbergen (Figure 1.2). It is hard to imagine why only ice wedges and pingos should leave permanent and useful traces after a climatic change.

Climate

Despite some gaps in the record climatological data are available from 1911 (Figure 1.1 & Table 1.1). Svalbard has an arctic maritime climate due to the moderating effects of the northerly flow of the Gulf Stream which keeps the west coast of Spitsbergen ice free longer than other areas of comparable latitude. Within the region there are great climatic differences caused by topography, continentality, sea ice and sea current conditions (Steffensen, 1969; Åkerman, 1978, 1980). As general surveys of the climate and its recent variations in the region have been given in several publications (Birkeland, 1930; Spinnanger, 1968; Steffensen, 1969; Baranowski, 1975; Vinje, 1977–1983; Svensson, 1978; Åkerman, 1978, 1980) only some basic figures concerning air temperatures will be given here.

Air temperatures are characterised by the relatively high mean values and great temperature fluctuations during the winter. The difference between the highest and lowest monthly means in January-February is about 22 °C at Isfjord Radio and Longyearbyen. Among the stations in Spitsbergen, Longyearbyen has the most distinctive continental climate with winter temperatures c. 2 °C lower, and summer temperatures c. 2 °C higher, than Isfjord Radio on the west coast (Table 1.1).

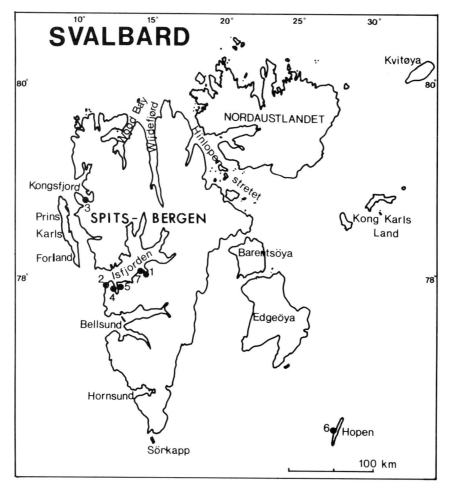

Figure 1.1. Location of sites in Svalbard.
1. Longyearbyen, 2. Kapp Linne and Isfjord Radio,
3. Ny Ålesund, 4. Green harbour, 5. Barentsburg,
6. Hopen and 7. Svalbard lufthamn.

The best indicator of both the intensity and the duration of cold temperatures is the freezing degree day index (cf. Harris, 1980, 1982). Longyearbyen has a mean annual freezing degree day index of 2467 °C days, and Isfjord Radio has 1944 °C days. These two stations are well within the zone of permafrost (cf. Harris, 1980, p. 89) but climatologically they are slightly anomalous compared with other stations at this latitude. If we compare the present day climate with the estimated conditions in western Europe during the last glaciation we find correlations which are good enough to permit the use of Spitsbergen as an area where we can search for analogues (Figure 1.3).

Permafrost

In North America there is good relation between the present-day mean annual air temperature and the permafrost distribution (Brown, 1960, 1963, 1972, 1973a & b). Permafrost occurrence, thickness, and temperature conditions are affected by many climatological factors, not only air temperature. Other factors are: local and micro climate, geological material and structure, vegetation, slope inclination and aspect, hydrology, geothermal activity, glaciers, fire and human activities (Brown & Péwé, 1973). The relationship of mean annual air temperature and permafrost in Arctic North America (Brown & Péwé, 1973) and Asia (Baranow, 1964),

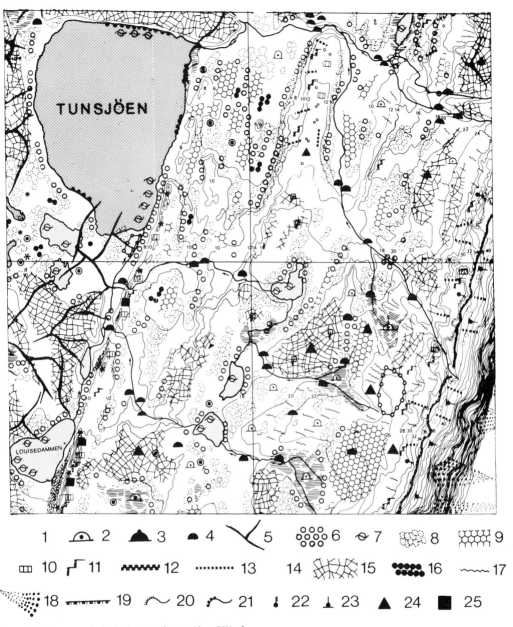

Figure 1.2. Geomorphological map of area 4 km SW of Kapp Linné, west Spitsbergen showing features which are typical of the strandflats of west Spitsbergen (after Åkerman 1980). 1. Hummock 2. Pals or group of palsas 3. Frost blister (large) 4. Frost blister (small) 5. Ice-wedge polygon 6. Sorted circle 7. Sorted circle below water level 8. Sorted net 9. Sorted polygons 10. Sorted polygons (small) 11. Sorted steps 12. Sorted stripes 13. Sorted stripes (small) 14. Non-sorted circle 15. Soil wedges 16. Non-sorted polygons 17. Non-sorted stripes 18. Talus cones 19. Gelifluction sheets 20. Gelifluction lobe (non-sorted) 21. Gelifluction lobe (sorted) 22. Ploughing block 23. Braking block 24. Ventifacts 25. Wind abraded rock surface. *Scale:* the grid is 1 km × 1 km.

Table 1.1 Annual and monthly means of air temperature at some stations within the Svalbard region.

	J	F	M	A	M	J	J	A	S	O	N	D	Year	Period
1. Longyearbyen	−12.1	−15.3	−14.4	−10.7	−3.2	2.8	6.3	5.1	0.8	−5.2	−9.2	−12.4	−5.8	1957–75
2. Isfjord Radio	−11.5	−11.7	−12.5	−9.3	−3.4	1.7	4.7	4.3	1.0	−3.5	−7.1	−9.6	−4.7	1951–75
3. Ny Ålesund	−12.8	−13.9	−13.1	−11.1	−3.8	2.1	5.2	4.1	0.1	−5.5	−9.7	−11.7	−5.8	1971–80
4. Green Harbour	−11.4	−14.1	−12.9	−9.7	−3.0	1.2	5.4	4.7	0.7	−5.2	−8.7	−11.0	−5.3	1911–30
5. Barentsburg													−4.5	?
6. Hopen	−13.7	−13.0	−13.9	−10.9	−4.7	−0.3	2.0	2.3	0.6	−3.0	−7.5	−10.6	−6.1	1951–80
7. Svalbard Lufthamn	−16.7	−17.3	−16.0	−12.7	−4.4	1.9	6.3	4.9	−0.1	−5.5	−9.7	−13.5	−6.8	1976–80
8. Björnön	−7.9	−7.4	−7.5	−5.4	−1.4	2.0	4.4	4.5	2.7	−0.3	−3.1	−6.0	−2.1	1951–80

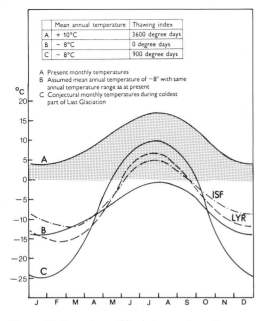

	Mean annual temperature	Thawing index
A	+ 10°C	3600 degree days
B	− 8°C	0 degree days
C	− 8°C	900 degree days

A Present monthly temperatures
B Assumed mean annual temperature of −8° with same annual temperature range as at present
C Conjectural monthly temperatures during coldest part of Last Glaciation

Figure 1.3. Present monthly air temperature at standard meteorological height at Isfjord Radio (ISF) and Longyearbyen (LYR) compared with present and conjectural monthly air temperatures in central England (partly after Williams, 1975, Figure 2).

indicates that Spitsbergen has a milder climate than that generally expected for permafrost regions. All observations, however, indicate that the entire Svalbard region lies well within the zone of continuous permafrost (Liestøl, 1977, pp. 9–10). This is also indicated on maps showing the distribution of permafrost in the northern hemisphere (e.g. Péwé 1969, p. 5; Washburn, 1979, p. 25). Therefore climatic variables other than the mean annual air temperature must be taken into account. In this situation the use of freeze/thaw indices can explain the complex nature of climate/process connections in the periglacial environment (Harris, 1980).

Permafrost data show that the thickness of permafrost can vary between 75 and 450 m (Liestøl, 1977; cf. also Orvin, 1944). The variations are probably a result of the presence of comparatively warm water along the west coast, areas with extensive glaciers, the variable topography, the geothermal activity, and the great local climatological differences (Salvigsen & Elgersma, 1985).

Ground ice

Pingos
In the majority of early observations and on old maps pingos are classified as some type of moraine.

After Müller's paper on pingos in East Greenland several reports of pingos in Spitsbergen appeared (Friend, 1959; FitzPatrick, 1960; Wirtman, 1964; Harland, 1965; Autenboer & Loy, 1966; Piper & Porritt, 1966; Svensson, 1971; Åhman, 1973). These and some new observations were reviewed by Liestøl (1977).

Pingos occur in Svalbard mainly in the valley bottoms of central Spitsbergen, especially between Isfjorden and Van Mijenfjorden. In other areas of the Archipelago they appear to be less common (Liestøl, 1977). The distribution is probably connected with lithology, morphology and permafrost-hydrology rather than with climatic conditions. The majority of the pingos are of the open system type (Svensson, 1970; Åhman, 1973; Liestøl, 1977), but those in the lower parts of the large valleys, very low delta surfaces, and in the estuaries are probably of the closed system type (Svensson, 1970).

Ice wedges
Together with pingos, ice wedges are indicative of permafrost. Their widespread occurrence and distinctive surface manifestation make them one of the most characteristic features of the periglacial landscape.

In Svalbard most of the low relief, poorly drained tundra surfaces along the coasts and in the valley bottoms are characterised by distinctive polygonal patterns (Figure 1.4). These patterns are often the surface manifestation of ice wedges. The average dimensions of the polygons range from 10 to 40 m, but patterns as wide as 150 m can be found (Svensson, 1969, 1970, 1973; Åkerman, 1980). From the investigations of Svensson (1969, 1970, 1973, 1976b) we know that the polygons on the vegetation-covered valley bottom of the Adventdalen valley, and in similar valleys of central Spitsbergen, are ice-wedge polygons. The ice wedges are active and have been used as indicators of recent climatic fluctuations (Svensson, 1976a). Péwé (1966) has concluded that ice wedges develop in areas where the mean annual temperature is −6 °C or colder. Taking into consideration local conditions the climate in the valley bottoms of Spitsbergen will fall within this limit.

It is difficult to determine the distribution of ice wedges in Spitsbergen. From studies by Jahn (1961, 1963) from Hornsund in the south and my own observations along the strandflats of west Spitsbergen it is clear that ice and soil-wedge polygons are commonly confused. Polygons of 10–20 m across are one of the most characteristic features in the landscape along the strandflats, and on raised

Figure 1.4. Large ice wedge polygon furrow 3 km SW of Kapp Linné, west Spitsbergen. Prof. Alfred Jahn for scale.

beach ridges all around the region. They are commonly classified as ice-wedge polygons. However, on the well-drained, raised beach ridges there are also soil wedges which are confined to the active layer and the upper 10–50 cm of the permafrost (Jahn, 1963, 1975; Åkerman, 1980) (Figure 1.5). Further research on the characteristics and distribution of the ice wedge and soil-wedge polygons in Spitsbergen is required before a clear picture can be given.

Icings

Icings (naled, Aufeis) formed by extrusive ice are a fairly common periglacial feature in Svalbard. There are several references to icings in the literature but specific studies have only been carried out by Orvin (1944), Liestøl (1977) and Åkerman (1980, 1982b). More than a hundred observations of different types of icings make it possible to classify them into major groups based upon their genesis.

Spring icings include those formed from groundwater springs in bedrock as well as from the soil cover. The springs may originate from water-bearing strata below the permafrost, as well as from intra-permafrost taliks. They vary greatly in size, from very small temporary features to large perennial or semi-perennial icings covering several km^2.

Thermal spring icings are rare in Spitsbergen, the largest ones being those associated with the thermal springs in the Woodfjorden and from Sörkapp Land north of the Oslokbreen glacier. Typical of this type of icing is that it is normally found at some distance from the source as it takes a longer time for the water to cool to the freezing point.

Pingo icings are quite common and are represented by small icings that are formed on and around pingos. Most of the pingos in Spitsbergen are of the 'open system' type which often have an artesian flow discharging water all the year around.

River or stream icings are numerous in the valleys of Spitsbergen. They often cover large areas of the floodplains of braided streams but they melt early in the summer. They are rarely seen in air photographs which are normally taken in August.

100 m

Figure 1.5. Aerial photograph of raised beach ridges with soil wedges and ice wedges in an area between Lake Linné and the Isfjorden 10 km east of Kapp Linné, west Spitsbergen. Detail from Norsk Polarinstitutt air photo No. S69 2436.

Glacier icings are the most common type in the region (Figure 1.6). The sub-polar glaciers that dominate the region normally discharge water also during the cold season, and therefore many of them have icings in their terminal areas. The glaciers also cut unfrozen aquifers and insulate the ground so that no permafrost exists beneath them. Most of the icings in front of the glaciers are not fed by water from the glacier itself, but rather from groundwater 'released' by the direct or indirect action of the glacier. Such icings are often of a considerable size and are of great importance to the geomorphological processes in front of glaciers.

Icings are directly or indirectly responsible for the formation of pavements, icing hollows, icing depressions, disturbed stream profiles and distinctive drainage patterns (Kozarski, 1975; Åkerman, 1980, 1982*b*). The formation of esker-like ridges in channels upon or inside icings or transverse ridges upon river beds has been described by Cegla & Kozarski (1977), Humlum (1979) and Åkerman

(1980, 1982). Icings may also provide information about recent climatic variations (Åkerman, 1980).

Palsa-like mounds

Apart from notes of turf hummocks in bogs and vegetation-covered valley bottoms (Jersak, 1968; Jahn, 1975) the number of observations of palsa-like features from Spitsbergen is small (Åkerman, 1973, 1980, 1982*a*; Salvigsen, 1977; Åhman, 1977). The palsa-like features in Spitsbergen include a variety of forms which resemble the traditional palsa but may have a completely different genesis. Observations show that four types can be distinguished (Åkerman 1982*a*, p. 47).

(a) Palsas – found in bog areas on the strandflats or the wide valley bottoms. The features are generally small, not exceeding 1.3 m in height and 10 m in diameter, and they are more or less circular (Figure 1.7). They are built up by ice layers (2–15 cm thick) of segregation ice, and the material

Figure 1.6. Icing in front of Pedersenbreen Glacier,
Kongsfjorden 10 km east of Ny Ålesund, Spitsbergen
(Part of Norsk Polarinstitutt aerial photo
No. S69 2436. Approximate scale 1:2500.

Figure 1.7. Palsa in a small bog 3 km south of Kapp Linné, Spitsbergen.

from the surface down to the bog bottom is peat with a low but increasing amount of mineral particles with depth.

The bogs of the region often show several examples of collapsed palsas. Small circular pools on the bog surface or peat ramparts with small pools in the centre are common.

(b) Frost blisters – this type can have the same size, form, and general appearance as the palsa. Generally frost blisters have steeper sides and cracks occur more frequently on the surface. Their position in the terrain is different from the palsas as they are generally found in the marginal part of a bog, along streams, lake and pond shores or near springs. The association with flowing water and/or a hydrological soil or ground-water gradient is often a diagnostic criterion. The internal structure is dominated by a massive ice core of injection ice (Figure 1.8). The peat cover is generally thin, 10–30 cm, and in the very characteristic surface cracks the ice is often visible. The form appears to be less stable than the palsas as melting and collapsing forms are frequently found.

(c) Active layer mounds – have been found on the vast grass and moss covered valley bottoms with an ice-wedge polygon pattern. Their form and general appearance can be similar to those of the palsas but they are in most cases smaller and their internal structure is different. They often lack a distinct peat layer, and they are exclusively found in the wet central parts of low centre ice-wedge polygons. Their internal structure is characterised by a massive ice core of segregation ice situated between the vegetation or a thin peat mat and the underlying mineral soil. Cracks and ruptures are common and the form is unstable, as a rule surviving only one or a few summers (French, 1971, pp. 32–38).

(d) Vegetation peat mounds – are quite different from the other three types since frost and ground ice formation are not responsible for their formation. The general appearance, size, and form are often similar to the palsas, and the peat material also shows similarities to the palsa. The position in the terrain is, however, different. They are generally found in dry localities, upon raised beach ridges

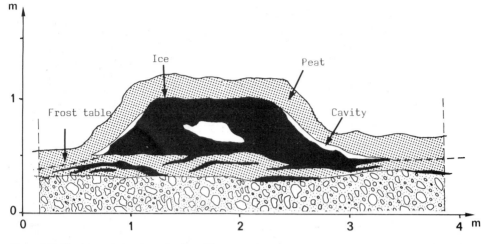

Figure 1.8. The internal structure of a frost blister formed by injection ice at the margin of a small bog 4 km south of Kapp Linné, Spitsbergen.

and other exposed places without any connection with running water. This position in the terrain is generally a diagnostic criterion. An excavation often shows a piece of driftwood, a whale bone, or some other animal remains. The salts and minerals released have accelerated the growth of mosses and grasses. When about 30 cm thick the insulating effect of the peat is strong enough to permit the formation of a frozen core with segregation ice which will enhance mound formation (Figure 1.9). The form is apparently stable as no signs of degenerated forms have been observed. The term 'bird-perches' which is commonly used for similar

forms can also be conveniently used in this case.

Unfortunately palsas and mounds of the types described above cannot be expected to survive a dramatic climatic change or leave any significant trace of value in the study of fossil periglacial environments.

Thermokarst

The term thermokarst which was first used to describe an irregular, hummocky terrain due to the melting of ground ice is now applied to the process of melting ground ice, irrespective of origin, and the landforms resulting from it. The term is used not

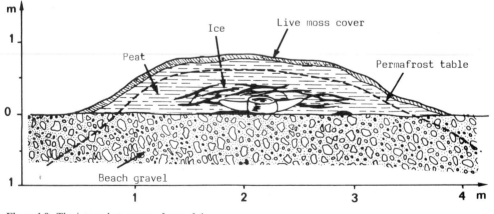

Figure 1.9. The internal structure of one of the 'vegetation peat mounds' on a raised beach ridge 4 km east of Kapp Linné, Spitsbergen. The feature in the centre of the mound is a vertebra from a whale.

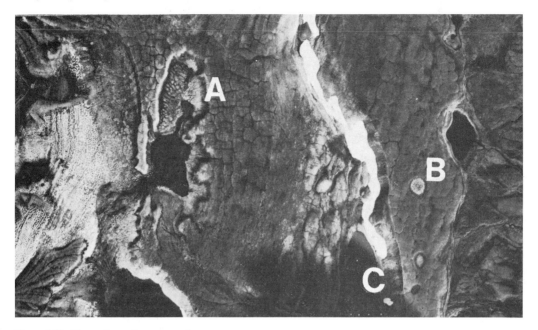

Figure 1.10. Thermokarst features on the Vardeborgsletta plain, 12 km east of Kapp Linné, Spitsbergen. A. Thermokarst basin B. Thermokarst doline and C. Thermal erosion slope along a small stream. Enlargement of Norsk Polar-institutt airphoto No. S69 2436. Approximate scale 1:2500.

only for processes of subsidence and collapse, but also for processes like thermal abrasion, thermal erosion, and thermo-erosional wash.

The complex of thermokarst processes is regarded as a dominant process operating on the periglacial landscape. All land surfaces which earlier were underlain by permafrost have to some extent been affected by thermokarst while the area was exposed to postglacial climatic change. Thermokarst is also one of the most common results of man-induced disturbance of the ground surface in permafrost environments. The principal effects of thermokarst are collapse features, surface pits, basins, ponds, funnel-shaped sinks and dolines (cf. Popov, 1956; Kachurin, 1962; Dylik, 1964). A detailed discussion of the range of thermokarst forms is given by Czudek & Demek (1970, 1971, 1973).

There are not many studies or reports directly concerning thermokarst in Spitsbergen. However, thermokarst processes, and forms resulting from them can be seen almost everywhere. In some areas like the Vardeborgsletta plain on the west coast thermokarst processes completely dominate the landscape (Figure 1.10). This area is probably also affected by traditional karst processes (Salvigsen &

Elgersma, 1985). Svensson (1970) has reported thermokarst in ice-wedge polygon nets due to thermo-erosion by flowing water along the polygon furrows in the Adventdalen valley. Similar features have been observed in several of the wide valleys of central Spitsbergen and also in the strandflat areas of the west coast. Thermokarst in association with pingos has been described by Liestøl (1977), Svensson (1970) and Åhman (1973). Their observations show thermokarst induced primarily by the cracking of the pingo during growth, but also by rivers and coastal erosion. Ponds and lakes of thermokarst origin with some resemblance to orientated lakes have been observed in the lower parts of some of the widest valleys of central Spitsbergen. Thermokarst processes give rise to ravines, niches, undercuts, slumps, earth flows, and rapid coastline retreat along steep shores (Dineley, 1953). Intensified thermokarst along the coast could be an indicator of current isostatic subsidence within the region.

Patterned ground

Patterned ground is one of the most characteristic features of the periglacial environment and has been used as a tool for gaining understanding of

Figure 1.11. Well developed sorted circles and sorted
nets on the southern shore of the Tunsjöen Lake
5 km S of Kapp Linné, Spitsbergen.

Figure 1.12. Large sorted polygons 3.5 km east of
Kapp Linné, Spitsbergen. The diameter of the
polygons varies between 4 and 12 metres.

active processes under different environmental controls. The different forms provide us with information on the lithological, hydrological and climatological situation when they formed and are of value for the reconstruction of past environmental conditions.

Patterned ground is extremely common and well developed in the Svalbard region and especially on the strandflat areas along the west and north coasts (Figures 1.11 & 1.12). It is impossible to go into any detail regarding patterned ground in this paper except to consider the abundance of patterned ground features in this periglacial area and the scarcity of fossil forms in western Europe and southern Scandinavia. Generally it is agreed that the majority of patterned ground forms are too small, too dynamic, or too fragile to leave traces that could be useful. However, it is very difficult to understand why some of the forms and structures would disappear without leaving any traces. It might be that we have not yet looked in the right places or with the correct methods.

Wind action

The direct and indirect action of wind may be of great value when reconstructing past periglacial environments (Johnsson, 1960, 1978; Svensson, 1972; Jahn, 1975; French, 1976; Washburn, 1979). Disregarding the extremely important indirect effects of the wind, like the distribution and redistribution of the snow cover, wind action is important in the discussion about environmental reconstruction, mainly because of formation of ventifacts, stone pavements, frosted sand grains, block and rock polish, loess and other aeolian deposits. All these features have a good potential for being preserved and therefore provide information about past environmental conditions.

Signs of direct wind action in the form of ventifacts and stone pavements are very common in Spitsbergen (Figure 1.13). In fact almost all ice-free surfaces (including nunataks) that are exposed to the wind during the winter months show some kind of wind effect. Some areas like the strandflats with exposed raised beach ridges and rock outcrops,

Figure 1.13. Ventifact with polish and surface facets showing a wind direction from north-north east. The ventifact is one of several upon a raised beach ridge just north of Lake Linné, Spitsbergen.

exposed mountain walls, and some of the flat mountain plateaus, have ventifacts and wind-abraded surfaces as one of their main geomorphological features. The dominant morphogenetic wind direction apart from local deviations, is from the north east (Åkerman 1980). A large number of ventifact observations are from sites where the presence of wind transported mineral particles is very unlikely. In these cases the abrasive material must be wind transported snow and ice crystals. Experiments performed in the field around Isfjord Radio have verified this theory (Åkerman, 1980, 1983).

Aeolian deposits of any significance like dunes or thick cover-sands have not been reported, but minor areas with dunes, loess and sand accumulations can be found along the coast and on river and outwash plains. The erosion and transport of fines in suspension is, however, apparently fairly high (Baranowski & Pekala, 1982; Czeppe, 1968; Åkerman, 1980, pp. 242–244). The very common stone and pebble pavements which can be found mainly at low level along the coast support this statement.

Slope processes

There is no one slope form or group of slope forms which may be regarded as unique to the periglacial environment but many mass wasting processes and slope forms reach their greatest intensity and efficiency under periglacial conditions. For example almost no other geomorphologic feature is as well developed and widespread in Spitsbergen as the talus slope. This may indicate that the conditions for talus formation today are extremely favourable in the region.

There is fairly detailed knowledge of large scale slope processes in Spitsbergen (Rapp, 1960; Jahn, 1960; Bibus, 1975; Swett et al., 1980; Larsson, 1982; Åkerman, 1984; Lindner & Marks, 1985). A recent review including the latest results from Spitsbergen is given by Rapp (1985b). Recent research on talus slopes has concentrated on secondary processes like debris flows and avalanches. Debris flows are widespread and well developed in Spitsbergen especially on north and north east facing slopes and in narrow valleys (Figure 1.14; Åkerman, 1984). The debris flows observed in central Spitsbergen are mainly triggered by intense rainfall (Thiedig &

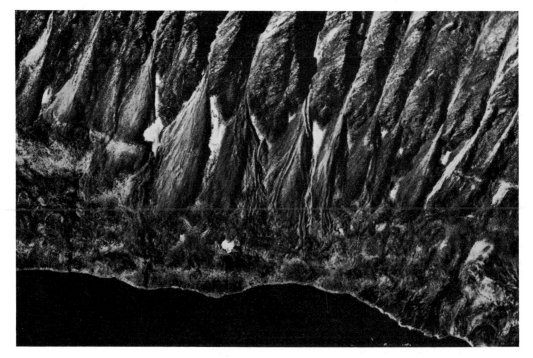

Figure 1.14. Talus cones with debris flow tracks on the east facing slope of the Griegaksla mountain ridge, 10 km east of Kapp Linné, Spitsbergen. Enlargement of Norsk Polarinstitutt air photograph no. S69 2438 (Aug. 19, 1969). Approximate scale 1:10 000.

Figure 1.15. Gelifluction sheet on the west facing side of the Griegaksla mountain ridge. Enlargement of Norsk Polarinstitutt air photograph no. S69 2438.

Kresling, 1973; Larsson, 1982; Åkerman, 1984; cf. also Rapp 1985*a*).

Gelifluction operates together with soil creep and slope wash on the slopes. The most important forms produced by this process are gelifluction sheets and gelifluction lobes (Figure 1.15). These forms and several other minor ones are widespread but in general smaller and less significant than at lower latitudes. This can be explained partly by the shallow active layer and the sparse vegetation. Few data concerning gelifluction rates have been published from Spitsbergen. Jahn (1960, 1961) reports rates between 3 and 12 cm/year from gelifluction lobes in Hornsund, south Spitsbergen and Åkerman (1973) has found rates up to 18 cm/year in gelifluction lobes and in the front of gelifluction sheets in west Spitsbergen.

Conclusions

If we are looking for recent analogues to the environment in western Europe during the late stages of the last glaciation, Spitsbergen has a lot to offer. Despite the great latitudinal differences there are close climatic similarities between Spitsbergen today and western Europe some 20,000 to 10,000 years ago. Spitsbergen contains almost all known periglacial processes and features, and detailed geodetic, climatic and geologic background data. What is lacking is more quantitative process data. Most studies have concentrated on surface forms and features and often little is known about the internal structure, and cryogenic processes. This is not satisfactory as the surface forms are the first to disappear if/when the environmental conditions and the active processes change.

References

Åhman, R. (1973). Studier av pingos i Adventdalen och i Reindalen på Spetsbergen, *Lunds Universitet Naturgeografiska Institution, Rapporter och Notiser* **25**, 27–44.

—(1977). Palsar i Nordnorge, *Meddelanden Från Lunds Universitet Geografiska Institution Serie Avhandlingar* LXXVIII. 165 p.

Åkerman J. (1973). Palsstudier vid Kapp Linné, Spetsbergen. In *Studier i Periglacial geomorfologi på Spetsbergen* (Ed. H. Svensson) pp. 51–68, Lunds Universitet Naturgeografiska Institution. Rapporter och Notiser nr 15.

—(1978). Meteorologiska undervisningsmodeller – några enkla exempel från arktisk miljö. *Geografiska Notiser* 1:1978, 12–19.

—(1980). Studies on Periglacial Geomorphology in West

Spitsbergen, *Meddelanden från Lunds Universitets Geografiska Institution Serie Avhandlingar* LXXXIX, 297 p.

—(1982a). Observations of palsas within the continuous permafrost zone in east Siberia and in Svalbard, *Geografisk Tidskrift* **2**, 45–51.

—(1982b). Studies on naledi (icings) in west Spitsbergen, *Proc. 4th Canadian Permafrost Conf. Calgary 1982*, 189–202.

—(1983). Notes concerning the vegetation on deflation surfaces, Kapp Linné, Spitsbergen, *Polar Research 1* n.s., 161–169.

—(1984). Notes on talus morphology and processes in Spitsbergen. *Geogr. Annlr.*, **66A** (4), 267–284.

Autenboer, Van T. and Loy, W. (1966). Pingos in Northwest Spitsbergen, *Norsk Polarinstitutts Årsbok* 1965, Oslo 1966.

Baranov, I.Y. (1964). Geographical distribution of seasonally frozen ground permafrost, *Canada Natl. Research Council Tech. Translation* 1121.

Baranowski, S. (1975). The climate of west Spitsbergen in the light of material obtained from Isfjord Radio and Hornsund, *Acta Univ. Wratislaviensis.* **251**, 21–34.

Baranowski, S. & Pekala, K. (1982) Nival-eolian processes in the tundra area and in the nunatak zone of the Hans Werenskiold glaciers SW Spitsbergen, *Acta Univ. Wratislaviensis* **525**, 11–27.

Bibus, von E. (1975). Geomorphologische Untersuchungen zur Hang- und Talentwicklung in zentralen West-Spitsbergen, *Polarforschung* **45**, 102–19.

Birkeland, B.J. (1930). Temperaturvariationen auf Spitsbergen, *Meteorologische Zeitschrift*.

Brown. R.J.E. (1960). The distribution of permafrost and its relation to air temperature in Canada and the USSR, *Arctic* **13**, 163–77.

—(1963). *The relation between mean annual air and ground temperatures in the permafrost region of Canada*. National Research Council, Canada. Division of Building Research, Ottawa.

—(1972). Permafrost in the Canadian Arctic Archipelago, *Z. Geomorph. N.F. Suppl.*, Bd **13**, 102–30.

—(1977a). Influence of climatic and terrain factors on ground temperature at three locations in the permafrost region of Canada. In *North American Contribution, Second Int. Permafrost Conf. Yakutsk, USSR*, pp. 27–34. Nat. Acad. Sci., Washington D.C.

—(1973b). Ground ice as an indicator of landforms in permafrost regions. In *Research in Polar and Alpine geomorphology; Guelph Symposium on Geomorphology* (Eds. B.D. Fahey and R.D. Thompson), pp. 25–42, Geo Abstracts, Norwich, England.

Brown, R.J.E. and Pewe, T.L. (1973). Distribution of permafrost in North America and its relationship to the environment; A review 1963–1973. In *North American Contribution Second Int. Permafrost Conf. Yakutsk, USSR.*, pp. 71–100 Nat Acad. Sci., Washington D.C.

Cegla, I. and Kozarski, S. (1977). Sedimentary and geomorphological consequences of the occurrence of naled sheets on the outwash plain of the Gås glacier, Sörkapp Land, Spitsbergen, *Acta Univ. Wratislaviensis.* 387. Wroctaw 1977.

Czeppe, Z. (1968). *Movements of Soil due to frost on the North Coast of Hornsund.* Polish Acad. of Science III, I.G.Y. Com. Warshava 1968.

Czudek, T. and Demek. J. (1970). Thermokarst in Siberia and its influence on the development of lowland relief, *Quarternary Research 1*, 103–20.

—(1971). Der Thermokarst in Ostteil des Mitteljakutischen Tieflandes, *Scripta Facultat is Scientarum naturalium Univ. Purkynianse Brunensis Geographica* I, 1–19.

—(1973). Die Reliefentvicklung während er Dauerfrostbodendegradation, *Ceskoslovenské Akademie Ved Rosspravy Rada Matematickuch a Prirodick Ved.* **83**(2), 69.

Dineley, D.L. (1953). Investigations in Vestspitsbergen, *J. of Glaciology.* **2**, 379–80.

Dylik, J. (1964). Le thermokarst phenomene neglige dans les études der Pleistocene, *Annals. Geogr.* **73**, 513–23.

Fitzpatrick, E.A. (1960). Geomorphic notes from Vestspitsbergen. *Biul. Perygl.* **7**, 159–64.

French, H.M. (1971). Ice cored mounds and patterned ground, southern Banks Island, Western Canadian Arctic, *Geog. Annlr.*, **53A**, 32–8.

—(1976). *The Periglacial Environment*, Longman, London 309 p.

Friend, P.F. (1959). Cambridge Spitsbergen Expeditions 1958, *Polar Record*, **9** (62), 463–4.

Harland, W.B. (1965). Cambridge Spitsbergen Expedition 1964, *Polar Record*, **12** (80), 589–91.

Harris, S.A. (1980). Climatic relationship of permafrost zones in areas of low winter snowcover. *Biul. Perygl.* **28**.

—(1982). Distribution of zonal permafrost landforms with freezing and thawing indices. *Erdkunde Band* 35 Heft 2, 81–90.

Humlum, O. (1979). Icing ridges, A sedimentary criterion for recognizing former occurrence of icing. *Bull. geol. Soc. Denmark*, **28**, 11–16.

Jahn, A. (1960). Remarks on evolution of slopes on Spitsbergen, *Zeitschrift für Geomorphologie.* Suppl. 1, 49–58.

—(1961). Quantitative analysis of some periglacial processes in Spitsbergen. *Universytet Wroclawski 1M. Boleslawa Bierutn Zeszytg Nankowe. Seria B.* Nr. 5 Warszawa 1961.

—(1963). Origin and development of patterned ground in Spitsbergen, *Int. Permafrost Conf. (Lafayette, Indiana) Proc. National Acad. of Science. National Res. Council, Publ.* 1287, pp. 140–5.

—(1975). *Problems of the periglacial zone*, PWN, Polish Scientific Publishers, Warszawa 223 p.

Jersak, J. (1968). *Moss rings in Sörkapp land, West Spitsbergen.* In (Ed. K. Birkenmajer) Polish Spitsbergen Expeditions 1957–60. Polish Academy of

Sciences, III IGY/IGC Committee. Warszawa 1968.

Johnsson, G. (1960). Periglacial wind and frost erosion at Klågerup, SW Scania. *Geog. Annlr.* XL, no. 3–4.

—(1978). De omdiskuterade isräfflorna inom Hardeberga-Dalbyområdet och vid Rönnarp (NO Landskrona). En glacial morfologisk studie. SGÅ **54**, 28–52.

Kachurin, S.P. (1962). Thermokarst within the territory of the USSR, *Biul. Perigl.*, **11**, 49–55.

Kozarski, S. (1975). Orientated kettle-holes in outwash plains, *Quaestiones Geographicae* **2**, 99–112.

Larsson, S. (1982). Geomorphological effects on the slopes of Longyear valley, Spitsbergen after heavy rainstorm in July 1972. *Geogr. Annlr.*, **64A**: 105–25.

Liestøl, O. (1977). Pingos, Springs and permafrost in Spitsbergen, *Norsk Polarinstitutt, Årbok 1975*, Oslo 1977, 7–29.

Lindner, L. & Marks, L. (1985). Types of debris slope accumulations and rock glaciers in south Spitsbergen, *Boreas* **14**, 139–53.

Orvin, A.K. (1944). Litt om kilder pa Svalbard. Norges Svalbards og Ishavsundersökelser. Meddelelse nr 59. Oslo 1944, 24 p.

Péwé, T.L. (1966). Ice wedges in Alaska – classification distribution and climatic significance. In *Proceedings, 1st International Permafrost Conference*. National Academy of Science-National Research Council of Canada. Publication 1287, 76–81.

—(1969) (ed.). *The Periglacial Environment*, Montreal, McGill-Queens University Press, 485 p.

Piper, D.J.W. and Porritt, C.J. (1965). Some Pingos in Spitsbergen, *Norsk Polarinstitutt Årbok 1965.*

Popov, A.I. (1965). Le Thermokarst, *Biul., Perigl.* **4**, 319–30.

Rapp, A. (1960). Talus slopes and mountain walls at Tempelfjorden, Spitsbergen, *Norsk Polarinstitutt Skrifter* nr 119. Oslo 1960.

—(1985a). Extreme rainfall and rapid snowmelt as causes of mass movements in high latitude mountains. In *Field and Theory. Lectures in geocryology* Eds M. Church and O. Slaymaker Vancouver 1985. 213 p.

—(1985b). Slope processes in high latitude mountains. In press.

Salvigsen, O. (1977). An observation of palsa-like forms in Nordostlandet, Svalbard, *Norsk Polarinstitutt Årbok 1976*, 364–7.

Salvigsen, O. & Elgersma, A. (1985). Large scale karst features and open taliks at Vardeborgsletta, outer

Isfjorden, Svalbard, *Polar Research* 3 n.s., 145–53.

Spinnanger, G. (1968). Global radiation and duration of sunshine in northern Norway and Spitsbergen, *Meteorologiske Annlr.*, **5**, (3) Oslo 1968, 137 p.

Steffensen, E. (1969). The climate and its recent variations at the Norwegian Arctic stations, *Meteorologiske Annlr.*, **5**, (8) Oslo 1969, 349 p.

Svensson, H. (1969). A type of circular lakes in northernmost Norway, *Lunds Studies in Geography, Ser. A.* **45**, 12 p.

—(1970). Thermokarst, *Svensk Geografisk Arsbok* nr 46. Lund 1970, 114–26.

—(1971) Pingos i yttre delen av Adventfjorden, *Norsk Polarinstitutt Årbok 1969*, 168–74.

—(1972). Vindaktivitet på Laholmsslätten, *Svensk Geografisk Årsbok* nr 48. Lund 1972, 65–85.

—(1973). Isfält, 'Naledi' in Cherskiybergen, *Svensk Geografisk Årsbok* nr. 49. Lund 1973, 225–7.

—(1976a). Iskilar som klimatindikator, *Svensk Geografisk Årsbok* nr. 52. Lund 1976.

—(1976b). *Observations on polygonal fissuring in non-permafrost areas of the Norden countries.* Abhandlungen d. Akad, d. Wiss. in Göttingen, Symp. Band.

—(1978). Ice wedges as a geomorphological indicator of climatic changes, *Danish Meteorological Institute, Climatological papers* **4**, 9–15.

Swett, K., Hambrey, M. & Johnson, D. (1980). Rock glaciers in northern Spitsbergen *Journal of Geology* **88**, 475–82.

Thiedig, von F. & Kresling, A. (1973). Metorologische und geologische Bedingungen bei der Entstehung von Muren im Juli 1972 auf Spitsbergen, *Polarforschung* 43 Jg. no 1/2, 1972, 40–9.

Vinje, T. (1977–83). Radiation Conditions in Spitsbergen, *Norsk Polarinstitutt, Årbok 1975 to 1979.*

Washburn, L.A. (1979). *Geocryology. A survey of periglacial processes and environments*, Arnold, London, 396 p.

Williams, R.B.G. (1975). The British climate during the last glaciation; an interpretation based upon periglacial phenomena. In *Ice ages: Ancient and Modern* (Eds A.E. Wright, F. Moseley), pp. 95–120, Liverpool, Seel House Press. 320 p.

Wirtman, W. (1964). *Die Landformed de Edge-Insel in Sydost Spitsbergen. Ergebnisse der Stauterland-Expedition 1959/60 (2)*, Wiesbaden.

2 · Periglacial processes and landforms in the Western Canadian Arctic

H.M. FRENCH

Abstract

On the basis of climate, topography and Quaternary history, a number of contemporary periglacial environments can be recognised in Western Arctic Canada. These include (a) polar desert and semi-desert regions of the High Arctic islands, (b) ice-rich tundra lowlands of the Mackenzie Delta and Yukon Coastal Plain, (c) unglaciated British and Ogilvie Mountains, (d) unglaciated interior pediments of Old Crow Basin, and (e) unglaciated interior uplands of Klondike (Yukon) Plateau. While no one region provides a convincing and complete analogue for the periglacial conditions which the British Isles experienced during the Pleistocene, each provides insight upon the roles played by lithology and moisture availability in determining the efficacy of cryogenic processes and the variability of permafrost conditions.

Introduction

Pleistocene environmental reconstructions which use relict or fossil periglacial phenomena are, by necessity, based upon the nature and present distribution of comparable features in modern periglacial environments (Washburn, 1979, 29). Probably the most critical features are those indicative of permafrost (e.g. Washburn, 1980) or perennially frozen ground (i.e. ground that remains at or below 0 °C for at least two years); other cold-climate phenomena are generally less informative as to their environmental and climatic significance (e.g. French, 1976, 227–49).

If the alpine periglacial regions of middle latitudes are excluded, the majority of modern periglacial regions possess three characteristics: (1) they are located in high (i.e. Arctic or Subarctic) latitudes, (2) they have been heavily glaciated during the Pleistocene, and (3) they are underlain, to varying degrees, by permafrost. Accordingly, the aim of this paper is to assess the suitability of parts of the Western Canadian Arctic as possible analogues for the periglacial conditions in the British Isles during the Pleistocene. Attention focusses not only upon the relatively well known environments of the High Arctic islands and the Mackenzie Delta but also upon unglaciated terrain of the subarctic interior and northern Yukon.

General considerations

In the British Isles much periglacial research in the last twenty years has been conducted within the framework of Quaternary studies, often using techniques based on the biological and physical sciences (West, 1985). The most frequently used analogues have been the high latitude environments of the Canadian Arctic, Spitzbergen and northern Alaska (e.g. Chandler, 1972; Waters, 1962; Watson, 1977; Williams, 1975). However, a major problem is presented by the lack of geological situations analogous to those which exist in the British Isles. Other concerns relate to the climatic conditions, especially the higher sun angle experienced in middle latitudes. In addition, seasonal fluvial and nival (i.e. snowmelt) conditions would have been more extended than in high latitudes where discharge is restricted to a brief period of summer thaw. Finally, there is the strong probability that the Pleistocene British Isles would have been influenced by a different global circulation system to that of today, characterised by blocking anticyclones, displaced westerlies, strong pressure gradients and precipitation anomalies.

The fact that most high-latitude periglacial environments have been glaciated at one time or another during the Pleistocene also complicates the use of such environments as modern analogues. Much of

27

northern Canada, for example, has only recently emerged from beneath continental ice sheets. More often than not, in these areas periglacial processes are merely transporting and re-working glacial sediments. The term 'paraglacial' is sometimes applied to these transition conditions (Church and Ryder, 1972). In such environments, it may be difficult to unambiguously assess the role of different periglacial processes, and to identify the critical factors influencing landform evolution.

A final consideration is the presence or absence of permafrost. Its aggradation and degradation, usually associated with either the formation or melt of ground ice, produces unique landforms such as ice-wedge polygons, perennial frost mounds (i.e. pingos) and thermokarst features. Equally important is the active layer, subject to two-sided freezing, frost heave and moisture migration through freezing and frozen soils in response to temperature gradients (e.g. Mackay, 1983; Smith, 1985). In this respect, the formation of ice-rich layers at the base of the active layer and thaw consolidation processes now explain the seemingly anomalous rapid mass movements characteristic of periglacial regions today (e.g. Capps, 1919; McRoberts and

Morgenstern, 1974a, b). Thus, emphasis no longer need be placed exclusively upon either the search for analogous geological situations or for regions of marked climatic similarity. Instead, a more thorough understanding of the dynamics of permafrost aggradation and degradation may explain many puzzling Pleistocene phenomena.

In temperate latitudes during the Pleistocene, permafrost conditions probably varied both in time and space, and continuous, discontinuous and sporadic permafrost might all have been present at one or several times at any locality. If discontinuous permafrost conditions existed, taliks (i.e. layers or bodies of unfrozen ground) and perennial water outlets (i.e. springs) would have assumed localised geomorphic importance, forming seasonal frost mounds, icings and other phenomena (e.g. Pollard and French, 1984; van Everdingen, 1978, 1982). If deep seasonal frost rather than permafrost existed, then one-sided freezing of the seasonally frozen layer would result in fundamental differences in terms of ice segregation, frost heave and cryoturbation.

Collectively, these generalisations suggest that few, if any, high latitude periglacial environments

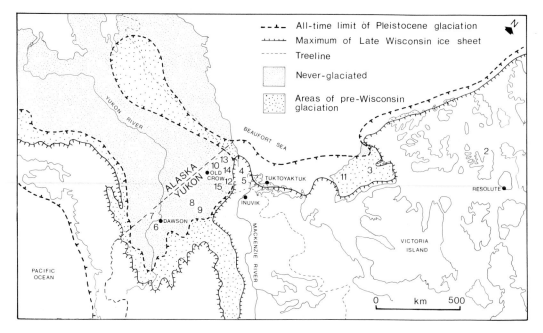

Figure 2.1. Location map of Western North American Arctic showing localities mentioned in text and generalised limits of glaciation (after Dyke *et al.*, 1982; Hughes *et al.*, 1983; Vincent, 1983). Numbers refer to locations of Figures 2.2–2.15 referred to in text.

Table 2.1 *Selected climatic data, Western Canadian Arctic*

Physiographic Region:	Northern Interior Yukon		Mackenzie Delta		High Arctic
Location:	Dawson City	Old Crow	Inuvik	Tuktoyaktuk	Resolute Bay
Latitude:	64° N	68° N	69° N	69° 30′N	74° N
Ecological Region:	Northern Boreal	Northern Subarctic	Northern Subarctic	Low Arctic	High Arctic
Elevation (m):	325	245	60	18	64
Mean Temperature (°C)					
Annual	− 4.7	− 10.0	− 9.6	− 10.7	− 16.4
January	− 28.6	− 31.7	− 29.0	− 27.2	− 32.6
July	+ 15.5	+ 14.4	+ 13.2	+ 10.3	+ 4.3
Average Frost-free Period:	92	30	45	55	9
Average Precipitation					
Annual (mm)	328	203	260	130	136
June–August (mm)	141	96	93	64	69
Snowfall (cm)	132	81	174	56	78

provide complete analogues for the Pleistocene periglacial environments of the British Isles. On the other hand, high latitudes provide insight into the roles played by lithology, climate and moisture availability in determining the efficacy of certain cryogenic processes, and the influence which frozen, freezing and thawing soils exert upon geomorphic processes and landform evolution. In theory, it can be hypothesised that the most informative environments might be:

(a) those in subarctic latitudes (i.e. 60–70° N/S) where both seasonal and diurnal temperature rhythms are present, and where permafrost bodies exist, either in response to present climatic conditions, or as relict phenomena, and where a range of geological materials occur; and,

(b) those at or beyond the limits of Pleistocene glaciation, where cryogenic processes have been able to operate without interruption for much of Quaternary time, and where landscapes might reasonably be regarded as being in equilibrium.

Regional considerations

The Western Canadian Arctic (Figure 2.1) is a vast region within which cryogenic, i.e. cold-climate, processes are a major control on landscape evolution. It extends from the subarctic latitudes of central Yukon (64° N) to the high latitudes of the Queen Elizabeth Islands (79° N).

Climatic conditions

Periglacial environments in the Western Canadian Arctic range from boreal forest and alpine shrub tundra in the south to tundra and polar desert north of treeline. Climates range from subarctic continental to high arctic in nature. Summaries of annual meteorological data for selected localities are given in Table 2.1.

Quaternary history

Although the majority of northern Canada was glaciated during the Pleistocene, large areas of the western Arctic either lay beyond the limits of the last glaciation, or escaped glaciation completely during the Pleistocene (see Figure 2.1). For example, it appears that the north west corner of Banks Island was never glaciated while much of central Banks Island lay beyond the limits of the last two glaciations (Vincent, 1983). Even more extensive areas of unglaciated terrain exist in the northern interior Yukon (Hughes, 1972; Hughes *et al.*, 1983; Rampton, 1982).

The High Arctic islands

It is relatively easy to argue that the High Arctic islands, located between 70–80° N, are not a good modern analogue for the periglacial conditions which must have existed during the Pleistocene in the British Isles, located between 52–54° N. As outlined above, the reasons are primarily related to the more severe, polar climate and the influence which this climate has upon the magnitude and frequency aspects of certain geomorphic processes (e.g. freeze-thaw, snowcover, surface run-off, etc.). In addition, there are paraglacial considerations. Nevertheless, the High Arctic is informative since it emphasises the fact that Arctic landscapes are controlled dominantly by geology.

Our understanding of cryogenic bedrock weathering is limited, in spite of a number of laboratory and experimental studies. With notable exceptions (e.g. Dixon *et al.*, 1984; St Onge, 1959; Washburn, 1969; Watts, 1983), few detailed studies of cryogenic weathering processes and landforms have been undertaken. Thus, the basic relationship between rock structure and relief in periglacial regions is not fully understood. For example, although hydration shattering has been proposed to explain the extensive occurrence of angular rock-rubble (Figure 2.2), a consensus still remains that the most acceptable explanation is frost wedging (Washburn, 1979, 74). These uncertainties regard-

ing cryogenic weathering seriously weaken any Pleistocene palaeo-environmental reconstruction which relies mainly upon morphological and/or sedimentological evidence.

Since the High Arctic islands are underlain by cold and thick permafrost, they also serve to emphasise the relationship between lithology and frozen ground, especially the occurrence of ground ice in weakly lithified shales, clays and mudstones. For example, Mesozoic shales of the Kanguk and Christopher Formations outcrop widely in the Sverdrup Basin and possess high ground ice contents (French *et al.*, 1986; Hodgson, 1982; Stangle *et al.*, 1982). In years of exceptionally warm summers, thaw consolidation and high pore-water pressures in the active layer result in 'skin-flows' or active-layer-failures, often on very low-angled slopes (Figure 2.3). These phenomena provide a process explanation for the periglacial mudslides and failures described from the shales and clays of

Figure 2.2. Many of the polar desert and semi-desert land-scapes of the High Arctic islands have a veneer of angular rock rubble, derived from the cryogenic weathering of bedrock. Sandstone terrain, Stockes Range, Bathurst Island, N.W.T. Photo: H.M. French.

Figure 2.3. Ice-rich and unconsolidated shales and clays are often subject to rapid failure confined to the active layer and caused by thaw consolidation processes, especially frequent in years of exceptionally rapid summer thaw and/or heavy summer precipitation. Shale of the Christopher Formation, Thomsen River area, northern Banks Island. The scarp on the left is about 1 m high. Photo: H.M. French.

southern England (e.g. Ackermann and Cave, 1967; Chandler, 1972; Chandler *et al.*, 1976; Harris, 1981; Hutchinson and Gostelow, 1976).

It must be recognised that modern High Arctic environments do not necessarily possess conditions exactly analogous to those of Pleistocene Europe. However, the influence which lithology exerts upon weathering processes and permafrost conditions in this region suggests that these considerations are fundamental to paleo-environmental reconstructions. This is particularly true of areas such as the British Isles, which possess a wide variety of geological settings.

The Mackenzie Delta

Both the Mackenzie Delta and adjacent Yukon Coastal Plain are well known in the periglacial literature, primarily on account of their excellent permafrost and ground ice exposures (e.g. Mackay, 1963, 1979; Mackay and Black, 1973; Rampton and Mackay, 1971).

The modern Mackenzie Delta provides a useful analogue for Pleistocene deltaic and alluvial periglacial environments, such as might have existed on floodplains, river terraces or in poorly drained areas. However, it must be remembered that the Mackenzie Delta is a relatively unique periglacial environment occupying only a fraction of the permafrost terrain of the Western Canadian Arctic. Moreover, not only is the profusion of pingos, the size and frequency of occurrence of ice wedges, and the massive dimensions of ground ice bodies rarely matched elsewhere in the world, but these features are mostly associated with the Pleistocene Delta (see Mackay, 1963) and reflect locally limited thermal and hydrological conditions. For these reasons, use of the Mackenzie Delta, as a modern analogue, must be with caution and precision.

The Mackenzie Delta area does provide however an opportunity to observe massive ground ice bodies and ice-rich permafrost in coastal sections (Figure 2.4). To those involved in Pleistocene

Figure 2.4. Bodies of massive segregated ice and icy sediments, several metres thick, occur within unconsolidated Quaternary sediments of the Mackenzie Delta and Yukon Coastal Plain. Sabine Point, northern Yukon coast. Photo: H.M. French.

palaeo-geographic reconstructions, it can serve, therefore, as a reminder of the importance of ground ice and thermokarst to periglacial landscape evolution. In many areas, especially those underlain by silty unconsolidated sediments, thermokarst processes were probably widespread during the waning stages of Pleistocene permafrost conditions. The self-destroying nature of many thermokarst processes, however, means that simple, morphological evidence may be lacking and diagnostic sedimentary structures hard to identify. For example, the sediments and taliks which exist beneath thaw lakes today (e.g. Black, 1969; French and Harry, 1983) are still insufficiently understood and it is virtually impossible to recognise them in their relict form in now-unfrozen terrain. Pingo scars (Flemal, 1976) are also ambiguous since they imply the former existence of taliks and hydrological conditions which are now often difficult to demonstrate. The possibility also exists that some pingo scars are the remnants of seasonal, rather than perennial, frost mounds, and need not imply the former existence of permafrost. On the other

hand, the occurrence of involuted structures ('cryoturbations') in parts of the British Isles (e.g. Williams, 1975) and Europe (e.g. Edelman *et al.*, 1936; Eissman, 1981; Vandenberghe and van de Broek, 1982) may be associated with the degradation of permafrost and dewatering effects as large ground ice bodies thawed, rather than with freezing and thawing processes (i.e. cryoturbation *senso stricto*; see Mackay, 1980; Zoltai *et al.*, 1978) in the active layer. Equally, the widely reported cambering and valley bulging phenomena (e.g. Ackermann and Cave, 1967; Chandler *et al.*, 1976; Hollingworth *et al.*, 1944; Horswill and Horton, 1976) and gulls (e.g. Hawkins and Privett, 1981) are best interpreted in terms of the degradation of ice-rich permafrost. In the Mackenzie Valley, the *in-situ* creep of frozen ground has now been measured (Savigny, 1980) giving credence to this mechanism. Only ice-wedge casts seem reasonably well understood in terms of their permafrost significance (e.g. Black, 1976; Seddon and Holyoak, 1985) but even here, modern large ice wedges (Figure 2.5) are usually typical only of poorly drained localities,

Figure 2.5. Large epigenetic ice wedges are the most widely distributed type of nearly pure ground ice to be found in the permafrost regions of the world. King Point, northern Yukon Coast. Photo courtesy of D.G. Harry (Geological Survey of Canada).

and the absence of ice-wedge casts in a region does not necessarily imply the former absence of permafrost conditions. Furthermore, permafrost conditions do not always produce ice wedges since their growth is controlled by a variety of factors, including moisture availability and lithology of enclosing sediments, in addition to ground thermal regime. For example, the ice-rich shale of the Christopher Formation on Eastern Melville Island, N.W.T., is noted for its virtual absence of ice wedges (French *et al.*, 1986).

Unglaciated periglacial terrain of Northern Yukon

The Northern Interior Yukon is important to Pleistocene periglacial reconstructions because large areas remained unglaciated throughout Quaternary time and relict permafrost is widespread. Numerous faunal remains preserved within the permafrost indicate that the area was part of the south eastern Bering refugium. The range of permafrost and associated hydrologic conditions, and the antiquity of much of the landscape provides the

opportunity to identify mature cryogenic landscapes, unaltered by major climatic fluctuations. However, its Cordilleran nature and subarctic latitude suggests its significance is more relevant to continental areas of mid-latitudes, such as central Europe and the interior plains of North America, rather than the British Isles. Three subdivisions of this region are discussed below.

Klondike Plateau
The Klondike (Yukon) Plateau forms an intermontane upland between 1000–1300 m a.s.l. developed mainly in Palaeozoic high-grade metamorphic rocks. It is deeply dissected by V-shaped valleys possessing rounded slopes and interlocking spurs (Figure 2.6). The valleys often possess high level benches or terraces suggesting a history of multi-cyclic valley development. Intervening ridges have uniform elevations and are presumed to be the remnants of an ancient uplifted erosion surface (Tempelman-Kluit, 1980). Valley bottoms are typically infilled with several metres of silty, organic-rich colluvium ('muck') which appears to have been

Figure 2.6. View along Bonanza Creek, near Dawson City, Klondike District, Yukon Territory, showing V-shaped valley, interlocking spurs and high level benches. Note the old gold placer workings in the valley bottom and the modern placer activity exploiting high level gravels. Photo: H.M. French.

transported by mass wasting processes from higher elevations at times of greater humidity during the Pleistocene. Permafrost has aggraded into these sediments and ice wedges and massive icy bodies have formed (e.g. French and Pollard, 1986). At higher elevations on the Klondike Plateau, tors (Figure 2.7) and cryoplanation terraces (Hughes *et al.*, 1972) are well developed, especially on old high-grade metamorphic shales and quartzites (see French and Heginbottom, 1983, 58–63). The growth of lichens on the tor surfaces, and the absence of freshly weathered rock debris, suggest that they are relict Pleistocene phenomena, not forming under today's climate.

The presence of discontinuous and relict permafrost gives rise to important hydrologic characteristics. Where present, permafrost presents a relatively impermeable barrier to groundwater flow. Where topographic gradients are encountered, as on hillslopes, substantial hydrostatic head may develop. In the Klondike, the unusual nature of groundwater flow is shown by disrupted

drainage in the Dawson City townsite, numerous icings along the Dempster Highway, groundwater icings in placer mining operations, and the presence of several open system pingos in the Klondike valleys. The latter are some of several hundred pingos known in the central Yukon and interior Alaska (e.g. Hughes, 1969).

On the basis of geology, relief and periglacial features, the Klondike Plateau has a certain similarity with parts of upland Britain, such as central Wales and Dartmoor, where tors, altiplanation terraces, solifluction (head) deposits and pingo scars have all been described (e.g. Mottershead, 1977; Palmer and Nielson, 1962; Waters, 1962; Watson and Watson, 1974). The usefulness of such an analogue is limited by recognition of (1) the more continental and arid nature of the climate of the Klondike today and the apparent inactivity of many frost-action processes, (2) the probability that periglacial phenomena in the Klondike formed during moister periods of the Pleistocene and (3) the many subtle controls over permafrost distri-

Figure 2.7. Tors occur at higher elevations on the deeply dissected Klondike (Yukon) Plateau in especially resistant high-grade metamorphic shales and quartzites. Photo: H.M. French.

bution and its associated hydrologic conditions. On the other hand, the degree of continentality of Devensian climates in Britain may have been high and the Klondike analogue may yet prove to be of great assistance. For example, halophytes commonly found in the cold stage floras of the Devensian indicate saline soils, possibly induced by high summer temperatures and evaporation rates, as in central Yakutia today. In addition, the relatively high percentage of *Artemesia* pollen and steppe species in certain pollen spectra also indicate continentality (e.g. Bell, 1969; West *et al.*, 1974).

Northern Ogilvie Ranges

The Northern Ogilvie Ranges consist of steeply dipping limestones and shales of Cambro-Ordovician age, and rise to 1700 m a.s.l. Distinct slope form assemblages occur in these unglaciated mountains (Figure 2.8). The limestones and shales have experienced mechanical weathering such that valley walls consist of block (scree) slopes close to the maximum angle of repose. Typically, upper hillslopes are convex and debris flow aprons are

common at the foot of gullies. Castellated tors appear as cliff remnants and isolated but numerous tors can occur in valleyside positions (Figure 2.9). The occurrence of tors in the Ogilvie Mountains, and on Klondike Plateau as previously described, suggest downwasting by solifluction rather than scarp retreat as the mechanism of formation since many tors occur without immediate association with cryoplanation terraces. Field investigation shows that most tors occurs where rock is more resistant to weathering and erosion. For example, intrusions, widely spaced joints and bedding planes, and secondary alteration (e.g. silicification) all lead to locally more resistant strata, and tor formation (Hughes *et al.*, 1972, 28–29).

Perennial groundwater discharges are a characteristic of many mountainous regions of the northern Yukon, even where permafrost is regarded as continuous. In most cases they reflect open hydrothermal taliks related to sub-permafrost systems which take advantage of fractures in bedrock or highly permeable strata such as limestone. In the Northern Ogilvies, for example, highly sulphurous

Figure 2.8. Smooth convex-concave slopes occur widely on limestones in the unglaciated Northern Ogilvie Ranges. They are veneered with angular rock debris. Engineer Creek area, Dempster Highway. Photo: H.M. French.

Figure 2.9. Valleyside tors surrounded by debris (scree) slopes are common in limestones of the Ogilvie Ranges. Perennial springs may discharge through the limestone aquifers. Castles' Hill, Ogilvie River Gorge. Photo: H.M. French.

Figure 2.10. The well known annual Babbage River icing, Barn Ranges, is associated with perennial discharge through sandstones and limestones of Triassic age, and can last well into August. The ice is 3–4 m thick. Photo: late June 1985. H.M. French.

Figure 2.11. Icing mounds can occur in winter months at locations where high hydraulic potentials develop, often associated with restricted hydraulic conductivities in open sub-channel taliks. Big River, central Banks Island. The mound is about 2.5 m high. Photo: April 1979, courtesy of D. Nasagaloak, Sachs Harbour.

perennial springs discharge from shales along Engineer Creek (Harris *et al.*, 1983) while fresh-water discharge at a rate of $1.4 \, m^3/s$ has been measured from limestones at Castles' Hill in the Ogilvie River Gorge. In both localities substantial icings occur during the winter months. Further north, in the British Mountains, and in certain of the High Arctic islands, icings and related phenomena occur along major rivers (Figures 2.10, 2.11). All are related to perennial groundwater discharges from limestone and sandstone aquifers or from open sub-channel taliks in permeable sediments. By acting as storage for winter baseflow, and by melting slowly throughout the summer months, icings reduce the extreme seasonal fluctuations of discharge characteristic of many rivers in permafrost environments.

No localities in the British Isles are readily apparent as Pleistocene analogues when consider-ing the Northern Ogilvie Ranges. However, the numerous recent descriptions of periglacial river sediments from southern England (e.g. Clarke and Dixon, 1981; Gibbard *et al.*, 1982; Green *et al.*, 1983), often believed to have been deposited at times of 'sustained regional permafrost' (Seddon and Holyoak, 1985), rarely consider the baseflow component of the hydrograph. In all probability, substantial icings would have formed in the proximity of springs issuing from the base of the Chalk escarpments. For example, there is evidence for springs issuing from Chalk in East Anglia with subsequent collapse and infilling by Devensian sediments (R.G. West, pers. comm.). Other occurrences would have been in the Hampshire and London Basins, and the scarp and vale topography of central England, wherever hydro-geological conditions were favourable.

Figure 2.12. Angular rock rubble veneers many of the upland surfaces of the interior plateaus and mountain ranges of the unglaciated northern Yukon. Large, inactive non-sorted circles and nets are common, as here. Barn Ranges, British Mountains. Photo: H.M. French.

Barn Ranges and Old Crow Pediments

The Barn Ranges form part of the British Mountains of the extreme northern Yukon and rise to over 1000 m from near sea level. They are flanked by extensive pediment-like surfaces, especially to the south. Distinct periglacial landform assemblages can be recognised at micro-, meso- and macro-scales.

At the micro-scale, angular rock rubble veneers many of the upland surfaces and large non-sorted circles are common (Figure 2.12). At higher elevations and adjacent to snowbanks, solifluction processes are active (e.g. Rampton, 1982, 33–34). At the meso-scale, in the adjacent Buckland Hills, tors and bedrock (i.e. cryoplanation) terraces exist at higher elevations (Figure 2.13). There is no obvious relationship between the tors and the terraces, and all appear unrelated to any geological control, although they are best preserved upon particularly resistant granites and conglomerates. As in the central Yukon, these features and the angular frost rubble surfaces show little sign that they are forming under today's climate.

At the macro-scale, the broad structural (i.e. geological) control over landscape is very apparent. Many of the Barn Ranges, for example, are formed from gently folded Mesozoic-age shale and sandstone formations. They possess a relative relief of 300–600 m and consist of impressive in-and-out-facing escarpments and isolated synclinal mountain masses formed in the sandstones, surrounded by extensive low angled pediments and broad valleys formed in the shales. Sleepy Mountain is the best known of these inselberg-like mountains (Figure 2.14).

Extensive and flat pediment-like surfaces are especially well developed on the interior (south-facing) side (Figure 2.15). They form a distinct physiographic region termed the Old Crow Pediments (Wiken *et al.*, 1981). The pediment surfaces are covered with a veneer of colluvium derived from local parent rock and form gently concave slopes,

Figure 2.13. Bedrock (i.e., cryoplanation) terraces exist at high elevations in the unglaciated northern Yukon, as at Sixty Mile (Boundary) on the Yukon (Klondike) Plateau and here, Buckland Hills, Barn Ranges, British Mountains. Photo: H.M. French.

Figure 2.14. The conical inselberg-like hill known as Sleepy Mountain, is capped by Mesozoic age sandstone and flanked by low-angled pediments and valleyside slopes formed in shales. Barn Ranges, British Mountains. Photo: H. M. French.

Figure 2.15. The Old Crow Pediments cover ≈ 50,000 km² and form low-angled concave surfaces veneered with bedrock-derived colluvium and shallow integrated drainage systems. Photo: H.M. French.

with angles of between 4–9°. The pediments possess an integrated shallow drainage pattern, only recognisable from the air.

It is not clear whether these surfaces are epigene palaeoforms (i.e. exposed since their formation) or etch forms (i.e. initiated as part of a weathering front and then exposed through the stripping of the saprolite). Hughes (1972) refers to these surfaces as cryopediments, and similar surfaces exist in Siberia (Czudek and Demek, 1973). Their great antiquity, and their similarity in form with other palaeosurfaces of the world, suggest that long term cryogenic landscape evolution is essentially no different to that of landscape evolution in other semi-arid regions. Notwithstanding the rather different geologic, topographic and scale considerations, it is tempting to conclude that if periglacial conditions in the British Isles had not been interrupted by alternating periods of glaciation and warmer climates during the Pleistocene, landscapes similar to those of the interior Yukon might have evolved.

Conclusions

It is clear that no one region in the Western Canadian Arctic provides a convincing and complete analogue for the periglacial conditions which the British Isles experienced during the Pleistocene. Instead, the different environments described provide insight into the roles played by lithology and climate in determining the efficacy of geomorphic processes, the nature and variability of permafrost conditions, and the evolution of cryogenic landscapes. Although Worsley (1977, 217) concludes that 'the key to the past may not necessarily be the present', a knowledge of the present is essential if the correct key is to be selected.

Acknowledgements
Fieldwork in the Western Canadian Arctic has been supported by the Natural Sciences and Engineering Research Council; the Polar Continental Shelf Project, The Geological Survey of Canada, and The Earth Physics Branch of the Department of Energy, Mines and Resources, Ottawa; and the Inuvik Scientific Resource Centre, Inuvik. Dr D.G. Harry (Geological Survey of Canada) and Professor R.G. West (University of Cambridge) made useful comments on the manuscript.

References

Ackermann, K.J. and Cave, R. (1967). 'Surficial deposits and structures, including landslip, in the Stroud District, Gloucestershire,' *Proceedings, Geologists Association*, **78**, 567–86.

Bell, F.G. (1969). 'The occurrence of southern steppe and halophyte elements in Weichselian (Last Glacial) floras from southern Britain'. *New Phytologist*, **68**, 913–22.

Black, R.F. (1969). 'Thaw depressions and thaw lakes: A review,' *Biuletyn Peryglacjalny*, **19**, 131–50.

Black, R.F. (1976). 'Periglacial features indicative of permafrost: ice and soil wedges,' *Quaternary Research*, **6**, 3–26.

Capps, S.R. (1919). 'The Kantishna Region, Alaska,' *United States Geological Survey*, Bulletin **687**, 7–112.

Chandler, R.J. (1972). 'Periglacial mudslides in Vestspitsbergen and their bearing on the origin of fossil "solifluction" shears in low angled clay slopes,' *Quarterly Journal Engineering Geology*, **5**, 223–41.

Chandler, R.J., Kellaway, G.A., Skempton, A.W., and Wyatt, R.J. (1976). 'Valley slope sections in Jurassic strata near Bath, Somerset,' *Philosophical Transactions Royal Society of London A*, **283**, 527–55.

Church, M.A. and Ryder, J. (1972). 'Paraglacial sedimentation: a consideration of fluvial processes conditioned by glaciation,' *Bulletin, Geological Society of America*, **83**, 3059–72.

Clarke, M.R. and Dixon, A.J. (1981). 'The Pleistocene braided river deposits in the Blackwater Valley area of Berkshire and Hampshire, England,' *Proceedings, Geologists Association*, **92**, 139–58.

Czudek, T. and Demek, J. (1973). 'The valley cryopediments in Eastern Siberia,' *Biuletyn Peryglacjalny*, **22**, 117–30.

Dixon, J.C., Thorn, C.E. and Darmody, R.G. (1984). 'Chemical weathering processes on the Vantage Peak nunatak, Juneau Icefield, southern Alaska,' *Physical Geography*, **5**, 111–31.

Dyke, A.S., Dredge, C.A. and Vincent, J.S. (1982). 'Configuration and dynamics of the Laurentide ice sheet during the late Wisconsinan maximum,' *Géographie Physique et Quaternaire*, **36**, 5–14.

Edelman, C.H., Florschutz, F. and Jesweit, J. (1936). 'Ueber spatpleistozane und fruhholozane kryoturbate Ablagerungen in den ostlichen Niederlanden,' *Geologisch-Mijnbouwkundig Genortschap voor Nederland en Kolonien*, Varhandelingen Geologisch Series **11**, 301–60.

Eissman, L. (1981). 'Periglaziare processe und permafrost-strukturen aus sechs kaltzeiten des Quartars,' *Altenburger Naturwissenschaftliche Forschungen*, Allenburg **1**, 3–171.

van Everdingen, R.O. (1978). 'Frost mounds at Bear Rock near Fort Norman, N.W.T., 1975–1976,' *Canadian Journal of Earth Sciences*, **15**, 263–76.

van Everdingen, R.O. (1982). 'Management of groundwater discharge for the solution of icing problems in the Yukon,' in *The Roger J.E. Brown Memorial Volume, Proceedings Fourth Canadian Permafrost Conference* (Ed. H.M. French), National Research Council of Canada, Ottawa, 212–28.

Flemal, R.C. (1976). 'Pingos and pingo scars: their characteristics, distribution and utility in reconstructing former permafrost environments,' *Quaternary Research*, **6**, 37–53.

French, H.M. (1976). *The periglacial environment*, Longmans, London and New York, 309 pp.

French, H.M. and Harry, D.G. (1983). 'Ground ice conditions and thaw lake evolution, Sachs River lowlands, Banks Island, Canada,' *Mesoformen der heutigen Periglazialraumes, Abhandlungen der Akademie des Wissenschaften in Gottingen* (Eds. H. Poser and E. Schunke), **35**, 70–81.

French, H.M. and Heginbottom, J.A. (1983). 'Northern Yukon Territory and Mackenzie Delta, Canada. Guidebook to permafrost and related features,' *Fourth International Conference on Permafrost, Fairbanks, Alaska*, Division of Geological and Geophysical Surveys, College, Alaska, 186 pp.

French, H.M. and Pollard, W.H. (1986). 'Ground ice investigation, Klondike District, Yukon Territory,' *Canadian Journal of Earth Sciences*, **23**, 450–460.

French, H.M., Bennett, L. and Hayley, D.W. (1968). 'The ground ice geology of Eastern Melville Island, N.W.T., Canada,' *Canadian Journal of Earth Sciences*, **23**, 1389–1400.

Gibbard, P.L., Coope, G.R., Hall, A.R., Preece, R.C. and Robinson, J.E. (1982). 'Middle Devensian deposits beneath the "Upper Floodplain" terrace of the River Thames at Kempton Park, Sunbury, England,' *Proceedings, Geologists Association*, **93**, 275–90.

Green, C.P., Keen, D.H., McGregor, D.F.M., Robinson, J.E. and Williams, R.B.G. (1983). 'Stratigraphy and environmental significance of Pleistocene deposits at Fisherton, near Salisbury, Wiltshire,' *Proceedings, Geologists Association*, **94**, 17–22.

Harris, C. (1981). *Periglacial Mass-wasting: A Review of Research*, B.G.R.G. Research monograph 4, GeoAbstracts, Norwich, 204 p.

Harris, S.A., van Everdingen, R.O. and Pollard, W.H. (1983). 'The Dempster Highway – Dawson to Eagle Plain,' in *Northern Yukon Territory and Mackenzie Delta, Canada, Guidebook to Permafrost and related features, Fourth International Conference on Permafrost, Fairbanks, Alaska* (Eds. H.M. French and J.A. Heginbottom), Division of Geological and Geophysical Surveys, College, Alaska, 65–86.

Harris, S.A., Heginbotton, J.A., Tarnocai, C. and van Everdingen, R.O. (1983). 'The Dempster Highway – Eagle Plain to Inuvik,' in *Northern Yukon Territory and Mackenzie Delta, Canada, Guidebook to permafrost and related features, Fourth International Conference on Permafrost, Fairbanks, Alaska* (Eds. H.M. French and J.A. Heginbottom), Division of Geological and Geophysical Surveys, College, Alaska, 87–111.

Hawkins, A.B. and Privett, K.D. (1981). 'A building site on cambered ground at Radstock, Avon,' *Quarterly Journal Engineering Geology, London*, **14**, 151–67.

Hodgson, D.A. (1982). 'Surficial materials and geomorphological processes, Western Sverdrup and adjacent islands, District of Franklin,' *Geological Survey of Canada*, Paper 81–9, 44 pp.

Hollingworth, S.E., Taylor, J.H. and Kellaway, G.A. (1944). 'Large scale superficial structures in the Northampton Ironstone Field,' *Quarterly Journal of the Geological Society of London*, **100**, 1–44.

Horswill, P. and Horton, A. (1976). 'Cambering and valley bulging in the Gwash valley at Empingham, Rutland' (with an appendix by P.R. Vaughn: The deformations in the Empingham valley slope), *Philosophical Transactions Royal Society of London, A*, **283**, 427–61.

Hughes, O.L. (1969). 'Distribution of open system pingos in central Yukon Territory, with respect to glacial limits,' *Geological Survey of Canada*, Paper 69–34, 8 pp.

Hughes, O.L. (1972). 'Surficial geology of northern Yukon Territory and northwestern District of Mackenzie, Northwest Territories,' *Geological Survey of Canada*, Paper 69–36, 11 pp.

Hughes, O.L., van Everdingen, R.O. and Tarnocai, C. (1983). 'Regional setting – physiography and geology,' in *Northern Yukon Territory and Mackenzie Delta, Canada, Guidebook to permafrost and related features, Fourth International Conference on Permafrost, Fairbanks, Alaska* (Eds. H.M. French and J.A. Heginbottom), Division of Geological and Geophysical Surveys, College, Alaska, 5–34.

Hughes, O.L., Rampton, V.N. and Rutter, N.W. (1972). 'Quaternary geology and geomorphology, southern and central Yukon,' in *Guidebook for field excursion A-11, 24th International Geological Congress, Montreal*, 59 pp.

Hutchinson, J.N. and Gostelow, T.P. (1976). 'The development of an abandoned cliff in London Clay at Hadleigh, Essex,' *Philosophical Transactions Royal Society of London, A*, 283, 557–604.

Mackay, J.R. (1963). 'The Mackenzie Delta area, N.W.T.,' *Geographical Branch Memoir*, **8**, Ottawa, 202 pp.

Mackay, J.R. (1979). 'Pingos of the Tuktoyaktuk Peninsula area, Northwest Territories,' *Géographie Physique et Quaternaire*, **33**, 3–61.

Mackay, J.R., (1980). 'The origin of hummocks, western Arctic coast, Canada,' *Canadian Journal of Earth Sciences*, **17**, 996–1006.

Mackay, J.R. (1983). 'Downward water movement into frozen ground, western Arctic coast, Canada,' *Canadian Journal of Earth Sciences*, **20**, 120–34.

Mackay, J.R. and Black, R.F. (1973). 'Origin, composition and structure of perennially frozen ground and ground ice: A review,' in *North American Contribution, Permafrost, Second International Conference, Yakutsk, U.S.S.R., 13–28 July, 1973*, Washington, D.C., National Academy Science Publication **2115**, 185–92.

McRoberts, E.C. and Morgenstern, N.R. (1974a). 'The stability of thawing slopes,' *Canadian Geotechnical Journal*, **11**, 447–69.

McRoberts, E.C. and Morgenstern, N.R. (1974b). 'Stability of slopes in frozen soil, Mackenzie Valley, N.W.T.,' *Canadian Geotechnical Journal*, **11**, 554–73.

Mottershead, D.N. (1977). 'Southwest England,' *X INQUA Congress, Guidebook for excursions A6 and C6, GeoAbstracts Ltd.*, 59 pp.

Palmer, J. and Nielson, R.A. (1962). 'The origin of granite tors on Dartmoor, Devonshire,' *Proceedings, Yorkshire Geological Society*, **33**, 315–40.

Pollard, W.H. and French, H.M. (1984). 'The groundwater hydraulics of seasonal frost mounds, North Fork Pass, Yukon Territory,' *Canadian Journal of Earth Sciences*, **21**, 1073–81.

Rampton, V.N. (1982). 'Quaternary geology of the Yukon coastal plain,' *Geological Survey of Canada*, Bulletin **317**, 49 pp.

Rampton, V.N. and Mackay, J.R. (1971). 'Massive ice and icy sediments throughout the Tuktoyaktuk Peninsula, Richards Island and nearby areas,' *Geological Survey of Canada*, Paper 71–21, 16 pp.

Savigny, K.W. (1980). 'In-situ analysis of naturally occurring creep in ice-rich permafrost soil,' Ph.D. Thesis, Department of Civil Engineering, The University of Alberta, Edmonton, 449 pp.

Seddon, M.B. and Holyoak, D.T. (1985). 'Evidence of sustained regional permafrost during deposition of fossiliferous Late Pleistocene river sediments at Stanton Harcourt (Oxfordshire, England),' *Proceedings, Geologists Association*, **96**, 53–71.

Smith, M.W. (1985). 'Observations of soil freezing and frost heave at Inuvik, Northwest Territories, Canada,' *Canadian Journal of Earth Sciences*, **22**, 283–90.

St-Onge, D.A. (1959). 'Note sur l'érosion du gypse en climat périglaciaire,' *Revue Canadienne de Géographie*, XIII, 155–62.

Stangle, K., Roggensack, W.D. and Hayley, D.W. (1982). 'Engineering geology of surficial soils, eastern Melville Island,' in *The Roger J.E. Brown Memorial Volume, Proceedings Fourth Canadian Permafrost Conference* (Ed. H.M. French), National Research Council of Canada, Ottawa, 136–50.

Templeman-Kluit, D.J. (1980). 'Evolution of physiography and drainage in southern Yukon,' *Canadian Journal of Earth Sciences*, **17**, 1189–203.

Vandenberghe, J. and van den Broek, P. (1982). 'Weichselian convolution phenomena and processes in fine sediments,' *Boreas*, **11**, 299–315.

Vincent, J-S. (1983). 'La géologie du Quaternaire et la géomorphologie de l'Ile Banks, Arctique Canadien,' *Geological Survey of Canada*, Memoir **405**, 118 pp.

Washburn, A.L. (1969). 'Weathering, frost action and patterned ground in the Mesters Vig district, Northeast Greenland,' *Meddelellser öm Gronland*, **176**, 303 pp.

Washburn, A.L. (1979). *Geocryology: a survey of periglacial processes and environments*, John Wiley and Sons, London and New York, 406 pp.

Washburn, A.L. (1980). 'Permafrost features as evidence of climatic change,' *Earth Science Review*, **15**, 327–402.

Waters, R.S. (1962). 'Altiplanation terraces and slope development in West Spitzbergen and southwest England,' *Biuletyn Peryglacjalny*, **11**, 89–101.

Watson, E. (1977). 'The periglacial environment of Great Britain during the Devensian,' *Philosophical Transactions Royal Society of London*, B, **280**, 183–98.

Watson, E. and Watson, S. (1974). 'Remains of pingos in the Cletwyr basin, southwest Wales,' *Geografiska Annaler*, **56A**, 213–25.

Watts, S.H. (1983). 'Weathering pit formation in bedrock near Cory Glacier, southeastern Ellesmere Island, Northwest Territories,' *Geological Survey of Canada*, Paper 83–1A, 487–91.

West, R.G. (1985). 'The future of Quaternary research,' *Proceedings, Geologists Association*, **96**, 193–98.

West, R.G., Camilla A. Dickson, J.A., Catt, A.H. Weir. and B.W. Sparks. 1974. 'Late Pleistocene deposits at Wretton, Norfolk. II Devensian deposits'. *Philosophical Transactions Royal Society of London*, B, **267**, 337–420.

Wiken, E.B., Welch, D.M., Ironside, G.R. and Taylor, D.G. (1981). 'The Northern Yukon: an ecological land survey,' *Ecological Land Classification Series*, 6, Lands Directorate, Environment Canada, Ottawa, 197 pp.

Williams, R.B.G. (1975). 'The British climate during the last glaciation: an interpretation based on periglacial phenomena,' in *Ice Ages: Ancient and Modern* (Eds. A.E. Wright and F. Moseley), Seel House Press, Liverpool, 95–120.

Worsley, P. (1977). 'Periglaciation,' in *British Quaternary Studies: recent advances* (Ed. F.W. Shotton), Oxford University Press, 203–19.

Zoltai, S.C., Tarnocai, C. and Pettapiece, W.W. (1978). 'Age of cryoturbated organic materials in earth hummocks from the Canadian Arctic,' in *Proceedings, Third International Conference on Permafrost, Edmonton, Alberta*, National Research Council of Canada, Ottawa, Volume One, 325–31.

3 · Periglacial phenomena of northern Fennoscandia

MATTI SEPPÄLÄ

Abstract

Northern Fennoscandia is located at the southern edge of the zone of the discontinuous permafrost. The mean annual air temperature ranges from $-1\,°C$ to $-4\,°C$. During the winter in the eastern part the temperature can fall below $-50\,°C$. Permafrost features such as palsas, pingos and rim-ridge lakes are present and periglacial phenomena formed by seasonal frost include gelifluction, frost sorting, stone polygons, boulder depressions, stone pits, nonsorted circles, tundra polygons, pounus, and thufurs. Special attention is paid to the distribution, morphology and origin of these periglacial phenomena, keeping in mind possible analogues for British Pleistocene deposits and landforms.

Introduction

The search for analogues is recommended when studying sedimentary structures and landforms of palaeoclimatic origin. Before one is able to ascertain the origin and palaeoenvironmental significance of Pleistocene periglacial phenomena one needs to know not only their morphological and structural similarities to active phenomena but also the conditions under which they form today.

The closest regions to the British Isles with active frost phenomena and permafrost exist in northern Fennoscandia, also called Lapland (Figure 3.1). Most of this region is to the north of the Arctic Circle. This means that during summer the angle of incidence of solar radiation is more gentle than in Britain; in the middle of winter the incoming radiation is dispersed and the amplitude of the diurnal air temperature depends on winds, not sunshine, which is absent.

This paper discusses some active periglacial features found in northern Fennoscandia. Special attention is paid to their morphology, distribution, and origin. The aim is that British colleagues will achieve more accurate interpretations when investigating Pleistocene frost phenomena. This short article does not try to cover all observed frost phenomena or all the periglacial literature published in Norden but picks examples.

Climate

Due to the Gulf Stream the mean annual air temperature is 6 to $10\,°C$ higher than in other regions on the same latitude. The climate on the Norwegian coast is maritime, with a difference of 12 to $14\,°C$ between the mean temperatures of the coldest and warmest months (Wallén, 1960). The amplitude of mean temperatures increases towards the east.

The isotherms of the mean annual air temperature in northern Norway in general follow the coast line. Near the coast the annual mean is about $+4\,°C$ decreasing rapidly inland (Åhman, 1977). On the high mountains of Sweden the mean annual air temperature is about $-4\,°C$ rising to $+1\,°C$ towards the Gulf of Bothnia. In northern Finland (Utsjoki, Enontekiö, Inari) the mean annual temperature is from -1 to $-3\,°C$ in the palsa region. Inland, the mean temperature of February ranges from -10 to $-15\,°C$ and in July from $+10$ to $+14\,°C$ (Atlas över Sverige, 1953–1971; Atlas of Finland, 1960).

The mean annual precipitation on the coast of Norway exceeds 2000 mm and in mountains along the border between Norway and Sweden about 1600 mm (Atlas över Sverige, 1953–1971, p. 32) decreasing rapidly towards the east to 450 mm and even below 350 mm (Karesuando) along the border between Sweden and Finland. The depth of snow cover decreases in the same way from the Swedish fjells towards the east from 130 cm to less than 60 cm (Atlas över Sverige, 1953–1971, p. 1) and ranges in Finnish Lapland from 50 to 70 cm towards the east (Atlas of Finland, 1960). Forty to fifty percent of precipitation is snow, and snow

45

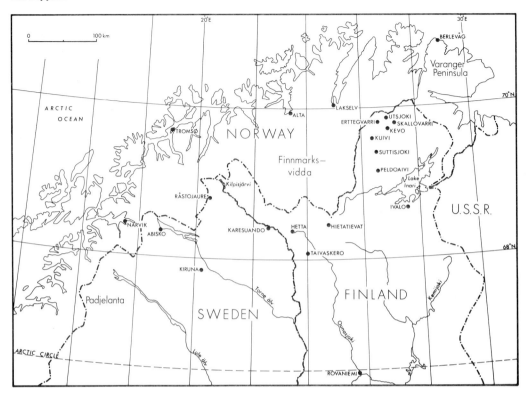

Figure 3.1. Northern Fennoscandia, showing places mentioned in the text.

cover lasts from 180 to 220 days a year (Andersson, 1976, p. 27).

Distribution of permafrost

The distribution of permafrost in Fennoscandia has been recorded mainly on the basis of landform morphology (e.g. Rapp, 1982). Palsas in northern mires have been described as permafrost features (e.g. Kihlman, 1890) and also ice-cored moraines on the high fjells (Østrem, 1964). Recently the existence of permafrost over vast areas of the high mountains has been described. It occurs in sediments and bedrock (King, 1983, 1984). Massive permafrost has been found in glacial till (Lagerbäck and Rodhe, 1985).

Seasonal frost

The road and building constructors in Fennoscandia have for a long time paid attention to frost. In central Finnish Lapland, north of the Arctic Circle, the mean date of the first ground frost is the 15th of October and it thaws between the 10th and 20th of June. Thus in mineral soils the frost season is some

8 months in duration (Soveri and Varjo, 1977). Further north, towards the Arctic Ocean, the frost season gets shorter. It depends not only on the air temperature but also on the thickness of snow cover and type of soil. Locally, in places with thin snow cover, frost is able to penetrate to a depth of over 3 m in mineral soil (Seppälä, 1976) while in northernmost Finland, on mires with normal snowcover, the average depth of frost penetration is 40–50 cm (Seppälä, 1982a, 1983).

Slope processes

On steep slopes both rapid and slow mass movements take place. Rock slides, partly due to frost shattering, are rather common on high fjells in northern Fennoscandia (Rapp, 1960; Söderman, 1980). Very well developed hundred metre high talus cones can be found under many vertical cliffs in northern Norway, for example in the Alta river valley, in Lakselv, and in Sandfjord close to Berlevåg (Åhman *et al.*, 1982).

Debris flows are especially active during snow and frost melt when the surface material is fully saturated by water and slides over the frost table. Heavy summer rains also cause debris flows on fjell slopes (Rapp, 1985; Nyberg, 1985).

One special type of rapid mass movement in periglacial conditions is the slush flow, an avalanche of wet snow which transports debris downslope and forms typical, chaotic poorly sorted deposits (Nyberg, 1985).

Gelifluction and solifluction are characteristic phenomena on the fjell slopes above the timberline. In Kärkevagge valley, Sweden, Strömquist (1983, p. 252) has recorded a rate of movement of gelifluction which is 100–350 times larger than surface wash. The median surface movement was 30 mm y^{-1} for 16 years. This corresponds well with observations from north western Finnish Lapland of 20–60 mm y^{-1} (Seppälä, 1979a). Slow mass movements form gelifluction lobes and terraces (steps) at lower levels. In Finnish Lapland the vertical height at their lower edge ranges from 1 to 1.5 m (Seppälä, 1982b).

One must keep in mind that all these slope processes can take place with only seasonal frost and permafrost is not needed for them to remain active.

Frost sorting

In wind-exposed places with silty till, where the ground water table is close to the surface, frost penetrates deeply into the ground and heaves stones and till. This process forms sorted stone polygons which are found on the summits of many fjells. On the fjell slopes, with an inclination of more than a few degrees, sorted stripes can be several hundreds of metres long and a few metres wide (Seppälä, 1972b, 1982b). Stone polygons are irregular in shape and have a diameter of 3 to 6 m, in some cases up to 10 m. Typical material of these large polygons is coarse till. The fine fraction is located in the central part and surrounded by large blocks and stones. Most sorted stone polygons at altitudes lower than 550 m are now inactive (Seppälä, 1982b).

The sorting of stone polygons is more active on the bottom of very shallow ponds which are dry for part of the year. There the water level is very close to the ground surface and can be seen many times between the stones during the summer. The bottom material is usually silty till with blocks. Even at low altitudes (100 m a.s.l.) in the birch forest zone frost activity is very strong at these sites (Seppälä and

Figure 3.2. Stone polygons 1 to 3 m in diameter on a terrace of the Vaskojoki river, Finnish Lapland. Note the well rounded stones.

Rastas, 1980; Seppälä, 1982*b*). Underwater polygons are also frequently observed.

Stone polygons occur on glaciofluvial gravel which contains some fine material. The stones are well rounded and sorted. This type of polygon, with a diameter up to 3 m, has been found on a terrace of the River Vaskojoki, Finnish Lapland (Seppälä, 1982*b*) (Figure 3.2).

In regions of deep seasonal frost boulder depressions are evidence of frost sorting. In small basins with a high ground water table boulders have been heaved to the ground surface. The dimension of these block concentrations vary from a few up to hundreds of metres (Seppälä, 1982*b*). The largest single boulder depression found in southern Finland is 10–20,000 square metres in area (Söderman, 1982). They occur throughout Finland (Piirola, 1969; Aartolahti 1969) and in Sweden (Lundqvist, 1951). Large areas with boulder depressions exist in the Lake Inari basin. In most places they are inactive but in northern Lapland the blocks are still in motion. Inactive forms can be easily reactivated when environmental conditions change and frost penetrates

deeper. Moving blocks normally lack lichens (Seppälä, 1982*b*).

Active small boulder depressions can be called stone pits and they are found everywhere in northern Fennoscandia on the edges of mires with thin peat cover. They are normally 1 to 3 m in diameter and less than 1 m deep. Fine material is washed out and the ground water table can often be seen in between the stones.

Frost heave and patterned ground

Frost heave is a well known phenomenon in Fennoscandia. Every spring stones are heaved in the fields. In northern Finland measurements every winter show that roads may heave as much as 50 cm.

Frost heaves boulders to the ground surface in a short time. For example, in Skallovarri, Utsjoki, Finland, the heaving of a big block was observed for several years. At first only a small corner was visible. Five years later the whole stone, about 50 × 60 × 80 cm, was lying on the surface (Figure 3.3).

In the upland region where silty till exists above

Figure 3.3. Frost heaved block. Skallovarri, Finnish Lapland. 27 August, 1975.

Figure 3.4. Patterned ground with raised centre free of snow about 30 cm above the surrounding stone circle (under snow). Below the surface, 6–10 cm is unfrozen. The material is silty till Peldoaivi, Finnish Lapland. 26 April 1969.

the timberline (*regio alpina*) (Seppälä and Rastas, 1980) there are nonsorted circles with diameter up to 3 m lacking vegetation (Figure 3.4). These are bounded by small cracks at the surface (Seppälä, 1982*b*) and are similar in character to those described by Washburn (1979, Figure 5.5) in NE Greenland. One of the largest fields of nonsorted circles is some hundred metres in diameter and is found in W Utsjoki north of the fjell Kuivi (Seppälä, 1982*b*). The effect of reindeer, digging their feeding pits in snow during the winter, on the formation of these nonsorted circles, is unknown.

Seasonal frost cracking and sand wedges

Frost cracks and frost-crack polygons can be found in sand dunes in northern Fennoscandia (Aartolahti, 1972; Seppälä, 1982*b*). On vegetation-covered deflation surfaces lying between sand dunes, the polygons are bounded by furrow-like depressions in the ground with a 5 to 15 cm deep open fissure in the middle of them. The polygons are irregular in shape. The length of their sides varies from 1 to 12 m. Most crack junctions are at angles of about 120° (Seppälä, 1982*b*). The depth of the crack is less than 70 cm. Of importance for the formation of seasonal frost cracks is the fact that at least in spring, the ground water table lies close to the surface of the deflation basin (Seppälä, 1982*b*).

A type of sand-wedge polygon is found on Hietatievat esker, Finnish Lapland (Seppälä, 1966, 1982*b*). On the upper part of the esker sand dunes exist with blow-outs (Figure 3.5). In some blow-outs deflation has exposed stratified silt (Figure 3.6). The silt surface is dissected by fissures filled with aeolian sand. Also found are open cracks with depths ranging from 0.5 to 2.5 cm in the centre of the aeolian filling. The wedges are between 35 and 50 cm deep. Their width at the surface varies from 30 to 60 cm and tapers rapidly downwards (Figure 3.7). The most likely origin of these sand-wedge polygons with diameters from 2 to 4 m is that they are connected with seasonal frost cracking of the silt (frost contraction). Desiccation may not be a possibility, because the polygons are so large. Once open, the cracks are filled with aeolian sand transported on the surface of the blow-out. During winter the silt is deeply frozen but the sand wedge itself is dry (Seppälä, 1982*b*).

Figure 3.5. Sand dunes destroyed by deflation on Hietatievat, Finnish Lapland. July, 1965.

Large (10–20 m in diameter) non-sorted polygons have been discovered in northern Sweden (Rapp and Clark, 1971; Melander, 1976, 1977). They occur mainly above the tree line on flat areas of till or outwash gravel in wind-exposed valley bottoms from 650 to 1000 m a.s.l. Similar large tundra polygons are found on coarse gravel deltas and raised marine terraces in windy places in northern Norway (Svensson, 1962, 1963). On the surface in shallow depressions are often found open cracks 1 to 3 cm wide and 10 to 20 cm deep (Svensson, 1969a). These soil wedges are rarely deeper than one metre (Åhman et al., 1982). It is problematic whether the features are active (i.e. seasonal frost crack phenomena) or inactive (i.e. reflecting an earlier stage of permafrost) like the ice-wedge casts in southern Finland (Aartolahti, 1970) or southern Sweden (Johnsson, 1981).

Frost mounds

Northern Fennoscandia is a classic region for palsa studies (Ruuhijärvi, 1960; Ohlson, 1964; Vorren, 1967; Åhman, 1977; Seppälä, 1979b; Seppälä (in press); Rapp, 1982). Palsas are the most typical permafrost features in northern regions with mean annual air temperature less than − 1 °C.

A palsa is a permafrost cored peat hummock rising from a mire (Seppälä, 1972c). The diameter of palsas range from a few metres to several tens of metres and their height from less than 1 m to 7 m. They may be dome shaped or hundreds of metres long ridges (Åhman, 1977) (Figure 3.8). Palsa complexes, also called peat plateaus, have diameters of hundreds of metres and a rather flat character. They may contain thermokarst hollows (Seppälä, 1979b, 1982b). The inner structure of the palsa is mostly composed of segregated ice and frozen peat with small ice crystals. Palsas also may have a minerogenic core below the peat cover. The boundary between the peat and the minerogenic soil is very sharp. Clayey silt with segregated ice (both vertical and horizontal ice lenses are found) is the typical material. In the upper part of the core the ice content is often more than 100% of the dry weight of the soil (Åhman, 1976).

Palsas form in places where wind thins the snow cover on a mire, so that frost can penetrate deeply into the peat. This causes initial upheaval of the surface, and during subsequent winters the hump has a greater tendency to become snow-free and the thickness of the frozen layer increases (Fries and Bergström, 1910). This has been experimentally

Figure 3.6. Sand wedge field in a blow-out on
Hietatievat, Finnish Lapland. 12 July, 1965.

Figure 3.7. Cross section of a sand wedge on
Hietatievat. Shorter side of the compass is
6.5 cm. 12 July, 1965.

Figure 3.8. About 3 m high collapsing palsa. Erttegvarri, northern Finland. 11 July, 1972.

tested in the field by clearing the mire surface of snow several times during the winter (Seppälä, 1982a). The end point of the cyclic development of a palsa is a rounded open pond or group of ponds on the mire. The pond might be surrounded by a low (0.5 to 2 m) rim ridge of peat (Seppälä, 1979b, 1982a, 1982b, in press).

It is possible to confuse pingo remnants with palsas. For example, the 'fossil' pingo described by Dylik (1961) near Lódź (Jozefow) in Poland has the characteristics of a buried palsa with side crackings in a 0.5 m thick peat layer (Seppälä, in press).

Rapp and Rudberg (1960) first described the circular lakes in the Abisko region, northern Sweden, and suspected them to be 'remains of small pingos'. On the plateau of Finnmarksvidda in the northernmost part of Norway (Figure 3.1) small ponds have been found with a circular or oval shape (Svensson, 1969b) which are less than 50 m in diameter and occur in groups (Svensson, 1976). In Finnish Lapland circular ridges of mineral material have been observed which resemble ramparts found in western Europe and called pingo-like remnants (Pissart, 1963; Watson, 1971).

Svensson (1964) described traces of pingo-like frost mounds but later came to the conclusion that 'true pingos in active formation do not exist in the Scandinavian peninsula' (Svensson, 1976). However, ice-cored mounds with a massive permafrost core (at least 8 m thick) have recently been described in Råstojaure, northernmost Sweden (Lagerbäck and Rodhe, 1985). The height of these mounds range from about 2 m to slightly more than 7 m and the diameters from 20 to 80 m. They are located in a basin at an altitude of 700 to 800 m and well above the tree-line. The mean annual temperature of the region is about $-3.5\,°C$. Lagerbäck and Rodhe (1985) conclude that these frost mounds may be open-system type pingos.

Peat and earth hummocks are very common features in the high Arctic where they cover large areas. They are not rare in Fennoscandia, but several types of peat and earth hummock of a seasonal frost origin have been found.

Peat hummocks (in Finnish called *pounu*(s)), are typical of mires and edges of palsa bogs (Figure 3.9). They have been described in detail by Salmi (1972), and are normally less than 1 m high and up to 1.5 m in diameter. The peat is often less than 60 cm thick and there may be a mineral core compressed upwards. Normally there is very little peat or just mineral soil around a *pounu*. *Pounus* rise above the

Figure 3.9. A group of *pounus* (*pounikko*) close to Skallovarri, Utsjoki, Finland. 30 July, 1985.

snow cover during the winter and therefore frost penetrates deep into their core. On these frost mounds the growing conditions are good for several mire plants and this means that the thickness of peat increases. Under the peat can often be found an ice lens some 10 to 20 cm thick which thaws before the end of the thawing season. *Pounus* occur normally in groups which are called *pounikko* (a Finnish word meaning a group of *pounus*) (Ruuhijärvi, 1960, pp. 220–222).

Earth hummocks, the so-called *thufurs* (an Icelandic term), which are mineral and humus knobs with a height and diameter of 10 cm to some decimetres, can be found in northern Fennoscandia especially on mountain slopes with silty material where the ground water table is close to the surface (Seppälä, 1982*b*).

The distribution of *pounus* or *thufurs* has not been systematically mapped: their small size makes them unidentifiable using remote sensing techniques.

Sand dunes and deflation

In the same periglacial environment where palsas occur we find active deflation on glaciofluvial and aeolian sands as well as on the edges of eskers and deltas (Seppälä, 1971, 1972*a*). The larger deflation basins are about 10 m deep and hundreds of metres in diameter. Only small remnants of the early postglacial periglacial parabolic dunes remain (Seppälä, 1973) (Figure 3.5).

Discussion and conclusions

In regions with seasonal frost lasting at least 7 months it is possible to find a rich selection of geomorphic phenomena produced by ground frost. The formation of most of these does not require permafrost.

Periglacial processes are an effective morphological agent in northern Fennoscandia. However, small scale periglacial features have little influence on the postglacial landscape. More significant effects are found on steep slopes.

Returning to the analogue theme one can pose a question to colleagues studying Pleistocene periglacial phenomena in Central and Western Europe: 'Are inactive periglacial features such as ice-wedge casts, frost cracks, collapsed mounds with rim ridges and solifluction slope deposits, which are found in "favourable" places, really indicative of continuous permafrost or could they have formed under sporadic permafrost and/or deep seasonal frost, as happens today in northern Fennoscandia?' In answer, it must be emphasized that favourable conditions for formation of many periglacial phenomena require only: 1) a winter sufficiently cold, 2) adequate moisture in ground, 3) thin snow cover and 4) suitable soil for movement of capillary water during freezing. It is of course more fascinating to imagine thick and massive permafrost as in North America and the USSR where periglacial phenomena are ubiquitous. In Central and Western Europe, however, their distribution is scattered. During colder periods of the Pleistocene in UK or during the transition from cold, non-glacial to warmer, interglacial or post-glacial conditions, there may have been a zone of sporadic permafrost or deep seasonal frost similar to that present in northern Fennoscandia today. A similar suite of landforms might be expected but, surprisingly, the UK literature does not indicate this. It may be that the mountains in the west of Fennoscandia collect precipitation from the Atlantic Ocean and keep summers relatively dry. In western Europe this climatic barrier was missing and the UK climate may have been more humid. On the other hand, pollen studies suggest that much of the UK Devensian period had a continental, cold climate which is counter to the precipitation arguments previously advanced. One must conclude that the significance and utility of the northern Fennoscandian analogue for Pleistocene periglacial conditions in the UK is ambiguous.

References

Aartolahti, T. (1969). On patterned ground in southern Finland. *Ann. Acad. Sci. Fennicae*, Ser. AIII, **104**, 30 pp.

Aartolahti, T. (1970). Fossil ice-wedges, tundra polygons and recent cracks in southern Finland. *Ann. Acad. Sci. Fennicae*, Ser. AIII, **107**, 26 pp.

Aartolahti, T. (1972). Dyynien routahalkeamista ja routahalkeamapolygoneista. (Summary: Frost cracks and frost crack polygons on dunes in Finland). *Terra*, **84**, 124–31.

Åhman, R. (1976). The structure and morphology of minerogenic palsas in northern Norway. *Biul. Perygl.*, **26**, 25–31.

Åhman, R. (1977). Palsar i Nordnorge. *Medd. Lunds Univ. Geogr. Inst., Avhandl.*, **78**, 165 pp.

Åhman, R., Seppälä, M. and Svensson, H. (1982). Periglacial excursion in northern Finland and Norway 1–8 September 1979. *Biul. Perygl.*, **29**, 261–73.

Andersson, T. (1976). Klimat, in *Norden i text och kartor* (Ed. H.W. Ahlmann), pp. 26–27, Generalstabens Litografiska Anstalts Förlag, Stockholm.

Atlas of Finland 1960, Geographical Society of Finland, Helsinki.

Atlas över Sverige. (1953–1971). National Atlas of Sweden Svenska Sällskapet för Antropologi och Geografi, Stockholm.

Dylik, J. (1961). Guide-book of excursion C, The Lódź region. *VIth INQUA Congress Publ.*, 84 pp.

Fries, T. and Bergström, E. (1910). Några iakttagelser öfver palsar och deras förekomst i nordligaste Sverige. *Geol. Fören. Stockholm Förh.*, **32**, 195–205.

Johnsson, G. (1981). Fossil patterned ground in southern Sweden. *Geol. Fören. Stockholm Förh.*, **103**, 79–89.

Kihlman, A.O. (1890). Pflanzenbiologische Studien aus Russisch Lappland. *Acta Soc. pro Fauna Flora Fennica*, 6:3, 263 pp.

King, L. (1983). High mountain permafrost in Scandinavia. *Permafrost, Fourth Intern. Conf. Proc.*, pp. 612–617, Nat. Acad. Press, Washington, D.C.

King, L. (1984). Permafrost in Scandinavia. Untersuchungsergebnisse aus Lappland, Jotunheimen und Dovre/Rondane. *Heidelberger Geogr. Arb.*, **76**, 174 pp.

Lagerbäck, R. and Rodhe, L. (1985). Pingos in northernmost Sweden. *Geogr. Annlr.*, **67A**, 239–45.

Lundqvist, G. (1951). Blocksänkor och några andra frostfenomen. *Geol. Fören. Stockholm Förh.*, **73**, 505–12.

Melander, O. (1976). *Geomorfologiska kartbladet 29J Kiruna.* SNV PM 741.

Melander, O. (1977). *Geomorfologiska kartbladet 30I Abisko, etc.* SNV PM 857.

Nyberg, R. (1985). Debris flows and slush avalanches in northern Swedish Lappland. *Medd. Lunds. Univ. Geogr. Inst., Avhandl.*, **97**, 222 pp.

Ohlson, B. (1964). Frostaktivität, Verwitterung und Bodenbildung in den Fjeldgegenden von Enontekiö, Finnisch-Lappland. *Fennia*, **89**:3, 180 pp.

Østrem, G. (1964). Ice-cored moraines in Scandinavia. *Geogr. Annlr.*, **46**, 282–337.

Piirola, J. (1969). Frost-sorted block concentrations in western Inari, Finnish Lapland. *Fennia*, **99**, 35 pp.

Pissart, A. (1963). Les traces de 'pingos' au Pays de Galles (Grande Bretange) et du Plateau des Hautes Fagnes (Belgique), *Zeit. Geomorph.* N.F., 7, 147–65.

Rapp, A. (1960). Recent development of mountain slopes in Kärkevagge and surroundings, northern Scandinavia. *Geogr. Annlr.*, **42**, 73–200.

Rapp, A. (1982). Zonation of permafrost indicators in Swedish Lappland. *Geogr. Tidsskr.*, **82**, 37–8.

Rapp, A. (1985). Extreme rainfall and rapid snowmelt as causes of mass movements in high latitude mountains, in *Field and theory. Lectures in geocryology.* (Eds. M. Church and O. Slaymaker), pp. 36–56, Univ. British Columbia Press, Vancouver.

Rapp, A. and Clark, G.M. (1971). Large nonsorted polygons in Padjelanta national park, Swedish Lappland. *Geogr. Annlr.*, **53A**, 71–85.

Rapp, A. and Rudberg, S. (1960). Recent periglacial phenomena in Sweden. *Biul. Perygl.*, **8**, 143–54.

Ruuhijärvi, R. (1960). Uber die regionale Einteilung der Nordfinnischen Moore. *Ann. Bot. Soc. 'Vanamo'*, **31**, 360 pp.

Salmi, M. (1972). Present development stages of palsas in Finland. *Proc. 4th Intern. Peat Congr.*, **1**, 121–41.

Seppälä, M. (1966). Recent ice-wedge polygons in eastern Enontekiö, northernmost Finland. *Publ. Inst. Geogr. Univ. Turku*, **42**, 274–87.

Seppälä, M. (1971). Evolution of eolian relief of the Kaamasjoki-Kiellajoki river basin in Finnish Lapland. *Fennia*, **104**, 88 pp.

Seppälä, M. (1972a). Location, morphology and orientation of inland dunes in northern Sweden. *Geogr. Annlr.*, **54A**, 85–104.

Seppälä, M. (1972b). Peat at the top of Rouhttir fell, Finnish Lapland. *Rep. Kevo Subarctic Station*, **9**, 1–6.

Seppälä, M. (1972c). The term 'palsa'. *Zeit Geomorph. N.F.*, **16**, 463.

Seppälä, M. (1973). On the formation of periglacial sand dunes in northern Fennoscandia. *Ninth Congr. INQUA (Christchurch), Abstracts*, 318–19.

Seppälä, M. (1976). Periglacial character of the climate of the Kevo region (Finnish Lapland) on the basis of meteorological observations 1962–71. *Rep. Kevo Subarctic Sta.*, **13**, 1–11.

Seppälä, M. (1979a). A new technique to measure the rate of mass movement on slopes. *Studia Geomorph. Carpatho-Balcanica*, **13**, 221–4.

Seppälä, M. (1979b). Recent palsa studies in Finland. *Acta Univ. Oulu, Ser. A*, **82**, 81–7.

Seppälä, M. (1982a). An experimental study of the formation of palsas, in *The Roger J.E. Brown Memorial Volume. Proc. Fourth Can. Permafrost Conf.*, Calgary, 36–42.

Seppälä, M. (1982b). Present-day periglacial phenomena in northern Finland. *Biul. Perygl.*, **29**, 231–43.

Seppälä, M. (1983). Seasonal thawing of palsas in Finnish Lapland. *Permafrost, Fourth Intern. Conf. Proc.*, pp. 1127–32. Nat. Acad. Press, Washington, D.C.

Seppälä, M. (in press). Palsas and related forms, in *Advances in periglacial geomorphology*, (Ed. M.J. Clark), Wiley, Chichester.

Seppälä, M. and Rastas, J. (1980). Vegetation map of northernmost Finland with special reference to subarctic forest limits and natural hazards. *Fennia*, **158**, 41–61.

Söderman, G. (1980). Slope processes in cold environments of northern Finland. *Fennia*, **158**, 83–152.

Söderman, G. (1982). Södra Finlands blocksänkor. *Geogr. Tidskr.*, **82**, 77–81.

Soveri, J. and Varjo, M. (1977). Roudan muodostumisesta ja esiintymisestä Suomessa vuosina 1955–1975. (Summary: On the formation and occurrence of soil frost in Finland 1955 to 1975). *Publ. Water Res. Inst. Nat. Board of Waters, Finland*, **20**, 66 pp.

Strömquist, L. (1983). Gelifluction and surface wash, their importance and interaction on a periglacial slope. *Geogr. Annlr.*, **65A**, 245–54.

Svensson, H. (1962). Note on a type of patterned ground on the Varanger peninsula, Norway. *Geogr. Annlr.*, **44**, 413.

Svensson, H. (1963). Tundra polygons. Photographic interpretation and field studies in North-Norwegian polygon areas. *Årb. Norges Geol. Unders.*, 223.

Svensson, H. (1964). Traces of pingo-like frost mounds. *Svensk Geogr. Årsb.*, **40**, 93–106.

Svensson, H. (1969a). Open fissures in a polygonal net on the Norwegian Arctic coast. *Biul. Perygl.*, **19**, 389–98.

Svensson, H. (1969b). A type of circular lakes in northern-most Norway. *Geogr. Annlr.*, **51A**, 1–12.

Svensson, H. (1976). Pingo problems in the Scandinavian countries. *Biul. Perygl.*, **26**, 33–40.

Vorren, K-D. (1967). Evig tele i Norge. *Ottar*, **51**, 3–26.

Wallén, C.C. (1960). Climate, in *A geography of Norden* (Ed. A. Sømme), pp. 41–53, J.W. Cappelens Forlag, Oslo.

Washburn, A.L. (1979). *Geocryology. A survey of periglacial processes and environments*. Arnold, London, 406 pp.

Watson, E. (1971). Remains of pingos in Wales and the Isle of Man. *Geol. Jour.*, **7**, 381–92.

4 · Spatial and temporal trends in alpine periglacial studies: implications for paleo reconstruction

COLIN E. THORN AND DEBORAH S. LOEWENHERZ

Abstract

Due to similarities in their glacial histories, the Colorado Front Range, U.S.A., represents a feasible analogue for reconstructions of previous periglacial activity in the British uplands. A model of landform evolution based on the relationship between climatic conditions and energy regime can be used to evaluate the general response of the landscape to periods of deglaciation and subsequent intervals of climatic stability and/or climatic amelioration/deterioration. Examples drawn from the Colorado Front Range illustrate the contribution of topography to the interaction of periglacial landforms with local ground climate. This interaction can be identified at macro-, meso-, and microscales and appears to place a strong spatial imprint on the temporal patterns of periglacial landform evolution observed in mid-latitude alpine environments.

Introduction

The uplands of Great Britain exhibit most of the periglacial landforms found in other alpine, periglacial regions; although, with the exception of the smaller forms, the British features are inactive today. The presence of inactive forms inevitably invites the use of analogues, both by those interested in the features themselves and those interested in their usefulness for paleo-reconstructions. The creation of analogues is an oft-trodden path in Quaternary and earth sciences and one fraught with difficulties; nevertheless, with careful forethought and a flexible perspective, analogues still represent one of the best techniques currently available to geomorphologists. In this paper we attempt to extract and synthesize from the literature on the alpine, periglacial regime of the Front Range, Colorado, U.S.A. some salient geomorphic attributes that might serve those investigating the British periglacial landscapes.

Undoubtedly the mountains of Great Britain have experienced multiple glaciations (e.g. King, 1976; Sissons, 1974). However, in upland regions the ice appears to have been so erosive that the only widely available and undisputed field evidence relates to the late-Devensian glaciation, which had apparently left most of Scotland deglaciated long before 11,000 BP (Sissons, 1981), and also to the Loch Lomond (Re) Advance (Sissons, 1980) which produced small glaciers in the Lake District, North Wales (Gray, 1982) and southern Scotland, as well as a large ice mass in the western Highlands of Scotland.

The larger periglacial features in the uplands of Britain generally lie outside the most recent glacial limit. This is most commonly interpreted to mean not only that earlier periglacial features were obliterated by glacial erosion, but that the existing forms also were created during late-Devensian and/or Loch Lomond Advance times. This is a logical possibility, perhaps even probability, but given the known emergence of periglacial features intact from beneath glacial ice elsewhere (e.g. Whalley *et al.*, 1985) it is important to appreciate that at least some periglacial features might be much older (Sugden, 1971). Many smaller periglacial forms require less severe climatic regimes and are found throughout the uplands, in some cases having been shown to be active even today (e.g. Tufnell, 1972).

There are a number of broad similarities between the periglacial histories of the British uplands and the Front Range of Colorado, but there are also some equally important differences. Large scale valley glaciation (there appears to have been no overriding ice cap) ended in the Front Range with termination of the Pinedale glaciation between 15,000 and 12,000 BP (Madole, 1986). Subsequently there were three distinct periods of Neoglaciation between 5,000 and 100 BP (Benedict, 1973*a*). The present periglacial landform assemblages represent larger scale features formed during colder phases, plus smaller features that are presently active. Thus both regions exhibit periglacial features in glaciated valleys and on unglaciated interfluves, although in Britain ancient glaciation of interfluves and the possibility of more recent protective ice-carapaces cannot be overlooked.

Perhaps the most important dissimilarity between the two regions is the extremely continental climate of Colorado versus the maritime climate of Great Britain; a contrast that is exacerbated by latitudinal differences. Williams (1975) noted the apparently unusual character of the paleo-periglacial climate in Britain and thought that present day analogues might not exist. Sugden (1971) also remarked on the extremely narrow temperature range ($\sim 2°$ C) that appears to separate the largely inactive periglacial regime of the Cairngorm Mountains today from periods of full scale glaciation. The discrepancy between the unglaciated Front Range interfluves and glaciated British upland interfluves must not be overlooked, especially as the precise nature of the late-Devensian ice cover is still debatable. Each region also has potentially important peculiarities. Recent work in the Front Range has led to a heavy emphasis being placed on aeolian influx (Thorn and Darmody, 1985). In upland Britain man's modification of the environment is of considerable importance (Tufnell, 1985), and particular emphasis needs to be placed on the importance of sheep grazing in modifying the microenvironments in which presently active forms develop.

A model

Perhaps the most pressing issue when creating any kind of geomorphic model or framework is identification of appropriate scales. At present it does not seem that such issues are well defined in periglacial geomorphology and precise definitions are beyond the scope of this paper. We will use macroscale to refer to landscape elements of the magnitude of individual valleys and interfluves, or larger; mesoscale to characterize such features as an individual rock glacier or talus; microscale to denote single solifluction lobes, stone stripes, and the like.

While introduction of the concepts of magnitude and frequency (Wolman and Miller, 1960) was a quite fundamental contribution to geomorphology their relevance has been considerably enhanced by the addition of the notions of 'healing time' (Wol-

man and Gerson, 1978) and 'sequence' (Church, 1980). It is now clear that it is appropriate to distinguish between those events that initiate landforms and those that sustain them. At a macroscale periglacial processes appear unlikely to have created any landforms in recently glaciated alpine regions, while they may sustain them. At a mesoscale some periglacial landform initiation occurs; for example some, but not all, rock glaciers. At microscales all stages of landform development may be dominated by periglacial activity. We suspect that the widespread disequilibrium that occurs during a paraglacial period (Church and Ryder, 1972) is disproportionately important in deglaciated periglacial environments because it is rich in landform-initiating events; while the subsequent periglacial regime is characterized largely by non-catastrophic, sustaining processes such as sheetwash erosion, rockfall and frost creep.

The distinction between erosional and depositional forms is also relevant. The absence of any direct erosional record means that interpretation of erosional forms for paleo-reconstructions is particularly hazardous. In periglacial regions the nivation hollow is a favourite, but often abused, example (Thorn, in press). For this reason our ideas are largely restricted to depositional forms.

A final concern is the relationship between climatic variability and the development, maintenance, and decay of periglacial forms. We believe that this issue is best considered as interaction between ground climate and landform, and that the distinction between 'air or meteorological screen' and ground climates is increasingly important as spatial scale decreases. Clearly air and ground climates are linked but there are also many complicating factors that are frequently profoundly important in periglacial regimes. Bearing in mind our use of 'climate' to mean ground climate, we now turn to this issue.

The evolutionary model presented in Figure 4.1 employs climatic conditions as the independent variable that determines the energy regime characterizing a geomorphic environment. The term 'energy regime' is used here to refer to the capacity for material breakdown and transport within the geomorphic system. In a glacial environment the mechanical erosion and transport mechanisms associated with mobile ice are generally much more effective than those available after deglaciation. Therefore, we represent the glacial landscape as being characterized by a higher energy regime.

Juxtaposed to the relationship between climatic conditions and energy regime is the response of the

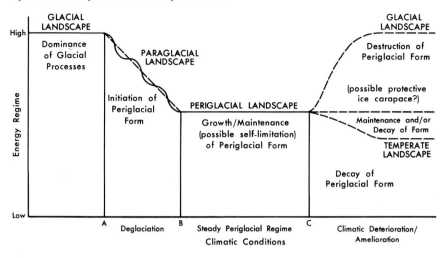

Figure 4.1. Potential behaviour of periglacial landforms under changing environmental conditions. For the sake of clarity we have only shown what we believe to be the most likely pattern of behaviour. Protective, as opposed to erosive, ice would certainly change the pattern; it is even possible that certain kinds of temperate regime would represent higher, rather than lower, energy than a periglacial one. This diagram is partially derived from Graf (1977).

landscape to the environment. In alpine regions, the onset of a periglacial regime is usually associated with the deglaciation of a landscape (point A in Figure 4.1). During the ensuing paraglacial period (extending from point A to B), relaxation occurs as the land surface attempts to equilibrate within the altered environment. These internal adjustments often propagate as disruptions within the slope sediment flux system and lead to the initiation of periglacial forms, both erosional and depositional. Past glacial activity may precondition the landscape, providing energy (e.g. gravitational potential) and materials for the formation of periglacial landforms.

If environmental conditions remain relatively constant, periglacial forms will continue to develop and be maintained via geomorphic events which transfer material through the forms. This timespan represents the segment from point B to C on the diagram and is associated with steady state forms in equilibrium with the periglacial environment. Achievement of a steady state is scale dependent and much more likely to occur in microscale phenomena than macroscale ones.

The pattern of development and maintenance exhibited by a particular form will be a function of the magnitude, the frequency and the sequence of sediment transfer events which either contribute or remove material from the form. In certain cases, landform development can only proceed to a predetermined limit before feedback mechanisms prevent further growth and either the form is maintained at that stage or a process of decay is initiated. This latter pattern of internally-imposed growth and decay appears to control the development of solifluction lobes under stable environmental conditions (Price, 1974).

A change in climatic conditions (point C) will generally result in the degeneration of periglacial forms, which may follow one of several paths. Climatic deterioration which produces a reglaciation of the landscape will usually cause the destruction of periglacial forms (especially depositional ones) over a relatively brief span of time as the environment returns to a higher energy regime. However, there is evidence that periglacial forms may potentially survive glaciation, so that in certain cases other models of landform evolution may be possible (e.g. Rapp, 1984). Climatic amelioration which leads to a more temperate environment will result in a gradual modification and decay of periglacial forms as the surface readjusts to lower energy conditions. Particular forms will exhibit varying degrees of resilience to climatic change, with some being altered/modified very little and others degenerating rapidly, leaving no evidence of past periglacial conditions. In many cases, the degeneration of form will result from a reversal of formative processes; i.e. erosional features may be "smoothed out" by depositional processes, while depositional periglacial forms may be eroded.

In the model of periglacial landform evolution presented in Figure 4.1 changing climatic conditions alter the energy regime which, in turn, affects rates of material transfer. However, changes in climate are not directly dependent on any fixed time scale; therefore, time is not an explicit variable within the model. The model thus exhibits the characteristics of a 'floating equilibrium' model as discussed by Thornes and Brunsden (1977). The amount of time associated with each segment cannot be uniquely determined as changing environmental regimes are treated as external conditions that cause the landscape to proceed through the proposed sequence. It is recognized that the elapsing of time will significantly affect the response of the landscape to a particular set of environmental conditions. In most cases equilibrium 'conditions' will only be established in the periglacial landscape if the environmental conditions are relatively constant for a sufficient period of time. However, it is the stability of the environment rather than the passage of a finite amount of time which allows the periglacial landscape to be developed and maintained in a state of equilibrium.

The contribution of topographic context to the interaction of climate and landform evolution (topoclimate) must also be considered. On the macroscale, altitudinal variations along a transect could potentially provide a spatial analogue for temporal changes in the periglacial landscape associated with climatic variations (e.g. Madole, 1972). However, such patterns can only be broadly distinguished and much of the meso- and microscale geomorphic activity of interest in the present analysis is obscured at that scale. At meso- and micro-scales, the significance of topoclimate may be evaluated in terms of two sets of issues: 1) process stratification associated with relative slope position; and 2) microclimatic variations associated with aspect and snow accumulation patterns. The importance of slope position in determining the dominance of specific periglacial processes has been comprehensively modelled by Caine (1974, 1982, 1986). The effects of aspect on rates of periglacial mass wasting have also been recognized (e.g. Benedict, 1970; White, 1981; Olyphant, 1985), as has been the importance of snow accumulation patterns in the production of micro-environmental variability (Thorn, 1978; 1983). Since periglacial

processes appear to operate most effectively at meso- and microscales, the following treatment of potential paleo-environmental indicators will attempt to highlight the significance of topoclimate as a set of environmental conditions which substantially control spatial patterns of landscape evolution; this will be followed by a review of temporal aspects of the situation.

Present-day process geomorphology

The Indian Peaks, Front Range, Colorado contain some large erosional remnants (e.g. Niwot Ridge) that have probably never been glaciated (Madole, 1982) as well as glaciated valleys (e.g. Green Lakes valley) that experienced multiple glaciations of generally decreasing extent throughout the Quaternary. A comprehensive regional description may be found in White (1982), while contemporary alpine wasting has been summarized by Thorn and Loewenherz (in press). The greater portion of the research discussed here has been conducted on Niwot Ridge and in the Green Lakes valley, so it is important to appreciate that periglacial features within the valley have been glacially preconditioned, while those on the ridge crest have not.

Caine (1974, 1982, 1986) has produced a particularly interesting model of this area which synthesises the typical periglacial rate data available for individual landforms (e.g. turf-banked lobes and lobate rock glaciers) into a basin-wide scale. In doing this, individual process-form studies are given a context while detailed regional denudation estimates are provided. Caine has divided the landscape into two morphological subsystems (hillslopes and drainage network) and three cascading subsystems (coarse debris flux (grain-size > 8 mm); fine sediment flux (grain-size < 8 mm); geochemical flux). Within the hillslope subsystem individual landform elements are: interfluve; freeface; talus; talus foot; valley floor. The drainage network has alpine lakes as an important component, as well as streams.

At present, coarse debris transfer dominates the free-face/talus/talus foot complex, but the transfer is internal and does not deliver material to the drainage network. Many of the individual elements within this system have been studied separately and will be discussed in the next section. Transfers of coarse debris on the interfluve are extremely localized and overwhelmingly associated with their incorporation in a matrix of fines which is being mobilized primarily by frost creep and solifluction (Benedict, 1970).

Transfers of fine sediment dominate the interfluve. Benedict (1970) suggested that frost creep is the dominant process under the current regime and that solifluction is important only where high soil saturation occurs during fall freeze-up. More recently (Burns, 1980a), pedogenetic studies have revealed the great significance of aeolian influx (Thorn and Darmody, 1985) onto the alpine tundra and Caine (1974) has suggested that it is the only material currently moving across the entire landscape and being deposited into alpine lakes. The salient result from Caine's synthesis is determination of extremely low rates of clastic transfer in the Front Range compared to other alpine areas; however geochemical action appears to be greater than is commonly recognized.

Geochemical transfers are clearly tied very closely to the movement of near surface waters, a poorly understood topic in periglacial regimes. Caine (1982) has made a preliminary consideration of it at a basin scale using the upper Green Lakes valley, while Dixon (1983, 1986) has completed the first detailed soil chemistry studies in the area. We will not attempt to incorporate geochemical concepts in this paper as, despite their great significance in denudation, their spatial variability is still poorly known.

Coarse debris flux and forms

Alpine valley glaciation often produces widespread oversteepening of valley sides which, upon deglaciation, promotes unloading. This combination represents glacial preconditioning, but the ensuing geomorphic events usually run their course in a periglacial regime that commonly begins with a paraglacial period (Church and Ryder, 1972). Free-face genesis is not uniquely glacial, but in this presentation we will only consider alpine valley-side development derived from glacially modified free-faces.

Upon deglaciation, an instability series is initiated which is comprised of a degenerating free-face and an accumulating debris pile. The nature of the debris pile is variable, but not random (Madole, 1972; White, 1981). In the Front Range of Colorado, Madole (1972) has suggested that there is a set of mutually exclusive facies, with each component representing a unique depositional environment. The facies are: talus; talus with a protalus rampart; talus with incipient lobate rock glacier; lobate rock glacier; tongue-shaped rock glacier; till. The set responds to environmental change in such a fashion that the normal rules of horizontal and vertical facies relationships pertain. This postulated sequence appears to be broadly

valid, although detailed use of it requires careful consideration of the influence of both topoclimate as well as reaction and relaxation times.

Talus occupies a broad depositional zone (Madole, 1972; White 1981), exhibiting several primary subtypes and numerous secondary features. The principal subdivision of talus is into rockfall, alluvial and avalanche categories (White, 1981); each has a distinctive morphology whose origins may be partially related to the orientation and morphology of the surface above the free-face (White, 1981). It is also possible to assign distinct environmental significance to the presence of protalus ramparts at the talus foot. The genesis of protalus ramparts has not been a contentious matter and according to Madole they represent the severest environment in which talus will accumulate. Nevertheless, it is apparent that hybrid forms, intermediate between rampart and lobate rock glacier, are common.

Lobate rock glaciers represent flow in the talus foot zone due to ice-cementation. Olyphant (1983) has attempted to model this flow and concluded that it is best represented by a power law if time-dependent behaviour is the primary interest. Cliff weathering rates one to two orders of magnitude greater than those occurring above talus appear necessary to initiate rock glaciers, although they may be maintained by lower rates. Tongue-shaped rock glaciers have been much more contentious forms than lobate rock glaciers, and apparently have multiple origins (e.g. White 1981). Madole (1972) postulated that they represent an environment that is not quite harsh enough to produce glaciation, although both Benedict (1973b) and White (1981) suggest subtle, but important, alternative explanations for their formation.

Fine sediment flux and forms

The crest of Niwot Ridge is largely unglaciated and covered by regolith in which a variety of microscale periglacial forms have developed. Unlike valley-side forms, those on the gently rolling alpine tundra of the interfluve do not stem from glacial preconditioning. Nevertheless, Benedict (1970) demonstrated that processes and forms on the ridge crest exhibit some important topoclimatic attributes analogous to Madole's Neoglacial facies.

Benedict (1970) investigated two primary processes, frost creep and solifluction (gelifluction of Washburn, 1980) and four principal forms: turf-banked lobes and terraces, stone-banked lobes and terraces. By carefully monitoring the spatial and temporal patterns of the two processes Benedict

(1970, 219–223) was able to determine much about the domain and nature of each one, as well as much about their interaction. In general, frost creep dominates in drier contexts and favours the movement of coarser material. On the other hand, solifluction requires soil saturation during fall freeze-up (springtime saturation alone being inadequate) and under the present regime exceeds frost creep only in very specific locations. Near surface soil movement rates on Niwot Ridge are presently controlled primarily by the depth to groundwater during the fall freeze-up with slope gradient playing a secondary role; differences in soil texture and temperature play only minor and indirect roles.

In investigating the specific relationships between individual processes and individual forms Benedict found important variations. On Niwot Ridge what would commonly be called solifluction lobes are actually driven by both solifluction and frost creep. Hence Benedict's preference for morphological terminology, e.g. turf-banked lobe rather than solifluction lobe. He found that where solifluction predominates fines move more rapidly than coarse fragments, but where frost creep predominates the relationship is reversed. However, all four forms investigated require snow accumulation slopes, plus a break in slope that locally reduces downslope movement rates. The preceding appear to be necessary requirements, but they may not be sufficient ones; for example stone stripes and stone-banked lobes also require a supply of coarse debris in addition to a frost creep dominated micro-environment. In turn, these findings indicate that caution is necessary when paleo-forms are interpreted in process terms.

Bendict (1970) mapped the spatial distribution of all four forms, as well as their 'vertical' position (i.e. superimposition of one on another); in conjunction with this work he also monitored present-day process rates and estimated paleo-rates from excavation and radio-carbon dating (Benedict, 1966). This combination enabled him to identify 'catenary' (Benedict, 1970, 174–175) sequences of periglacial forms, as well as infer environmental variability from the changes in form type.

The highly specific micro-environments required to generate turf-banked lobes and terraces, as well as stone-banked lobes and terraces mean that substantial areas of interest may be devoid of them. At one end of the spectrum increasing snowfall will lead to snow accumulation sufficient to generate permanent snow patches, while at the other end windswept conditions should create xeric tundra fellfields, Thorn (1978, 1983) has already attempted to show that snow accumulation patterns afford a useful perspective from which to view the organization of surficial geomorphic processes within alpine tundra and Bovis and Thorn (1981) have illustrated that significant differences in sediment transfer exist even when overt landforms do not.

One area where mechanical transfer of fine sediments and geochemical processes are known to produce discernible spatial patterns is in pedogenesis. Burns (1980a) and Burns and Tonkin (1982) present both a map and a conceptual model for alpine soil distributions in the alpine tundra zone of the Front Range. In using the K-cycle model they placed their pedologic study in a framework that is directly comparable to the Dynamic Metastable Equilibrium model (Schumm, 1979) used in many geomorphological studies. The soil steady state in the alpine zone of the Colorado Front Range is assumed to be represented morphologically by an A/B/C horizon sequence with a cambic horizon. The ridge-top tundra zone is assumed to have been stable (with the exception of periglacial processes) for a sufficient period that soil differences reflect spatial attributes such as snow accumulation and catenary position (Burns and Tonkin, 1982).

Within this conceptual framework Burns and Tonkin recognized seven micro-environments producing distinctive soils: extremely windblown; windblown; minimal snowcover; early-melting snowbank; late-melting snowbank; semi-permanent snowbank; wet meadow. This sequence was called a Synthetic Alpine Slope (SAS) model as it was envisaged as forming a catena on leeward slopes, although it was never identified on any single slope. Soils in these seven micro-environments may also be placed in a relative developmental sequence reflecting their progress towards the optimal morphology outlined above.

The soils described above correlated strongly (Burns, 1980a) with alpine vegetation communities mapped by Komárková and Webber (1978). Using a different classification scheme for plant communities, Webber and May (1977) determined that alpine communities are controlled by substrate moisture, snow cover, and substrate disturbance (in this order). Although there are some discrepancies between the two botanical approaches they overlap sufficiently to allow us to assert that there is substantial overlap between alpine plant communities, pedogenesis, and surficial soil loss; all of which are primarily controlled by the direct and indirect influences of seasonal snowpack accumulation.

Thus stratification by plant community may be an important tool (Frank and Thorn, 1985), although one that is of limited paleo-significance.

Temporal Behaviour

An appreciation of topoclimatic influences permits a researcher to extract the spatial component from his/her landscape interpretation and more clearly evaluate the temporal facets. Nevertheless, a wide range of temporal perspectives remains and interpretations might vary accordingly.

Relative age dating of coarse debris (e.g. Carroll, 1974) permits approximate dating of talus, protalus ramparts, and rock glaciers (Madole, 1972). Such dating, combined with horizontal and vertical stratigraphic concepts has revealed some broad environmental shifts. However, theoretical modelling of rock glacier behaviour (Olyphant, in press) suggests many complicating factors. Olyphant (1983) found bedrock fracture density in the freeface (a spatial factor) to exhibit the strongest relationship to rock glacier distribution. Thus, temporal behaviour may well be secondary and Olyphant (1983) has shown that it is certainly complex, with significantly different relaxation times at the rock glacier head and snout, a more rapid response to input increases than decreases, plus great variations in relaxation periods with size. Large rock glaciers may have relaxation periods > 1,000 yr with imperceptible changes occurring at the snout (a common measurement site). All of these attributes suggest that rock glaciers are very stable during ameliorating climatic conditions, making them potentially good long-term, but poor short-term, indicators.

Fine debris forms have been dated absolutely and relatively (Benedict, 1966, 1970) and, in combination with their stratigraphic relationships, may be used for paleo-environmental interpretations. Lobe and terrace initiation appears to have occurred primarily during the waning phases of glaciation in the Indian Peaks (Benedict, 1970, p. 221) and subsequent movement may have varied as much as eightfold during Neoglaciation alone. This again suggests great morphological stability over a wide range of micro-environmental conditions.

Accepting the possibility of successfully linking geochemistry to pedogenesis, available pedogenic data offer much promise. Burns (1980*b*) has identified buried soils beneath snowpatches, and Shroba and Birkeland (1983) have broadly delimited the duration of periods of soil horizon development in the alpine zone of the Colorado Rocky Mountains.

At present, two things appear to dominate our temporal perspective: 1) the apparent stability or extremely slow degeneration of certain periglacial forms during climatic amelioration; and 2) a general lack of sophisticated evolutionary models for individual landforms. Accordingly, it appears that presence/absence, while bearing a strong topoclimatic (spatial) imprint does provide us with an assured (but limited) paleo-environmental message that may be used in an essentially stratigraphic fashion. Landform size and/or supposed stage of development appear to bear an even heavier topoclimatic (spatial) imprint which, combined with our lack of evolutionary models and evidence for self-limitation (e.g. Price, 1974; Thorn, 1976), should serve both to caution against their use and stimulate research.

The distribution of fossil and active periglacial forms in the Front Range reflects strong spatial (topoclimatic) controls derived from macro-, meso- and microscales. Furthermore, much of the temporal record reflects the occurrence of conditions favourable to landform-initiating events at sometime or another. This combination would appear to place great emphasis on the paraglacial period while revealing little about the ensuing periglacial regime. If the latter is to be clarified, this thrusts to the forefront the need for better evolutionary models, because stage of development, once stripped of the spatial signal, becomes the primary source of temporal information. Consequently, more theory rather than fieldwork should be our first priority.

Many of these ideas are already used in British periglacial geomorphology; a recent example is Ballantyne's (1984) appraisal of Late Devensian periglaciation in upland Scotland in which he addresses on several occasions, spatial (topoclimatic) issues and their significance. Our intention is to emphasize the usefulness of carefully deciphering the spatial and temporal inputs to periglacial landforms, as well as to highlight the significance of landform assemblages themselves in paleo-interpretation.

Acknowledgements

We wish to extend our thanks to all the colleagues whose work made this paper possible. However, we are totally responsible for the contents of this paper. Professor Nel Caine (University of Colorado) kindly reviewed the paper, his comments were much appreciated.

References

Ballantyne, C.K. (1984). 'The Late Devensian periglaciation of upland Scotland', *Quat. Sci. Rev.*, **3**, 311–43.

Benedict, J.B. (1966). 'Radiocarbon dates from a stone-banked terrace in the Colorado Rocky Mountains, U.S.A.,' *Geogr. Annal.*, **48A**, 24–31.

Benedict, J.B. (1970). 'Downslope soil movement in a Colorado alpine region: Rates, processes and climatic significance', *Arctic and Alp. Res.*, **2**, 165–226.

Benedict, J.B. (1973a). 'Chronology of cirque glaciation, Colorado Front Range', *J. Quat. Res.*, **3**, 584–99.

Benedict, J.B. (1973b). 'Origin of rock glaciers', *J. Glaciol.*, **12**, 520–2.

Bovis, M.J. and Thorn, C.E. (1981). 'Soil loss variation within a Colorado alpine area', *Earth Surf. Proc. and Lndfrm.*, **6**, 151–63.

Burns, S.F. (1980a). *Alpine soil distribution and development, Indian Peaks, Colorado Front Range* (unpublished Ph.D. thesis): Boulder, University of Colorado.

Burns, S.F. (1980b). 'Using buried soils beneath perennial alpine snowbanks to date past climate changes', *J. Colorado-Wyoming Acad. Sci.*, **12**, 24–5.

Burns, S.F. and Tonkin, P.J. (1982). 'Soil geomorphic models and the spatial distribution and development of alpine soils', In *Space and Time in Geomorphology.* (Ed. C.E. Thorn), 25–43, George Allen and Unwin, Boston.

Caine, N. (1974). 'The geomorphic processes of the alpine environment', in *Arctic and Alpine Environments.* (Eds. J.D. Ives and R.G. Barry), 721–48, Methuen, London.

Caine, N. (1982). 'Water and sediment fluxes in the Green Lakes Valley, Colorado Front Range', In *Ecological Studies in the Colorado Alpine A Festschrift for John W. Marr: University of Colorado, Institute of Arctic and Alpine Research Occasional Paper No. 37.* (Ed. J.C. Halfpenny), 13–22.

Caine, N. (1986). 'Sediment movement and storage on alpine slopes in the Colorado Rocky Mountains' In *Hillslope Processes* (Ed. A.D. Abrahams), 115–37, Allen and Unwin, Boston.

Carroll, T. (1974). 'Relative age dating techniques and a late Quaternary chronology, Arikaree Cirque, Colorado', *Geology*, **2**, 321–5.

Church, M. (1980), 'Records of recent geomorphological events', in *Timescales in Geomorphology* (Eds. R.A. Cullingford, D.A. Davidson and J. Lewin), 13–29, Wiley, New York.

Church, M. and Ryder, J.M. (1972). 'Paraglacial sedimentation: a consideration of fluvial processes conditioned by glaciation,' *Geol. Soc. Am. Bull.*, **83**, 3059–72.

Dixon, J.C. (1983). *Chemical weathering of late Quaternary cirque deposits in the Colorado Front Range* (unpublished Ph.D. thesis): Boulder, University of Colorado.

Dixon, J.C. (1986). 'Solute Movement on Hillslopes in the Alpine Environment of the Colorado Front Range,' In *Hillslope Processes* (Ed. A.D. Abrahams), 139–59, Allen and Unwin, Boston.

Frank, T.D. and Thorn, C.E. (1985). 'Stratifying alpine tundra for geomorphic studies using digitized aerial imagery', *Arctic and Alp. Res.*, **17**, 179–88.

Graf, W.L. (1977). 'The rate law in geomorphology', *Am. J. Sci.*, **277**, 178–91.

Gray, J.M. (1982). 'The last glaciers (Loch Lomond Advance) in Snowdonia, N. Wales', *Geol. J.*, **17**, 111–33.

King, C.A.M. (1976). *Northern England*, Methuen, London.

Komárková, V. and Webber, P.J. (1978). 'An alpine vegetation map of Niwot Ridge, Colorado,' *Arctic and Alp. Res.* **10**, 1–29.

Madole, R.F. (1972). 'Neoglacial facies in the Colorado Front Range,' *Arctic and Alp. Res.*, **4**, 119–30.

Madole, R.F. (1982). *Possible origins of till-like deposits near the Summit of the Front Range in north-central Colorado*, U.S. Geol. Sur. Prof. Paper **1243**, 1–31.

Madole, R.F. (1986). 'Lake Devlin and Pinedale glacial history, Front Range, Colorado', *J. Quat. Res.*, **25**, 43–54.

Olyphant, G.A. (1983). 'Computer simulation of rock-glacier development under viscous and pseudoplastic flow,' *Geol. Soc. Am. Bull.*, **94**, 499–505.

Olyphant, G.A. (1985). 'Topoclimate and the distribution of Neoglacial facies in the Indian Peaks section of the Front Range, Colorado, U.S.A.,' *Arctic and Alp. Res.*, **17**, 69–78.

Olyphant, G.A. (in press). 'Theoretical estimates of the timing and magnitude of rock glacier response to abrupt changes in talus production,' In *Studies on Rock Glaciers* (Eds. J.R. Giardino and J.F. Schroder, Jr.) Allen and Unwin, Boston.

Price, L.W. (1974). 'The development cycle of solifluction lobes,' *Assoc. of Am. Geogers. Annals*, **64**, 430–8.

Rapp. A. (1984). 'Nivation hollows and glacial cirques in Söderasen, Scania, South Sweden,' *Geogr. Annal.*, **66A**, 11–28.

Schumm, S.A. (1979). 'Geomorphic thresholds: the concept and its application', *I.B.G. Trans.*, **4**, 485–515.

Shroba, R.R. and Birkeland, P.W. (1983). 'Trends in late-Quaternary soil development in the Rocky Mountains and Sierra Nevada of the western United States. In *Late-Quaternary Environments of the United States. Volume One, The Late Pleistocene.* (Ed. S.C. Porter), 145–56, Univ. Minnesota Press Minneapolis.

Sissons, J.B. (1974). 'The Quaternary in Scotland: a review', *Scott. J. Geol.*, **10**, 311–37.

Sissons, J.B. (1980). 'The Loch Lomond Advance in the Lake District, northern England', *Roy. Soc. Edinburgh Trans: Earth Sci.*, **71**, 13–27.

Sissons, J.B. (1981). 'The last Scottish ice-sheet: facts and speculative discussion', *Boreas*, **10**, 1–17.

Sugden, D.E. (1971). 'The significance of periglacial activity on some Scottish mountains,' *Geograph. J.*, **137**, 388–92.

Thorn, C.E. (1976). 'A model of stony earth circle development, Schefferville, Quebec,' *Assoc. Am. Geogers Proc.*, **8**, 19–23.

Thorn, C.E. (1978). 'The geomorphic role of snow,' *Assoc. Am. Geogers Annals*, **68**, 414–25.

Thorn, C.E. (1983). 'Seasonal snowpack variability and alpine periglacial geomorphology,' *Polarforschung*, **53**, 31–5.

Thorn, C.E. (in press). 'Nivation: a geomorphic chimera' in *International Perspectives in Periglacial Research* (Ed. M.J. Clark), Wiley, London.

Thorn, C.E. and Darmody, R.G. (1985). 'Grain-size distribution of the insoluble component of contemporary eolian deposits in the alpine zone, Front Range, Colorado,' *Arctic and Alp. Res.*, **17**, 433–42.

Thorn, C.E. and Loewenherz, D.S. (in press). 'Alpine Mass Wasting in the Indian Peaks, Front Range, Colorado: A Case Study', in *Geomorphic Systems of North America* (Ed. W.L. Graf), The Geological Society of America. Boulder, Colorado.

Thornes, J.B. and Brunsden, D. (1977). *Geomorphology and Time*, Halsted Press, New York.

Tufnell, L. (1972). 'Ploughing blocks with special reference to north-west England', *Biul. Peryglac.*, **21**, 237–70.

Tufnell, L. (1985). 'Periglacial landforms in the Cross Fell – Knock Fell area of the northern Pennines', in *Field Guide to the Periglacial Landforms of Northern England* (Ed. J. Boardman), pp. 4–14, Quaternary Research Association, Cambridge.

Washburn, A.L. (1980). *Geocryology a survey of periglacial processes and environments*, Halsted Press, New York.

Webber, P.J. and May, D.E. (1977). 'The magnitude and distribution of belowground plant structures in the alpine tundra of Niwot Ridge, Colorado,' *Arctic and Alp. Res.*, **9**, 157–74.

Whalley, W.B., Cordon, J.E., Gellatly, A.F., Ferguson, R.I. (1985). 'Glaciers of the southern Lyngen Peninsula, Norway', in *International Geomorphology 1985* (Ed. T. Spencer), p. 644.

White, S.E. (1981). 'Alpine mass movement forms (non-catastrophic): Classification, description and significance', *Arctic and Alp. Res.*, **13**, 127–37.

White, S.E. (1982). 'Physical and geological nature of the Indian Peaks, Colorado Front Range, in *Ecological Studies in the Colorado Alpine: A Festschrift for John W. Marr: University of Colorado, Institute of Arctic and Alpine Research Occasional Paper No. 37* (Ed. J.D. Halfpenny), pp. 1–12.

Williams, R.B.G. (1975). 'The British climate during the Last Glaciation; an interpretation based on periglacial phenomena', in *Ice Ages: Ancient and Modern* (Eds. A.E. Wright and F. Mosely), pp. 95–120, Seel House Press, Liverpool.

Wolman, M.G. and Gerson, R. (1978). 'Relative scales of time and effectiveness of climate in watershed geomorphology', *Earth Surf. Proc. and Lndfrm.*, **3**, 189–208.

Wolman, M.G. and Miller, J.P. (1960). 'Magnitude and frequency of forces in geomorphic processes', *J. Geol.*, **68**, 54–74.

(b) Pleistocene conditions in adjacent Europe

5 · Pleistocene periglacial conditions and geomorphology in north central Europe

JOHANNES KARTE

Abstract

The combination of mid-latitude climate, a higher degree of continentality than at present, tundra and forest-tundra like vegetation, lithology, pre-existing relief and preceding geomorphic evolution, especially the influence of several glaciations, and the time factor, determine the uniqueness of Pleistocene periglacial conditions and geomorphology in north central Europe. All types of fossil periglacial structures and landforms occur in the areas and their palaeo-environmental significance is discussed. Some features like pingo scars remain controversial. In addition, some specific deposits and structures like gravelly periglacial sands, giant diapiric upturnings and grèzes litées are presented. There is stratigraphic evidence for at least 12 phases of intense periglacial conditions with continuous permafrost in the Pleistocene, and several less intense periglacial phases of varying spatial extent have occurred. Using as an example the maximum of the Weichselian/Würmian glaciation the former extent and thickness of permafrost is reconstructed and its palaeo-climatic implications are discussed.

The uniqueness of Pleistocene periglacial conditions in north central Europe

The object of this paper is to review the Pleistocene periglacial conditions in north central Europe, i.e. the area between NW-Germany and Poland. In a broad sense the term 'Pleistocene periglacial conditions' implies the former climatic and non-climatic environmental factors. When considering the Pleistocene periglacial geomorphology even complex factors like the pre-existing relief, the preceding geomorphic evolution and the time factor have to be taken into account. In combination these controlling factors determine the uniqueness of Pleistocene periglacial conditions and geomorphology in north central Europe.

1. Due to its mid-latitude, moderately continental lowland location periglacial climatic conditions in north central Europe were substantially different from most present periglacial climates. Traditionally, the periglacial climates of Spitsbergen or Iceland have been regarded as modern analogues but now it is evident that both are unique even within the context of the present polar periglacial zone. Compared to Pleistocene periglacial Britain there is latitudinal similarity but it can be expected that the Pleistocene periglacial climate in north central Europe was more continental.

2. A fundamental difference between present polar periglacial geomorphic systems and Pleistocene mid-latitude periglacial geomorphic systems derives from the overall palaeo-climatic context of these environments. Pleistocene periglacial conditions in north central Europe have to be seen in the light of several cyclic changes from full glacial/periglacial to full interglacial conditions whereas in the present polar periglacial environment these changes have occurred from glacial to periglacial or between various degrees and intensities of periglacial conditions. In this sense the Pleistocene periglacial system of north central Europe was basically more unstable than that of the present periglacial zone.

3. Apart from these general considerations Pleistocene periglacial conditions have been influenced by glacial events and the pre-Quaternary geomorphic evolution of the area. In this respect north central Europe can be roughly subdivided into the Central Upland Zone between the Scandinavian and Alpine glaciations which apart from some local ice caps has never been glaciated and the Northern German-Polish lowlands which have been affected by 3 major inland ice-sheets and numerous shorter stages and oscillations since the Elsterian.

These glaciations were of different areal extent

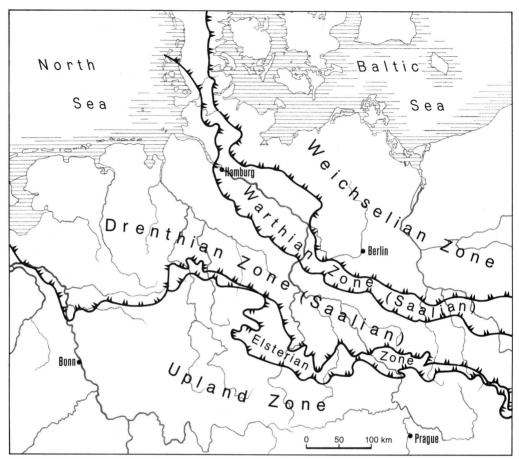

Figure 5.1. Glacial limits and periglacial zones in Central Europe (after Liedke, 1981).

with the oldest glaciation (i.e. the Elsterian) extending furthest to the south and each younger glaciation (i.e. the Saalian and Weichselian) covering successively smaller areas. Ideally, these preconditions existed only in East Germany and parts of southern Poland because in the western part the Saalian glaciation (Drenthe-substage) extended furthest to the south.

As a consequence of this, and on considering the time element involved, there are zones of decreasing periglacial impact from the unglaciated uplands towards the youngest morainic landscape along the Baltic Sea. However, this aspect of the varying duration and impact of periglacial periods is counteracted by the prevalence of hard rocks of varying lithology and pre-existing generally steeper relief in the uplands and the availability of loose, easily erodible glacial and glaciofluvial deposits in the lowlands.

Because of local factors in north central Europe it is difficult to identify true analogues in present and other past periglacial environments. Even though at the scale of former periglacial climates there are only gradual differences between Pleistocene Britain and north central Europe there are significant contrasts in pre-existing relief, preceding geomorphic evolution, lithology and vegetation as a whole. In many respects the search for analogues is a very valuable scientific approach but we should also consider more non-actualistic viewpoints. This goes for the periglacial environment as a whole but also for specific periglacial phenomena.

Indicators of former periglacial conditions

Besides soil-physical, soil-mechanical, pedological, palaeo-hydrological and geomorphic indicators for former periglacial conditions all types of hitherto known fossil periglacial structures occur in north-central Europe. As to the reconstruction of palaeo-periglacial climatic conditions and former conditions of frozen ground only the latter are regarded as diagnostic indicators.

Fossil frost crack structures like fossil frost cracks, soil wedges and ice-wedge casts are widespread. So far, in the literature too little distinction has been made between true ice-wedge casts and fossil soil wedges. The distinction is important as both may indicate different regimes of former frozen ground. Only ice-wedge casts, i.e. wedge-shaped structures exceeding the depth of the former active layer (0.5–2 m) are indicators of former permafrost whereas soil wedges may have been formed in seasonally frozen ground. Fossil sand wedges are rare in north central Europe and most occurrences can be explained by local environmental conditions.

Polygonal structures can be observed in exposures and on air photographs, especially of the Saalian till and meltwater sand areas (Christensen 1974; Svensson, 1976; Ehlers, 1978; Höfle, 1983). In recent years fossil frost crack structures have also been traced successfully at the bottom of the North Sea (Streif, 1985).

Cryoturbations and involutions occur in a great variety of forms. They are the most widespread of all periglacial structures but it is often not clear which are the modern analogues for all these types (thufur, earth hummocks, mudboils, nonsorted circles, active layer instabilities) and what exact significance they have as indicators for a former periglacial environment. As they do not necessarily require permafrost for their formation they are not diagnostic indicators of permafrost but if they show a flat bottom in permeable substrate or are stratigraphically related to ice-wedge casts they can be used as indicators for former permafrost.

Compared to these features, fossil sorted structures are rare, or at least have not been identified as such. Considering the availability of large areas with deposits susceptible to frost sorting and a former mid-latitude frozen ground regime with respective freeze-thaw activity this scarcity of fossil sorted structures is surprising and needs further investigation.

In the zone of younger morainic landscapes (i.e. Weichselian) closed depressions of all shapes and sizes of glacial origin (dead-ice topography) are typical. In the zones of older morainic landscapes most of them have been filled in by subsequent periglacial processes. But there are still tens of thousands of small and shallow closed depressions some of which have a rim and have been suggested to be of pingo origin (Garleff, 1968; Lade, 1980). As there are too few detailed studies into the internal structure of these features it is difficult to make a clear distinction between alternative possibilities of origin, and therefore the pingo origin remains as controversial as the idea of thermokarst origin. Most features claimed by Wiegand (1965) to be of pingo origin can also be explained by other mechanisms of formation.

A periglacial phenomenon widespread in the formerly glaciated areas is a gravelly sand (in German: Geschiebedecksand) which constitutes a layer up to 0.6 m thick of periglacially disturbed sands and loam with a typical enrichment of stones at the bottom. This distinct layer covers all sediments except Holocene fluvial and aeolian deposits. The exact origin and environmental significance is far from clear but it seems that it was formed by a complex of frost processes like cryoturbation and solifluction in combination with deflation/aeolian accumulation and slope wash (Liedtke, 1981).

All the periglacial phenomena presented so far were formed by processes related to former aggrading or existing permafrost or intense seasonally frozen ground. Although the fossilisation of most periglacial phenomena occurred on the degradation of frozen ground little attention has been paid to periglacial structures related to this process. It is suggested that some large involutions and giant diapiric upturnings have to be interpreted in this way. The latter are widespread as diapiric intrusions of lignite into overlying sediments within and outside the limits of the Scandinavian ice-sheets and attain thicknesses from several metres to several dozens of metres. It is assumed that they were formed by gravitational density inversions during the degradation of permafrost which was especially rich in ground ice in the lignite. They are also valuable indicators for the thickness of former permafrost (Eissmann, 1981; Strunk, 1983).

On slopes, especially in the Upland Zone, periglacial conditions are manifested by a widespread cover of solifluction debris, frequently overlying a zone of curved strata. In favourable locations, e.g. in depressions, this cover sheet of debris can be subdivided lithostratigraphically into layers with differing components related to solifluction, slope wash and aeolian (loess) accumulation (Altermann *et al.*, 1978; Fried, 1984; Richter, 1978; Semmel, 1968). Most of these deposits are of Late Weichselian to Younger Dryas age. On crystalline and volcanic/plutonic rock outcrops there are local blockfields, blockstreams and individually transported blocks.

In specific topographical and hydrological situations and on easily weathered shales thick stratified deposits of the grèzes litées type occur in the Central Upland Zone, especially in the Rhenish Shield (Karte, 1983). It must be emphasized that they are rare and local phenomena. In recent years it has become evident that similar rhythmically bedded deposits of sandy composition are widespread in the valley bottoms and on the lower slopes in the older morainic landscape. They indicate that besides solifluction, slope wash was an effective geomorphic agent on frozen ground without vegetation and in association with snow meltwater. Therefore, they are termed 'ablual' (slope wash) sediments by Liedtke (1983).

As mentioned earlier there is a variety of landforms in north central Europe indicating former periglacial conditions, e.g. frost riven cliffs on slopes, cryoplanation features (Goebel, 1978; Demek, 1983), cryopediments (Brunotte, 1978; Czudek, 1985), climatically induced asymmetrical valleys (Karrasch, 1970; Czudek, 1973) and dry valleys on permeable substrates. As most of these landforms are polygenetic and require a comparatively long time for their formation they are not diagnostic indicators of climatic conditions in a specific periglacial period. In a similar way this is also true for landforms and phenomena related to periglacial aeolian activity which is manifested by the Central European loess-belt along the northern margin of the Upland Zone, and by cover sands, ventifacts and dunes within the formerly glaciated terrain. They have been discussed in the light of periglacial wind conditions and vegetation but they do not indicate temperatures or frozen ground. Therefore, the following discussion will focus on the classical periglacial structures.

Stratigraphy of periglacial structures and reconstruction of former permafrost

In the literature opinions have varied widely as to the extent of former permafrost in Central Europe. Upon theoretical grounds, based on assumptions as to the former snow cover or temperatures reconstructed from the lowering of the former climatic snowline, there was only episodic, sporadic or no permafrost at all in Central Europe during the Pleistocene (Kostyaev, 1966; Morawetz, 1973; Velichko, 1985; Gullentops, 1977). Earlier reconstructions based on periglacial permafrost indicators led to the assumption of former permafrost extending as far as the Pyrenees in Western Europe (Kaiser, 1960). These reconstructions were based on the compilation of occurrences of periglacial structures irrespective of their exact age and based on existing knowledge of the environmental significance of periglacial phenomena. However, if periglacial features are to be used as indicators of the extent of the former periglacial environment and the conditions in a specific periglacial period, correct typological identification and exact dating is required. Poser (1948) followed this principle, and according to his reconstruction permafrost extended as far as Northern France, and underlay the whole of Central Europe during the Weichselian.

Usually, only relative dating is possible by dating of the host sediments or relating the fossil structures to landsurfaces of known age. In Central Europe the possibilities of dating are particularly good in the loess belt and fluvial terrace sediments which can be correlated with the glacial stratigraphy, (Table 5.1).

South of the glacial limits in East Germany there is evidence of at least 12 phases of intense periglacial conditions with permafrost as indicated by deep ice-wedge casts (Eissmann, 1981). There is a clear difference as to pre- and post-Elsterian time. Before the Elsterian glaciation there were only episodic and fairly short permafrost periods whereas afterwards permafrost existed for periods of thousands or even tens of thousands of years.

Within one glacial period, glacial and periglacial conditions developed asynchronously. Periglacial conditions existed in Central Europe during the build-up of ice-sheets in Scandinavia and for a long time before the ice-sheets crossed the Baltic and extended into north Germany and Poland. The advancing ice-sheets moved over permafrost as indicated by *en bloc*-glacial push structures which are only conceivable with frozen ground. It remains controversial as to whether permafrost was conserved underneath the ice-sheets or degraded. Most authors believe that permafrost melted underneath the ice-sheets and re-invaded the ice-free areas during deglaciation. Deglaciation occurred both in the form of oscillating and receding ice-fronts as well as stagnation. As a result of climatic warming during deglaciation periglacial phases in the deglaciated areas were considerably shorter than during the time of build-up of the ice-sheets.

Within the framework of a project initiated by S. Kozarski, Pozan, under the auspices of the former IGU Coordinating Committee for Periglacial Research and in cooperation with the INQUA-Commission 'Palaeo-geographic Atlas of the Quaternary', data have been compiled to enable reconstruction of permafrost during the maximum of the Weichselian glaciation, i.e. between post-

Table 5.1 *Quaternary stratigraphy and stratigraphical position of fossil periglacial structures in Northern Germany. (Size of dots indicate relative frequency of feature.)*

Stratigraphy	yrs. B.P.	Fossil Periglacial structures (frequence of occurrence)			
		Ice-wedge casts, soil wedges, frost cracks	Cryoturbations, Involutions	Pingo-scars	Large diapiric upturnings
Holocene	10,000				
Weichselian (Devensian)					
Late Glacial	14,000	•	•	•	
Maximum	25,000	•	•		•
Early Glacial	75,000	•	•		•
Eemian (Ipswichian)	?130,000				
Saalian (Wolstonian)					
Late Glacial		•	•		•
Warthe Stadial		•	•		•
Drenthe Stadial		•	•		•
	?240,000				•
Holsteinian (Hoxnian)	?320,000				
Elsterian (Anglian)					
Late Glacial		•	•		•
Maximum		•	•		
Early Glacial		•	•		•
	?575,000				
Cromerian					
Menapian Glacial (Beestonian)		•	•		•
Wallian (Pre-pastonian)					
Eburonian Glacial (Baventian)		•	•		
Tiglian					
Brossenian Glacial		•	•		
Preatiglian					

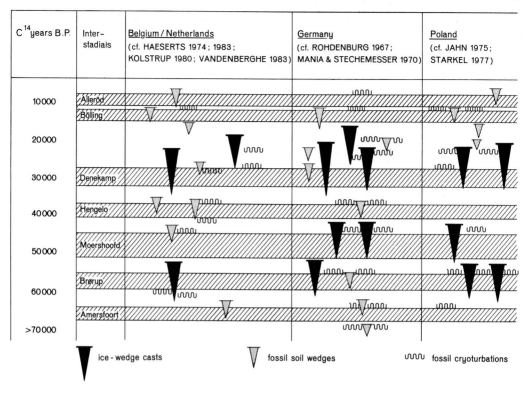

Figure 5.2. Stratigraphy of Weichselian periglacial structures in Central Europe.

Denekamp (about 30,000 B.P.) and pre-Bölling (about, 13,000 B.P.) (Karte, 1981). A schematic compilation of the stratigraphical position of ice-wedge casts and related cryoturbations shows several horizons within the Weichselian of which those at the Weichselian maximum are the most conspicuous (Figure 5.2). But even during the maximum of the Weichselian permafrost developed in a different way during several substages and phases. In principle this is compatible with the stratigraphy of periglacial structures in Belgium and the Netherlands where the stratigraphy, however, is more detailed (Haeserts, 1983; Langohr, 1983; Vandenberghe, 1983, 1985). Most of the large and deep ice-wedge casts were initiated early during the maximum of the late Weichselian glaciation. But there is also enough evidence from north eastern Germany, Poland and the alpine foreland that permafrost extended into the deglaciated younger morainic landscape for short periods during the Older and Younger Dryas (Lembke, 1954; Weinberger, 1954; Liedtke, 1957/58; Bachmann, 1966; Kliewe, 1968; Kozarski, 1974).

Palaeo-environmental and palaeo-climatic conclusions

On a map (Figure 5.3) locations of well-dated reliable permafrost indicators, mainly ice-wedge casts, have been plotted (Karte, 1981). Most of the plotted features are located within the loess belt which is not surprising because of the possibilities for dating and because loess is a deposit susceptible to ice-segregation and frost-cracking. There are, of course, considerably more permafrost indicators, but they had to be excluded because of uncertain dating.

From the distribution of ice-wedge casts it can be concluded that the whole of Central Europe was underlain by continuous permafrost during the maximum of the last glaciation. It is still open to question whether the lack of reliable Weichselian permafrost indicators in the Upper Rhine valley indicates absence of permafrost due to warmer conditions – the Upper Rhine valley is still today a particularly warm area – or merely gaps in knowledge. For older glaciations there is enough evidence for former permafrost even in this area

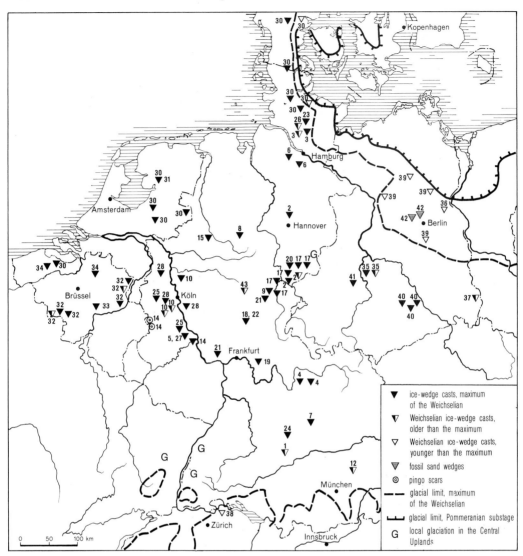

Figure 5.3. Indicators of permafrost at the maximum of the last glaciation in Central Europe.

Sources (references in KARTE, 1981):

1 BLEICH & GROSCHOPF (1959)
2 BRÜNING (1966)
3 DÜCKER (1954)
4 EMMERT (1965)
5 FRECHEN & ROSAUER (1959)
6 HAGEDORN (1961)
7 HAUNSCHILD (1967)
8 HENKE (1964)
9 HORN (1971)
10 KAISER (1958)
11 KAISER (1960)
12 KARRASCH (1970)
13 LÜTTIG (1960)
14 MÜCKENHAUSEN (1960)
15 MÜLLER (1978)
16 PICARD (1956)

17 ROHDENBURG (1967)
18 SABELBERG, MAVROCORDAT, ROHDENBURG & SCHÖNHALS (1976)
19 SCHIRMER (1967)
20 SELZER (1936)
21 SEMMEL (1968)
22 SABELBERG, ROHDENBURG & HAVELBERG (1974)
23 SVENSSON (1976)
24 ZEESE (1971)
25 LÖHR & BRUNNACKER (1974)
26 PICARD (1956)
27 SCHIRMER (1970)
28 THOSTE (1974)
29 LÜTTIG (1960)

30 KOLSTRUP (1980)
31 MAARLEVELD (1976)
32 HAESERTS (1974)
33 PAEPE & PISSART (1969)
34 VANDENBERGHE & GULLENTOPS (1977)
35 MANIA & STECHEMESSER (1970)
36 LEMBKE (1954)
37 SCHUBERT (1979)
38 BACHMANN (1966)
39 LIEDTKE (1957/58)
40 LIEBEROTH (1963)
41 RUSKE & WÜNSCHE (1968)
42 BLUME, HOFFMANN & PACHUR (1979)
43 Eigene Beobachtungen im Raume Winterberg

(Stäblein, 1968; Brüning, 1972; Semmel, 1974).

As mentioned earlier cryoturbations are the most widespread of periglacial structures. Even though they are not necessarily indicators of former permafrost they at least imply seasonally frozen ground and a mean annual air temperature below − 2 °C. If stratigraphically closely related to ice-wedge casts or with a flat bottom in permeable substrate they indicate former permafrost and the thickness of the former active layer. The latter varied between 0.5 and 2.0 m.

As to the thickness of former permafrost, inferences can be drawn from the thickness of fossil periglacial diapiric upturnings (Strunk, 1983). A compilation of such data reveals that during the Weichselian the permafrost thickness decreased rapidly from about 50 m in the NE to less than 10 m in the E and SW along the lower Rhine. For the whole Pleistocene there is a decrease in thickness from more than 100 m in the E and NE to about 10 m in the W and SW. As the thickness was a function of time, temperature and local factors these values have not yet been interpreted climatically but they clearly reflect increasingly intense periglacial conditions towards the E.

From the occurrences of ice-wedge casts a decrease of mean annual air temperature of 14 to 16 °C as compared with the present and considerably lower temperatures in the coldest month has been concluded (Karte, 1981). The latter implies a greater degree of thermal continentality in winter, which can be explained by the combined effect of the ice-sheets and sea-ice conditions, colder surface water temperatures and different ocean currents in the Atlantic W and NW of the British Isles (CLIMAP, 1976; Kellog, 1980), or by weather conditions with predominantly easterly or north easterly winds.

A present analogue to such conditions is hard to identify but should at best be expected in a subpolar lowland region with a similar degree of continentality and a tundra vegetation or with very little vegetation. It is suggested that the lowlands of northern Labrador-Ungava or western Alaska come close to such an analogue.

References

Altermann, M., Haase, G., Lieberoth, I. and Ruske, R. (1978). 'Lithologie, Genese und Verbreitung der Loess- und Schuttsedimente im Vorland der Skandinavischen Vereisungen', *Schriftenr. Geol. Wissensch* **9**, 231–55.

Bachmann, F. (1966). 'Fossile Strukturböden und Eiskeile auf jung-pleistozänen Schotterflächen im nordostschweizerischen Mittelland', *Arbeiten aus dem Geogr. Inst. der Universität Zürich, Serie A*, 172, Zürich.

Brüning, H. (1972). 'Das Rhein-Main-Gebiet in den quartäreiszeitlichen Periglazialbereichen', *Jahrbuch und Mitteilungen Oberrheinisch Geologischer Verein*, **54**, 79–100.

Brunotte, E. (1978). 'Zur quartären Formung von Schichtkämmen und Fußflächen im Bereich des Markoldendorfer Beckens und seiner Umrahmung', *Göttinger Geographische Abhandlungen*, **72**, Göttingen.

Christensen, L. (1974). 'Crop-marks revealing large-scale patterned ground structures in cultivated areas, southwestern Jutland, Denmark', *Boreas*, **3**, 153–80.

CLIMAP Project Members (1976). 'The surface of the ice-age earth', *Science*, **191**, 1131–7.

Czudek, T. (1973). 'Die Talasymmetrie im Nordteil der Moravská Brána (Mährische Pforte)', *Acta Sc. Nat. Brno*, **7**, Brno.

Czudek, T. (1985). 'Zum Problem der Talkryopedimente', *Acta Sc. Nat. Brno, Nova Series*, **19**, Brno.

Demek, J. (1983). 'Fossil periglacial phenomena in Czechoslovakia and their paleoclimatic evaluation', *Foldrajzi Kozlemenyek*, **31**, 258–65.

Ehlers, J. (1978). 'Die quartäre Morphogenese der Harburger Berge und ihrer Umgebung', *Mitteilungen der Geographischen Gesellschaft in Hamburg*, **68**, Hamburg.

Eissmann, L. (1981). 'Periglaziäre Prozeese und Permafroststrukturen aus sechs Kaltzeiten des Quartärs. Ein Beitrag zur Periglazialgeologie aus der Sicht des Saale-Elbe-Gebietes', *Altenburger Naturwissenschaftliche Forschungen*, **1**, Altenburg.

Fried, G. (1984). 'Gestein, Relief und Boden im Buntsandstein-Odenwald', *Frankfurter Geowissenschaftliche Arbeiten, Serie D, Physische Geographie*, **4**, Frankfurt.

Garleff, K. (1968). 'Geomorphologische Untersuchungen angeschlossenen Hohlformen ("Kaven") des Niedersächsischen Tieflandes', *Göttinger Geographische Abhandlungen*, **44**, Göttingen.

Goebel, P. (1978). 'Untersuchungen an Golezterrassen im Westharz', *Hercynia*, **15**, 29–50.

Gullentops, F. (1977). 'Fossil periglacial conditions in Western Europe', *10th INQUA Congress Abstracts*, **186**, Norwich.

Haeserts, P. (1983). 'Stratigraphic distribution of periglacial features indicative of permafrost in the Upper Pleistocene loesses of Belgium', *Permafrost Fourth International Conference, Proceedings*, 421–6, Washington.

Höfle, H.C. (1983). 'Periglacial phenomena', in *Glacial deposits in northwest Europe* (Ed. J. Ehlers), pp. 297–8, Rotterdam.

Jahn, A. (1975). *Problems of the periglacial zone*, US National Science Foundation Publication, Washington.

Kaiser, K.H. (1960). 'Klimazeugen des periglazialen Dauerfrostbodens in Mittel – und Westeuropa', *Eiszeitalter und Gegenwart*, **11**, 121–41.

Karrasch, H. (1970). 'Das Phänomen der klimabedingten Reliefasymmentrie in Mitteleuropa', *Göttinger Geographische Abhandlungen*, **56**, Göttingen.

Karte, J. (1981). 'Zur Rekonstruktion des weichselhochglazialen Dauerfrostbodens im westlichen Mitteleuropa', *Bochumer Geographische Arbeiten*, **40**, 59–71.

Karte, J. (1983). 'Grèzes litées as a special type of periglacial slope sediments in the German Highlands', *Polarforschung*, **53**, 67–74.

Kellog, T.B. (1980). 'Paleoclimatology and paleooceanography of the Norwegian and Greenland seas: glacial-interglacial contrasts', *Boreas*, **9**, 115–37.

Kliewe, H. (1968). 'Periglazialphänomene im Spätglazialgebiet der Weichselvereisung', *Przeglad Geograficzny*, **40**, 351–62.

Kostyaev, E.G. (1966). 'Über die Grenzen der unterirdischen Vereisung und die Periglazialzone im Quartär', *Petermanns Geographische Mitteilungen*, **110**, 253–61.

Kozarski, S. (1974). 'Evidences of late-Würm permafrost occurrences in north-west Poland', *Quaestiones Geographicae*, **1**, 65–86.

Lade, U. (1980). 'Quartärmorphologische und -geologische Untersuchungen in der Bremervörder-Wesermünder Geest', *Würzburger Geographische Arbeiten*, **50**, Würzburg.

Langohr, R. (1983). 'The extension of permafrost in Western Europe in the period between 18.000 and 10.000 years B.P. (Tardiglacial): information from soil studies', *Permafrost Fourth International Conference, Proceedings*, 683–8.

Lembke, H. (1954). 'Die Periglazialerscheinungen im Jungmoränengebiet westlich des Oderbruches bei Freienwalde', *Göttinger Geographische Abhandlungen*, **16**, 55–94, Göttingen.

Liedtke, H. (1957/58). 'Frostbodenstrukturen aus dem norddeutschen Jungmoränengebiet', *Wissenschaftliche Zeitschrift der Humboldt-Universität zu Berlin, Mathematisch-Naturwissenschaftliche Reihe*, **7**, 359–76.

Liedtke, H. (1981). 'Die nordischen Vereisungen in Mitteleuropa', *Forschungen zur deutschen Landeskunde*, **204**, Trier.

Liedtke, H. (1983). 'Periglacial slope wash and sedimentation in North-western Germany during the Würm (Weichsel-) glaciation', *Permafrost Fourth International Conference, Proceedings*, 715–18, Washington.

Morawetz, S. (1973). 'Permafrost-Schneegrenze-Periglaziales', *Arbeiten aus dem Geographischen Institut der Universität Salzburg*, **3**, 37–44, Salzburg.

Poser, H. (1948). Boden und Klimaverhalnisse in Mittel und Westeuropa der Würmeiszeit, *Erdkunde*, **2**, 53–68.

Richter, H. (1978). 'Die Bedeutung der Kaltzeiten für die Gestaltung des Reliefs der Mittelgebirge im unvergletscherten Gebiet', *Schriftenr. Geol. Wissensch.*, **9**, 309–17.

Semmel, A. (1968). 'Studien über den Verlauf jungpleistozäner Formung in Hessen', *Frankfurter Geographische Hefte*, **45**, 15–17, Frankfurt.

Semmel, A. (1974). 'Das Eiszeitalter im Rhein-Main-Gebiet', *Rhein-Mainische Forschungen*, **78**, Frankfurt.

Stäblein, G. (1968). 'Reliefgenerationen der Vorderpfalz', *Würzburger Geographische Arbeiten*, **23**, Würzburg.

Streif, H. (1985). 'Südliche Nordsee im Eiszeitalter. Überflutungen und Eisvorstöße', *Forschung. Mitteilungen der DFG*, **1**, 9–11.

Strunk, H. (1983). 'Pleistocene diapiric upturnings of lignites and clayey sediments as periglacial phenomena in Central Europe', *Permafrost Fourth International Conference, Proceedings*, 1200–4, Washington.

Svensson, H. (1976). 'Relict ice-wedge polygons revealed on aerial photographs from Kaltenkirchen, northern Germany', *Geografisk Tidsskrift*, **75**, 8–12.

Vandenberghe, J. (1983). 'Ice-wedge casts and involutions as permafrost indicators and their stratigraphic position in the Weichselian', *Permafrost Fourth International Conference, Proceedings*, 1298–302, Washington.

Vandenberghe, J. (1985). 'Paleoenvironment and stratigraphy during the last Glacial in the Belgian-Dutch Border Region', *Quaternary Research*, **24**, 23–38.

Velichko, A.A. (1975). 'Paragenesis of a cryogenic (periglacial) zone', *Biuletyn Peryglacjalny*, **24**, 89–110.

Weinberger, L. (1954). 'Die Periglazial-Erscheinungen im Österreichischen Teil des eiszeitlichen Salzach-Vorlandgletscher', *Göttinger Geographische Abhandlungen*, **15**, 17–90, Göttingen.

Wiegand, G. (1965). 'Fossile Pingos in Mitteleuropa, *Würzburger Geographische Arbeiten*, **10**, Würzburg.

6 · Weichselian periglacial structures and their environmental significance: Belgium, the Netherlands, and northern France

A. PISSART

Abstract

The paleo-climatic significance of periglacial structures known in Belgium, the Netherlands and northern France is reviewed. Their position in the stratigraphic sequence of the last glaciation is presented as well as a short summary of the main climatic variations of this cold period.

Resumé

La signification paléoclimatique des principales structures périglaciaires connues en Belgique, aux Pays-Bas et dans le nord de la France est examinée. La position de ces phénomènes dans la séquence stratigraphique de la dernière glaciation est donnée ainsi qu' un bref résumé des variations climatiques principales actuellement connues pendant cette période.

Introduction

The reconstruction of the climatic environment of Pleistocene periglacial times remains a difficult and hazardous task partly because our knowledge of the climatic significance of fossil periglacial features is incomplete. Moreover, the stratigraphy is still much in doubt and as a result, often we may be mixing features from different times. However, it is useful to review our present knowledge of this subject not only to make a contribution to the paleo-climatic reconstruction of Europe, but also to illustrate where further research on present-day periglacial phenomena is needed. In this paper, we briefly present what is known about the periglacial conditions of the last glaciation in Belgium, northern France and the Netherlands.

The difficulties encountered in the reconstruction of paleo-environments from fossil periglacial features are numerous. Karte (1979) has shown clearly that reliance on a single feature is not satisfactory and that we must consider several together and exclude atypical sites that were exceptionally favourable for the development of the features. Such a procedure is not easy in the study of fossil features. Complications arise because of the effect of other factors such as variations in vegetation, differences in geomorphological situations (e.g. Vandenberghe, 1985), and the nature of the soil

(e.g. Romanovsky, 1985). There is also the problem of determining the temperature under which periglacial features are formed. For areas with less than 50 cm of snow in winter, Harris (1982) has shown the existence of relationships between the formation of periglacial features, mean annual temperature and freezing and thawing indices. At present, it is not possible to apply his results in paleo-climatic research, but if we find a relationship between the distribution of zones of vegetation and the thawing index, it will be possible to deduce freezing indices and this will provide important paleo-climatic information.

Paleo-climatic indicators

Poser (1947 a and b; 1948 a and b) was probably the first to use the distribution of fossil periglacial phenomena to map past climates. Since his important contributions, more information has been gained about the significance of these phenomena.

Ice wedges

It is well known that the formation of modern ice wedges is partly dependent on temperature (e.g. Black, 1976). For instance, the highest mean annual air temperature which allows ice wedges to form in Alaska is between -6 and $-8\,°C$ by (Péwé, 1966). Similar values are reported by Brown and Péwé

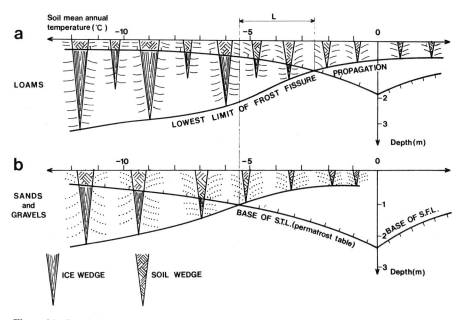

Figure 6.1. Correlation between ice and soil wedges with mean annual soil temperature in, a) loams and b) sands and gravels. S.T.L. = seasonally thawed layer; S.F.L. = seasonally frozen layer (from Romanovsky, 1985, p. 159 with small modifications).

(1973), and by Washburn (1980). A relationship also exists between the material in which ice wedges develop and mean annual temperature. Harris (1982) found that ice wedges formed in peat under a mean annual air temperature of $-3.5\,°C$, while in mineral soil the mean annual temperature had to be much lower ($-7.5\,°C$). Romanovsky (1985) specifies that the soil mean annual temperature favourable to the development of ice wedges is $-5.5\,°C$ in sands, $-2.5\,°C$ in loams (Figure 6.1) and $-2\,°C$ in peat. His paper confirms the idea presented by Goździk (1973) and Kolstrup (1980) that ice wedges grow at a higher temperature in loess than in sands. But the conversion from soil mean annual temperature to mean annual air temperature is hazardous. Gold and Lachenburch (1973) give a difference of 1 to $6\,°C$ between the two values, the difference being greater as the winter snow cover increases.

Although permafrost is necessary for the formation of ice wedges, it is not the only condition. Brutal drops in temperature (Lachenbruch, 1966) are needed to open frost cracks in the frozen ground. To be efficient, such temperature variations must occur when there is no thick snow cover insulating the ground surface. This is the main reason why ice wedges are better developed in continental than in maritime climates.

Soil wedges

Soil wedges, mainly described by Soviet authors, are formed by repeated frost cracking and infilling with mineral sediments. Because they grow in seasonally thawed layers, the ice melts in summer and these remain wedges of mineral soil (mainly sands) with a vertical lamination. The conditions necessary for the formation of these structures are not well known. The evidence reported by Romanovsky (1985) (Figure 6.1) shows that soil wedges, like ice wedges, have a more southerly limit in loams than in sands. The soil mean annual temperature for the formation of soil wedges in sands must be below $-0.5\,°C$. In loams, a temperature limit does not exist.

Frost mounds

As in the case of ice wedges, perennial mounds formed by accumulation of ice in the ground are proof of permafrost. For the closed system pingo, the maximum mean annual air temperature is $-5\,°C$ (Mackay, 1978) or $-6\,°C$ (Washburn, 1980). Open system pingos are found in locations where the mean annual air temperature is below $-2\,°C$ (Washburn, 1980).

Mineral palsas giving scars similar to pingo remnants were described in Canada by Pissart and

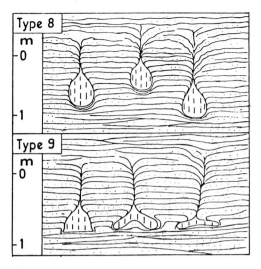

Figure 6.2. Cryoturbation of type 8 and 9 following the classification of Heyse (1983). Type 8 = drop-structures and spherical structures with no relation to permafrost; type 9 = clock-structures and boomerang structures with a flat base formed in association with a permafrost table.

Gangloff (1984). At present, they occur where the mean annual air temperature is below − 3 °C. On the other hand, for the formation of organic palsas, the mean annual air temperature must be below 0 °C (Washburn, 1980; Pissart, 1985; Dionne, 1984). Remnants of such features are unknown in Holland, Belgium and France, and these features are therefore no help in paleo-climatic reconstruction.

Involutions

It is generally agreed that fossil involutions are not necessarily related to the former occurrence of permafrost. Maarleveld (1981) found no relationship between the depth of modern involutions, the thickness of the active layer and the air temperature in July in present-day cold areas. For involutions which are remnants of large non-sorted polygons, Williams (1961) suggests that the mean annual air temperature, during the time of their formation, is below − 3 °C. On the other hand, Goldthwait (1976) said it was − 4 to − 6 °C, while Washburn (1980) suggests 0 °C for polygons with diameters of more than 2 m. These figures are not compatible.

Today in Belgium, the Netherlands and France, authors identify as proof of permafrost, involutions with a flat base (Figure 6.2) that probably corresponds to the permafrost table (Gullentops and Paulissen, 1978; de Moor, 1981, Vandenberghe and Vandenbroeck, 1982; Vandenberghe, 1983, 1985; Lautridou et al. 1985, Van Vliet-Lanoë, 1985). Such

involutions allow one to measure the thickness of the active layer if the level of the ground surface is known at the time of formation.

Stratigraphic position of periglacial structures

The determination of the significance of periglacial structures is not the only problem of paleo-climatic reconstruction. To be useful, the structures must be located unambiguously in the stratigraphic sequence which is based upon lithologic units, palynological studies and ^{14}C dates. The stratigraphic sequence in W. Europe is still uncertain because (a) ^{14}C dates are limited to the last 50,000 years (b) organic material for ^{14}C dating is uncommon when dealing with cold environments (c) the stratigraphy of the last glaciation is based mainly on loess deposits, and we now know that aeolian sedimentation did not occur throughout the glaciation but only for short periods; important gaps exist, (d) all the organic horizons from the last cold period were first regarded as proof of interstadials; it seems probable now that some organic layers are due to local thermokarst phenomena and are not related to climatic events.

To illustrate these uncertainties, the differences between the sequence of Paepe and Vanhoorne (1967) and that of Haesaerts (1984) (Figure 6.3) for the beginning of the last glaciation, are great. Also the age of the important lithostratigraphic horizon, the 'Kessel soil', is now thought to be about 23,000 years B.P. (Haesaerts & Van Vliet, 1981) and it is not now regarded as being equivalent to the Denekamp soil of 29,000 years B.P.

In *The Netherlands*, ice-wedge casts in sands are found from two periods in the last glaciation (Maarleveld, 1976; Vandenberghe, 1985). The more recent are dated at about 20,000 years B.P. (Kolstrup, 1980) and were formed at, or a little before, the time of the maximum of the last glaciation. The oldest ice wedges are older than 55,000 B.P.: Vandenberghe (1985) believes they probably formed between 62,000 and 70,000 B.P. by comparison with the Grande Pile diagram in the Vosges (Mook and Woillard, 1982). On the basis of the presence of ice-wedge casts in sands, it is likely that the mean annual air temperature was below − 6.5 °C.

Pingos which were described for the first time in the Netherlands by Maarleveld & Van der Toorn (1955) were also formed before 19,000 years B.P. (Paris *et al.*, 1979; De Gans, 1981; De Gans *et al.*, 1984). Because they were closed system pingos, they support the conclusion that the mean annual air temperature was below − 6 °C at this time.

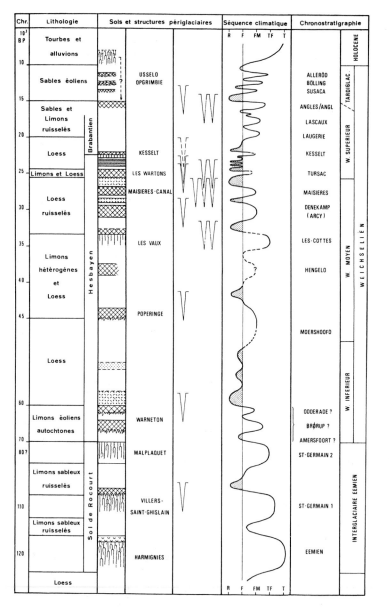

Figure 6.3. Paleo-climatic reconstruction of the last glaciation for the loess part of Belgium by Haesaerts (1984). R = rigorous with continuous permafrost; F = cold with discontinuous permafrost; FM = medium cold; TF = temperate cold; T = temperate; 1: leached soil (B + horizon); 2: leached soil to brown leached soil (sol brun lessivé); 3: Decalcified brown soil (B horizon); 4: eluvial horizon; 5: humic soil with bleached patches; 6: soil or humic deposits; 7: highly iron depleted horizon (tundra gley); 8: frequent ice wedges; 9: occasional ice wedges; 10: isolated ice wedges.

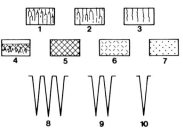

In the loess cover of *Belgium*, several levels of ice-wedge casts have been described. They are shown on the stratigraphic diagram of Haesaerts (1948) (Figure 6.3). The ice-wedge casts are well developed in the upper pleniglacial as was the case in the Netherlands. Typical ice-wedge casts were also discovered at other levels in the stratigraphic sequence where they are not known in the sands of the Netherlands. This distribution is completely in agreement with Romanovsky's diagram (1985) (Figure 6.1) which shows that the mean temperature may be higher for ice wedges in loams than in sands. The description of three levels of ice wedges in the very complex filling of the Flemish valley before 50,000 B.P. by De Moor (1983), proves that it is an oversimplification to speak of only two periods of permafrost during the last glacial period.

In the north of *France*, two levels of ice wedges have been described (Paepe and Sommé, 1970; Lautridou and Sommé, 1981). For all these countries, the evidence collected from periglacial phenomena is consistent but general. Precise stratigraphic correlations remain difficult and often impossible.

The short period of the Younger Dryas, between 11,000 and 10,000 years B.P., is easier to identify. Maarleveld (1976) has shown that during this period, soil wedges were formed in the Netherlands and because they were in sands they cannot be dessication cracks. Maarleveld (1976) believes that they indicate a mean annual temperature between 0 and $-6\,°C$.

Evidence of discontinuous permafrost in Belgium during Younger Dryas time is presented by De Moor (1981) and Heyse (1983). They describe involutions with an horizontal base in sandy ridges north of the Flemish valley. The thickness of the active layer as shown by these structures is about 1.5 m.

Features now interpreted as remnants of mineral palsas (and previously described as pingo remnants) (Figure 6.4) on the Hautes Fagnes plateau were formed during the Younger Dryas (Pissart and Juvigné, 1981; Pissart, 1983; Mullenders and Gullentops, 1969). These features probably formed outside the limit of continuous permafrost and indicate a mean annual temperature of $-3\,°C$ or lower. This value agrees with the observations

Figure 6.4. Remnant of a periglacial mound in the Hautes Fagnes (Belgium). Formerly interpreted as pingo scars, these features are now regarded as remnants of mineral palses (Pissart and Gangloff, 1984).

previously reported from the north of Belgium and the Netherlands, because the altitude of the Hautes Fagnes, about 600 m above sea level, gives a difference at present of 3 °C in mean annual temperature.

We have no information about the temperature of northern France during the Younger Dryas.

The stratigraphic sequence of the last glaciation in Belgium, The Netherlands and Northern France

Stratigraphic difficulties, especially those due to discontinuous sedimentation, make it virtually impossible to present a paleo-climatic reconstruc-

tion of the last glaciation based solely upon periglacial arguments. It is necessary to look for other observations and to combine profiles to try to obtain a more complete record of the glaciation.

As Haesaerts (1984) has shown, different records give similar views of the paleo-climatic succession. The palynological profile from Grande Pile in the Vosges (Figure 6.5) (Mook and Woillard, 1982) which was confirmed by the profile from Les Echets near Lyon (de Beaulieu and Reille, 1984), is now probably the best evidence that one could use in positioning our paleo-climatic phenomena. This curve is very similar to the curve obtained by Dansgaard *et al.* (1971) from isotopic studies of ice

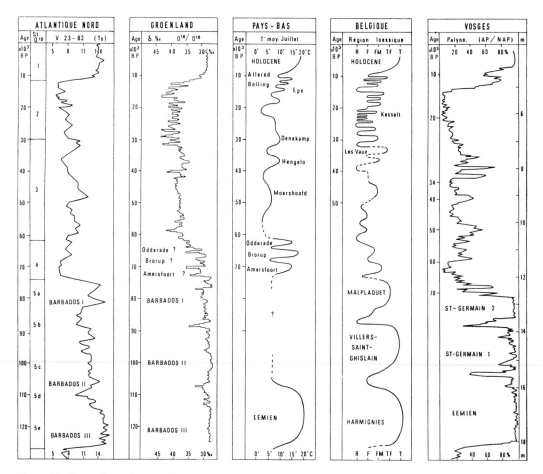

Figure 6.5. Comparison of some palaeo-climatic curves by Haesaerts (1984) 1. North Atlantic, foraminifera (Sancetta *et al.*, 1973); 2. Greenland, O^{18}/O^{16}, Camp Century (Dansgaard *et al.*, 1971); 3. The Netherlands – palynology – July Temperature (Zagwijn, 1975; Kolstrrup, 1980); 4. Loess part of Belgium (Haesaerts, 1984); 5. Vosges, La Grande Pile (France) palynology (Mook and Woillard, 1982).

at Camp Century in Greenland. The curve from Haesaerts (1984) is not only the most recent but also the best one as it is confirmed by all the observations made in loessic deposits of Belgium. The curve for the Netherlands given by Haesaerts is based upon the work of Zagwijn (1975) and Kolstrup (1980). Placed with the other curves, it identifies the gaps which probably exist in the stratigraphic sequence of the Netherlands (Figure 6.5).

After the Eemian (*sensu stricto*, Mook and Woillard, 1982), evidence of St Germain I and II interstadials is seen in the remnants of soils (Villers St Ghislain and Malplaquet) formed under forest (Haesaerts and Van Vliet, 1974, Haesaerts and Van Vliet-Lanoë, 1981). Between these soils, the first indication of permafrost is found (Figure 6.3). The stratigraphic position of these features is derived from a comparison with the Grande Pile curve and may therefore be questionable.

The next periglacial period begins between 70,000 and 60,000 years B.P. and develops a cold continental climate. Periods of better conditions (Amersfoort, Brørup, Odderade) produced humiferous soils (Warneton soil, Paepe 1964). The palynology shows that during these interstadials trees returned (Bastin, 1974; Paepe and Vanhoorne, 1967). The first cover of loess came around 50,000 years B.P. probably during a dry period.

The middle pleniglacial, from 50,000 to 25,000 B.P. corresponds to a wetter climate. During this period, permafrost occurred several times. Three climatic ameliorations, deduced by palynology, were called Moershoofd (50 to 45,000 B.P.), Hengelo (39 to 37,000 B.P.) and Denekamp (32 to 29,000 B.P.) (Zagwijn, 1975). Trees were not numerous. The herbaceous plants indicate that during the Denekamp in the Netherlands, the mean July temperature was below 10 °C (Kolstrup, 1980); large ice-wedge casts indicate continuous permafrost immediately after Denekamp time.

From 25,000 to 15,000 years B.P., during the upper pleniglacial, the climate was first dry and cold, allowing sedimentation of aeolian silt and coversands, but later from 20,000 to 15,000, it was cold and wet. Three climatic improvements are shown by palynology: the interstadials of Laugerie, Lascaux and Angle-sur-Langlin (Haesaerts and Bastin, 1977).

The late glacial, from 15,000 to 10,000 B.P., is the best known period with two climatic improvements: Bolling (12,300 B.P.) and Allerod (between 11,800 and 11,000 B.P.). Permafrost developed at the beginning of this period as demonstrated by ice-wedge casts. Discontinuous permafrost returned during Younger Dryas time (11,000 to 10,000 B.P.). The evidence of herbaceous plants suggests that the mean July temperature was + 11.5 °C during the Younger Dryas, and + 13 °C during the Allerod (Kolstrup, 1979). Van der Hammen *et al.* (1967), report + 10 °C and + 14 °C. As conditions became cold, pine disappeared and was replaced in northern Belgium by herbaceous cover with some lichens (Munaut and Paulissen, 1973; Damblon, 1974). A microfauna collected from a cave at Bomal-sur-Ourthe illustrates the complexity of the landscape (Cordy, 1974): coexisting were animals from cold steppes, wet grassland, swamps and also woodland, showing the existence of different types of vegetation in favourable places.

Conclusion

Some advances have occurred during the last few years which help us to attempt paleo-climatic reconstructions:

1. A better knowledge of the significance of periglacial features (a) the relation between the soil character and the mean annual temperature for ice and soil wedges (Romanovsky, 1985); (b) the distinction between remnants of palsas and pingos (Pissart, 1985); (c) flat-based involutions as an indication of permafrost (Gullentops and Paulissen, 1978).

2. A better understanding of the influence of local site factors on the different geomorphological processes, as Vandenberghe (1985) has demonstrated in Kempen.

3. The stratigraphic sequence is improved, and we now understand how important are the breaks in Weichselian aeolian sedimentation.

It is clear, however that we still need to improve our knowledge to obtain a better understanding of the paleo-climatic evolution of the last glaciation. Periglacial phenomena have proved to be valuable tools for this work.

Acknowledgements

The author thanks A. Roy for improving the English of the first draft and also, J. Boardman, H.M. French and R.B.G. Williams for numerous modifications made to a subsequent version.

References

Bastin, B. (1974). Recherches sur l'évolution du peuplement végétal en Belgique durant la glaciation du Würm. *Acta geographica Lovaniensia*, **9**, 136 p.

Black, R.F. (1976). Features indicative of permafrost. *Annual review of Earth and Planetary Science*, **4**, 75–94.

Brown, R.J.E. and Péwé, T.L. (1973). Distribution of permafrost in North America and its relationship to the environment: a review, 1963–1973. In, *Permafrost. North America Contribution to the second Intern. Conf.*, Natl. Acad. Sci., Washington.

Cordy, J.M. (1974). Etude préliminaire de deux faunes à rongeurs du Tardiglaciaire belge. *Ann. Soc. Géol. Belg.*, **97**, 5–9.

Damblon, F. (1974). Observations palynologiques dans la grotte de Remouchamps. *Bull. Soc. Roy. belge Anthrop. et Préhist.*, **85**, 131–5.

Dansgaard, W., Johnson, S.J., Clausen, H.B. and Langway, C.C., (1971). Climatic record revealed by the Camp Century ice core. In, *Late Cenozoïc Glacial Ages.* (Ed. K.K. Turekian), pp. 37–56, New Haven, Connecticut.

De Beaulieu, J.L. & Reille M. (1984). A long Upper Pleistocene pollen record from Les Echets, near Lyon, France. *Boreas*, **13** (2), 111–132.

De Gans, W. (1981). *The Drentsche Aa Valley System.* Doctor's thesis. Free University. Amsterdam. 132 p.

De Gans, W., Cleveringa, P. and Gongrijp, G. (1984). Een ontsluiting in de Wal van een pingoruine naby Papenvoort (Drente). *Report Rijksinstituut voor Natuurbeheer*, 84/6, Leersum, 53 p.

De Moor, G. (1981). Periglacial deposits and sedimentary structures in the Upper Pleistocene infilling of the Flemish Valley (NW Belgium). *Biul. Perygl.*, **18**, 277–90.

De Moor, G. (1983). Cryogenic structures in the Weichselian deposits of Northern Belgium and their significance. *Polarforschung*, **53** (2), 79–86.

Dionne, J.-Cl. (1984). Palses et limite méridionale du pergélisol dans l'hémisphère Nord: le cas de Blanc-Sablon, Québec. *Géogr. phys. et Quaternaire*, **38** (2), 165–84.

Gold, L.W. and Lachenbruch, A.H. (1973). Thermal conditions in permafrost. A review of North American literature. In, *Permafrost. North American Contribution to the Second Intern. Conf.*, pp. 3–23, Natl. Acad. Sci., Washington.

Goldthwait, R.P. (1976). Frost sorted patterned ground: a review. *Quaternary Research*, **6**, 27–35.

Goździk, J. (1973). Geneza i pozycja stratygraficzna struktur peryglacjalnych w Srodkowej Polsce. (summary: The genesis and stratigraphical position of periglacial structures in Central Poland). *Acta Geogr. Lodziensia*, **31**.

Gullentops, F. and Paulissen, E. (1978). The drop soil of the Eisden type. *Biul. Perygl.*, **27**, 105–15.

Haesaerts, P. (1984). Aspects de l'évolution du paysage et de l'environnement en Belgique au Quaternaire. Chapitre III: 'Peuples chasseurs de la Belgique préhistorique dans leur cadre naturel'. *Publication Inst. Roy. Sc. Nat. de Belg.*, 27–40.

Haesaerts, P. & Bastin, B. (1977). Chronostratigraphie de la fin de la dernière glaciation à la lumière des résultats de l'étude lithostratigraphique et palynologique du site de Maisières-Canal (Belgique). *Géobios*, **10**, 123–7.

Haesaerts, P. & Van Vliet, B. (1974). Compte rendu de l'excursion du 25 mai 1974 consacrée à la stratigraphie des limons aux environs de Mons. *Ann. Soc. Géol. Belg.*, **97**, 291–324.

Haesaerts, P. & Van Vliet, B. (1981). Phénomènes périglaciaires et sols fossiles observés à Maisières-Canal, à Harmignies et à Rocourt. *Biul. Perygl.*, **28**, 291–325.

Harris, S.A. (1982). Distribution of zonal permafrost landforms with freezing and thawing indices. *Biul. Perygl.*, **29**, 163–82.

Heyse, I. (1983). Fossil cryoturbation types in eolian Würm late glacial sediments in Flanders (Belgium). *Polarforschung*, **53** (2), 87–95.

Karte, J. (1979). Raumliche Abgrennzung und regionale Differenzierung des Periglaziärs. *Bochumer Geographisches Arbeiten*, Heft **35**, 211 p.

Kolstrup, E. (1979). Herbs as July temperature indicators for parts of the pleniglacial and Late Glacial in the Netherlands. *Geol. en Mijnbouw*, **58** (3), 377–80.

Kolstrup, E. (1980). Climate and stratigraphy in Northwestern Europe between 30.000 B.P. and 13.000 B.P. with special reference to the Netherlands. *Meded. Rijks Geol. Dienst*, 32–15, 181–253.

Lachenbruch, A.H. (1966). Contraction theory of ice wedge polygons: a qualitative discussion. *Permafrost International Conference (Lafayette, Ind., 11–15 Nov. 1963). Proceedings.* pp. 63–71, Natl. Acad. Sci. National Research Council Publication 1287.

Lautridou, J.P. & Sommé, J. (1981). L'extension des niveaux repères périglaciaires à grandes fentes de gel de la stratigraphie du Pléistocène récent dans la France du Nord-Ouest. *Biul. Perygl.*, **28**, 179–85.

Maarleveld, G.C. (1976). Periglacial phenomena and the mean annual temperature during the last glacial time in the Netherlands. *Biul. Perygl.*, **26**, 57–78.

Maarleveld, G.C. (1981). Summer thaw depths in cold regions and fossil cryoturbation. *Geologie en Mijnbouw*, **60**, 347–52.

Maarleveld, G.C. & Van der Toorn, J.V. (1955). Pseudo-sölle in Noord-Nederland. *Tijdschr. Kon. Nederl. Aardrijk. Genootschap*, **72**.

Mackay, J.R. (1978). Contemporary pingos: a discussion. *Biul. Perygl.*, **27**, 133–4.

Mook, W. and Woillard, G. (1982). Carbon-14 dates at Grande-Pile. Correlation of land and sea chronologies. *Science* (Washington, D.C.), **215**, 159–61.

Mullenders, W. and Gullentops, F. (1969). The age of the pingos of Belgium. *The periglacial environment; Past and Present.* (Ed. Troy L. Péwé), pp. 321–35, McGill Queen's University Press. Montreal.

Munaut, A.V. & Paulissen, E. (1973). Evolution et paléo-écologie de la vallée de la petite Nèthe au cours du post-Würm (Belgique). *Ann. Soc. Géol. Belg.*, **96**, 301–48.

Paepe, R. (1964). Les dépôts quaternaires de la plaine de la Lys. *Bull. Soc. belge Géol., Paléont. et Hydrol.*, **73**, 327–65.

Paepe, R. & Somme, J. (1970). Les loess et la stratigraphie du Pleistocène récent dans le N de la France et en Belgique. *Ann. Soc. Géol. du N.*, **90**, fasc. 4, 191–201.

Paepe, R. & Vanhoorne, R. (1967). *The stratigraphy and paleobotany of the Late Pleistocene in Belgium.* Mém. pour servir à l'explication des cartes géologiques et minières de la Belgique. **8**, Bruxelles, 96 p.

Paris, F.P., Cleveringa, P. and De Gans, W. (1979). The Stockersdobbe: geology and palynology of a deep pingo remnant in Friesland (The Netherlands). *Geologie en Mijnbouw*, **58** (1), 33–8.

Péwé, T.L. (1966). Paleoclimatic significance of fossil ice wedges. *Biul. Perygl.*, **15**, 65–73.

Pissart, A. (1983). Remnants of periglacial mounds in the Hautes Fagnes (Belgium): structure and age of the ramparts. *Geol. en Mijnbouw*, **62**, 551–5.

Pissart, A. (1985). Pingos et palses: un essai de synthèse des connaissances actuelles. *Inter-Nord.*, **17**, 21–32.

Pissart, A. & Gangloff, P. (1984). Les palses minérales et organiques de la vallée de l'Aveneau, près de Kuujjuaq, Québec subarctique. *Géogr. physique et Quaternaire*, **38** (3), 217–28.

Pissart, A. & Juvigne, E. (1981). Genèse et âge d'une trace de butte périglaciaire (pingo ou palse) de la Konnerzvenn, Hautes Fagnes, Belgique. *Ann. Soc. Géol. Belg.*, **103**, 73–86.

Poser, H. (1947a). Dauerfrostboden und Temperaturverhaltnijsse während der Würmeiszeit im nicht vereisten Mittel – und West Europa. *Naturwissenschaften*, **34**, 10–18.

Poser, H. (1947b). Auftautiefe und Frostzerrung im Bodem Mitteleuropas Während der Würm-Eiszeit. *Naturwissenschaften*, **34**, p. 323–8 & 262–7.

Poser, H. (1948a). Boden- und Klimaverhältnisse in Mittel- und Westeuropa während der Würmeiszeit. *Erdkunde*, **2**, 53–68.

Poser, H. (1948b). Äolische Ablagerungen und Klima des Spätglazials in Mittel und West Europa. *Naturwissenschaften*, **9**, 269–75, 302–12.

Romanovsky, N.H. (1985). Distribution of recently active ice and soil wedges in the U.S.S.R. *Field and Theory: Lectures in geocryology* (Eds. M. Church and S. Slaymaker), pp. 154–65, University of British Columbia.

Sancetta, C., Imbrie, J. and Kipp, N.G. (1973). Climatic record of the past 130,000 years in the North Atlantic deep-sea core V 28–32: correlations with terrestrial record. *Quaternary Research*, **3**, 110–16.

Vandenberghe, J. (1983). Ice-wedge casts and involutions as permafrost indicators and their stratigraphic position in the Weichselian. In, *Permafrost – Fourth Int. Conference*, pp. 1298–1302, Nat Acad. Sci., Washington.

Vandenberghe, J. (1985). Paleoenvironment and stratigraphy during the last glacial in the Belgian-Dutch Border Region. *Quaternary Research*, **24** (1), 23–38.

Vandenberghe, J. & Vandenbroeck, P. (1982). Weichselian convolution phenomena and processes in fine sediments. *Boreas*, **11**, 299–315.

Van der Hammen, T., Maarleveld, G.C., Vogel, J.C. & Zagwijn, W.H. (1967). Stratigraphy, climatic succession and radiocarbon dating of the last glacial in the Netherlands. *Geol. en Mijnbouw*, **46**, 79–95.

Van Vliet-Lanoe, B. (1985). Frost effects in soils. In, *Soils and Quaternary Landscape Evolution* (Ed. J. Boardman), pp. 117–58, Wiley and Sons, Chichester.

Washburn, A.L. (1980). Permafrost features as evidence of climatic change. *Earth-Sci. Rev.*, **15**, 327–402.

Williams, P.J. (1961). Climatic factors controlling the distribution of certain frozen ground phenomena. *Geogr. Annlr.*, **43**, 339–47.

Zagwijn, W.H. (1975). Chronostratigraphie en biostratigrafie, indeling van het Kwartaire op grond van veronderingen in vegetatie in Klimaat. In, *Toelichting by geologische overzichts-Kaarten van Nederland. Haarlem. Ryks geologische Dienst.* (Eds. W.H. Zagwijn and C.J. Van Staalduinen), pp. 109–14.

PART II

Britain and Ireland

7 · Permafrost stratigraphy in Britain – a first approximation

PETER WORSLEY

Abstract

Apart from limited occurrences of collapsed cryogenic mounds and fossil rock glaciers the only reliable indices of former permafrost are thermal contraction phenomena (ice-wedge casts and sand wedges). Since the former two are all of Devensian age (Last Glacial Stage), the recognition of earlier events is based entirely on structures arising from permafrost cracking. Uncertainty regarding the stratigraphy prevents a confident permafrost history but despite this we may claim its presence during at least five cold stages. Pre-Hoxnian permafrost occurs in the Anglian and Beestonian cold stages and probably involved several phases in each. At the Hoxnian type site post-Hoxnian permafrost events can be demonstrated shortly after the interglacial but elsewhere severe correlation problems arise. Three new sites provide evidence for permafrost shortly before the Ipswichian (Last Interglacial) Stage. In the Devensian the most complete record is in east Cheshire. Extensive permafrost was present throughout Britain in the Dimlington Stadial but in the Loch Lomond Stadial its status is unclear.

Introduction

One of the most important stimuli to the study of British periglaciation was the visit by the New Zealander Martin Te Punga in 1955. His report, presented to the British Association meeting in that year (Te Punga, 1956), highlighted the abundance and range of periglacial phenomena in southern England. Since that time, numerous workers have made detailed studies of various aspects of the periglacial legacy and the current trend, as expressed by the contributions to this volume, suggests that we may anticipate future significant advances in the understanding of former British periglacial environments.

In terms of the fluctuating climatic environments which have typified the Quaternary, at the simplest level two modal states are recognised, namely glacials and interglacials and these underpin the standard stages of the British Quaternary classification (Mitchell *et al.*, 1973). In the popular conception a glacial stage is equated with glacier ice activity and this is understandable since glaciation *per se* usually has a catastrophic impact on the landscape. Further the effects of glacial erosion and deposition are normally readily identified by the resultant landforms or sedimentary responses. By contrast the expression of cold but non-glacigenic processes is often more subtle and hence recognition requires a more refined understanding of contemporary cold climate environments. Matters are not eased by the fact that some of the processes operative in a periglacial environment and hence a glacial stage, have much in common with those in interglacials with consequent ambiguities in establishing their climatic significance.

An overlap of processes operative in interglacials and glacials has enabled Ballantyne (1987) to write on 'present day periglacial activity in British mountains' when stratigraphically we are in an interglacial. Thus we have the basis of what could easily become a sterile semantic debate on what the threshold conditions for periglaciation are, since in an earlier review (Worsley, 1977) the writer maintained the opinion that 'approximately 10,000 BP truly periglacial environments within the British Isles were abruptly terminated and have not since returned'. Clearly there is a spatial transition from temperate to cold environmental conditions and personal preferences will influence the perceived boundary. When examining an assumed periglacial rock record from a temporal perspective a paramount need is to eliminate as much ambiguity as possible, hence only those sediments containing evidence for former permafrost will be considered here.

Evidence for permafrost in the Pleistocene

What then constitutes valid evidence for inferring the former presence of permafrost? Here we are largely dependent upon the successful recognition of landforms and structures arising from the melting of ground ice which originally developed in conjunction with permafrost. The only features in Britain uniquely related to permafrost are fossil rock glaciers, decayed cryogenic mounds (see Worsley, (1986b)) and thermal contraction phenomena (ice and sediment wedges). At present the limited evidence related to rock glaciers and cryogenic mounds consists almost entirely of features at or close to the present day landsurface and hence is in all probability the last glacial stage in age i.e. Devensian. In contrast permafrost wedge structures are common in Devensian sediments but also occur in the pre-Devensian sedimentary record where they constitute the sole source of firm evidence.

A consideration of permafrost frequency is naturally going to be heavily dependent upon the precision accorded to the allied Quaternary stratigraphy. The schema compiled by Mitchell et al. (1973) is currently subject to critical appraisal and the correlation of certain key elements is in doubt. Although the oxygen isotope signature from deep sea sediments would appear to indicate numerous glacial and interglacial stages, the British terrestrial evidence as presently interpreted suggests a lesser number. The conventional wisdom recognises three major glaciations – Anglian, Wolstonian and Devensian, each being accorded stage status. Yet the view is gaining ascendancy that the products of what have hitherto been interpreted as totally separate Anglian and Wolstonian glaciations are in reality parts of a single glacial complex which in time corresponds to the Anglian Stage (Sumbler, 1983). This is not to deny the existence of at least one cold stage equivalent to the current 'Wolstonian' between the Hoxnian and Ipswichian Interglacials but rather that the rock record at Wolston which currently defines it should be correlated with the Anglian. Thus we have an emerging more simplified model of British glaciation history rather than an increasingly complex one, more in accord with the marine record. This has serious consequences for present purposes since it creates uncertainty over what have been assumed to be reliable regional stratigraphic units. Since interglacial deposits are relatively rare and re-stricted in their distribution, the practical means of correlation are the lithostratigraphic units, particularly the tills, since these have to be used to project spatially the interglacial biostratigraphic framework. Glacial stage biostratigraphy alone (and this of course embraces periglacial environmental evidence) is of limited use in correlation since 'cold' floras and faunas of different ages are usually very similar. As a result there are major problems in assigning ages to structures which appear to relate to what have hitherto been regarded as Wolstonian sediments.

Another problem concerns the identification of permafrost-related wedge structures. Remarkably Paterson's (1940) classic paper has remained, until the recent publication by Seddon and Holyoak (1985), a rare example of a British comparative study of modern and relict ice wedges based upon first hand experience of both. This highlights a serious difficulty with much work to date, a heavy reliance upon a sparse modern analogue literature. In addition there has been a tendency to interpret almost all wedge structures as ice-wedge casts. Despite Johnsson's (1959) timely early warning of the inherent pitfalls and later discussions e.g. Black (1976, 1983), a number of wedge structures of dubious parentage have been accepted as permafrost indicators in the British literature. However, the examples to be cited are, in the judgement of the writer, probably a consequence of thermal contraction although caution is recommended in a few cases.

The permafrost stratigraphy

The ensuing discussion of the stratigraphic distribution of fossil thermal contraction structures indicative of permafrost, will concentrate on those associated with reasonable dating contexts. The question of ice-wedge cast and sand wedge discrimination will be set aside since both kinds of structure are indicative of permafrost. Selectivity is necessary and will be primarily guided by utility in contributing towards the compilation of a Pleistocene permafrost history.

(a) Pre-Hoxnian

East Anglia contains the only extensive early and middle Pleistocene sequences in Britain and hence it is not surprising to discover that the oldest known permafrost structures occur in this region. Natural exposures along a long eroding coastline have provided much of the basic chronological framework. That part of the sequence lying below the oldest till has been subject to an authoritative multidisciplinary synthesis (including a consideration of periglacial stratigraphy) by West (1980) and this updates and amplifies the earlier part of his pioneer regional periglacial history (West, 1969).

The oldest cold stage sediments associated with permafrost are of Beestonian age. They outcrop at several localities in the Cromer area beneath Cromerian interglacial sediments but their stratigraphy is complex and the current understanding may be oversimplified. Some 13 structures have been identified as ice-wedge casts and interpreted as possibly signifying up to six permafrost events (West, 1980). However, the inferred palaeo-environment of a low relief landscape with shifting river channels, may have been associated with casting on a localised scale without recourse to periodic climatic changes. A striking fragment of a Beestonian ice-wedge cast polygonal network was visible on the upper part of the foreshore at West Runton in the 1960s. The casts penetrated marine silts assigned to the preceding Pastonian interglacial stage (West, 1968). Unfortunately, coastal defence work has (for the time being) obscured the exposure although a similar aged network occasionally emerges on the foreshore a few hundred metres east of the previous locality after major scour events associated with winter storms. Further south in the Paston–Mundesley area three wedge structures of pre-Cromerian age (?Beestonian) are recorded by West (1980).

At first encounter, a proposal that permafrost was present in the succeeding interglacial seems anomalous yet this is proposed with respect to pollen assemblage biozone Cr IVc of the Cromerian at West Runton (West, 1980; Rose *et al.*, 1985a). It is claimed that ice-wedge casts were coeval with an environment supporting a birch dominated woodland, a relationship which, by comparison with some contemporary permafrost areas, is not unreasonable. However, close inspection of West's excellent drawn sections shows that the dating is founded upon lithostratigraphic correlation along a coastal cliff with intermittent exposure and when the nature of the sedimentary facies are taken into account, confidence is further diminished. The permafrost evidence centres upon two wedge structures both of which are shallow and truncated and one of these (West, 1980, Figure 10, 216 m) could equally well be pre-Cromerian in age. As a consequence it is suggested that the evidence is unsatisfactory and the case for late Cromerian permafrost remains unproven.

In the same sections, but at a higher stratigraphic level, a further four wedge structures have been taken to indicate a slightly later permafrost phase. The structures were all truncated by the basal erosional surface of a sand unit immediately underlying the Cromer Till. The glacigenic sands and till are the first undisputed evidence for glaciation in the English succession and are correlated with the Anglian Stage. Thus these wedges are for the time being best ascribed to an inter Cromerian-Anglian age especially since this particular stratigraphic break may, in the future, be shown to bridge at least one glacial-interglacial stage cycle which is not currently part of the standard British succession.

The ice-wedge casts in the Anglian sub-till sand unit confirm that a permafrost environment prevailed prior to deposition of the Cromer Till. These structures were first noted by West and Donner (1958) and since that time a number of papers have added data. A major advance has been the recognition in southern East Anglia of an extensive soil stratigraphic unit which normally occurs immediately below the base of the Anglian till sheet. This is now formally named the Barham Soil (Rose *et al.*, 1985b) and is considered to be a buried palaeosol. Ice-wedge casts and sand wedges (sometimes glacio-tectonically deformed) contribute towards the total character of the Barham Soil horizon at some 10 localities although it is debatable whether these permafrost structures should be included as elements of the soil, for in contemporary permafrost environments, the zone of pedogenesis usually corresponds with the active layer. Temporary exposures of polygonal networks at the Barham Soil horizon have been described from two sites, Newney Green in Essex (Rose *et al.*, 1985b) and Corton Cliff, Suffolk (Gardner and West, 1975).

(b) '?Early Wolstonian'

As noted earlier, the stratigraphical definition of the Hoxnian-Ipswichian interval is currently problematic and therefore unless permafrost evidence can be directly related to deposits of these two limiting interglacials it is best to leave in abeyance any discussion of structures associated with the Wolstonian succession in the English Midlands. However, at the Hoxne interglacial type site, excavations have revealed wedge structures at two different horizons in sediments above the interglacial deposits and these are considered to represent two phases of permafrost (Gladfelter, 1975). The permafrost appears to relate to the cold stage which immediately followed the Hoxnian. This stage is best left unnamed for the present.

(c) '?Late Wolstonian'

Stratigraphic evidence consistent with a hitherto unrecognised interglacial intermediate in age between the Hoxnian and Ipswichian Stages has recently been forthcoming from several localities in southern England. At two of these, large ice-wedge casts are present and these appear to date from a cold stage between the 'new' interglacial and the Ipswichian.

First, at Stanton Harcourt in Oxfordshire, gravel pit workings have revealed a basal channel cut into a Jurassic clay infilled with biogenic sediments indicative of an interglacial environment. The channel was buried beneath 4–5 m of sandy gravels forming a terrace, the bluff of which stood 3 m above the adjacent low Floodplain Terrace of the River Thames (Briggs *et al.*, 1985). Regionally, terrace features a few metres above the Floodplain Terrace are grouped into a terrace system (Summertown-Radley) which in parts incorporates Ipswichian materials (see Figure 7.1A). Bryant (1983) has outlined the terrace sedimentology at Stanton Harcourt and concluded that the sandy

gravel facies represents braided stream alluvium with a maximum channel relief amplitude not exceeding 2 m. Intraformational truncated ice-wedge cast structures were regarded by him as the products of localised permafrost degradation caused by lateral channel migration in conjunction with talik extension. A detailed examination of the casts was later undertaken by Seddon and Holyoak (1985) who recognised normal, truncated and superposed reactivated cast types. Like Bryant, they argued for sedimentation in a sustained permafrost environment, the casting events having no regional climatic control since they were a product of sub-channel talik movement.

A problem with the talik extension hypothesis is that its validity is difficult to test and it can be argued that the probability of sub-channel taliks having developed is low in view of the previously noted restriction on bed relief which would favour seasonal freezeback to the bed. An alternative and possibly more plausible mechanism for casting on extensive low relief floodplains (periglacial sandar) might operate in association with the utilisation of

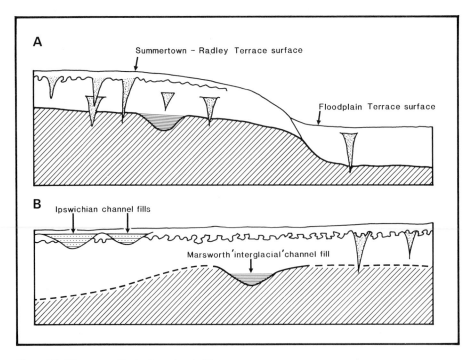

Figure 7.1. Diagrammatic stratigraphy. A. The Summertown-Radley and Floodplain Terraces at Stanton Harcourt, Oxfordshire. The 'interglacial' channel infill is shown beneath the terrace by the horizontal shading. B. The permafrost structures at Marsworth in relation to the Ipswichian and Marsworth interglacial deposits.

the troughs which typically overlie the sub-surface ice wedges. These troughs frequently carry melt-water drainage especially at the time of ice break-up; thus flowing or standing water can cause thermal erosion or induce thaw of the wedge ice. Sediments accumulating in the newly created voids can create casts of the ground ice geometry. What-ever the precise mechanism active casting in alluvial environments does not require climatic change as a prerequisite (this also applies to the Beestonian wedges noted previously).

Although Seddon and Holyoak appear cautious in assigning the Stanton Harcourt sandy gravels to a specific cold stage, the dating results lead them to infer a Devensian age for the permafrost and gravel aggradation. However, the two dating techniques in this instance yield divergent results and could well be misleading. Certainly, the long accepted mor-phostratigraphy is at variance with a Devensian age and on balance the evidence favours correlation of the permafrost event with an immediately pre-Ipswichian cold stage, a conclusion in accord with the views of Briggs *et al.* (1985).

Second, impressive evidence substantiating a cold stage of similar age was exposed in a quarry at Marsworth (Pitstone) in Buckinghamshire. Cur-rently only an outline stratigraphy is available (Green *et al.*, 1984). Above chalk, a cover of late Pleistocene deposits up to 8 m thick consisting of chalky muds passed upwards into coombe rock indicative of former extensive solifluction. Locally, channels cut into the chalk lay beneath the peri-glacial sediments, and the channel fills included clasts of travertine containing the impressions of maple leaves (i.e. interglacial material). Above the coombe rock, a shallow channel fill yielded a rich large vertebrate faunal assemblage which appears diagnostic of the Ipswichian. Just beyond the area described by Green *et al.* the chalk-rich periglacial sediments were penetrated by large ice-wedge casts and in the late 1960s when the surficial sediments were being stripped, these wedges were seen to correspond with linear features forming a large scale patterned ground network. Crucial evidence for dating the permafrost event is provided by an extensive horizon of involution structures devel-oped in the upper horizons of the coombe rock. These are truncated by the erosive base of the upper channel (Ipswichian). The involutions extend across the wedge infill sediments and clearly post-date the casting event. Since the travertine clasts in the lower channel have yielded Uranium Series dates in the 150–175 ka range, there are good grounds for assigning the permafrost event to an immediately pre-Ipswichian cold stage (see Figure 7.1B).

Finally, mention of ice-wedge cast – Ipswichian relationships at Maxey in Cambridgeshire is apposite. A 4–5 m thick sandy gravel succession overlay Jurassic clay and, in the middle of the gravels, were shallow channels containing Ipswi-chian biogenic sediments (French, 1982). These interglacial channels were seen by the writer to directly truncate ice-wedge casts in the lower part of the gravels giving an undoubted pre-Ipswichian age for the basal succession and associated per-mafrost structures. It is salutary to note that without knowledge of the interglacial channels, which are of restricted extent, there would be no reason to suspect that the total gravel aggradation did not belong to a *single* cold stage. The lower gravels are probably the result of cold stage aggrad-ation immediately antedating the Ipswichian.

(d) Devensian

In east Cheshire it has been possible to reconstruct a number of phases of permafrost development and to date this area possesses the most detailed record available in Britain (Worsley, 1966). A schematic update on the stratigraphic distribution of per-mafrost related structures is shown in Figure 7.2. The Devensian sequence comprises a fluvio-aeolian succession (Chelford Sands Formation) overlain unconformably by glacigenic sediments (Stockport Formation) associated with Late Devensian glaci-ation, i.e. Dimlington Stadial of Rose (1985). Whilst no evidence has yet been forthcoming which un-equivocally demonstrates that the bulk of the Chelford Sands are of Devensian age, it is current wisdom to assume that this is the case. The Farm Wood Peat Member (Chelford Interstadial) is probably of Early Devensian age (Worsley 1985, 1986a).

In the Chelford area the interstadial deposits occupied a palaeo-channel system and marginal to it a buried contemporaneous landsurface was re-cognised. This horizon was characterised by a soil consisting of in situ rootlets overlain by a thin organic-rich layer or irregular lags of pebble–size clasts which possessed either a high degree of polish or facets. From the palaeosol horizon ice-wedge casts descended but the age of these with respect to the interstadial was difficult to establish with certainty as the landsurface appears to have been essentially stable whilst the palaeo-channel was cut and infilled. Cast structures just above the palaeo-channel base and directly below the interstadial organics suggest that a permafrost phase immedi-

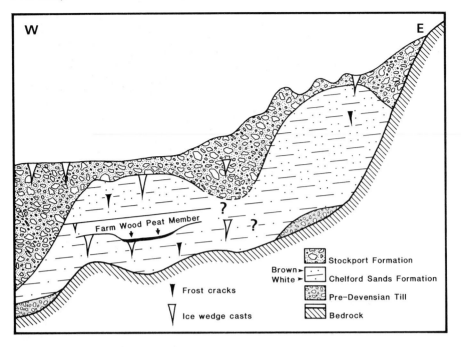

Figure 7.2. A schematic west-east cross-section through the Pleistocene succession of east Cheshire showing the stratigraphical distribution of probable Devensian ice-wedge casts. The casts within the Stockport Formation are in both till and sand lithologies.

ately antedates the interstadial. No ice-wedge casts have been seen immediately above the interstadial sequence but features reminiscent of thermo-erosional niches (Jahn, 1975 p. 113) cut into the uppermost organic fill suggest at least deep freezing immediately after the cessation of organic accumulation. We probably have evidence for a permafrost episode immediately before the Chelford Interstadial and possibly after it.

A change from white to brown coloured sands occurred at a horizon above the interstadial and was marked by an erosional disconformity. An episode of ice-wedge growth and decay followed by truncation of the resultant cast structures intervened prior to the aggradation of the brown sands. Thus only the lower tips of the casts were preserved within the white sands (see Figure 7.3). Within the brown sands sporadic minor wedge structures are ascribed to frost cracking processes or incipient ice wedges (ice veins). At some localities the terminal depositional surface of the brown sands appeared to be preserved and from this ice-wedge casts descended. Since sediment from the overlying Stockport Formation occurred within the fills it

appears likely that the casting post-dated burial by the Dimlington Stadial ice sheet.

The recognition that much of the hummocky terrain and allied sediments in the east Cheshire lowlands is diagnostic of a supraglacial landform-sediment association has strengthened the previous conclusion that permafrost was present before, during and after the glacial ice advance to the Late Devensian maximum limit. At least one of the structures previously reported (Worsley, 1966 pp. 362–3) is now interpreted as a soft rock deformation structure analogous to what have been termed 'till wedges' – see discussions by Dreimanis (1973), Mörner (1972) and Worsley (1973). Other structures are still regarded as true ice-wedge casts and maintain the pattern of permafrost presence which has previously been inferred.

The only other locality with possible Early Devensian ice-wedge casts was discovered at Wretton on the eastern Fenland margin (West *et al.*, 1974). A 6 m thick succession of sands and sandy gravels forming a low terrace bordering the River Wissey overlay undoubted Ipswichian sediments. When exposed, the succession contained small

Figure 7.3. A truncated ice-wedge cast within white sands and unconformably overlain by brown sands. Outcrop in the Chelford Sands Formation formerly exposed in the Catchpenny Quarry, near Chelford (Grid ref. SJ 812711).

enclosed basins a few metres across at two levels and these were interpreted as the products of seasonal ground ice mound decay; a direct association with permafrost was considered unproven. An ice-wedge cast horizon apparently lay *between* the two basin levels and another was close to the present day surface. It is the lower of these two cast horizons which potentially is the more significant since pollen within both levels of basin fill suggested the occurrence of woodland substages – i.e. two interstadials separated by an intervening permafrost event. Unfortunately there is an unsolved

Figure 7.4. A complex Devensian ice-wedge cast in
gravels at Baston, Lincolnshire. Two phases of growth
with an intervening casting phase are evident. Axial
plane of former wedge lay at an angle of 45° to the
quarry face. Height of section 2.8 m.

dichotomy between the pollen evidence and that from included Coleopteran faunas since the latter indicate a treeless environment during basin infilling. Hence the suggested correlation of the upper level of basin fills with the Chelford Interstadial is questionable. Therefore at Wretton there is only a possibility of a permafrost event with a pre-Chelford Interstadial age.

After the Chelford Interstadial until the Dimlington Stadial the evidence for permafrost environments having prevailed is fairly common, for a large number of sites with ice-wedge casts are known, usually in river terrace contexts. Sporadic organic lenses yielding floral and faunal evidence pertinent to climatic reconstructions are occasionally exposed and two basic types have been identified (a) stadial with open tundra-type habitats, and (b) interstadial with largely treeless conditions but warm summers. Unfortunately, inter-site correlation has poor precision being dependent upon either radiocarbon dating, a technique which is beset with severe problems in the 25–50 ka range (and beyond) or morphological relationships. It is the practice to accept an age of just over 40 ka for the interstadial (Upton Warren *sensu stricto*) and taking this as a datum it is evident that most, if not all the ice-wedge casts post-date it.

A number of maps have been compiled showing the distribution of alleged ice-wedge cast structures in Britain and the latest is that of Rose *et al.* (1985a). A pioneering attempt at understanding distribution patterns led Williams (1965) to suggest a palaeo-climatic significance to a concentration in the eastern half of England. Another early concept was that the Dimlington Stadial ice maximum was probably synchronous with the main permafrost event outside the ice limit. An implication arising was that all surface structures were of a similar age, however it soon became clear that not only was permafrost a recurrent phenomena in the Devensian, but the presence of surface structures within the glacial limit showed it to have extended

Figure 7.5. Two Devensian ice-wedge casts in gravels at Baston, Lincolnshire. The differing widths are mainly due to varying axial trends.

throughout most of the area affected by Dimlington Stadial glaciation. Watson (1977) commented upon the human factor in influencing the density of sites and a concentration in central Wales is testimony to his work in that area.

Perhaps the most pressing current issue concerns whether or not permafrost capable of developing ice wedges was present during the Loch Lomond Stadial. Certainly the distribution maps show large blank areas in western Britain largely corresponding to where Loch Lomond aged glaciers are thought to have existed. One or two wedge structures have been described as penetrating Loch Lomond Stadial end moraines e.g. Sissons (1974) but in the absence of details the validity of these as permafrost indicators is questionable. Seemingly, the best evidence to date was presented by Rose (1975) who described two deep wedge structures penetrating gravels forming a raised shoreline ridge lying at 34 m O.D. The site was at Old Kilpatrick on the north bank of the River Clyde west of Glasgow where the shoreline chronology is ambiguous but nevertheless does not deny a possible Loch Lomond Stadial age for these structures. Caution is also urged over the interpretation of the structures as ice-wedge casts especially in the light of a 'rounded structure' between the two wedges and the detailed irregularities shown by the wedge terminations. It is conceivable that they are all soft-rock deformations, with the wedges being genetically related to clastic dykes. A claim by Gemmell and Ralston (1984) that polygon networks in north east Scotland were of Loch Lomond age brought forth a critical response from Armstrong and Paterson (1985) who stressed that they could equally well date from the end of the Dimlington Stadial. Although there is good evidence for the presence of at least localised permafrost in England and Wales during the Loch Lomond Stadial (this is expressed by rock glaciers and cryogenic ridges and hollows – see Bryant and Carpenter, 1987), no undoubted ice-wedge casts are known which date from this short duration cold period even though circumstantial evidence suggests that appropriate conditions for their formation might have prevailed. Therefore until structures associated with firm stratigraphical contexts are discovered an open mind is appropriate when considering ice-wedge casts of potential Loch Lomond Stadial age.

Conclusion

From the foregoing account it is clear that we are currently some way from achieving a full understanding of British permafrost history. Much depends upon an improved dating resolution for the middle and upper Pleistocene rock record. In Britain, unlike many areas, we are hampered by a lack of a known long sedimentation sequence and the acuteness of this situation is exemplified by the absence of a basic succession consisting of an Ipswichian sequence superposed on one from the Hoxnian. Biostratigraphical advances are likely to be mainly concentrated on the floras and faunas associated with interglacial sediments rather than those from the glacial stages. Periglacial biota are notoriously similar in character creating problems in chronological differentiation. In the immediate future we may anticipate a better understanding of the environmental conditions accompanying the permafrost and a precurser to this is the kind of study presented by Seddon and Holyoak (1985). Advances of this nature, together with a more reliable absolute chronology for the Devensian will give us a better insight into cold stage variability. Pre-Devensian events will be dependent upon new findings similar to those at Marsworth and Stanton Harcourt plus further work on sites with evolving exposures such as that by Rose *et al.* (1985*b*) on the Barham palaeosol. At present we may claim permafrost development in parts of the last five known cold stages in Britain.

References

Armstrong, M. & Paterson, I.B. (1985). Some recent discoveries of ice-wedge cast networks in north-east Scotland – a comment. *Scott. J. Geol.*, **21**, 107–8.

Ballantyne, C.K. (1987). The present day periglaciation of upland Britain. In, *Periglacial Processes and Landforms in Britain and Ireland* (Ed. J. Boardman), pp. 113–26, Cambridge University Press.

Black, R.F. (1976). Periglacial features indicative of permafrost: Ice and soil wedges. *Quat. Res.*, **6**, 3–26.

Black, R.F. (1983). Pseudo-ice-wedge casts of Connecticut, northeastern United States. *Quat. Res.*, **20**, 74–89.

Briggs, D.J., Coope, G.R. & Gilbertson, D.D. (1985). The chronology and environmental framework of early man in the upper Thames Valley A new model. *Brit. Archaeol. Rept. Brit. Ser.*, **137**, 176pp.

Bryant, I.D. (1983). Facies sequences associated with some braided river deposits of late Pleistocene age from southern Britain. *Spec. Publs. Inst. Ass. Sediment.*, **6**, 267–275.

Bryant, R.H. and Carpenter, C.P. (1987). Ramparted ground ice depressions in Britain and Ireland. In, *Periglacial Processes and Landforms in Britain and Ireland* (Ed. J. Boardman), pp. 183–90 Cambridge University Press.

Dreimanis, A. (1973). The first report on 'till wedges' in Europe – a reply. *Geol. Fören. Stockh. Förh.*, **95**, 156–7.

French, C.A.I. (1982). An analysis of the molluscs from an Ipswichian interglacial river channel deposit at Maxey, Cambridgeshire, England. *Geol. Mag.*, **119**, 593–8.

Gardner, K. & West, R.G. (1975). Fossil ice-wedge polygons at Corton, Suffolk. *Bull. Geol. Soc. Norfolk*, **27**, 47–53.

Gemmell, A.M.D. & Ralston, I.B.M. (1984). Some recent discoveries of ice-wedge cast networks in north-east Scotland. *Scott. J. Geol.*, **20**, 115–18.

Gladfelter, B.G. (1975). Middle Pleistocene sedimentary sequences in East Anglia (United Kingdom). In, *After the Australopithecines: Stratigraphy, Ecology and Cultural Change in the Middle Pleistocene.* (Eds. K.E. Butzer and G.L. Isaac), pp. 225–58, Mouton, The Hague.

Green, C.P., Coope, G.R., Current, A.P., Holyoak, D.T., Ivanovich, M., Jones, R.L., Keen, D.H., McGregor, D.F.M. & Robinson, J.E. (1984). Evidence of two temperate episodes in late Pleistocene deposits at Marsworth, U.K. *Nature*, **309**, 778–81.

Jahn, A. (1975). *Problems of the Periglacial Zone.* Polish Scientific Publishers, Warszawa.

Johnsson, G. (1959). True and false ice wedges in southern Sweden. *Geogr. Annlr.*, **41**, 15–33.

Mitchell, G.F., Penny, L.F., Shotton, F.W. & West, R.G. (1973). A correlation of Quaternary deposits in the British Isles. *Geol. Soc. Lond., Special Rept.*, No 4, 99 pp.

Mörner, N-A. (1972). The first report on till wedges in Europe and Late Weichselian ice flows over southern Sweden. *Geol. Fören. Stockh. Förh.*, **94**, 581–7.

Paterson, T.T. (1940). The effects of frost action and solifluxion around Baffin Bay and in the Cambridge District. *Q. Jl. Geol. Soc. Lond.*, **96**, 99–130.

Rose, J. (1975). Raised beach gravels and ice wedge casts at Old Kilpatrick near Glasgow. *Scott. J. Geol.*, **11**, 15–21.

Rose, J. (1985). The Dimlington Stadial/Dimlington Chronozone: a proposal for naming the main glacial episode of the Late Devensian in Britain. *Boreas*, **14**, 225–230.

Rose, J., Boardman, J., Kemp, R.A. & Whiteman, C.A. (1985a). Palaeosols and the interpretation of the British Quaternary stratigraphy. In, *Geomorphology and Soils*, (Eds. K.S. Richards, R.R. Arnett and S. Ellis), pp. 348–75, George Allen & Unwin, London.

Rose, J., Allen, P., Kemp, R.A., Whiteman, C.A. & Owen, N. (1985b). The early Anglian Barham Soil of eastern England. In, *Soils and Quaternary Landscape Evolution.* (Ed. J. Boardman), pp. 197–229. John Wiley, Chichester.

Seddon, M.B. & Holyoak, D.T. (1985). Evidence of sustained regional permafrost during deposition of fossiliferous Late Pleistocene river sediments at Stanton Harcourt (Oxfordshire, England). *Proc. Geol. Ass.*, **96**, 53–71.

Sissons, J.B. (1974). The Quaternary in Scotland: a review. *Scott. J. Geol.*, **10**, 311–37.

Sumbler, M.G. (1983). A new look at the type Wolstonian glacial deposits of central England. *Proc. Geol. Ass.*, **94**, 23–31.

Te Punga, M.T. (1956). Periglaciation in southern England. In, *The Earth its crust and atmosphere.*, (Ed. J.B. Hol), pp. 401–12, E.J. Brill, Leiden.

Watson, E. (1977). The periglacial environment of Great Britain during the Devensian. *Phil. Trans. R. Soc. Lond. Ser. B*, **280**, 183–98.

West, R.G. (1968). Evidence for pre-Cromerian permafrost in East Anglia. *Biul. Perygl.*, **17**, 303–4.

West, R.G. (1969). Stratigraphy of periglacial features in East Anglia and adjacent areas. In, *The Periglacial Environment.* (Ed. T.L. Péwé), pp. 412–15, McGill-Queen's University Press, Montreal.

West, R.G. (1980). *The pre-glacial Pleistocene of the Norfolk and Suffolk coasts.* Cambridge University Press, Cambridge.

West, R.G. & Donner, J.J. (1958). A note on Pleistocene frost structures in the cliff section at Bacton, Norfolk. *Trans. Norfolk & Norwich Nat. Soc.*, **18**, 8–9.

West, R.G., Dickson, C.A., Catt, J.A., Weir, A.H. & Sparks, B.W. (1974). Late Pleistocene deposits at Wretton, Norfolk. II Devensian deposits. *Phil. Trans. R. Soc. Lond. Ser. B*, **267**, 337–420.

· Williams, R.G.B. (1965). Permafrost in England during the last glacial period. *Nature*, **205**, 1304–5.

Worsley, P. (1966). Some Weichselian fossil frost wedges from East Cheshire. *Mercian Geol.*, **1**, 357–65.

Worsley, P. (1973). The first report on 'till wedges' in Europe – a discussion. *Geol. Fören. Stockh. Förh.*, **95**, 152–5.

Worsley, P. (1977). Periglaciation. In, *British Quaternary Studies recent advances.* (Ed. F.W. Shotton), pp. 205–219, Clarendon Press, Oxford.

Worsley, P. (1985). Pleistocene history of the Cheshire-Shropshire Plain. In, *Geomorphology of north-west England.* (Ed. R.H. Johnson), 201–21, Manchester University Press. Manchester.

Worsley, P. (1986a). On the age of wood in till at Broughton Bay. *Quat. Newsl.* **49**, 17–19.

· Worsley, P. (1986b). Periglacial environment. *Prog. Phys. Geogr.* **10**, 266–74.

8 · Periglacial periods in Ireland

WILLIAM P. WARREN

Abstract

Periglacial features include thick deposits of head on the south and south west coasts, ice-wedge casts, probable pingo ramparts and cryoturbation features. Their stratigraphic distribution indicates that periglacial conditions, probably with permafrost, obtained with a high degree of frequency through the last cold period, the Fenitian (Midlandian) Stage. It is difficult to date these events precisely or to estimate their duration owing to a lack of dated stratigraphic units. The distribution of these features cannot be used to substantiate the traditional limit of the Fenitian ice sheets as (a) it begs the question of the age of the glacial deposits, (b) the features transcend the proposed boundaries, (c) factors other than age, such as bedrock geology, topography and the character of the Quaternary sediments may have influenced distribution and (d) clustering of particular features may simply reflect the number of areas studied in detail. An attempt is made, on the basis of stratigraphic occurrence, to indicate when periglacial activity took place in Ireland.

Introduction

Non-glacial features indicative of cold climate conditions have long been recognised in Ireland. Kinahan (1894) first identified what have come to be called protalus ramparts (Watson, 1966) and correctly interpreted their origin. In 1908 Kilroe (in Wilkinson *et al.*, 1908) described what is clearly an ice-wedge cast and attributed it to infill from above into a fissure in frozen gravel (Colhoun, 1970). Wright and Muff (1904) recognised the probability that the head deposits of the south coast were periglacial in that they favoured frost action is the agent which produced the angular clasts. The occurrence of soliflucted debris in a sedimentary sequence was used, along with palynological evidence, to distinguish a cold phase within lateglacial climatic oscillations by Jessen and Farrington (1938). From the late 1950's the distribution of features indicative of cold climate conditions has commonly been used as an aid in delimiting the extent of last glaciation ice (Mitchell, 1957, 1972; Mitchell *et al.*, 1973; Orme *et al.*, 1964; Stephens, 1970; Stephens and Synge, 1965; Synge, 1968, 1970). But Farrington (1963) urged caution in the use of cryoturbation features as supportive evidence for a pre last glaciation age for their host sediments.

The best general climatic inference that can be made in interpreting periglacial features in the geological record is that climatic conditions were such as to leave clear and unambiguous evidence of frost action while specific features such as ice-wedge casts suggest a specific mean annual maximum temperature. This is close to Washburn's (1979, 2) definition; '...a climate characterised by intense frost action and snow-free ground for part of the year'. With the possible exception of some highland areas, such conditions are incompatible with the present Irish climate and the periglacial record must generally relate to previous periods of much colder climate. In addition to features indicative of frost activity, such periods will produce sedimentary and morphological features which can form under a variety of climatic regimes. Lewis (1985) has interpreted landslides and tors as periglacial but, whereas they may have formed under periglacial conditions, they are not diagnostically periglacial.

During the past decade three review papers dealing with the Irish periglacial record have appeared in the scientific literature. Two (Lewis, 1978, 1985) dealt chiefly with the occurrence and distribution of periglacial features and one (Mitchell, 1977) dealt with periglacial activity during the last cold stage, the Fenitian of Warren (1985). Mitchell concluded that periglacial conditions occurred twice in Ireland during the Fenitian Stage. Mitchell (1977) considered frost conditions (particularly permafrost) incompatible with deglaciation and suggested that it was improbable that the development of ice sheets would coincide with conditions suitable for the production of periglacial features.

In this paper an attempt is made to relate the periglacial features to the established stratigraphic record with reference to the model proposed by Warren (1985). The relationship with earlier strati-graphic and morpho-stratigraphic models is also considered.

The stratigraphic model

The stratigraphic model to which the periglacial features and events are related (Warren, 1985) is illustrated in Figure 8.1. It recognises deposits of

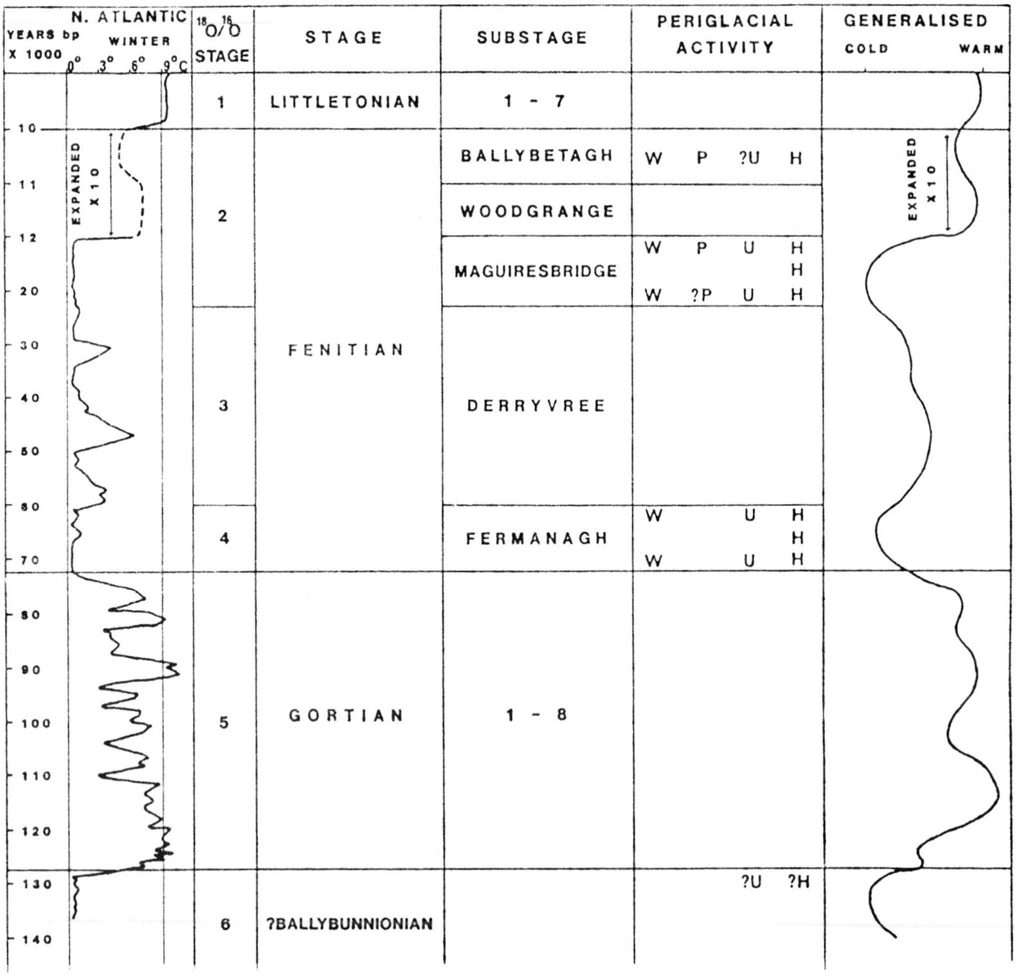

YEARS bp X 1000 / N. ATLANTIC WINTER 0° 3° 6° 9°C	18/16 O/O STAGE	STAGE	SUBSTAGE	PERIGLACIAL ACTIVITY				GENERALISED COLD — WARM
10	1	LITTLETONIAN	1 – 7					
11	2	FENITIAN	BALLYBETAGH	W	P	?U	H	
12			WOODGRANGE					
20			MAGUIRESBRIDGE	W	P	U	H	
							H	
				W	?P	U	H	
30	3		DERRYVREE					
40								
50								
60	4		FERMANAGH	W		U	H	
70							H	
				W		U	H	
80	5	GORTIAN	1 – 8					
90								
100								
110								
120								
130	6	?BALLYBUNNIONIAN				?U	?H	
140								

Figure 8.1. Periglacial activity as indicated by the occurrence of periglacial features in the Irish Quaternary stratigraphic record (Warren, 1985). The North Atlantic palaeo-temperature curve for winter surface water is based on oxygen isotope data from a deep-sea borehole (V23–82) at 52°35′ N and 21°56′ W (Sancetta *et al.*, 1973) and the generalised curve, also based on the deep-sea $^{18}O/^{16}O$ record, is from Emiliani (1966). In the diagram W represents the occurrence of ice-wedge casts, P pingo ramparts, U involutions and H head. The position of the symbol suggests the probable development of the feature at that time. A ? suggests a possible, less preferred, alternative occurrence as discussed in the text.

but one interglacial, the Gortian, which is regarded as last interglacial in age and referred to $^{18}0/^{16}0$ Zone 5, (Shackleton, 1969). The Courtmacsherry Raised Beach of the south and south west coasts belongs to this interglacial. The overlying head, the Main Head and Upper Head of Wright and Muff (1904), and till, where it occurs, belong to the last cold stage (the Fenitian). Deposits of an earlier cold stage are recognised at Ballybunnion, County Kerry. This, the Ballybunnionian, is of uncertain age, but predates the Gortian (interglacial) Stage.

No periglacial features have been recognised of which it can be said with confidence that they predate the Fenitian Stage. It is possible that some high altitude features such as block fields may predate the last glacial period but this cannot be demonstrated to be the case. Mitchell (1977) doubted whether periglacial structures could have survived the last interglacial.

Mitchell (1977) and other (Mitchell *et al.*, 1973) regard the Southern Irish End Moraine of Lewis (1894) and Charlesworth (1928) or its more recent, modified, line (Synge, 1979) as the southern limit of last glaciation ice yet there is no evidence of deep weathering in glacial sediments to the south of this line. Mitchell (1977) also referred to patterned ground and head outside the moraine. However, in the south of Ireland outside the mountainous areas and parts of north Kerry, north Cork and west Limerick the large quantities of head (the Main Head of Wright and Muff, 1904) generally *underlie till* which Mitchell *et al.* (1973) placed in the penultimate glaciation. There is very little evidence of soliflucted debris overlying these tills. The Upper Head of Wright and Muff (1904) and Farrington (1966) overlies, in places, the tills of the south coast and is generally in the region of 1 m in thickness. Both the Upper Head and the Main Head (Fenit Formation) are regarded here as deposits of the Fenitian Stage.

Mitchell *et al.* (1973) equated the Upper Head of the south coast with the upper head facies between Fenit and Spa, County Kerry. However, Mitchell (1977) regarded the Fenit-Spa upper facies as 'Wolstonian' in age and seemed to place the Upper Head of the south coast in the 'Devensian'. Clearly Mitchell (1977) used Devensian and Wolstonian in place of the Midlandian and Munsterian of Mitchell *et al.* (1973).

Periglacial features in pre-Fenitian sediments

At Ballybunnion (Figure 8.2), the stratotype of the Ballybunnion Formation, 2–3 m of raised beach

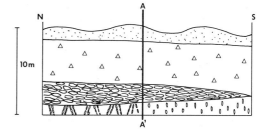

Interpretative section at A A'

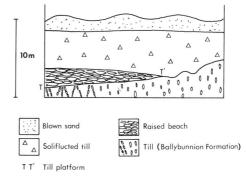

	Blown sand		Raised beach
	Soliflucted till		Till (Ballybunnion Formation)

T T'   Till platform

Figure 8.2. Schematic diagram showing the units exposed at Ballybunnion.

gravel and sand rest on 1–1.5 m of exposed till and are overlain by 4–6 m of head. The head is a soliflucted facies of the underlying till. The raised beach deposits lie between 7.0 m and 10.0 m OD (4.2 m and 7.2 m MSL). The beach sediment unit has been correlated with the Courtmacsherry Raised Beach Formation of the south coast (Warren 1981, 1985). There is no *in situ* till overlying the beach sediments so that the head (soliflucted till) and overlying recent blown sand represent the total visible post-beach sedimentation in the area.

The till underlying the raised beach deposits forms a raised marine-cut platform and exhibits consistent evidence of frost disturbance where it underlies the beach. The 1–1.5 m of till exposed in vertical section shows lateral sorting and vertical stones with most of the larger clasts arranged in columns and erected on either a vertical 'a' or 'b' axis. Very many of the clasts which were originally subangular to subrounded have been shattered. Where exposure is deepest (about 1.5 m) the vertical line of erected stones begins to give way downwards to what seems to be the base of a festoon. The raised beach sediments remain undisturbed except where they become incorporated into the base of the overlying head.

The periglacial features in the till are taken to be

involutions of the regular type described by French (1976, 279) and may have related to sorted stripes as suggested by French. It is difficult, however, to determine whether they were formed before or after the platform was cut. Features such as these elsewhere in Ireland rarely exceed 2.0 m in depth (Colhoun, 1970; Farrington, 1966; Quinn, 1975; Lewis, 1974; Warren, 1978), and it seems unlikely that the platform was cut following their formation. If it was, then we might speculate that less than 1.0 m of till was removed in the process. It seems likely, both from the thickness of soliflucted till on top of the beach deposit and the thickness of the till unit on either side of the beach exposure, that a minimum of 2.5 m of till were removed to form the platform and that the periglacial structures therefore post-date the cutting of the platform. The lack of periglacial disturbance in the beach suggests that either sea level fell to allow frost action to take place following the cutting of the platform and then rose again to cover the surface with sand and gravel, or that sea level remained high at the onset of the cold period which produced the involutions but that as the beach sedimentation was active it did not retain any disturbed structures; the structures preserved in the platform formed in what was the intertidal area but was later covered by beach material possibly relating to a slightly lower sea level.

The occurrence of head resting on the marine-cut rock platform but underlying the Courtmacsherry Raised Beach Formation on the south coast of County Cork, led Farrington (1966) to suggest that a period of low water intervened between the cutting of the rock platform there and the deposition of the beach. The situation may be analogous to that at Ballybunnion.

Thus both at Ballybunnion and on the south coast there is evidence of periglacial conditions either predating or penecontemporaneous with the final deposition of the Courtmacsherry Raised Beach. They relate either to a period very early in the Fenitian Stage or to an earlier cold stage.

The only other evidence of pre-Fenitian periglacial activity is a reference by Mitchell et al. (1973, 80) to the 'Gort Lower Solifluction Gravel' at Gort, County Galway, underlying the interglacial sediments at the Gortian stratotype, giving reference to Jessen et al. (1959). However, Jessen et al. (1959, 13) described this as 0.9 m of 'Reddish non-calcareous sandy stony clay' and there is reference to 'pebbles of sandstone and quartzite' towards the bottom of the overlying 'light brown and reddish fine-sandy clay' but there is no direct reference to periglacial activity. In the text the deposits underlying the

interglacial sediments are referred to simply as 'local wash' (p. 11). Nevertheless, periglacial conditions probably obtained in the period immediately preceding the Gortian as the palynology indicates a transition from almost subarctic conditions through temperate interglacial conditions. Thus it is likely that the local colluvium was deposited under periglacial conditions.

There is, therefore, little evidence of periglacial conditions prior to the Gortian Interglacial and no specific period of periglacial activity can be identified. There was an earlier cold stage during which the Ballybunnion Till Formation was deposited and it is likely therefore that there was a period or periods of periglacial activity. These will only be identified if and when further stratigraphic evidence becomes available.

At Courtparteen, County Cork, near Kinsale on the south coast 'a wedge of gravel over a foot (0.3 m) wide and 3 feet (0.9 m) deep' occurs in the Courtmacsherry Raised Beach Formation, the top of which is 'churned' to a depth of 0.5 m (Farrington 1966, 202). Although Farrington did not specifically interpret it as such, and it has not been

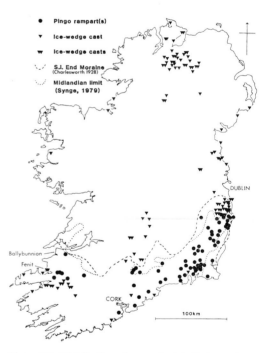

Figure 8.3. Distribution of permafrost indicators – ice wedge casts and pingo ramparts. Based on references cited, the author's field observations and personal communication from P.O'Callaghan, the late F.M. Synge, G.F. Mitchell, H. Saul, A.M. McCabe, P. Coxon and R. Devoy.

described or illustrated any more fully than above, this feature has been interpreted as an ice-wedge cast (Lewis, 1978, 1985; Warren, 1981). It is indicated in Figure 8.3 (west of Cork Harbour) as an ice-wedge cast, yet there must be some doubt as to this interpretation. If this feature is an ice-wedge cast then it is the only evidence of permafrost predating the accumulation of the Main Head of Wright and Muff (1904) named the Fenit (Head) Formation by Warren (1985).

The Fenit (Head) Formation

Thick deposits of head occur very commonly along the south coast of Ireland (Wright and Muff, 1904; Farrington, 1966). Similar deposits occur along parts of the south west coast in County Kerry (Bryant, 1966; Mitchell, 1970; Lewis, 1974; Warren, 1977, 1981). Wright and Muff (1904) distinguished a 'Main Head' and an 'Upper Head'. They recognised that stratigraphically the Main Head overlies the Courtmacsherry raised beach deposits and that the Main Head and Upper Head are separated by a till unit or units. The Upper Head, though common, is more frequently absent from the sequence than present and, as stated above, is generally in the region of 1.0 m thick. At Fenit (Warren, 1981), at the western end of the Peninsula of Corca Dhuibhne, County Kerry (Bryant, 1966; Lewis, 1974) and at Ballybunnion (Warren, 1985) there is no till unit overlying the Courtmacsherry Raised Beach Formation. In each case a head deposit overlies the raised beach sediments and it is likely that in these areas both the Upper and Lower Heads are incorporated in a single unit. This area of north Kerry appears therefore not to have been glaciated during the Fenitian Stage (see Warren, 1985) but the full extent of the area that lay outside the ice limit has not yet been identified.

The complete head unit as exposed at Fenit is termed the Fenit (Head) Formation (Warren, 1985). Its stratotype is the exposed cliff section between Fenit and Spa on the northern shore of Tralee Bay where it directly overlies the Courtmacsherry Raised Beach Formation. Here at Ballymakegogue a thin layer of peat lies between the beach deposits and the base of the head (Mitchell, 1970). The peat, which contains a pollen suite that reflects an open pine wood with grasses and heather and may represent either late interglacial or interstadial conditions, produced a ^{14}C date of 42,000 years B.P. (Mitchell, 1970). The head is composed of angular clasts of local Carboniferous shale with varying amounts of Devonian sandstone erratics in a silty matrix. Generally the coarser upper parts of

the deposit are clast-supported and the lower parts are matrix-supported. At the base of the unit, immediately above the peat is a grey silt unit which contains peaty organic lenses and interdigitates with the base of the head. The head is interpreted as a geliflucted deposit derived from locally gelifracted Carboniferous shale together with Devonian sandstone glacial erratics (Warren, 1981; but see Mitchell, 1970). The silt probably represents distal fines washed downslope during the early stage of gelifluction activity (cf. Watson and Watson, 1970). Although the erratics of Devonian sandstone occur throughout the deposit they are small and dispersed in the finer basal part of the head. They become both more plentiful and larger up through the deposit until a little more than half way towards the top Devonian sandstone boulders (many frost shattered but many also well striated) predominate. In many places along the section they form a distinct line of boulders. The upper part of the head contains fewer, though still common, erratics.

Ice-wedge casts have been recorded in the head at the level at which the sandstone erratics become dominant (Mitchell, 1970, 1976; Warren, 1981) and involutions are common in the upper 1–1.5 m of the section (Mitchell, 1970).

The upper part of the head at Fenit has been correlated with the Upper Head of the south coast (Mitchell *et al.*, 1973). However, the tills that separate the Upper Head and Main Head on the south coast are absent from the sequence at Fenit. There is, therefore, no clear common datum upon which to compare the upper part of deposits at Fenit with those of the south coast. Furthermore, it is possible that the slope process continued unabated at Fenit while the tills were being deposited on the south coast. Alternatively the erratic boulder concentration, interpreted previously as a lag layer representing a change in the dynamics of the mass wasting process (Warren 1981, 1985), may have formed while till was being deposited in the glaciated area. The occurrence of involutions in the Main Head, underlying the Ballycroneen Till Formation at Ballycrenane (Farrington, 1966), suggests that the slope process which formed the head had halted there before the tills were deposited. Involuted head also underlies a till unit at Newtown, County Waterford (Mitchell, 1962). This may reflect a change in slope process similar to that at Fenit, but the resumption of gelifluction may have begun earlier at Fenit than on the south coast. The upper head facies at Fenit may be largely a lateral equivalent of the tills of the south coast.

The head deposit at Fenit (Fenit Head Formation) is taken to represent the total period of periglacial deposition of the last cold period, the Fenitian Stage. This stage is correlated with Zones 4, 3 and 2 of the $^{18}0/^{16}0$ record, with the upper soil horizon representing Zone 1 (Warren, 1985). The erratic boulders are derived from an earlier till which is probably equivalent to the till at Bally-bunnion. The lower part of the head (below the concentration of erratic boulders) represents a period of gelifraction and gelifluction which also involved a considerable amount of water flow as indicated by frequent well washed or sorted units. The boulder concentration is interpreted as a lag layer where fines were removed and mass movement was not so dynamic. The upper head facies represents a renewal of gelifluction. The ice-wedge casts indicate a period of permafrost just prior to, or at the beginning of, the period of formation of the lag layer. Involutions in the upper 1–2 m of sediment suggest stable slope conditions after gelifluction had ceased.

Both the Main Head and Upper Head of the south coast are generally regarded as gelifluction deposits (Wright, 1937; Mitchell, 1960; Farrington, 1966; Mitchell et al., 1973). The base of the Main Head in places interdigitates with raised beach deposits (Farrington, 1966; Warren, 1978) but it is not clear that this implies contemporaneity of beach and head formation, for frequently it is clear that the beach material has been reworked by slope processes.

Periglacial structures in buried Fenitian sediment

Periglacial involutions and ice-wedge casts occur in each of the major sedimentary units overlying the Courtmacsherry Raised Beach Formation in the south and south west of the country. At Newtown, County Waterford 2–3 m of head resting on a wave-cut platform and underlying a till of inland provenance is cryoturbated (Mitchell, 1962; Quinn, 1984). This is probably the Main Head. At Bally-crenane on the coast west of Youghal in County Cork the top of the Main Head is cryoturbated. It is here overlain by till of the Ballycroneen Formation (Farrington, 1966). An ice-wedge cast occurs within the Main Head at Ballyeelinan in County Waterford (Quinn, 1984). Ice-wedge casts in the head deposit at Fenit have been referred to above (Mitchell 1970, 1976). Ice-wedge casts in gravel of the Brittas glacial event at Ballinascorney, County Dublin, are overlain by gravels of the Gilltown glacial event; and gravels associated with the Gormanstown Glaciation, also underlying gravels

of the Gilltown event at Loughanstown, County Dublin contain cryoturbation structures (Hoare and McCabe, 1981). Ice-wedge casts appear to occur within gravels of last glaciation age near Tempo, County Fermanagh (Hoare and McCabe, 1981; McCabe et al., 1978).

These occurrences indicate the persistence or recurrence of permafrost conditions and/or conditions suitable for the development of cryoturbation structures through the Fenitian Stage.

Periglacial structures in the surface deposits of the Fenitian Stage

Periglacial structures are widespread in the surface Pleistocene deposits of Ireland. Figure 8.3 might seem to support the view that their distribution is more concentrated to the south of the Southern Irish End Moraine than to the north. But, as has been remarked elsewhere (Lewis, 1978; Warren, 1985), their distribution to a large extent reflects areas where detailed studies have been carried out. Ironically, studies inside this moraine (Colhoun, 1970; Hoare and McCabe, 1981; Lewis, 1977), if taken at face value, suggest a greater concentration of ice-wedge casts inside the moraine and its suggested equivalents (Synge, 1979) than outside.

The Southern Irish End Moraine is often regarded on morphostratigraphic grounds as the southern limit of last glaciation ice (Charlesworth 1928; Mitchell et al., 1973). But the application of standard stratigraphic principles suggests that it is not (Bowen, 1973; Warren, 1979, 1985). The suggestion that the inferred relative intensity of periglacial activity can be used to delineate or substantiate this line as the limit of last glaciation ice fails any objective test. The only acceptable means of indicating that two sets of glacial deposits belong to separate cold stages is to indicate evidence of an intervening warm stage. To suggest that periglacial features outside a given glacial limit owe their greater intensity over those inside the limit to the fact that they were not obliterated by the ice of that event, as were those inside the limit, is acceptable reasoning if the facts are accurate. To conclude that this substantiates the line as the limit of last glaciation simply begs the question of the age of the glacial deposits outside it. But if the facts are inaccurate then even the time relationship between the deposits inside the line and the periglacial event or events outside it remains unclear. That this is the case in Ireland is indicated below.

In 1965 Stephens and Synge drew a line between Moville and Dunaff Bay in Inishowen, County Donegal. They regarded this as the northern limit of last glaciation ice on the basis of evidence of deep cryoturbation (1–1.8 m) and ice-wedge casts outside the line. However Colhoun (1970) has shown that, in the area north of the Sperrin Mountains, in County Londonderry, well within the limit of Stephens and Synge (1965) similar features are very common. He recorded involutions with depths of 1–3 m and ice-wedge casts 1–4 deep and 0.2–0.1 m wide.

In the south west, involutions extending to a depth of 2.0 m in south and west Iveragh, County Kerry, notably at An Trá Bhán (White Strand), have been used to suggest that the glacigenic sediments in which they occur predate the last glaciation (Quinn, 1975; Bryant, 1977). However, well developed and almost identical involutions of the festoon type (French, 1976) occur in sediments of the Killumney moraine complex (see Farrington, 1954). They occur in a till unit 2–3 m thick resting on planar bedded outwash gravels at Ovens, County Cork. This moraine complex, described by Lewis (1894), has been regarded as the end moraine of the Kerry-Cork ice cap of the last glaciation (Farrington 1954; Mitchell *et al.*, 1973; Synge, 1970) and is generally accepted as a deposit of the last glaciation.

North of the MacGillycuddy's Reeks, in County Kerry, ice-wedge casts are widely dispersed in the deglacial sediments (Wright, 1920) but cryoturbation structures appear to be confined to the sediments of the outer suite of moraines (Warren, 1977). These are generally regarded as deposits of the last glaciation (Synge, 1979).

In County Wicklow, Lewis has shown that ice-wedge casts occur in morainic gravel deposits of all Synge's (1973) glacial phases for the area with the sole exception of those he attributed to the lateglacial phase.

Figures 8.3 and 8.4 clearly show that cryoturbation structures and ice-wedge casts are widespread inside and outside Synge's (1979) limits for last glaciation ice. They are, however, by no means ubiquitous, so that their present distribution must reflect factors other than the periglacial conditions under which they formed. Certainly there is no logical means by which the ages of the major sedimentary suits can be determined from the distribution of these periglacial structures.

As can be seen in Figure 8.3, the distribution of presumed pingo ramparts is not as widespread as the other features (Figures 8.3 and 8.4). The type of feature here referred to as pingo ramparts include those of the type described by Mitchell (1973) and further discussed by Bryant and Carpenter (1987).

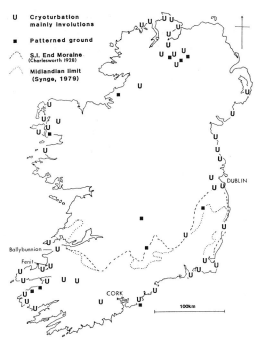

Figure 8.4. Distribution of cryoturbation features, mainly involutions of the festoon type, and patterned ground features. From sources quoted in the text.

Those recorded to date occur in the southern part of the country and, as has been observed by others (Mitchell, 1977; Lewis, 1978), many, but not all, occur outside Synge's (1979) ice limits of the last glaciation. Mitchell (1977) concluded that the pingos and other periglacial features south of Synge's (1977, 1979) last glaciation ice limit formed, in the main, before the last glaciation reached its maximum extent. This conclusion was however, based on the assumption that periglacial structures are better developed '…on a scale unmatched anywhere…' on deposits outside the last glaciation limit (Mitchell, 1977, 205). As has been seen this thesis is not sustainable except in the case of pingo remnants. Mitchell (1977) did, however, concede that some pingos may have formed during the Ballybetagh Substage in the lateglacial period. This is the Nahanagan Stadial of Mitchell *et al.* (1973).

It is possible to relate the known distribution of the ramparts to features other than the once established ice limit. Indeed, assuming that they are pingo ramparts, they are probably all of the open-system type (French, 1976) and factors influencing the local hydro-geological regime must have been important. They occur entirely within two specific structural/morphological regions of the south of

Ireland recognised by Orme *et al.* (1964), the Caledonian Province and the Armorican Ridge and Valley Province. These are areas where there is considerable variation in bedrock-controlled relief and they exclude the whole of the midland area which is underlain by Carboniferous limestone, retaining within them only small outliers or narrow marginal stretches of Carboniferous limestone usually flooring synclinal valleys. Also these regions are characterised by a generally thin Quaternary sediment cover which is patchy in distribution and generally thicker in valley floors than on ridges. Mitchell (1973) suggested that their distribution might be controlled by the distribution of solifluctted till. In contrast, the area to the north and west of these provinces, the South Central Lowlands, is characterised by large spreads of glaciofluvial gravels and tills which can achieve thicknesses in excess of 50 m. Relief in the midlands is very strongly controlled by glacial and glaciofluvial features. As the above factors directly affect groundwater flow characteristics and would have affected the nature of permafrost any or all of them may have influenced the favoured location of pingo ramparts. In addition it is important to note that it is probable that pingos, if they occurred among the deglacial features that characterise the midlands, would be much more difficult to detect than in areas of dominantly thin and featureless Quaternary cover.

Sorted stone features have been recorded at many upland sites: Curraun, County Mayo (Flatrès, 1957); Ballydesmond (formerly Kingwilliamstown), County Cork (Mitchell, 1957); the Sperrin Mountains (Colhoun, 1970); Knocknadobar, County Kerry (Lewis, 1974; Quinn, 1975); Stookaniller, Country Kerry (Warren, 1978); Truskmore, Country Sligo (P. Coxon, pers. comm.). These features are generally inactive but some of the smaller stone polygons on Knocknadobar may be active at present (Quinn, 1975, 1987).

Discussion

There is no certain evidence of periglacial activity in the period predating the Fenitian Stage. Cryoturbation structures in the Ballybunnion Till Formation and head underlying the Courtmacsherry Raised Beach Formation may however predate the Gortian Interglacial.

The Fenitian (Cold) Stage has, on the other hand, left ample evidence of prolonged and often severe periglacial activity. This stage is based on the Fenit (Head) Formation which lies outside the area glaciated during the Fenitian. This deposit suggests a continuous process of gelifraction and gelifluction with only one probable major period of reduced slope activity, or total stability, throughout the Fenitian Stage.

If the feature in the Courtmacsherry Raised Beach at Courtparteen described by Farrington (1966) is an ice-wedge cast, the Fenitian Stage began with a period of cold so intense that it produced permafrost in south County Cork. The cryoturbation structures in the till at Ballybunnion may reflect this event. Solifluction then commenced and proceeded at Fenit until the period when ice-wedge casts were formed in association with, or slightly before, the establishment of the boulder horizon there.

It is not clear whether or not permafrost persisted during the early formation of the head, but the ice-wedge cast in the head at Ballyeelinan, County Waterford, may point to such a conclusion. This cast though not obviously syngenetic with the head may be associated with an horizon or discontinuity above it that might suggest a former surface and therefore a halt or change in the solifluction process. The casts at Fenit occur below a distinct horizon marking the base of a sand bed which lies above them, the integrity of which suggests that they had become casts by the time the overlying sand layer and head were deposited (see Mitchell, 1970).

The ice-wedge casts at Fenit, County Kerry, Ballyeelinan, County Waterford and Ballinascorney, County Dublin, may in fact relate to the same permafrost event. And the involutions in the Main Head underlying till units at both Newtown, County Waterford, and Ballycrenane, County Cork, indicating a period of slope stability prior to glaciation, may relate to the same event, as may the involutions at Loughanstown, County Dublin.

At Fenit the ice-wedge development was followed by the reactivation of the solifluction process while at Loughanstown, Ballinascorney, Newtown and Ballycrenane glaciation ensued. After the withdrawal of glacial ice from the south coast periglacial slope processes produced occasional patches of head.

All of the surface deposits, with the exception of those of the Ballybetagh Substage, the Upper Head, tills and gravels south of the Southern Irish End Moraine, tills and gravels north of the moraine, and periglacial deposits in areas apparently unglaciated during the Fenitian Stage, display evidence of frost disturbance, and ice-wedge casts and pingo remnants attest to the occurrence of permafrost after the uppermost glacial and periglacial sediments had been deposited. It is not known when these features formed. Colhoun (1970) and Hoare and McCabe (1981) suggested that a permafrost table followed the retreating ice fronts during the dissolution of last glaciation ice. But Mitchell (1972) thought glacial retreat and permafrost development were incompatible. It seems clear that conditions during the Woodgrange Substage were inimical to permafrost development and periglacial activity generally (Watts, 1985). Mitchell (1977) suggested that the Ballybetagh Substage was both sufficiently cold and sufficiently long for the development of pingos. While it is difficult to reconcile conditions conducive to general deglaciation of the country with the maintenance of permafrost, it is possible that periods of intense cold did punctuate the milder conditions it is assumed are necessary for general ice retreat. Little is known about the conditions necessary for the production of involutions (Washburn, 1979) but they may also have developed at this time.

Conclusion

Evidence at Fenit indicates that in the areas unglaciated during the Fenitian Stage, gelifluction processes operated with the exception of one period during which the process was arrested or all but arrested. This period during which the sandstone boulder concentration developed in the head, may correspond to the Derryvree Substage which in turn is attributed to $^{18}O/^{16}O$ Stage 3 of the oxygen isotope record (Warren, 1985). This being the case the lower part of the head would refer to the Fermanagh Substage (Stage 4) and the upper part to the Maguiresbridge Substage (Stage 2). The evidence of frost structures suggests between two and five periods of permafrost and either three or four periods of cryoturbation. It is possible that permafrost persisted for most of the Fenitian Stage, although it must have dissipated during the Woodgrange Substage and probably during the Derryvree Substage (Mitchell, 1977). It is likely that when the pingos, and probably the ice-wedges in the present surface deposits, were being formed the permafrost was discontinuous.

It is difficult to date many of the sedimentary units within the Fenitian Stage. Some of the surface tills, particularly those of the southern part of the country, may have been deposited during the Fermanagh Substage but this is not certain and it is possible that all Fenitian lowland tills were deposited during the Maguiresbridge Substage (Warren, 1985). It is therefore difficult to date periglacial

features associated with the units. In Figure 8.1 a best fit is attempted.

If the feature at Courtparteen is an ice-wedge cast it indicates the occurrence of permafrost at the beginning of the Fermanagh Substage. The ice-wedge casts at Fenit indicate permafrost at the end of this Substage, and those at Ballinascorney probably formed in permafrost at the beginning of the Maguiresbridge Substage. The ice-wedges and pingos at the surface formed after deglaciation had set in and possibly indicate permafrost towards the end of the Maguiresbridge Substage and during the Ballybetagh Substage. Involutions formed at Ballybunnion either at the end of a cold stage preceding the Fenitian or at the beginning of the Fenitian. They also formed just before the tills at Newtown, County Waterford, and Ballycrenane, County Cork, were deposited (either mid to late Fermanagh Substage or late Derryvree to early Maguiresbridge Substage) and again either in the late Maguiresbridge Substage or in the Ballybetagh Substage, or both.

The lack of certainty as to when many of these features were formed reflects the paucity of correlative data in Irish Pleistocene sediments. This is due in large measure to the vigour of both the glacial and periglacial processes that operated.

References

Bowen, D.Q. (1963). The Pleistocene Succession of the Irish Sea. *Proc. Geol. Assoc.*, **84**, 249–72.

Bryant, R.H. (1966). The 'pre-glacial' raised beach in south-west Ireland. *Ir. Geogr.*, **5**, 188–203.

Bryant, R.H. (1977). Bantry to Waterville. In, *South and Southwest Ireland* Guidebook for excursion A15, INQUA X Congress, (Ed. D.Q. Bowen), pp. 23–29, Norwich.

Bryant, R.H., and Carpenter, C.P. (1987). Ramparted ground ice depressions in Britain and Ireland. In, *Periglacial Processes and Landforms in Britain and Ireland* (Ed. J. Boardman), pp. 183–90, Cambridge University Press.

Charlesworth, J.K. (1928). The Glacial retreat from central and southern Ireland. *Q. Jl Geol. Soc. Lond.*, **84**, 293–342.

Colhoun, E.A. (1970). Early record and interpretation of ice wedge pseudomorph in County Londonderry, Northern Ireland, by J.R. Kilroe. *J. Glaciol.*, **9**, 391–92.

Emiliani, C. (1966). Palaeotemperature analysis of Caribbean cores P6304–8 and P6304–9 and a generalised temperature curve for the past 425,000 years. *J. Geol.*, **74**, 109–23.

Farrington, A. (1954). A note on the correlation of the Kerry–Cork glaciations with those of the rest of Ireland. *Ir. Geogr.*, **3**, 47–53.

Farrington, A. (1963). Cryoturbation. *Ir. Nat. Jour.*, **14**, 178–9.

Farrington, A. (1966). The Early-Glacial Raised Beach in County Cork. *Scient. Proc. R. Dubl. Soc.*, **2A**, 197–219.

Flatrès, P. (1957). La Péninsule de Corran Comté de Mayo Irlande. *Bull. de la Soc. Geol. et Mineralog. de Britagne* (N.S.), **1**, 1–63.

French, H.M. (1976). *The Periglacial Environment.* Longman, London.

Hoare, P.G. and McCabe, A.M. (1981). The periglacial record in east–central Ireland. *Biul. Perygl.*, **28**, 57–78.

Jessen, K., Andersen, Th. and Farrington, A. (1959). The interglacial deposits near Gort, County Galway, Ireland. *Proc. R. Ir. Acad.*, **60**, 1–77.

Jessen, K. and Farrington, A. (1938). The bogs at Ballybetagh, near Dublin with remarks on Late-glacial conditions in Ireland. *Proc. R. Ir. Acad.*, **44B**, 205–60.

Kinahan, G.H. (1894). The recent Irish Glaciers. *Ir. Nat.*, **3**, 236–40.

Lewis, C.A. (1974). The glaciations of the Dingle Peninsula, County Kerry. *Scient. Proc. R. Dubl. Soc.*, **5A**, 207–35.

Lewis, C.A. (1977). Ice-wedge casts in north east County Wicklow. *Scient. Proc. R. Dubl. Soc.*, **6A**, 17–35.

Lewis, C.A. (1978). Periglacial features in Ireland: an assessment 1978. *J. Earth Sci. R. Dubl. Soc.*, **1**, 135–42.

Lewis, C.A. (1985). Periglacial features. In, *The Quaternary History of Ireland* (Eds. K.J. Edwards and W.P. Warren), pp. 95–113, Academic Press, London.

Lewis, H.C. (1894). *Papers and notes on The Glacial of Geology of Great Britain and Ireland.* Longmans, Green and Company, London.

McCabe, A.M., Mitchell, G.F., and Shotton, F.W. (1978). An inter-till fresh water deposit at Hollymount, Maguiresbridge, Co. Fermanagh. *Proc. R. Ir. Acad.*, **78B**, 77–89.

Mitchell, G.F. (1957). The Pleistocene Epoch. In, *A View of Ireland* (Eds. J. Meenan and D.A. Webb), pp. 32–39, Hely's Ltd. Dublin.

Mitchell, G.F. (1960). The Pleistocene history of the Irish Sea. *Adv. Sci.*, **17**, 313–25.

Mitchell, G.F. (1962). Summer field meeting in Wales and Ireland. *Proc. Geol. Ass.*, **73**, 197–213.

Mitchell, G.F. (1970). The Quaternary deposits between Fenit and Spa on the North Shore of Tralee Bay, Co. Kerry. *Proc. R. Ir. Acad.*, **70B**, 141–62.

Mitchell, G.F. (1972). The Pleistocene history of the Irish Sea: second approximation. *Scient. Proc. R. Dubl. Soc.*, **4A**, 59–68.

Mitchell, G.F. (1973). Fossil pingos in Camaross Townland, Co. Wexford. *Proc. R. Ir. Acad.*, **73B**, 269–82.

Mitchell, G.F. (1976). *The Irish Landscape.* Collins, Glasgow.

Mitchell, G.F. (1977). Periglacial Ireland. *Phil. Trans. R. Soc. Lond. B*, **280**, 199–209.

Mitchell, G.F., Penny, L.F., Shotton, F.W., and West, R.G. (1973). A correlation of Quaternary deposits in the British Isles. *Geol. Soc. Lond.*, Special Report No. 4.

Orme, A.R., Davies, G.L., and Synge, F.M. (1964). The Physique of the South of Ireland. In, *Field Studies in The British Isles* (Ed. J.A. Steers), pp. 482–99, Nelson, London.

Quinn, I.M. (1975). *Glacial and Periglacial features in north-west Iveragh, Co. Kerry.* Unpublished M.A. Thesis, University College, Dublin.

Quinn, I.M. (1984). *The Glaciation of County Waterford.* Field guide for the Geographical Society of Ireland, Maynooth.

Quinn, I.M. (1987). The significance of periglacial features on Knocknadobar, south west Ireland. In, *Periglacial Processes and Landforms in Britain and Ireland* (Ed. J. Boardman), pp. 287–94, Cambridge University Press.

Sancetta, C., Imbrie, J., and Kipp, N.G. (1973). Climatic Record of the Past 130,000 years in North Atlantic Deep-Sea Core V23–82; Correlation with the Terrestial Record. *Quat. Res.*, **3**, 110–16.

Shackleton, N.J. (1969). The last interglacial in the marine and terrestial records. *Proc. R. Soc. Lond.*, B, **174**, 135–54.

Stephens, N. (1970). The West Country and Southern Ireland. In, *The Glaciations of Wales and Adjoining Regions* (Ed. C.A. Lewis), pp. 267–314, Longman, London.

Stephens, N. and Synge, F.M. (1965). Late-Pleistocene Shorelines and Drift Limits in North Donegal. *Proc. R. Ir. Acad.*, **64B**, 131–53.

Synge, F.M. (1968). The Glaciation of West Mayo. *Ir. Geogr.*, **5**, 372–86.

Synge, F.M. (1970). The Irish Quaternary: Current views 1969. In, *Irish Geographical studies in honour of E. Estyn Evans* (Eds. N. Stephens and R.E. Glasscock), pp. 34–48, Department of Geography, The Queen's University, Belfast.

Synge, F.M. (1973). The glaciation of south Wicklow and the adjoining parts of the neighbouring counties. *Ir. Geogr.*, **6**, 561–9.

Synge, F.M. (1977). Introduction. In, *South and South West Ireland.* Guidebook for excursion A14, INQUA X CONGRESS (Ed. D.Q. Bowen), pp. 4–8, Norwich.

Synge, F.M. (1979). Glacial Landforms. In, *Atlas of Ireland.* Royal Irish Academy, Dublin, Plate 21.

Warren, W.P. (1977). North East Iveragh. In, *South and South West Ireland.* Guidebook for excursion A15, INQUA X CONGRESS (Ed. D.Q. Bowen), pp. 37–45, Norwich.

Warren, W.P. (1978). *The glacial history of the MacGillycuddy's Reeks and adjoining area in parts of* the baronies of *Iveragh, Dunkerron North and Magunihy, Co. Kerry*. Unpublished Ph.D. thesis, National University of Ireland.

Warren, W.P. (1979). The stratigraphic position and age of the Gortian Interglacial deposits. *Geol. Surv. Ire. Bull.*, **2**, 315–32.

Warren, W.P. (1981). Features indicative of prolonged and severe periglacial activity in Ireland, with particular reference to the south-west. *Biul. Perygl.*, **28**, 241–8.

Warren, W.P. (1985). Stratigraphy. In, *The Quaternary History of Ireland* (Eds. K.J. Edwards and W.P. Warren), pp. 39–65, Academic Press, London.

Washburn, A.L. (1979). *Geocryology, A survey of periglacial processes and environments*. Arnold, London.

Watson, E. (1966). Two nivation cirques near Aberystwyth, Wales. *Biul. Perygl.*, **15**, 79–101.

Watson, E. and Watson, S. (1970). The coastal periglacial slope deposits of the Cotentin Peninsula. *Trans. Inst. Br. Geogr.*, **49**, 125–144.

Watts, W.A. (1985). Quaternary vegetation cycles. In, *The Quaternary History of Ireland* (Eds. K.J. Edwards and W.P. Warren), pp. 155–185, Academic Press, London.

Wilkinson, S.B., McHenry, A., Kilroe, J.R., and Seymour, H.J. (1908). *The Geology of the Country around Londonderry. Mem. Geol. Surv. Ireland.* Dublin.

Wright, W.B. (1920). Minor periodicity in Glacial Retreat. *Proc. R. Ir. Acad.*, **35B**, 95–105.

Wright, W.B. (1937). *The Quaternary Ice Age* (2nd edition). MacMillan, London.

Wright, W.B., and Muff, H.B. (1904). The Pre-Glacial Raised Beach of the South Coast of Ireland. *Scient. Proc. R. Dubl. Soc.*, **10**, 250–324.

9 · The present-day periglaciation of upland Britain

COLIN K. BALLANTYNE

Abstract

The present climate of British uplands is characterised by extreme wetness and strong winds rather than severe cold, and this is reflected in the range of active periglacial processes and landforms. Because of limited frost penetration, active patterned ground features (sorted circles and stripes, earth hummocks) are small and solifluction is shallow and slow, though the wet conditions seem to favour widespread ploughing boulder movement and (locally) frequent debris flow activity. The strong winds promote a rich variety of wind-related features, including deflation surfaces, niveo-aeolian sand deposits and several types of wind-patterned ground and turf-banked terrace. Nivation and avalanche activity appears limited, and active talus formation is localised. The lower limit of active periglaciation apparently declines westwards and northwards across Highland Scotland in response to increased exposure and precipitation, but the range of features in any area is largely dictated by regolith characteristics and therefore lithology. Current mass-transport rates are comparable with (and sometimes exceed) those of some alpine and low-arctic mountain environments.

Introduction

The earliest accounts of active periglacial phenomena on British mountains were published over half a century ago, and concerned sorted patterned ground (e.g. Ward, 1876; Gregory, 1930; Simpson, 1932), turf-banked terraces (Peach et al., 1913), deflation features (Crampton, 1911) and high-level blown sand deposits (Peach et al., 1913). Particularly outstanding was the work of Hollingworth (1934), who discussed the characteristics and genesis of a wide range of frost action and mass-movement features in the English Lake District. Despite this long history of research, however, some British geomorphologists remain sceptical regarding both the current effectiveness of periglacial activity on British mountains and the 'periglacial' status of the present upland environment (e.g. Worsley, 1977, p. 217).

The aim of this review is to suggest that high ground in Great Britain does indeed constitute a truly active 'periglacial' environment, albeit one that in its climatic and geomorphological characteristics is rather different from those of arctic or alpine areas. This view is only tenable, however, if one adopts an eclectic definition of 'periglacial' that does not require the presence of permafrost. Here Washburn's (1979, p. 4) widely-accepted definition is adopted; the term is used to designate '... non-glacial processes and features of cold climates characterised by intensive frost action, regardless of age or proximity to glaciers'. 'Periglacial environment' therefore refers to an environment in which cold climate non-glacial processes (particularly those dependent on or influenced by ground freezing) have produced distinctive landforms and deposits. Aspects of present periglaciation on British mountains are considered below. Localities mentioned in the text are depicted in Figure 9.1.

The present climatic environment on British mountains

In comparison with arctic and alpine environments, high ground in Britain experiences a relatively mild temperature regime that reflects both proximity to the sea and the moderating influence of the North Atlantic Drift. Mean annual air temperature on the highest British summit (Ben Nevis, 1343 m) is fractionally above 0 °C (Manley, 1971a), and mean monthly air temperatures are below freezing for only four months of the year at altitudes below 800–900 m and for no more than six months on the highest peaks (Figure 9.2). Absolute minima are unremarkable: the lowest recorded screen temperature during 20 years of observations at the summit of Ben Nevis was − 17.3 °C, and data for various mountain areas indicate that screen

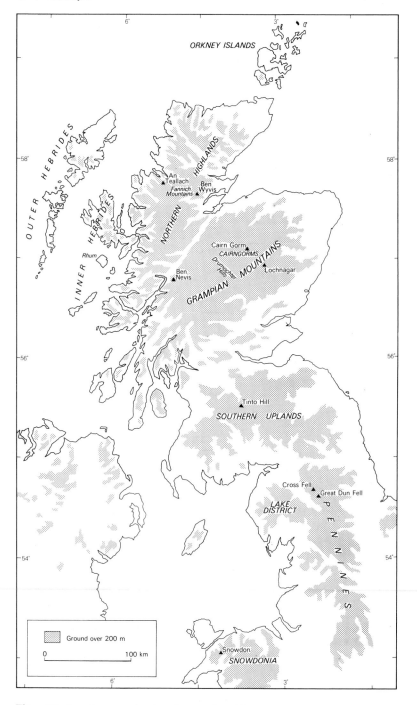

Figure 9.1. Location map showing sites mentioned in the text.

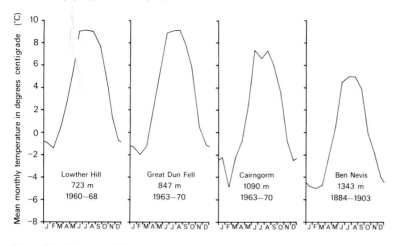

Figure 9.2. Mean monthly screen temperature regime at four stations on British mountains.

temperatures below $-10\,°C$ are infrequent. The limited data available suggest that at 600–800 m there are on average 30–40 ambient (air) freezing cycles per year, the majority probably related to the alternation of warm and cold air masses during periods of cyclonic activity rather than diurnal heating and nocturnal cooling (Ballantyne, 1981).

Permafrost is absent, though at higher altitudes there may be in some years an annual ground freezing cycle of 2–4 months duration, with ground freezing to depths of at least 0.5 m (Ragg and Bibby, 1966) or more (Halstead, 1974). Diurnal freeze-thaw cycles, however, penetrate no more than 50–60 mm into the ground and are ineffective in causing ground freezing under all but the shallowest cover of snow. Snow also mitigates the effect of longer ('cyclonic') freezing cycles; available data suggest that only 4–5 freeze-thaw cycles per year penetrate to depths exceeding 100 mm at 650–750 m altitude in the Southern Uplands (Halstead, 1974; Ballantyne, 1981).

Westerly airstreams and frontal structures rise sharply on meeting the mountain barrier of western Britain, giving rise to increased cloud cover and heavy precipitation (Taylor, 1976). Precipitation gradients are steep (Ballantyne, 1983), so that above 600 m all but the most easterly uplands experience over 2000 mm y^{-1} mean annual precipitation, with some western mountains receiving more than 4000 mm y^{-1} (Meteorological Office, 1977). Cyclonic and (less frequently) summer convectional rainstorms with intensities exceeding 50 mm/24 h are common. Duration of winter snow-lie increases

approximately linearly with altitude. In the Scottish Highlands average snow-lie ($> 50\%$ cover) generally exceeds 100 d y^{-1} at 600 m and ranges from *c.* 150 to *c.* 180 d y^{-1} at 900 m, with 200–220 d y^{-1} snow-lie on the very highest peaks. Farther south snow-lie is rather less prolonged: the equivalent figures are 105 d y^{-1} for the summit area (*c.* 880 m) of Cross Fell in the Pennines and *c.* 70 d y^{-1} for 900 m on Snowdon (Manley, 1971b).

Perhaps the most notable feature of upland climate in Britain is the strength of the wind. Westerly airflow is concentrated and accelerated in its passage over mountain barriers, and during 13 years of observations on Ben Nevis there was an average of 261 gales exceeding 50 mph (82 km h^{-1} or 22.7 ms^{-1}) per year (Pearsall, 1968). Even on Great Dun Fell (847 m) in the Pennines gusts exceeding 180 km h^{-1} (50 ms^{-1}) occur every few years whilst the strongest gusts recorded annually on Cairngorm (1215 m) range from 167 to 232 km h^{-1} (46.5 to 64.4 ms^{-1}).

In summary, then, the severity of the present climatic environment on British mountains relates not so much to extreme cold, frequent freezing cycles or deeply-frozen ground as to extreme wetness, intense precipitation, prolonged snow-cover and frequent very strong winds. Climatically, the British uplands experience a distinctive *maritime periglacial* regime that is markedly different from arctic and alpine areas where there are much greater extremes of cold. This climatic distinction inevitably affects the nature and range of present periglacial activity.

The range and characteristics of present-day periglacial processes and landforms on British mountains

Age and activity of upland periglacial phenomena

Although it is widely agreed that British mountains support both relict periglacial phenomena formed under severe climatic conditions during the Late Devensian and features active at present, there is less consensus regarding which features are relict and which active. An interesting 'provisional' age classification of periglacial features in Snowdonia (Ball and Goodier, 1970) left many areas of uncertainty. More recently, Ballantyne (1984) differentiated Late Devensian relicts from active Holocene forms on Scottish mountains using four criteria: (i) the distribution of periglacial features in relation to the limits of the glaciers that occupied upland areas during the Loch Lomond Stadial of *c.* 11,000–10,000 B.P., the last period of stadial conditions to affect the British Isles; (ii) radiocarbon dating and pollen analysis of organic horizons buried under periglacial deposits; (iii) measurements of present activity; and (iv) the present appearance of upland periglacial phenomena (many relict features support mature zonal soils or a virtually complete cover of vegetation and/or peat). The range of active Holocene features identified by Ballantyne (1984, p. 315) is illustrated in Figure 9.3 and forms the framework of the following discussion.

Periglacial weathering

The marked contrast in the degree of frost shattering of rock inside and outside the mapped limits of Loch Lomond Stadial glaciers (e.g. Sissons, 1967; Thorp, 1981; Ballantyne, 1982) and the apparent

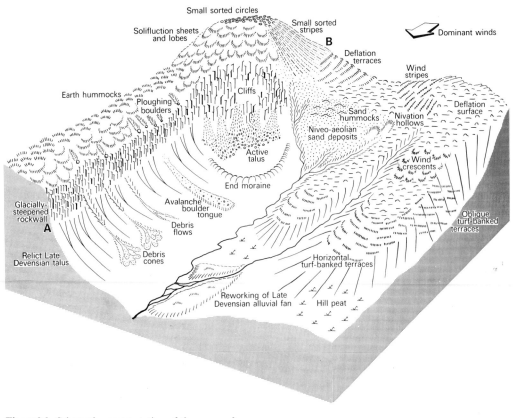

Figure 9.3. Schematic representation of the range of active periglacial phenomena on British mountains. Those depicted to the left of an imaginary line linking A and B are characteristic of frost-susceptible 'Type 3' regolith; those to the right of this line are typical of cohesionless sandy 'Type 2' regolith.

absence of *in situ* frost-weathered detritus in the form of blockfields and other mountain-top detritus within these limits (Ballantyne and Wain-Hobson, 1980; Ballantyne, 1981, 1984) strongly suggests that large-scale frost wedging of rock (macrogelivation) has been largely inoperative on British mountains since the end of the Loch Lomond Stadial. Some researchers (e.g. Godard, 1959, 1965; King, 1968; Hills, 1969) have maintained that limited frost splitting operates on certain lithologies under present conditions, but substantive evidence for this is lacking.

Conversely, microgelivation (mechanically-induced granular disintegration and flaking of rock under cold conditions) is certainly active at present, but its effects are highly discriminatory with respect to rock type. Judged in terms of the roundness of exposed rock surfaces and abundance of recent granular detritus, some sandstones and granites appear most susceptible to granular disaggregation under present conditions (Galloway, 1958; King, 1968; Ballantyne, 1981) but the present effect of microgelivation on fine-grained igneous and metamorphic rocks such as quartzite, porphyrite, felsite and lavas appears very limited. Rocks with well-developed cleavage (e.g. schists, shale and slate) are subject to periodic flaking. The marked contrast in rounding between exposed and buried rock and clast surfaces (Ballantyne, 1981, 1984) indicates that the effects of current microgelivation are limited to exposed surfaces, so that the process is constrained by the cover of soil, peat and vegetation that mantles much high ground in Britain. Although the lack of clay and silt in upland periglacial deposits has been interpreted by some researchers (e.g. Ragg and Bibby, 1966) as indicative of limited chemical weathering activity, the present role of chemical weathering has not been rigorously investigated.

Active patterned ground features

Small-scale active sorted patterned ground has been reported to occur in virtually all parts of upland Britain, including Snowdonia (Tallis and Kershaw, 1959; Ball and Goodier, 1970), the Lake District (Hollingworth, 1934; Hay, 1936, 1943; Caine, 1962, 1963a, 1963b, 1972; Warburton, 1985), the Pennines (Tufnell, 1969), southern Scotland (Gregory, 1930; Miller *et al.*, 1954), the Hebrides (Godard, 1958, 1965; Ryder and McCann, 1971; Birks, 1973) and various parts of the Scottish Highlands (Simpson, 1932; Kelletat, 1970a). A number of common characteristics are evident from the above-cited accounts. First, active sorted patterns are common on a limited range of lithologies, particularly volcanics, slate, schist and felsite, rocks that tend to have weathered to yield a diamicton consisting of fairly small clasts embedded in a relatively fine-grained frost-susceptible matrix (Caine, 1972; Ballantyne, 1984; Warburton, 1985). Excavation of frozen fine stripes has revealed segregated ice lenses (Caine, 1962, 1963b; Ballantyne, 1981). Secondly, although many authors have described active sorted 'polygons' and stripes, all of the supposed 'polygons' known to the author or illustrated by previous researchers (e.g. Hollingworth, 1934; Godard, 1958; Tallis and Kershaw, 1959; Ball and Goodier, 1970) are circular, oval or irregular in plan and lack straight edges, hence are more accurately described as sorted circles or nets (*sensu* Washburn, 1979). Thirdly, although reported dimensions vary considerably, active sorted circles do not normally exceed 0.6 m and stripes 0.7 m in width or 'repeat distance', and depth of sorting is invariably shallow (0.2 m or less). Several authors have cited the maximum size of sorted clasts as 130–160 mm (e.g. Miller *et al.*, 1954; Godard, 1958; Caine, 1963b; Ryder and McCann, 1971) or less (e.g. Tallis and Kershaw, 1959), which suggests that there is a limit to the size of material capable of being sorted under present conditions of shallow freezing. Fourthly, sections cut through active sorted circles and stripes reveal a common structure consisting of an undulating surface of fines with variable stone content. The crests of the undulations mark the locations of circle centres or fine stripes and the troughs contain clasts (often aligned vertically or downslope) that define the circle margins or coarse stripes. This structure has been interpreted by Caine (1963b) and others as reflecting the lateral migration of upfrozen clasts from the crests to the troughs. Finally, available data indicate that sorted patterns may form or re-form rapidly. Miller *et al.* (1954) reported complete re-formation of sorted stripes over disturbed ground on Tinto Hill over two winters, and observations by the author at the same site revealed that under favourable winter conditions both circles and stripes could re-form within a few winter weeks. Conversely, Tallis and Kershaw (1959) have shown that more fragile sorted patterns may be rapidly destroyed by high winds and heavy rain. Rates of downslope surface clast movement on sorted stripes are rapid: Caine (1963a) reported median rates of 70–254 mm over one winter on 9–19° slopes in the Lake District, and on a 23° slope on Tinto Hill nearly all marker clasts monitored by the author moved over 1.0 m downslope between November 1977 and May 1980. Such rates are comparable to the most rapid recorded for any periglacial environment (cf. Washburn, 1979, p. 154). Subsurface movement, however, is much slower, and extends to depths of only 100–140 mm (Caine, 1963a; Ballantyne, unpublished). Caine concluded that frost creep and sliding of clasts during thaw are the main agents of movement, but on Tinto Hill creep due to needle ice growth and collapse and possibly surface wash is also important.

Sorted patterned ground genesis has been variously attributed to needle ice (Hay, 1936, 1943) and differential frost heave (Caine, 1962, 1963b). On Tinto Hill the author has witnessed the formation *ab initio* of small sorted circles without intermediate polygon development, which suggests an origin independent of ground cracking (Washburn, 1979), and the occurrence of adjacent sorted circles of widely different cell diameters appears to support the notion of formation through upfreezing and outfreezing of clasts from randomly-spaced concentrations of frost-susceptible fines (cf. Goldthwait, 1976). Hay (1936) observed that active stripes in the Lake District give way upslope to a subsurface system of parallel rills, and observations by the author on Tinto Hill suggest that such rills are of fundamental importance in initiating the troughs in which clasts accumulate.

Supposedly active non-sorted patterned ground features in the form of small dome-shaped vegetation-covered earth hummocks in the N.W. Pennines have been described, classified and analysed in terms of their dimensions and distribution by Tufnell (1975), and similar but rather flatter forms on low ground in northern England have been described by Pemberton (1980). In dismissing other (biogenic) modes of origin, both authors concluded that the features they described are frost-action phenomena analogous to the thufur of Iceland, but failed to provide positive evidence for this. Both also based their claims of recent activity on the grounds that hummocks have apparently developed on sites that probably experienced disturbance within recent historical times, but *conclusive* evidence of such disturbance and current activity seems lacking.

Tufnell (1975) also maintained that earth hummocks are of limited distribution in upland Britain, but forms similar to those he described are fairly widespread on frost-susceptible regolith on Scottish mountains (Birks, 1973; Ballantyne, 1981, 1984, 1987; Chattopadhyay, 1982). Unlike the Pennine features, however, the hummocks described on Scottish hills often give way to hummocky stripes and relief stripes (*sensu* Nicholson, 1976) with

increasing gradient, and the presence of mature undisturbed podzolic soil horizons within these structures suggests that they are relict features. It therefore appears that British mountains may support both recent and long-inactive earth hummocks, though in the author's view the periglacial origin of supposedly active hummocks requires to be more convincingly demonstrated. Despite the assertions of Tufnell (1975), the dome-shaped forms he described and particularly those illustrated by Pemberton (1980) are morphologically quite unlike the closely-spaced knob-like forms of arctic lowlands or indeed Icelandic thufur.

Solifluction features

On the upper slopes of many British mountains landforms produced by slow mass-movement of regolith form a complex morphological continuum of sheet-like, terrace-like and lobate forms. Here the term 'sheet' refers to a detritus mantle that is terminated downslope by a long step or riser. On slope crests (6–10°) such risers are usually fairly straight in plan, but with increasing gradient they become progressively more lobate or crenulate until on steep slopes (> 25°) overlapping of lobate sheets produces the appearance of isolated lobe forms. The 'solifluction lobes' referred to by many writers are often simply lobate extensions of much more extensive detritus sheets (King, 1972; Ballantyne, 1981).

Although many of the sheets and lobes on British hills are Late Devensian relics (e.g. Galloway, 1961; Kelletat, 1970b; Sissons, 1976, 1980; Shaw, 1977; Ballantyne, 1984), active solifluction features appear to be widespread above *c.* 550 m (e.g. Tufnell, 1969; Ball and Goodier, 1970; Kelletat, 1970a). Four criteria may be used to differentiate active and relict forms. First, active lobes are generally smaller than their Late Devensian counterparts (Galloway, 1961; Ball and Goodier, 1970; Kelletat, 1970a, 1970b; Sugden, 1971; Sissons, 1976). In particular, riser heights rarely exceed 1.0 m (Ballantyne, 1981; Chattopadhyay, 1982) whereas those of relict lobes may be as much as 5.9 m high (Shaw, 1977). Secondly, unlike Late Devensian features, active lobes sometimes occur within the mapped limits of Loch Lomond Stadial glaciers (Sissons, 1977; Chattopadhyay, 1982). Thirdly, excavation of apparently active lobes has invariably revealed a structureless brown soil consisting of angular stones embedded in a dominantly sandy but frost-susceptible matrix and overlying organic soil horizons or peat fragments containing Flandrian pollen (Mottershead and White, 1969;

Ballantyne, 1981; Chattopadhyay, 1982). Radiocarbon dating of over-ridden organic material has yielded dates ranging from 5440 ± 55 B.P. to 2680 ± 120 B.P. (Sugden, 1971; Mottershead, 1978), indicating at least intermittent lobe movement during the Late Flandrian. In contrast, Late Devensian lobes often contain many boulders, often lack a true matrix and are sometimes vertically sorted; buried organic horizons are usually absent, although some small, vertically-sorted Late Devensian solifluction lobes are apparently active at present and have over-ridden soils containing Flandrian pollen (Ballantyne, 1981, 1984; Chattopadhyay, 1982). Finally, whereas the risers of relict features are often degraded, those of active sheets and lobes are steep (often around 45°) and sometimes bulging. Measured rates of current activity are low, however, surface movements of two steep lobes on Ben Wyvis over a single year (1976–7) did not exceed 17.4 mm and 10.4 mm (Ballantyne, 1981), and on a lobe in the Drumochter Hills, Chattopadhyay (1982) recorded only 50 mm surface displacement over three winters, declining to zero at 20 mm depth. Such rates are low in comparison with those recorded in other periglacial environments (cf. Benedict, 1976).

Intimately associated with the solifluction features described above are ploughing boulders located at the downslope end of vegetation-covered furrows. Such furrows, together with the 'bow-waves' of turf and soil pushed up downslope of the boulders, indicate downslope movement of the boulders at a rate exceeding that of the surrounding regolith. Ploughing boulders have been reported in virtually all parts of upland Britain, and their distribution appears to coincide almost exactly with that of active solifluction sheets and lobes (Kelletat, 1970a; Ballantyne, 1981) though isolated examples have been reported as low as 450 m (Tufnell, 1972; Shaw, 1977).

Various authors have summarised and analysed the morphological characteristics of ploughing boulders and associated microforms and have monitored current rates of boulder movement (Tufnell, 1972, 1976; Shaw, 1977; Ballantyne, 1981; Chattopadhyay, 1982, 1983). Average recorded rates of movement of individual boulders vary widely (0.4–64 mm y^{-1} on the Pennines; 0.3–8.7 mm y^{-1} on Lochnagar; 6–34.5 mm y^{-1} on the Fannich Mountains; 1.5–7.0 mm y^{-1} on the Drumochter Hills) and at the latter two sites are strongly related to gradient. Tufnell (1972) suggested that movement may result from insolation creep (*sensu* Statham, 1977), frost creep, freezing of water

trapped upslope of boulders or sliding of boulders over a frozen substrate during thaw. Ballantyne (1981), however, challenged the adequacy of these mechanisms and proposed that boulder movement accompanies the thawing of ice lenses under boulders during thaw of the surrounding frost-susceptible sediments. Although this explanation requires further verification, it would appear to account for the observed close association of ploughing boulders with active solifluction features.

Rockfall, talus, debris flows and avalanche activity

The majority of taluses investigated in upland Britain display features characteristic of unmodified rockfall accumulations: an upper straight slope and basal concavity, maximum gradients of around 36° and some degree of fall-sorting and preferred downslope orientation of surface clasts (Andrews, 1961; Statham, 1973, 1976a; Shaw, 1977; Ballantyne, 1981; Ballantyne and Eckford, 1984). Many taluses (particularly those outside the limits of Loch Lomond Stadial glaciation) are, however, largely or entirely vegetation-covered and have been modified by gullying, debris flows and translational slides. These characteristics suggest that such taluses are essentially relict Lateglacial accumulations on which erosion is currently the dominant mode of geomorphic activity (Ball, 1966; Tufnell, 1969; Ball and Goodier, 1970; Ryder and McCann, 1971; Ballantyne and Eckford, 1984). This conclusion is supported by calculations which indicate that rockwall retreat rates during the Loch Lomond Stadial were about two orders of magnitude higher than those associated with relict talus at present (Ballantyne, 1984). The latter average 0.015 mm y^{-1}, is similar to rates measured in some arctic areas but much less than those in alpine environments (Ballantyne and Eckford, 1984; Stuart, 1984).

Inside the limits of the stadial glaciers, however, talus cones that must have developed entirely during the Holocene often present a much fresher and less 'mature' appearance. Such cones are commonly overlooked by steep, high cliffs, and fresh debris is often strewn over their sparsely vegetated slopes. It would appear that current rockfall activity in such localities is much greater than that associated with relict talus outside the stadial glacier limits. Within a corrie on An Teallach, for example, the author has recorded an average of *c.* 0.6 rockfalls per hour. Although most were of very small magnitude, disruption of painted boulders on an active talus cone in the same corrie indicates that larger-scale events are not infrequent (Ballantyne, 1981). Such evidence suggests that talus accumulation may still be appreciable, but only at favourable sites within the limits of stadial glaciation.

Also of localised (but rather more widespread) importance as an agent of current mass-transport on British mountains is debris flow activity triggered by intense precipitation (Common, 1954, Baird and Lewis, 1957). Most frequent are hillslope flows (*sensu* Brunsden, 1979), though valley-confined flows that issue from rock or drift gullies also occur (e.g. Statham, 1976*b*). When stabilised, individual flows take the form of paired levées aligned downslope and terminating on lower gradients in one or more lobes of debris. Where successive flows have followed the same track, the flow deposits have often accumulated as steep, poorly-sorted debris cones, spectacular examples of which flank the floors of some glacial troughs (e.g. Glencoe). Although debris flows affect all types of frost-weathered debris and drift, they tend to be most abundant on regolith with a cohesionless sandy matrix, such as that developed on sandstone or granite mountains (Ballantyne, 1981; Innes, 1982). In such areas hillslope flows may cover entire mountainsides and flow events may be frequent: in the Lairig Ghru, a steep-sided, high-level glacial breach in the Cairngorms, at least 71 flows were mobilised between 1970 and 1980 (Innes, 1983). Although the great majority of such flows transport $< 30 \, m^3$ of debris (Innes, 1985), they represent the major form of current mass-transport activity in areas of abundant activity. Innes (1983) concluded from lichenometric evidence that most hillslope flows in the Scottish Highlands occurred within the last 500 years, and cited burning and overgrazing as potential triggers of accelerated activity. This conclusion seems questionable on two counts: first, at several of the sites he investigated, some of the flow sources are rock gullies unlikely to have been affected by overgrazing and burning; secondly, later flows often obscure earlier ones, thus introducing a possible bias into the lichenometric dating of such features.

Finally, it is worth noting that although most snow avalanches in Britain are small and full-depth avalanches rare (Ward, 1984), in the Lairig Ghru avalanches have locally eroded and transported debris flow deposits, forming in at least one case a small, recent avalanche boulder tongue. Such features, however, appear to be extremely rare, and it seems likely that outside of the Cairngorms snow avalanches are presently of negligible geomorphic importance.

Aeolian and niveo-aeolian features

The strong winds that scour the higher parts of British mountains have given rise to a number of distinctive landforms. The effectiveness of wind action as a geomorphic agent is, however, conditioned by regolith type and hence lithology; all of the features described below tend to be well developed on (but not exclusive to) regolith with a coarse sandy matrix, usually developed on sandstone or granitic rocks. On exposed plateaux underlain by such rocks, strong winds have often stripped virtually all vegetation cover and have winnowed away all exposed sand-size particles to create extensive deflation surfaces carpeted by a lag deposit of fine gravel. The archetypal examples are the great granite plateaux of the Cairngorms and Lochnagar, together with those of Torridon Sandstone mountains in N.W. Scotland. Deflation surfaces are, however, also developed at only 400 m on some windswept islands such as Rhum, Orkney and Shetland.

Complementing such extensive deflation is the accumulation of windblown sand deposits in the form of vegetation-covered 'sand sheets' on lee slopes (Peach *et al.*, 1913; Godard, 1965; Ball and Goodier, 1974; Goodier and Ball, 1975). Research on the Torridon Sandstone massif of An Teallach in N.W. Scotland (Ballantyne, 1981) has shown that these are currently accumulating through sand blown from unvegetated plateaux becoming trapped in the winter snowpack downwind. As the snow ablates, the sand is lowered on to the underlying vegetation, which grows through the accumulating deposit and thus stabilises it. Thufur-like 'sand hummocks' are sometimes developed on the surface of the accumulating niveo-aeolian sand as a result of selective wash between vegetation tussocks (Ballantyne, 1987). Radiocarbon dating and pollen analysis of organic horizons within and at the base of such deposits has demonstrated that sand has been accumulating since the Early Flandrian, reaching thicknesses of up to 4 m. Present accumulation declines with distance downwind of the plateau source area and ranges from 10 to 300 g $m^2 \, y^{-1}$, but this is balanced to some extent by retreat of the unvegetated margins of the sand sheets at rates averaging 25–30 mm y^{-1}.

Commonly associated with deflation surfaces are three forms of wind-patterned ground: (i) stripes of vegetation aligned parallel with dominant wind direction on otherwise unvegetated terrain; (ii) crescents of vegetation aligned across dominant wind direction on otherwise unvegetated terrain; and (iii) elongate scars of vegetation-free ground on otherwise vegetated surfaces. Less regular and transitional forms also exist (Crampton, 1911; Kelletat, 1970a; Ball and Goodier, 1974; Goodier and Ball, 1975; Ballantyne, 1981). King (1971) provided evidence that elongate deflation scars migrate slowly through a combination of erosion at the downwind end and vegetation colonisation at the upwind end. Although it is generally agreed that wind-patterned ground reflects the joint action of frost (particularly needle ice) and deflation, probably operating on a formerly complete vegetation mat, the erosive process is poorly documented. Nor is it known: (i) whether frost action alone was responsible for the initial disruption of vegetation cover; (ii) when this occurred; and (iii) why some wind patterns display remarkable regularity of spacing.

Closely related to the wind patterns that form on gentle gradients are turf-banked terraces, step-like features with gently-sloping, largely unvegetated treads and steep well-vegetated risers. Such forms occur throughout upland Britain (e.g. Galloway, 1961; Tufnell, 1969; Ball and Goodier, 1970; Kelletat, 1970a) though are again most widespread on sandstone or granite terrain. The attitude and form of turf-banked terraces is clearly a response to dominant wind direction (Ball and Goodier, 1974; Goodier and Ball, 1975). Three types may be differentiated: (i) horizontal 'deflation terraces' aligned parallel to dominant wind direction and apparently formed by creep operating on the treads of deflation scars cut across vegetated slopes (King, 1971); (ii) other horizontal terraces formed on lee slopes, possibly by the accumulation of creeping debris dammed by vegetation 'crescents' (Hollingworth, 1934); and (iii) oblique terraces that dip steeply upwind on otherwise vegetation-free slopes and which appear to reflect the progressive anchoring of creeping debris by vegetation sheltering in the lee of boulders (Ballantyne, 1981). The latter two types commonly intersect at transitional sites. The horizontal types are characteristically 3–20 m in length (across-slope) with tread widths (downslope) of 0.5–4.0 m and riser heights of 0.1–1.2 m. Oblique terraces are often longer and broader, with riser heights of 1–3 m, and dip across slope at angles of 10–30°. They also tend to occupy steeper slopes (up to 36°) than the horizontal types (6–31°). Movement of debris on terrace treads and around the relatively immobile risers seems to be dominated by frost creep (Hollingworth, 1934), averag-

ing a few millimetres per year at the surface and declining rapidly to zero at depths of 140 mm or less (Ballantyne, 1981), though solifluction may also be responsible for terrace movement on frost-susceptible regolith.

Nivation

There are conflicting opinions regarding the current effectiveness of nivation processes on British mountains. Tufnell (1971) suggested that nival meltwater contributes to accelerated boulder movement and that headward erosion is associated with late-lying snowbeds in the Pennines, but the corroborative evidence he presented seems to the present author too speculative and localised to support his claim that 'snow is a major element in the current development of the landscape of the area' (p. 497), though others have endorsed this view (Vincent and Lee, 1982). In contrast, observation and measurements made at snowbed sites in the northern Highlands (mainly small nivation hollows formed in niveo-aeolian sands) indicated no increase in freeze-thaw activity, chemical weathering or mass-movement, and showed that although snowcreep occurs it is of negligible importance as a transportation agent (Ballantyne, 1985). Indeed, snowpatch-related activity at the study sites was restricted to the localised redistribution of cohesionless sandy sediments by surface wash, and as this process is apparently ineffective on vegetation-covered ground its importance is likely to be restricted to areas of unvegetated sand-rich regolith.

Some aspects of the distribution of active periglacial phenomena

Local controls

At a local scale, the dominant controls affecting the distribution of active periglacial features on mountains of uniform lithology are altitude, vegetation cover, aspect and gradient. The first two of these variables mainly reflect climatic severity, and are more usefully considered in terms of regional controls (see below). Aspect exerts a strong influence on the distribution of aeolian features, most of which display a marked directional preference dictated by dominant wind direction (Figure 9.3), but otherwise appears to be unimportant. Gradient exercises a strong control on local distribution (Figure 9.4); most noticeable is a transition at 5–7.5° from features not affected by mass-movement (sorted circles, wind-patterned ground) to those that are (sorted stripes, solifluction sheets, plough-

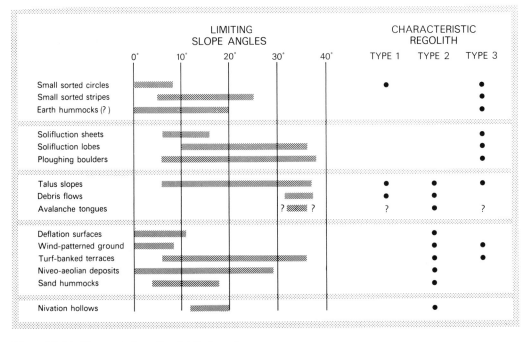

Figure 9.4. Limiting controls on the distribution of active periglacial phenomena on British mountains: limiting gradients and characteristic regolith type. Note that the limiting gradients for debris flows and avalanche tongues refer to the angle at which movement is initiated; both features may descend on to much lower gradients.

ing boulders and turf-banked terraces).

On a slightly broader scale, lithology (or more specifically, the response of different lithologies to Late Devensian periglacial weathering) has exercised a powerful control on the distribution of active periglacial phenomena. Ballantyne (1984) identified three general categories of weathered regolith on British mountains: (i) openwork block deposits developed on rocks such as quartzite, microgranite and granulite (Type 1); (ii) diamictons consisting of clasts embedded in a coarse cohesionless sandy matrix and typical of many sandstones and granites (Type 2); and (iii) diamictons relatively rich in silt and fine sand, formed by the weathering of rocks such as mica-schist, shale, slate and lavas (Type 3). The landforms characteristic of each regolith type are summarised in Figure 9.4. Apart from slope-foot forms (talus, debris flows and possibly avalanche tongues) and occasional sorted circles where fines reach the surface, Type 1 regolith rarely supports active periglacial features. Type 2 regolith, being cohesionless but rarely frost-susceptible, tends to be dominated by deflation and aeolian features. In contrast, frost-susceptible Type

3 regolith usually supports forms that are dependent on ice segregation, such as sorted patterned ground and solifluction features. Although some rocks (particularly granite) have variable weathering characteristics, lithology is unquestionably the dominant influence on the *range* of periglacial phenomena found on any mountain, such that nearby mountains of similar altitude and relief but different lithology may support utterly different associations of periglacial features (cf. Ballantyne, 1984, Figures 8 and 9).

Regional controls

There is at present insufficient information to establish the nature of the altitudinal distribution of all active periglacial phenomena across upland Britain. Galloway (1958) pointed out, however, that the minimum altitude to which several periglacial features descend appears to decline northwards and especially westwards across Scotland, a trend he related to increased exposure and a corresponding decline in the altitude at which unvegetated ground occurs. The work of Kelletat (1970a) strongly supported this proposition. Further support is

Table 9.1 *Comparative rates of mass transport activity in three mountain environments*[1]

Process Set	An Teallach, N. Scotland (Ballantyne, 1981)	Karkevagge, N. Sweden (Rapp, 1960)	San Juan Mts., Colorado (Caine, 1976)
Rockfall	1.689	0.405	0.133
Avalanches	0.0	0.453	0.001
Landslides and debris flows	0.560	1.997	0.362
Frost creep and so‖fluction	0.036[2] 0.175	0.166	0.109
Surface wash	localised	slight	0.147
Wind action	0.394	—	—
Solute transport	9.017[3]	2.828	0.104

[1] All values are expressed in W km^{-2}.

[2] 0.036 represents value for sites supporting turf-banked terraces: 0.175 represents unterraced sites.

[3] Probably a considerable over-estimate, as it includes the solute input of incident precipitation.

provided by data on the lowest altitude at which patterned ground occurs (Figure 9.5). Significantly, the 'anomalous' figures of 400 m and 370 m in Figure 9.5 represent sites where vegetation has been artificially removed (Ballantyne, 1981), which suggests that the dominant *regional* altitudinal control on active patterned ground distribution is not temperature or precipitation but simply the availability of vegetation-free sites on suitable regolith. This conclusion is further supported by Spence's (1957) description of active frost-sorted patterned ground near sea-level in Shetland (on serpentine soils inimical to vegetation colonisation) and by the author's successful experiments in 'growing' sorted circles in suitable regolith under open air conditions near sea-level at St. Andrews. A general westward decline in the altitude of deflation and aeolian features from *c.* 800 m in the Cairngorms to *c.* 400 m on Rhum probably reflects similar controls, but the more gradual westwards decline in the minimum altitude of solifluction features documented by Kelletat (1970*a*) may be a response to increased precipitation.

Comparative rates of current mass-transport activity

Some attempt has been made in preceding sections to present representative rates of current mass-transport activity, but the measurements cited do not permit direct comparison of the effectiveness of different transport processes. This has been attempted for only one British mountain, the Torridon Sandstone massif of An Teallach (1,062 m) in N.W. Scotland. For comparative purposes, the mass transport rates measured on An Teallach have been converted to a common unit, watts per square kilometre (W km^{-2}). This unit represents potential energy loss over a uniform time interval and standard area of 1 km^2 (Caine, 1976); details of the calculations are given in Ballantyne (1981).

The results (Table 9.1) must be treated with some caution, as An Teallach is a fairly high, steep mountain, exposed to high precipitation (*c.* 3,600 mm y^{-1} at 670 m) and very strong winds that have stripped plateau areas and most upper slopes of all but a patchy vegetation cover. The rates measured (especially for rapid mass transport and

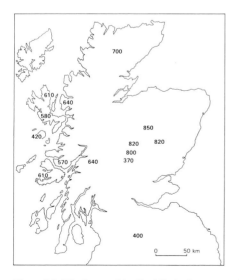

Figure 9.5. The lower altitudinal limits in metres of active sorted patterned ground at various sites in Scotland (Ballantyne, 1981).

wind action) are therefore likely to be above average for most British mountains. Comparison of the An Teallach figures highlights four features: (i) the greater effectiveness of rapid mass-transport processes (rockfall and debris flow) compared with creep and solifluction; (ii) the slower creep rates on slopes supporting turf-banked terraces, which confirms that such terraces (unlike solifluction lobes) reflect retardation rather than acceleration of slow mass-movement (cf. Hollingworth, 1934); (iii) the importance of solute transport, even though the figure cited is certainly an over-estimate; and (iv) the effectiveness of wind transport, though this represents optimal circumstances and is not representative of most other mountains. For all process sets except avalanches, the An Teallach rates are of the same order of magnitude as (and sometimes exceed) those measured by Rapp in northern Scandinavia, and in all cases for which data are available exceed those measured by Caine in the alpine environment of the San Juan Mountains. It is also notable that the relative effectiveness of different agents (i.e. solute transport > rapid mass-movement > slow mass-movement) is similar for An Teallach and Karkevagge.

In sum, the figures indicate that, admittedly under favourable circumstances, rates of mass transport under the maritime periglacial conditions of upland Britain are not dissimilar to (and in some cases exceed) those on mountains subject to more extreme periglacial conditions. Much more data are required, however, to substantiate the relative importance of different forms of mass-transport activity on a country-wide basis.

Conclusions

Five general conclusions emerge from this review.
1. The climate of the maritime periglacial environment of upland Britain is characterised by extreme wetness, intense precipitation, strong winds, absence of extreme cold and consequently relatively shallow ground freezing.
2. The range of current periglacial activity and resultant landforms reflects the climatic regime. Patterned ground forms are small, with a shallow depth of sorting; solifluction features are also shallow; extreme wetness seems to favour ploughing boulder movement; intense rainstorms generate (locally) frequent debris flow activity; and strong winds promote the development of a rich variety of aeolian and niveo-aeolian phenomena.
3. Available data indicate that, across Highland Scotland at least, there is a westwards and

northwards decline in the lower limit of current periglaciation. This appears to be partly due to increased exposure and a consequent decline in the lower limit of vegetation-free ground (allowing the formation of sorted patterned ground and aeolian features) and probably also to increased wetness that permits solifluction and possibly debris flow activity at lower altitudes.
4. At the local scale, regolith characteristics and thus lithology exercise a powerful control on the range of periglacial phenomena present.
5. Despite the relative mildness of the climatic regime, under favourable conditions many forms of mass-transport activity operate at rates comparable to those measured in some arctic or alpine periglacial environments.

Acknowledgements

The author thanks Bert Bremner for preparing the diagrams and Marie Dewar for typing the manuscript.

References

Andrews, J.T. (1961). 'The development of scree slopes in the English Lake District and central Quebec-Labrador', *Cah. Geogr. Quebec*, **10**, 219–30.

Baird, P.D. and Lewis, W.V. (1957). 'The Cairngorm floods, 1956: summer solifluction and distributary formation', *Scott. Geogr. Mag.*, **73**, 91–100.

Ball, D.F. (1966). 'Late-glacial scree in Wales', *Biul. Peryglac.*, **15**, 151–63.

Ball, D.F. and Goodier, R. (1970). 'Morphology and distribution of features resulting from frost action in Snowdonia', *Field Studies*, **3**, 193–217.

Ball, D.F. and Goodier, R. (1974). 'Ronas Hill, Shetland: a preliminary account of its ground pattern features resulting from the action of frost and wind', in *The natural environment of Scotland* (Ed. R. Goodier), pp. 89–106, Nature Conservancy Council, Edinburgh.

Ballantyne, C.K. (1981). *Periglacial landforms and environments on mountains in the Northern Highlands of Scotland*, unpub. Ph.D. thesis, Univ. Edinburgh.

Ballantyne, C.K. (1982). 'Depths of open joints and the limits of former glaciers', *Scott. J. Geol.*, **18**, 250–2.

Ballantyne, C.K. (1983). 'Precipitation gradients in Wester Ross, North West Scotland', *Weather*, **38**, 379–87.

Ballantyne, C.K. (1984). 'The Late Devensian periglaciation of upland Scotland', *Quaternary Sci. Rev.*, **3**, 311–43.

Ballantyne, C.K. (1985). 'Nivation landforms and snowpatch erosion on two massifs in the Northern Highlands of Scotland', *Scott. Geogr. Mag.*, **101**, 40–9.

Ballantyne, C.K. (1987). 'Nonsorted patterned ground

on mountains in the Northern Highlands of
Scotland', *Biul. Peryglac.* **30**, 15–34.

Ballantyne, C.K. and Eckford, J.D. (1984).
'Characteristics and evolution of two relict talus
slopes in Scotland', *Scott. Geogr. Mag.*, **100**, 20–33.

Ballantyne, C.K. and Wain-Hobson, T. (1980). 'The
Loch Lomond Advance on the Island of Rhum',
Scott. J. Geol., **16**, 1–10.

Benedict, J.B. (1976). 'Frost creep and gelifluction
features: a review', *Quaternary Res.*, **6**, 55–76.

Birks, H.J.B. (1973). *Past and present vegetation of the
Isle of Skye: a palaeocological study*, Cambridge
University Press.

Brunsden, D. (1979). 'Mass movements', in *Process in
Geomorphology* (Eds. C. Embleton and J. Thornes),
pp. 130–86, Arnold, London.

Caine, N. (1962). *The effect of frost action on low angle
scree slopes and sorted stripes in the Lake District*,
unpub. M.A. thesis, Univ. Leeds.

Caine, N. (1963a). 'Movement of low angle scree slopes
in the Lake District, Northern England', *Rev.
Géomorph. Dyn.*, **14**, 171–7.

Caine, N. (1963b). 'The origin of sorted stripes in the
Lake District, northern England', *Geogr. Annlr.*, **45**,
172–9.

Caine, N. (1972). 'The distribution of sorted patterned
ground in the English Lake District', *Rev. Géomorph.
Dyn.*, **21**, 49–56.

Caine, N. (1976). 'A uniform measure of subaerial
erosion', *Bull. Geol. Soc. Am.*, **87**, 137–40.

Chattopadhyay, G.P. (1982). *Periglacial geomorphology
of parts of the Grampian Highlands of Scotland*,
unpub. Ph.D. thesis, Univ. Edinburgh.

Chattopadhyay, G.P. (1983). 'Ploughing blocks on the
Drumochter Hills in the Grampian Highlands,
Scotland: a quantitative report', *Geogr. J.*, **149**, 211–
15.

Common, R. (1954). 'A report on the Lochaber, Appin
and Benderloch floods', *Scott. Geogr. Mag.*, **70**, 6–20.

Crampton, C.B. (1911). *The vegetation of Caithness
considered in relation to the geology*, Edinburgh.

Galloway, R.W. (1958). *Periglacial phenomena in
Scotland*, unpub. Ph.D. thesis, Univ. Edinburgh.

Galloway, R.W. (1961). 'Solifluction in Scotland', *Scott.
Geogr. Mag.*, **77**, 75–87.

Godard, A. (1958). 'Quelques observations sur le
modelé des regions volcaniques du nord-ouest de
l'Ecosse', *Scott. Geogr. Mag.*, **74**, 37–43.

Godard, A. (1959). 'Contemporary periglacial
phenomena in Western Scotland', *Scott. Geogr.
Mag.*, **75**, 55.

Godard, A. (1965). *Recherches de Géomorphologie en
Ecosse du Nord-Ouest*, Masson, Paris.

Goldthwait, R.P. (1976). 'Frost sorted patterned
ground: a review', *Quaternary Res.*, **6**, 27–35.

Goodier, R. and Ball, D.F. (1975). 'Ward Hill, Orkney:
patterned ground features and their origins', in *The
natural environment of Orkney* (Ed. R. Goodier),
pp. 47–56, Nature Conservancy Council, Edinburgh.

Gregory, J.W. (1930). 'Stone polygons beside Loch
Lomond', *Geogr. J.*, **76**, 415–18.

Halstead, C.A. (1974). 'Soil freeze-thaw recording in the
Southern Uplands of Scotland', *Weather*, **29**, 261–5.

Hay, T. (1936). 'Stone stripes', *Geogr. J.*, **87**, 47–50.

Hay, T. (1943). 'Notes on glacial erosion and stone
stripes', *Geogr. J.*, **102**, 13–20.

Hills, R.C. (1969). 'Comparative weathering of granite
and quartzite in a periglacial environment', *Geogr.
Annlr.*, **51A**, 46–7.

Hollingworth, S.E. (1934). 'Some solifluction
phenomena in the northern part of the Lake
District', *Proc. Geol. Assoc.*, **2**, 167–88.

Innes, J.L. (1982). *Debris flow activity in the Scottish
Highlands*, unpub. Ph.D. thesis, Univ. Cambridge.

Innes, J.L. (1983). 'Lichenometric dating of debris-flow
deposits in the Scottish Highlands', *Earth Surf. Proc.
Landforms*, **8**, 579–88.

Innes, J.L. (1985). 'Magnitude-frequency relations of
debris flows in northwest Europe', *Geogr. Annlr.*,
67A, 23–32.

Kelletat, D. (1970a). 'Rezente Periglazialerscheinungen
im Schottischen Hochland' *Göttinger Geogr.
Abhand.*, **51**, 67–140.

Kelletat, D. (1970b). 'Zum Problem der Verbreitung,
des Alters und der Bildingsdauer alter (inaktiver)
Periglazialerscheinungen im Scottischen Hochland',
Z. Geomorph., **14**, 510–19.

King, R.B. (1968). *Periglacial features in the Cairngorm
Mountains, Scotland*, unpub. Ph.D. thesis, Univ.
Edinburgh.

King, R.B. (1971). 'Vegetation destruction in the sub-
alpine and alpine zones of the Cairngorm
Mountains', *Scott. Geogr. Mag.*, **87**, 103–15.

King, R.B. (1972). 'Lobes in the Cairngorm Mountains,
Scotland', *Biul. Peryglac.*, **21**, 153–67.

Manley, G. (1971a). 'Scotland's semi-permanent snows',
Weather, **26**, 458–71.

Manley, G. (1971b). The mountain snows of Britain',
Weather, **26**, 192–200.

Meteorological Office (1977). *Average annual rainfall:
northern Britain*, 1:625,000 map, Ordnance Survey,
Southampton.

Miller, R., Common, R. and Galloway, R.W. (1954).
'Stone stripes and other surface features of Tinto
Hills', *Geogr. J.*, **120**, 216–19.

Mottershead, D.N. (1978). 'High altitude solifluction
and postglacial vegetation, Arkle, Sutherland', *Trans.
Bot. Soc. Edinb.*, **43**, 17–24.

Mottershead, D.N. and White, I.D. (1969). 'Some
solifluction terraces in Sutherland', *Trans. Bot. Soc.
Edinb.*, **40**, 604–20.

Nicholson, F.H. (1976). 'Patterned ground formation
and description as suggested by Low Arctic and
Subarctic examples', *Arctic and Alpine Res.*, **8**, 329–
44.

Peach, B.N., Gunn, W., Clough, C.T., Hinxman, L.W.,
Crampton, C.B. and Anderson, E.M. (1912). 'The
geology of Ben Wyvis, Carn Chuinneag, Inchbae

and the surrounding country', *Mem. Geol. Surv. Scot.*, Edinburgh.

Peach, B.N., Horne, J., Gunn, W., Clough, C.T., Hinxman, L.T., Cadell, H.M., Greenly, E., Pocock, T.I. and Crampton, C.B. (1913). 'The geology of the Fannich Mountains and the country around upper Loch Maree and Strath Broom', *Mem Geol. Surv. Scot.*, Edinburgh.

Pearsall, W.H. (1968). *Mountains and Moorlands*, Collins, Glasgow.

Pemberton, M. (1980). 'Earth hummocks at low elevation in the Vale of Eden, Cumbria', *Trans. Inst. Br. Geogr.*, New Series, **5**, 487–501.

Ragg, J.M. and Bibby, J.S. (1966). 'Frost weathering and solifluction products in southern Scotland', *Geogr. Annlr.*, **48**, 12–23.

Rapp, A. (1960). 'Recent development of mountain slopes in Karkevagge and surroundings, northern Scandinavia', *Geogr. Annlr.*, **42**, 65–200.

Ryder, R.H. and McCann, S.B. (1971). 'Periglacial phenomena in the Island of Rhum in the Inner Hebrides', *Scott. J. Geol.*, **7**, 293–303.

Shaw, R. (1977). *Periglacial features in part of the south-east Grampian Highlands of Scotland*, unpub. Ph.D. thesis, Univ. Edinburgh.

Simpson, J.B. (1932). 'Stone polygons on Scottish mountains', *Scott. Geogr. Mag*, **48**, 37.

Sissons, J.B. (1967). *The evolution of Scotland's scenery*, Oliver and Boyd, Edinburgh.

Sissons, J.B. (1976). *The geomorphology of the British Isles: Scotland*, Methuen, London.

Sissons, J.B. (1977). 'The Loch Lomond Readvance in the northern mainland of Scotland', in *Studies in the Scottish Lateglacial environment* (Eds. J.M. Gray and J.J. Lowe), pp. 45–59, Pergamon, Oxford.

Sissons, J.B. (1980). 'The Loch Lomond Advance in the Lake District, northern England', *Trans. R. Soc. Edinb: Earth Sci.*, **71**, 13–27.

Spence, D.H.N. (1957). 'Studies on the serpentine vegetation of Shetland, 1: the serpentine vegetation on Unst', *J. Ecol.*, **45**, 917–45.

Statham, I. (1973). 'Scree slope development under conditions of surface particle movement', *Trans. Inst. Br. Geogr.*, **59**, 41–53.

Statham, I. (1976a). 'A scree-slope rockfall model', *Earth Surf. Proc.*, **1**, 43–62.

Statham, I. (1976b). 'Debris flows on vegetated screes in the Black Mountain, Carmarthenshire', *Earth Surf. Proc.*, **1**, 173–80.

Statham, I. (1977). *Earth surface sediment transport*, Clarendon, Oxford.

Stuart, H.A. (1984). *A comparative study of Lateglacial and Holocene talus slopes in Snowdonia*, unpub. B.Sc. thesis, Univ. St. Andrews.

Sugden, D.E. (1971). 'The significance of periglacial activity on some Scottish mountains', *Geogr. J.*, **137**, 388–92.

Tallis, J.H. and Kershaw, K.A. (1959). 'Stability of stone polygons in North Wales', *Nature*, **183**, 485–6.

Taylor, J.A. (1976). 'Upland climates', in *The climate of the British Isles* (Eds. T.J. Chandler and S. Gregory), pp. 264–87, Longman, London.

Thorp, R.W. (1981). 'A trimline method for defining the upper limit of Loch Lomond Advance glaciers: examples from the Loch Leven and Glencoe areas', *Scott. J. Geol.*, **17**, 49–64.

Tufnell, L. (1969). 'The range of periglacial phenomena in northern England', *Biul. Peryglac.*, **19**, 291–323.

Tufnell, L. (1971). 'Erosion by snow patches in the north Pennines', *Weather*, **26**, 492–8.

Tufnell, L. (1972). 'Ploughing blocks with special reference to north-west England', *Biul. Peryglac.*, **21**, 237–70.

Tufnell, L. (1975). 'Hummocky microrelief in the Moor House area of the northern Pennines, England', *Biul. Peryglac.*, **24**, 353–68.

Tufnell, L. (1976). 'Ploughing block movements on the Moor House Reserve (England), 1965–75', *Biul. Peryglac.*, **26**, 313–17.

Vincent, P.J. and Lee, M.P. (1982). 'Snow patches on Farleton Fell, South-East Cumbria', *Geogr. J.*, **148**, 337–42.

Warburton, J. (1985). 'Contemporary patterned ground (sorted stripes) in the Lake District' in *Field Guide to the periglacial landforms of northern England*, (Ed. J. Boardman), pp. 54–62, Quaternary Research Association, Cambridge.

Ward, J.C. (1876). 'The geology of the northern part of the English Lake District', *Mem. Geol. Surv.*, London.

Ward, R.G.W. (1984). 'Avalanche prediction in Scotland: 1. a survey of avalanche activity', *Applied Geog.*, **4**, 91–108.

Washburn, A.L. (1979). *Geocryology: a survey of periglacial processes and environments*, Arnold, London.

Worsley, P. (1977). 'Periglaciation' in *British Quaternary Studies: recent advances* (Ed. F.W. Shotton), pp. 205–19, Clarendon, Oxford.

(b) Weathering and soils

10 · Frost weathered mantles on the Chalk

R.B.G. WILLIAMS

Abstract

Chalk in Britain is often weathered near the surface into thin, platy fragments and chalk 'paste' that contrast with the unweathered cubical or rectangular joint blocks beneath. Although much of the weathering seems to be due to periglacial frost action, it is often very different in character from the shattering that is produced when chalk samples are experimentally frost weathered in the laboratory. There is therefore conflict between field and laboratory evidence.

History of investigations

Geologists in the nineteenth century made few studies of rock weathering (Tinkler, 1985), and these were mainly concerned with chemical processes, especially limestone solution. One of the earliest accounts of mechanical weathering was provided by De la Beche (1835). In an introductory field manual for geologists, he pointed out that limestones and other rocks in Britain are often broken up near the surface. In a sketch section, he showed unweathered, jointed bedrock passing upwards into a rubble of angular rock fragments covered by a thin soil. He noted that the fragments generally become smaller and more disturbed towards the surface.

De la Beche's observations had little immediate impact. Even by the end of the century, little progress had been made in studying the mechanical weathering of rock outcrops. Whitaker (1889, p. 75) noted that the Upper Chalk is weathered into "thin irregular platy fragments, which strongly contrast with the dull-white nodular or lumpy chalk beneath", but he made no detailed investigation. Most writers considered that frost contributed to the mechanical weathering of Chalk (see, for example, Whitaker 1867 and Woodward 1887), but they seemed to regard it as a contemporary, rather than a periglacial phenomenon, which was strange because they had no difficulty accepting a periglacial origin for Coombe Rock and other valley infills composed of transported weathered debris. In a now classic paper, Reid (1887) argued that frosts in winter during the Glacial Period broke up the surface layers of the Chalk. Summer rains then washed the debris into the valleys,

depositing it as Coombe Rock. Although Reid was not explicit, he seems to have thought of the frost as attacking only the surface of the ground, and to have imagined that the debris was removed as fast as it was shaved from the bedrock. Neither he nor his supporters mentioned the existence of a mantle of rubbly Chalk beneath the present soil; still less did they suggest that it might be the result of periglacial frost shattering.

Woodward (1912) went much further than his contemporaries in emphasising that mechanically weathered mantles were widely developed on limestones and other rocks. In his book, *The Geology of Soils and Substrata*, he included a striking photograph of a rubbly surface layer on Portland Stone in Dorset, and gave descriptions for the Chalk, Oolite, and Liassic limestone, but he did not say if the weathering was a fossil feature or still developing.

The next important advance was in 1936 when Bull published a short paper on the geomorphology of the South Downs in which he pointed out that the Chalk in a few localities is broken to great depths below the surface. As an example, he cited the major dry valley that is cut by the sea cliffs at Birling Gap, near Eastbourne. The Chalk is very deeply weathered under the valley floor, but is only shallowly affected beneath the valley sides. Bull suggested that the deep weathering was the work of periglacial frosts. In 1940 he went on to suggest that periglacial frosts also produced the shallow weathering mantles that are common on the Chalk. He did not explain why the weathering should be shallow in one place but deep in another.

It was a tragedy for British geomorphology that

most of Bull's contemporaries were obsessed with the study of erosion surfaces and were not greatly interested in geomorphological processes. Even those who stressed the importance of past periglaciation were often unaware of the widespread existence of mechanically weathered mantles on Chalk and other limestones. For example, in his *Geology of Oxford* (1947), Arkell stressed that there had been much periglacial frost shattering of bedrock, but he suggested that the debris had been quickly deposited in the valleys by solifluction and other processes. He seems not to have grasped that the shattered bedrock might still be preserved *in situ* in many places.

It was not until the 1950's that Bull's ideas began to permeate mainstream British geomorphology. They received important support from Pinchemel (1954) who identified frost-shattered Chalk at sites in southern England and northern France. Further insight was provided by Tricart (1956). The first British geomorphological textbook to emphasise the importance of mechanical weathering on Chalk and other rocks was Dury's influential *The Face of the Earth* (1959). Since the 1950's geomorphologists have taken more note of weathering mantles on British limestones, but published descriptions have tended to be brief, and the origin of the mantles has

received surprisingly little discussion. Engineering geologists have carried out much more detailed research than geomorphologists, but have concentrated on geotechnical matters, particularly the strength properties of the weathered mantles (Meigh and Early, 1957; Higginbottom, 1965; Ward *et al.*, 1968; Higginbottom and Fookes, 1970).

Description of the weathering

Unweathered Chalk is usually traversed by three sets of joints set approximately at right angles to each other. Where the Chalk is horizontal or only gently dipping, one set of joints follows the bedding planes while the other two sets intersect the bedding planes vertically or near vertically. The spacing of the vertical joints varies considerably, but generally averages between 50 and 250 mm, although much wider spacing occurs at certain horizons, for instance in the Melbourn Rock in southern Cambridgeshire. Although most of the vertical joints are quite short and often curved, semi-planar master joints may cut through a considerable number of beds and extend laterally for hundreds of metres. It is these master joints that control the sculpture of many sea cliffs, for example at Flamborough Head in Yorkshire and at the Seven Sisters in Sussex.

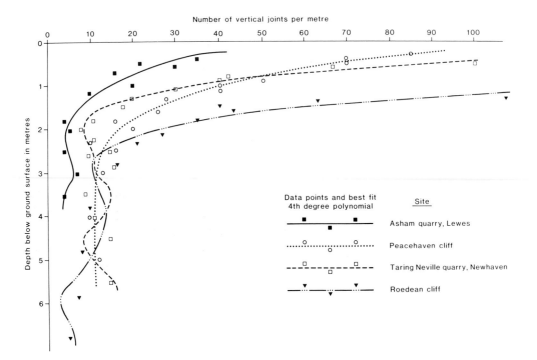

Figure 10.1. Variation of joint spacing with depth: four sites on the chalk in East Sussex.

In the weathered mantle, the joints are generally five to ten times more closely spaced than in the unweathered bedrock (Figure 10.1). Most of the new joints created by the weathering lie parallel to the ground surface, but smaller numbers are developed normal to the ground surface, both at right angles and parallel to the line of slope. In many exposures, the joints paralleling the ground surface outnumber other types of joints by a factor of two to one.

In the lower part of the weathered mantle, the new joints are relatively tight, some forming mere hair-line cracks. The joints divide up the rock into roughly cubical or rectangular blocks. Nearer the surface, the joints are more open and separate the rock into tabular or platy fragments that parallel the ground surface and fit only loosely together. The fragments become smaller in an upwards direction, and tend to be more rounded. Their porosity is no greater than that of the unweathered Chalk. It seems that mechanical weathering was concentrated along existing joints and large internal flaws but did not affect the fabric of the remainder of the rock.

Immediately below the surface soil, the Chalk is sometimes highly pulverised. Isolated, rounded fragments are embedded in a powdery groundmass, in which no bedding or jointing can be distinguished. This pulverised material has been called 'putty chalk,' (Meigh and Early, 1957, Higginbottom, 1965), and 'Grade V, mélange chalk' (Ward *et al.*, 1968). In this upper zone the Chalk has evidently succumbed to a process of disaggregation or remoulding in place of, or in addition to, brittle fracturing.

At many places there is a relatively rapid transition between the mantle and the unweathered bedrock (for an excellent photograph see Higginbottom and Fookes, 1970), but sometimes the transition is more gradual and it is not possible to define the base of the mantle with much precision. In eastern and southern England, the combined thickness of the mantle and the surface soil is typically about 1 to 2.5 m.

The weathered mantle can be difficult to identify where the Chalk is heavily jointed as a result of diagenetic or tectonic stresses. The problem is that the new joints created by the weathering are not clearly distinguishable from the old ones.

The weathered mantle can be identified with

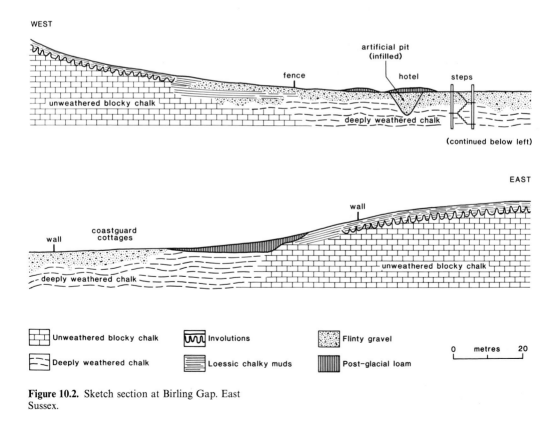

Figure 10.2. Sketch section at Birling Gap. East Sussex.

greatest confidence at sites where (1) the beds of Chalk were originally only sparsely jointed, (2) the exposure is long and deep, and (3) the ground slope cuts across the bedding so that the mantle is developed on a succession of beds. The frost resistance of the Chalk (Williams, 1980) is also seemingly important. Examination of Chalk outcrops in Sussex suggests that the weathering is most clearly developed on the hardest varieties of Chalk, notably the *Micraster* Chalk, and is relatively inconspicuous on weak Chalks, such as those of the *Marsupites* and *Offaster* fossil zones.

The mantle is best developed on gentle slopes and flat ground. It is absent from many steep slopes on the escarpments, although it is occasionally found even where the angle reaches 25 or 30 degrees. On dip slopes, it can often be traced more or less continuously over very large areas. It is well developed, for example, at the top of the sea-cliffs between Brighton and Eastbourne. The total length of the cliffs, excluding areas of Tertiary cover, is about 22 km, and the mantle is present over at least 80% of this distance. It is found even on the steep sides of the asymmetrical valleys of the Seven Sisters.

Deep mechanical weathering on the Chalk is well developed only beneath the floors of the larger dry valleys. The case of Birling Gap has already been mentioned (Figure 10.2). The Chalk beneath the valley sides is massive and unweathered, except next to the surface where there is a shallow weathering mantle with conspicuous involutions. Flinty gravels of presumed periglacial origin underlie the floor of the valley. The chalk beneath this infill is shattered to depths of 10 m or more. Large lumps of Chalk are embedded in a pasty groundmass. The material is very unlike that found in the normal, shallow mantle and resembles Coombe Rock, but is more or less *in situ*. The flint bands in the unweathered, massive Chalk on either side of the valley can be traced horizontally into the weathered zone below the valley floor. The bands first become wavy, and then are almost completely disrupted, the individual flints lying scattered within the weathered Chalk. The junction of the flinty gravels and the weathered Chalk is very uneven, possibly because of frost heaving.

Similar deep weathering is found beneath some of the other large dry valleys in the South Downs, for example at Rottingdean and Saltdean. The deep weathering is absent or only feebly developed under the shallower dry valleys, such as those seen in cross-section in the sea cliff at the Seven Sisters. Outside Sussex, large-scale deep weathering has

been identified in Yorkshire (Lewin, 1969), Kent and the Isle of Wight.

Origin of the weathering

The shallow mechanically weathered mantles on the Chalk are often assumed to be due to frost action during periglacial periods. However, some writers, while agreeing that frost is the prime agent, suggest that other processes of weathering have contributed to the disintegration (see, for example, Dury, 1959 and Williams, 1980). Rodda *et al.* (1976) have even suggested that some of the jointing is not a weathering phenomenon in the strict sense, but is caused by pressure release accompanying the removal of overlying rocks by erosion. Since there has been little previous discussion, it is important to review the evidence for the frost theory:

(1) Mechanically weathered mantles are overlain by periglacial deposits in many places. As Kerney (1964) has shown, shattered Chalk is often found beneath soliflucted chalk muds and rubbles deposited during the Late Glacial. It is also found under many earlier solifluctional deposits. Shattered Chalk underlies loess at Pegwell Bay, Kent (Kerney, 1964), and at other sites in south east England. In East Anglia, coversands of periglacial origin are frequently found resting on mechanically weathered Chalk.

These facts suggest that much of the weathering occurred before periglacial conditions ended.

(2) Patterned ground structures of presumed periglacial origin are often found within the weathered mantle. For example, wind-blown sand, soliflucted muds and other superficial deposits frequently descend in pockets into the weathered Chalk, forming festoons or involutions. In eastern England it is common to find large-scale polygons and stripes within the weathered mantle (Williams, 1973). When the patterned ground developed, the weathered fragments were moved around within the mantle, often developing a distinct vertical orientation, as if affected by frost heaving. The frosts that are presumed to have created the patterned ground may also have caused the weathering of the mantle, although this cannot be regarded as proven.

(3) The weathered mantle is often overlain by Post-glacial hillwashes. Furthermore, it is absent from slopes formed during the Post-glacial, or is at best only feebly developed. In the Ouse and Cuckmere valleys in Sussex, for instance, river cliffs that were formed at some time during the Post-glacial and are now degraded have no mechanically weathered mantle. The mantle is well developed,

however, on other slopes in the valleys that were formed in Late glacial or earlier times.

This pattern of distribution is consistent with a periglacial origin for the mantle. It suggests that contemporary mechanical weathering beneath the surface soil is slow or non-existent.

(4) Field observations and laboratory experiments have established that most types of chalk are very vulnerable to frost action (Williams, 1980; Lautridou *et al.*, 1986). Cycles of freezing and thawing quickly break up all but the hardest chalks. Under periglacial conditions, seasonal frost weathering could have been intense and have extended to a depth equal to that of the mantle. Contemporary frosts, even in the severest winters, scarcely penetrate more than a metre into the Chalk (Williams, 1980). They may have caused some fragmentation in the upper part of the mantle, but they cannot have created the fragmentation lower down.

(5) The weathering that created the mantle was successful not only in opening existing joints but also in creating large numbers of new joints. Frost would seem to be the only weathering process capable of such a major transformation. Repeated wetting and drying can crack impure chalks with more than 2% insoluble residue, but most chalks are very pure and are unaffected by moisture changes. Plant roots are effective at wedging open existing joints, but they are unlikely to be capable of creating new joints, except perhaps in the softest chalks. Infiltrating water could be expected to enlarge unopened joints by washing out debris and gradually dissolving the walls. However, there is no evidence that any new joints have been formed by water flow. As already mentioned, many joints in the mantle are developed parallel to the ground surface. If infiltrating water had caused the mantle, it would have selectively enlarged vertical or near vertical joints as it descended to the water-table.

(6) The theory that many of the joints are due to pressure release fails to stand up to close scrutiny. It is true that one set of joints in the mantle parallels the ground surface and becomes more widely spaced with depth, which is a characteristic of stress relief joints. Most authorities, however, consider that stress relief joints are confined to igneous and metamorphic rocks that have been deeply buried, such as granite, gneiss or marble (Sparks, 1971). Unlike Chalk, many of these rocks expand during quarrying, sometimes explosively. The arching up of rock shells, which is indicative of stress release, has not been observed in Chalk. Furthermore, if stress relief had been important, one would expect

the weathered mantle to be relatively poorly developed on high ground where the removal of overburden has been least, but in fact it is often on high ground that the mantle is most conspicuous. Another difficulty with the theory is that it does not explain why the mantle is so highly fragmented but generally very shallow. Where stress relief joints have developed in granites or similar rocks they are much more widely spaced and extend to considerably greater depths below the surface.

This brief review has shown that the frost theory is well supported by the evidence, and that the alternative theories would seem at best to provide only a partial explanation for the weathering. Although the evidence is only circumstantial, the presumption must be that the mantle mainly results from periglacial frost action. The widespread preservation of the mantle and its frequent preservation under Late Glacial deposits suggests that it mostly developed towards the end of the Devensian and that the Chalk land surface has been little modified in Post-glacial times. During earlier periglacial episodes, mantles were doubtless created, but have been largely eroded away.

The general shallowness of the mantle would seem to indicate that it was formed by seasonal freezing and thawing, possibly in an active layer over permafrost. The presence of an active layer has already been suggested as a result of an examination of the involutions and other structures (Williams, 1975). The often abrupt transition between the mantle and the underlying rock could be interpreted as marking the base of a former active layer. Nevertheless, it would be unwise to assume that the mantle formed exclusively in the presence of permafrost. During the periglacial periods, there may well have been frequent occasions when the temperatures were just low enough to permit frost weathering but too high to allow the formation of permafrost.

The weathering of the bedrock under larger dry valleys extends to depths of 20 m or more, far beyond the probable limits of seasonal freezing and thawing in periglacial times. The most likely explanation is that the weathering developed while permafrost formed (Lewin, 1969). The Chalk beneath the major valleys was probably much wetter than elsewhere, and therefore more susceptible to frost action. At drier sites, the permafrost may have developed without causing much damage, leaving the active layer as the main target of weathering.

The high transmissibility of the Chalk beneath major valleys (Ineson, 1962) may be caused by the deep frost weathering, which has created a multiplicity of joints that facilitate the flow of water.

Deficiencies of laboratory experiments

Although laboratory experiments demonstrate that most chalks are highly susceptible to frost weathering, they yield debris that is generally of finer calibre then that of the mantle. The softest chalks are reduced to a paste or wet slurry after a single cycle of freezing and thawing. The harder chalks weather more slowly, releasing small quantities of pulverised material with each cycle. Angular fragments of intact chalk are produced somewhat sparingly, and usually disintegrate rapidly during the following cycles. All this contrasts with the weathering of the mantle which has left large numbers of chalk fragments and usually only a small quantity of fines. The fragments can be assumed to be the end-product of innumerable cycles of freezing and thawing, rather than just a transient stage at the start of weathering.

The results of the laboratory experiments are undeniably embarassing. At first sight, they might appear to undermine the theory that frosts have created the mantle. It is far more likely, however, that the fault lies with the experiments rather than with the theory.

One major limitation of the experiments is that they often use very artificial temperature cycles. The so-called 'Siberian' cycle, for instance, has long been a favourite with investigators, yet it subjects the rock specimens in a few days to a temperature range equalling the annual cycle of a continental Arctic area. The rates of freezing are almost certainly more rapid than those that occurred in Britain during the periglacial periods.

If a porous rock is wetted and then slowly frozen, large ice crystals can develop in a small number of widely scattered pores. The crystals feed on the pore water and may become big enough to enlarge the pores and cause fracturing of the rock. Quick freezing, by contrast, promotes the development of myriads of small crystals in large numbers of pores. A rock that can be destroyed by slow freezing may be able to withstand quick freezing because none of the small crystals may be capable of exerting enough pressure to open up the pores. With the softer varieties of Chalk, however, quick freezing generally proves fatal. The small ice crystals have enough strength to rupture large numbers of pores simultaneously, effectively pulverising the rock. It is this large-scale pore bursting which is perhaps a rather unrealistic feature of many laboratory experiments. Had slow freezing been used, the result

might have been the production of coarse debris rather than general collapse.

In many freezing experiments the rock specimens are kept submerged in water-filled containers to ensure that they remain reasonably saturated from cycle to cycle. This procedure is somewhat extreme and artificial. Partly immersing the specimens might produce coarser debris, more akin to that found in the weathered mantle.

The small size of the rock specimens selected for laboratory experimentation is another serious limitation. No one should expect small intact specimens to weather in the same way as large outcrops divided up by pre-existing joints and bedding planes. The scale of the laboratory experiments helps ensure that the specimens will not weather in the same coarse manner as an outcrop in the field.

The joints in the mantle that parallel the ground surface may well result from ice lens formation. Lenses up to 25 mm thick develop in Chalk in hard winters. Like the joints, they tend to follow the ground surface and become more widely spaced with depth. Unfortunately, in laboratory experiments it is very difficult to create similar systems of ice lenses. One would need to experiment with massive blocks of Chalk, freezing them slowly from the top downwards to allow the pore water time to migrate upwards towards the freezing front.

Frost weathering in the field in present cold winters produces a very different style of debris compared with laboratory experiments. Vertical faces of Chalk quarries often undergo surface spalling. Sheets, sometimes only a few millimetres thick and up to 0.1 square metres in surface area, become detached and fall to the ground, generally disintegrating on impact. Large blocks lying on quarry floors also tend to weather by spalling, but smaller blocks, more in contact with the ground and hence generally wetter, tend to crack into small pieces. The fragmentation resembles that found in the upper part of the weathered mantles. Fines are produced in quantity only in very wet places, for example around rainwater pools on the quarry floors.

Small lumps of frozen chalk picked up in winter on quarry floors or on the surface of ploughed fields are often found to be sheathed in ice that has been extruded from the pores. The centres of the lumps are generally quite dry. On thawing, the outer layers of the lumps tend to slough off, leaving the centres intact. It is possible that this freeze-dry weathering provides a model for the peculiar shattering found below the deeper dry valleys. As permafrost spread downwards into the Chalk, it may have tended to penetrate most rapidly along the joints and bedding planes, drawing water from the centres of the joint blocks, so enabling them to survive as intact lumps. Laboratory experiments are planned that will try to simulate this freeze-dry process.

Acknowledgement
The author is greatly indebted to Dr R.N. Mortimore for many helpful comments on a first draft of this paper.

References
Arkell, W.J. (1947). *The Geology of Oxford*, Oxford University Press, Oxford.

Bull, A.J. (1936). 'Studies in the geomorphology of the South Downs', *Proc. Geol. Ass.*, **47**, 99–129.

Bull, A.J. (1940). 'Cold conditions and land forms in the South Downs', *Proc. Geol. Ass.*, **51**, 63–71.

De la Beche, H.T. (1835). *How to Observe: Geology*, Knight, London.

Dury, G.H. (1959). *The Face of the Earth*, Penguin, Middlesex.

Higginbottom, I.E. (1965). 'The engineering geology of Chalk' in 'Chalk in Earthworks and Foundations', *Proc. Symp. Instn. Civ. Engrs. London* (1966), 1–14.

Higginbottom, I.E. and Fookes, P.G. (1970). 'Engineering aspects of periglacial features in Britain', *Q. Jl. Engrg. Geol.*, **3**, 85–117.

Ineson, J. (1962). 'A hydrogeological study of the permeability of the Chalk', *J. Inst. Water Eng.*, **16**, 449–63.

Kerney, P. (1964). 'Late-Glacial deposits on the Chalk of South-East England', *Phil. Trans. Roy Soc.*, B **246**, 203–54.

Lautridou, J.P., Letavernier, G., Linde, K., Etlicher, B. and Ozouf, J.C. (1986). 'Porosity and frost susceptibility of flints and chalk', in *The Scientific Study of Flint and Chert* (Ed. G. Sieveking), Cambridge University Press, Cambridge.

Lewin, J. (1969). 'The formation of Chalk dry valleys: The Stonehill Valley, Dorset', *Biul. Peryglacjalny*, **19**, 345–50.

Meigh, A.C. and Early, K.R. (1957). 'Some physical and engineering properties of Chalk', *Proc. Fourth Int. Conf. Soil Mech.*, **1**, 68–73.

Pinchemel, P. (1954). *Les Plaines de Craie du Nord-Ouest du bassin Parisien et du Sud-Est du bassin de Londres et leur bordures: Étude de Géomorphologie*, Colin, Paris.

Reid, C. (1887). 'On the origin of dry valleys and of Coombe Rock', *Q.J. Geol. Soc.*, **43**, 364–373.

Rodda, J.C., Downing, R.A., and Law, F.M. (1976). *Systematic Hydrology*, Newnes-Butterworths, London.

Sparks, B.W. (1971). *Rocks and Relief*, Longmans, London.

Tinkler, K.J. (1985). *A Short History of Geomorphology*, Croom Helm, London.

Tricart, J. (1956). 'Étude expérimentale du problème de la gélivation', *Biul. Peryglacjalny*, **4**, 282–318.

Ward, W.H., Burland, J.B. and Gallois, R.W. (1968). 'Geotechnical assessment of a site at Mundford, Norfolk, for a large proton accelerator, *Géotechnique*, **18**, 399–431.

Whitaker, W. (1867). 'On subaerial denudation, and on cliffs and escarpments of the Chalk and the Lower Tertiary Beds', *Geol. Mag.*, **4**, 447–83.

Whitaker, W. (1889). *The Geology of London, and of part of the Thames Valley*, Memoirs of the Geological Survey, H.M.S.O., London.

Williams, R.B.G. (1973). 'Frost and the works of Man', *Antiquity*, **47**, 19–31.

Williams, R.B.G. (1975). 'The British climate during the Last Glaciation: an interpretation based on periglacial phenomena' in *Ice Ages: Ancient and Modern* (Eds. A.E. Wright and F. Moseley), pp. 95–120, *Geol. J. Sp. Issue 6*.

Williams, R.B.G (1980). 'The weathering and erosion of Chalk under periglacial conditions', in *The Shaping of Southern England* (Ed. D.K.C. Jones), pp. 225–48, Academic Press, London.

Woodward, H.B. (1887). *The Geology of England and Wales* (2nd Edition) Philip, London.

Woodward, H.B. (1912). *'The Geology of Soils and Substrata'*, Arnold, London.

11· Frost and salt weathering as periglacial processes: the results and implications of some laboratory experiments

L.C. JERWOOD, D.A. ROBINSON AND R.B.G. WILLIAMS

Abstract

Cubes of chalk from the south of England have been wetted with distilled water or salt solutions and subjected to simulated frost weathering under three different freeze–thaw regimes. Monitoring has shown that internal rock temperatures lag behind air temperatures by a varying but often considerable amount. Even under intense freezing regimes there are time delays of several hours before the centres of cubes are frozen. Delays under milder regimes may be such that cubes remain below 0 °C throughout successive cycles. The temperatures at which salt solutions crystallise and freeze depend on their type and concentration, and under some freeze–thaw regimes salts increase the time lag. Frost damage is likely to be at a maximum at the eutectic temperature when solidification is complete. The minimum temperature attained by a rock during freezing in a salt solution may therefore be of considerable importance in determining the degree of weathering.

Introduction

In recent years many laboratory experiments have investigated the weathering of rocks by frost. Much of the research has focused on the effects of different temperature cycles on the rate of rock breakdown (see, for example, Potts, 1970; Lautridou and Ozouf, 1978; Williams, 1980). The minimum temperature reached during the cycles, and the rate of freezing, have been shown to be important in controlling the amount of debris produced. It has also been shown that the presence of salts such as mirabilite ($NA_2SO_4.10H_2O$), thenardite (Na_2SO_4) and halite (NaCl), which are frequently encountered in dry periglacial regions, greatly affects the susceptibility of rocks to frost weathering (Goudie, 1974; Williams and Robinson, 1981; McGreevy, 1982).

In most experiments it is the air temperatures in the freezing apparatus which are controlled and recorded. There are good theoretical reasons for believing that rock temperatures lag far behind air temperatures, particularly while the rocks are actually freezing and thawing. This has been demonstrated in the laboratory by a few measurements of internal rock temperatures made during freezing experiments by Lautridou and Ozouf (1978). However, the time lags which occur will be different for different temperature cycles and will also depend upon the efficiency of the freezing cabinet used. The present paper describes some experiments to study the lag effects that occur inside rocks during three contrasting temperature cycles. Data are presented on the temperature regimes in samples of dry rock and samples fully or partly immersed in distilled water or salt solution. Data on rates of rock breakdown are not presented.

Equipment and materials

The rock selected for the experiments was freshly quarried *Micraster* Chalk from Upper Beeding Cement Works, Shoreham, Sussex. This chalk, which is one of the most resistant to frost weathering (Williams, 1980), has a dry density of about $1710 \, kg \, m^{-3}$ and a porosity of around 32 per cent.

Large joint blocks were cut into 76 mm (3 inch) cubes, and 5 mm diameter holes were drilled from the tops of the cubes to the centres. Each cube was oven-dried, then put into a separate plastic box measuring 130 mm deep and 100 mm square. A thermistor (EU-type) was placed in the hole in each cube and sealed in with pulverised chalk. Some of the cubes were kept completely dry; the others were allowed to stand in water or a salt solution for over 36 hours, either fully immersed, or partly immersed to a depth of 20 mm with the top 56 mm exposed. The boxes containing the fully immersed cubes were insulated at the sides and base by a 55 mm layer of expanded polystyrene to try to ensure that freezing took place from the top downwards. Half of the boxes holding the dry cubes were insulated in the same way; the other half and the boxes for the partly immersed cubes were insulated solely at the base by a 25 mm layer of polystyrene. After an initial run of experiments it was found necessary to place polythene caps on the boxes containing salt solutions to avoid cross-contamination of salts due to vapour pressure differences.

A Fisons Climatic Cabinet (Type FE 1000H/ MU/R40 – IND LH FRIDGE) was used for the experiments, enabling accurate control of air temperatures to within 0.5 °C. For the first experiments the temperatures were recorded manually at one hour intervals by connecting each thermistor in turn to an Edale Digital Thermometer (Type D515). Later, the temperatures were recorded automatically at 15 minute intervals by connecting the thermistors to two different multi-channel loggers attached to a BBC B microcomputer. The air temperature read-out on the Cabinet agreed with Cabinet air temperatures recorded by the thermistors.

Temperature cycles

Three cycles were used to investigate temperature lags. Cycle A lasted 83 hours. For the first 12 hours the air temperature was lowered from + 15 °C to − 40 °C at a uniform rate of 4.58 °C an hour. It was maintained at − 40 °C for 34 hours, then raised back to + 15 °C, at 5.00 °C an hour, for 8 hours until 0 °C was reached and thereafter at 2.14 °C an hour. For the remaining 22 hours of the cycle the temperature was held at + 15 °C.

Cycle B lasted 72 hours. During the first 12 hours the air temperature was lowered from + 15 °C to − 25 °C at a uniform rate of 3.33 °C an hour. It was held for 24 hours at − 25 °C, and then raised at a steady 3.33 °C an hour for 12 hours until it was back to + 15 °C. During the remaining 24 hours the temperature was held at + 15 °C.

Cycle C was of 24 hours duration. The air temperature was held at + 7 °C for 6 hours before being lowered at a uniform rate of 2.33 °C an hour over 6 hours to a minimum of − 7 °C. This minimum was then maintained for 6 hours before the temperature was raised at a uniform 2.33 °C an hour back to + 7 °C.

Cycles A and B were chosen as modifications of the four day + 15 °C to − 30 °C 'Siberian cycle' used by Tricart (1956), Potts (1970) and others to simulate annual temperature changes in continental Arctic areas. The mean temperature of the coldest month is around − 40 °C in northern Siberia and about − 25 °C in subarctic areas of southern Siberia. It should be noted, however, that under natural conditions the temperature does not change as violently as in Cycles A and B.

Cycle C was designed to approximate to the one day + 7 °C to − 6 °C 'Icelandic cycle' introduced by Tricart to model diurnal temperature changes in maritime Arctic areas.

Lautridou and Ozouf (1982) have used a 2.5 day + 18 °C to − 28 °C cycle to simulate continental Arctic temperatures. This roughly resembles Cycle B, except for the shorter freezing period, about 26 hours as against 39. They have also used a one day cycle from + 18 °C to − 8 °C to replicate maritime Arctic temperatures. This differs from Cycle C in its much higher maximum temperature.

Results of the experiments

1. Lag effects with dry rocks

The dotted lines in Figures 11.1 to 11.6 record the average temperatures of the centres of the dry cubes during Cycles A, B and C. The air temperatures are shown as solid lines.

When dry rocks are cooled, two distinct lag effects can be distinguished. The first, which will be called the *alpha component*, becomes apparent immediately the air temperatures are lowered. At first, the rock temperatures lag increasingly behind the air temperatures, but in 1 to 3 hours the lags assume a constant value. This value depends on the mass of the rock samples, their thermal properties (specific heat and conductivity), the insulating effect of the surrounding containers (if any), and the rate of circulation of air within the freezing apparatus. The Fisons Climatic Cabinet has a forced draught and is able to cool rock samples faster than an ordinary deep freeze that lacks a circulatory fan or ventilation system. The Cabinet simulates a moving air environment rather than a still air environment.

The second component of lag will be called the *omega component*. It arises only after the air temperatures have reached the minimum level. As the temperature within the rock samples approaches this minimum, the rate of fall becomes steadily less in accordance with Newton's Law of Cooling, which states that the rate of loss of heat from a hot body is proportional to the temperature difference

Table 11.1 *Estimated values (in hours), of Alpha, Beta and Omega for rocks in the dry state and immersed in water. (All figures are means of 4 to 8 different cubes.)*

| | Cycle A Dry | | | | Cycle B Dry | | | | Cycle A Distilled Water | | | | Cycle B Distilled Water | | | |
| | Fully insulated | | Partly insulated | | Fully insulated | | Partly insulated | | Fully immersed | | Partly immersed | | Fully immersed | | Partly immersed | |
	Cooling	Warming	Cooling	Warming	Cooling	Warming	Cooling	Warming	Cooling	Warming	Cooling	Warming	Cooling	Warming	Cooling	Warming
Alpha	1.63	2.50	1.00	2.00	1.75	2.00	1.13	1.23	3.79	4.14	0.84	1.84	4.75	3.63	0.84	2.38
Beta	—	—	—	—	—	—	—	—	4.25	14.83	3.25	6.44	8.13	14.11	3.94	4.75
Omega	2.75	2.25	2.25	0.63	1.25	1.25	0.50	0.77	4.32	7.71	1.84	4.44	6.00	7.38	1.18	2.94

Table 11.2 *Estimated values (in hours), of Alpha, Beta and Omega for rocks immersed in salt solutions. (All figures are means of 4 to 8 different cubes.)*

| | Cycle A Sodium Chloride (1 molar) | | | | Cycle B Sodium Chloride (1 molar) | | | | Cycle A Sodium Sulphate (1 molar) | | | | Cycle B Sodium Sulphate (1 molar) | | | |
| | Fully immersed | | Partly immersed | | Fully immersed | | Partly immersed | | Fully immersed | | Partly immersed | | Fully immersed | | Partly immersed | |
	Cooling	Warming	Cooling	Warming	Cooling	Warming	Cooling	Warming	Cooling	Warming	Cooling	Warming	Cooling	Warming	Cooling	Warming
Alpha	3.70	2.45	1.88	1.44	3.83	—	1.94	1.25	3.80	4.70	0.84	2.13	4.75	3.67	0.84	1.69
Beta-1	4.63	8.67	2.25	2.88	4.83	12.83	1.38	2.13	1.70	—	0.79	—	1.42	—	1.22	—
Beta-2	1.17	1.88	0.75	1.13	0.00	4.00	1.88	1.25	3.40	11.80	2.62	4.50	7.08	16.17	4.00	4.19
Omega	3.38	9.92	2.51	3.56	14.17	8.67	2.86	1.38	6.00	8.40	1.44	5.31	6.58	6.50	0.81	2.60

between the body and the surrounding air. This reduction in the rate of rock temperature fall results in an increase in time lag. The size of the omega component at any given temperature can be calculated by subtracting the estimated alpha component from the total time lag. The component reaches its maximum value as the rock temperatures attain the minimum air temperature, or come so close that there is no longer any measurable difference.

During the second half of each temperature cycle, the two components of lag reappear. The alpha component develops as soon as the air temperatures are raised above the minimum. As the rock temperatures approach the maximum air temperature, the omega component is added.

Estimated values of alpha and omega for Cycles A and B are shown in Table 11.1. The values of alpha are somewhat greater during heating than during cooling. This may be because the rocks chill the air in the boxes while they are heating and the heavier chilled air is only slowly dissipated from within the boxes despite the forced draught. During cooling, the warm air in contact with the rocks will tend to rise and be displaced by colder air from the Cabinet.

2. Lag effects with distilled water
The temperatures recorded during Cycle A at the centres of the cubes that were partly or fully immersed in water are plotted as lines of dots and dashes in Figures 11.1 and 11.2. During both cooling and heating, the rock temperatures lag most strongly behind the air temperatures at about $-0.5\,°C$ when the rock temperature curves flatten to form a bench or plateau whilst the air tempera-

tures continue to change at the planned rate. The fully immersed cubes undergo a more prolonged temperature arrest than the partly immersed ones because they contain a greater volume of water (about 630 ml as against about 200 ml). The arrest within both sets of cubes is longer during thawing than during freezing.

Alpha and omega components can be distinguished as with dry rock. The water and ice in the rock increase the thermal conductivity, which reduces the alpha component, but they also have a larger specific heat than air and this greatly increases the alpha component. The net result is that alpha is appreciably larger for the fully immersed cubes than for the partly immersed and dry cubes.

During freezing, the alpha component is augmented by a further lag effect, which will be referred to as the *beta component*. It is caused by the release of latent heat $(83\,cal\,gm^{-1})$ during the phase change of water to ice. Normally this would occur at $0\,°C$, but there is a slight supercooling effect probably due to the smallness of the pores within the rock. The initial size of the beta component, as measured by the width of the bench on the rock temperature curve, is controlled by both the volume of water present and the efficiency of the freezing apparatus. The beta component for an unventilated rock sample in still air will be much greater than for a sample in a forced draught.

Once freezing is complete or near complete, the rock temperatures start falling again. The partly immersed cubes cool relatively quickly and the beta component is steadily reduced until eventually little more than the alpha component remains. In contrast, the fully immersed cubes cool relatively slowly because of their greater insulation and larger

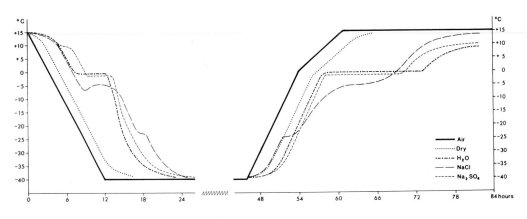

Figure 11.1. Rock temperature curves – cycle A – fully immersed cubes.

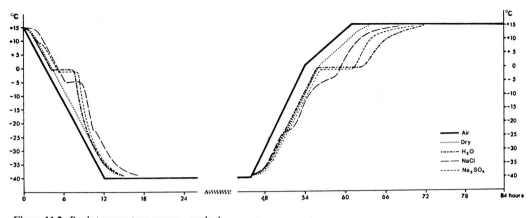

Figure 11.2. Rock temperature curves – cycle A – partly immersed cubes.

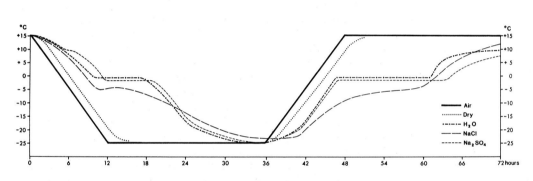

Figure 11.3. Rock temperature curves – cycle B – fully immersed cubes.

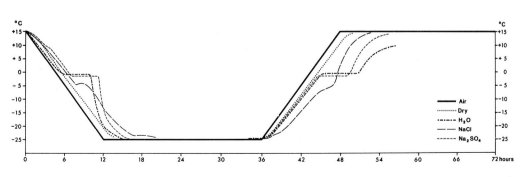

Figure 11.4. Rock temperature curves – cycle B – partly immersed cubes.

volume of water. The beta component is still important even when the rocks reach the minimum temperature of $-40\,°C$.

During thawing, latent heat is absorbed when the ice melts. The resulting time lag, or beta component, can again be measured by the width of the bench on the rock temperature curve.

Estimated mean values of alpha, beta and omega are shown in Table 1. Beta is much smaller during freezing than during thawing presumably because the difference between the rock and air temperatures is much larger during the cooling part of the cycle than during the warming part. In the case of the fully immersed cubes, for example, the tempera-

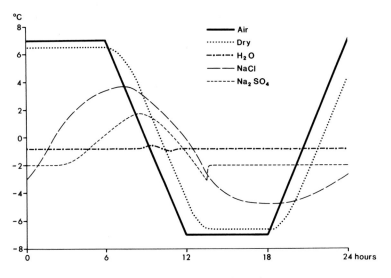

The curves shown are those repeated from the 6th cycle onwards

Figure 11.5. Rock temperature curves – cycle C – fully immersed cubes.

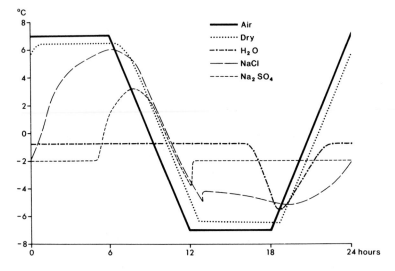

The curves shown are those repeated from the 6th cycle onwards

Figure 11.6. Rock temperature curves – cycle C – partly immersed cubes.

ture differential approaches 40 °C as the cubes finish freezing but during thawing never exceeds 15 °C.

Rock temperature curves for Cycle B are shown in Figures 11.3 and 11.4, and Table 1 gives estimates of alpha, beta and omega. The values of beta on cooling are greater than for Cycle A because of reduced temperature differentials. Beta values on warming are similar for both cycles, except for partly immersed cubes where the increased warming rate, and therefore greater temperature differential, effectively reduces beta.

In Cycle B, the periods of maximum and minimum temperature are only just long enough for the time lags of the fully immersed cubes to be contained within each cycle. The cubes thaw so slowly that they approach the maximum temperature only as the cycle ends. In Cycle C the time lags are so long relative to the length of the cycle, that they accumulate from one cycle to the next. As a result, the rock temperature curves have little or no resemblance to the air temperature curve. After a few cycles, the temperature curve for the fully immersed cubes remains fairly steady at about −0.5 °C (Figure 11.5). The temperature curve for the partly immersed cubes has a rather greater amplitude (Figure 11.6). The temperatures of both sets of cubes are unable to rise above freezing because melting is incomplete at the end of each cycle. In the case of the fully immersed cubes, the lack of a downturn in the rock temperature curve indicates that freezing is also incomplete.

3. Effects of salts

One group of cubes was fully or partly immersed in a one molar solution of sodium chloride (5.5% NaCl). During Cycle A the temperature curves of the cubes displayed marked inflections at −4 to −5 °C and −23 to −25 °C (Figures 11.1 and 11.2). The curves can be explained as follows. When a solution of less than 29% sodium chloride is cooled, no crystallisation occurs until the temperature falls to the freezing point of the solution. For a one molar solution this is at −3.5 °C. At this temperature, water in the solution begins to turn to ice and latent heat is generated. As this heat is removed and the temperature lowered further, ice continues to form. The separation of the ice changes the composition of the solution, increasing the concentration of sodium chloride. At −21 °C, the eutectic point, the remaining solution has a concentration of 29% sodium chloride. Ice and sodium chloride dihydrate ($NaCl.2H_2O$) then crystallise out simultaneously to form the cryohydrate (Bowden, 1960),

releasing still more latent heat until solidification is complete.

The inflections on the temperature curves mark the onset of freezing and the final crystallisation at the eutectic. However, the temperatures are depressed by around 1 °C at the onset of freezing and 2 to 4 °C at the eutectic. Measurement error can be discounted because identical results have been obtained using three separately calibrated sets of thermistors connected to different recording devices. The delay in the onset of freezing is due to supercooling, as evidenced by the small but definite overshoot followed by a temporary rise in temperature. The apparent lowering of the eutectic temperature may also be partly due to supercooling. When freezing sodium chloride in cement paste, Litvan (1975) found that the heat generated at the eutectic, measured by Differential Thermal Analysis, occurred at −25 °C, not −21 °C. He suggested that the small size of the pores in his paste caused supercooling. In the present experiments the small pores in the chalk cannot be the sole cause of the lowering of the eutectic temperature because a depression of 1 to 2 °C occurs when solutions alone are frozen in the boxes. The lowering of the eutectic may be partly because crystallisation occurs under non-equilibrium conditions in which the temperature is continually being lowered.

During the warming part of the cycle, the two stage crystallisation is reversed, with the cryohydrate melting after the temperature has risen to near the eutectic, and ice alone melting as the temperature continues to rise.

Table 11.2 compares the time lags in Cycles A and B. The beta component has contributions from two distinct sources: the crystallisation above the eutectic (*beta-1*) and the crystallisation at the eutectic (*beta-2*). Beta-1 is the increase in the time lag measured when crystallisation starts and during the descent to the eutectic, while beta-2 is the further increase recorded at the eutectic. The total beta components are generally larger for Cycle B than for Cycle A because of smaller temperature differentials. The minimum temperature in Cycle B is only a little below the eutectic, and there must be some doubt as to whether the cycle is long enough to allow complete solidification.

A second group of cubes was fully or partly immersed in a one molar solution of sodium sulphate (12.5%). The temperatures recorded in the cubes during Cycles A and B (Figures 11.1 to 11.4) are also explained by the phase reactions of this salt. When a one molar solution of sodium sulphate is cooled from 15 °C, the solution rapidly becomes saturated and crystallisation of the decahydrate starts to occur at about 10 °C. Latent heat is given out causing an inflection in the temperature curve. The alpha component is augmented by a beta-1 component. Crystallisation of the decahydrate continues until the temperature reaches the eutectic point at -1.2 °C, when all the remaining solution solidifies as cryohydrate (ice + decahydrate). The latent heat released at the eutectic is sufficient to arrest the drop in temperature temporarily, and a marked bench occurs before the temperature curves again start to fall. The beta-2 component equals the width of this bench.

The temperatures of the cubes in the two salt solutions during Cycle C are plotted in Figures 11.5 and 11.6. The sodium chloride curves have a larger amplitude than the sodium sulphate curves and more faithfully echo the air temperatures. This is especially true of the partly immersed cubes. The greater responsiveness of the sodium chloride curves to the changing air temperatures is due to the lower eutectic point of the salt and its high solubility at low temperatures. No salt crystallises during Cycle C, and smaller volumes of ice form than in the distilled water experiments. Sodium sulphate solution, on the other hand, crystallises completely during Cycle C, generating heat when solidifying and absorbing heat when melting.

4. Subsidiary experiments

Several of the experiments have been repeated using Ardingly Sandstone which is a soft, porous sandstone of Lower Cretaceous age. Results are very similar to those for the chalk samples. Experiments on different sized cubes of chalk have shown that the lags increase with the size of cubes. Investigations have also been carried out to determine the effects of different concentrations of salts. Details of all these experiments will be published elsewhere (Jerwood, in preparation).

Implications for weathering experiments

The present study confirms that rock temperatures can lag considerably behind air temperatures during freeze-thaw experiments. Laboratory experimenters striving to simulate natural conditions will unfortunately encounter more difficulties with time lags than experimenters who adopt a more simplistic and artificial approach. For example, selecting large rock samples, might be thought to be more realistic than selecting miniature samples, but they will not follow the planned temperature cycles as closely. Surrounding the sides and base of the samples with insulation may help to ensure freezing from the top downwards, as in nature, but it greatly increases the time lag.

It is important for experimenters to record both the air and internal rock temperatures. Rock freezing and thawing rates cannot be predicted directly from air cooling and warming rates. Rates of freezing and thawing are related to temperature differentials, and these in turn are dependent on the point at which freezing and thawing begin and end, as determined by the experimental conditions.

The harsher temperature regime of the Siberian Cycle is less seriously affected by time lags than those of the Icelandic type. This is partly due to the faster air cooling rate and the lower minimum temperature. Even so, care must be taken to ensure that thawing is complete at the end of each cycle. The Icelandic type of cycle would seem to be plagued by uncertainties. Small changes in the experimental conditions, such as in the volume of liquid, may greatly change the length of the time lags. Freezing and thawing may affect the entire rock sample or just the outer skin. The difficulty of controlling the rock temperatures in the Icelandic cycle may be one reason why experimenters have disagreed about its effectiveness in producing weathered debris. Some have claimed that it produces more debris than the Siberian cycle, whereas others have claimed the opposite (for discussion, see Potts, 1970). As experimenters have used samples of varying mass, and varying amounts of liquid and insulation, this disagreement is scarcely surprising.

The effects of salts on rates of frost weathering depend on the composition and concentration of the salts and the minimum temperature reached by the rocks. At temperatures only a little below freezing and concentrations below saturation, some salts such as sodium chloride will actually inhibit frost weathering. With all salts maximum frost weathering is likely to occur only if the minimum temperature falls below the eutectic point and remains there long enough to allow complete solidification. Above the eutectic, liquid will be present in the pores which may limit the amount of damage. Further experiments are being undertaken to test these ideas.

Acknowledgements

Grateful thanks are due to Mr Stubbings and Mr M. Wingfield for help in the preparation of the chalk cubes and with the laboratory work; to Dr M. Ford-Smith for many useful discussions, and to Miss S. Rowland for drawing the diagrams. The research was carried out while the first author was in receipt of a NERC postgraduate studentship.

References

Bowden, S.T. (1960). *The Phase Rule and Phase Reactions*, pp. 230–236, MacMillan, London.

Goudie, A.S. (1974). 'Further experimental investigation of rock weathering by salt crystallisation and other mechanical processes', *Zeitschrift fur Geomorphologie, Supp. Band.* **21**, 1–12.

Lautridou, J.P. and Ozouf, J.C. (1978). 'Relations entre la gelivite et les proprietes physiques (porosite, ascension capillaire) des roches calcaires', *RILEM/UNESCO Symposium, Paris, Deterioration and preservation of stone monuments.*

Lautridou, J.P. and Ozouf, J.C. (1982). 'Experimental frost shattering: 15 years of research at the Centre de Geomorphologie du CNRS', *Progress in Physical Geography* **6**, 215–32.

Litvan, G.G. (1975). 'Phase transitions of adsorbates: VI, effect of deicing agents on the freezing of cement paste', *Journal of the American Ceramic Society* **58** (1–2), 26–30.

McGreevy, J.P. (1982). 'Frost and salt weathering: further experimental results', *Earth Surface Processes and Landforms*, **7**(5), 475–88.

Potts, A.S. (1970). 'Frost action in rocks: some experimental data', *Transactions of the Institute of British Geographers*, **49**, 109–124.

Tricart, J. (1956). 'Etude experimentale du probleme de la gelivation,' *Biuletyn Peryglacjalny*, **4**, 285–318.

Williams, R.B.G. (1980). 'The weathering and erosion of chalk under periglacial conditions', in *The Shaping of Southern England* (Ed. D.K.C. Jones), pp. 225–48, Academic Press, London.

Williams, R.B.G. and Robinson, D.A. (1981). 'Weathering of sandstone by the combined action of frost and salt', *Earth Surface Processes and Landforms*, **6**(1), 1–9.

12 · Effects of the Devensian cold stage on soil characteristics and distribution in eastern England

J.A. CATT

Abstract

Excluding the small areas of Holocene alluvial, marine and lacustrine deposition, almost all the soils on the present land surface of eastern England south of the Devensian glacial limit are influenced by processes of periglacial deposition, erosion or disturbance. Soils formed partly or entirely from loess or coversands are widespread, and almost all slopes have some soils derived from gelifluction deposits. Devensian gelifluction is also partly responsible for the restriction of strongly altered (paleo-argillic) soils to level plateaux and terrace remnants. The effects of frost action are seen in cryoturbations, polygonal patterns of ice-wedge casts, the downward tonguing of loessial E into paleo-argillic Bt horizons, the formation of coarse, bleached ped coatings (skeletans), and the disruption of argillans, but it is often difficult to relate these features to the Devensian Stage with any confidence.

Introduction

The main event of the Devensian Stage in Britain was the slow development of a thick glacial cover over northern parts of the country and adjacent areas that are now beneath the sea. The rates of ice accumulation and expansion of the ice sheet are uncertain, but in eastern England the final southward or south westward advance to a limit inland of the present Yorkshire, Lincolnshire and Norfolk coasts (Figure 12.1) is known to have occurred between 18,500 and about 14,000 radiocarbon years B.P. (Penny *et al.*, 1969) in the later part of the Dimlington Stadial. This resulted in the deposition of two tills and associated glaciofluvial sediments, which thin rapidly inland from the present coast to a feather-edge on the rising surface of Mesozoic bedrock or pre-Devensian glacial deposits (Madgett and Catt, 1978). The ice sheet must have also eroded any earlier soils from these areas, as buried soils are almost unknown beneath the Late Devensian glacial deposits.

The soils of areas outside the Late Devensian glacial limit have various profile characteristics, which can be explained in terms of:

(a) features inherited from pre-Devensian warm stages (the palaeo-argillic horizons of Avery, 1980), which occur mainly on level plateaux and terraces that escaped significant periglacial erosion in the Devensian,

(b) periglacial aeolian deposition of silt (loess) and sand (coversand),

(c) mass movement often associated with seasonally frozen ground or permafrost (gelifluction as defined by Baulig, 1956),

(d) fluvial activity in the cold environment of the Devensian and in later (Holocene) temperate conditions,

(e) disturbance by frost action,

(f) various processes of temperate soil development in the Holocene,

(g) slopewash of cultivated soil material in the late Holocene.

The nature and origin of paleo-argillic soils in Britain have been considered by Bullock (1974), Bullock and Murphy (1979), Catt (1979, 1985*a*, 1985*b*), Sturdy *et al.* (1979), Chartres (1980), Atkinson and Burrin (1984), Avery (1985) and Kemp (1985), and their distribution is shown on numerous maps of the Soil Survey of England and Wales, including the 1:250,000 map of the whole country (Soil Survey of England and Wales, 1983). The distribution of loess based on recent soil mapping was reviewed by Catt (1985*c*), and Perrin *et al.* (1974). Catt (1977), Wilson *et al.* (1981) and Douglas (1982) have discussed the stratigraphy, origin and distribution of coversands. In this paper I shall therefore consider only the effects of Devensian periglacial mass movement, periglacial fluvial

145

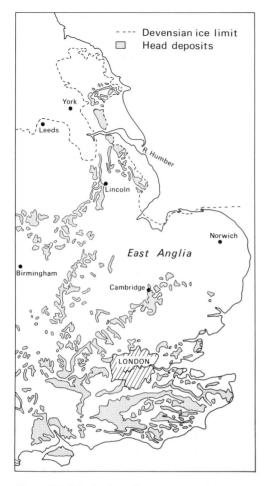

Figure 12.1. Distribution of head deposits in eastern England, based on 1:250,000 soil map (Soil Survey of England and Wales, 1983).

activity and various forms of frost disturbance on the soils of the present land surface in eastern England.

Head deposits

The term 'head' has been used by British geologists for deposits of variable composition, derived from local formations, which are 'clearly the result of slow flow, from higher to lower ground, while oversaturated with water from melting snow or ice, rain, or lines of springs or seepages' (Dines *et al.*, 1940). This definition implies that gelifluction and temperate solifluction are the main processes involved, but locally other processes of periglacial mass movement are also included (Harris, 1987). Figure 12.1, based on the 1:250,000 soil map of England (Soil Survey of England and Wales, 1983), shows the distribution of the main soil associations

thought to be wholly or mainly derived from these deposits. The associations included are Panholes (map symbol 511c), Swaffham Prior (511e), Coombe 511f, 511g), Grove (512d), Charity (571l, 571m), Whimple (572d, 572e, 572f), Dunnington Heath (572g), Oxpasture (572h), Ratsborough (572r), Wickham (711e, 711f, 711g, 711h, 711i) and Hense (871b). Almost all are slightly or moderately stony; usually there is little difference in stone content between topsoil and subsurface horizons, though a distinct stone line often occurs at the base of thin head deposits overlying stoneless substrata.

The head deposits occur typically on lower scarp and valley slopes and overlie various bedrock types, including Chalk, other limestones, sands and clays. Some, such as the thick Coombe Deposits on the floors of dry chalkland valleys, are mainly composed of frost-shattered bedrock which has been transported down slopes > 2° by rolling, frostcreep or mass sliding over the upper surfaces of melting ice lenses or a permafrost table (gelifluction). However, the most extensive are thin spreads of stony fine loams on the floors of clay vales, such as the outcrops of the Weald Clay in south east England, the Tertiary clays of the London and Hampshire Basins, the Upper Jurassic clays of the Vale of Aylesbury and the Lias in west Lincolnshire. These clay vale head deposits often occur on extremely gentle slopes (frequently < 1°) or virtually level ground, yet contain stones derived from hard rock escarpments several kilometres distant. Their mode of deposition was probably different from Coombe Deposits. In many areas they seem to grade laterally into thicker gravels of low river terraces, and the distal portions of some were perhaps partly deposited or reworked by extensive overbank flooding during episodes of rapid thawing. But fluvial activity cannot explain the thicker proximal accumulations towards scarp slopes bordering the clay vales. These are probably cold climate mudflows initiated on steeper slopes (7–10°) above the scarp foot. Rock debris eroded in various ways from the upper scarp was mobilised and progressively mixed with clay saturated beyond the liquid limit in an active layer over permafrost during thawing of a seasonally frozen layer (Worsley, 1977), or possibly on a poorly vegetated surface not significantly influenced by ground ice. The long distances over which many of the mudflows have moved is possibly explained by the mechanism of undrained loading (Hutchinson and Bhandari, 1971) over the frozen and vegetation-free clay bedrock. A few of the clay vale drifts are sandy clays apparently extruded from the scarp face at the boundary between the clay and thin unconsolidated sandy formations above (Catt *et al.*, 1975); such mixtures were probably extruded under pressure when the weight of the sandy overburden was increased by the accumulation of ground-ice.

Many of the areas delimited as head in Figure 12.1 coincide with those shown as loess-covered (Catt. 1985c) on the basis of the same 1:250,000 source map. This is because loess is a common component of many English head deposits (Mottershead, 1971; Catt *et al.*, 1974). Where head deposits are thick (e.g. at the foot of steep coastal slopes), the loess often forms discrete lenticles and streaks, but elsewhere it is intermixed as part of the fine matrix around larger clasts, and may be concentrated in soil horizons if the clasts (e.g. chalk) are removed by weathering. Some of the loess could have been incorporated directly in the head deposits by fall-out from the atmosphere during accumulation of the head, but most was probably derived from pre-deposited loess upslope.

The head deposits shown in Figure 12.1 are probably all Devensian in age because none of the soils mapped on them has paleo-argillic horizons. Pre-Devensian head deposits do occur locally in eastern England, for example in fans near the foot of the Chalk scarp in Berkshire (Horton *et al.*, 1981), but they are either overlain by Devensian deposits or crop out over areas too small to include in Figure 12.1. Areas of head covered by later deposits, such as the Holocene slopewash on the floors of dry chalkland valleys and the peat and alluvial sediments in many river valleys, are also too small to show separately and have been included as head.

Figure 12.1 confirms the observation of Williams (1968) that periglacial slope deposits are less extensive in East Anglia than elsewhere in southern England. As in Lincolnshire and Humberside, they occur mainly on the Chalk outcrop as either thick valley-floor accumulations or thin interfluve patches composed of frost-shattered chalk and flint mixed with loess, or locally in Cambridgeshire and Lincolnshire with coversand. This type of distribution in areas close to the Devensian glacial limit undoubtedly reflects the extreme susceptibility of chalk to frost disruption. The more extensive spreads on other substrata occur 80 kilometres or more from the ice limit, and there is a strong tendency for them to increase in extent and frequency southwestwards. Williams (1968) attributed this increase to the greater frequency of steep slopes (> 8°) in southwestern areas, the gentler slopes of East Anglia resulting from earlier glacial erosion.

However, the abundance of head deposits on numerous very gently sloping surfaces throughout southern England shows that slope angles < 8° did not limit movement of debris in any way. It is more likely that during the Devensian the main type of mass movement on slopes resulting in head deposits was the saturated mudflow, and that these were more common in the wetter and slightly less cold areas away from the glaciated area.

Periglacial fluvial deposits

These occupy much smaller areas than the head deposits, and occur mainly as small patches and narrow strips (low terraces) along the middle and upper reaches of river valleys, such as the Thames above Kew Bridge, the Medway above Maidstone, the Great Ouse above St Ives, the Cam above Waterbeach, the Nene above Whittlesey, the Trent above Newark and the Ouse above Selby. The soil associations involved (Soil Survey of England and Wales, 1983) are Badsey (map symbols 511h, 511i), Milton (512f), Wick (541 r), Newnham (541 w), Efford (571s), Sutton (571u, 571v), Hucklesbrook (571w), Bishampton (572t), Waterstock (573a), Wigton Moor (831c), Kelmscot (832), Hurst (841b), Swanwick (841c), Shabbington (841d) and Clayhythe (872b). Many of these are moderately to extremely stony, but loamy surface horizons commonly occur above the gravels. These are usually formed from thin layers of loess, coverloam or colluvial sediment deposited after terrace aggradation ceased, but a few are the accumulated residues from decalcification of limestone-rich gravels, and some may be fine fluvial overbank sediments.

The abundance of stones in the Devensian fluvial sediments indicates that the river valleys of eastern England were occupied usually by seasonal braided streams carrying large bedloads of mainly frost-shattered bedrock material. Peak flows were usually strong enough to carry most of the fine sand, silt and clay in suspension beyond the present coastline, but the thin superficial layer of fine overbank sediments suggests that the final episode of aggradation before renewed downcutting was sometimes one of decreased but more continuous flow under temperate climatic conditions, in which the river was confined to a single channel.

Evidence for frost disturbance *in situ* without appreciable lateral movement

Although most of the evidence for frost disturbance in English soils is too small in scale to influence soil patterns portrayed on published Soil Survey maps, and some is indeed microscopic, a few isolated features can be seen on 1:25,000 maps. These include thermokarst depressions > 1 km across, such as the two peat-filled hollows at the western Fenland margin south of Peterborough (Burton, 1976, 1987). Smaller ground-ice depressions 10–120 m across also occur, for example at Walton Common and other sites on the eastern Fenland margin (Sparks et al., 1972); many of these were formed in chalky head deposits and contain peaty infills.

Patterns of non-sorted frost-wedge polygons and stripes affect large areas of the Chalk outcrop in eastern England, including many parts covered by Coombe Deposits. They are most clearly seen as soil and crop marks in aerial photographs. In the Brecklands, south Cambridgeshire and east Hertfordshire, the polygonal wedge casts are 1–5 m wide and filled with coversand, giving deep coarse loamy argillic brown earths (Moulton series) with shallower brown rendzinas (Newmarket series) and brown calcareous earths (Swaffham Prior series) in the polygonal areas between the cracks. The polygons occur on level or gently sloping surfaces and are 10–150 m across, though with no clear reason for the distribution of different sizes. The smaller polygons give way to stripes 2–5 m wide on slopes steeper than 1°, but there are no patterns on slopes exceeding 7° (Evans, 1972). Further north the patterns on the Lincolnshire and Yorkshire Wolds are mainly stripes 30 cm to 10 m wide, which are usually formed by differences in the thickness of loess over chalk or chalky head (Evans, 1976; Ellis, 1981), though there is some coversand in north Lincolnshire and Humberside. The coversand west of the Lincolnshire Wolds has been dated to the final cold episode of the Devensian (the Loch Lomond Stadial) between approximately 10,800 and 10,000 B.P. (Buckland, 1982), suggesting that the patterns could not have originated earlier. But the same age does not necessarily apply to the loess-covered stripes, as the loess has been dated by thermoluminescence to the Dimlington Stadial (26,000–13,000 B.P.) (Wintle and Catt, 1985). In the Brecklands periglacial soil patterns are more extensive and also occur at lower levels (12–46 m O.D.) than on other parts of the Chalk outcrop, possibly because the late Devensian climate was slightly more continental in the Brecklands (Evans, 1976).

Away from the Chalk outcrop the areas of polygons are smaller and less frequent. Locally they affect Devensian gelifluction deposits and river gravels, many pre-Devensian formations and interglacial (paleo-argillic) soils. The age of those cutting earlier deposits and soils is often uncertain, but many of the truncated wedge casts and polygonal patterns of bleached cracks affecting upper parts of paleo-argillic horizons are filled with Devensian loess and were probably formed during or after the Dimlington Stadial. These wedge casts and cracks in paleo-argillic soils occur on Chalk plateaux and interfluves, especially on the Chiltern Hills and North Downs, on the Hythe Beds dipslope in west Kent, and on older terraces of the Thames, Kennet and other rivers. The very irregular boundary formed initially between the loess and the truncated paleo-argillic Bt horizon by Devensian frost action was subsequently accentuated by Holocene clay illuviation, to give downward tongues of E horizon penetrating the Bt.

Involutions or cryoturbations are probably more common in eastern England than frost-wedge polygons, but it is likely that some are not periglacial in origin. They range from gentle undulations of the boundaries between contrasting deposits to festoons of vertically orientated stones and sharply-bounded flask-shaped structures containing loess or coversand and piercing Chalk (Williams, 1975), pre-Devensian tills (Douglas, 1982), head and other deposits. Most occur at the same stratigraphic level as undoubted periglacial features, such as the ice-wedge casts at the boundary between paleo-argillic horizons and overlying loessial layers, but a few of the irregular contortions seen in deeper subsoil horizons are water-escape structures in sands or differential load structures formed under temperate climatic conditions.

Many moderately or slightly stony soils in eastern England show tendencies for the stones to become more abundant but smaller and more angular upwards, which can probably be attributed to frost-shattering and heaving mainly during the Devensian. These effects are especially evident in stony clays such as the flinty paleo-argillic soils on Chalk plateaux (Batcombe, Hornbeam, Carstens and Winchester series), in which the occasional flints at depth are either unfractured nodules similar to those in the Chalk itself or large (> 10 cm) fragments of such nodules, but those in the top 70–100 cm are mainly angular fragments < 5 cm across. There is often a marked concentration of small flints near the top of the paleo-argillic horizon, suggesting that most of the heaving and fracturing occurred before deposition of loess. A similar concentration at 25–60 cm depth in some Moulton and other soils derived from Coombe Deposits may indicate a period of surface stability with frost-heaving between two separate episodes

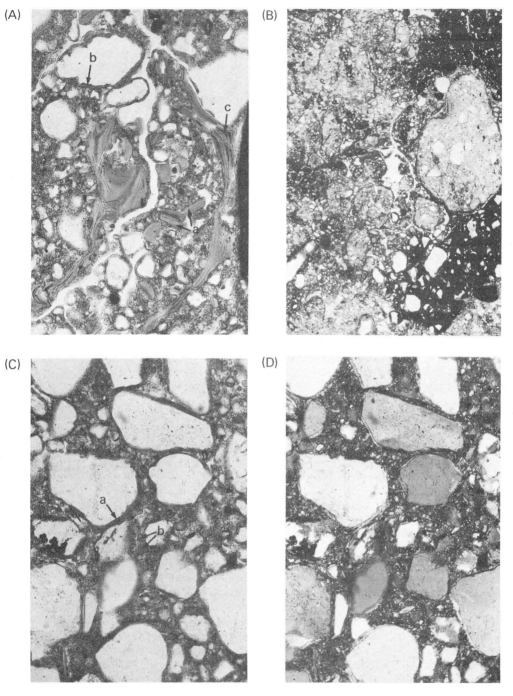

Figure 12.2. Some microscopic effects of Devensian frost action in an English paleo-argillic brown earth (Berkhamsted series at SP 401138, originally described by Bullock and Murphy, 1979) (Photos: C.P. Murphy) A. Disrupted void argillans (papules) (a) and grain argillans (b) embedded in the soil matrix; undisrupted Holocene illuvial clay coats and fills some pores (c). Plane polarised light; frame height 5.225 mm.

B. Rounded fossil aggregates, the largest (right) intruded into a red, haematitic mottle formed earlier by interglacial iron segregation. Plane polarised light; frame height 5.225 mm.
C. Grain argillans (a) and silt-sized papules (b) embedded in soil matrix. Plane polarised light; frame height 1.348 mm.
D. The same field as C, polarisers partially crossed.

of gelifluction, or after gelifluction but before a second phase of coversand or loess deposition.

A feature quite commonly seen in clayey profiles in eastern England, especially fine-grained paleo-argillic soils, is the accumulation of bleached coarse particles (sand or coarse silt) on ped surfaces in the subsoil. These coatings of skeleton grains (or skeletans) have often been attributed to direct illuviation of particles from a superficial cover of aeolian sand or loess into contraction cracks formed by frost or desiccation. But it is now thought that percolating meltwater from snow and ground ice can disperse the soil on surfaces of aggregates (Van Vliet-Lanoë, 1985), so that sand and silt particles devoid of clay can accumulate between peds. This process could have occurred before deposition of loess or coversand.

Fragipans (Avery, 1980, 24–25) and compact platy aggregates are often formed in periglacial soils by repeated growth of ice lenticles (Van Vliet-Lanoë, 1985), but they are not very common in eastern England. Weak fragipans sometimes occur in the upper parts of paleo-argillic horizons derived from sandy or loamy deposits, and have also been reported from soils in loamy Tertiary beds in north Kent (Fordham and Green, 1976), but they are far less common than in western and northern Britain. Avery et al. (1982) found compact silty aggregates in brickearth filling a doline at Gaddesden Row on the Chiltern Hills, and Derbyshire et al. (1985) reported similar fabrics in Devensian glacial and other sediments from the floor of the North Sea, which was presumably exposed to periglacial conditions at the end of the Devensian before the area was drowned by the eustatic rise of sea-level. However, despite the assertion of Derbyshire et al. (1985, 274) that compact platy aggregates may be widespread in southern England, they seem to be much rarer than on the mainland of north west Europe (Van Vliet and Langohr, 1981), though there is no obvious reason for this.

The main microscopic evidence for frost action in the soils of eastern England is the occurrence of sharply defined papules, formed by disruption of pre-Devensian void argillans and incorporation of the angular fragments in the soil matrix. These are an extremely common feature in thin sections from upper parts of all palaeo-argillic horizons (Figure 12.2), but are virtually unknown in soils formed on Devensian or Holocene deposits. This distribution strongly suggests formation by Devensian or earlier frost action rather than by any other process of temperate soil disturbance, such as root penetration, burrowing, tree-fall or cultiva-

tion. Bullock and Murphy (1979) tentatively attributed clusters of rounded soil aggregates seen in thin sections of a clayey paleo-argillic soil in Oxfordshire to disruption in the lower parts of an active layer, but suggested that they were formed in a pre-Devensian cold period because they occurred deeper in the profile than other evidence of frost action.

Other microscopic effects of frost in soils described by Van Vliet-Lanoë (1985), such as vesicles and silty cappings on stones and peds, have yet to be identified in the surface soils of eastern England, though they seem to be quite common elsewhere in Britain. As with the scarcity of fragipans and compact platy peds, the absence of these features could be more apparent than real, and in time examples may be found. But the routine field and micromorphological descriptions of soil profiles by the Soil Survey of England and Wales has been no less intensive in eastern England than elsewhere, suggesting that the Devensian climate did not favour development of these features as much as in other parts of Britain and north west Europe.

Periglacial erosion

Evidence for interglacial soil development (paleo-argillic horizons) in the surface soils of Britain is restricted to level or very gently sloping plateau, interfluve and higher terrace remnants south of the Devensian glacial limit. The absence of such evidence from scarp slopes, valley sides and floors south of the ice limit can be attributed to Devensian periglacial erosion, which was probably mainly by mass movement (gelifluction, mudflows and frost-creep), though runoff from precipitation and melting snowbeds could also have contributed. In addition there must have been widespread slight erosion even on the level plateaux and terraces, because the paleo-argillic soils all lack the thick clay-depleted E horizons implied by the large amounts of papules. The E horizons were removed before deposition of loess in the Late Devensian, and it is likely that the erosion of any interglacial soils on slopes also occurred earlier than the later part of the Late Devensian (i.e. before about 18,000 B.P.) This would account for the fact that, although some head deposits on valley floors contain transported reddish paleo-argillic soil material, many do not. The existing head deposits were often derived from slopes that had already lost their interglacial soil mantles.

Conclusions

Through widespread aeolian, fluvial or slope deposition, erosion, or disturbance *in situ* by frost action, the Devensian cold stage affected all soils south of the Devensian glacial limit in eastern England, except those derived from Holocene sediments on valley floors and in areas recently emerged from beneath lakes or the sea. During the Devensian the climate was cold enough in Britain for frost-wedges, involutions, etc. to form on at least five separate occasions (Catt, 1979). The known evidence for some of the earlier episodes is entirely buried, and the periglacial features seen in soils on the present land surface of eastern England are likely to date from the last two or three occasions only, probably mainly from the penultimate episode, i.e. the Dimlington Stadial. The Dimlington Stadial was also the time of most periglacial erosion and deposition, though considerable erosion occurred on steep Chalk scarp slopes and localised deposition of coversand occurred in many areas during the final cold episode (the Loch Lomond Stadial). The best evidence for *in situ* frost disturbance is from the upper parts of paleo-argillic horizons on flat interfluves and terrace remnants, because these were the most stable parts of the land surface through later periods of the Devensian. In such areas, as in many northern and western parts of Britain, soil features inherited from episodes of Devensian frost action often controlled the depth to which the subsequent effects of Holocene pedogenic processes could penetrate.

By removing much of the earlier strongly weathered soil mantle and by extensively replacing it with loess and other deposits formed mainly by processes of physical weathering, the Devensian cold stage was responsible for a major rejuvenation of British soils. Together with the subsequent change to a temperate humid climate in the Holocene, this explains why southern parts of the country are one of the world's most productive farming regions.

References

Atkinson, T. and Burrin, P. (1984). Rubification, palaeosols and the Wealden Angular Chert Drift. *Quaternary Newsletter* **44**, 21–8.

Avery, B.W. (1980). *Soil classification for England and Wales (Higher Categories)*. Soil Survey Technical Monograph 14, Harpenden, 67 pp.

Avery, B.W. (1985). Argillic horizons and their significance in England and Wales, in *Soils and Quaternary Landscape Evolution* (Ed. J. Boardman), pp. 69–86, J. Wiley and Sons, Chichester.

Avery, B.W., Bullock, P., Catt, J.A., Rayner, J.H. and Weir, A.H. (1982). Composition and origin of some brickearths on the Chiltern Hills, England. *Catena* **9**, 153–74.

Baulig, H. (1956). Pénéplaines et pédiplaines. *Bulletin de la Société Belge d'Etudes Géographique* **25**, 25–58.

Buckland, P. (1982). The coversands of north Lincolnshire and the Vale of York. In, *Papers in Earth Studies, Lovatt Lectures* (Eds. B.H. Adlam, C.R. Fenn and L. Morris), pp. 143–78, GeoAbstracts, Norwich.

Bullock, P. (1974). The use of micromorphology in the new system of soil classification for England and Wales. In, *Soil Micromorphology* (Ed. G.K. Rutherford), *Transactions of the 4th International Congress on Soil Micromorphology*, pp. 607–31, The Limestone Press, Kingston, Ontario.

Bullock, P. and Murphy, C.P. (1979). Evolution of a paleo-argillic brown earth (Paleudalf) from Oxfordshire, England. *Geoderma* **22**, 225–52.

Burton, R.G.O. (1976). Possible thermokarst features in Cambridgeshire. *East Midland Geographer* **6**, 230–40.

Burton, R.G.O. (1987). The role of thermokarst in landscape development in eastern England. In, *Periglacial Processes and Landforms in Britain and Ireland* (Ed. J. Boardman), pp. 203–8, Cambridge University Press.

Catt., J.A. (1977). Loess and coversands. In, *British Quaternary Studies Recent Advances* (Ed. F.W. Shotton), pp. 221–9, Clarendon Press, Oxford.

Catt, J.A. (1979). Soils and Quaternary Geology in Britain. *Journal of Soil Science* **30**, 607–42.

Catt, J.A. (1985*a*). Soils and Quaternary stratigraphy in the United Kingdom. In, *Soils and Quaternary Landscape Evolution* (Ed. J. Boardman), pp. 161–78, J. Wiley and Sons, Chichester.

Catt, J.A. (1985*b*). The nature, origin and geomorphological significance of Clay-with-flints. In, *The Scientific Study of Flint and Chert* (Eds. G. de G. Sieveking and M.B. Hart), pp. 151–9, Cambridge University Press.

Catt, J.A. (1985*c*). Soil particle size distribution and mineralogy as indicators of pedogenic and geomorphic history: examples from the loessial soils of England and Wales. In, *Geomorphology and Soils* (Eds. K. Richards, R. Arnett and S. Ellis), pp. 202–18, G. Allen and Unwin, London.

Catt, J.A., King, D.W. and Weir, A.H. (1975). The soils of Woburn Experimental Farm I. Great Hill, Road Piece and Butt Close. *Rothamsted Experimental Station Report for 1974*, Part 2, 5–28.

Catt, J.A., Weir, A.H. and Madgett, P.A. (1974). The loess of eastern Yorkshire and Lincolnshire. *Proceedings of the Yorkshire Geological Society* **40**, 23–39.

Chartres, C.J. (1980). A Quaternary soil sequence in the Kennet Valley, central southern England. *Geoderma* **23**, 125–46.

Derbyshire, E., Love, M.A. and Edge, M.J. (1985). Fabrics of probable segregated ground-ice origin in some sediment cores from the North Sea Basin. In, *Soils and Quaternary Landscape Evolution* (Ed. J. Boardman), pp. 261–80, J. Wiley and Sons, Chichester.

Dines, H.G., Hollingworth, S.E., Edwards, W., Buchan, S. and Welch, F.B.A. (1940). The mapping of head deposits. *Geological Magazine* **77**, 198–226.

Douglas, T.D. (1982). Periglacial involutions and the evidence for coversands in the English Midlands. *Proceedings of the Yorkshire Geological Society* **44**, 131–43.

Ellis, S. (1981). Patterned ground at Wharram Percy, North Yorkshire: its origin and palaeoenvironmental implications. In, *The Quaternary in Britain* (Eds. J. Neale and J. Flenley), pp. 98–107, Pergamon Press, Oxford.

Evans, R. (1972). Air photographs for soil survey in lowland England: soil patterns. *Photogrammetric Record* **7**, 302–22.

Evans, R. (1976). Observations on a stripe pattern. *Biuletyn Peryglacjalny* **25**, 9–22.

Fordham, S.J. and Green, R.D. (1976). Soils in Kent III Sheet TQ 86 (Rainham). *Soil Survey Record* **37**, Harpenden, x + 166 pp.

Harris, C. (1987) Solifluction and related periglacial deposits in England and Wales. In, *Periglacial Processes and Landforms in Britain and Ireland* (Ed. J. Boardman), pp. 209–23, Cambridge University Press.

Horton, A., Worssam, B.C. and Whittow, J.B. (1981). The Wallingford Fan Gravel. *Philosophical Transactions of the Royal Society of London* **B293**, 215–55.

Hutchinson, J.N. and Bhandari, R.K. (1971). Undrained loading, a fundamental mechanism of mudflows and other mass movements. *Géotechnique* **21**, 353–8.

Kemp, R. (1985). The Valley Farm Soil in southern East Anglia, in *Soils and Quaternary Landscape Evolution* (Ed. J. Boardman), pp. 179–96, J. Wiley and Sons, Chichester.

Madgett, P.A. and Catt, J.A. (1978). Petrography, stratigraphy and weathering of late Pleistocene tills in East Yorkshire, Lincolnshire and north Norfolk. *Proceedings of the Yorkshire Geological Society* **42**, 55–108.

Mottershead, D. (1971). Coastal head deposits between Start Point and Hope Cove, Devon. *Field Studies* **3**, 433–53.

Penny, L.F., Coope, G.R. and Catt, J.A. (1969). Age and insect fauna of the Dimlington Silts, East Yorkshire. *Nature, London* **224**, 65–7.

Perrin, R.M.S., Davies, H. and Fysh, M.D. (1974). Distribution of late Pleistocene aeolian deposits in eastern and southern England. *Nature, London* **248**, 320–4.

Soil Survey of England and Wales (1983). *Soil Map of England and Wales Scale 1:250,000.* Soil Survey of England and Wales, Harpenden.

Sparks, B.W., Williams, R.B.G. and Bell, F.G. (1972). Presumed ground-ice depressions in East Anglia. *Proceedings of the Royal Society of London* **A327**, 329–43.

Sturdy, R.G., Allen, R.H., Bullock, P., Catt, J.A. and Greenfield, S. (1979). Paleosols developed on Chalky Boulder Clay in Essex. *Journal of Soil Science* **30**, 117–37.

Van Vliet-Lanöe, B. (1985). Frost effects in soils. In, *Soils and Quaternary Landscape Evolution* (Ed. J. Boardman), pp. 117–58, J. Wiley and Sons, Chichester.

Van Vliet, B. and Langohr, R. (1981). Correlation between fragipans and permafrost with special reference to silty Weichselian deposits in Belgium and northern France. *Catena* **8**, 137–54.

Williams, R.B.G. (1968). Some estimates of periglacial erosion in southern and eastern England. *Biuletyn Peryglacjalny* **17**, 311–35.

Williams, R.B.G. (1975). The British climate during the Last Glaciation; an interpretation based on periglacial phenomena. *Geological Journal Special Issue* **6**, 95–120.

Wilson, P., Bateman, R.M. and Catt, J.A. (1981). Petrography, origin and environment of deposition of the Shirdley Hill Sand of southwest Lancashire, England. *Proceedings of the Geologists' Association* **92**, 211–29.

Wintle, A.G. and Catt, J.A. (1985). Thermoluminescence dating of Dimlington Stadial deposits in eastern England. *Boreas* **14**, 231–4.

Worsley, P. (1977). Periglaciation. In, *British Quaternary Studies Recent Advances* (Ed. F.W. Shotton), pp. 205–19, Clarendon Press, Oxford.

13 · Periglacial features in the soils of north east Scotland

E.A. FITZPATRICK

Abstract

There is a wide range of relic periglacial features in north east Scotland. Parts of the area may not have been glaciated during the Devensian. A patchy and discontinuous cover of till rests on rocks chemically weathered during the Tertiary period. Because of the undulating topography, solifluction was the predominant process which reworked and removed most of the till on the upper and middle slopes thus exposing and soliflucting the underlying weathered rock. Where the rocks are chemically unweathered they have been severely frost shattered and also soliflucted down the slope. Many of the soils have a marked discontinuity at about 30–50 cm. Below the discontinuity is the well known indurated layer which is regarded as a relic of former permafrost. Above the discontinuity the soil usually has a much higher content of silt and fine sand. This is interpreted as a late stage solifluction deposit and not loess which is conspicuously absent. Other relic features include vertically orientated stones on flat sites, stone polygons and ice-wedge casts.

Introduction

The geomorphological evolution of north east Scotland probably dates from at least the mid-Tertiary period. This is suggested by the fact that many ground surfaces are underlain by deeply weathered rocks (FitzPatrick, 1963; Hall, 1982). There is evidence for glaciation, but most conspicuous are the intensely developed, ubiquitous, relic, periglacial features (FitzPatrick, 1958; Galloway, 1961). The duration of the periglacial period is unknown because of the lack of datable stratigraphic markers. This has led to different interpretations of the evidence and the formulation of conflicting hypotheses about the Pleistocene geomorphology of the area.

Many workers suggest repeated glaciation including the Devensian (Clapperton and Sugden, 1975, 1977). However, Synge (1956) has suggested that a part of north east Scotland was unglaciated during this period. The area known as 'moraineless Buchan' was so named by Charlesworth (1956) who investigated the area but could find no evidence for morainal forms. However, there are some moraines that have been modified by periglacial processes and are difficult to identify morphologically; the material can only be established as of glacial origin when deep sections are exposed.

When the Buchan area is carefully examined it is generally only possible to find deposits for one and

sometimes two glaciations, but at Kirkhill to the east of Strichen, is a site which shows stratigraphic evidence for three glaciations (Connell *et al.*, 1982). Here the uppermost till is presumed to be early Devensian, but could be pre-Devensian because it underlies Late Devensian till further to the east. This indicates that the Kirkhill area might have been unglaciated during the Devensian. The Moray Firth and North Sea coast are generally regarded as having been covered by late Devensian ice and consequently the topography is distinguished by morainal forms which also show periglacial features but generally not as intense as within the Buchan area. This review covers the area below about 600 m, but periglacial features also extend onto the higher ground to the west (Ballantyne, 1984). The following are the main relic periglacial features:

1 Solifluction deposits
2 Evidence for former permafrost
3 Frost heave, stone nets and involutions
4 Frost shattering
5 Ice-wedge casts
6 Tors

Solifluction deposits

The solifluction deposits can be divided into four types; those developed in tills, those developed in

Table 13.1 *Clashindarroch particle size distribution*
(Percentage mineral material – range in μm.)

| HORIZON | | | | | | | | | | | | | | |
Depth (cm)	Symbol	> 2000	2000 to 1000	1000 to 500	500 to 200	200 to 100	100 to 50	50 to 20	20 to 10	10 to 5	5 to 2	2 to 1	1 to 0.5	< 0.5
0–18	Ml	32	2	2	3	4	13	21	11	10	10	3	3	17
18–28	(AtSq)	22	1	2	4	4	13	25	11	10	9	2	3	16
28–46	(AtSq)	43	1	3	7	7	20	29	10	6	6	1	2	8
46–75	1In	68	7	12	12	12	22	23	7	3	1	< 1	1	3
75–130	2In	57	8	8	13	12	19	27	4	4	1	0	1	3

chemically deeply weathered rocks, those developed in frost shattered rocks and those formed in old soils (FitzPatrick, 1958; Galloway, 1961). The result is that the nature of solifluction deposits is very varied.

The tills, have in most places been disturbed by periglacial processes; this is sometimes evident through stone orientation but in many cases the field morphology is not distinctive. On many slopes the till has been removed but there may be intercalations or thin seams in the solifluction deposits from weathered rocks. These intercalations are easily recognised by their greater particle size range and rock fragments of mixed lithology. Solifluction

Figure 13.1. Solifluction of weathered granite. Note the two discontinuities, the uppermost is at the change between the dark topsoil and the weathered granite with the solifluction arcs. The lower discontinuity is shown by the dark line separating the soliflucted material from the *in situ* weathered granite.

has been so intense that many valleys contain three or more metres of soliflucted till derived from adjacent slopes.

Usually the solifluction deposits have two discontinuities. The upper discontinuity at 50–60 cm is sharp and represents the junction between the former active layer and the underlying permafrost with the characteristic features described below. This upper discontinuity is easily recognised because the upper part of the former permafrost layer is usually paler in colour and harder than the active layer above.

Figure 13.2. Strongly frost shattered sandstone.

The second discontinuity occurs at about 2 m and is within the former permafrost layer. This is not as distinct as the upper discontinuity but is usually recognised by the down-slope orientation of stones or solifluction strata.

Above the upper discontinuity, on all types of material, there is a higher content of silt and fine sand than the material below as shown in Table 13.1. This increase in silt and fine sand is difficult to explain but on the basis of texture it appears to be an addition of loess. Since there is no evidence for loess on flat sites this fine material is tentatively considered to be a late Pleistocene slope wash which has been incorporated and mixed into the active layer by cryoturbation.

Between the discontinuities there is clear evidence of mass movement. Chemically weathered materials are curved and drawn down the slope as shown in Figure 13.1. Chemically unweathered slates and fine grained sandstones have been shattered into sharp angular fragments also with the formation of arcs and their protraction down the slope to give well developed stone orientation as shown in Figures 13.2 and 13.3.

The conventional hypothesis is that solifluction is a freeze-thaw process resulting in a down-slope movement of the material (French, 1976). While this process may have taken place in the active layer it is unlikely to have caused the mass movement between the two discontinuities. In the Arctic it is extremely doubtful if summer thawing exceeds 1 m. However, periglacial conditions in north east Scotland would have been different and it is suggested that the movement *en masse* of the material in the former permafrost layer took place in the frozen state when ice occupied all of the pores and would have constituted at least 50% and probably 60–65% of the permafrost.

It is possible that two processes operated in the original permafrost causing the movement. In its upper metre the annual temperature range would have been as much as 15–20 °C and would cause considerable expansion and contraction because the coefficient of expansion of ice is 10^{-6} cm/°C which is very high for a solid. This expansion and contraction would gradually lead to a down-slope displacement. It is possible also to think of permafrost on slopes as being similar to dirty glaciers with flow occurring by plastic deformation at depth and freeze-thaw in the active layer above the upper discontinuity. The lower discontinuity is regarded as the depth to which slope movement took place.

A third possibility is that the movement is due to sliding. This is doubtful because the material

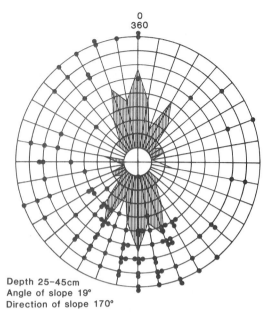

Depth 25–45cm
Angle of slope 19°
Direction of slope 170°

Figure 13.3. Stone orientation pattern at Clashindarroch. The stones are oriented normal to the contour and more or less parallel to the slope.

between the discontinuities shows an increasing amount of displacement from bottom upwards, thus slow differential movement seems more likely.

Solifluction has led to distinctive slope sequences of soils in most parts of the north east of Scotland (FitzPatrick, 1969). Up to an elevation of about 600 m the up-slope positions tend to have lost a considerable amount of material by solifluction and the soil is composed predominantly of angular frost-shattered rock. In the mid-slope situation there is a finer textured topsoil overlying a sharp discontinuity to the underlying material which may be weathered rock (Figure 13.1) or frost shattered rock (Figure 13.2). In the valleys there are thick accumulations of soliflucted glacial drift with varying amounts of weathered or frost shattered material which has been removed from the slopes. This slope sequence is accompanied by a textural sequence with the material becoming progressively finer down the slope often being a clay loam in the valleys. It should be mentioned at this point that the clay content of the soil has been largely inherited from the deeply weathered rock of the Tertiary period (Wilson *et al.*, 1984).

Only in the gently undulating eastern part of the Buchan area are glacial drifts of mixed lithology the dominant parent materials. It is common to find that the crests and upper slopes of undulations have shallow soils with frost-shattered rock while most of the slopes and valleys have soliflucted glacial till. Seldom within the Buchan area is it possible to find an unbroken spread of glacial drift 1 km² in extent because it has been strongly reworked by periglacial processes.

Evidence for former permafrost

The nature of the evidence for permafrost varies with the particle-size distribution of the material. It is in freely draining medium to coarse textured materials that the two discontinuities in the profile are best seen. In these situations the permafrost layer is usually harder than the overlying material and contains less fine material. It has a unique combination of properties including the following: massive or lenticular structure with discontinuous vesicular pores, bulk density of about two and silt cappings on the upper surface of stones (Figure 13.4).

All of these features are attributed to freezing during which gas bubbles were released from the water to form the vesicular pores, the stones developed a sheath of ice which left a cavity above the stone when the ice melted and into which silt and fine sand were deposited. These features may extend to a depth of many metres and below the

depth of the second discontinuity (FitzPatrick, 1956, 1976).

In fine textured materials a distinct subcuboidal structure is found and is very well shown in the Old Red Sandstone derived tills and lacustrine deposits around Tipperty and Cruden Bay.

The very coarse textured glaciofluvial deposits do not preserve very well the influence of permafrost except where there were ice wedges, then the evidence in the form of ice-wedge casts is quite clear.

Frost heave, stone nets and involutions

On flat sites the stones in soils usually tend towards vertical orientation. This may not be a conspicuous feature in the field because of the nature of the material but repeated stone orientation measurements have shown that nearly all of the superficial deposits, namely glacial drifts, glaciofluvial materials and raised beaches, have vertically orientated stones as shown in Figures 13.5 and 13.6. One of the best examples is at Windy Hills, a site about which there is much controversy but might be a Tertiary raised beach (Flett and Read, 1921; Kesel and Gemmell, 1981; Hall, 1982). Frost heaving causes stones to move up through the active layer and to accumulate at the surface giving

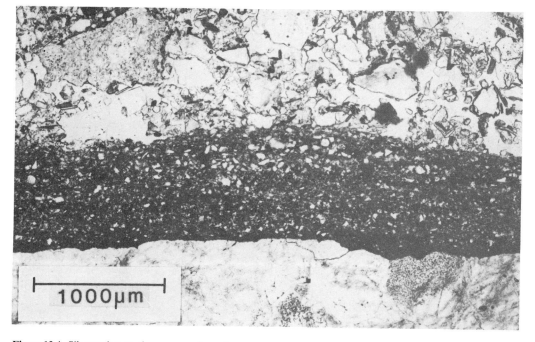

Figure 13.4. Silt capping on the upper surface of a quartzite stone at Windy Hills.

Figure 13.5. Vertically oriented stones in a soil profile
at Windy Hills. All of the stones in the middle and
lower part of the soil have silt cappings on their upper
surfaces. Note that a stone just right of centre has the
outline of a thin iron pan on its surface with no pan in
the adjacent soil.

(a)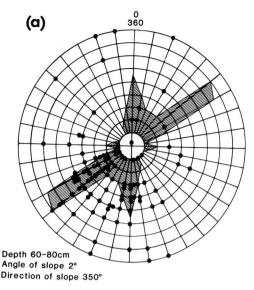

(b)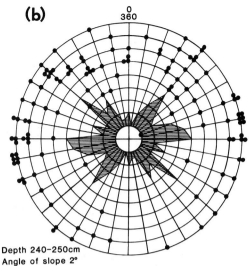

Depth 60–80cm
Angle of slope 2°
Direction of slope 350°

Depth 240–250cm
Angle of slope 2°
Direction of slope 350°

Figure 13.6. Stone orientation pattern at Windy Hills.
(a) Strong vertical orientation near the surface.
(b) The original orientation in the subsoil.

many profiles two stone maxima. Also associated with stone orientation are involutions and frost shattering.

Stone nets should be expected but they have only been seen at the hill of Dudwick. They are probably easily destroyed by cultivation, by wind throw and by earthworms. In many situations, at a depth of about 15–20 cm, there is a concentration of stones which seem to have been heaved to the surface by periglacial processes and then buried by earthworm activity during the Holocene. In very acid materials such as the quartzites of Dudwick and Windy Hills there seems never to have been any earthworm activity so that there is still a stone maximum and nets preserved at the surface.

Involutions are not very common, probably because of the lack of stratified fine materials which hold large amounts of water that would lead to involutions upon freezing. They can be found associated with vertically oriented stones in some stratified materials but their presence has to be interpreted with caution because slump and other displacement mechanisms might have been the operative processes.

Frost shattering

Frost shattering of both rock fragments and individual mineral grains is very common, the type of rock having a marked influence upon the degree of frost shattering. Granites, gabbros, felsites and gneisses seem to be the most resistant, but in pre-glacial or interglacial materials they have been broken down into angular fragments. This is particularly conspicuous in the case of core stones or boulders, numerous fragments of which may be close to each other or moved apart by frost heave or solifluction. Slates and phyllites are easily shattered and in places form a thick mantle dominated by angular material. Likewise quartzite has been severely shattered into angular fragments. Flint is particularly sensitive and the flint cobbles in the quartzite gravels of Windy Hills and elsewhere have been shattered into numerous fragments.

In the deeply weathered granularly disintegrated rocks in which permafrost developed, some of the minerals show two stages of weathering. Initially the chemical weathering formed embayments in some of the grains particularly the feldspar. Later, water freezing in the embayments caused the grains to fracture physically as shown in Figure 13.7.

On flat sites there is an evolutionary sequence that is shown in Figure 13.8. At stage 1 there is a glacial deposit with horizontally orientated stones. At stage 2 an active layer (gelon Gn) and permafrost horizon (cryon Cy) have formed, the latter with the characteristic lenses of frozen soil and bifurcating veins of ice. At stage 3 the stones have become vertically orientated in the active layer and some are frost shattered. At stage 4 there is further shattering of the stones especially at the surface.

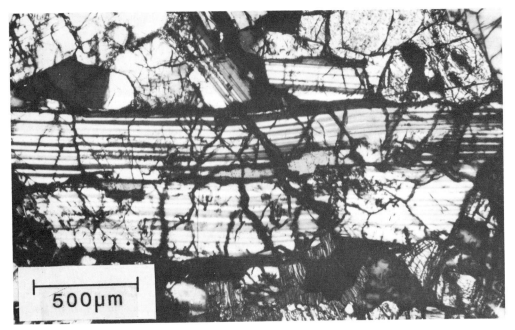

Figure 13.7. Frost shattered feldspar grain in granularly disintegrated gabbro at the Cabrach – circularly polarised light.

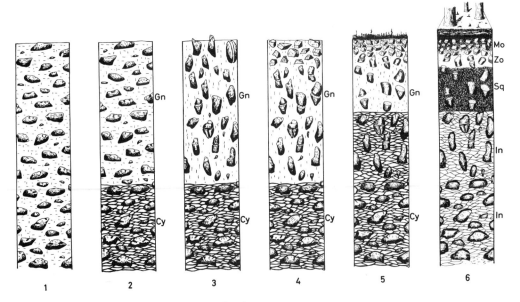

Figure 13.8. Soil evolutionary stages on some flat sites. The horizon symbols and names are as follows with Soil Taxonomy equivalents in brackets.
Gn—Gelon (Ah ochric epidedon), Cy—cryon (permafrost),
Mo—modon (Ah horizon), Zo—zolon (E, albic horizon),
Sq—sesquon (Bs, spodic horizon), In—ison (fragipan).

Stage 5 shows further shattering and heaving, causing a concentration of shattered stones at the surface. There is also the colonisation by vegetation which acts an an insulator and reduces the depth of summer thawing causing the permafrost table to move closer to the surface. Finally at stage 6 climatic improvement caused a Podzol to form. The profile has two discontinuities, the upper is at the junction between the Sq (spodic horizon) and the In (fragipan). The lower discontinuity is not as clearly shown and occurs where there is a change in stone orientation from horizontal to vertical. Within the profile evidence for former periglacial conditions includes a fragipan (ison: In) with its abrupt upper boundary, vertically orientated and shattered stones, and the accumulation of shattered stones at the surface.

Ice-wedge casts

The presence of ice-wedge casts is usually used as a criterion to indicate the degree of coldness of an area. Since the formation of ice wedges seems to require a mean annual air temperature of less than -6 to $-8\,°C$, their presence is indicative of very cold conditions (Péwé, 1966). Throughout the area numerous ice-wedge casts occur in alluvial and glaciofluvial deposits, and fields of ice-wedge casts have been reported by Gemmell and Ralston (1984). Most of the deposits in which they occur are of Devensian age such as those in the Dee valley but a few are in glaciofluvial deposits of a previous glaciation. Extensive fields also occur around Kintore, in the lower Don valley, which seems not to have been glaciated during the last major glacial phase but aggraded over a long period of time such that there is now a wide spread of alluvial material and a well developed terrace system. Sometimes it is possible to count 20 or more casts in one of the large sand quarries. An interesting feature of the sites in the lower Don valley is that very often there seems to have been a pause during the aggradation of the material when some wedges formed, later to be covered by a further aggradational phase. The ice-wedge casts start at about 2 m below the surface. It would seem that much of the aggradational material in the Don valley was derived from late glacial solifluction deposits higher up the valley and laid down by moderately fast flowing rivers. The material is mainly coarse sand and gravel with some stony material forming individual layers or lenses.

Tors

Tors are conspicuous features in many parts of north-east Scotland particularly on granite and gabbro. They are most distinctive on the high ground (Ballantyne, 1984) but many occur at about 600 m on the gabbro in the region around the Cabrach. Often they are surrounded by a mass of core stones. They are believed to have formed as a result of an initial phase of deep chemical weathering followed by the removal of the weathered rock by solifluction (Linton, 1955).

Dating the fossil periglacial features

The absence of stratigraphic markers makes dating of these features extremely difficult but there are a number of fragments of evidence upon which a chronology might be based. Four sites seem to play key roles, they are Teindland, Windy Hills, Kirkhill and Crossbrae. At Teindland a buried Podzol underlies Late Devensian deposits (FitzPatrick, 1965). The organic matter at the top of the profile gives a radio-carbon date of 28,000 BP, but pollen analysis suggests that it may have developed during the last interglacial period (Edwards *et al.*, 1976). This soil shows the initial stages of solifluction, the top 20–30 cm having been moved slightly down slope. The data seems to mark to onset of the Late Devensian in the north east, suggesting that solifluction had started just prior to burial. It is also suggested that the moraines extending eastward from this area represent the Late Devensian ice maximum. Thus the area to the south may have experienced periglacial processes through the Late Devensian, sufficient to have destroyed the interglacial soils and formed all of the present solifluction deposits. If, however, the area was unglaciated during the Devensian some of the periglacial features may be inherited from a previous cold period because the site at Kirkhill clearly shows pre-Devensian periglacial processes in buried soils.

At Windy Hills the present soil has a distinctive thin iron pan which characteristically runs through the quartzite stones in its path. However, some stones containing a thin iron pan occur in the zone of former permafrost and are almost vertically orientated, but there is no iron pan in the adjacent soil. This indicates that these stones were at one time a part of a soil containing a thin iron pan which was frost churned, destroying the iron pan. Since these stones are still present and are fairly close to the surface, it seems unlikely that there was either erosion or deposition of material at Windy Hills during the Devensian period. This is possibly one of the best lines of evidence for the absence of glaciation and for a long period of periglacial processes. The third site at Kirkhill has a number of superimposed glacial and periglacial deposits with the uppermost weathered till occurring beneath Late Devensian till at sites along the coast (Connell et al., 1982). This again indicates that Kirkhill was probably not glaciated during the Devensian.

The fourth and final site at Crossbrae (Hall, 1984) shows soliflucted till overlying peat dated at 22–26,000 BP and having interstadial pollen and macrofossils; this in turn overlies till. Therefore, it would seem that the intensity of the periglacial processes, the common occurrence of fossil periglacial features and the probable absence of Late Devensian till in at least three situations, suggest that the Buchan area was unglaciated during the last major ice advance and possibly the whole of the Devensian stage. Whether that be the case or not, the soils in the north east of Scotland certainly show the ubiquity of periglacial features. These have often helped to direct the course of subsequent soil development, and in many cases influence to some extent land use practices; in particular the indurated layer (ison) is an effective barrier to water movement and root penetration. Much wind damage to forests can be attributed to shallow rooting due to the presence of this indurated layer.

Acknowledgement

I should like to thank Dr A.M.D. Gemmell for reading the manuscript and making many useful suggestions for its improvement.

References

Ballantyne, C.K. (1984). The Late Devensian periglaciation of upland Scotland. *Quaternary Science Review* 3, 311–43.

Charlesworth, J.K. (1956). The Late-Glacial history of the Highlands and Islands of Scotland. *Transactions of the Royal Society of Edinburgh* 62, 769–928.

Clapperton, C.M. and Sugden, D.E. (1975). The glaciation of Buchan: a reappraisal, in *Quaternary Studies in north-east Scotland*. (Ed. A.M.D. Gemmell), pp. 19–22, Aberdeen University.

Clapperton, C.M. and Sugden, D.E. (1977). The Late Devensian glaciation of north-east Scotland, in *Studies in the Scottish Lateglacial Environment* (Eds. J.M. Gray and J.J. Lowe), pp. 1–13.

Connell, E.R., Edwards, K.J. and Hall, A.M. (1982). Evidence for two pre-Flandrian paleosols in Buchan, north-east Scotland. *Nature* 297, 570–2.

Edwards, K.J., Caseldine, C.J. and Chester, D.K. (1976). Possible interstadial and interglacial floras from Teindland, Scotland. *Nature*, 264, 742–4.

FitzPatrick, E.A. (1956). An indurated soil horizon formed by permafrost. *Journal of Soil Science* 7, 248–54.

FitzPatrick, E.A. (1958). An introduction to the periglacial geomorphology of Scotland. *Scottish Geographical Magazine* 74, 28–36.

FitzPatrick, E.A. (1963). Deeply weathered rock in Scotland, its occurrence, age, and contribution to the soils. *Journal of Soil Science* 14, 33–43.

FitzPatrick, E.A. (1965). An interglacial soil at Teindland, Morayshire. *Nature* 207, 621–2.

FitzPatrick, E.A. (1969). Some aspects of soil evolution in north-east Scotland. *Soil Science* 107, 403–8.

FitzPatrick, E.A. (1976). Cryons and isons. *Proceedings of the north of England Soils Discussion Group* (1974) 11, 31–43.

Flett, J.S. and Read, H.H. (1921). Tertiary gravels of the Buchan district of Aberdeenshire. *Geological Magazine* 58, 215–25.

French, H.M. (1976). *The Periglacial Environment*. Longman, London.

Galloway, R.W. (1961). Periglacial phenomena in Scotland. *Geografiska Annlr.*, 43, 348–53.

Gemmell, A.M.D. and Ralston, I.B.M. (1984). Some recent discoveries of ice-wedge cast networks in north-east Scotland. *Scottish Journal of Geology* 20, 115–18.

Hall, A.M. (1982). The 'Pliocene' Gravels of Buchan: A Reappraisal: Discussion. *Scottish Journal of Geology* 18, 336–8.

Hall, A.M. (Ed.) (1984). *Buchan Field Guide*. Quaternary Research Association, Cambridge, pp. 120.

Kesel, R.H. and Gemmell, A.M.D. (1981). The 'Pliocene' gravels of Buchan: a reappraisal. *Scottish Journal of Geology*, 17, 185–203.

Linton, D.L. (1955). The problem of tors. *Geographical Journal* 212, 470–86.

Péwé, T.L. (1966). Palaeoclimatic significance of fossil ice wedges. *Biul. Perygl.*, 15, 65–73.

Synge, F.M. (1956). The glaciation of north-east Scotland. *Scottish Geographical Magazine* 72, 129–43.

Wilson, M.J., Bain, D.C. and Duthie, D.M.L. (1984). The soil clays of Great Britain: II. Scotland. *Clay Minerals* 19, 709–35.

14 · Characteristic ratios of width to depth-of-sorting for sorted stripes in the English Lake District

JEFF WARBURTON

Abstract

Rayleigh convection cell modelling of sorted stripe regularity implies a range of characteristic width to depth-of-sorting ratios of 2.68 to 3.81, A field experiment was conducted to test this hypothesis and examine possible variations of characteristic ratios with parent materials. Measurements of stripe width and depth based on a systematic grid-point scheme are considered for two stripe sites, of uniform slope, in the English Lake District. The two stripe fields are developed on the Borrowdale Volcanics (n = 180) and the Skiddaw Slates (n = 150). Mean ratios from the two sites (volcanics, 3.54; slates, 3.49) are within the implied range. Sample variance is greater for the slates ($\rho^2 = 0.82$) than for the volcanics ($\rho^2 = 0.65$). Variation in the characteristic ratio is chiefly due to variations of width across-slope and increasing depth downslope. Downslopes trends are thought to be explained by a joint hypothesis relating the effects of rill action and mass movements to stripe morphology.

Introduction

Rayleigh convection cell modelling of sorted stripe regularity implies a range of characteristic width to depth-of-sorting ratios of 2.68 to 3.81 (Ray et al., 1983a; Gleason, 1984). This paper describes a field experiment designed to test this hypothesis and examine possible variations of characteristic ratios with parent materials. This experiment is structured into several sections which are characteristic of this type of inquiry (Church, 1984).

Several reasons justify this study: few measurements of the width to depth-of-sorting ratio for sorted stripes exist; variations of width to depth-of-sorting ratios in stripe sets have not been evaluated; and measurements should be useful in testing the validity of the model in environments different from those investigated so far (c.f. Gleason, 1984; Ray et al., 1983b).

Measurements of stripe width and depth are considered for two active stripe sets, of uniform slope, in the English Lake District: one on Helvellyn and the other on Skiddaw. This area was chosen for study because sorted stripes are abundant, their small size allows intensive excavations of multiple stripe sets, and data, from a pilot study, suggests large variations in width to depth-of-sorting ratios within this area. The two stripe fields are developed on contrasting lithologies, the Borrowdale Volcanics and the Skiddaw Slates, and both occur at

above 800 m O.D. Active layer depths (the depth of seasonal frost) vary between about 15 and 30 cm.

Conceptual model and hypothesis generation

The Rayleigh convection model for sorted patterned ground regularity (Ray et al., 1983a and 1983b) was developed on a theoretical basis. It has been verified indirectly by field tests on patterned ground in the Rocky Mountains (Gleason, 1984; Ray et al., 1983b). The fundamentals of this model have been discussed at length elsewhere (Ray et al., 1983a). Therefore only a brief description of the model in relation to sloping media and sorted stripe development is needed.

The Rayleigh free convection cell model predicts that the width to depth-of sorting ratio of sorted stripes will vary between 2.68 and 3.81 depending on the slope angle and the magnitude of sub-surface flows within the active layer at the time of initiation. The Rayleigh free convection model suggests that under some critical conditions convective water flows, driven by unstable density stratification in the active layer, result in uneven melting of the ice-front during thawing of frozen ground (Figure 14.1A). The resulting undulatory ice-front with regular spaced peaks and troughs provides the regularity observed in sorted patterned ground (Ray et al., 1983a). In the case of stripes, the resultant corrugated ice-surface with regularly

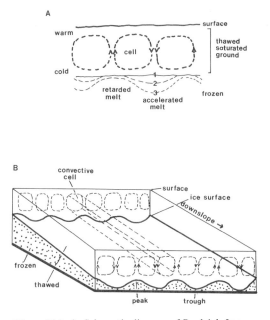

Figure 14.1. A. Schematic diagram of Rayleigh free convection and the development of an undulatory ice-front.
B. Diagram of sloping deformed ice-front.

spaced ridges and troughs provides a structure over which subsequent sorting occurs (Ray *et al.*, 1983*a*) (Figure 14.1B).

Before fluid convection can take place certain thresholds must be exceeded. These can be expressed as the dimensionless Rayleigh number (Ra) for a porous medium (soil). This is the ratio of the buoyancy force divided by the product of the shearing viscosity and thermal conductivity

critical value
Ra > 27·1 →
convection.

$$Ra = \frac{\rho_c{}^2 Cp\beta\Delta TKgL}{\lambda_s u}$$

buoyance force
shearing viscosity
thermal conductivity.

where ρ_c is the density of the fluid at its reference temperature (water at 273 °K), Cp is the heat capacity of water, β is the thermal expansion coefficient of water, ΔT is the temperature difference imposed across the active layer depth L, K is the permeability of the soil, g is gravitational acceleration, λ_b is the thermal conductivity of the soil, and u is the shear viscosity of the fluid, water at temperature T. Any variable that makes Ra large therefore, contributes to the onset of convection. The critical value for Ra, above which convection occurs, was originally determined theoretically to be 27.1 (Ray *et al.*, 1983*a*). Linear stability analysis shows that the critical wavelength (defining the spacing of active layer undulations) at the inception of Rayleigh convection is 3.81 times the active layer

depth. This theoretical result implies that for flat terrain the undulatory ice-front should have ice peaks at intervals of 3.81 active layer depths. On slopes convection cells transform into roll cells oriented downslope (Figure 14.1B). Theory predicts the width to depth-of-sorting, in this case, will vary between 2.68 and 3.81 dependent on slope.

This model only describes a mechanism for initial regularity which is exacerbated by sorting mechanisms in the active layer. In that the model does not assert that convection directly produces sorting, measurements of width and depth are therefore only an indirect estimate of original regularities.

Constant width to depth-of-sorting ratios can be produced by two possible active layer geometries: regular width and depth or; irregular width and irregular depth varying together. Measurements should determine which is the case.

In generating testable hypotheses an *a priori* knowledge of the field relations is desirable. Results from a pilot study suggest that width to depth-of-sorting ratios show considerable variation beyond the predicted range and lithology may be an important control on pattern geometry. Lithology has been cited previously as an important control on the distribution (Caine, 1972) and form (Hollingworth, 1934) of sorted stripes in this area. Based on these suggestions three hypotheses will be tested: 1) There is no significant difference in the width to depth-of-sorting ratios in the downslope direction of a sorted stripe field. 2) There is no significant difference in the width to depth-of-sorting ratios in the across-slope direction of a sorted stripe field. 3) There is no significant difference in width-to-depth of sorting ratios between the Helvellyn and Skiddaw stripe sets.

Hypotheses 1) and 2) test for within-sample variance while hypothesis 3) tests for between-sample variance of width to depth-of-sorting ratios predicted by the Rayleigh free convection model. The appropriate statistical analyses are: one-way analyses of variance (ANOVA) to test the multiple sample hypotheses of within-site variations; and a two-way ANOVA which considers the separate effects of the two independent variables (distance downslope and lithology) and also their joint effects. The two-way ANOVA is useful since it tests for variations (in width/depth ratios) within and between the two sites, and considers these effects jointly. In addition to these tests, correlation and variance measures are considered since these are useful in interpreting the results from hypothesis testing.

Table 14.1 *Site characteristics, measurements and width to depth-of-sorting parameters.*

Site	Helvellyn			Skiddaw		
Location						
Grid reference	NY 337158			NY 264258		
Elevation (m)	810			880		
Lithology	Borrowdale volcanics			Skiddaw slates		
Slope angle (degrees)	11 – 12			12		
Sampling grid						
Downslope sampling distance	20 cm			11 cm		
Number of measurements downslope	15			15		
Number of measurements across-slope	12			10		
Sample size (n)	180			150		
Morphological variables						
variables	mean	σ^2	cv	mean	σ^2	cv
Width (cm)	35.73	56.16	21.0	23.30	11.74	19.6
Depth (cm)	10.46	5.09	21.6	6.95	1.85	14.7
Width/depth (ratio)	3.54	0.65	22.8	3.49	0.82	25.9

Site selection

Careful pre-screening of sites minimizes the influence of factors not addressed directly in the hypotheses. Therefore selected sites (Table 1) were: 1) comparable in gradient, 2) unvegetated, 3) free of large boulders, 4) of uniform slope morphology, and 5) removed from obvious human interference. Climate was assumed equivalent at the two sites and aspect was not considered important (Caine, 1972). Any remaining variability is probably due to lithological controls on grain-size, thermal conductivity, permeability and frost susceptibility.

Measurement procedure

Two properties are of interest, the width measured between stripes and the depth of assumed frost sorting. Width is measured by stretching a tape from the centre of one stripe to the centre of the next adjacent fine stripe, ignoring the intervening rocky border. The procedure for measuring depth is to excavate a trench across-slope exposing the pattern in cross-section. Depth of sorting is then measured as the vertical distance from the stretched tape to a point at the base of the coarse border (Figure 14.2). This approximates the depth of active sorting which is usually well-defined but sometimes may need to be determined from stone orientations. This is not always simple since slope fabrics may overshadow orientation due to frost action. These

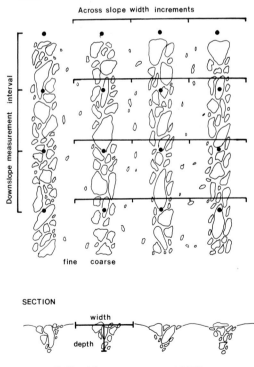

Figure 14.2. The measurement scheme (not drawn to scale).

measurements are arranged into a formalised scheme based on systematic grid-sampling (Figure 14.2).

The systematic grid is referred to a straight-line datum, which follows the line of maximum slope, and comprises a series of trenches excavated across-slope orthogonal to the datum. Therefore the grid is flexible in the across-slope dimension (since point sampling is dependent on stripe width) whereas the downslope sampling interval is arbitrarily determined as half the mean stripe width exposed in the first trench. These equally spaced data can be used to determine serial dependence in downslope observations and allow preliminary evaluations of spatial characteristics within sorted stripe fields. Ten stripes were considered at the Skiddaw site and twelve stripes at the Helvellyn site. Only stripes which were continuous over the sampling grid were included in the statistical analyses. Stripes which terminated within the grid (e.g. two stripes at the Helvellyn site, Figure 14.8) were not included in the statistical analyses.

Results

It is apparent from the data (Figure 14.3) that mean width to depth-of-sorting ratios fall within the predicted range and are equivalent statistically (Table 14.2). The two sites however, show considerable scatter; 35 per cent of the ratios, at the Helvellyn site, and 29 per cent at the Skiddaw site plot outside the predicted range. The majority of observations which plot outside the predicted range have width/depth ratios greater than expected. Variance estimates, of the width/depth ratio, for the two samples are equivalent since a two-tailed variance ratio test for the null hypothesis of the equivalency of the two site variances is accepted (F = 1.36; $\alpha = 0.10$; d.f. = 179:149). This implies that the sample variances at the two sites can be assumed estimates of the same population variance. However, t-tests, testing the equivalency of means at the two sites (Table 14.2), suggest measurements of width and depth are not equivalent. This lends indirect support to the Rayleigh free convection hypothesis which predicts a constant width to depth-of-sorting ratio, regardless of the depth of sorting, due to dimensional scaling of the convection cells in the active layer.

Comparisons of coefficients of variation (Table 14.1) show approximately equal values for width and depth (21.0 and 21.6) at Helvellyn whereas Skiddaw has a 5 per cent greater variation in depth than width (19.6 and 14.7). These results agree with width to depth-of-sorting variance estimates which

Table 14.2 *Results of two sample 't' tests between the Helvellyn and Skiddaw sites.*

Null hypothesis	t	α	d.f.	Null hypothesis
$W_H = W_S$	19.66	0.05	328	reject
$D_H = D_S$	16.73	0.05	328	reject
$WD_H = WD_S$	0.55	0.05	328	accept

t = 't' test statistic
α = level of significance
d.f. = degrees of freedom
W, D, WD = sample means of width, depth and the width/depth ratio respectively.
H, S = Helvellyn site and Skiddaw site.

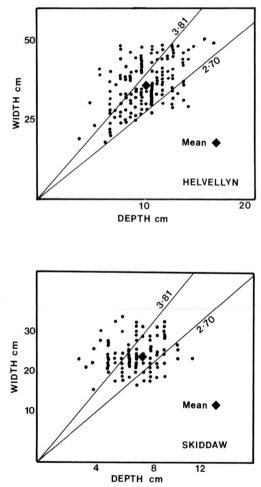

Figure 14.3. Width versus depth at the Helvellyn and Skiddaw sites.

Table 14.3 *Results of analysis of variance procedures.*

One-Way

source of variation

site	slope direction	F	d.f.	α
Skiddaw	downslope	4.88	9	0.001
	across-slope	2.60	14	0.002
Helvellyn	downslope	4.18	11	0.001
	across-slope	3.42	14	0.001

Two-Way

source of variation

		F	d.f.	
	stripes	6.44	9	0.001
	lithology	1.30	1	0.254
	interaction	3.58	9	0.001

F = variance ratio
d.f. = degrees of freedom
α = level of significance

Table 14.4 *Correlation coefficients for sorted stripe fields.*

	Distance downslope		Distance across-slope	
	r	(signif.)	r	(signif.)
Helvellyn				
width	0.17	(0.008)	− 0.35	(0.001)
depth	0.52	(0.001)	− 0.29	(0.001)
width/depth	− 0.39	(0.001)	0.05	(0.266)
Skiddaw				
width	− 0.13	(0.049)	− 0.01	(0.479)
depth	0.42	(0.001)	0.29	(0.001)
width/depth	− 0.37	(0.001)	0.25	(0.001)

r = correlation coefficient
(signif.) = level of significance

are somewhat greater at the Skiddaw site (Skiddaw, 0.82, Helvellyn, 0.65).

Results from the one-way ANOVA (Table 14.3) show that the two hypotheses of no significant difference in the mean width to depth-of-sorting ratios in both the downslope and across-slope directions, for a significance level of 0.05, are clearly rejected at the two sites. Therefore significant variation in the width/depth ratios, between stripes and trenches, does occur. Results of the two-way

ANOVA (Table 14.3) are in agreement with the hypotheses tested above since the hypothesis of no significant difference between stripes, for a F ratio test, is clearly rejected; the hypothesis of no significant difference between lithologies is accepted; and the interaction hypothesis between stripe and lithology is rejected. This suggests variations within sites (between stripes) are important and variations between sites (between lithologies) are important when considered in the interaction term.

Simple linear correlations (Table 14.4) are useful for assessing overall trends in the data which may account for a proportion of the variance in the samples. The most interesting suggestions from these coefficients are: width shows no marked downslope trends; depth tends to increase in a downslope direction and at the Helvellyn site across-slope width and depth tend to decrease away from the centre of the slope. Because width shows no marked trend in the downslope direction, and the planform of the stripe sets seem evenly spaced (Figure 14.8), the increasing depth produces lower width/depth ratios downslope. Figure 14.4 supports this suggestion since linear regressions for individual stripes indicate: (1) width shows no marked trend downslope, (2) depth increases and consequently (3) there is a consistent downslope decrease in width/depth ratios. Therefore the surface pattern (width) may appear constant while sub-surface structure (depth) varies.

These observed trends have implications for sampling since isolated determinations of width-depth ratios may give a misleading impression if the population variance is not known *a priori* and mean width/depth ratios vary dependent on the location of trenching, which is the usual method of data collection. Therefore use of more comprehensive sampling schemes is strongly advocated.

Discussion

If stripe morphology can be taken to reflect sorting over the initial oscillations in the ice surface, then these results suggest that cell dimensions may have varied substantially on a slope (at a site) and differences between lithologies (between sites) seem slight. However, the close correspondence in the width to depth-of-sorting mean values and variances, at the two sites, are intriguing, especially since tests of significance for width and depth measured separately show these values not to be equivalent (Table 14.2). Therefore a better indicator of material influences is the absolute size of patterns. This is supported by a number of independent studies which relate pattern dimensions to

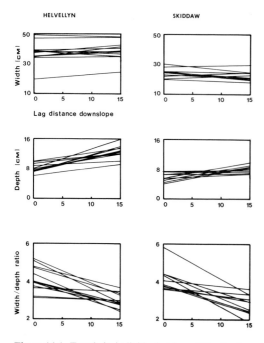

Figure 14.4. Trends in individual stripe width, depth and width to depth-of-sorting ratios in the downslope dimension. For downslope lag distance corresponds to downslope sampling interval, Table 14.1.

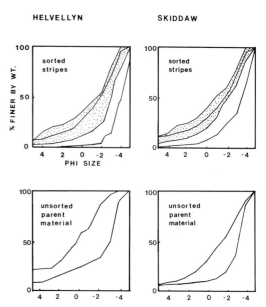

Figure 14.5. Textural properties of sorted stripes and underlying parent materials. Curves define an envelope of grain-size curves based on 7–8 samples. Stippling refers to the grain-size envelope of the fine stripe samples.

material properties (Hollingworth, 1934; Goldthwait, 1976; Büdel, 1982; and Bailey, 1983). A common statement in these studies is to the effect that stripe width is a function of clast size which reflects the relationship between soil physical properties and the degree to which the soil is sorted.

Some physical properties can be used to explain the differences in absolute cell-size dimensions. A comparison of the two soil types (Figure 14.5) shows the Helvellyn sorted stripe soils to be coarser than the Skiddaw soils. This suggests that the Helvellyn soils would have a higher thermal diffusivity since increased grain-size is associated with a general increase in thermal diffusivity (Farouki, 1981, p. 25 Figure 23.). This relationship is consistent when comparing relatively dry soils, but thermal diffusivity varies with moisture content (Harris, 1981, p. 26 Figure 12.). Therefore during thaw, when saturated conditions may be assumed, the Helvellyn soil being coarser will have a higher moisture content. This implies that thermal diffusivity will be greater in the Helvellyn soils, except at the very highest soil moisture contents. Therefore the active layer at the Skiddaw site should be shallower due to lower thermal diffusivity leading to reduced frost penetration and thaw depths.

These suggestions are consistent with the observed data: Skiddaw mean depth, 6.95 cm; Helvellyn mean depth, 10.46 cm. As we have already seen, Helvellyn mean width is greater than Skiddaw mean width (Helvellyn, 35.73 cm; Skiddaw, 23.30 cm). This suggests that as depth increases, width (stripe spacing) becomes greater (e.g. Ray et al., 1983a). Only convective models (Ray et al., 1983b, invoking fluid convection; Hallet et al., 1985, with soil convection) which relate cell-size to active layer depth predict such a relationship.

Variation within the predicted width/depth range depends partly on the magnitude of sub-surface water flows. The slightly coarser texture of the Helvellyn soils is likely to enhance permeability which may more readily promote the onset of convection since increased pore interconnections reduce resistance to water flow. However these effects are not easily evaluated since field conditions at the onset of convection cannot be reconstructed but the high mean values of the width/depth ratios suggest flows may have been substantial.

Interpretations of width to depth-of-sorting ratios in sorted stripes are difficult due to a lack of observations and of understanding of frost sorting over a tilted undulatory ice-surface and the effects of slope processes. However, the effects of slope processes can be reasonably well hypothesised from field observations. Two main effects are thought to modify the width/depth ratio in the downslope direction:

1) Eluviation of the coarse gutters (Caine, 1963).
2) Frostcreep and mass movements of the fine stripes.

Eluviation of the coarse gutters occurs during saturated soil conditions such as during intense rainstorms or at the time of thaw. This effect removes basal fines causing collapse of the overlying clast structure and a deepening of the gutter relative to the fine stripe. This effect may be intensified downslope due to increased discharge. Frost creep and gelifluction (during thaw) produce a net sediment flux downslope which will increase the height of fine stripes in this direction.

Both these processes act in a downslope direction with opposing trends (Figure 14.6B) i.e. both fine stripe height and coarse stripe depth increase (Figure 14.6A). Width changes little since fine stripe and coarse stripe processes are mutually exclusive: fines washed laterally into the gutters will be eluviated and coarse clasts moved laterally into the fine stripes, will be heaved back in winter. Freeze-thaw also accentuates stripe relief through time (Muir, 1983). This hypothesis is summarised in Figure 14.6A which is a temporal transformation of the observed spatial distribution, showing the width/depth ratio to decrease downslope (Figure 14.6C). This effect is important since width/depth ratios tend to be high (Figure 14.3).

Spatial variability within sorted stripe fields is evident; this presents problems for sampling. Single point measurements are inappropriate for determining representative width/depth ratios for sorted stripes. Similarly, the excavation of a single stripe or across-slope trench may also be poor estimates depending on the sampling position on the slope (Figure 14.4). Determination of variability is therefore an important pre-requisite for the interpretation of width/depth ratios.

The semivariogram is an important way of expressing the spatial dependence of equally spaced observations and the distance at which they become statistically independent (Nortcliff, 1984). The semivariogram is a plot of semivariance versus a series (e.g. a series of depth measurements downslope) and it can be used for estimating spatial variability in serial data. This method has proved very useful in the spatial analysis of soils (Burgess and Webster, 1980) and is equally suitable for assessing spatial dependence in sorted stripe fields. Results, from the two sites (Figure 14.7), indicate: (1) widths at the Helvellyn sites show a greater downslope dependence (lag 5–6) than at the Skiddaw site; (2) depth, at both sites, has low serial dependence due to downslope trends; and

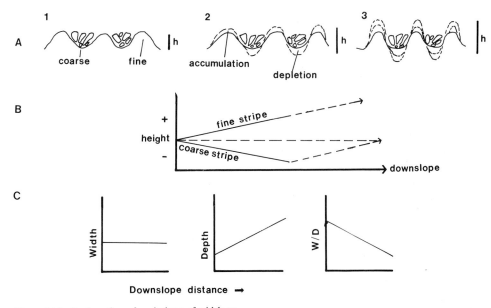

Figure 14.6. Explanation of variations of width to depth-of-sorting ratios.

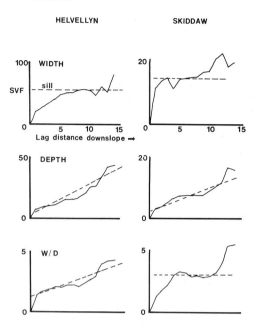

Figure 14.7. Semivariograms of width, depth and the width to depth-of-sorting ratio. Semivariance plotted against lag distance downslope.

(3) width/depth ratios, due to the trend in depth, also have low serial dependence. Therefore, there is a lack of statistical dependence in apparently regular stripes. However, mapped coarse gutters (Figure 14.8) suggest width is relatively stable even in the presence of a large perturbation. Helvellyn stripes show large crenulations focused around the termini of the two short stripes. Immediately downslope of this point is a large buried boulder (35 cm long axis). It may be argued on the basis of Rayleigh free convection that this boulder represents an obstruction to convective water flows which will inhibit stripe development downslope of the boulder. Alternatively the boulder may represent a perturbation in the ground thermal regime and associated sorting mechanisms around the boulder but this would not explain the apparent regularity in the stripes.

Conclusion

This experiment has shown that the means of the width to depth-of-sorting index, for the two sites, fall within the range predicted by the Rayleigh free convection model (Ray *et al.*, 1983*a*). Although mean width/depth ratios for Skiddaw and Helvel-

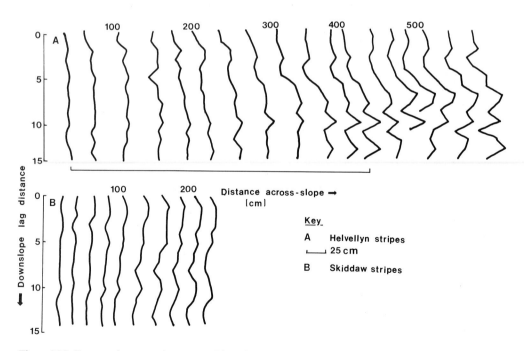

Figure 14.8. Pattern of coarse stripe gutters. Plotted lines are the centre.

lyn are equivalent, mean width and mean depth parameters are not. This suggests sorted stripes show some form of crude dimensional scaling depending on a depth of the active layer. Considerable scatter in the data suggests these values should be evaluated cautiously. Trends, both downslope and across-slope, are responsible for some of this variation. Downslope trends show a decrease in the width/depth ratio. This is an important consideration for sampling design if representative width/depth ratios are to be collected.

A combined hypothesis of rill action and slope mass movements, acting in a downslope direction, provide a plausible explanation of these trends. If these trends are explicable in terms of this hypothesis it would seem that width/depth values would have initially been higher. This would imply that the majority of ratios would originally have been greater than the Rayleigh model prediction of less than 3.81.

Rayleigh free convection may have been important in the dimensional scaling of Lake District sorted stripes but this is masked by the effects of secondary slope processes acting on the assumed regular initial structure. Realistically frost action may be important in the initiation of these features but slope movements and the effect of running water are probably more important as time progresses. Further work is needed to study sediment movements in sorted stripe fields since the ridge-trough micro-topography may be an efficient sediment transport system. Therefore as an indicator of frost action sorted stripes should not be considered as important as sorted circles, polygons and nets.

Acknowledgements

This work has been financially supported by the National Science Foundation (Grant No. DPP-8210156) and carried out while the author was at the Institute of Arctic and Alpine Research, University of Colorado. Nel Caine and Dave Furbish are thanked for their valuable comments on early versions of this paper. I am also very grateful to an anonymous reviewer whose comments were much appreciated.

References

Bailey, P.K. (1983). 'Periglacial Geomorphology in the Kokrine-Hodzana Highlands of Alaska', *Proceedings Fourth International Permafrost Conference* Fairbanks, Alaska, pp. 34–39.

Büdel, J. (1982). *'Climatic Geomorphology'* Princeton University Press, Princeton, New Jersey. 443 pp.

Burgess, T.M. and Webster, R. (1980). 'Optimal interpolation and isarithmic mapping of soil properties I. The semivariogram and punctual kriging'. *Journal of Soil Science* **31**, 315–31.

Caine, T.N. (1963). 'The origin of sorted stripes in the Lake District, Northern England', *Geogr. Annlr.*, **45**, 172–9.

Caine, T.N. (1972). 'The distribution of sorted patterned ground in the English Lake District', *Revue de Geomorphologie Dynamique* 21 Année No. 2, 49–56.

Church, M.A. (1984). 'Experimental method in Geomorphology', In *Catchment experiments in fluvial geomorphology*, (Eds. Burt T.P. and D.E. Walling), 563–580, Geobooks, Norwich, 591 pp.

Davis, J.C. (1973). *'Statistics and Data Analysis in Geology'*. John Wiley and Sons, New York, 550 p.

Farouki, O.T. (1981). 'Thermal Properties of Soils', *CRREL Monograph* 81–1, 136 pp.

Gleason, K.J. (1984). *'Nonlinear Boussinesq Free Convection in Porous Media: Application to Patterned-Ground Formation'*, Unpublished M.Sc. Thesis, Department of Chemical Engineering, University of Colorado, Boulder, 175 pp.

Goldthwait, R.P. (1976). 'Frost sorted patterned ground: a review', *Quaternary Research* **6**, 27–35.

Hallet, B., Prestrud, S., Gregory, C. and Stubbs, C. (1985). 'Halos of Stone'. In: Weisbud S. *Science News* No. **127**, 42–4.

Harris, C. (1981). *'Periglacial mass-wasting: a review of research'*, BGRG Monograph No. 4, Geobooks, Norwich, 204 pp.

Hollingworth, S.E. (1934). 'Some solifluction phenomena in the Northern Lake District', *Proceedings of the Geological Association* **45**, 167–88.

Muir, M.P. (1983). 'The role of pre-existing corrugated topography in the development of stone stripes', *Proceedings Permafrost Fourth International Conference*, Fairbanks, Alaska, pp. 877–82.

Nortcliff, S. (1984). 'Spatial analysis of soils – Progress Report', *Progress in Physical Geography* **8**, No. 2, 261–9.

Ray, R.J., Krantz, W.B., Caine, T.N. and Gunn, R.D. (1983*a*) 'A model for patterned ground regularity', *Journal of Glaciology*, **29**, 317–37.

Ray, R.J., Krantz, W.B., Caine, T.N. and Gunn, R.D. (1983*b*). 'A mathematical model for patterned ground: sorted polygons and stripes, and underwater polygons', *Proceedings Fourth International Permafrost Conference*, Fairbanks, Alaska, pp. 1036–41.

15 · Rock platform erosion on periglacial shores: a modern analogue for Pleistocene rock platforms in Britain

A.G. DAWSON, J.A. MATTHEWS AND R.A. SHAKESBY

Abstract

The processes responsible for rock platform development in periglacial coastal and lacustrine environments have never been studied in detail. Information is presented here on rates and processes of rock platform erosion at a former glacier-dammed lake at Böverbrevatnet, southern Norway. Shore platforms in metamorphic bedrock up to 5.3 m in width were produced during a 75–125 year period at an average rate of 2.6–4.4 cm/yr. A model of rock platform development by frost-wedging below lake level is proposed. Emphasis is placed on deep penetration of the annual freeze–thaw cycle, movement of lake water towards the freezing plane, and the growth of segregation ice in bedrock fissures. It is suggested that this mechanism provides a modern analogue for the rapid erosion of rock platforms in the British Pleistocene. Support is given to the theory of R.W. Fairbridge that mid-latitude coastal rock platforms were eroded under periglacial conditions and not in interglacials by wave action alone.

Introduction

In recent years the nature of rock platform development in periglacial environments has been the subject of considerable debate (Fairbridge, 1977; Trenhaile, 1983). Most attention has focused on the genesis of coastal rock platforms (e.g. Sissons, 1974; Dawson, 1979). The proposal that rock platforms are produced rapidly in periglacial coastal environments has largely been inferred from studies of relict (Late Pleistocene) shore platforms (cf. Sissons, 1974). This view has been supported by several studies in which shore platforms have been described from polar coastlines (e.g. Jahn, 1961; Sollid et al., 1973; Moign, 1976). However, in the absence of detailed measurements, the origins of polar coastal rock platforms remain ambiguous. It is not surprising therefore that some authors, who have noted an absence of platforms in certain polar areas, have suggested the contrary view that platform erosion in polar coastal environments occurs extremely slowly (e.g. Zenkovich, 1976; King, 1972).

The processes of platform erosion on periglacial lake shorelines are equally unknown although here the existence of rock platforms on the shorelines of former ice-dammed lakes demonstrates unequivocally that platforms can be produced rapidly in such environments. The presence of rock platforms on the shores of former ice-dammed lakes provides an excellent opportunity not only to measure rates of platform erosion with some accuracy, but also to study the processes of platform erosion. This information, in turn, should contribute to our knowledge of analogous erosional processes on polar coastlines.

This paper describes rock platforms on a shoreline of a former ice-dammed lake near Böverbreen, southern Norway. A comprehensive account of the ice-dammed lake (Böverbrevatnet) and the rock platforms is given in Matthews et al. (1986). In this paper, attention is focused upon the rates and processes of rock platform erosion at Böverbrevatnet and their implications for Pleistocene rock platforms in the British Isles.

Location, site and environment

Böverbreen (8° 05′ E: 61° 33′ N) forms the western outlet of the Smörstabbreen ice cap in the Jotunheimen mountains of southern Norway and lies east of the Sognefjell. The Böverbrevatnet lake lies about 1 km from the glacier snout at an altitude of 1374 m and is dammed by a moraine ridge (M3 in Figure 15.1). Temperatures and precipitation at the

Table 15.1 *Rock platform erosion rates associated with the main lake shoreline*

Profile	Platform width (m)	Cliff height (m)	Cross sectional area removed (m²)	Erosion rates* Width/year (cm/yr)	Erosion rates* Volume/year/metre (m³/yr/m)
1	5.30	1.10	2.75	4.24–7.07	0.022–0.037
2	1.70	1.55	1.26	1.36–2.27	0.010–0.017
3	3.15	1.40	2.07	2.52–4.20	0.017–0.028
4	2.25	1.25	1.43	1.80–3.00	0.011–0.019
7.	3.95	1.25	2.26	3.16–5.27	0.018–0.030
x̄	3.27	1.31	1.95	2.62–4.36	0.016–0.026

*All rates assume 125 years (first value) and 75 years (second value) as the age of the platforms.

site, estimated from meteorological data from Fannaråken (2062 m) are: mean annual temperature, −1.2 °C; mean annual precipitation, approximately 1000 mm. Geologically, the site lies along the boundary of the Jotunheimen massif on the partly mylonitised gabbros of the north west boundary fault zone (Battey & Bryhni, 1981; Gibbs & Banham, 1979).

The rock platforms

Rock platforms are found along the north western and south western former shores of the ice-dammed lake. Platform widths in bedrock range from 1.7 to 5.3 m (n = 5), they slope towards the lake at angles of 5–12° (n = 5), and the inner edges of the platforms (cliff-platform junctions or 'notches') lie between 1.8 and 2.6 m (n = 9) above

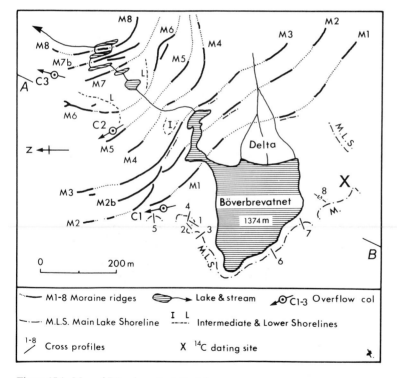

Figure 15.1. Map of Böverbrevatnet, the lake shorelines and the end moraine sequence. AB represents the line of projection for the height-distance diagram in Figure 15.3 (after Matthews *et al.*, 1986). Reproduced by permission of Universitetsforlaget.

Figure 15.2. Rock platforms along the shoreline of Böverbrevatnet. In (A) the figure is standing above a zone of shattered bedrock and at the probable level of the former lake surface. The development of a prominent cliff (left) is related to the dominant dip of the bedrock joints from left to right. In (B) the figure is standing at the cliff-platform junction. The platform surface is strewn with angular rock fragments and the low-angle cliff is related to bedrock joints dipping from right to left.

present lake level, with an average height of 2.32 m. Bedrock on the platforms has a shattered appearance while angular rock fragments and slabs up to boulder size and in various states of attachment to the bedrock, litter the irregular surface. The breakdown of these rocks by frost-shattering appears to be achieved through the loosening and subsequent breakdown of joint-bounded blocks (Figure 15.2).

Several other types of feature indicate the existence of a former shoreline (the main lake shoreline) above the present lake level. These include: benches eroded in moraines and till slopes; overflow channels, littoral boulder pavements and ice-push ridges; lacustrine silt deposits; a perched delta; vegetation trim lines and lichen zonation.

The heights of these features were surveyed from a temporary bench mark close to a former shoreline, using an automatic level, with a maximum closing error of 0.02 m. The results are summarised in the height-distance diagram (Figure 15.3). The overall average height of the benches eroded in till, trimlines and lichen limits lies 0.97 m (n = 20)

above the height of the cliff-platform junctions, which indicates that the platforms were formed *below* the surface of the ice-dammed lake.

Dating and chronological control

Lichenometry,[14]C dating and historical information have been combined to define the time period during which the rock platforms were eroded. The long axes of the largest individuals of *Rhizocarpon geographicum* agg. were recorded above and below the former lake shoreline at six sites so that maximum comparability was ensured with lichenometric dating studies carried out on the moraines of Storbreen, some 10 km to the east (Matthews, 1974). The substitution of lichen size data from the shoreline in the families of lichenometric curves previously published for Storbreen produced predicted dates for the lake shoreline and hence drainage of the lake ranging from A.D. 1822 to A.D. 1830 with a mean prediction of A.D. 1826.

Mapping and levelling the lake shoreline established that moraine M 3 is the youngest moraine in which the shoreline is eroded. It can be inferred,

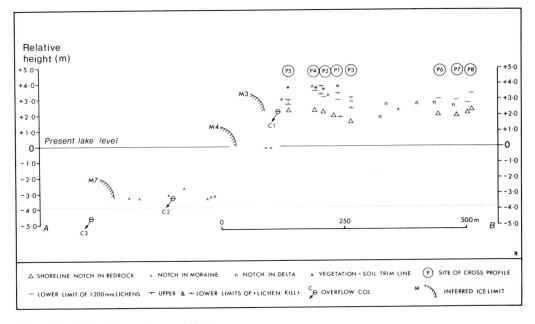

Figure 15.3. Height-distance diagram of features associated with the lake shorelines at Böverbrevatnet. The line of projection (AB) is shown in Figure 15.1. Cliff-platform junctions are termèd shoreline notches in this figure. The figure also shows the altitude of two lower shorelines, which are discussed in Matthews *et al.* (1986). Reproduced by permission of Universitetsforlaget.

therefore, that the level of the ice-dammed lake fell to that of the present lake after the deposition of M 3 but prior to the deposition of M 4. These moraines were also dated with reference to the Storbreen lichenometry curves and thus a second estimate of the date of the lake shoreline was bracketed by the mean predicted dates of A.D. 1817 (M 3) and A.D. 1830 (M 4).

In an attempt to define further the age of the ice-dammed lake, organic material from above (sample 1) and below (sample 2) the lacustrine silts was ^{14}C dated. Sample 1 was from the basal 1 cm of the overlying peaty turf. Sample 2 was composed of compressed moss plants that occur beneath 24 cm of lake silts. The samples provided ^{14}C ages of 15 $\pm$ 55 radiocarbon years B.P. (CAR-781) and 305 $\pm$ 60 radiocarbon years B.P. (CAR-782) respectively. According to the high precision calibration curve of Stuiver (1982) these dates indicate that the deposition of the silts began after about A.D. 1440 (p = < 0.05).

Although the sub-morainic topography is unknown, the impounding of the ice-dammed lake Böverbrevatnet must have occurred after the glacier advanced beyond the position of col 2 (Figure 15.1) and before it reached its 'Little Ice Age' maximum limit at M 1. It seems most likely that in common with many other southern Norwegian glaciers, Böverbreen attained its 'Little Ice Age' maximum extent about A.D. 1750 (cf. Matthews, 1977, 1982). By analogy with other glaciers in southern Norway, most notably the outlet glaciers of the Jostedalsbreen ice cap (about 40 km to the west of Böverbreen) it seems probable that the advance of Böverbreen to its 'Little Ice Age' limit was much more rapid than its subsequent retreat (Hoel and Werenskiold, 1962; Østrem *et al.*, 1976). Accepting a date of about A.D. 1750 for M 1, the retreat of the glacier from M 1 to M 3 is estimated, on the basis of lichenometry, to have taken about 75 years. It is thus reasonable to assume that the advance over the same ground took less than 50 years. This places the initiation of ice-dammed Böverbrevatnet between A.D. 1700 and A.D. 1750. Retreat of the glacier from M 3 in about A.D. 1826 allowed the surface of the lake to fall to its present level. It is therefore concluded that the former ice-dammed lake Böverbrevatnet existed for between 75 and 125 years.

Rock platform erosion rates
Estimates of the rate of development of rock platforms and associated bedrock erosion rates were based on five cross-profiles (see Matthews

et al., 1986) representing the best-developed visible rock platforms.

Rates of rock platform erosion (Table 15.1) have been expressed in two ways: (1) as an estimate of platform extension (increase in width per year); and (2) as a volumetric estimate of rock eroded per year per metre of shoreline. Both estimates for each profile have been expressed as a range of values. Each range assumes that the lake shoreline developed over a period of 75 years (upper value) or 125 years (lower value). Erosion rates were found to be greatest at site 1 (Figure 15.1) where the platform is estimated to have been cut at a rate of 4.24–7.07 cm/yr while bedrock was removed at a rate of 0.022–0.037 m^3/yr/m. Values averaged over all five sites suggest that a platform of width 3.3 m and with a cliff 1.3 m high would have been eroded at a rate of 2.63–4.36 cm/yr and 0.016–0.026 m^3/yr/m.

Since the date of cessation of shoreline development is well-defined, the most important limitation of these estimates is the uncertainty involved in dating the onset of lake shoreline development (see above). A second limitation involves the possibility that the lake shoreline was not active for the whole of the 75–125 year time span. Ice-dammed lake levels are far from static (e.g. Shakesby, 1985) and this one may have experienced intervals of subglacial drainage when its level could have been considerably lower than the lake shoreline. If so, then the period of shoreline development must have been less than the number of years of existence of the lake. Under such circumstances, the erosion rates in Table 15.1 must be regarded as minimum rates. A third limitation concerns the possibility that the lake shoreline may have been active earlier in the Holocene (cf. Matthews & Shakesby, 1984). However, there is no evidence for higher shorelines and it seems unreasonable to suppose that any earlier ice and moraine configurations were precisely equivalent to those of the 'Little Ice Age'. Thus, it is unlikely that the surface of any previous lake would have coincided precisely with the level of the 1826 lake shoreline.

The process of platform erosion
The appearance of the bedrock, the angularity of the slabs and smaller rock fragments that comprise the boulder pavements, and the irregularity of the platform surface (Figure 15.2) all point to an origin by frost-shattering. However, the appearance of exposed rock surfaces above the level of the former lake surface indicates that frost-shattering was, and is today, largely ineffective above the lake surface. Thus rock platform production appears to have

taken place below lake level in association with the growth of lake ice. Application of the Stephan formula (Harris, 1981) to estimate lake ice thickness at Böverbrevatnet during the 'Little Ice Age' indicates a maximum possible lake-ice thickness of 1.4 m (cf. Matthews *et al.*, 1986). It is envisaged that the growth of segregation ice (Harris, 1981) within bedrock joints and other foci of weakness near the lake-ice/bedrock interface loosened rock slabs by ice wedging (Washburn, 1979) and hence led to the development of rock platforms. Furthermore, platform erosion below lake level would have been promoted in those areas characterised by a high

degree of water saturation and susceptibility to freezing (cf. Taber, 1950).

Owing to the greater thermal diffusivity of rock than water (Harris, 1981), the freezing plane would have penetrated to greater depths in the bedrock than in the adjacent lake (Figure 15.4). Unfrozen lake water would tend therefore to move towards an inclined freezing plane. However, since the hydraulic conductivity of rock would limit the penetration of such water, the growth of segregation ice would be concentrated in the surface layers of the bedrock. Above the lake level, water would not be as freely available whilst beneath the

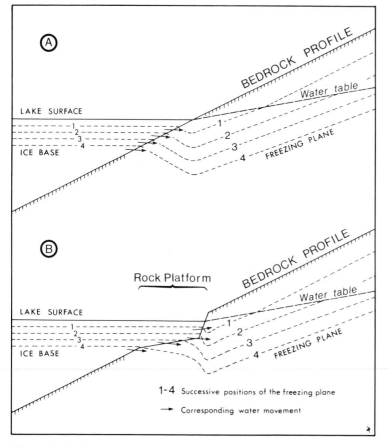

Figure 15.4. Rock platform development by frost shattering at the interface between bedrock and lake ice; a semi-quantitative model (A) Lake-ice thickening, frost penetration into bedrock and the movement of unfrozen water towards the freezing plane during an annual freezing cycle. (B) the same process superimposed on a rock platform with similar dimensions to those observed at the main lake shoreline of Böverbrevatnet. Further explanation in text (after Matthews *et al.*, 1986). Reproduced by permission of Universitetsforlaget.

lake ice, water would not freeze. The zone of frost-shattering activity would therefore occur at the level of the platform surface and cliff base and planation would occur over a height interval defined by optimal moisture and temperature conditions.

A consequence of this hypothesis is that the outer (offshore) edge of each platform is equated with the lower limit of frost penetration and that the average height of the cliff-platform junction lies 0.5 m above this level and 0.9 m below the presumed lake surface. Thus, steeply inclined freezing planes are indicated near the cliff base (Figure 15.4) and imply that in the latter area the short distance between the unfrozen lake water and the freezing plane would promote locally intense growth of segregation ice. Given that the winter ice surface may not correspond precisely with the summer lake level, that the value of 1.4 m thickness of ice would vary annually according to winter temperature and snow cover, and that the zone of frost-shattering might be extended by lake level fluctuations, the model appears to be a reasonable explanation of the *in situ* frost weathering process. Clearly, however, the secondary processes of lake-ice push and pull are important in removing blocks (or at least moving them) and hence in a full explanation of platform formation (Dionne, 1979). At Böverbrevatnet, however, such processes of removal appear to be inefficient, possibly partly as a result of the small size of the lake.

Implications for British Pleistocene rock platforms

Lake shores

The above conclusions imply that rock platforms should have been produced on the shores of lakes in Britain during periods of Pleistocene cold climate. To date, only two studies have reported the occurrence of relict rock platforms along lake shores. Sissons (1978) described a rock platform eroded in metamorphic rocks along the shoreline of a former ice-dammed lake in Glen Roy, Scotland. He noted that the platform is up to 12 m wide with a cliff up to 5 m high and argued that it was produced as a response to the cold climate of the Loch Lomond Stadial (Younger Dryas). Although this stadial is generally considered to have lasted from *c.* 11,000 to 10,000 yrs B.P., the platform, owing to ice-dammed lake level fluctuations, must have formed during a much shorter time interval. Sissons (1978:242) attributed rock platform formation in Glen Roy to '···powerful frost action in the critical

environment of a slightly varying lake level.' Firth (1984) has described a relict rock platform in schist bedrock along the shoreline of a former proglacial lake of Loch Lomond Stadial age in Loch Ness, Scotland. Firth concluded that the platform, which is up to 20 m wide and has a cliff 3–5 m high, was also produced by periglacial processes during this period. Future research may confirm the prediction that rock platform development was widespread along other British lake shores during this and other Pleistocene cold phases.

Coasts

The results from Böverbrevatnet suggest the need for a shift in existing views on the nature of frost shattering processes along polar coastlines (cf. Trenhaile, 1983). Most importantly, many hypotheses of polar shore erosion have attributed great importance to subaerial frost shattering and diurnal freeze-thaw on cliffs (e.g. Nansen, 1922; Jahn, 1961; Moign, 1974). We suggest here that these processes are relatively ineffective agencies of cliff erosion largely due to an inadequate supply of moisture and to shallow penetration of the freezing plane. We would stress instead the importance of the annual freeze-thaw cycle which, through the promotion of segregation ice growth in the bedrock beneath nearshore pack (analogous to lake ice), may penetrate to considerable depths below a specific datum and loosen large slabs of rock.

Sissons (1974) was the first to suggest that a pronounced coastal rock platform could have been produced rapidly in Scotland under Late-Pleistocene periglacial conditions. He described a raised rock platform, typically 50–150 m wide with a cliff 15–25 m high, eroded in a wide variety of rock types, that is well-developed along considerable stretches of the coastline of western Scotland. Sissons referred to the feature as the Main Lateglacial Shoreline and concluded that it was produced during the Loch Lomond Stadial by severe frost action assisted by wave action (see also Gray, 1978; Sutherland, 1981). However, the rates of rock platform erosion estimated for this period are high. Dawson (1980) calculated, for example, that in parts of the Scottish Inner Hebrides, cliff retreat rates in quartzite bedrock during this period may have been as high as 7 cm/yr. In a later study, Sissons (1981) proposed that the high rock platform fragments of western Scotland, which generally occur between 18 and 51 m O.D. were also produced by periglacial coastal processes during the last and previous glaciations. These platforms are eroded in a wide variety of rock types and are locally up to 1 km wide with cliffs up to 90 m high (see also Dawson, 1983*b*).

The rapid rates of coastal cliff retreat inferred to have taken place during the Loch Lomond Stadial are particularly remarkable since they are of an order of magnitude greater than comparable inland rockwall retreat rates estimated for the same period (cf. Ballantyne, 1984). The reasons for this have never been understood and since little information was available on processes and rates of rock platform erosion in periglacial environments, it has proved impossible until now to attribute the rapid coastal erosion of bedrock to a specific geomorphic process with any degree of certainty (cf. Gray, 1978; Sutherland, 1981). The Böverbrevatnet study therefore represents a possible breakthrough in our understanding of rock platform development for two reasons. First, although it describes bedrock erosion in a freshwater environment, it clearly demonstrates that platform extension can take place rapidly in periglacial environments and at rates similar to those inferred for the Loch Lomond Stadial. Second, it provides a new model that may explain the formation of rock platforms on polar coastlines.

On current interpretations most (although not all) relict rock platforms in Scotland are generally considered to have formed in former periglacial environments. However, there are many other parts of the British coastline where relict rock platforms are conspicuous features of the landscape (e.g. Wright & Muff, 1904; Stephens, 1957; Keen, 1978). In order to account for the origin of such features, some of which exceed 1 km in width, it has often been proposed that the platforms were produced during successive periods of interglacial marine erosion (e.g. Kidson, 1977). This hypothesis has been based on the assumptions that platforms were cut by wave action and required the relatively high sea levels characteristic of interglacials. However, the inferred patterns of climatic change derived from oxygen isotope studies suggest rapidly fluctuating Pleistocene sea levels (Shackleton & Opdyke, 1973). As a result, it is difficult to envisage the former occurrence of prolonged periods of stable interglacial sea level necessary for rock platform formation by wave action alone. Furthermore, rapidly fluctuating global environmental changes may allow the simultaneous existence of high sea levels and cold climate due, for example, to sea level change lagging behind a major climatic deterioration.

Fairbridge (1977) suggested that early and mid-Pleistocene cold-phase sea levels were in fact higher than present due to a secular decline in Pleistocene world sea level. In conjunction with this hypothesis Fairbridge (1977) proposed an alternative model of rock platform formation by periglacial shore erosion to explain the origin of the raised rock platforms of middle and high latitudes, including southern Britain. However, apart from his study, formation of these rock platforms by periglacial coastal processes has not been given any consideration – partly because most researchers have not regarded periglacial shore erosion of bedrock as an effective geomorphic process. The Böverbrevatnet data show clearly that the opposite is true and imply that many traditional views on the origins of coastal rock platforms in Britain and elsewhere are in need of a major reassessment.

Conclusions

Investigations of the rock platforms developed on the shoreline of former ice-dammed lake Böverbrevatnet have led to the following conclusions:

1. The rock platforms in gabbro were produced rapidly between A.D. 1700/1750 and *c*.A.D. 1826. Thus platform formation was limited to between 75 and 125 years. Rates of erosion calculated from cross profiles of the platforms indicate that platform extension occurred at a mean rate of 2.62–4.36 cm/yr (maximum rate 4.24–7.07 cm/yr).

2. A model of rock platform development by frost shattering below lake level at the interface between the lake ice and bedrock is proposed. The outer (offshore) edge of the platform is considered to correspond to the base of the lake ice. The model emphasises deep penetration of the annual freeze-thaw cycle, the movement of unfrozen lake water towards the freezing plane and the growth of segregation ice in interconnected fissures within the platform and at the cliff base. At Böverbrevatnet, the cliff-platform junction is estimated to lie about 0.9 m (range 0.6–1.2 m) *below* the former lake surface.

3. The Böverbrevatnet results imply that the shorelines of periglacial lakes are the foci of active rock platform development. If this interpretation is correct there are important implications for our understanding of Pleistocene rock platforms in Britain and elsewhere. First, rock platforms are likely to have been produced on the shores of numerous Pleistocene periglacial lakes in Britain. Second, there is also now a case to be made for the interpretation of many relict

rock platforms along the coasts of Britain as being periglacial in origin. This, in turn, casts doubts on the traditional interpretation of some relict rock platforms in Britain as interglacial phenomena.

Acknowledgements

The work at Böverbrevatnet was carried out on the University College Cardiff and University College Swansea, Joint Jotunheimen Research Expedition, 1984. We are grateful to all those who supported the expedition and assisted with the fieldwork. Particular thanks must go to the Royal Geographical Society and the British Sugar Corporation for financial support in the form of a British Sugar Award.

References

Ballantyne, C.K. (1984). The Late Devensian periglaciation of Upland Scotland. *Quaternary Science Reviews* 3, 311–344.

Battey, M.H. & Bryhni, I. (1981). Berggrunnen og landskapet. *Jotunheimen. Norges Nasjonalparker* **10**, (Eds. T.T. Garmo and E. Marker), pp. 21–33, Oslo.

Dawson, A.G. (1979). Polar and non-polar shore platform development. *Papers in Geography, Department of Geography, Bedford College, University of London* No. 6. 28pp.

Dawson, A.G. (1980). Shore erosion by frost: an example from the Scottish Late glacial. *Studies in the Lateglacial of North-West Europe* (Eds. J.J. Lowe, J.M. Gray and J.E. Robinson), pp. 45–53, Pergamon, Oxford.

Dawson, A.G. (1983a). Glacier-dammed lake investigations in the Hullet lake area, South Greenland, *Meddelelser om Grønland. Geoscience* **11**, 3–22.

Dawson, A.G. (1983b). *Quaternary Research Association Field Guide: Islay and Jura, Scottish Hebrides*, 31pp.

Dionne, J.C. (1979). Ice action in the lacustrine environment. A review with particular reference to Subarctic Quebec, Canada. *Earth Science Reviews* **15**, 185–212.

Fairbridge, R. (1977). Rates of sea-ice erosion of Quaternary littoral platforms. *Studia Geologica Polonica* **52**, 135–42.

Firth, C.R. (1984). *Raised shorelines and ice-limits in the Inner Moray Firth and Loch Ness areas, Scotland.* Unpublished Ph.D. thesis, Coventry Polytechnic.

Gibbs, A.D. & Banham, P.H. (1979). *Sygneffell Berggrunnsgeologisk kart, 1518 III, 1:50,000.* Foreløpig utgave Norges Geologiske Undersøkelse.

Gray, J.M. (1978). Low-level shore platforms in the south west Scottish Highlands: altitude, age and correlation. *Trans. Inst. Brit. Geogr., New series*, **3**, 151–64.

Harris, C. (1981). *Periglacial Mass-Wasting: A Review of Research.* (British Geomorphological Research Group, Research Monograph No. 4), 204 pp. Norwich.

Hoel, A. & Werenskiold, W. (1962). Glaciers and snowfields in Norway. *Skr. Nor. Polarinst.*, **114**, 1–291.

Jahn, A. (1961). Quantitative analysis of some periglacial processes in Spitsbergen. *Universytet Wroclawski im. Boleslawa Bieruta, zeszyty naukowe, nauki przyrodnicze, Ser. B5 (Nauk o Ziemi II)*, 1–34.

Keen, D.H. (1978). The Pleistocene deposits of the Channel Island. *Rep. Inst. Geol. Sci.*, 78/26.

Kidson, C. (1977). The coast of southwest England. *Quaternary History of the Irish Sea*, (Eds. C. Kidson and M.J. Tooley), pp. 257–98, Seal House Press, Liverpool.

King, C.A.M. (1972). *Beaches and Coasts* (2nd edition). Edward Arnold, London.

Matthews, J.A. (1974). Families of lichenometric dating curves from the Storbreen gletschervorfeld, Jotuneheimen, Norway. *Norsk Geogr. Tidsskr.*, **28**, 215–35.

Matthews, J.A. (1977). A lichenometric test of the 1750 end-moraine hypothesis, Storbreen gletschervorfeld, southern Norway. *Norsk Geogr. Tidsskr.*, **31**, 129–36.

Matthews, J.A. (1982). Soil dating and glacier variations: a reply to Wibjörn Karlén. *Geogr. Annlr.*, **64A**, 15–20.

Matthews, J.A. & Shakesby, R.A. (1984). The status of the 'Little Ice Age' in southern Norway: relative-age dating of Neoglacial moraines with Schmidt hammer and lichenometry. *Boreas* **13**, 333–46.

Matthews, J.A., Dawson, A.G. & Shakesby, R.A. (1986). Lake shoreline development, frost weathering and rock platform erosion in an alpine periglacial environment, Jotunheimen, southern Norway. *Boreas* **15**, 33–50.

Moign, A. (1974). Geomorphologie du strandflat au Svalbard: problems (age, origine, processus) methodes de travail. *Inter-Nord* **13–14**, 57–72.

Moign, A. (1976). L'action des glaces flottantes sur le littoral et les fonds marins du Spitzberg central et nord-occidental. *Rev. Geogr. Montreal* **30**, 51–64.

Nansen, F. (1922). The strandflat and isostasy. *Videnskapsselskapet Skrifter 1921 I. Mat.-Nat. Kl.* **2** (ii), 313 pp. (Norges Videnskaps Akademie i Kristiania).

Østrem, G. Liestøl, O. & Wold, B. (1976). Glaciological investigations at Nigardsbreen, Norway. *Norsk Geogr. Tidsskr.*, **30**, 187–209.

Shackleton, N.J. & Opdyke, N.D. (1973). Oxygen isotope and palaeomagnetic stratigraphy of the Equatorial Pacific core V28–238: oxygen isotope temperatures and ice volumes on a 10^5 and 10^6 year scale. *Quat. Res.* **3**, 39–55.

Shakesby, R.A. (1985). Geomorphological effects of jökulhlaups and ice-dammed lakes, Jotunheimen, Norway. *Norsk Geogr. Tidsskr.* **39**, 1–16.

Sissons, J.B. (1974). Late-glacial marine erosion in Scotland. *Boreas* **3**, 41–8.

Sissons, J.B. (1978). The parallel roads of Glen Roy and adjacent glens, Scotland. *Boreas* **7**, 229–44.

Sissons, J.B. (1981). British shore platforms and ice-sheets. *Nature* **291**, 473–5.

Sollid, J.L. *et al.* (1973). Deglaciation of Finnmark, North Norway. *Norsk Geogr. Tidsskr.*, **27**, 233–325.

Stephens, N. (1957). Some observations on the "Interglacial" platform and the Early Post-glacial raised beach on the east coast of Ireland. *Proc. Roy. Irish Acad.*, **58**, 129–49.

Sutherland, D.G. (1981). *The raised shorelines and deglaciation of the Loch Long/Loch Fyne area, western Scotland.* Unpublished Ph.D. thesis, University of Edinburgh.

Taber, S. (1950). Intensive frost action along lake shores. *Am. J. Sci.* **248**, 784–93.

Trenhaile, A.S. (1983). The development of shore platforms in high latitudes. *Shorelines and Isostasy* (Eds. D.E. Smith and A.G. Dawson), pp. 77–93, London & New York.

Washburn, A.L. (1979). *Geocryology: a survey of periglacial processes and environments.* Edward Arnold, 406pp.

Wright, W.B. and Muff, H.B. (1904). The preglacial raised beach of the south coast of Ireland. *Scient. Proc. Roy. Dublin Soc. n.s.* **10**, 250–324.

Zenkovich, V.P. (1967). *Processes of Coastal Development.* Oliver and Boyd, Edinburgh.

(c) Permafrost and ground ice

16·Ramparted ground ice depressions in Britain and Ireland

R.H. BRYANT AND C.P. CARPENTER

Abstract

Relict ground ice depressions exhibiting rampart development occur widely in England, Wales and southern Ireland. Recent discoveries include those in west Surrey and Cumbria. Analysis of the location and siting of all ramparted depressions reveals similar controls of relief and substrate, but anomalies exist between British and Irish distributions in relation to glacial limits. The diversity of detailed morphological characteristics is attributable to ground slope, the degree of clustering and sediment type. Attempts to determine the origin of these features are complicated by the range of analogous present-dry arctic forms which include hydraulic and hydrostatic pingos and seasonal frost mounds.

Introduction

Enclosed depressions of periglacial origin which possess fully or partly surrounding ramparts have been reported from southern Britain and Ireland (Figure 16.1). Following their initial recognition in central Wales by Pissart (1963), nearly all have been interpreted as pingo scars. However, in present-day arctic and sub-arctic environments, pingos are only one of a series of active frost mound features which include frost blisters (Van Everdingden, 1978), icing mounds (Pollard and French, 1984), and minerogenic palsas (Pissart, 1987) which may give rise to similar relict forms. They have in common an active phase which involves cryogenic uplift of the centre leading to an accumulation of overburden material at the periphery in the relict phase. These distinctions have not so far been applied to the relict forms of Britain and Ireland. We do not presume here to re-interpret the ramparted ground ice depressions found in these islands, but rather, our purpose is to highlight salient data, factors and problems which may lead to their better understanding.

In this paper we use the term 'ramparted ground ice depression' as a general term for all British and Irish features which either possess identifiable ramparts, or which can be shown to have had ramparts. Non-ramparted depressions such as alases are excluded by the term. Some of the ramparted depressions may be the remnants of true pingos, and where this can be reasonably demonstrated, we use the term pingo scar, following Flemal (1976) and De Gans (in press).

Factors of distribution

The overall distribution of British and Irish ramparted ground ice depressions exhibits two regional concentrations: a west British or 'Gaelic' province, including those in south-west Wales (Pissart, 1963; Watson, 1971; Watson and Watson, 1974), and southern Ireland (Mitchell, 1973; Coxon and O'Callaghan, 1987), and an assemblage of forms in eastern England where they occur mostly in valleys of the Chalk plateau (Sparks et al., 1972). This bimodal distribution led Watson (1977a) to postulate, in the belief that the features are all pingo scars, a zone of discontinuous permafrost across southern Britain at the time of their formation. Other recent discoveries have shown that ramparted features are even more widespread than had been previously suspected. Sites have been recognised from the Whicham Valley, Cumbria (Bryant et al., 1985) and from the Elstead area of west Surrey (Carpenter and Woodcock, 1981). Possible pingo scars have also been located beneath central London (Hutchinson, 1980).

Ramparted forms appear to be entirely absent from Scotland and from considerable areas of northern England. It has been generally assumed that this situation is a product of the Devensian glaciation; by the time ice had retreated, climate had ameliorated sufficiently to inhibit the form-

Devensian Limit (Britain)
Midlandian Limit (Ireland)

Limit of Maximum Glaciation

● Ramparted ground ice depressions
○ Other periglacial depressions

Figure 16.1. Generalised distribution of ramparted ground ice depressions and other periglacial depressions in Britain and Ireland. Each symbol represents several individual features. Numbers and authorship for ramparted features in Britain listed in Table 16.1. Other periglacial depressions in Britain after Hutchinson (1980). Irish distribution based on Mitchell, Coxon and O'Callaghan, Quinn, and Warren as cited in the bibliography or personal communication.

Table 16.1 *Data for main groups of ramparted ground-ice depressions in England and Wales.*

No	Location	Author	Methods Employed	Morphological Situation	Association	Substrate	External Diameter	Size Rampart Height	Depth of infill	System	Age*	Related Phenomena
1.	Whicham Valley Cumbria	Bryant et al. (1985)	Geomorphology Stratigraphy Pollen	Gently sloping valley floor	Several well spaced individuals	Lacustrine clay over-lying fluvio glacial outwash sands and gravels	65 m	Max. 2 m	3 m	Hydraulic	Probably Loch Lomond Stadial	Dry gully system
2.	Elstead, West Surrey	Carpenter & Woodcock (1981)	Geomorphology Stratigraphy Pollen	Gently sloping valley floor less than 5°	9 separated remnants in a clustered group	Unconsolidated Cretaceous Sands (L. Greensand)	100 m	Max. 1 m	Max 4.2 m	Hydraulic	Dimlington Stadial	None
3.	Central London	Hutchinson (1980)	Geomorphology Stratigraphy	River Thames flood plain	25 separated remnants broadly clustered	London Clay (Eocene)	20–150 m	–	12 m	Hydraulic	Devensian; possibly earlier	None
4.	Llangurig, Powys Mid-Wales	Pissart (1963)	Geomorphology Pollen Radiometric dating	Gently sloping valley floor in association with alluvial fan	Large group of overlapping remnants plus second group of 4 adjacent forms	Periglacial slope deposits and poorly sorted alluvial gravels	Max. 120 m	1.6 m	6.5 m	Hydraulic	Within Dimlington Stadial glacial limits	Rampart material shows imbrication; Solifluction
5.	East Anglia: Walton and Foulden Commons	Sparks et al. (1972)	Photogrammetry Geomorphology Stratigraphy Pollen Plant Macro	Gently sloping ground	Many in clustered and overlapping association	Solifluected chalk rubble and chalk sand	10–120 m	Not given but 2 m +	Usually less than 3 m	Hydraulic	Subdued forms: Dimlington Stadial Fresh forms: Loch Lomond Stadial	Sorted stone stripes
6.	Ballaugh, Isle of Man	Watson (1971)	Geomorphology	Located on slope of alluvial fan (2°)	9 separated remnants within clustered group	Platy alluvial gravels	Max 140 m	Absent	Not given	Hydraulic	Late Dimlington Stadial	Fan gravels show well developed imbrication
7.	South west Wales	Watson (1971, 77a, 77b) Watson & Watson (1974)	Geomorphology Photogrammetry Stratigraphy Pollen	Lower valley slopes less than 4°.	Many remnants clustered & overlapping	Gravelly clay inc. reworked glacial deposits	Rounded forms: 60–125 m Elongated max length: 165 m	Max 7 m	max recorded infill 11.8 m	Hydraulic	Late Dimlington Stadial	Solifluction

* Dimlington Stadial: 26,000–13,000 BP (Rose, 1985)   Loch Lomond Stadial 11,000–10,000 BP

ation of permafrost. However, in England and Wales the last glacial limit as conventionally defined (Figure 16.1) does not appear to restrict the distribution in this way. The Whicham Valley is well inside the limit, as are the majority of Welsh features. Only in Ireland do nearly all the examples lie outside the Midlandian (Late Pleniglacial) limit. If this is the time-stratigraphic equivalent of the Devensian limit, then there is an apparent anomaly in the distribution of ramparted depressions between Britain and Ireland. There may be a number of possible explanations for this, including differences in hydrological conditions, and temperature variations between Wales and Ireland during the period of retreat of Late-Pleniglacial ice, although there are no firm data bearing on this point. Alternatively, the Midlandian limit in Ireland may not represent the maximum extent of the last glaciation, but is instead a retreat phase (Warren, 1979).

The absence of these features from much of the English Midlands and southern England is striking. Whilst climate is undoubtedly important in determining the distribution of frost mounds, it is only one of a more complex set of environmental factors which influence the critical ground water pressure gradient. With favourable conditions prevalent in west Britain, East Anglia and in local areas of south east England, it is difficult to envisage a total lack of suitable sites over so wide an area of southern Britain. It seems more likely that such sites remain undiscovered, or perhaps have been destroyed. Worsley (1977) has suggested that the known distribution reflects more the interests of the particular field worker in each area. It remains, however, possible that the extremities of south west England were climatically unsuitable to the development of permafrost (Williams, 1975).

Site characteristics for British and Irish ramparted ground ice depressions are summarised in Table 16.1. From the data it can be seen that there is a clear preference for gently sloping ground within valley systems. This relationship is particularly marked in south west Wales. In west Surrey the depressions are aligned along the floor of a shallow valley in a similar relationship to that noted in the Netherlands (De Gans, 1981). In the Camaross district of Southern Ireland, Mitchell (1973) noted that what he regarded as open-system pingos had developed extensively on the flanks of open, gently-sloping valleys. He noted an absence of any scars at the bottom of the valley where changes in substrate conditions created an adverse hydrological environment. Nevertheless, in almost all cases British and Irish examples are restricted to slopes of less than 5°.

Another important control in location is the nature of the substrate, since this will inevitably influence local hydrological conditions. Although the data show that British and Irish examples have developed on substrates ranging from soliflucted clay-rich till to unconsolidated sand, most of these materials are sufficiently permeable to allow for the subsurface migration of groundwater. One apparent exception is the Whicham valley, where pingo scars have developed on impermeable glacial-lacustrine clays. However, here their development is likely to have been related to groundwater movement within underlying sand formations which had caused injection of ice into the superjacent clay layer, possibly in association with diapiric structures (Bryant et al., 1985).

Morphological characteristics

The principal morphological characteristics of British and Irish features are noted in Table 16.1. External diameters range from only 10 m in the case of examples in East Anglia (Sparks et al., 1972) and in west Surrey, to 140 m on the Isle of Man (Watson, 1971), although in general they range from 40–120 m. In Wales, elongated forms may reach a length of 210 m (Watson, 1977b). In Ireland, recorded diameters range from 20 m in the Drum Hills, County Wexford, to 100 m at Castleisland, County Kerry (Mitchell, 1971). Some of these dimensions lie outside typical morphological criteria suggested for true pingo scars by De Gans (in press).

Most British and Irish depressions show a marked degree of asymmetry, and clear cut circular or oval forms are in the minority. Generally there is a pronounced downslope deformation, with an increase in slope bringing a corresponding elongation in overall form. On steeper gradients (3–4°), ramparts survive as horse-shoe or crescent-shaped forms, whilst only on the rather rare flat sites in the valley floors do ramparts tend to completely surround symmetrical basins.

Watson (1977a) found that in the majority of cases in south west Wales, the basins were deepest on the downslope margin. This asymmetry reaches its most extreme form in the linear features of the Glantre Valley where they are developed on slopes of around 3°. Watson believed, however, that linear forms required more than a mere increase in slope gradient. He found that the valleys in which linear scars occurred also had a significantly greater longitudinal gradient, and suggested that in order to develop, they needed a down-valley migration of groundwater. This would merit further investigation.

The overall form of the ramparted depression is directly influenced by proximity to its neighbours. Solitary examples are very rare, both in Britain and Ireland. Almost all occur in loose communities, as in the case of the west Surrey group, or in complex masses of mutually interfering forms as predominate is south west Wales (Watson 1971; Watson and Watson, 1972) and East Anglia, in particular at Walton Common (Sparks *et. al.*, 1972). The complex grouping of ramparted depressions appears to be a distinctive feature of British and Irish examples, and its origin is not yet well understood. It may indicate the development of systems over a relatively long time period, involving several distinct generations within one area. In cases where the features are true pingo scars, multiple complexes would seem inherently much more likely to occur in open-system situations, where the causative hydrological factors remain similar over long periods of time, than in closed-system environments, which favour isolated forms.

The discovery of subdued ramparted depressions in Surrey suggests that there may be others in central and southern England (Figure 18.1). The recognition of further features should not be hampered by the popular conception of an archetypal circular or oval form with pronounced ramparts. Irregular active pingo forms have been well documented by Pissart and French (1976) and French and Dutkiewicz (1976). In unconsolidated materials, ramparts may be weakly developed in their original state or considerably subdued by later erosion. Nor would it seem wise at present to place strict minimum or maximum size limits on particular features, as has been suggested for pingo scars by De Gans (in press). If we follow Pissart (in press) in accepting that an active pingo is a hill or mound in (largely) minerogenic materials pushed up by an ice lens which does not disappear seasonally, then pingos can in theory be quite small, perhaps only 10 m or so in diameter. Conversely, seasonal frost mounds may reach up to 40 m in diameter.

Rampart form

The presence of a surrounding rampart or ringwall has always been a critical factor in the recognition of ground-ice depressions as pingo scars, and yet in common with other morphological characteristics, they show considerable variation. Many ramparts in west Britain and west Ireland reach 2–3 m above adjacent ground, and in south west Wales, Watson

(1971) records a rampart 7 m in height. One of the examples at Snugborough in Co. Wicklow (Ireland) is of similar dimensions. In contrast, many ramparted depressions on the Drenthe plateau in the Netherlands (De Gans, 1981) are difficult to detect amongst loessic terrain. In certain areas there appears to exist a direct relationship between site gradient and the development of ramparts, as in south west Wales, where Watson and Watson (1974) concluded that in many cases the upslope section of the rampart tended to collapse into the basin, producing an asymmetrical form. A similar situation has been noted in west Surrey (Carpenter and Woodcock, 1981). However, rampart asymmetry may result from the morphology of the original subsurface ice-lens, although it would be very difficult to determine its shape from a fossil feature. In yet other cases it is possible to envisage almost all of the rampart material collapsing back into the basin, producing a subdued depression with low ramparts. Such depressions occur quite widely, and have been noted in association with sharper forms in East Anglia (Sparks *et al.*, 1972) and in west Surrey.

In both British and Irish examples there is a strong correlation between the height of the rampart and its composition. At sites visited by the authors, ramparts possessing greatest amplitude are formed from clay-rich soliflucted till, as in south west Wales, or from glacio-lacustrine clay as in the Whicham Valley. In contrast, ramparts composed of unconsolidated sand in the Surrey area show only a very restricted morphological expression, seldom exceeding 1 m in height. In this respect the west Surrey examples present a strong parallel with the Dutch features.

For areas outside Britain and Ireland, considerable discussion has centred on the presence of deformation structures within the sediments of the rampart wall (Washburn, 1979; De Gans, 1981). Pissart and French (1976) found on the slopes of contemporary pingos on Banks Island in the Canadian Arctic, that the upper layers of the overlying sediment, especially those in the active layer, are frequently deformed by frost creep and solifluction. Given the likely processes involved in the decay stages of all frost mounds, such deformation features ought to be frequently present. To date, they have been observed in few British or Irish examples. Despite extensive trenching, they are conspicuously absent from the rampart walls of the Whicham valley features (Bryant *et. al.*, 1985); neither have they been recognised in west Surrey. In both cases the material throughout the rampart walls exhibits a high degree of homogeneity. The present evidence indicates that the composition of the sediments forming the rampart walls is critical in determining the preservation of deformation structures. For this reason the presence of such structures should not be regarded as crucial to the recognition of pingo scars.

Dating

Largely on the basis of presumed ice-wedge casts, there is considerable evidence to suggest that permafrost existed quite widely in Britain during many of the cold stages of the Quaternary. It is, however, unlikely that any of the visible British and Irish ramparted depressions predate the Devensian, with the possible exception of the somewhat problematic features below Central London (Hutchinson, 1980).

Within the context of the last *c.* 25,000 years, ramparted features have proved very difficult to date with any precision. No suitable organic material from beneath a rampart, which would allow absolute dating of the maximum age of the feature, has yet been located, in contrast to the studies undertaken in the Netherlands by De Gans (1981). British and Irish workers have relied on palynological and radiometric data from material taken from *within* the depressions, together with general stratigraphic relationships.

From the available evidence it seems as if there were phases of active development of ground ice mounds in Britain and Ireland both at the time of maximum glacial advance in the Devensian/Midlandian, and also during the Loch Lomond Stadial. Areas outside the glacial limits may possess indications of both ages of growth. In East Anglia, Sparks *et. al.* (1972) recorded two generations of depressions. They recognised an older generation of subdued forms which are probably of Late Devensian i.e. Dimlington Stadial age, and fresher features of Loch Lomond Stadial age. A similar relationship has been noted in Ireland by Mitchell (1973).

For areas inside the Last Glacial limits, ramparted ground ice depressions are most likely to date from the Loch Lomond Stadial since the environment was almost certainly harsh enough to allow for at least the local development of permafrost, albeit for a relatively short time (Watson, 1977a). The preceding Windermere Interstadial (*c.*13,000– 11,000 B.P.) appears to have been a time of little or no significant periglacial activity. However, there is also the possibility of local or regional ground-ice formation during the 'paraglacial' phase immediately following the retreat of the Dimlington Stadial ice sheet. Some of the ramparted forms may date from this period, but such a suggestion is speculative, pending the discovery of some firm dating evidence.

The lack of precision in establishing a stratigraphic framework for the development of ramparted ground ice depressions in Britain and Ireland remains an important area of difficulty. Any potential for these features to form part of the framework of palaeo-environmental reconstruction cannot be realised until this problem is resolved. There is a need for the systematic re-investigation of many of the already identified sites, with one of the prime objectives being an attempt to locate datable material beneath the enclosing ramparts.

Discussion

Of the various types of relict periglacial depressions so far identified in Britain and Ireland, those with ramparts are by far the most common. This is perhaps not surprising, given the obvious morphological expressions of the rampart itself, although as we have already pointed out, this is not diagnostic of the precise conditions of formation. Essentially, we are dealing here with a problem of equifinality. In Britain and Ireland, evidence for the origin of ramparted ground-ice depressions has been based largely on morphological criteria, with some supporting sedimentological data in a few cases. Pissart (in press) has rightly pointed out that identification of true pingo scars must include a convincing demonstration of the origin of the formative ground-ice. Such a condition is very difficult to meet. From the morphological and environmental evidence so far available it seems likely that if many of the British and Irish ramparted forms are pingo scars, then they are of the 'open-system' hydraulic type (as defined by Mackay, 1979). Watson and Watson (1972) have shown that a strong parallel exists between the fossil structures observed in south west Wales and the actively developing forms in Alaska and the Yukon. Such parallels should, however, be applied with caution as the environment of Britain during the Devensian may have been climatically very different to that of the present day discontinuous permafrost regions in North America. In addition, relatively little is known about modern open-system pingos; far more has been published on the closed-system (hydrostatic) types. In relation to modern arctic landforms, Sparks *et. al.* (1972) regarded the East Anglian scars as very atypical, in as much as they were too small and too closely packed to be pingo remnants in an exact sense; indeed, they used the term 'ground-ice depression'. Despite this, the formative processes described by them are similar to those of Mackay's (1979) hydraulic type. It still does not seem possible to say whether the East Anglian features are an aberrant pingo form or something else. No pingo scars suggestive of hydrostatic formation have been recorded so far in either Britain or Ireland. Nevertheless, it has been demonstrated that it may well be possible for pingos to develop from pore water expulsion produced by encroaching regional permafrost. Such a modified hydrostatic type could conceivably have operated in Britain, and the possibility has been suggested for the Whicham Valley (Bryant *et al.*, 1985).

Seasonal frost mounds of various types have been widely reported from arctic North America, and there is considerable evidence to suggest that they may be capable of developing scars similar to those formed by small pingos (Pollard, in press). In particular, frost blisters result from increased hydraulic potential within the supra-permafrost ground water of the active layer during the winter freeze back (Pollard and French, 1983). Frost blisters have been shown to range in basal diameter from 3 m to 70 m, and may well persist from year to year, experiencing on occasions, multi-year growth (Pollard and French, 1984).

Pollard and French (1983), have shown that frost blisters commonly occur at or below the break of slope between the valleyside and floodplain. They conclude that the break in slope is hydrologically significant, representing the approximate intersection point between the water table and the ground surface. Hydrological environments of this type are a common site characteristic of many British and Irish ramparted ground ice depressions.

Seasonal frost mounds have also been recorded from non-permafrost areas characterised by long cold winters and deep seasonal frost (Pollard, in press). Under such conditions, they develop where bedrock or other sediments with a low permeability exist near the ground surface. Again, such substrate conditions have been noted in association with British and Irish ramparted depressions. The possibility that some, at least, of these features were formed by frost blisters has already been suggested (French, 1979; Pollard, in press). The unequivocal recognition of such phenomena would have important implications for the Late-Quaternary environmental reconstruction for this part of Europe.

The precise origins of British and Irish ramparted ground ice depressions remains problematical. A key missing link is an understanding of the way in which fossil scars and their internal structures survive and develop from active ground ice mounds. Stress has been laid in this discussion on the variety of such forms existing in present-day arctic environments. Equally, it needs to be emphasised that each type of active feature can be found in a range of climatic environments. This applies not only to seasonal frost mounds but also to pingos. A true pingo scar may be taken as indicative of the former existence of permafrost, but mapping of modern 'hydraulic' open-system pingos shows that they form under a wide range of climatic and terrestrial conditions, from polar deserts to arctic maritime margins. The implication is that even if the causative mechanism of a relict feature in Britain and Ireland can be reasonably determined by analogy, extreme caution needs to be exercised in any palaeo-climatic interpretation. Finally, there is the wider context of latitudinal comparison. The problem of insolation differences between high and middle latitudes is liable to be particularly acute in the understanding of the development and degradation of the surface ground ice features with which this paper has been concerned.

Acknowledgements
The authors are grateful for the comments of Drs John Boardman and Wim De Gans on an earlier draft of this paper. To the latter appreciation is also expressed for many valuable discussions in the field. The helpful suggestions of Professor Hugh French, are also acknowledged.

References
Bryant, R.H., Carpenter, C.P. and Ridge, T.S. (1985). Pingo scars and related features in the Whicham Valley, Cumbria. In, *Field Guide to the Periglacial Landforms of Northern England* (Ed. J. Boardman), pp. 47–53 Quat. Res. Assoc., Cambridge.

Carpenter, C.P. and Woodcock, M.P. (1981). A detailed investigation of a pingo remnant in Western Surrey. *Quaternary Studies* 1, 1–26.

Coxon, P. and O'Callaghan, P. (1987). The distribution and age of pingo remnants in Ireland. In, *Periglacial Processes and Landforms in Britain and Ireland* (Ed. J. Boardman) pp. 195–201, Cambridge University Press.

De Gans, W. (1981). *The Drentsche Aa Valley System. A study of Quaternary Geology.* Vrije Universiteit te Amsterdam. 132 pp.

De Gans, W. (in press). Pingo scars and their identification. In, *Advances in Periglacial Geomorphology* (Ed. M.J. Clark), John Wiley, Chichester.

Flemal, R.C. (1976). Pingos and Pingo scars: their characteristics, distribution, and utility in reconstructing former permafrost environments. *Quat. Res.*, **6**, 37–53.

French, H.M. (1979) Periglacial geomorphology. *Progress in Physical Geography* **3**, 264–73.

French, H.M. and Dutkiewicz, L. (1976). Pingos and pingo-like forms, Banks Island, Western Canadian Arctic. *Biul. Perygl.*, **26**, 211–22.

Hutchinson, J.N. (1980). Possible Late Quaternary pingo remnants in Central London. *Nature* **284**, 253–5.

Mackay, J. (1979). Pingos of the Tuktoyaktuk Peninsula Area, Northwest Territories. *Geogr. Phys. Quat.*, **33**, 3–61.

Mitchell, G.F. (1971). Fossil pingos in the south of Ireland. *Nature*, **230** 43–4.

Mitchell, G.F. (1973), Fossil pingos at Camaross Townland, County Wexford. *Proc. R. Irish Acad.* **73**, 269–82.

Pissart, A. (1963). Les traces des 'pingos' du Pay de Galles (Grande Bretagne) et due plateau des Hautes Fagnes (Belgique). *Z. Geomorph.* **71**, 147–65.

Pissart, A. (in press). Pingos: an overview of the present state of knowledge. In, *Advances in Periglacial Geomorphology* (Ed. M.J. Clark), John Wiley. Chichester.

Pissart, A. (1987). Weichselian periglacial structures and their significance: Belgium, the Netherlands and northern France. In, *Periglacial Processes and Landforms in Britain and Ireland* (Ed. J. Boardman), pp. 77–85. Cambridge University Press.

Pissart, A., and French, H.M. (1976). Pingo investigations, north-central Banks Island, Canadian Arctic. *Can. J. Earth Sci.* **13**, 937–46.

Pollard, W.H. (in press). Seasonal frost mounds. In, *Advances in Periglacial Geomorphology*. (Ed. M.J. Clark), John Wiley, Chichester.

Pollard, W.H. and French, H.M. (1983). Seasonal frost mound occurrence, North Fork Pass, Ogilvie mountains, northern Yukon, Canada. In, *Permafrost: Fourth International Conference, Proceedings*. Washington D.C.

Pollard, W.H. and French, H.M. (1984). The groundwater hydraulics of seasonal frost mounds, North Fork Pass, Yukon Territory. *Can. J. Earth Sci.* **21**, 1073–81.

Rose, J. (1985) The Dimlington Stadial/Dimlington Chronozone: a proposal for naming the main glacial episode of the Late Devensian in Britain. *Boreas* **14**, 225–30.

Sparks, B.W., Williams, R.B.G., and Bell, F.G. (1972). Presumed ground-ice depressions in East Anglia *Proc. R. Soc. Lond. A* **327**, 329–43.

Van Everdingen, R.O. (1978). Frost mounds at Bear Rock, near Fort Norman, Northwest Territories, 1975–76. *Can. J. Earth Sci.* **15**, 263–76.

Warren, W. (1979). The stratigraphic position and age of the Gortian interglacial deposits. *Bull. Geol. Surv. Ire.*, **2**, 315–32.

Warren, W. (1981). Features indicative of prolonged and severe periglacial activity in Ireland, with particular reference to the South West. *Biul. Perigl.*, **28**, 241–8.

Washburn, A.L. (1979). *Geocryology: a survey of Periglacial Processes and Environments*. Arnold, London.

Watson, E. (1971). Remains of pingos in Wales and the Isle of Man. *Geol. J.*, **7**, 381–92.

Watson, E. (1977a). The periglacial environment of Great Britain during the Devensian. *Phil. Trans. Roy. Soc. Lond. B* **280**, 183–98.

Watson, E. (1977b). *Mid and North Wales*. INQUA – X Congress – Excursion Guide C9, GeoAbstracts Limited, Norwich, 48 pp.

Watson, E. and Watson, S. (1972). Investigation of some pingo basins near Aberystwyth, Wales. *Rep. 24th Int. Geol. Congr. (Montreal)*. Section **2**, 212–33.

Watson, E. and Watson, S. (1974). Remains of pingos in the Cletwr Basin, South West Wales. *Geog. Annlr.* **56A**, 213–25.

Williams, R.B.G. (1975). The British climate during the last glaciation; an investigation based on periglacial phenomena. In, *Ice Ages: Ancient and Modern* (Eds. A.E. Wright and F. Moseley), pp. 95–120, Seal House Press.

Worsley, P. (1977). Periglaciation. In, *British Quaternary Studies – Recent Advances* (Ed. F.W. Shotton), pp. 205–19., Clarendon Press, Oxford.

17·Origin of small hollows in Norfolk

R.G. WEST

Abstract

The origin of small hollows in Norfolk could include one or more of the following: ground ice, icings and solution processes. Investigation of the origin needs details of the stratigraphy of the infill, of the form of the base of the infilling and of the nature and structure of the sediments in which the hollow occurs and below the hollow. Examples of the problems of origin of hollows are discussed.

Small hollows with an infill of organic sediments are not uncommon in the valleys or on the valley slopes of west and central Norfolk. They also occur concealed beneath solifluction or fluviatile sediments. The origin of these hollows has been a matter of discussion for some time. Those at Walton Common were studied by Sparks *et al.* (1972). This site (see Figure 17.1 for location of sites) is in an area of low-lying Chalk where springs rise at present. Sparks *et al.* (1972) discussed in detail the possible origins of such hollows and concluded that they resulted from the formation of ground-ice in the Late Devensian and its subsequent melting, with the hollows filled by Flandrian organic sediments. Raised rims around some of the hollows gave evidence for the sloughing-off of surface sediments raised by ground-ice formation. Other similar hollows have been noted by Bradshaw (1981) at and near Oxborough, Norfolk.

In further investigations of small hollows elsewhere, both at the surface and concealed, problems of origin are again encountered. Origins could include one or more of the following: ground-ice, icings and collapse or solution of underlying sediments. Investigation of the origin needs details of the stratigraphy of the infill, of the form of the base of the infilling and of the nature and structure of the sediments in which the hollow occurs and below the hollow. Thus a study of a hollow at Thelnetham, west Suffolk, led Coxon (1978) to suggest an icing origin on the basis of morphology, presence of a spring, terrace age and Devensian late-glacial age of basal sediments in the hollow.

The following five examples illustrate some hollows and their infilling and allow discussion of

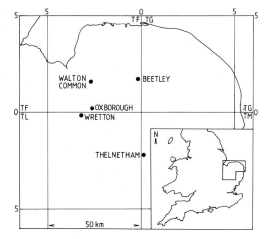

Figure 17.1. Location of sites.

possible origins in each case. The sections discussed are shown in Figure 17.2.

Present hollows

Beetley N (TF 98551773)
This water-filled hollow is about 40 m diameter and a spring issues within it, draining through a gap on its eastern side into the valley of the White Water stream. The area around the hollow is irregular with many smaller shallower hollows. There is a rim around the eastern side of the hollow towards the valley, but it is not raised above the general level of the area around the western part of the hollow.

Figure 17.2 shows a section through the north west margin of the hollow. The hollow is filled with

191

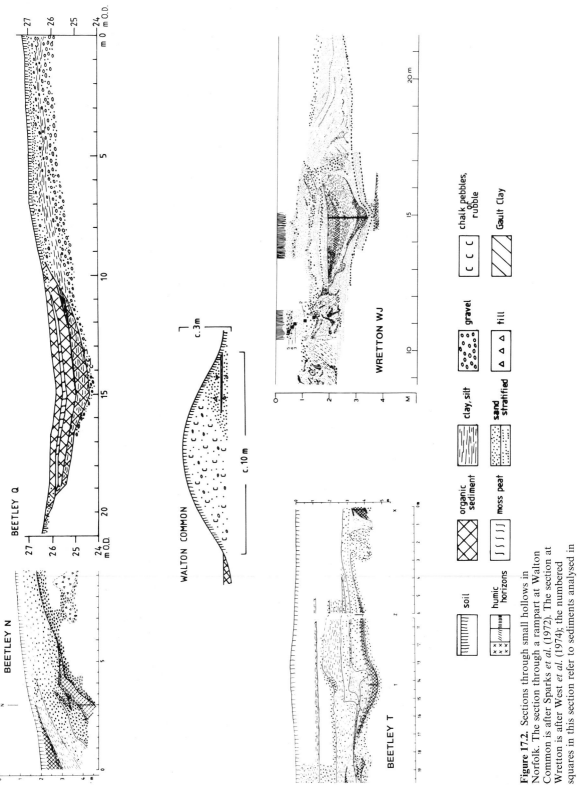

Figure 17.2. Sections through small hollows in Norfolk. The section through a rampart at Walton Common is after Sparks *et al.* (1972). The section at Wretton is after West *et al.* (1974); the numbered squares in this section refer to sediments analysed in

Flandrian organic sediment. Below it is a sandy clay, probably of Late or Middle Devensian age. Near the base of the section is a further organic sediment, which pollen analysis indicates is of Early Devensian age. The till in the gravel below is of Anglian age, but is likely to have been disturbed by subsequent periglacial action. The Chalk is some 15 m below the bottom of the section (see Auton, 1982).

The configuration of the sediments within the hollow indicates an Early Devensian hollow in which the lower organic horizon formed. The change of angle of this filling and the steeply dipping and interdigitated sediments above it indicate a collapse of the hollow in a subsequent period. Later the hollow filled with Late or Middle Devensian inorganic sediments and Flandrian organic sediments. Boreholes across the hollow would greatly amplify this outline history, but access is very difficult.

It seems likely that the origin of this hollow is partially at least through collapse in the underlying Chalk. The present spring may be of great antiquity and be the cause of solution. From the evidence of the section it is not possible to say whether ground-ice or icings played an important part in its formation.

Beetley Q (TF 98551770)

This hollow is about 10 m in diameter and is filled with water in the winter. A section through the hollow is shown in Figure 17.2. There is no raised rim around the hollow. It lies on a narrow terrace to the west of the White Water stream and is underlain by gravels which are Middle Devensian or older. At first sight the hollow might be thought to be related to an icing at the time of deposition of the gravels (see e.g. Coxon, 1978), since there is an intermittent spring in the hollow at present. However, the basal organic sediments in the filling of the hollow are shown by pollen analysis to belong to the *Betula* pollen assemblage zone of the early Flandrian.

There is thus a considerable gap in time between the beginning of the filling and the terrace formation. Since the Chalk is some 15 m below the base of the hollow, a shallow collapse may again be the cause of hollow formation. The downward warping of the gravel/fines interface at 11 to 8 m on the section suggests such a cause. Even though collapse may be the main cause of hollow formation, it may be that ground-ice formation in the Devensian and its subsequent melting aided the processes leading to collapse; but any such ground-ice was not sufficient to result in a raised rim on melting. It

seems unlikely that an icing related to the spring allowed a hollow to develop at the time of terrace formation, since a hollow so formed should contain sediments much older than early Flandrian.

Walton Common (TF 736164)

The shallow hollows of Walton Common have been described and thoroughly discussed by Sparks *et al.* (1972). Some of the hollows have very marked ramparts. A generalized section through a rampart, given by Sparks *et al.*, is shown in Figure 17.2. Here the situation is totally different from that described for the Beetley hollows. The configuration of the hollows and ramparts indicates the strong growth of ground-ice in the Late Devensian, related to springs from the underlying Chalk. This resulted in the sloughing-off of surface chalk rubble and sand, leaving ramparts when the ground-ice melted. The thin organic seams and sand to the right of the section are probably sediments of the depressions between the rising ground-ice mounds, as suggested by Sparks *et al.* (1972).

Concealed hollows

Beetley T (TF 98581790)

The section in Figure 17.2 shows a shallow depression filled with early or mid-Devensian organic sediments overlain by fluviatile sands and then 2 to 3 metres of solifluction deposits. The base of the organic filling is telmatic peat and the upper part is limnic mud, indicating a rise in water level in the course of deposition. The margins of the hollow show deformation which appears to have occurred soon after the beginning of the deposition of the fluviatile sands. The deformation is probably associated with the release of hydrostatic pressure through the more permeable inorganic sediments at the margin of the hollow filling, which movement also resulted in the accentuation of the hollow. A question then arises about the origin of the hydrostatic pressure. The area is near the foot of a slope which bears springs at the present time, indicating artesian pressures. Such pressure may have been strengthened by the development of frozen ground unslope, leaving an open system under pressure below (for present possibly similar conditions see Pollard & French, 1984). A detailed survey of the surrounding geology, together with a study of the palaeo-climate conditions through palaeontological analyses, would be needed to support such an explanation.

The hollow was evidently present before the deformation. Its origin is uncertain. Possibly it is a small thermokarst lake, with the organic sequence showing a reversed hydrosere. Or it may be a depression of a type found with low-centred polygons; a wedge cast was observed to the right of the section. The first would require ground-ice or frozen ground, the second permafrost.

Wretton WJ (TL 678994)

This section, shown in Figure 17.2, is described in detail by West *et al.* (1974). It lies in the low Devensian terrace of the River Wissey. The section shows a hollow surrounded by a rampart, both later submerged by the deposition of fluviatile sands and gravels. The terrace sediments all rest on Gault Clay. Possible origins of the structure were discussed as follows. Seasonal down-freezing or permafrost penetrated through the coarser sediments of the terrace, more slowly through the clayey sediments of a channel filling in the terrace. Different rates of down-freezing in the channel and adjacent deposits would then produce a closed system, with hydrostatic pressures developing in and beneath the channel fill. In these conditions ground-ice would form and raise a mound, sloughing-off the overlying sediments to later form the ramparts. Alternatively, or at the same time, segregation ice in the clayey sediments might have acted as a nucleus for the growth of ground-ice, and the hydrostatic pressures might have been augmented by a supply of water under open-system conditions. Superficially similar hollows with rims have been described from Banks Island by French and Dutkiewicz (1976), who suggested they might be the result of freezing of localized taliks within a braided channel system.

Conclusions

From this brief survey of five hollows it will be seen that the solution of the problems of origin can only lie in detailed studies of stratigraphy and palaeontology, both of the filling of the hollows and the configuration and nature of the sediments in which they lie. They are associated with processes of Devensian age, and so can be considered periglacial. But all are not necessarily associated with permafrost. All except the hollow at Wretton are associated with areas where springs rise at the present day. Ground-ice is certainly involved at Walton Common and Wretton, but not necessarily at the other sites. Collapse seems a major cause at two of the sites. It cannot be demonstrated that icings were the cause at any of the five sites described, though such an origin has been suggested for the hollow at Thelnetham described by Coxon (1978). A more certain icing origin for sediments might be demonstrated if late-glacial or older Devensian sediments were in a basin of sedimentation not now visible in a hollow, but once held up by an icing in a valley.

Acknowledgements

I am indebted to numerous colleagues for discussions on these matters in the field and to the owners of the Beetley gravel pit, Barker's, for generous access.

References

Auton, C.A. (1982). *A preliminary study of the sand and gravel deposits of part of Central Norfolk (1:25,000 sheets TF 91,92 and TG 01).* Institute of Geological Sciences, Keyworth.

Bradshaw, R.H.W. (1981). Quantitative reconstruction of local woodland vegetation using pollen analysis from a small basin in Norfolk, England. *Journal of Ecology,* **69**, 941–55.

Coxon, P. (1978). The first record of a fossil naled in Britain. *Quaternary Newsletter,* **24**, 9–11.

French, H.M. and Dutkiewicz, L. (1976). Pingos and pingo-like forms, Banks Island, Western Canadian Arctic. *Biul. Perygl.,* **26**, 211–222.

Pollard, W.H. and French, H.M. (1984). The groundwater hydraulics of seasonal frost mounds, North Fork Pass, Yukon Territory. *Canadian Journal of Earth Science,* **21**, 1073–81.

Sparks, B.W., Williams, R.B.G. and Bell, F.G. (1972). Presumed ground-ice depressions in East Anglia. *Proceedings of the Royal Society of London,* A, **327**, 329–43.

West, R.G., Dickson, C.A., Catt, J.A., Weir, A.G. and Sparks, B.W. (1974). Late Pleistocene deposits at Wretton, Norfolk. II. Devensian deposits. *Philosophical Transactions of the Royal Society of London,* B, **267**, 337–420.

18 · The distribution and age of pingo remnants in Ireland

P. COXON AND P. O'CALLAGHAN

Abstract

A map of all known occurrences of structures believed to be pingo remnants in Ireland is presented and their origin, distribution and age is examined. The possibility of a polygenetic origin for the Irish pingo remnants is discussed as is their distinct distributional pattern (mostly outside of the Midlandian glacial limits) and their relationship to topography and other environmental factors. A number of sites with pingo remnants are shown to have been active during the Nahanagan Stadial although previous activity cannot be discounted.

Introduction

This study attempts to locate, map and date a range of features that resemble the ramparts and associated depressions left by melted ground-ice lenses as described by numerous authors (e.g. Pissart, 1963; Watson, 1971; Mitchell, 1971). One of us (PO'C) has been responsible for collecting the records of pingo remnants and interpreting the aerial photographs. The other (PC) prepared the discussion below and carried out the palaeo-environmental work.

The terminology poses a problem because the origin of the ramparted structures is open to question (cf. Sparks *et al.*, 1972). However, since the most likely origin of the features appears to be the collapse of a pingo, we have referred to them as pingo remnants although it should be emphasised that we appreciate that they may be of varied origin (cf. Bryant and Carpenter, 1987; West, 1987).

Pingos are ice-cored mounds produced by the intrusion of water under pressure (which freezes) or by the growth of segregated ice lenses (French, 1976). Pingo mounds are variable in form (from conical features to asymmetric and elongate forms) as well as size (ranging in height from 3 m − 70 m and in diameter from 30 m − 600 m). Muller (1959) proposed that two types of pingos could be recognized:

i. Open-system pingos which occur on low angled slopes or on valley floors in areas of thin or discontinuous permafrost. These grow by the intrusion of water through the thin permafrost where a hydrostatic head exists.

ii. Closed-system pingos which occur on low lying land in areas of continuous permafrost and are formed by advancing permafrost in previously unfrozen sediments (usually at the site of a former lake) pushing pore water towards a developing ice lens.

In both open- and closed-system pingos the ice lens continues to grow, stretching and over-steepening the 'skin' of the pingo. Eventually, mass wasting from the pingo's sides and rupture of the 'skin' expose the ice-core and melting commences leading to the formation of a central depression surrounded by a rampart (De Gans, 1981).

Low circular or crescentic ramparts enclosing shallow depressions have been widely described in north-western Europe as fossil pingos, pingo remnants, 'pingo-like' features and 'ground-ice depressions' (e.g. Maarleveld, 1965; Watson and Watson, 1972; De Gans, 1981 and references in French, 1976, p. 246). Most of the pingo remnants in Europe are believed, on morphological and distributional grounds to have been open-system type pingos during their formation (French, 1976).

The close association of the ramparted structures of the Irish pingo remnants with spring lines at the foot of south-facing slopes (e.g. near Castleisland, County Kerry: site 1 on Figure 18.1) strongly suggests that at many of the localities the features were dependent on particular local conditions such as the availability of ground water and a thinning of the permafrost through which it could pass. The Irish pingo remnants (e.g. Camaross, County Wexford: site 2 on Figure 18.1) also exhibit the

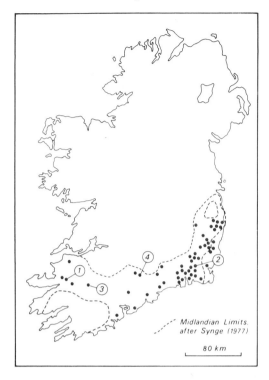

Figure 18.1. The location of pingo remnants in Ireland from original mapping and numerous other sources including the field mapping of G.F. Mitchell and F.M. Synge. The numbered sites are referred to in the text.

Features mapped as pingo remnants

The melting of a pingo's ice-core may leave a recognisable trace of the original feature. Usually such a trace is a depression (or scar) surrounded, at least in part, by a rampart. In this study only features with an obvious rampart have been included because isolated depressions in an area recently glaciated may be kettle holes (the product of dead glacial ice wastage). We have used 'pingo remnant' to refer to a shallow depression at least partially enclosed by a rampart. Sites located on aerial photographs have been checked in the field and features of uncertain origin have been excluded from the distribution data.

The distribution of the Irish pingo remnants

Figure 18.1 shows the distribution of pingo remnants in Ireland. The data have been collected from a number of sources and from detailed inspection of the Geological Survey of Ireland's 1:30,000 aerial photographs.

This distribution map may be prone to error for two main reasons: firstly there has been a lack of detailed Quaternary field mapping in Ireland and secondly, within the limits of the Last (Midlandian) Glaciation, it is possible that pingo remnants have been excluded because they have been mistaken for kettle holes even though the latter features have no ramparts. Caution has to be used when interpreting the map which should be considered as a preliminary source of information. The first constraint suggests that the mapped distribution is an under estimate. However fieldwork by a number of workers in northern, western and east-central Ireland, within the Midlandian ice limits, as well as inspection of aerial photographs, has failed to produce additional records of pingo remnants (e.g. Hoare and McCabe, 1981).

Accepting the fact that additional examples will probably be found as further work is carried out, the following observations can be made:

1. There is a strong concentration of pingo remnants outside of the limits of the Last Glaciation.
2. The pingo remnants are more numerous in the eastern part of their range although large groups are found centrally (e.g. Meenskeha Townland, County Cork, site 3 on Figure 18.1) and in the west (e.g. Ballyegan Townland, Castleisland, County Kerry, site 1).
3. Many of the clusters of pingo remnants are found in wet areas, usually along valley floors, near to the base of a slope or actually at spring sources.

overlapping and clustering forms typical of open-system pingos (French, 1976).

The large size range in Irish pingo remnants (c. 10 m – 100 m in diameter) and the occurrence of remnants as individuals, small groups (sometimes widely separated) and large clusters could mean that the fossil features are polygenetic: perhaps the type of ground-ice was controlled by local climatic and hydrological conditions. It is possible that some of the smaller forms, less than 25 m in diameter, which are clustered around springs near valley sides, may have formed as seasonal frost mounds (cf. Pollard and French, 1983, 1984). Such seasonal features form where groundwater from perennial springs freezes during the winter freezeback. Features such as the 'mineral palsas' of Pissart (1984) also cannot be excluded as one possible modern analogue.

Palaeo-environmental reconstructions using landforms classified as 'pingo remnants' are likely to be inaccurate because the conditions required to produce pingos *sensu stricto* may be quite different to those required to produce other cryogenic mounds in the periglacial landscape.

4. The features occur on a wide variety of bedrock and there is no apparent rock control of the distribution. However many sites do have a variable depth (e.g. at Camaross, Ballyegan and Meenskeha it is *c.* 1–1.5 m) of a diamicton, possibly solifluction deposits, in which the original pingos formed.

5. The altitude of the pingo remnants is normally below 150 m and they occur at low altitudes (*c.* 20 m O.D.) in both east and west.

6. A large number of the pingo remnants lie on the northern side of valley floors or along, or at the base of, gentle (1–7°) south-facing slopes.

The almost complete lack of pingo remnants from within the limits of the Midlandian Glaciation may represent a strong bias by Quaternary workers in their search for such features. If however the map is taken at its face value then a number of reasons might be proposed for that distribution. Firstly, the formation of Irish pingos may have been limited by the availability of permeable solifluction deposits. Secondly, the initiation of pingo growth may have occurred at 18–20,000 years B.P. when the ice sheets are believed to have reached their maximum. Thirdly it is possible that beyond the glacial limits permafrost had formed during the Midlandian and because this area remained unglaciated the permafrost was more stable or better developed than elsewhere. If the cryogenic mounds we are dealing with require permafrost (and open-system pingos do require discontinuous permafrost) then this factor may have had a strong influence on ground-ice development.

No one explanation is really satisfactory. Not enough is known about the relationship of the pingo remnants to substrate and it is likely that suitable deposits exist within the ice limits for the growth of cryogenic mounds. The second explanation can only be tested when datable material is recovered from below the ramparts of some of these features (see below). The final hypothesis is hard to test because we know little about permafrost conditions or how important permafrost was to the formation of the Irish ground-ice features.

The concentration of pingo remnants in eastern areas may reflect more continental conditions or lower snowfall (or both) in this region.

The fact that aspect and hydrological conditions are important in controlling the distribution shows the importance of micro-climate and water supply. These limiting factors suggest ground-ice formed most frequently where the permafrost was slightly thinner or where seasonal melting provided a readily available source of water to feed ice lenses.

Previous dating of pingo remnants in Ireland

Mitchell's work (1971 and 1973) showed that pingo scars in County Wexford (near Camaross, site 2, Figure 18.1), like their counterparts in Wales (Watson, 1975), did not begin to accumulate sediment until the end of Zone III (based on biostratigraphic correlation to Jessen's (1949) tripartite Late Glacial stratigraphy – see Table 18.1). This suggested that the pingos had been active (i.e. ice lenses had been present in what are now the pingo scars) during Zone III of the Late Glacial. An outline of the chronostratigraphy and biostratigraphy of the Irish Late Glacial and Early Post Glacial is given in Table 18.1.

Zone III of the Late Glacial in Ireland has been informally accepted as being equivalent to the Nahanagan Stadial, a phase during which glaciers readvanced at Lough Nahanagan in the Wicklow Mountains (Colhoun and Synge, 1980), although direct comparisons of Jessen's scheme and modern pollen assemblages are not perfect. The glacier readvance occurred after 11,500 B.P. (Colhoun and Synge suggest the period *c.* 11,000–10,500 B.P. for the renewed glaciation) and the Stadial probably spans the period between *c.* 11,000–10,200 B.P. The Nahanagan Stadial is a period in which there was widespread deposition of inorganic sediments in lake basins throughout Ireland. Sediments at many such sites are now dated e.g. L. Aisling, County Mayo, P. Browne pers. comm.) and there are terrestrial deposits dated to this phase at Old Head, County Mayo (Mitchell, 1977) and Drumurcher, County Monaghan (Coope, *et al.*, 1979). Protalus ramparts believed to date to the Nahanagan Stadial have been described by Colhoun (1981) and Coxon (1985).

The Nahanagan Stadial is frequently represented on pollen diagrams by an assemblage in which *Artemisia* is the characteristic plant (Watts, 1977), with a preceding Cruciferae peak possibly indicating the demise of grassland due to solifluction in a deteriorating climate. The end of the Stadial is marked by a Gramineae-*Rumex* peak followed by a *Juniperus-Filipendula* assemblage at the beginning of the Post Glacial (Watts, 1977).

In order to add to Mitchell's dating of the Wexford pingo remnants the authors have visited a large number of the Irish sites to test for datable material either within (or below) the ramparts or in the rampart enclosed hollows. Many sites (e.g. in the Burncourt area, County Tipperary, site 4,

Table 18.1 Correlation table for the Late Midlandian Glaciation. (*After Jessen 1949, Mitchell et al. 1973, Mangerud et al. 1974 and Watts 1977, 1985). Figures are years B.P.*

Continental north west Europe			Ireland					Pollen assemblages		Jessen's (1949) tripartite scheme the Late Glacial
Stage	Substage		Chronozone	Stage	Substage					
Flandrian	Early Flandrian	8,000 / 9,000–8,000 / 10,000–9,000 / 10,000	Boreal / Preboreal	Littletonian	Early Littletonian	8,000 / 8,000 Early Post Glacial / 10,000		*Corylus* phase / *Salix – Betula* phase	8,500– / 9,500–8,500	
								Second Juniper peak	10,000–9,500	
Weichselian	Late Weichselian	11,000–10,000 / 11,800–11,000 / 12,000–11,800 / 13,000–12,000 / 13,000	Younger *Dryas* / Allerød / Older *Dryas* / Bølling		Late Midlandian	10,000 Late Glacial / 13,000	Nahanagan S. / Woodgrange I/S	Gramineae – *Rumex* peak	10,200–10,000	III
								Artemisia phase	10,900–10,200	II
								Grass phase	11,800–10,900	
								Erosion phase	12,000–11,800	
								First Juniper peak	12,400–12,000	I
								Rumex – Salix assemblage	13,000–12,400	
	Middle Weichselian			Midlandian	Middle Midlandian	26,000				

Figure 18.1) with impressive pingo remains simply contained diamictons of local origin formed by mass movement of part of the pingo rampart into the depression. Post-depositional disturbance of enclosed sediments was a potential problem and local flax treatment may have led to the clearing out of sediment from the latter site. At sites in County Wexford, clusters of small rampart-enclosed hollows were found that contained small lakes. However, the sediments (which presumably contained some peat) had been cut out, probably to provide fuel in an area where such a resource is rare.

No site to date has yielded organic sediments from within or below the ramparts which would provide a date for the collapse of the original pingo mound. However, two sites (Ballyegan Townland, near Castleisland, County Kerry and Meenskeha Townland, near Millstreet, County Cork) had pingo remnants that contained Late Glacial/Early Post Glacial sediments and these sites are discussed below.

Further evidence on the age of the Irish pingo remnants

Meenskeha Townland
The site of the pingo remnants at Meenskeha Townland is at grid reference W 273973 (Irish O.S. 1/2 inch sheet 21) 7.5 km north of Millstreet and 300 m north of the N27 (Rathmore to Mallow) road. The locality is shown as site 3 on Figure 18.1 and Figure 18.2 is a detailed map of the site taken

from Coxon (1986). Figure 18.2 is based on fieldwork and Geological Survey of Ireland 1:30,000 scale aerial photographs.

The pingo remnants lie along a spring line at the foot of a south-facing slope (the break of slope is just below the 152.4 m contour on Figure 18.2) and exhibit the overlapping and clustered form typical of open-system pingo development (French, 1976). The preserved ramparts suggest that over 25 pingos existed at some time along the base of the south-facing slope. In one field, where sedges had been cleared, a polygonal network, presumed to be produced by frost cracking under periglacial conditions, was visible on aerial photographs (site 4 on Figure 18.2). The slope on and below which the pingo remnants lie forms part of a ridge trending east-west. In this area, Carboniferous Coal Measures are overlain by an unsorted deposit over 1 m thick which is probably a till or solifluction deposit.

The pingo ramparts, which are now somewhat subdued due to the infilling of the associated hollow, are in the order of 1–2 m high and 3–4 m wide and composed of the unsorted deposit referred to above. One large circular rampart (site 2 on Figure 18.2) is 100 m across, another (site 3 on Figure 18.2) is almost 80 m in diameter. The pingo remnants are more usually 50 m in diameter although the fragmented forms of the residual ramparts makes measurement difficult.

A number of the depressions in the area were investigated to find an undisturbed and long sedimentary record and site 1 (Figure 18.2) was

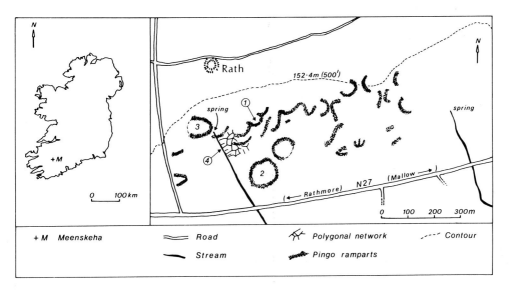

Figure 18.2. Pingo ramparts at Meenskeha, County Cork.

sampled using a Livingstone piston sampler (Wright, 1967).

The ramparts enclosed a shallow depression which contained 3 m of sediment.

The detailed sedimentological and palynological results are only briefly referred to here and have been published in full elsewhere (Coxon, 1986). Three samples for radiocarbon dating were submitted to the Subdepartment of Quaternary Research in Cambridge in order to provide dating control for the pollen diagram and the results were as follows:

Sample ref.	Depth in core	Cambridge ref.	Date
MRC3	160–170 cm	Q-2453	8290 +/− 120 B.P.
MRC2	220–228 cm	Q-2454	9420 +/− 150 B.P.
MRC1	280–288 cm	Q-2455	9740 +/− 150 B.P.

The sedimentary record suggests an initial input into the hollow of coarse, poorly sorted debris, similar to the material that forms the ramparts, followed by a period of lacustrine deposition which may at first have been influenced by unstable conditions. Organic deposition began at *c.* 288 cm and this sediment was dated (MRC 1 above). The increasing volume of organic material found in the upper parts of the core (and the wood fragments) suggest that the lake was being infilled with debris from trees growing in or around the hollow.

The earliest pollen assemblage recorded here (Cyperaceae-Gramineae with a diverse herb flora including *Rumex*) is replaced by an assemblage with rapidly increasing percentages of pollen of *Juniperus* and the appearance of *Salix*. This succession is similar to those described from numerous sites (Mitchell, 1976; Watts, 1977; Craig, 1978) and the open Gramineae and Cyperaceae vegetation probably represents the latter part of the Nahanagan Stadial and the beginning of the Littletonian at *c.* 10,000–10,200 years B.P. (see Table 18.1). This assumption is supported by the radiocarbon sample MRC1, from immediately above this zone, with its age of 9,740 years B.P.

Ballyegan Townland

The pingo remnants in this area have not been studied in as much detail as those at Meenskeha but preliminary findings are presented below.

The Ballyegan pingo remnants form several distinct clusters in Maglass, Coolgarriv, Crag and Ballyegan Townlands centred on grid reference

Q 960117 (Irish O.S. 1/2 inch sheet 21) 5 km north west of Castleisland on the T28 (Castleisland to Tralee) road.

Most of the pingo remnants lie along a spring line at the foot of a south west facing slope at between 50–60 m O.D. There are four distinct clusters of five or six scars with diameters of between 30 and 50 m and there are also larger individual remnants one of which is over 100 m in diameter and straddles the T28 road. The pingo ramparts are composed of a limestone rich diamicton and the area on which the remnants lie is underlain by Carboniferous Limestone.

One pingo scar in Ballyegan Townland was sampled using a Hiller Corer and the basal sediment, a calcareous clay with some organic detritus overlying sandy clay with angular limestone fragments, was analysed for its pollen content. The highly calcareous sediment was unsuitable for radiocarbon dating.

The earliest pollen assemblage recorded here was, as at Meenskeha, Cyperaceae-Gramineae with a diverse herb flora including *Rumex*. An assemblage containing 40% pollen of *Juniperus* succeeds the lower assemblage. As at Meenskeha the open Gramineae and Cyperaceae vegetation probably represents the latter part of the Nahanagan Stadial and the beginning of the Littletonian at *c.* 10,000–10,200 years B.P.

The biostratigraphic and chronostratigraphic data from the two pingo remnants at Ballyegan and Meenskeha suggest that deposition began in the pingo scars during the transition from the Late Glacial into the Early Post Glacial. This indicates that at least two groups of pingos, in addition to Mitchell's in Wexford, were active during the latter part of the Late Glacial in the Nahanagan Stadial and their basins were not available for sediment deposition until after *c.* 10,200–10,000 B.P.

Conclusions

This analysis of the distribution of pingo remnants in the Irish landscape provides a basis for further work. The map we have produced is probably an under representation of the true distribution but it gives preliminary information about the environmental controls on the location of pingo remnants.

Because of a lack of information regarding the internal structure of the pingo remnants and because of the lack of modern analogues there is doubt about the origin of the mounds. Although it is highly likely that many sites represent open-system pingo growth a polygenetic origin cannot be discounted.

The pingos appear to have been active at several sites during the Nahanagan Stadial although we can only say that this was their last period of activity. The Midlandian Glaciation was a long and complex event with cold conditions prevailing for over 70,000 years. With such conditions it is probable that the pingos were active much earlier than the Nahanagan Stadial but as yet we can provide no evidence.

Acknowledgements

The authors would like to acknowledge the assistance of numerous people who have brought cryogenic mounds to their attention including G.F. Mitchell, W.P. Warren and the late F.M. Synge. They would also like to thank Sybil Watson for commenting on a draft of this paper and Dr W. De Gans for very helpful criticism and suggestions.

Note

Since this chapter was written, one of the authors (PC) has discovered sediments of Woodgrange Interstadial age within a pingo remnant which is inside the limits of the Midlandian Glaciation (near Snugborough, grid reference T 244783) proving that at least some pingos were active in Ireland prior to the Nahanagan Stadial.

References

Bryant, R.H. and Carpenter, C.P. (1987). Ramparted ground ice depressions in Britain and Ireland. In, *Periglacial Processes and Landforms in Britain and Ireland* (Ed. J. Boardman), pp. 183–90 Cambridge University Press.

Colhoun, E.A. (1981). A protalus rampart from the western Mourne Mountains, Northern Ireland, *Irish Geography* 14, 85–90.

Colhoun, E.A. and Synge, F.M. (1980). The cirque moraines at Lough Nahanagan, County Wicklow, Ireland, *Proc. R. Ir. Acad.*, **80B**, 25–45.

Coope, G.R., Dickson, J.H., McCutcheon, J.A. and Mitchell, G.F. (1979) The Late Glacial and Early Postglacial deposit at Drumurcher, Co. Monaghan, *Proc. R. Ir. Acad.*, **79B**, 63–85.

Coxon, P. (1985) Gleniff – Protalus rampart. In, *Sligo and West Leitrim. Irish Association for Quaternary Studies Field Guide No. 8. (1985)* (Ed. R.H. Thorn), IQUA. Dublin.

Coxon, P. (1986). A radiocarbon dated Early Post Glacial pollen diagram from a Pingo remnant near Millstreet Co, Cork. *Ir. J. Earth Sci.*, **8**, 9–20.

Craig, A.J. (1978). Pollen percentage and influx analyses in South-east Ireland: A contribution to the ecological history of the Late Glacial period, *Journal of Ecology* **66**, 297–324.

De Gans, W. (1981). *The Drentsche Aa Valley System*, Rodopi, Amsterdam, 132pp.

French, H.M. (1976). *The Periglacial Environment*, Longman, 309pp.

Hoare, P.G. and McCabe, A.M. (1981). The periglacial record in east-central Ireland, *Biuletyn Peryglacjalny* **28**, 57–78.

Jessen, K. (1949). Studies in late Quaternary deposits and flora-history of Ireland, *Proc. R. Ir. Acad. B* **52**, 85–290.

Maarleveld, G.C. (1965). Frost Mounds, *Mededelingen van de Geologische Stichting* **17**, 3–16.

Mangerud, J., Andersen, S.T., Berglund, B.E. and Donner, J.J. (1974). Quaternary stratigraphy of Norden, a proposal for terminology and classification, *Boreas* **3**, 109–27.

Mitchell, G.F. (1971). Fossil pingos in the south of Ireland. *Nature Lond.*, **230**, 43–4.

Mitchell, G.F. (1973). Fossil pingos in Camaross Townland, Co. Wexford. *Proc. R. Ir. Acad.*, **73B**, 269–82.

Mitchell, G.F. (1976). *The Irish Landscape*, Collins, London, 240pp.

Mitchell, G.F. (1977) Periglacial Ireland, *Phil. Trans. R. Soc. Lond.*, **B280**, 199–209.

Mitchell, G.F., Penny, L.F., Shotton, F.W. and West, R.G. (1973). A correlation of Quaternary deposits in the British Isles, *Geol. Soc. Lond. Spec. Rep.*, **4**, 99pp.

Muller, F. (1959). Beobachtungen uber pingos, *Meddelelser om Gronland* 153, 3, 126pp. National Research Council of Canada Technical Translation **1073**, **1963**, 177pp.

Pissart, A. (1963). Les traces de pingos du Pays de Galles (Grande Bretagne) et du plateau des Hautes Fagnes (Belgique), *Zeitschrift fur Geomorphologie* **7**, 147–65.

Pissart, A. (1984). Les Palses minerales et organiques de la Vallee de L'Aveneau, pres de Kuujjuaq, Quebec Subarctique, *Géographie physique et Quaternaire* **38**, 217–28.

Pollard, W.H. and French, H.M. (1983). The occurrence of seasonal frost mounds, North Fork Pass, Ogilvie Mountains, Yukon Territory. In, *Proceedings, Fourth International Conference on Permafrost. Vol. 1*, pp. 1000–1004, National Academy Press, Washington, DC.

Pollard, W.H. and French, H.M. (1984). The groundwater hydraulics of seasonal frost mounds, North Fork Pass, Yukon Territory, *Can. J. Earth Sci.*, **21**, 1073–81.

Sparks, B.W., Williams, R.B.G. and Bell, F.G. (1972). Presumed ground-ice depressions in East Anglia, *Proc. R. Soc. Lond.*, **A327**, 329–43.

Synge, F.M. (1977) Introduction. In, *Guidebook for excursion A15, South and South West Ireland.* (Ed. C.A. Lewis), INQUA.

Watson, E. (1971). Remains of pingos in Wales and the Isle of Man, *Geol. J.*, **7**, 381–92.

Watson, E. (1975). *Guide to field excursions. Periglacial Symposium IGU, Aberystwyth.*

Watson, E. and Watson, S. (1972). Investigations of some pingo basins, near Aberystwyth, Wales, *Rep. 24th Int. Geol. Cong., Canada, Sect. 12*, 212–23.

Watts, W.A. (1977). The Late Devensian vegetation of Ireland, *Phil. Trans. R. Soc. Lond.* **B, 280,** 273–93.

Watts, W.A. (1985). Quaternary vegetation cycles. In, *The Quaternary History of Ireland* (Eds. K. Edwards and W.P. Warren), pp. 155–85, Academic Press, London.

West, R.G. (1987). Origin of small hollows in Norfolk. In, *Periglacial Processes and Landforms in Britain and Ireland* (Ed. J. Boardman), pp. 191–4 Cambridge University Press.

Wright, H.E. (1967). A square-rod piston sampler for lake sediments, *J. Sediment. Petrol.*, **37**, 975–6.

19 · The role of thermokarst in landscape development in eastern England

RODNEY G.O. BURTON

Abstract

A number of near circular depressions, about a kilometre in diameter, and arcuate topographical features that occur along the western side of the Fenland of eastern England are described. They have been excavated through thin Devensian terrace deposits into a Jurassic clay substrate. The presence of polygonal ice-wedge cast patterns in the terraces indicates a large ground-ice content and their formation is ascribed to Late Devensian thermokarst processes. They are similar to modern alases and alas valley systems in Yakutia. Their widespread occurrence indicates the importance of thermokarst in landscape development in the Fenland. Other large depressions have been noted in the southern Vale of York. Along the eastern side of the Fenland the different hydrological and geological conditions caused a large number of small ground-ice depressions to form.

Introduction

The shallow Fenland basin of Eastern England, floored mainly by Jurassic and Cretaceous clays, is thought to have been excavated by an advancing Anglian ice-sheet (Perrin *et al.*, 1979). Rivers entering the Fenland from narrow upland valleys have at various times during the Pleistocene formed extensive spreads of gravels, interrupted by periods of incision. The gravels form a discontinuous rim around the basin and cap high ground within the Fenland (Figure 19.1). They are now assigned to First and Second Terraces (Gallois, 1980; Wyatt, 1984). All ground up to 3.7 m O.D. has been covered by peat during the Flandrian but the buried surfaces are slowly being exhumed by peat wastage following drainage for agriculture.

Some terraces display a polygonal network at the modern ground surface highlighted as differential crop growth patterns on summer aerial photography. This network is interpreted as consisting of epigenetic ice-wedge casts, features associated with a rigorous climate with permafrost (e.g. Péwé, 1966). Figure 19.1 also shows the distribution of a number of large, near circular or oval depressions, of remarkable symmetry, associated with the occurrence of terraces.

The depressions

Conington Fen

A pair of oval depressions excavated into Oxford Clay and thin superficial drift at the western edge of the Fenland (centred at grid ref. TL 190850 and TL 200850), were the first to be detected and described (Burton, 1976). They are both about 1000 m long by 825 m wide, with a topographic depth of 7.5 m, separated by a 125 m wide 'rampart'. They have flat floors and are infilled with Flandrian peat with its base dated palynologically to the Atlantic period (Zone VIIa). Both depressions have drainage outlets at the downslope end, that of the eastern depression being only 60 m wide. They bear little resemblance to previously published descriptions, but on the evidence available they were thought to have had a thermokarstic origin in a periglacial environment, probably by the melting of large ice lenses. A patchy distribution of thin silty aeolian drift was noted on the slopes and considered to postdate the formation of the depressions.

Farcet Fen

Eight km to the north in Farcet Fen (TL 220935) near Peterborough, a peat-filled oval depression

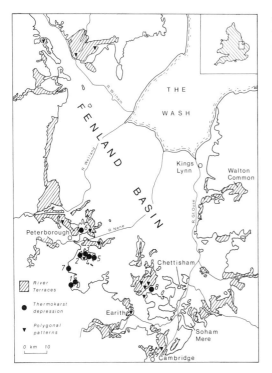

Figure 19.1. The Fenland Basin, eastern England, showing the distribution of terraces, large thermokarst depressions and polygonal patterns.
Depressions: 1 Conington Fen; 2 Farcet Fen; 3 White Hall Farm; 4 Homestead Farm; 5 Underwood's Farm; 6 Eyebury Farm; 7 Stilton Fen; 8 Mepal Fen.

within a raised terrace remnant overlying Oxford Clay was investigated after its discovery on aerial photographs (Burton, 1978). The depression is of comparable size to those in Conington Fen, 1000 m by 750 m and 6 m deep, and also has a narrow outlet through which the whole depression drains. The presence of polygonal ice-wedge cast patterns in the terrace suggests that here thermal erosion was initiated in a manner similar to that described for modern alases in Yakutia (Czudek and Demek, 1970). The ice in the wedges combined with pore ice could have provided the large ground ice content necessary for thermokarst degradation without the need to postulate a lens of massive segregation ice, although the presence of this cannot be ruled out.

The lithostratigraphic investigation revealed solifluction deposits masking the slopes of Oxford Clay both within the depression and around the outer edges of the raised terrace outlier. They can be separated into a coarser-textured component

overlain by a finer-textured layer. A thin silty veneer covers the whole of the raised terrace surface. It also covers the upper slopes but down-slope the bed is a silty clay or clay, and resembles the Oxford Clay country rock. This corresponds to the Crowland Bed of the British Geological Survey (Booth, 1982, p. 8; Wyatt, 1984), composed of silt and clay with occasional stones and interpreted by these authors as the final stage of terrace aggradation.

This depression differs from those in Conington Fen in that the evidence is more complete; it is better preserved, perhaps fossilised by the disappearance of permafrost. The drift-covered dividing 'rampart' in Conington Fen is merely a remnant of the former inter-alas terrace in which ice-wedges could have developed, rather than a true rampart formed by radial thrust from an expanding ice lens or by sloughing off a pingo mound.

Other depressions in the Conington/Farcet area

In present permafrost areas alas or thaw lake depressions form in groups in flat lowland areas rich in ground ice. Recent soil surveys along a 16 km section of the western Fenland have revealed other similar landforms. These are shown in Figure 19.2 by plotting isopachytes of thickness of Flandrian deposits now filling most of the Fenland basin, a crude but effective means of mapping the configuration of the Fenland floor without levelled data. The terrace at 3.2 m O.D. in Farcet Fen dips gently to the east to be covered by Flandrian peat and estuarine alluvium up to an elevation of about 0 m O.D. Three less complete depressions occur near White Hall Farm (TL 237938), Homestead Farm (TL 247930) and Underwood's Farm (TL 269935). White Hall and Homestead Farm depressions are connected by a 50 m wide, 1 m deep channel floored by Crowland Beds. At Milby two curvilinear slopes isolate a 200 m-wide spur capped by terrace deposits. In Stilton Fen to the south (TL 184893) an 800 m-wide peat-filled hollow forms the head to a deeply incised valley abutting against the upland at Holme (TL 195882) (Burton and Seale, 1981, peat depth map). Near Eyebury Farm (TF 220020), Peterborough, an irregularly shaped alluvial-filled depression etched into Oxford Clay has two narrow outlet gullies. Solifluction or mudflow clay similar to the slope deposits at Farcet Fen has been traced seaward and in a channel south of Pondersbridge (at TL 270905) was seen in a pipeline trench to overlie bedded gravels which extended to − 6.3 m O.D.

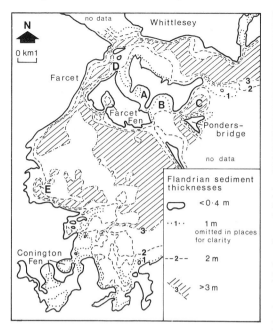

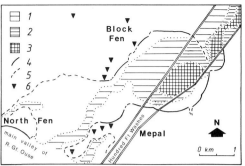

Figure 19.2. The western margin of the Fenland south of Whittlesey, Cambridgeshire. Isopachytes of Flandrian sediment thickness show the approximate configuration of the Fenland floor, outlining large thermokarst depressions.
A White Hall Farm; B Homestead Farm;
C Underwood's Farm; D Milby; E Stilton Fen.

Figure 19.3. Large thermokarst depression and connecting valleys at Mepal Fen, (TL 440380), Cambridgeshire.
1,2 and 3 Flandrian sediment thicker than 1,2 and 3 metres respectively; 4 sharply defined micro-scarp; 5 less distinct slope bounding valley; 6 known distribution of polygonal patterns from aerial photographs.

Mepal Fen

In Mepal Fen (TL 440830) micro-scarps encircle a depression 2.2 km in diameter. In plan they are not of constant curvature, comprising seven distinct arcuate sections (Figure 19.3) clearly visible as pale tones on bare ground aerial photographs. The depression is cut into a (Middle?) Devensian terrace that is broadly assigned to Terrace 1–2 (Gallois, 1980), of similar age to that described at Earith, 8 km to the south west, by Bell (1970). North east of the depression in Block Fen, the terrace at about 1 m O.D. displays a polygonal pattern of crop marks over presumed ice-wedge casts. Its surface has a thin covering of aeolian silt and fine sand beneath which has formed a soil with a well-developed textural B horizon of clay translocation (Seale, 1975a, soil profile No. TL48/3332). On its south-eastern side the depression abuts against Jurassic Ampthill Clay near the village of Mepal.

Reconnaissance mapping of this newly detected feature has revealed that within the depression at about − 1 m O.D., there is an infilling of Flandrian peat and estuarine alluvium to a maximum thickness centrally of 1.6 m on agricultural land subject to peat wastage. Crossing the depression is a strip of pasture land, the Hundred Foot Washes flood relief reservoir, which has been less prone to peat wastage with peat thicknesses to 3.6 m being found. Flooring most of the depression is a clay, with a maximum proven thickness of 1.4 km, interpreted here as a solifluction or mudflow deposit, overlying coarser-textured deposits of unknown thickness. The source of the mudflow clay is believed to be the Ampthill Clay which it closely resembles and for which it can be mistaken. A description and particle-size analysis of it is given by Seale (1975a, soil profile no. TL48/4533).

Along the south western side a shallow 900 m-wide outlet, also bounded by arcuate micro-scarps in places, links the depression to the main incised valley of the Flandrian river Great Ouse. This 3 km-long connecting valley has a thin silty covering over coarser terrace deposits or over thin mudflow clay along the main axis. In the north east the line of the micro-scarp has not yet been proved by augering through the thick deposits of the Washes, but an aerial photograph (V3 58 RAF 9669 no. 0063) clearly shows sharp vegetational differences along the same line of curvature as on either side. A narrow deep outlet also floored by clay solifluction deposits has been found on the eastern side of the depression. It extends beneath the Washes and widens out to the north east.

The formation of the features outlined in Mepal Fen is ascribed to a combination of periglacial processes. Initiation probably occurred as Late Devensian thermokarst subsidence on terraces with a large ground ice content in ice wedges.

Table 19.1 *Location and dimensions of arcuate bluffs flanking valleys in the Fenland.*

			Curvature	
Valley	Location	Grid ref	angle	radius
Gt Ouse	North Fen	TL 400814	62°	1000 m
Gt Ouse	Manea	TL 463875	32°	2250 m
Cam	Swaffham Prior Fen	TL 542680	138°	450 m
Cam	Bottisham Fen	TL 530663	174°	275 m
Nene	Milby	TL 220947	49°	1060 m
Nene	Crowland	TF 220083	29°	1700 m

Subsequent rapid retrogressive thermal erosion produced thaw flowslides resulting in thermocirques (cf. Czudek and Demek, 1970, p. 106). This provided the very fluid mudflow clay that on very gentle slopes covered most low lying ground leaving now-fossilised arcuate micro-scarps. Drainage of the depression was by narrow outlets on opposite sides, a configuration typical of alas valleys that have wide sections and narrow connecting sections. The initiation of thermokarst development may have been influenced by the marginal terrace site against higher ground of impervious Ampthill Clay at Mepal and the introduction of massive segregation ice from an artesian source, and hence greater potential thermal instability. From the shape it seems unlikely to have formed by lateral migration of river meanders along an existing valley.

Arcuate topography

Arcuate bluffs forming the contact between low gravel terraces and Flandrian floodplain deposits have been noted in the valleys of several Fenland rivers (Table 19.1). Although morphologically resembling a short section of depression wall or micro-scarp, they probably represent Late Devensian or early Flandrian meander scars formed during the period of low sea level by fluvio-thermal or mechanical processes respectively, and prior to the accumulation of peat and alluvium. One studied at Milby had similar solifluction deposits masking the scarp to those occurring in the nearby Farcet Fen depression, but with an Oxford Clay surface slope of 45°.

Older features

Much elevated ground in the Fenland is capped by glacial or terrace deposits, remnants of levels once more extensive. Due west of Chettisham village, 3 km north of Ely, Cambridgeshire, is a depression (TL 540830) enclosed on the north, east and west sides by high ground capped by chalky till (Burton, 1978, p. 70). To the south a shallow break in the enclosing ridge is filled by thin drift deposits while in the north a deep but narrow gully forms a drainage outlet for the depression. The floor of the depression is formed in Kimmeridge Clay with scattered pockets of sandy gravelly drift.

The oval basin, partly occupied by the former lake, Soham Mere (TL 570730), possesses a curved enclosing upland capped by till and Third Terrace (R. Snail) gravels of Ipswichian age (Worssam and Taylor, 1969, p. 77). The basin is 5.5 by 3 km and contains Second and First Terrace deposits (Devensian). Thus excavation of the basin seems to have occurred between Third and Second Terrace times, i.e. Early to Middle Devensian. Did similar thermokarst depressions form on the Fenland plain in earlier periglacial periods?

Southern Vale of York

A very large circular depression occurs at West Moor (SE 650065), 8 km north east of Doncaster, S. Yorks (Gaunt, 1976; Jarvis, 1973). It has a diameter of 2.5 km and is formed in thin glaciofluvial or deltaic drift (Old River Gravel) over Triassic Bunter Sandstone, with the rock at higher elevations around the rim. This is referred to as the Lower Periglacial Surface (Gaunt, 1981), of Devensian age. The floor of the depression is occupied by '25-ft Drift' deposited in Lake Humber which gained access by way of two gullies at the eastern end. A soil formed in the '25-ft Drift' within the depression and covered by blown sand and peat yielded a ^{14}C date of 11,100 years B.P. (Gaunt *et al.*, 1971) and was equated with the Windermere Interstadial (Zone II). Gaunt (1976) considered the flanking rampart not to be an accumulated ridge created by a pingo but a remnant of the former land surface, concluding that the landform should be equated with a fossil alas.

Alases are unlikely to develop in isolation, and in fact Gaunt mentioned a second probable example, 1 km in diameter and also occupied by '25-ft Drift' on the eastern side of Belton, Isle of Axholme (SE 790065) and other less distinctive anomalous low areas including the alluvial area south west of Beltoft (SE 805060). Jarvis (1973, p. 1) also noted small enclosed depressions near West Moor 'where ridges converge like pincers'. These are Branton Moor (SE 637020) 1100 m by 750 m, Black Carr (SE 632008) 550 m by 600 m and Mill Hill, Auckley (SE 647002) 450 m by 500 m. Straw (1979, p. 42) suggested these were collapsed ground ice features, developed during melting of large ice lenses or massive ice bodies, formed as ground water under artesian pressure froze.

Discussion

From the evidence of the large depressions outlined above and their relationship with the terraces along the western side of the Fenland, it is suggested that thermal degradation of the ground was initiated in association with a polygonal network of ice wedges forming alases or thaw lake depressions. Although there is no firm evidence for the presence of other massive ice bodies, they cannot be excluded as a possible contributory factor. There was probably further incision by retrogressive thermal or fluvio-thermal processes to produce arcuate micro-escarpments, the headwalls of ground ice slumps or thermocirques, as in Mepal Fen. Removal of the contents of the depressions, such as a thermokarst lake, was probably by catastrophic emptying that operated preferentially along a furrow above a major ice wedge, as would appear to be the case in Farcet Fen. This gully too could be widened by fluvio-thermal erosion to give a more open depression. With the exception of Farcet Fen, the coalescing of depressions and the widening of the interlinking gullies has largely destroyed the individual features but the alas valley systems so produced are a previously unconsidered factor in the shaping of the Fenland basin floor.

Thin depositional layers can be detected and mapped by routine soil surveys and characterised by soil profile sampling. Fieldwork in the Fenland has revealed a widespread occurrence in different physiographic situations of soil with a high silt content (usually greater than 50%), also observed by Baden-Powell (1934). Its composition and location accord with the silt-sand province of aeolian drift of Perrin *et al.* (1974) and it is common on low-lying ground between Peterborough and Mepal. The local distribution of this silt-rich soil is given in publications of the Soil Survey of England & Wales, e.g. Seale (1975*b*) and Burton and Seale (1981). On indirect evidence, Catt (1977) linked the loess cover of southern and eastern England to the Dimlington Stadial (Rose, 1985). Since then, Wintle (1981) has confirmed this age by dating samples from southern England by thermoluminescence techniques to 14,500 –18,800 B.P., although with a $+/-20\%$ error. With the described relationships of silt-rich soil to the depressions, their formation is thought to be penecontemporaneous with or to predate loess deposition in southern and eastern England.

The initiation of the thermokarst degradation cannot be ascribed to any particular local or regional cause, or to any general climatic amelioration as these processes are a part of terrain evolution even in a stable climate with permafrost.

Along the whole eastern side of the Fenland extending from south west of Cambridge to King's Lynn, small ground-ice collapse features are common. They occur as 'hummock and hollow' topography in sandy or chalky drift overlying Lower and Middle Chalk. Fresh forms, well exemplified by the group at Walton Common, Norfolk (Sparks *et al.*, 1972) were dated to the Loch Lomond Stadial based on contained deposits. With diameters of 10 to 120 m, ramparts up to 3 m high and generally lacking a drainage outlet they have been considered to result from the melting of ground-ice lenses along a zone of spring discharge when permafrost was thin or discontinuous. Worsley (1977) considered them to be equivalent to open-system pingos. Taylor (1978) ascribed the formation of hollows with ramparts near Cambridge to thermokarst subsidence of segregated ice formed in poorly drained substrates. According to West (1987), one or more processes could have been involved in the formation of small hollows in Norfolk during the Devensian. He concludes that detailed stratigraphical and palaeontological studies of both the infilling and the material in which the hollow is formed are required to solve the problems of origin of each one. There are also subdued forms with little or no relief, the circular and vermiform soil patterns of Evans (1972), sometimes at higher elevations. These have formed earlier than the fresh forms in thin sandy drift over frost susceptible Chalk and may possibly date from a period of the Late Devensian.

Conclusions

During the Late Devensian the Fenland was a complex thermokarst terrain with, to the east, repeated eruptions of open-system pingos or seasonal ground-ice mounds along poorly drained ground with springs, forming small hollows bounded by ramparts upon collapse. Further west in gravel terraces overlying Jurassic clays large near circular depressions without ramparts may have been caused by the random melting of ground rich in ice wedges or local occurrences of massive segregated ice.

Common features of depressions within the Fenland are:

1. large size, about 1000 m major diameter or larger;
2. enclosed by high ground except for an outlet, at some sites as narrow as 60 m, towards which the whole depression drains;
3. form the source of some of the deeply incised channels crossing the Fenland floor;
4. bordered by Devensian 1st and 2nd Terrace surfaces with evidence of a polygonal network of ice wedges, which bestowed a large ground-ice content to the sands and gravels;
5. excavated through the terrace deposits into the underlying Jurassic clay to form a flat or very gently concave floor;
6. slopes masked by a drift sequence of coarser deposits overlain by finer solifluction deposits with a loessic component.

These depressions were probably linked by channels to form alas valley systems.

References

Baden-Powell, D.F.W. (1934). 'On the marine gravels at March, Cambridgeshire', *Geol. Mag.*, **71**, 193–219.

Bell, F.G. (1970). 'Late Pleistocene floras from Earith, Huntingdonshire', *Phil. Trans. R. Soc. Lond. B*, **258**, 347–78.

Booth, S.J. (1982). 'The sand and gravel resources of the country around Whittlesey, Cambridgeshire: description of 1:25,000 sheets TF 20 and TL 29', *Miner. Assess. Rep. Inst. Geol. Sci.*, No. 93.

Burton, R.G.O. (1976). 'Possible thermokarst features in Cambridgeshire', *E. Midl. Geogr.*, **6**, 230–40.

Burton, R.G.O. (1978). *Thermokarst in eastern England*, unpubl. M.Sc. dissertation, City of London and North London Polytechnics.

Burton, R.G.O. and Seale, R.S. (1981). *Soils in Cambridgeshire I: 1:25,000 sheet TL18E/28W (Stilton)*. Soil Surv. Rec. No. 65, Harpenden.

Catt, J.A. (1977). 'Loess and coversands', in *British Quaternary Studies: recent advances* (Ed. F.W. Shotton), pp. 221–9, Clarendon Press, Oxford.

Czudek, T. and Demek, J. (1970). 'Thermokarst in Siberia and its influence on the development of lowland relief', *Quat. Res.* **1**, 103–20.

Evans, R. (1972). 'Air photographs for soil survey in lowland England: soil patterns', *Photogramm. Rec*, **7**, 302–22.

Gallois, R.W. (1980). *Ely*, British Geological Survey 1:50,000 sheet 173, Ordnance Survey, Southampton.

Gaunt, G.D. (1976). *The Quaternary geology of the southern part of the Vale of York*, unpubl. Ph.D. thesis, Univ. of Leeds.

Gaunt, G.D. (1981). 'Quaternary history of the southern part of the Vale of York', in *The Quaternary in Britain* (Eds. J. Neale and J. Flenley), pp. 82–97, Pergamon, Oxford.

Gaunt, G.D., Jarvis, R.A. and Matthews, B. (1971). 'The Late Weichselian sequence in the Vale of York', *Proc. Yorks. Geol. Soc.* **38**, 281–4.

Jarvis, R.A. (1973). *Soils in Yorkshire II: 1:25,000 Sheet SE 60 (Armthorpe)*. Soil Surv. Rec. No. 12, Harpenden.

Perrin, R.M.S., Davies, H. and Fysh, M.D. (1974). 'Distribution of late Pleistocene aeolian deposits in eastern and southern England', *Nature*, **248**, 320–4.

Perrin, R.M.S., Rose, J. and Davies, H. (1979). 'The distribution, variation and origins of pre-Devensian tills in eastern England', *Phil. Trans. R. Soc. Lond. B.*, **287**, 535–70.

Péwé, T.L. (1966). 'The palaeoclimatic significance of fossil ice wedges', *Biul. Peryglacj.*, **15**, 65–72.

Rose, J. (1985). 'The Dimlington Stadial/Dimlington Chronozone: a proposal for naming the main glacial episode of the Late Devensian in Britain', *Boreas*, **14**, 225–30.

Seale, R.S. (1975a). *Soils of the Ely district*. Mem. Soil Surv. Gt Br., Harpenden.

Seale, R.S. (1975b). *Soils of the Chatteris district*. Soil Surv. Spec. Rec. No. 9, Harpenden.

Sparks, B.W., Williams, R.B.G. and Bell, F.G. (1972). 'Presumed ground-ice depressions in East Anglia', *Proc. R. Soc. Lond. A*, **327**, 329–43.

Straw, A. (1979). 'Eastern England', in *Eastern and Central England*, A. Straw and K.M. Clayton, pp. 1–139, Methuen, London.

Taylor, A. (1978). 'Thermokarst depressions in southern Cambridgeshire', *Quat. Newsl*, **26**, 1–2.

West, R.G. (1987). Origin of small hollows in Norfolk. In, *Periglacial Processes and Landforms in Britain and Ireland* (Ed. J. Boardman), pp. 191–4 Cambridge University Press.

Wintle, A.G. (1981). 'Thermoluminescence dating of late Devensian loesses in southern England', *Nature*, **289**, 479–80.

Worsley, P. (1977). 'Periglaciation', in *Britain Quaternary Studies: recent advances*, (Ed. F.W. Shotton), pp. 205–19, Clarendon Press, Oxford.

Worssam, B.C. and Taylor, J.H. (1969). *The geology of the country around Cambridge*. Mem. Geol. Surv. Gt Br.

Wyatt, R.J. (1984). *Peterborough*, British Geological Survey 1:50,000 sheet 158, Ordnance Survey, Southampton.

(d) Slopes, sediments and mass wasting

20 · Solifluction and related periglacial deposits in England and Wales

CHARLES HARRIS

Abstract

Three major categories of periglacial slope deposit or 'head' are identified on the basis of parent materials: head derived from non-argillaceous bedrock, head derived from till, and head derived from argillaceous bedrock. Clay content is shown to have been of major importance in controlling the processes responsible for head accumulation. The silty and sandy heads derived from non-argillaceous bedrock and tills have low Liquid Limits and Plasticity Indices. Here downslope displacement of sediment was by gelifluction. Clay-rich heads, derived from clay bedrock and clayey tills, show much higher Liquid Limits and Plasticity Indices, and slope failure occurred by shallow mudsliding rather than gelifluction. Head has often accumulated on slopes with gradients well below the threshold for stability under present day conditions. The high pore water pressures necessary to induce mass movements on these low angled slopes resulted from thaw consolidation of ice-rich active layers during seasonal thawing.

Periglacial slope deposits, generally referred to as 'head', are widespread in England and Wales. Head deposits are variable in composition since they may incorporate a wide variety of regoliths and pre-existing superficial sediments. Although De la Beche (1839) inferred no specific origin when introducing the term, subsequent workers have often assumed solifluction to have been the dominant mechanism of downslope movement (Ball and Goodier, 1970; Higginbottom and Fookes, 1971). However, the precise mechanism of mass movement may be difficult to determine, and heads formed over clay substrates have often suffered translational sliding over laterally extensive shear planes during periglacial phases rather than solifluction. Head may therefore be defined as slope deposits accumulated through various periglacial mass movement processes. Slope wash deposits are excluded, and should be referred to as colluvium, though they often occur in association with head, reflecting variation in the relative importance of slope wash and mass movement.

Many head deposits consist of matrix supported diamictons with a very variable clast content. Where derived from frost weathering of local bedrock, clasts are angular and slabby, but where derived from till, clasts show edge rounding due to glacial abrasion. Jones and Derbyshire (1983) de-scribed head as often resembling till, but having a higher void ratio, looser fabric, higher permeability and lower mechanical strength.

Head deposits derived from non-argillaceous bedrock

To the south of the Pleistocene ice limits the relationship between head materials and underlying bedrock lithology is generally clear. In south west England for instance, McKeown et al. (1973) described diamictons consisting of angular clasts set in a blue-grey silty clay matrix overlying slaty and shaly facies of the Devonian and Carboniferous rocks in north Cornwall and west Devon, while the more arenaceous Bude formation gives a yellowish brown silty diamicton, locally clayey or sandy. Over the Permian outcrop is spread a cover of brownish gravelly silts, and the clayey head overlying the adjacent Carboniferous rocks is reddened up to 275 m beyond the boundary between the two rock types. Similarly Edmonds et al. (1968) showed that on the northern flanks of Dartmoor, granite head may extend well beyond the boundary with the surrounding metamorphic rocks.

A brief case study of a coastal section from Whitesands Bay, south Cornwall, is presented here to serve as an example of typical head deposits derived from non-argillaceous parent material.

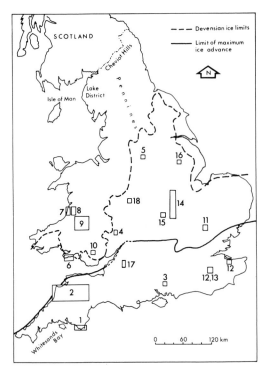

Figure 20.1. Location map of studies referred to in text. 1. Start Point to Hope Cove coastal sections (Mottershead, 1971). 2. Carboniferous mudstone bedrock, N. Cornwall and Mid Devon (Grainger and Harris, 1986). 3. Chalk dry valley near Petersfield, Hampshire (Shakesby, 1975). 4. Deposits south-east of Hereford (Shakesby, 1981). 5. Vale of Edale, Derbyshire (Wilson, 1981). 6. South Gower Coast (Henry, 1984a, b). 7. Morfa-bychan (Watson and Watson, 1967). 8. Peithnant Valley (Watson, 1976). 9. Mid Wales (Potts, 1971). 10. S. Wales Coalfield (Harris and Wright, 1980). 11. Cam Valley, Essex (Baker, 1975). 12. Periglacially sheared Weald Clay and Gault Clay (Weeks, 1969). 13. Lower Greensand escarpment and Weald Clay vale, Sevenoaks, Kent (Skempton and Weeks, 1976). 14. Periglacially sheared Lias Clay (Chandler, 1970a, b 1976). 15. Periglacially sheared Lias Clay (Biczysko, 1981). 16. Periglacially sheared Lias Clay (Penn et al., 1983). 17. Periglacially sheared Fullers Earth (Chandler, et al., 1976). 18. Periglacially sheared Carboniferous marl (Hutchinson et al., 1973).

However, as indicated above, variation in the lithology and jointing of bedrock will lead to variation in matrix/clast ratios.

Whitesands Bay lies to the west of Plymouth Sound (Figure 20.1) and consists of a sweeping south-west facing cliffline formed in Lower Devonian slates. The bevelled cliff profile has a coastal slope of around 15° (Figure 20.2) which is mantled with head (Figure 20.3a).

An exposure on a small headland at the western end of the bay was logged and sampled (Figure 20.2). Three units of slope deposits were identified (Figure 20.3a) overlying shattered bedrock. The latter showed creep deformation, with beds bending over in a downslope direction. The three sedimentary units were diamictons with silty sand matrix containing platy angular clasts. Unit 1 showed a matrix/clast ratio by weight of 1.32:1 (matrix taken as material finer than 2 mm), Unit 2, 0.47:1 and Unit 3, 1.78:1. Grain-size distributions were all positively skewed and the poorly sorted nature of the sediment was reflected in standard deviation values ranging from 3.57 to 3.82 (Figure 20.2). Clay contents were less than 1% of the total weight of Unit 2, and 5% of the total weight of Units 1 and 3, these values corresponding to 2% of the matrix in Unit 2, 7% in Unit 1 and 8% in Unit 3 (Figure 20.4).

Sand grain roundness was assessed against Powers charts (Powers, 1958) by observing grains under low magnification in thin sections made from impregnated undisturbed samples (Figure 20.2). Clasts were allocated a value of 1 to 6 in each Powers category and a simple average roundness value was calculated which resembled closely Folk's 'rho' scale (Folk, 1955; Matthews and Petch, 1982). Mean roundness of clasts fell in the very angular category for units 1 and 2 and the angular category for unit 3 (Table 20.1 and see Figure 20.3b). Sand grains in Units 1 and 2 at Whitesands Bay were consistently angular, with mean roundness values slightly higher than the clasts contained in these two units (Table 20.1).

The organisation of elongate clasts is illustrated in Figure 20.2, where macrofabrics for units 1 and 2 are shown as rose diagrams and polar plots. The latter show the low angle of dip of these platy clasts, with most stones dipping at a lower angle than the surface slope, in an imbricate fashion (see also Figure 20.3b). Such macrofabrics are typical of diamicton head deposits in England and Wales and are generally interpreted as indicating gelifluction (Stephens, 1961; Kirby, 1967; Watson and Watson, 1967; Kidson, 1971; Mottershead, 1971; Potts, 1971; Harris and Wright, 1980; Wilson, 1981; Douglas and Harrison, 1983; Henry, 1984a, b). Similar downslope preferred orientations and low angles of dip are widely reported from gelifluction sediments in the modern periglacial zone (see Harris, 1981). Elongate sand grains measured from thin section cut in the vertical plane parallel to the line of greatest slope also show a strong preferred apparent dip, with grains tending to lie in an

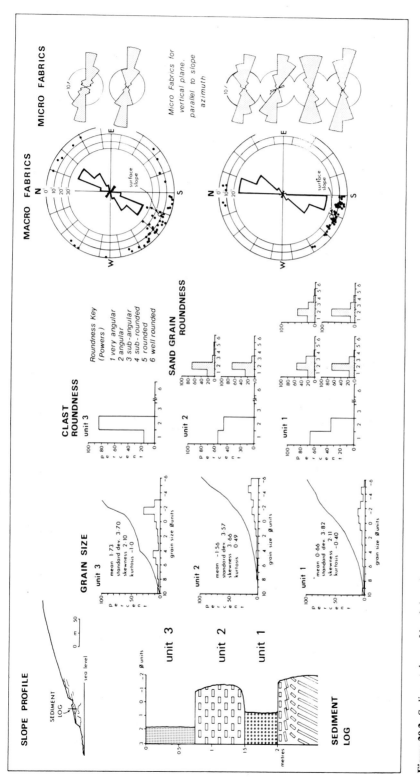

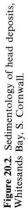

Figure 20.2. Sedimentology of head deposits, Whitesands Bay, S. Cornwall.

(a)

(b)

Figure 20.3. a. Section described in text from
Whitesands Bay, Cornwall. Bottom of the hammer
handle marks the boundary between Units 1 and 2.
Unit 3 comprises uppermost more matrix-dominated
material.
b. Close-up of Unit 2, showing angular slabby clasts
with low angle of dip.

Table 20.1. *Roundness data from Whitesands Bay and South Devon coastal exposures.*

Site	Mean roundness of clasts	Nominal Class (Power)	Mean roundness of sand grains	Nominal Class (Power)
Whitesands Unit 1	1.34	Very angular	2.07	Angular
Unit 2	1.46	Very angular	1.86	Angular
Unit 3	1.85	Angular		
Start Point to Hope Cove	2.06	Angular		
(Mottershead, 1971)	2.04	Angular		
Green Schist	2.36	Angular		
	2.28	Angular		
	2.00	Angular		

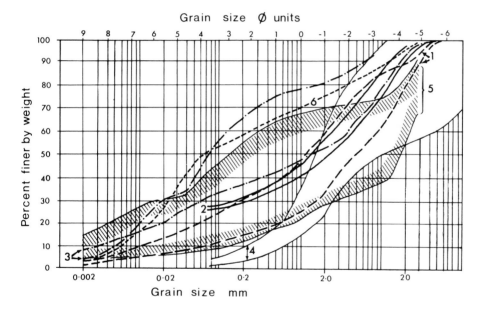

Figure 20.4. Grain-size distributions for non-argillaceous heads. 1. Whitesands Bay, Units 1 and 2. Bedrock Devonian slate. 2. Falmouth, Cornwall, Devonian slaty siltstones (data supplies by J. Harris of F.W. Sherrell, Consulting Geologists, Tavistock). 3. Head derived from Carboniferous mudstones and sandstones, North Cornwall. 4. Envelope for chalk head, Hampshire Downs (Shakesby, 1975). 5. Envelope for head derived from Carboniferous Grits and Shales, Vale of Edale (Wilson, 1981). 6. Soliflucted till, Nant Myddlyn Valley, South Wales (Harris and Wright, 1980).

imbricate fashion relative to the surface slope (Figure 20.2). Harris and Ellis (1980) have described similar imbricate low angled dips of sand grains in gelifluction lobes and terraces in northern Norway.

The majority of the head deposits in southern Britain are of the Whitesand Bay type. Variation in size and frequency of clasts may, however, result from lithological variation in the source area upslope, temporal variations in the intensity of frost weathering, and variations in the input of fine grained slope wash material (Kidson, 1971; Mottershead, 1977). Waters (1964) described two facies of granite head in valley bottoms on Dartmoor, with finer clasts present in the lower unit, overlain by head containing many large boulders. Waters postulated two phases of sediment supply, with near surface layers of regolith containing finer rock fragments being spread over the slopes below first, followed by the downslope mass-movement of the coarser detritus from lower in the weathering profile, giving the upper layer of coarser head.

In coastal exposures between Hope Cove and Start Point in South Devon (Figure 20.1), Mottershead (1971) reported a tendency for material to become finer grained at greater distances from the bedrock source areas, this change being associated with a transition from positively skewed grain-size distributions to negatively skewed distributions. Mottershead explained this decrease in clast size and frequency as resulting from progressive comminution of clasts during transport. In these South Devon head deposits developed on schists, clay content of the matrix ranged from 3% to 14% (Figure 20.5).

Where mudstones and shales predominate, higher clay contents occur. For instance, Grainger and Harris (1986) report that the matrix of head derived from upper Carboniferous mudstones in Cornwall and Devon consists of silty clay, with silt/clay ratios of between 1.4:1 and 1:1 (Figure 20.5).

Even the periglacially weathered and solifluced chalk or 'coombe rock' (Bromehead in Dewey *et al.*, 1924) is sedimentologically similar to the non-argillaeous heads (Figure 20.4), with angular chalk clasts set in a silty matrix (Small *et al.*, 1970; French, 1973; Shakesby, 1975). French (1973) stressed the low angle of north east-facing slopes in asymmetrical chalk valleys is southern and south eastern England, where gradients of 5° may be underlain by up to 3 m of coombe rock. In a dry valley in the Hampshire Downs, Shakesby (1975) identified two sedimentary units on the lower valley side slopes and the valley bottom, an upper white

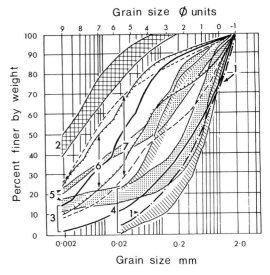

Figure 20.5. Grain-size envelopes for matrix from non-argillaceous heads. 1. Limit of frost susceptibility (Beskow, 1935). Sediments finer than this limiting curve are susceptible to ice segregation. 2. Weathered mudstone, N. Cornwall and Mid Devon (Grainger and Harris, 1986). 3. Head from south Devon coast (Mottershead, 1971). 4. Head derived from Silurian Limestones and shales, Herefordshire (Shakesby, 1981). 5. Head from Barber Booth and Grindsbrook, Vale of Edale, Derbyshire (Wilson, 1981). 6. Morfabychan heads derived from mudstones (Watson, 1976). 7. Peithnant Valley heads, derived from reworked till and local mudstones (Watson, 1976).

chalky matrix containing chalk clasts, and a lower buff-coloured matrix containing chalk clasts, marcasite nodules, ironstone fragments and shattered flints. Below about 2.2 m the angular chalk clasts became increasingly large. The matrix in both units contained less than 12% clay and both units showed strong preferred orientation of elongate clasts parallel to the valley-side slopes.

Further north, and closer to the Devensian ice limits, periglacial weathering and mass-movement of Silurian limestones and shales south east of Hereford (Figure 20.1) has produced diamicton deposits with silty or sandy matrix and angular to subangular clasts (Shakesby, 1981). Clay contents were less than 3% of the total and between 0.5% and 24% of the matrix (Figure 20.5). Elongate clasts showed strong downslope preferred orientations. Similar valley fill deposits in the Vale of Edale, North Derbyshire were described by Wilson (1981), where deposits were derived from Carboniferous grits, sandstones and shales. They contained 30% to 70% gravel, 17.9% to 37.9% sand, 3.9% to 23.6% silt and 4.6% to 17.6% clay, with clay content of the matrix ranging from 11% to 27% (Figures 20.4 and 20.5). Occasional crude stratification was noted by Wilson, indicating accumulation in discrete layers, and clasts were again strongly oriented downslope. Both Shakesby and Wilson assign a Late Devensian age to these head deposits, Shakesby arguing for a major Loch Lomond Stadial contribution while Wilson concluding that its importance remains debatable.

In south Gower, beyond the Devensian ice limits, recent work by Henry (1984*a*, *b*) at Hunts Bay and Horton (Figure 20.1) has identified five facies of head and related deposits, ranging from clast dominated scree to colluvial silts. The main head unit, referred to as Hunts Breccia, consists of locally derived angular limestone clasts set in a silty matrix. Silt content of the matrix ranged from 7.4% to 63.7% with clay content from 2.1% to 30.6%. Incorporation of pre-Devensian till introduced rounded erratics into certain head facies, notably the Western Slade Diamicton, giving matrix dominated head, the matrix containing up to 55.2% silt, and up to 16.6% clay. Fabrics showed the expected very strong downslope preferred orientation and low angle of dip (mean dip ranging from 6° to 23°).

In West Wales the thick head succession at Morfa-bychan in Cardigan Bay (Figure 20.1) has been described in detail by Watson and Watson (1967). The siltstones of the Aberystwyth Grits produced silty head with frost susceptible matrix (Figure 20.5) containing angular clasts which are strongly oriented downslope. The Blue Head facies at Morfa-bychan, however, contains rounded and striated clasts which may have been originally glacially eroded (Vincent, 1976). Slope wash produced distinct lenses and layers of sand and silt, and left bands of head depleted of fines. This suggests a progressive accumulation of these sediments layer by layer rather than massive landsliding.

The head deposits of the Palaeozoic and Mesozoic non-argillaceous rocks of England and Wales, therefore, form a readily identifiable sediment type and show remarkable similarity over a wide range of bedrock types. All are poorly sorted, usually bimodal in grain-size distribution, with a silty or sandy matrix. Most are matrix supported, the matrix being frost susceptible. Many are crudely bedded, the bedding dipping roughly parallel to the surface gradient. Thawing of an ice-rich active layer is generally considered to have caused downslope displacement of the regolith, though slopewash, promoted by active layer saturation and lack of vegetation, frequently contributed to downslope

sediment transfer, introducing irregular layers or lenses of relatively well sorted silts or fine sands.

Head derived from till

Much of Wales, the Midlands, northern and eastern England is mantled with tills which are commonly affected by some degree of periglacial reworking. On slopes, downslope mass movement has produced smooth-surfaced concave sheets containing a variable admixture of locally weathered rock. Such solifluction sheets or terraces have been described in Wales (Crampton, 1965; Crampton and Taylor, 1967; Ball *et al.*, 1969; Lewis, 1970; Potts, 1971; Wright and Harris, 1980; Harris, 1981), the Lake District and northern Pennines (Dines *et al.*, 1940; Tufnell, 1969; Boardman, 1985), the Isle of Man (King, 1976; Thomas, 1977) and the Cheviots (Douglas and Harrison, 1983; Douglas and Harrison, 1987).

In the Peithnant Valley, of the upper Rheidol, mid Wales (Figure 20.1), Watson (1976) observed reworked till incorporated with locally derived frost shattered bedrock in the main solifluction deposit. Typical surface gradients of 4° to 8° were associated with smooth concave valley side profiles. Strongly developed downslope preferred orientation of elongate clasts were associated with low angles of dip, clasts tending to show imbrication relative to the slope gradient. The matrix was frost susceptible (Figure 20.5), its granulometry resembling the heads of south west England. Potts (1971) described very similar valley bottom solifluction sheets in mid Wales. He interpreted these sediments as reworked till on the basis of high fines content (mainly in excess of 40%) and the presence of striated clasts. Again macrofabrics showed strong preferred orientations parallel to the valley side gradients.

In South Wales, Harris and Wright (1980) reported up to 7 m of head overlying a tough grey lodgement till in the Nant Myddlyn Valley, near Pontypridd (Figure 20.1). Lithology, shape and roundness of clasts were similar in both deposits but the lodgement till fabric showed downvalley orientation while in the overlying head, clasts were strongly oriented down the valley side, approximately perpendicular to the fabric of the underlying till (Figure 20.6). The head showed crude bedding picked out by clasts which dipped approximately parallel to the ground surface, plus irregular sandy lenses where silts had been washed out. Loss of silt was reflected in a sandier matrix in the head, silt content averaging 23% of the matrix compared with 47% in the parent till. Clay contents were

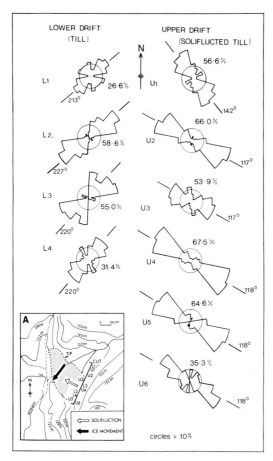

Figure 20.6. Macrofabrics from lodgement till and overlying head, Myddlyn Valley, near Pontypridd, S. Wales (Harris and Wright, 1980). Percentage values refer to two-dimensional vector magnitudes.

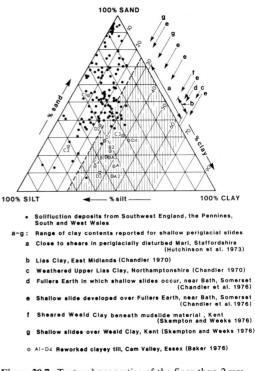

- • Solifluction deposits from Southwest England, the Pennines, South and West Wales
- a–g : Range of clay contents reported for shallow periglacial slides
  - a   Close to shears in periglacially disturbed Marl, Staffordshire (Hutchinson et al. 1973)
  - b   Lias Clay, East Midlands (Chandler 1970)
  - c   Weathered Upper Lias Clay, Northamptonshire (Chandler 1970)
  - d   Fullers Earth in which shallow slides occur, near Bath, Somerset (Chandler et al. 1976)
  - e   Shallow slide developed over Fullers Earth, near Bath, Somerset (Chandler et al. 1976)
  - f   Sheared Weald Clay beneath mudslide material, Kent (Skempton and Weeks 1976)
  - g   Shallow slides over Weald Clay, Kent (Skempton and Weeks 1976)
  - ⊘   A1–D4 Reworked clayey till, Cam Valley, Essex (Baker 1976)

Figure 20.7. Textural properties of the finer than 2 mm fractions of head deposits. Arrows indicate clay contents of mudslide materials. Shaded area of graph shows range within which mudslide material may fall.

around 4% in both sediments (Figure 20.4).

The head deposits in the Cheviots are sedimentologically similar to the deposits described above (Harrison and Douglas, 1987), as are the heads from the Isle of Man, the Lake District and the northern Pennines. However, in contrast to tills in these upland areas, the chalky tills of East Anglia are generally clay-rich and their response to periglaciation was similar to that of the clay bedrocks of southern and eastern England rather than the silty tills of western and northern England. Baker (1976) showed that Devensian reworking by periglacial slope processes has affected the till in different ways, according to its clay content. Where clay contents were high (samples A1, A2, A3, D3, Figure 20.7) the till had undergone little internal reorganisation, but suffered large scale landslipping into the valleys.

Where clay contents were lower (samples C1, C2, D1, D2, Figure 20.7) clasts were re-oriented, though not in a downslope direction but orthogonal to the slope direction. Baker suggested that such fabrics might result from granular disaggregation and reorganisation associated with basal flowage in an earth flow type of failure.

Some distinction may therefore be drawn between tills with a silty or sandy matrix and those with a high clay content in terms of their mechanisms of slope failure under periglacial conditions.

Head derived from argillaceous bedrocks

Periglacial weathering of clays in southern England and the East Midlands resulted in extensive brecciation and softening, and on slopes the high water contents generated during thaw initiated extensive shallow translational slides affecting the whole or part of the active layer. Planar slip surfaces roughly parallel to the ground surface may be preserved beneath the clay heads, often giving problems of slope instability during engineering works (e.g. Weeks, 1969). Weeks described shear planes lying between 0.9 m and 4.5 m below the surface in heads developed on Weald Clay, Gault Clay and London Clay in Kent (Figure 20.1). Surface gradients were as low as 3°. Residual shear strength parameters for Weald Clay (ϕ_r' 15°–16°, c_r' 1.4–2.1 kN/m²), and for Gault Clay (ϕ_r' 12.4°, c_r' 0), indicated that slopes in excess of 7° are necessary for landsliding under present day climates. Weeks concluded that the high pore water pressures necessary for failures on slopes as low as 3° were associated with thawing of ice-rich soils under periglacial conditions.

The area to the south of the Lower Greensand escarpment, near Sevenoaks, Kent, was subsequently described in more detail by Skempton and Weeks (1976). Two clearly defined sheets of clayey head were observed extending south of the escarpment over the Weald Clay Vale (Figure 20.8). The lower sheet extended as a smoothly concave surface of gradient 4° to 2° for up to 1 km, and within 300 m of the escarpment was overridden by the upper sheet which was clearly defined morphologically by a lobate frontal bank. Trial pits and boreholes proved the presence of extensive planar slip surfaces beneath both head units. Several well defined slip surfaces to depths of 3 m, were observed in the brecciated clay of the lower unit. An organic soil which developed on the surface of the lower head unit was buried by the advance of the upper head (Figure 20.8), and gave a radiocarbon age of 12,250 ± 200 radiocarbon years B.P. The soil is therefore of Windermere Interstadial age, the underlying head of Late Devensian age, and the upper head of Loch Lomond Stadial age. Both head units consist of brown silty sandy clay containing chert fragments, and the upper head is overlain by slopewash deposits. Clay contents averaged 24% in the upper

head, and in the lower unit 33% (Figure 20.7). Skempton and Weeks show that under residual strength conditions ($c_r' = 1$ kN/m², $\phi_r' = 14°$) slopes greater than 8° are needed for sliding under temperate conditions. They concluded that thawing of an ice-rich active layer over permafrost released these mudslides, displacement continuing down to gradients as low as 2°.

The Lias Clay of Northamptonshire and Lincolnshire also suffered degradation by periglacial mudslides (Chandler, 1970a, b, 1976; Biczysko, 1981; Penn *et al.*, 1983) (Figure 20.1). In Northamptonshire, Chandler (1970a) described shallow slickensided slip surfaces approximately parallel to the ground surface beneath clayey head. Gradients ranged from 4° to 6.75° and the slip surfaces penetrated the upper few cm of underlying Lias Clay. A slope greater than 12° is necessary to initiate sliding under residual strength conditions ($\phi_r' = 16°$, $c_r' = 0$). Further north in the Lias Clay outcrop Chandler (1970b) described similar shallow mudslides underlain by polished planar slip surfaces at depths of between 1.5 m and 2 m. Slope gradients of 9° were close to the limiting angle and in places landsliding was still active. However in both cases initiation of widespread instability was considered to have occurred under periglacial conditions.

In the Gwash valley, east of Oakham, Chandler (1976) described large scale landsliding in the Lias Clay. However the depth of disturbance suggested an absence of permafrost, and this major phase of instability was considered to have occurred during a Devensian interstadial. Shallow clay head underlain by slip surfaces subsequently partly covered the

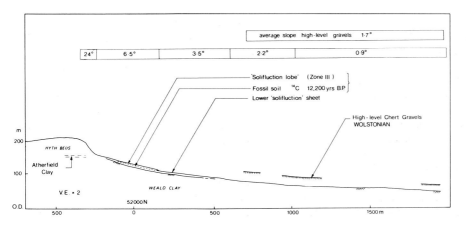

Figure 20.8. North–south section through the Lower Greensand escarpment near Sevenoaks Weald, Kent (Skempton and Weeks, 1976).

landslides, and radiocarbon dating of a buried soil indicated that these shallow mudslides were active during the Loch Lomond Stadial. Similar shallow mudslides were reported by Biczysko (1981) at Daventry, Northampton where road construction reactivated a planar slip surface at a depth of 3 m. The shear plane penetrated the Lias clay but underlay 2.5 m of head.

In the Swainswick Valley, a tributary of the River Avon in Somerset, Chandler *et al.* (1976) described slopes of around 9° mantled with up to 4 m of clayey head containing fragments of limestone. The head overlay Fullers Earth, a Jurassic Clay, and continuous shear surfaces extended through its base. In the Horescombe Vale, also a tributary of the River Avon, head derived from Fullers Earth extended over an earlier limestone head, and a buried soil between the two units contained mollusca indicating Windermere Interstadial age. The Fullers Earth mudslides therefore, were of Loch Lomond Stadial age, while the underlying limestone head accumulated during the Late Devensian.

The final example of periglacial mudsliding over clay-rich bedrock is from the Carboniferous marls of Staffordshire. At Bury Hill, near Wolverhampton, Hutchinson *et al.* (1973) described a large landslide in head and colluvium of thickness up to 10 m. The area was outside the Devensian ice limits, and the strongly frost susceptible marl suffered extensive shallow, active-layer failures under Devensian periglacial conditions. Excavation beyond the landslide, on an apparently stable slope of 11° to 12°, revealed a planar polished slip plane 3.2 m below the surface, above which the head exhibited mudflow fabric, with lumps of weathered clay in a remoulded clayey silt matrix. Clay content along the slip surface was 50% (Figure 20.7). Two phases of periglacial activity on this slope were recognised, an earlier phase dominated by frost heaving with limited lateral displacements, followed by the phase of shallow periglacial mudsliding.

Periglacial slope stability
Ice segregation during freezing of fine grained soils draws water towards the freezing plane (Taber, 1929, 1930; Konrad and Morgenstern, 1980, 1981, 1982). Thawing of the resulting ice-rich soil releases larger volumes of meltwater from ice lenses than can be accommodated in the normal pore space. With drainage impeded by the underlying frozen ground, consolidation of the thawing mass results in transfer of stress from grain contacts to pore water, generating pore water pressures in excess of

hydrostatic (Taber, 1943; Morgenstern and Nixon, 1971). Such pore pressures reduce the frictional strength of the soil, leading to failures on very gentle slopes.

Coventional slope stability analysis of Pleistocene head deposits in England and Wales indicates that high pore water pressures were necessary to initiate and maintain mass movements on slopes with gradients below the limiting angles for stability under temperate conditions (see Harris, 1981, p. 97). Since the matrix of most head deposits is frost susceptible (Figure 20.5), ice segregation was likely to occur during winter freezing of the active layer, leading to potentially high pore pressures and loss of strength during subsequent thaw.

The one-dimensional thaw consolidation theory (Morgenstern and Nixon, 1971) combines the two time-dependent factors, rate of thaw and rate of consolidation to give the thaw consolidation ratio R, such that

$$R = \frac{\alpha}{2\sqrt{C_v}} \qquad (1)$$

where C_v is the coefficient of consolidation and α is the thaw parameter in the Newman equation:

$$X = \alpha\sqrt{t} \qquad (2)$$

X being the depth of thaw in time t.

The thaw consolidation theory has been applied to the prediction of slope stability using the infinite slope model by McRoberts and Morgenstern (1974) who provide a graphic solution for a soil with $\phi' = 25°$ and specific gravity of particles 2.7. For soil moisture contents greater than 20%, when R is greater than 0.5 instability is predicted on slopes of less than 10°, and when R exceeds 1.0, gradients of 5° or less are likely to be unstable.

Influence of parent material on soil properties
The nature of both weathering products and tills are largely controlled by the lithology of parent materials (Dreimanis and Vagners, 1971), so that sandstones give sandy regoliths and relatively coarse till matrix, while mudstones yield silty sediments. Over much of upland Britain rocks break down to give arenaceous or silty weathering products and tills, and these in turn produce head deposits of similar granulometry. However, as described above, the argillaceous rocks of the Midlands and southern England yield clay soils and in East Anglia and Lincolnshire clay-rich tills (Figure 20.7). The clay content and mineralogy influences the geotechnical properties of a sediment

significantly, and therefore its response to variation in moisture status and shear stress.

In general, sands and silts have high frictional strength but little cohesion while clays have lower frictional strength but are cohesive. Sands have low porosity and void ratio, and consequently low saturation water content while clays have higher void ratio and higher saturated water content (Terzaghi and Peck, 1967). These properties are, to a greater or lesser degree, reflected in the Atterberg Limits of a soil, which give an indication of consistency under different moisture conditions. If the moisture content exceeds the Liquid Limit

(Liquidity Index greater than 1), disturbance of the soil transforms it into a viscous slurry (Terzaghi and Peck, 1967). Clay mineralogy influences index properties, and the 'activity' of clay minerals was defined by Skempton (1953) as the ratio of Plasticity Index to the percent clay fraction. This ratio is more or less constant for a given clay mineral, so that as clay content increases, the value of the Plasticity Index also increases. Despite variations in clay mineralogy and therefore activity, a general increase in Plasticity Index and Liquid Limit as clay content increases is revealed for head deposits in England and Wales (Figure 20.9), the clay heads

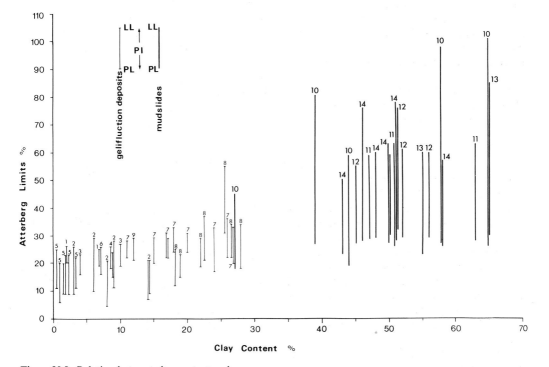

Figure 20.9. Relation between clay content and Atterberg limits for matrix material of head. 1. Whitesands Bay, Cornwall. 2. S. Devon coast (Mottershead, 1971). 3. Wembury, S. Devon (Harris, 1981). 4. Seaton, Cornwall. 5. Herefordshire (Shakesby, 1981). 6. S. Wales (Harris and Wright, 1980). 7. Vale of Edale, Derbyshire (Wilson, 1981). 8. Head derived from Carboniferous sandstones and shales near Launceston, Cornwall (data supplied by J. Harris of F.W. Sherrell, Consulting Geologists, Tavistock). 9. Head derived from Devonian slates, near Plymouth (data supplied by J. Harris). 10. Jurassic clay head near Bath, Somerset (Chandler *et al.*, 1976). 11. Lias Clay head, Gwash Valley, near Oakham, Rutland (Chandler, 1976). 12. Lias Clay, Northamptonshire (Chandler, 1970*b*). 13. Weald Clay, Sevenoaks Weald (Skempton and Weeks, 1976). 14. Etruria Marl, Staffordshire (Hutchinson *et al.*, 1973).

showing significantly higher values than the poorly sorted diamicton soils. Skempton (1957) has shown a direct linear relationship between Plasticity Index and the undrained shear strength when pore pressures reduce effective stresses to zero.

The plasticity chart (Casegrande, 1948; British Standards 1377:1975) provides a means of classifying soils according to their index properties (Figure 20.10), with clays tending to fall slightly above the A line and silts slightly below. Data from head deposits in England and Wales show a marked distinction between the low plasticity head derived from non-argillaceous bedrock and till, and the mainly high or very high plasticity clay-rich heads (Figure 20.10). Data from modern gelifluction lobes and sheets in Norway (Harris, 1977), and Greenland (Washburn, 1967) are also plotted in Figure 20.10, and clearly correspond to the non-argillaceous diamicton heads rather than the sheared clays.

The low Liquid Limit and Plasticity Index of the heads derived from non-argillaceous bedrock and tills make them particularly sensitive to changes in water content, and susceptible to loss of strength and flowage when water contents are high. Such conditions are widespread in the active layer of periglacial regions. The release of meltwater from segregation ice plus inputs from snowmelt, generate high water contents in the thawing active layer, often leading to artesian pore water pressures (Harris, 1977). Disturbance of the soil structure during thaw consolidation may then initiate viscous flow (gelifluction). It is therefore concluded that gelifluction was responsible for the accumulation of the majority of the poorly sorted head deposits described in this paper. The crude stratification commonly reported, and the absence of evidence for large scale mudflows or landslides indicates a gradual accumulation of material, layer by layer, as suggested by Wilson (1981).

The clay-rich heads on the other hand, with Liquid Limits in excess of 45% and Plasticity Index greater than 20% (Figure 20.10) retain their cohesive strength even when pore pressures reduce effective stresses to zero, and failure is much more likely to be by sliding over distinct slip surfaces rather than thixotropic flow. The presence of the permafrost table restricted the depth of landsliding to the thickness of the active layer and produced the laterally extensive shear planes commonly reported within and beneath these argillaceous head deposits. The disturbed material above the slip surfaces generally shows a mudflow fabric (Hutchinson, 1970) with brecciated clay fragments set in

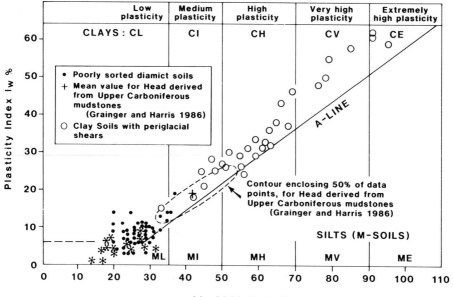

Figure 20.10. Plasticity Chart. Data from modern gelifluction deposits Norway (Okstindan Mountains, Harris, 1977) and Greenland (Target Line 7, Mesters Vig, N.E. Greenland, Washburn, 1967), indicated by*.

Table 20.2 *Classification of head deposits in England in Wales in terms of grain size, Atterberg Limits and mass movement process*

Matrix Grain Size	Liquid Limit (%)	Plasticity Index (%)	Mode of failure under periglacial conditions	Post Glacial slope stability
sand plus silt	20–35	0–15	gelifluction	high permeability, generally stable
silt plus clay	30–55	15–25	gelifluction	groundwater may induce shallow translational slides on slopes greater than about 15°
clay	45–100	25–80	shallow mudslides	groundwater may reactivate fossil periglacial shears on slopes greater than 7° to 9°

a remoulded clayey matrix. It would appear therefore that there was some degree of internal deformation during sliding.

Intermediate soils, such as those derived from weathered mustones in Cornwall and Devon, described by Grainger and Harris (1986) show Atterberg Limits mid-way between the two extremes discussed above (Figure 20.10). Clay contents in the weathered Carboniferous mudstones described by Grainger and Harris were as high as 40% to 50% (Figure 20.5), although the clay was predominantly of non-swelling clay mineralogy with low activity (Grainger and Witte, 1981). These soils are liable to shallow translational landslides today, but under Devensian periglacial conditions "plastic or ductile flow was a much more important mechanism" (Grainger and Harris, 1986), giving head deposits with completely reorganised fabrics. A classification of slopes in England and Wales on the basis of mass movement mechanisms and soil properties is given in Table 20.2.

Conclusions

Slope deposits resulting from periglacial mass-wasting of non-argillaceous regoliths or tills are recognised as constituting a distinctive sediment type. The deposits are characteristically matrix supported diamictons with low Liquid Limits and Plasticity Indices. Clasts show consistent low angle dips approximately parallel or slightly imbricate to the ground surface and macrofabrics are strongly orientated parallel to the direction of maximum slope. Irregular bands and lenses of silt and fine sand may interrupt otherwise massive units, marking phases of increased slope wash activity. Valley side slopes are often smoothly convexo-concave, with valley bottom gradients decreasing to 4° or 5°.

Rivers cut through these sheets of head to form terrace-like landforms. Similar smooth-surfaced aprons of head often extend seawards from fossil coastal cliffs, particularly in south west England and parts of South Wales.

In contrast, clayey tills and clay bedrocks suffered softening and brecciation under periglacial conditions, and on slopes extensive planar slip surfaces developed over which sliding of the active layer occurred. Reorganisation and remolding of the clay-rich head did take place during translational sliding, but was incomplete, in contrast to the more arenaceous heads. Slopes as low as 2° may have suffered instability. Two distinct generations of mudslide deposits may occur, the lower dating to the main Devensian or possibly earlier cold phases, the upper to the Loch Lomond Stadial.

Whilst permafrost was probably present during periods of clay head accumulation, preventing deep seated slides, other evidence, such as ice-wedge casts or cryotrubation structures, must be sought to prove its presence during accumulation of the poorly sorted gelifluction deposits, since gelifluction may occur in areas of deep seasonal freezing, as well as in areas of permafrost (Harris, 1977; Gamper, 1983).

References

Baker, C.A. (1976). 'Late Devensian periglacial phenomena in the upper Cam valley, north Essex', *Proc. Geol. Ass.*, **87**, 285–306.

Ball, D.F., Mew, G. and Macphee, W.S.G. (1969). 'Soils of Snowdon', *Field Studies*, **3**, 193–218.

Biczysko, S.J. (1981). 'Relic landslip in west Northamptonshire', *Q.J. eng. Geol. London*, **14**, 169–74.

Boardman, J. (1985). 'Field guide to the periglacial

landforms of northern England', *Quaternary Research Association*, Cambridge, 82pp.

British Standards 1377 (1975). 'Methods of test for soils for engineering purposes', British Standards Institution, London.

Casagrande, A. (1948). 'Classification and identification of soils', *Trans. Am. Soc. Civ. Eng.*, **113**, 901–92.

Chandler, R.J. (1970a). 'The degradation of Lias Clay slopes in an area of the East Midlands', *Q.J. eng. Geol. London*, **2**, 161–81.

Chandler, R.J. (1970b). 'A shallow slab slide in the Lias Clay near Uppingham, Rutland', *Géotechnique*, **20**, 253–60.

Chandler, R.J. (1976). 'The history and stability of two Lias clay slopes in the upper Gwash valley, Rutland', *Phil. Trans. R. Soc. Lond.*, **283A**, 463–91.

Chandler, R.J., Kellaway, G.A., Skempton, A.W. and Wyatt, R.J. (1976). 'Valley slope sections in Jurassic strata near Bath, Somerset', *Phil. Trans. R. Soc. Lond.*, **283A**, 527–55.

Crampton, C.B. (1965). 'An indurated horizon in soils of South Wales', *J. Soil Sci.*, **16**, 230–41.

Crampton, C.B. and Taylor, J.A. (1967). 'Solifluction terraces in South Wales', *Biul. Perygl.*, **16**, 15–36.

De la Beche, H.T. (1839). 'Report on the geology of Cornwall, Devon and West Somerset', *Mem. Geol. Survey*.

Dewey, H., Bromehead, C.E.N., Chatwin, C.P. and Dines, H.G. (1924). 'The geology of the country around Dartford', *Mem. Geol. Surv.* HMSO London.

Dines, H.G., Hollingworth, S.E., Edwards, W., Buchan, S. and Welch, F.B. (1940). 'The mapping of head deposits', *Geol. Mag.*, **77**, 198–226.

Douglas, T.D. and Harrison, S. (1983). 'Solifluction sheets – a review and case study from the Cheviot Hills', *Newcastle upon Tyne Polytechnic, School of Geography and Environmental Studies*, Occasional Series in Geography, 7, 35pp.

Douglas, T.D. and Harrison, S. (1987). Late Devensian periglacial slope deposits in the Cheviot Hills. In, *Periglacial Processes and Landforms in Britain and Ireland* (Ed. J. Boardman), pp. 237–44, Cambridge University Press.

Dreimanis, A. and Vagners, U.J. (1971). 'Bimodal distribution of rock and mineral fragments in basal tills', in *Till: a symposium* (Ed. R.P. Goldthwait), pp. 237–50, Ohio State University Press.

Edmonds. E.A., Wright, J.E., Beer, K.E., Hawkes, J.R., Williams, M., Freshney, E.C. and Fenning, P.J. (1968). 'Geology of the country around Okehampton', *Mem. Geol. Surv.* HMSO London.

Folk, R.L. (1955). 'Student operator error in determination of roundness sphericity and grain size', *J. Sedim. Petrol.*, **25**, 297–301.

French, H.M. (1973). 'Cryopediments on the chalk of southern England', *Biul. Perygl.*, **22**, 149–56.

Gamper, M.W. (1983). 'Controls and rates of movement of solifluction lobes in the eastern Swiss Alps', *Proc. 4th Int. Conf. Permafrost, Fairbanks,* *Alaska*, pp. 328–33. National Academy Press, Washington.

Grainger, P. and Harris, J. (1986). 'Weathering and slope stability on Upper Carboniferous mudrocks in southwest England', *Q. J. eng. Geol. London.*, **19**, 155–74.

Grainger, P. and Witte, G. (1981). 'Clay mineral assemblages of Namurian shales in Devon and Cornwall', *Proc. Ussher Soc.*, **5**, 168–78.

Harris, C. (1977). 'Engineering properties, groundwater conditions, and the nature of soil movement on a solifluction slope in north Norway', *Q.J. eng. Geol. London*, **10**, 27–43.

Harris, C. (1981). *Periglacial Mass-Wasting: A Review of Research*, B.G.R.G. Research Monograph No. 4, Geo Abstracts, Norwich, 204pp.

Harris, C. (1987). 'Mechanics of mass movement in periglacial environments'. In. *Slope Stability* (Eds. M.G. Anderson and K.S. Richards), pp. 531–59, Wiley, Chichester.

Harris, C. and Ellis, S. (1980). 'Micromorphology of soils in soliflucted materials, Okstindan, northern Norway', *Geoderma*, **23**, 11–29.

Harris, C. and Wright, M.D. (1980). 'Some last glaciation drift deposits near Pontypridd, South Wales', *Geol. J.*, **15**, 7–20.

Henry, A. (1984a). *The Lithostratigraphy, Biostratigraphy and Chronostratigraphy of Coastal Pleistocene Deposits in Gower, South Wales*, Unpubl. Ph.D., University of Wales, 517pp.

Henry, A. (1984b). 'Gower' in *Quaternary Research Association Field Guide, Wales: Gower, Preseli, Fforest Fawr* (Ed. D.Q. Bowen), pp. 19–32.

Higginbottom, I.E. and Fookes, P.G. (1971). 'Engineering aspects of periglacial features in Britain'. *Q.J. eng. Geol. London*, **3**, 85–117.

Hutchinson, J. (1970). 'A coastal mudflow on the London Clay cliffs at Beltinge, North Kent', *Géotechnique*, **20**, 412–38.

Hutchinson, J.N., Somerville, S.H. and Petley, D.J. (1973). 'A landslide in periglacially disturbed Etruria Marl at Bury Hill, Staffordshire', *Q.J. eng. Geol. London*, **6**, 377–404.

Jones, P.F. and Derbyshire, E. (1983). 'Late Pleistocene periglacial degradation of lowland Britain: implications for civil engineering', *Q.J. eng. Geol. London*, **16**, 197–210.

Kidson, C. (1971). 'The Quaternary history of the coasts of South West England, with special reference to the Bristol Channel coast', in *Exeter Essays in Geography* (Eds. K.J. Gregory and W.L.D. Ravenhill), pp. 1–22, Exeter.

King, C.A.M. (1976). *Northern England*, Methuen, London.

Kirby, R.P. (1967). 'The fabric of head deposits in South Devon', *Proc. Ussher Soc.*, **1**, 288–90.

Konrad, J-M. and Morgenstern, N.R. (1980). 'A mechanistic theory of ice lens formation in fine-grained soils', *Can. Geotech. J.*, **17**, 473–86.

Konrad, J-M. and Morgenstern, N.R. (1981). 'The segregation potential of a freezing soil', *Can. Geotech. J.*, **18**, 482–491.

Konrad, J-M. and Morgenstern, N.R. (1982). 'Prediction of frost heave in the laboratory during transient freezing', *Can. Geotech. J.*, **19**, 250–9.

Lewis, C.A. (1970). 'The upper Wye and Usk regions' in, *The Glaciation of Wales* (Ed. C.A. Lewis), pp. 147–74, Longmans, London.

Matthews, J.A. and Petch, J.R. (1982). 'Within valley asymmetry and related problems of Neoglacial lateral moraine development at certain Jotunheimen glaciers, southern Norway', *Boreas*, **11**, 225–47.

McKeown, M.C., Edmonds, E.A., Williams, M., Freshney, E.C. and Masson Smith, D.J. (1973). 'Geology of the country around Boscastle and Holsworthy', *Mem. Geol. Surv.*

McRoberts, E.C. and Morgenstern, N.R. (1974). 'The stability of thawing slopes', *Can. Geotech. J.*, **11**, 447–69.

Morgenstern, N.R. and Nixon, J.F. (1971). 'One dimensional consolidation of thawing soils', *Can. Geotech. J.*, **8**, 558–65.

Mottershead, D.N. (1971). 'Coastal head deposits between Start Point and Hope Cove, Devon', *Field Studies*, **5**, 433–53.

Mottershead, D.N. (1977). *South-West England, Guidebook for Excursion A6 and C6, INQUA, 10th Congress, 1977.*

Penn, S., Royce, C.J. and Evans, C.J. (1983). 'The periglacial modification of the Lincoln Scarp', *Q.J. eng. Geol. London*, **16**, 309–18.

Potts, A.S. (1971). 'Fossil cryonival features in Central Wales', *Geogr. Annlr.*, **53A**, 39–51.

Powers, M.C. (1958). 'A new roundness scale for sedimentary particles', *J. Sedim. Petrol.*, **23**, 117–9.

Shakesby, R.A. (1985). 'An investigation into the origin of the deposits in a chalk dry valley of the South Downs, Southern England', *Univ. Edinburgh Dept. Geography Research Discussion Paper*, **5**, 25pp.

Shakesby, R.A. (1981). 'Periglacial origin of slope deposits near Woolhope in the Welsh Borderland', *Cambria*, **8**, 1–16.

Skempton, A.W. (1957). 'Discussion: the planning and design of the new Hong Kong airport', *Proc. Inst. Civil Engrs. London*, **7**, 305–7.

Skempton, A.W. and Weeks, A.G. (1976). 'The Quaternary history of the Lower Greensand escarpment and Weald Clay Vale near Sevenoaks, Kent', *Phil. Trans. R. Soc. Lond.*, **283A**, 493–526.

Small, R.J., Clark, M.J. and Lewin, J. (1970). 'The periglacial rock-stream at Clatford Bottom, Marlborough Downs, Wiltshire', *Proc. Geol. Ass.*, **81**, 87–98.

Stephens, N. (1961). 'Pleistocene events in North Devon', *Proc. Geol. Ass.*, **72**, 469–72.

Taber, S. (1929). 'Frost heaving', *J. Geol.*, **37**, 428–61.

Taber, S. (1930). 'The mechanisms of frost heaving', *J. Geol.*, **38**, 303–17.

Taber, S. (1943). 'Perennially frozen ground in Alaska: its origin and history', *Bull. Geol. Soc. Am.*, **54**, 1433–548.

Terzaghi, K. and Peck, R.B. (1967). *Soil Mechanics in Engineering Practice*, Wiley, New York, 729pp.

Thomas, G.S.P. (1977). 'The Quaternary of the Isle of Man', in *The Quaternary History of the Irish Sea* (Eds. C. Kidson and M.J. Tooley), Geological Journal Special Issue No. 7.

Tufnell, L. (1969). 'The range of periglacial phenomena in northern England', *Biul. Perygl.*, **19**, 291–323.

Vincent, P. (1976). 'Some periglacial deposits near Aberystwyth, Wales, as seen with a scanning electron microscope', *Biul. Perygl.*, **25**, 59–64.

Washburn, A.L. (1967). 'Instrumental observations of mass-wasting in the Mesters Vig District, Northeast Greenland', *Med. om. Grønland*, 166, **4**, 296pp.

Waters, R.S. (1964). 'The Pleistocene legacy to the geomorphology of Dartmoor' in, *Dartmoor Essays* (Ed. I. Simmons), pp. 73–96, University of Exeter, Exeter.

Watson, E. (1976). 'Field excursions in the Aberystwyth region, 1–10 July 1975', *Biul. Perygl.*, **26**, 79–112.

Watson, E. and Watson, S. (1967). 'The periglacial origin of the drifts at Morfa-bychan, near Aberystwyth', *Geol. J.*, **5**, 419–40.

Watson, E. and Watson, S. (1970). 'The coastal periglacial slope deposits of the Cotentin Peninsula', *Trans. Inst. Brit. Geogr.*, **49**, 125–44.

Weeks, A.G. (1969). 'The stability of slopes in south-east England as affected by periglacial activity', *Q.J. eng. Geol. London*, **5**, 223–41.

Wilson, P. (1981). 'Periglacial valley-fill sediments at Edale, North Derbyshire', *East Midlands Geographer*, **7**, 263–71.

Wright, M.D. and Harris, C. (1980). 'Superficial deposits in the South Wales Coalfield', in *Cliff and Slope Stability in South Wales* (Ed. J. Perkins), pp. 193–205, Dept. Extra Mural Studies, University College Cardiff.

21· Periglacial sediments and landforms in the Isles of Scilly and West Cornwall

J.D. SCOURSE

Abstract

The Pleistocene stratigraphy of the Isles of Scilly and West Cornwall is dominated by solifluction sediments deposited under periglacial conditions. For these sediments facies are defined on the basis of granulometry, fabric and structure and are incorporated into a facies model illustrating lateral and vertical relationships and sequential development. Consideration is given to the influence of bedrock in relation to the character of the sediments. Periglacial structures, including thermal contraction cracks, ice fissures, involutions and festooning are described from areas of slate bedrock, especially the Camel Estuary. Reasons for the absence of such structures from areas of granite bedrock are discussed. The close relationship between these sediments and granite tors in the Isles of Scilly is noted and, based on a revised Pleistocene stratigraphy for the region, a recent age for tor exhumation proposed. The importance of periglacial processes in the landscape evolution of the region is stressed.

Introduction

South West England has been well represented in the periglacial literature. The widely used term 'head' was first proposed by de la Beche (1839) to describe angular rubble drift exposed in coastal sections in the region, and Whitley (1916) recorded similarities between sediments being actively deposited in Siberia and those of Cornwall. His paper represents one of the earliest uses of a periglacial analogue. In the 1950s Te Punga (1956, 1957) recognised the region as a relict periglacial landscape, and during the second half of the same decade intense geomorphological controversy was generated over the origin of the Dartmoor and Bodmin Moor granite tors (Linton, 1955, 1964; Palmer and Radley, 1961; Palmer and Nielson, 1962).

This paper reviews new evidence on periglacial sediments and landforms from the Isles of Scilly and West Cornwall, the westernmost extremity of the South West Peninsula (Figures 21.1 and 21.2). Though the database is local, the conclusions reached are nevertheless significant for a much wider area of southern Britain.

Stratigraphic models

Field observations of coastal sections have enabled the simplification of the Pleistocene stratigraphy of

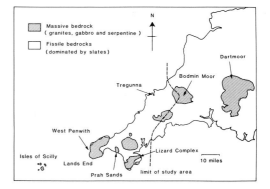

Figure 21.1. West Cornwall and the Isles of Scilly; limit of study area, and areas of massive and fissile bedrock.

the region into two models, one each for the Isles of Scilly and West Cornwall (Figure 21.3 and Scourse, 1985). The depositional environments of the various units have been interpreted from detailed field and laboratory analyses and their stratigraphical relationships have permitted chronological reconstructions of glacial, periglacial, vegetational and sea level events. In terms of the number and variety of sedimentary units, the quantity of material and the amount of time

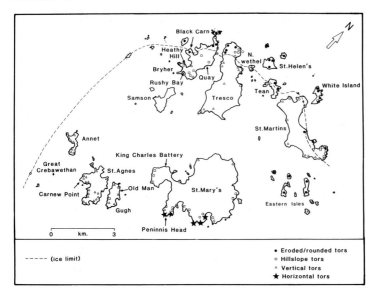

Figure 21.2. The Isles of Scilly; sites mentioned in the text, ice limit (taken as the southern limit of the Hell Bay Gravel) and tor morphology distribution.

represented, periglacial processes have been predominant in the region during the Late Pleistocene.

Solifluction deposits

Terminology

As also adopted by other workers (Henry, 1984), the term 'breccia' is used here in preference to 'head' as the former is specifically non-genetic. Though de la Beche did not intend the term head to be genetic, it has become so through usage. Some 'heads' as described may not be the product of solifluction over permafrost, or indeed of mass movements in general. 'Solifluction' as a term used in isolation refers to mass movement phenomena usually, but not necessarily, associated with permafrost. 'Solifluction breccia' is therefore used to denote coarse angular accumulations formed by mass movements, probably, but not by definition, over permafrost.

Lithological variability

Solifluction deposits are represented by the Porthloo and Bread and Cheese Breccia units in the

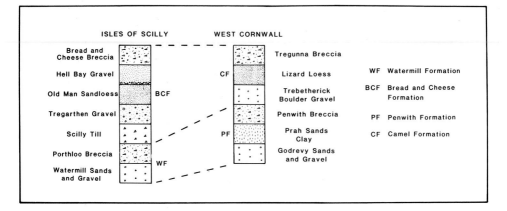

Figure 21.3. Stratigraphic models for the Isles of Scilly and West Cornwall, and their correlation; units on models are of member status.

Scillies, and the Prah Sands Clay, Penwith and Tregunna Breccias in West Cornwall (Figure 21.3). The Hell Bay Gravel is also of solifluction origin, but is largely derived from reworked glacigenic sediments rather than weathered bedrock. It is not considered in detail below.

Solifluction breccias derived from granitic and other massive bedrocks (including gabbro and serpentine) differ in a number of critical respects from those derived from slate bedrocks (Figure 21.1). The Penwith Breccia contains both granitic and slaty variants. The Scillies being exclusively granite, the Porthloo and Bread and Cheese Breccias are of the granitic type, and the limited outcrop of the Tregunna Breccia in the Camel Estuary is dominantly slaty in character. The Prah Sands Clay is a special form of solifluction deposit and is discussed briefly below.

The granitic breccias are dominantly very poorly sorted (Figure 21.4) with a wide range of clast sizes and contain a high matrix/clast ratio except in specific situations (see below). The matrix is dominated by coarse quartz and feldspar granules. The slate derived breccias, on the other hand, are usually clast supported with a very low matrix/clast ratio, the clasts being dominated by discoid forms. The matrix is usually silty and relatively well sorted. Secondary structures related to ground ice are

absent in the granitic breccias but extremely common in the slaty breccias in which they obscure any primary downslope clast fabric.

These sedimentological differences between the breccia variants are the result of three factors:

i) the way the different bedrocks respond to the primary frost-heave process, and the resultant nature of the fractured material;
ii) differences in behaviour during solifluction, and
iii) a differential susceptibility to ground ice.

Fissile slates break down into discoid clasts and silt under frost-heave whilst massive granites break into large angular blocks and 'growan', coarse sand and granules. These differences have subsequent effects on gelifluction and frost creep during solifluction, and on the efficacy of ground ice processes.

Periglacial structures in slaty breccias
Ice-wedge casts have been documented from a number of sites within the region (Clarke, 1973) but some of these must be regarded as conjectural. Whilst some of these 'casts' constitute zones of rhizome penetration from the contemporary land surface which have subsequently become preferred axes of chemical alteration, two undoubted thermal

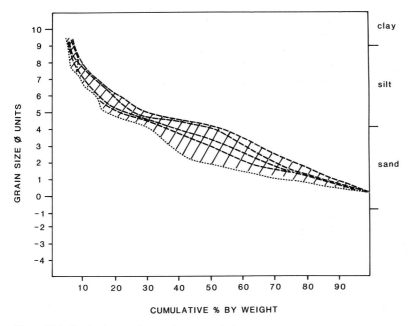

Figure 21.4. Grain-size envelope and some typical cumulative frequency distributions for facies D granitic breccia from the Isles of Scilly.

Figure 21.5. Section at Tregunna in the Camel Estuary, north Cornwall. One of the two thermal contraction cracks visible at this site can be seen to the left of the spade, penetrating slaty Penwith Breccia (below) and the coarse Trebetherick Boulder Gravel (above). Photograph: R.G. West.

contraction cracks can be seen in section at Tregunna (Figure 21.5; Clarke, 1973; Scourse, 1985). In section the cracks are over a metre in depth, but are truncated towards their base by the present shore platform. The cracks penetrate the Trebetherick Boulder Gravel and the Penwith Breccia. The tops of the cracks, which reach a width of 0.5m, are near the present land surface. The cracks are filled with silts and vertically orientated slate discs, and the clasts marginal to the cracks are upturned. The cracks can be seen extending laterally across the wave-cut platform. The small size, form and sedimentary context of these features suggest that they formed as active layer soil wedges (French, 1976). However, they are of uncertain total depth. If these features prove to be deeper than about 1.5 m their origin as soil wedges must be in doubt and an ice-wedge cast invoked. This hypothesis would be supported by the marginal clast upturning (A. Pissart, pers. comm., 1985). The features are thought to be Late Devensian in age based on the overall stratigraphic scheme (Figure 21.3). If these

features are interpreted as Late Devensian ice-wedge casts this implies the presence of permafrost (Washburn, 1973; Seddon and Holyoak, 1985) further south and west in southern Britain than previously considered (Williams, 1969).

Other characteristic periglacial structures also occur within the slaty Penwith Breccia at this site, and also at Porthleven. These include small ice fissures, tens of centimetres in length but less than a centimetre in width. Where these occur in groups, marginal clast upturning produces festooning. Involution structures are also extremely common within the slaty breccia.

The common occurrence of such structures in slaty breccias and their almost total absence from granitic breccias can be accounted for in two ways:

i) the enhanced efficacy of ground ice processes in weathered slate compared with weathered granite, and
ii) the visual enhancement of the structures within slaty breccias because of the linear, discoid clast shape, and lack of matrix.

The high proportion of silt within the slaty breccia matrices enhances ice segregation through small interstices causing high pore-water pressures (Taber, 1929, 1930; Mackay, 1971). Slaty breccia is therefore frost susceptible and favours the development of ground ice bodies. In the coarser granitic breccia, however, only low pore water pressures can be sustained in the larger interstices, and pore ice develops.

Facies model – granitic breccia

Examination of many sections of granitic solifluction breccia, and other soliflucted material derived from massive bedrocks including gabbro and serpentine, has enabled the definition of five facies, one of which can be subdivided into two subfacies. These have been incorporated into a model (Figure 21.6) which illustrates the stratigraphic and sequential relationships between the facies.

Facies A as a whole may be termed 'deformation' breccia by analogy with deformation till (Dreimanis, 1976). It is subdivided into two subfacies, Aa and Ab, and always occurs at the base of the soliflucted material. Subfacies Aa occurs at sites where the mass movement sheet/lobe has overridden unconsolidated, usually Pleistocene raised beach sediments (Watermill and Godrevy Sands and Gravel members, Figure 21.3), and Ab where the unit rests on solid bedrock. Subfacies Aa represents the entrainment of basal material into the downslope flow. Structurally this entrainment takes the form of flames or tongues when seen in three dimensional view (Figure 21.7a) and can eventually lead to the formation of plications. Bryan (1946) noted that the downslope movement itself can produce deformation or drag structures owing to differential lateral movements, and Jahn (1956) has illustrated stages in the development of

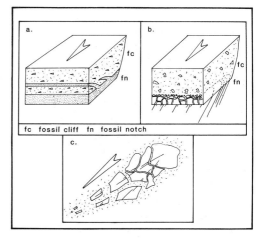

Figure 21.7. a. Facies Aa 'deformation breccia' b. Facies Ab 'deformation breccia' c. Clast-trail structure, common in facies D. Arrow indicates direction of flow of solifluction lobe/sheet.

such forms, the final stage being characterised by roll-like or cylindrical forms. Such structures, when only seen in two-dimensional view, can be misinterpreted. Where the entrained sediments are dominantly beach sands they may be distinguished from *in situ* material by silt/clay ingestion, slump and flow structures, and where rounded pebbles and cobbles, by being matrix supported and with distinctive dip into the flow direction (see Facies D below). Subfacies Aa is extremely common.

Subfacies Ab represents the frost-heave of the bedrock, the production of discrete clasts, often related to bedrock discontinuities, and their entrainment downslope into the solifluction flow proper (Figure 21.7b). Similar structures are reported by Waters (1971) who interprets them as formed by a two-stage process of slopewash over a

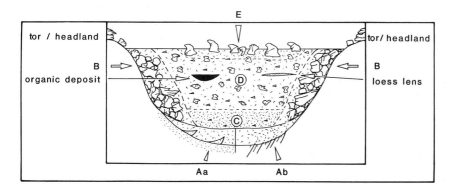

Figure 21.6. Granitic breccia facies model illustrating stratigraphic and sequential development.

former land surface followed by subsequent solifluction. An alternative explanation of contemporaneous frost-heave and solifluction is preferred. The resultant deformation of weathered bedrock, involving the downslope deflection of inclined strata has been reported underlying solifluction deposits throughout South West England (Mottershead, 1971; Green and Eden, 1973), elsewhere (Penck, 1953; FitzPatrick, 1963; Jahn, 1969; J. Hutchinson, pers. comm. 1985) and has recently been subject of a geotechnical study within West Cornwall (Cresswell, 1983). Cresswell believes the deformation structures to be the result of high pore fluid pressures associated with confined aquifers in the active layer.

Subfacies Aa and Ab are most commonly observed close to the fossil cliff line (Figure 21.7). Away from the fossil cliff line in thick sequences the basal facies is most commonly C.

Close to bedrock headlands, facies B predominates (Figure 21.6). This consists of extremely large clasts with 'a' axes in excess of 10 m and estimated

Figure 21.8. Section at St Loy, near Land's End, Cornwall. Structurally chaotic facies B granitic breccia containing extremely large granite clasts (scale given by spade, bottom right). The section is immediately to the left of a prominent hillslope tor.

to weigh over 100 tonnes (Figure 21.8). These boulders are usually clast supported whilst the matrix is extremely poorly sorted and structurally chaotic. The facies represents the frost-heave of enormous blocks from hillslope tors and other exposed bedrock, transported short distances by solifluction. Facies B sometimes contains practically no matrix and resembles rock-fall deposits; with more matrix it approximates to blockfield or felsenmeer deposits (French, 1976).

Facies C is usually crudely stratified, matrix-supported with only occasional clasts, the matrix being dominated by granules. It represents an early stage of solifluction with the removal of fine material from the upslope land surface, including soil and weathered bedrock. Such fine, crudely stratified horizons have been reported from South Wales, where associated reddening is thought to represent the solifluction of rubified soil (Bowen, 1971). The proximity of easily weathered bedrock variants may cause facies C to comprise largely stony clay; the Prah Sands Clay (Figure 21.3) is thought to represent such material, felsite elvan dyke and associated metasediments having weathered to clay upslope. Such clayey deposits have also been reported from South Wales, including the Pwll Du red beds at Hunt's Bay, Gower (Bowen, 1970, 1971), and the grey-green weathering horizon at Abermawr, Preseli (Davies, 1969). In many places facies C appears to have been either partially or totally removed by and incorporated into the overlying facies, D.

Facies D represents the most commonly observed variant of granitic breccia. It commonly overlies facies A, B or C in section (Figure 21.6), and consists of matrix supported angular clasts set in an extremely poorly sorted silty sand with small amounts of clay; the matrix is commonly coarse-skewed (Figure 21.4). Lobate structures in section are common, with stone accumulations marking lobe margins. Facies D is characterised by a classic solifluction fabric (Figure 21.9; Washburn, 1973; French, 1976). The clasts display a distinctive downslope preferred orientation and dip into the slope. Such angles of dip of between 5° and 45° from the horizontal can be explained in terms of penecontemporaneous upfreezing and the mass movement of material under gravity processes in the seasonally thawed layer (French, 1976).

Contemporaneous frost-heave and mass movement explains what can be described as 'clast-trail' structures common in facies D (Figure 21.7c). Large clasts have been frost-heaved into a number of smaller clasts and then strung out to form a trail

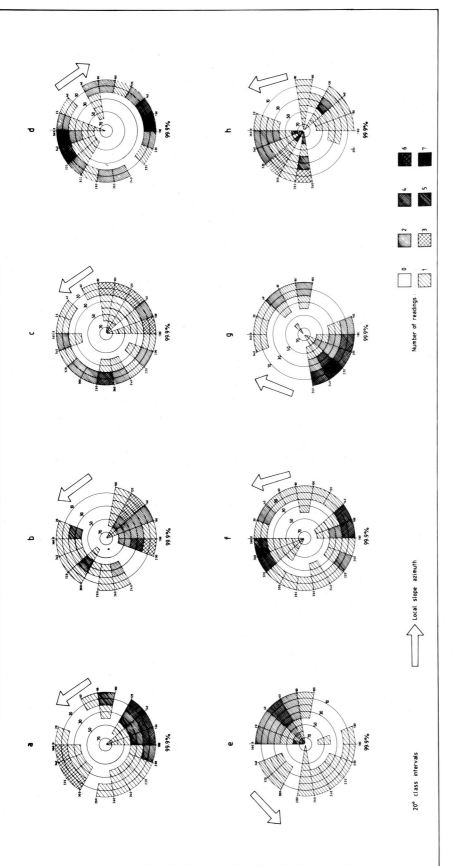

Figure 21.9. Three-dimensional plots of fabric data from granitic breccia facies D in the Isles of Scilly. All fabrics are significant at the 99.9% level.
a, b, c—King Charles Battery (St Mary's)
d—Quay (Bryher) e—Rushy Bay (Bryher) f, g—Heathy Hill (Bryher) h—Black Carn (Bryher)

by subsequent solifluction. The smaller clasts can often be joined together to form the parent clast, so fresh are the products. Such clast-trail structures, like the fabric characteristics, can therefore be related to the seasonal cycle of frost-heave and mass movement.

Facies D contains occasional lenses of loessic material and organic sequences representing ponding associated with nalyedi (Brown, 1967) or solifluction processes. These have proved critical in dating the sequences (see below).

Facies E forms the most consistant capping of the sections (Figure 21.6). The upper parts of the Penwith, Porthloo and Bread and Cheese Breccias most commonly consist of this material (Figure 21.3). It consists of extremely large blocks of granite set in a granular matrix, with a distinctive lack of material in the pebble/cobble grade (Figure 21.10). Deposits of this sort have previously been described from the region (Mitchell and Orme, 1967; Brown, 1977).

Three hypotheses can be invoked to explain the occurrence of the large boulders in facies E:

 i) mudflow transport,
 ii) solifluction rafts, and
 iii) ploughing blocks.

High energy mudflows can raft large boulders, as documented by Broscoe and Thompson (1972) in the St Elias mountains, Alaska. Large boulders thought to have rafted on the surface of solifluction sheets and lobes have been invoked to explain the striking 'rock streams' of Wiltshire and Dorset (Williams, 1968; Small *et al.*, 1970). However, large actively moving blocks and boulders lying on the surface of solifluction sheets and lobes have been extensively reported from contemporary periglacial environments where they have been described as 'ploughing blocks' (Tufnell, 1972) because they move faster than the solifluction deposits they rest on, and as a result produce an upslope depression and downslope mound. The essential difference between rafted and ploughing blocks is therefore the velocity of the boulder in relation to the movement of the underlying material.

Figure 21.10. Section at Carnew Point, St Agnes, Isles of Scilly. Fossil ploughing block partially buried at the top of the section. A horizontal tor can be seen to the right, and the scale is given by the rucksack in the right foreground.

Some of the facies E boulders overlie deformational structures in the underlying material thought to result from the loading of the sediment by the boulder. Such deformational relationships are probably indicative of rafting. Other boulders, however, exhibit erosional basal contacts suggestive of ploughing behaviour. It is therefore thought that at least some of the facies E boulders represent fossil ploughing blocks; such blocks have not been readily identified in fossil situations (an exception is Lyford *et al.*, 1963).

The blocks are usually found only semi-buried at the top of the sections, rarely fully embedded within the underlying material. This phenomenon also requires explanation and two hypotheses can be invoked:

i) upfreezing to the surface, and
ii) penecontemporaneous frost-heave of boulders during solifluction.

The well-documented tendency for large objects to upfreeze in the periglacial environment would tend to lift or push such large boulders to the surface (French, 1976). Though this hypothesis may explain the situation of some smaller boulders, the penecontemporaneous frost-heave and break-up of the boulders during solifluction is thought to be the most likely general explanation. The ploughing and rafted blocks can be seen to be intimately related to the clast-trail structures described above. During the last phase of periglacial conditions large blocks of material would have been removed from summit and hillslope tors and other bedrock exposures, forming block and clitter fields on the surface of solifluction sheets and lobes. Individual blocks would constitute ploughing or rafted blocks moving in one of the four ways enumerated by Tufnell (1972). During cold periods these blocks would be subject to frost-heave, reduced in size and finally incorporated into the underlying solifluction proper. Ploughing and rafted blocks therefore represent a transitional stage between the breakdown of the solid bedrock and the formation of typical solifluction sediment i.e. facies D. The sudden climatic amelioration 10,000 years B.P. fossilised the blocks as they moved downslope on the land surface, where they have remained. Clast-trail structures accordingly represent partially destroyed ploughing and rafted blocks.

Facies E type material has been found to characterise the Loch Lomond Stadial of the Devensian Late-glacial on Bodmin Moor (Brown, 1977). Though no well-dated sites of this age have been reported from coastal sites in the study area, it is highly likely that the ploughing blocks of facies E were deposited at this time. The facies is most commonly represented in the uppermost solifluated units i.e. in superposition to the Old Man Sandloess and Lizard Loess (Figure 21.3). These latter units have been dated by thermoluminescence (TL) to 18,600 years B.P. and 15,900 years B.P. respectively (Wintle, 1981); so the emplacement of the facies E blocks must be later than these dates.

Sections where all the facies described above can be observed together are rare; the model is based on the frequency of repeating facies relationships at many sites. Where sequences of solifluated material are most commonly developed, it will be clear that a broadly coarsening upwards sequence occurs i.e. facies C-D-E (Figure 21.6). This characteristic has been observed within solifluction deposits elsewhere (Jessen and Milthers, 1928) and previously within South West England (Waters, 1964; Brunsden, 1964; Gregory, 1969). Waters (1964) attributes such coarsening upwards sequences to an inverted weathering sequence i.e. first the solifluction of weathered regolith and later the removal of freshly fractured bedrock. Mottershead (1971) and Green and Eden (1973) both dispute the validity of this observation. Green and Eden undertook a quantitative study of the location of blocks > 15 cm within solifluated material in sections on Dartmoor. They propose a less ordered pattern of solifluction, but with a general tendency towards a fining upwards sequence. Large blocks, they argue, occur most commonly in the basal sediments. From their discussion, however, it is clear that their analyses concentrated largely on facies A type material, deformation breccia, which, as stated above, often contains a high concentration of freshly heaved blocks. Had they considered a wider variety of sediments it is suggested that a coarsening upwards sequence would have emerged from their analyses. The detailed explanation for the facies variations given above largely agrees with the general model proposed by Waters (1964).

Solifluction and permafrost

The sedimentological characteristics of these deposits and their geomorphological context leave no doubt that they are the result of mass movements. They can therefore be accurately described as 'solifluction' deposits. Whether they were deposited in association with permafrost, however, is less easy to answer.

'Solifluction' in the periglacial context has been defined as a mass movement phenomenon involving the interaction of the frost-creep and gelifluction processes (French, 1976). The existence of permafrost and an active layer are necessary prerequisites for gelifluction *sensu stricto*. The number of features observed within these sequences that require explanation in terms of penecontemporaneous frost-heave and/or the presence of ground ice along with mass movement suggests a gelifluction origin. This is supported by the fact that high pore fluid pressures are necessary to explain many of the described features. An origin in terms of cold climate mudflows without any necessity for regional permafrost cannot, however, be ruled out.

If the sediment is of gelifluction origin, the great thickness (up to 30 m) preserved would suggest the accretion of multiple lobes or sheets based on the recorded maximal thickness of around 1.5 m for contemporary periglacial active layers. As the sediments accumulated so the permafrost table would have migrated progressively upwards through the previously deposited material. Structures within the sediments in conjunction with the presence of buried organic layers support this hypothesis of incremental growth.

Tors

Tor morphology and distribution in the Isles of Scilly

The term 'tor' is used here non-genetically to denote vertical or sub-vertical outcrops of bedrock exposed on summits or hillslopes. In this region the features are restricted to areas of granite bedrock (Figure 21.1).

Field mapping and aerial photograph interpretation has enabled the definition of four tor forms on the Isles of Scilly (Figure 21.11). The distribution of these is given in Figure 21.2.

Form A, horizontal tors, are characterised by large horizontal discontinuities separating large granite slabs which often touch at few points, thus resembling 'pedestal' features locally called 'logan' stones. This tor form has often been described as 'mammilated', 'castellated' or 'lamellar' (Waters, in discussion of Linton, 1955). Form B, vertical tors, are characterised by vertical discontinuities, granitic rubble often filling the voids. Form C, hillslope tors, are a slope or coastal variant of forms A and B. Form D can be described as smoothed, rounded or eroded, with all loose material completely removed.

These tor forms represent points along a continuum. This, combined with the difficulty of defining tors in coastal areas where much bare granite is exposed, make this tor classification and their mapping a largely subjective exercise. Nevertheless,

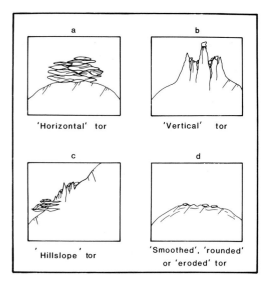

Figure 21.11. Tor morphological variations in the Isles of Scilly.

some trends can be discerned. Forms A, B and C are all concentrated well to the south of the ice limit on the Scillies (Figure 21.2), especially on the south side of St Mary's on St Agnes and the Western Rocks. The horizontal tors of Peninnis Head, St Mary's, represent some of the finest granite landforms to be seen in Britain. Form D tors are only found to the north of the ice limit; many of these, such as Round Island, resemble roche moutonnée features. Between these two zones very few tors of any kind occur. Instead, rounded hills without bare granite exposure predominate. Samson, with its distinctive rounded North and South Hills, is typical of this transitional zone.

The clear association between these landforms and the ice limit suggests that the smoothed form D is a product of glacial erosion; it is difficult to see how forms A-C could withstand overriding by ice despite the fact that some authors have interpreted elaborate tor forms as occurring within apparent former ice limits (Dahl, 1966; Sugden, 1968; Clapperton, 1970). It must be stressed that the ice limit shown on Figure 21.2 is constructed from independent sedimentary evidence (Scourse, 1985) and is not based on the tor forms themselves.

Landform – sediment association on the Scilly tors

The key to understanding the evolution of erosional landforms lies in the interpretation of their associated sediments. This holds for all the tor forms described above. As far as forms A-C are concerned, their intimate association with solifluc-ted sediments is critical. The close relationship between tors, solifluction deposits and cryoplan-ation terraces in South West England has been exhaustively described (Te Punga, 1956, 1957; Mottershead, 1971; Green and Eden, 1973), but the solifluction deposits have never been securely dated. On the Scillies twenty-nine ^{14}C dates from within the lower Porthloo Breccia indicate depo-sition within the late Middle and Late Devensian between 34,000 and 21,000 years B.P. (Scourse, 1985). Given that the tors and solifluction deposits are components of the same system this indicates that tor exhumation took place at this time. The solifluction sediments themselves bear no evidence of derivation from deep chemically weathered deposits so there is no need to invoke either interglacial or Tertiary deep weathering as a causal mechanism. The active processes of bedrock frost-heave, the production of ploughing and rafted blocks and solifluction were arrested by climatic amelioration 10,000 years ago. The features we see today are relics of the active process of tor formation.

Landscape evolution in the Scilly Isles and West Cornwall

Aside from the underlying structural control almost all the major geomorphological features of the Isles of Scilly and West Cornwall owe their existing form to cold climate processes. Any sugges-tion of major geomorphological activity during interglacial stages (Linton, 1955, 1964; Palmer and Nielson, 1962; Waters, 1965) must be critically questioned. Te Punga stated perceptively in 1955 that inter-periglacial erosion in southern England was unimportant away from streams.

Eakin (1916) was the first to recognise that cryoplanation terraces can develop under peri-glacial conditions at a variety of levels, and that these levels might have no significance in the denudational chronology of a region. Te Punga (1956, 1957) later expanded this thesis for South West England. With the exception of the Lizard and north Penwith platforms (Scourse, 1985) almost all flat surfaces in the region can be interpre-ted as either solifluction or cryoplanation terraces, and not erosion surfaces as Wooldridge (1950) suggested.

Acknowledgements

The research described in the Chapter was sup-ported by an N.E.R.C. Studentship, and the Chap-ter written during the tenure of a Research Fellow-ship at Girton College, Cambridge; both these sources are gratefully acknowledged. I should also like to thank Dr P.L. Gibbard, Dr R.W. Hey, Prof. J.N. Hutchinson, Prof. A. Pissart and Prof. R.G. West, F.R.S. for useful discussion, Dr R.C. Preece for critically reading an early draft of the manu-script, Dr J. Boardman and an anonymous referee for criticism and corrections, and Mr W. Rowntree (photography), Dr J.R.M. Allen (drawing) and Miss M. Couser (typing) for technical assistance.

References

de la Beche, H.T. (1839). *Report on the Geology of Cornwall, Devon and West Somerset*, Geol. Surv. Mem. (U.K.).

Bowen, D.Q. (1970). 'South-east and central South Wales', in *The Glaciations of Wales and Adjoining Regions* (Ed. C.A. Lewis), pp. 197–227, Longman, London.

Bowen, D.Q. (1971). 'The Quaternary succession of south Gower' in *Geological Excursions in South Wales and the Forest of Dean* (Eds. D.S. and M.G. Bassett), pp. 135–42.

Broscoe, A.J. and Thompson, S. (1972). 'Observations on an alpine mudflow, Steele Creek', in *Icefield Ranges Res. Proj. Scient. Results, Am. Geog. Soc. and Arctic Inst. N. America 3* (Eds. V.C. Bushnell and R.H. Rayle), pp. 53–60.

Brown, A.P. (1977). 'Late Devensian and Flandrian vegetational history of Bodmin Moor, Cornwall', *Phil. Trans. R. Soc.*, **B276**, 251–320.

Brown, R.J.E. (1967). 'Permafrost in Canada', *Canada, Geol. Surv. Map* **1246A**.

Brunsden, D. (1964). 'The origin of decomposed granite on Dartmoor', in *Dartmoor Essays* (Ed. I.G. Simmons), pp. 97–116, The Devonshire Association, Exeter.

Bryan, K. (1946). 'Cryopedology – the study of frozen ground and intrusive frost action with suggestions on nomenclature', *Am. J. Sci.*, **244**, 622–42.

Clapperton, C.M. (1970). 'The evidence for a Cheviot ice cap', *Trans. Inst. Br. Geog.*, **50**, 115–27.

Clarke, B.B. (1973). 'The Camel Estuary section west of Tregunna House', *Proc. Ussher Soc.*, **2**, 551–3.

Cresswell, D. (1983). 'Deformation of weathered profiles, below head, at Constantine Bay, north Cornwall', *Proc. Ussher Soc.*, **5**, 487.

Dahl, R. (1966). 'Blockfields, weathering pits and tor-like forms in the Narvik Mountains, Nordland, Norway', *Geogr. Annlr.*, **48**, 55–85.

Davies, D.P. (1969). Undergraduate thesis, University College of Wales, Aberystwyth, Geography Dept.

Dreimanis, A. (1976). 'Tills: their origin and properties', in *Glacial Till. An Interdisciplinary Study* (Ed. R.F. Legget), pp. 11–49, Roy. Soc. Canada Spec. Publ. **12**.

Eakin, H.M. (1916). 'The Yukon-Koyukuk region, Alaska', *U.S. Geol. Surv. Bull.*, **631**, 1–88.

FitzPatrick, E.A. (1963). 'Deeply weathered rock in Scotland, its occurrence, age and contribution to the soils', *J. Soil Science*, **14**, 33–43.

French, H.M. (1976). *The Periglacial Environment*, Longman, London.

Green, C.P. and Eden, M.J. (1973). 'Slope deposits on the weathered Dartmoor granite, England', *Zeit. f. Geomorphologie*, **18**, 26–37.

Gregory, K.J. (1969). 'Geomorphology', in *Exeter and its Region* (Ed. F. Barlow), pp. 27–42, Exeter.

Henry, A. (1984). *The lithostratigraphy, biostratigraphy and chronostratigraphy of coastal Pleistocene deposits in Gower, South Wales*, Unpublished Ph.D. thesis, University of Wales.

Jahn, A. (1956). 'Some periglacial problems in Poland', *Biul. Perygl.*, **4**, 164–94.

Jahn, A. (1969). 'Some problems concerning slope development in the Sudetes', *Biul. Perygl.*, **18**, 331–48.

Jessen, K. and Milthers, V. (1928). 'Stratigraphical and palaeontological studies of interglacial fresh-water deposits in Jutland and northwest Germany', *Danm. Geol. Unders.*, **48**.

Linton, D.L. (1955). 'The problem of tors', *Geogr. J.*, **121**, 470–87.

Linton, D.L. (1964). 'The origin of the Pennine tors; an essay in analysis', *Zeit. f. Geomorphologie*, **8**, 5–24.

Lyford, W.H., Goodlett, J.C. and Coates, W.H. (1963). 'Landforms, soils with fragipans, and forest on a slope in the Harvard Forest', *Harvard Forest Bull.*, **30**, 68 pp.

Mackay, J.R. (1971). 'The origin of massive icy beds in permafrost, western Arctic coast, Canada', *Can. J. Earth Sci.*, **8**, 397–422.

Mitchell, G.F. and Orme, A.R. (1967). 'The Pleistocene deposits of the Isles of Scilly', *Q.Jl. geol. Soc Lond.*, **123**, 59–92.

Mottershead, D.N. (1971). 'Coastal head deposits between Start Point and Hope Cove, Devon', *Field Std.*, **3**, 433–53.

Palmer, J. and Nielson, R.A. (1962). 'The origin of granite tors on Dartmoor, Devonshire', *Proc. Yorks. geol. Soc.*, **33**, 315–40.

Palmer, J. and Radley, J. (1961). 'Gritstone tors of the English Pennines', *Zeit. f. Geomorphologie*, **5**, 37–52.

Penck, W. (1953). *Morphological Analysis of Landforms*, London.

Scourse, J.D. (1985). *Late Pleistocene stratigraphy of the Isles of Scilly and Adjoining Regions*, Unpublished Ph.D. thesis, University of Cambridge.

Seddon, M.B. and Holyoak, D.T. (1985). 'Evidence of substained regional permafrost during deposition of fossiliferous Late Pleistocene sediments at Stanton Harcourt (Oxfordshire, England)', *Proc. geol. Ass.*, **96**, 53–72.

Small, R.J., Clark, M.J. and Lewin, J. (1970). 'The periglacial rock-stream at Clatford Bottom, Marlborough Downs, Wiltshire', *Proc. geol. Ass.*, **81**, 87–98.

Stephens, N. (1970). 'The west country and southern Ireland', in *The Glaciations of Wales and Adjoining Regions* (Ed. C.A. Lewis), pp. 267–314, Longman, London.

Sugden, D.E. (1968). 'The selectivity of glacial erosion in the Cairngorm Mountains, Scotland', *Trans. Inst. Br. Geog.*, **45**, 79–92.

Taber, S. (1929). 'Frost heaving', *J. Geol.*, **37**, 428–61.

Taber, S. (1930). 'The mechanics of frost heaving', *J. Geol.*, **38**, 303–17.

Te Punga, M.T. (1956). 'Altiplanation terraces in southern England', *Biul. Perygl.*, **4**, 331–8.

Te Punga, M.T. (1957). 'Periglaciation in southern England', *Tijdschrift Kon. ned. aardrijksk. Genoot.*, **74**, 400–12.

Tufnell, L. (1972). 'Ploughing blocks with special reference to north-west England', *Biul. Perygl.*, **21**, 237–70.

Washburn, A.L. (1973). *Periglacial Processes and Environments*, Arnold, London.

Waters, R.S. (1964). 'The Pleistocene legacy to the geomorphology of Dartmoor', in *Dartmoor Essays* (Ed. I.G. Simmons), pp. 23–31, Exeter.

Waters, R.S. (1971). 'The significance of Quaternary events for the landforms of south-west England', in *Exeter Essays in Geography* (Eds. K.J. Gregory and W.L.D. Ravenhill), pp. 23–31, Exeter.

Whitley, D.'G. (1916). 'The Cornish Quaternary deposits in the light of Siberian alluvial formations', *Trans. R. Geol. Soc. Corn.*, **15**, 143–60.

Williams, R.B.G. (1968). 'Some estimates of periglacial erosion in southern and eastern England', *Biul. Perygl.*, **17**, 311–35.

Williams, R.B.G. (1969). 'Permafrost and temperature conditions in England during the last glacial period', in *The Periglacial Environment* (Ed. T.L. Péwé), Montreal.

Wintle, A.G. (1981). 'Thermoluminescence dating of Late Devensian loesses in southern England', *Nature*, **289**, 479–80.

Wooldridge, S.W. (1950). 'The upland plains of Britain: their origins and geomorphological significance', *Advmt. Sci.*, **1**, 20–30.

22 · Late Devensian periglacial slope deposits in the Cheviot Hills

T.D. DOUGLAS AND S. HARRISON

Abstract

A period of periglacial conditions during the Loch Lomond Stadial has resulted in the formation of a landform-sediment association consisting of smooth slopes underlain by soliflucted debris. These solifluction sheets are characteristic forms that have developed in response to a periglacial climate acting on frost susceptible drifts. The sheets display a variety of forms with bluffs 3–20 m high and treads 20–300 m wide. Tread angles range from 5–30 degrees. The slope deposits display characteristic downslope macrofabrics. Three sedimentological components can be identified: 1, soliflucted till; 2, soliflucted growan (gruss); 3, soliflucted gelifractate. Clast shape and roundness characteristics are used to discriminate between these components.

Introduction

The Cheviot Hills straddle the border between England and Scotland (Figure 22.1). They form two dissected plateaux. The outer plateau stands at 450–500 m OD and is underlain mainly by andesite; small areas of rhyolite lavas, pyroclast beds and various dykes also occur. The inner plateau, composed predominantly of granite, rises to over 800 m OD. During the Devensian, the Cheviot Hills were affected by ice flowing northeast down Teviotdale and by ice from the Southern Uplands moving eastwards through the Tyne Gap. Till on the northern and southern flanks of the massif contains erratics, but in the central area, only locally derived materials occur, providing evidence for the former existence of a Cheviot ice cap (Clapperton, 1970). Lateglacial moraines have been described from the upper reaches of the College valley and it seems that only here were conditions suitable for Loch Lomond Stadial ice. However, the impact of the Stadial on the landscape is considered by the authors to be significant. Common (1954) noted 'small discontinuous benches, possibly due to periglacial conditions' in the College and Bowmont valleys, whilst Clark (1970) observed that many of the valleys are 'asymmetric in cross-section, east- and northeast-facing sides sloping more gently'. He also described 'large solifluction or debris terraces ... especially on the north-facing slopes of the Cheviot'. These features, which are found in

most of the Cheviot valleys as benches on the lower hillsides, are the most important morphological expression of former periglacial activity. We advocate the term 'solifluction sheet' rather than 'solifluction terrace', the latter having been used to describe a wide variety of forms. It is our view that these forms approximate closest to relict solifluction sheets as described in their active mode by Everett (1967) and French (1974).

These features in the Cheviot Hills are characterised by bluffs 3–20 m high and smooth treads 20–300 m wide (Figure 22.2). The tread angles lie between 5 and 30 degrees. Treads that are wide generally slope at a low angle and vice versa. Where the valleys are relatively broad, solifluction sheets are present on both sides of the river and may be continuous along large stretches of the valley. Conversely, when the valleys become sinuous and incised, the sheets are far less extensive, restricted to shallow slopes and enclaves. These features have an upper altitudinal limit of 500 m OD.

Similar forms have been noted elsewhere in upland Britain: in south and mid Wales (Crampton & Taylor, 1967; Watson, 1969, 1970; Potts, 1971; Humphries, 1979); in the Isle of Man (Thomas, 1976) and in the Howgill Fells (Harvey et al., 1984). In the Cheviot Hills many of these features have been mapped as glacial boulder clay by the Geological Survey although they often contain significant thicknesses of soliflucted material. Such slope forms

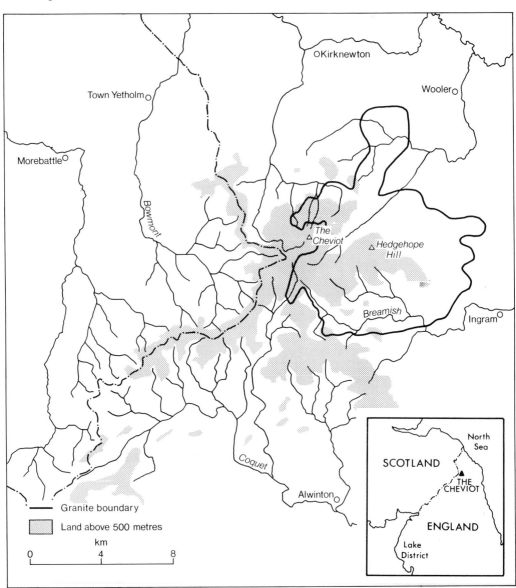

Figure 22.1. The Cheviot Hills.

may be seen as characteristic of upland valleys where landforms and frost-susceptible deposits of the valley glacier landform-sediment association have been subjected to solifluction (Eyles & Paul, 1983).

The sediments
Solifluction sheets may normally be identified by two common features – their smooth treads and the preferred downslope orientation of clasts within the deposit (Watson, 1967). Macrofabrics from soliflucted deposits in the Cheviots confirm their deposition by mass wasting processes (Figure 22.3). All these fabrics indicate statistically significant preferred orientations which are closely aligned with the direction of slope.

One of the main problems in the investigation of the sediments forming the solifluction sheets is to identify their various origins. In the Cheviots, these

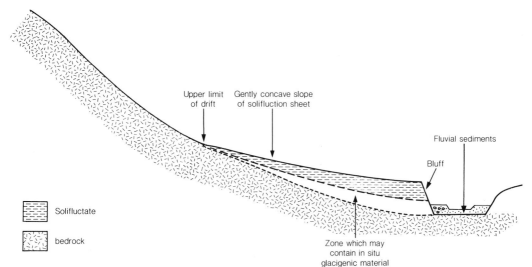

Figure 22.2. Schematic diagram of Cheviot solifluction sheet showing characteristic morphology.

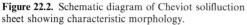

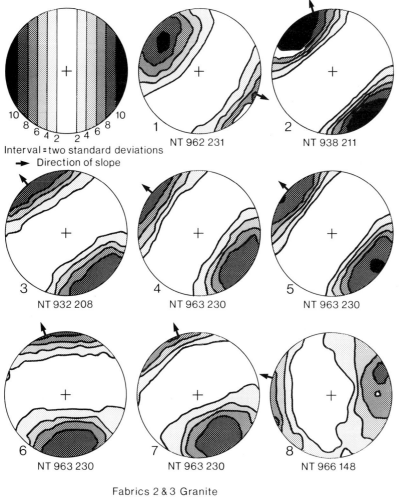

Fabrics 2 & 3 Granite
Fabrics 1,4,5,6,7 & 8 Andesite

Figure 22.3. Macrofabrics from Cheviot solifluctates (Harthope and Breamish valleys) Upper hemisphere projections.

Table 22.1 *Selected characteristics of sediments exposed at Makendon, Coquet Valley (see Figure 22.4).*

Unit	Interpretation	Macrofabric Preferred orientation (degrees)	Mean clast roundness	Clast shape % c/a ≤ 0.4	% silt & clay (< 2 mm fraction)
C	Soliflucted Gelifractate	39	2.81	68	24
B	Soliflucted Till	25	2.87	32	15
A	*In situ* till	95	2.30	32	20

sediments are composed of reworked till, weathered granite (growan or gruss), gelifracted detritus or a combination of these. The distinction between different sediments is made possible through the study of aggregate clast form characteristics. Granulometric analyses of sediments from sites within the Cheviots have shown that this technique does not always discriminate adequately between till and solifluctate (Douglas & Harrison, 1985). At Linhope Spout a site in the Breamish valley, 4 m of bedded solifluctate overlies till. The solifluctate is clearly derived from weathered granite upslope and contains less than 12% silt and clay (of the finer than 2 mm fraction); whereas the till has 29% silt and clay. However at Makendon in the Coquet valley, granulometric analyses fail to show any significant textural differences between the till and the overly-

ing solifluctate; identification being achieved through fabric and clast form.

In this paper measures of clast form are restricted to roundness and clast shape is measured by the relationships between the axial lengths.

At Makendon, situated at 300 m OD in the Coquet valley in an area largely underlain by Cheviot volcanics, 8 m of sediments are exposed in a gully section cut into a solifluction sheet which faces north. Three stratigraphic units can be identified (Figure 22.4). The sedimentological characteristics of these units are shown in Table 22.1. The fabrics in unit A show a downvalley orientation, whilst those of B and C are downslope. Similarities between the clast form characteristics of units A and B and the occurrence of facetted and striated clasts in both units are indicative of till or deriv-

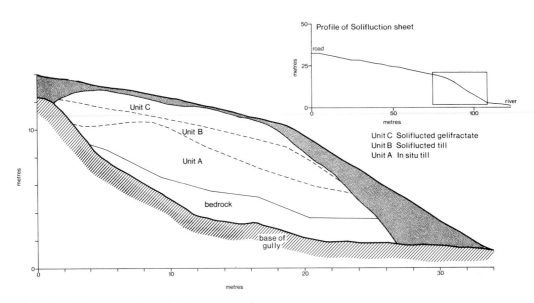

Figure 22.4. Makendon, gully section through edge of solifluction sheet.

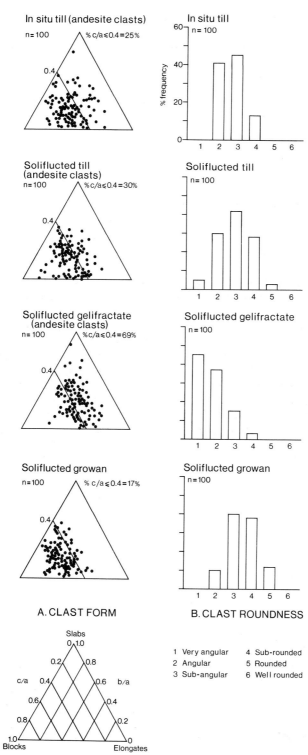

Figure 22.5. Clast characteristics for different sediments.

ation from till. Differences are however observed in clast roundness, with unit B having a slightly broader spread of values and a greater mean roundness, properties consistent with its interpretation as soliflucted till. Unit A which has a sharp upper boundary is interpreted as *in situ* till. The uppermost layer, unit C, shows a downslope fabric, similar mean roundness values to the soliflucted till, but can be differentiated on the basis of clast form. The low c/a ratios observed are typical of freshly weathered material derived from andesite. Evidence of edge-rounding and strong downslope fabrics for this unit suggest gelifraction of bedrock and subsequent downslope movement. The textural properties of all three units fall within the envelope for modern soliflucted sediments (Harris, 1981).

Examination of sites throughout the Cheviot area has confirmed that three distinct components can be recognised in the periglacial sediments, each with distinctive field characteristics:

Soliflucted till

On the lower slopes of the Cheviot valleys till is invariably covered by a veneer of solifluctate (Figure 22.2). The boundary between till and soliflucted till is often sharp and characterised by seepage promoted by the greater permeability of the reworked sediments. The till contains a greater proportion of fines and field tests with a shear vane have demonstrated substantially higher shear strengths in the *in situ* till than the soliflucted till.

Soliflucted growan

The second component observed in the region is restricted to the central granite massif. Soliflucted growan has been observed overlying massive till and granite. The solifluctate may contain occasional striated and facetted boulders and thus is likely to have come from more than one source. Crude banding in better sorted layers can be interpreted as being the result of slopewash under snowmelt conditions. The deposits are matrix-supported and predominantly sandy, with the fine fraction comprising as much as 90% sand. The presence of thicknesses of over 5 m of soliflucted growan overlying till is a clear indication of the extent of periglacial modification.

Soliflucted gelifractate

Lying on the sediments described above, is often a distinctive deposit up to 1 m in thickness and comprising relatively platy clasts with a variable matrix. This is unit C at the Makendon site

(Figure 22.4) and has been observed at many other locations, although is most frequent where andesite is the bedrock. This component can often be distinguished by its high clast/fines ratio, and for andesite clasts, a much higher percentage of platy clasts than is found in the tills or soliflucted tills (Figure 22.5). This component has also been observed to rest directly on bedrock. The edge-rounding of clasts implies transport and the form characteristics and lithological uniformity of the clasts indicate local upslope sources. It must be stressed that this component forms only a thin layer; the volume of soliflucted till and growan is far greater.

The forms

It is clear from examination of the literature, that little research has been published on the morphometry of fossil solifluction sheets. Most work has tended to concentrate on the preferred aspect of these landforms, about which there seems to be considerable disagreement (Crampton & Taylor, 1967; Watson, 1967; Potts, 1971). However, perhaps the most striking feature of the solifluction sheets in the Cheviots is the morphometric range which they exhibit. Figure 22.6 shows a series of Abney level profiles for slopes in the Harthope, Coquet and Bowmont valleys. Not surprisingly there is a clear relationship between distance upvalley and the width and steepness of the solifluction sheets. The narrow, steep sheets occurring in

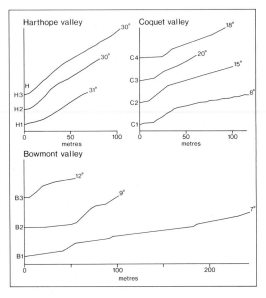

Figure 22.6. Selected Abney level profiles of solifluction sheets from three valleys.

the upper reaches of the Cheviot valleys where the drainage is more sharply incised. This is particularly well illustrated in the sequence from the Bowmont Valley (Figure 22.6), where the three profiles demonstrate the steepening and narrowing up-valley. Near Langlee, in the Harthope valley, the metamorphic aureole of the Cheviot granite has produced more resistant rocks and a constriction in the valley. Here, the narrow sheets (Figure 22.6, Hl-3) are composed of coarse, openwork, clast-dominated deposits and approach screes in angle although they are not backed by a free-face. Forms this steep are rare, but there is a clear trend towards coarser material underlying the steeper sheets.

The forms of the valley glacier landform-sediment association have been clearly modified to a recognisable periglacial landform-sediment association consisting of smoothed slopes underlain by soliflucted till and other debris. It would appear that hillslope processes have achieved little since the Lateglacial. The sheet bluff is an erosional rather than a depositional feature, having been trimmed by contemporary fluvial processes.

Although the tread surfaces of these landforms are smoothed, the sub-drift surface is often highly irregular. This is demonstrated in several places where first order streams cut through and across the sheet tread showing variable drift thicknesses. However, there is a general tendency for drift thicknesses to increase downslope (Figure 22.2), confirming the observations made by workers such as Galloway (1961) who remarked that solifluc-tion 'seems to have first swept any glacial till off the slopes and concentrated it in the valley bottoms'. It would appear that rather than being a deposit of uniform thickness covering the lower hillslopes, a relatively thin veneer of solifluctate has filled in hollows and the hummocky till surfaces have been smoothed.

Discussion

Periglacial processes have reworked a number of different regoliths from different lithologies and glacigenic material into a landform whose morphometry varies considerably. The possibility that slopewash and rapid mass movement may have contributed to these features may preclude the use of the term 'solifluction' to describe them unless this term is accepted in its widest sense. Many attempts to explain the uneven distribution of these land-forms have been made. Watson (1967), working in central Wales, stressed the role of aspect in the development of 'solifluction terraces'. In his opinion the local climate of cold north- or

northeast-facing slopes closely controlled the processes of solifluction over a frozen substratum. Crampton and Taylor (1967) put forward an alternative hypothesis namely that south or west facing slopes being relatively warm, had deep active layers, frequent freeze – thaw cycles and therefore accelerated rates of mass movement.

It has been demonstrated above that the Cheviot sheets are composed largely of re-worked till and growan with the element derived from gelifraction of rock being limited to a surface veneer or confined to the steeper slopes. Thus any control exerted by aspect is more likely to control the distribution of these sheets through its effect on solifluction rather than on gelifraction. The Cheviot examples are suitable for demonstrating the likely role of aspect as the pattern of valleys is a radial one, with all aspects being represented. However, no clear preferred orientation has been observed and the distribution of these features is probably simply a reflection of the availability of material for periglacial mass wasting after deglaciation and during the Loch Lomond Stadial. Where iceflow was predominantly downvalley, sheets are found on both valley sides; where iceflow was across the present drainage, glacial deposition has occurred on lee slopes whilst those facing up-ice have been glacially steepened. This pattern has been preserved with the redistribution of material during a periglacial phase.

Acknowledgement
Our thanks are due to Mr G. Haley for drawing the diagrams.

References
Clapperton, C.M. (1970). The evidence for a Cheviot ice cap. *Trans. Inst. Br. Geogr.*, **50**, 115–26.

Clark, R. (1970). Periglacial landforms and landscapes in Northumberland. *Proc. Cumberland Geol. Soc.*, **3** (1), 5–20.

Common, R. (1954). The geomorphology of the East Cheviot area. *Scott. Geogr. Mag.*, **70**(3), 124–38.

Crampton, C.B. & Taylor, J.A. (1967). Solifluction terraces in South Wales. *Biul. Perygl.*, **16**, 15–36.

Douglas, T.D. & Harrison, S. (1985). Periglacial landforms and sediments in the Cheviots, in *Field Guide to the Periglacial Landforms of Northern England* (Ed. J. Boardman), pp. 68–76, Quaternary Research Association, Cambridge.

Everett, K.R. (1967). Mass wasting in the Tasersiaq area, west Greenland. *Meddelelser om Gronland*, **165** (5), 1–32.

Eyles, N. & Paul, M.A. (1983). Landforms and sediments resulting from former periglacial climates, in *Glacial geology: an introduction for engineers and earth scientists* (Ed. N. Eyles), pp. 111–39, Pergamon.

French, H.M. (1974). Mass wasting at Sachs Harbour, Banks Island, NWT, Canada. *Arctic and Alpine Research* **6**(1), 71–8.

Galloway, R.W. (1961). Solifluction in Scotland. *Scott. Geogr. Mag.,* **77**(2), 75–87.

Harris, C. (1981). *Periglacial mass wasting: a review of research.* BGRG Research Monograph no. 4. Geo Books.

Harvey, A.M., Alexander, R.W. & James, P.A. (1984). Lichens, soil development and the age of Holocene valley floor landforms: Howgill Fells, Cumbria. *Geogr. Annlr.,* **66A**, 353–66.

Humphries, A.M. (1979). *The Quaternary deposits of the upper Severn basin and adjoining areas,* Unpublished PhD thesis, University College of Wales, Aberystwyth.

Potts, A.S. (1971). Fossil cryonival features in central Wales. *Geogr. Annlr.,* **53A**, 39–51.

Thomas, G.S.P. (1976). The Quaternary stratigraphy of the Isle of Man. *Proc. Geol. Assoc.,* **87**(3), 307–23.

Watson, E. (1967). *The Periglacial element in the landscape of the Aberystwyth region,* Unpublished PhD thesis, University College of Wales, Aberystwyth.

Watson, E. (1969). The slope deposits in the Nant Iago valley, near Cader Idris, Wales, *Biul. Perygl.,* **18**, 95–113.

Watson, E. (1970). The Cardigan Bay area, in *The Glaciations of Wales and Adjoining Regions* (Ed. C.A. Lewis), pp. 125–45, Longman.

23·Strongly folded structures associated with permafrost degradation and solifluction at Lyme Regis, Dorset

J.N. HUTCHINSON AND D.W. HIGHT

Abstract

The sequence of superficial deposits on coastal slopes north-east of Lyme Regis in Dorset is described and details are given of their geotechnical properties. The Cretaceous and Lias Heads at the top of the sequence are considered to be the product of periglacial solifluction in the active layer. A zone of Disturbed Lias, underlying the Lias Head and overlying the *in situ* Shales-with-Beef, is interpreted as representing the minimum former extent of permafrost, which penetrated at least 7 m below ground level. Shallow, strongly folded structures in the Disturbed Lias are exposed locally in the side scarps of a landslide. The overturned chevron folds are interpreted as being the result of compression at the toe of a translational slide which took place within the Disturbed Lias during its thawing. The intense folding is set in a periglacial context by the observation of shale intruded into the necks between boudins within the folds: a back-analysis of these intrusions leads to an estimated undrained strength of the shale which is much lower than the present strength and consistent with that to be expected in the freshly thawed state.

Introduction

Recent studies of the morphology and superficial deposits of inland slopes near the Dorset coast, in the vicinity of Lyme Regis and Charmouth, have been made by Brunsden and Jones (1972, 1976), Brown (1973), Denness *et al.* (1975) and Conway (1979). The landslides on these slopes and on the coast itself have been described by Jukes–Brown (1908), Lang (1928, 1955), Arber (1973), Conway (1974), Brunsden and Jones (1976) and Hutchinson (1984). The present paper describes the fossil periglacial solifluction features of the coastal slopes just north-east of Lyme Regis, previously studied by Conway (1979). It provides additional data on the geotechnical properties and structures of these, derived mainly from the recent investigation of two landslides at East Cliff, the deep slip of 1973/74 and the associated retrogressive shallow slip of 1976 (Figures 23.1 and 23.2). Attention is focused particularly on shallow, strongly folded structures near the foot of the slopes of a type which has not, apparently, been reported previously. These are interpreted as being due to the development of translational sliding in the Jurassic shales just beneath the active layer during their thawing.

Physical setting

The slopes under discussion lie immediately to the north-east of Lyme Regis (Figure 23.1) and fall from Timber Hill to the top of the coastal cliff by the East Cliff landslides, a vertical distance of about 150 m, at an average slope of around 9°.

The area is formed of Jurassic strata, overlain unconformably by the Gault and Upper Greensand, lying on the south-western flank of the Marshwood pericline (Wilson *et al.*, 1958). The regional dip is between 2° and 3° to the south or south-east, modified locally by shallow flexures. A map of the local solid geology, based on Lang (1914) and the Institute of Geological Sciences (1977), is shown in Figure 23.1. Although not glaciated during the Quaternary, the area was subjected to several periods of periglacial climate and hence to many cycles of freezing and thawing. As a result, sheets of debris have been moved downslope by periglacial solifluction to form the Lias Head and Cretaceous Head which mantle the area (Figure 23.2). The local stratigraphical succession is outlined in Figure 23.1.

Profile of the near-surface deposits

The Lyme Regis Head deposits have been described

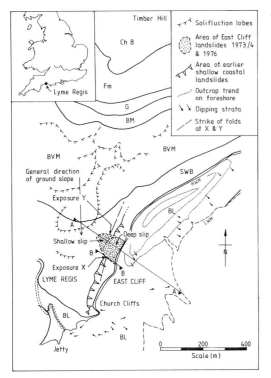

Figure 23.1. Location and plan of site. (ChB = chert beds, FM = Foxmould, G = Gault, BM = Belemnite Marls, BVM = Black Ven Marls, SWB = Shales-with-Beef, BL = Blue Lias, HWM = High Water Mark, LWM = Low Water Mark).

by Conway (1979). He divides them into an upper, Cretaceous Head, derived mainly from the Upper Greensand chert beds and Foxmould, and a lower, Lias Head, derived from the Lower Lias marls and shales down to and including the Shales-with-Beef (Beef is fibrous calcite). A description and classification of these and the other deposits at East Cliff (outside the coastal landslide area itself) is given in Table 23.1. We agree with Conway's indication that the Cretaceous Head tends to have ac-

cumulated in shallow valleys in the surface of the Lias Head, forming lobes. The distribution of Cretaceous Head is thus very irregular, both down- and cross-slope. It can also range from being predominantly cherty to quite clayey. We confirm also Conway's observation that slip surfaces are common at or near the base of the Lias Head. We also observed slip surfaces just below the Cretaceous Head.

While accepting the division of the Head deposits at Lyme Regis into Cretaceous and Lias varieties, we have found it necessary to introduce another category 'Disturbed Lias', between the base of the Lias Head and truly *in situ* material, in this case the Shales-with-Beef (SWB). In the Disturbed Lias mudslide fabric is generally absent, but a degree of disturbance is indicated by slight folding or rotation of the bedding and Beef layers and by a moderate enhancement of the water content (Table 23.2). Towards the foot of the slopes, the Disturbed Lias exhibits some remarkably strong local folding. The nature and mode of formation of this folding is discussed subsequently.

Geotechnical properties
Index properties, consolidation and compressibility coefficients and peak and residual shear strength parameters in terms of effective stresses are summarised for the relevant strata in Table 23.2. Undrained shear strengths (measured on samples 38 mm diameter and 76 mm high) in the Lias Head and the shaley parts of the Shales-with-Beef range between about 15 and $30\,kN/m^2$, and 110 and $135\,kN/m^2$, respectively. In the Disturbed Lias an undrained strength of $70\,kN/m^2$ was measured.

Strongly folded beds
Two exposures of strongly folded beds, shown as X and Y in Figure 23.1, were found on the side scarps of the deep and shallow slips. Both exposures involve the Shales-with-Beef, the lithology of

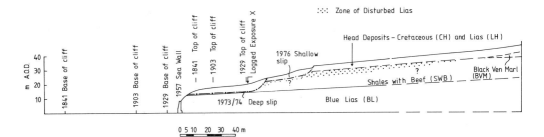

Figure 23.2. Section along line A–A on Figure 23.1.

Table 23.1 *Description and classification of superficial and solid geological beds at East Cliff, Lyme Regis (outside the area of the coastal landslides).*

Cretaceous Head (CH)	Orange-brown and pale grey sandy and clayey, fine to coarse chert GRAVEL and COBBLES, with rootlets.
Lias Head (LH)	Dark grey and yellow-brown slightly sandy CLAY with randomly oriented fine to coarse gravel-size clay clasts and fragments of Beef, occasional chert gravel, rootlets and pockets of yellow/green sand (i.e. with mudslide fabric).
Disturbed Lias (DL)	Blue-grey and yellow-brown CLAY, sometimes laminated, showing some disturbance of bedding and of Beef layers.
Shales-with-Beef (SWB)	Firm, fissured, shaly CLAY with thin bands of argillaceous limestones and fibrous calcite (Beef).
Blue Lias (BL)	Alternations of thin beds of hard argillaceous LIMESTONE and firm, shaly CLAY. Limestone bands vary from 10 to 40 cm and constitute 30 to 40% of total thickness. The junction with the SWB was taken as the top of a siltstone band, approximately 100 mm thick, which caps the sequence of limestone bands.

Table 23.2 *Summary of typical index properties and geotechnical parameters.*

Soil Type	Water content w	w_L	w_P	Mean PI (%)	Mean clay fraction (<2μ) (%)	Coeff. of consolidation c_v (m²/yr) (1)	Coeff. of compressibility m_v (m²/MN) (1)	Peak strength c' kN/m² (on 38×76mm samples)	Peak strength ϕ' (degrees)	Residual strength ϕ'_r (degrees) (2)	Mean bulk unit weight (kN/m³)
CH(4)						—	—	—	—	—	19.40
LH	29	66	26	44	68	15–0.2	0.27–0.08	0	25	14.0°	19.40
DL	25.5	78	28	40	52	14–1.1	0.10	22	25	10.2°–18.2°	19.13
SWB	22.5	65	25	50	52	8–0.8	0.06	(3)		12.3°–17.3°(5)	22.37
BL	18	58	23	35	44	10	0.01	(3)		12.3°–17.3°(6)	22.37

(1) From oedometer tests: stress level = $p'_0 + 100$ kN/m².
(2) Measured in a Bromhead ring shear apparatus at a normal effective stress of 50 kN/m², with $c'_r = 0$.
(3) Fissuring, calcite banding and rock layers prevented sample preparation for triaxial testing.
(4) Clayey Cretaceous Head: one measurement only.
(5) Back-analysis of the shallow slip in its later stages indicates, for $c'_r = 0$, $\phi'_r = 14.2°$ @ $\sigma'_n = 50$ kN/m².
(6) Back-analysis of the deep slip indicates, for $c'_r = 0$, $\phi'_n = 13.0°$ @ $\sigma'_n = 61$ kN/m².

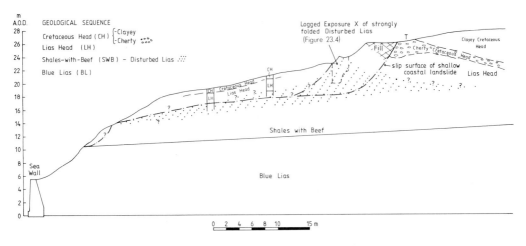

Figure 23.3. Section along line B–B on Figure 23.1.

which, with its alternating layers of brittle Beef with associated indurated marl and of relatively plastic shales, is ideally suited for the development and imprinting of the observed folding.

Exposure X

This is located on the south west face of the 1973/74 slide scarp in an area affected by recent fairly shallow slipping in the sea cliffs immediately to the south west (Figure 23.1). The relationship of this exposure to the slope generally is shown in the section of Figure 23.2. The section of Figure 23.3 illustrates in more detail its relationship to the associated landslide and solifluction features and to the solid geology.

A detailed log of the exposure is given in Figure 23.4. Strong folding is exposed in a near-vertical face over an area nearly 3 m wide and up to 4 m high. Unfortunately, it was not feasible to extend the exposure further and the base of the folding was not quite reached. The folds terminate downslope at an intermediate scarp of the recent shallow coastal landslides just mentioned (Figure 23.3). The folding may previously have extended some distance further downslope, but not as far as the next logged exposure (Figure 23.3), 9 metres away. In the upslope direction the strong folding is believed to die away near the rear scarp of the shallow coastal landslide.

The structures logged in Figure 23.4 are estimated to have been back-tilted bodily through about 25° and translated a couple of metres downslope, after their formation, as a result of the recent shallow coastal landslide (Figure 23.3). The folds

are of chevron type and, making this correction in attitude, it can be seen that they are to some extent overturned (Hills, 1963). The upper limbs tend to be thrust over the lower limbs at the fold hinges and the brittle layers of Beef and indurated marl exhibit boudinage (Ramsay, 1967) in places. A photograph showing over-thrusting in two adjacent fold hinges in the upper part of the exposure (Figure 23.4) is given in Figure 23.5. The fold hinges have a bearing of approximately 200° magnetic (Figure 23.1). Some of the discontinuities, particularly in the upper, upslope parts of the exposure, have the style of emergent passive shears. The total shortening involved in the exposed folding, making an appropriate allowance for boudinage, is estimated to be about 6 m. The minimum thickness of the Shales-with-Beef involved is difficult to estimate, but is unlikely to be less than about 2 m.

Exposure Y

This is located on the north east face of the 1976 slide scarp, just landward of the area affected by the associated earlier shallow coastal landslides immediately to the north east. Its relationship to these landslides and to Exposure X is shown in Figure 23.1.

A detailed log of the exposure is given in Figure 23.6. Moderate folding is exposed in an area between about 1 m and 1.8 m below ground level, over a width of around 2 m. It was not feasible to establish the possible further extent of these structures. The visible features have the geometry of kink bands (Ramsay, 1967) and bear at approximately 210° magnetic (Figure 23.1).

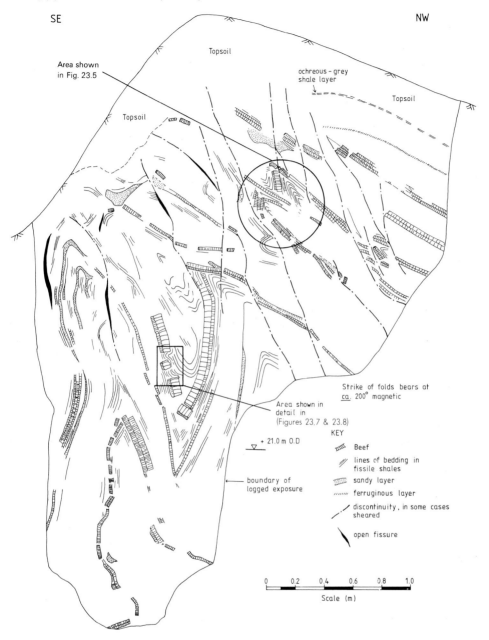

SE

NW

Area shown
in Fig. 23.5

Topsoil

ochreous – grey
shale layer

Topsoil

Topsoil

Strike of folds bears at
ca. 200° magnetic

Area shown in
detail in
(Figures 23.7 & 23.8)

KEY

▽ + 21.0 m O.D

Beef

lines of bedding in
fissile shales

boundary of
logged exposure

sandy layer

ferruginous layer

discontinuity, in some cases
sheared

open fissure

0   0.2   0.4   0.6   0.8   1.0

Scale (m)

Figure 23.4. Detailed log of Exposure X (Figure 23.3.)
looking south-west.

General

The strongly folded structures are located towards the foot of the present slopes. An etching by Roberts (1823) shows a hill just seaward of where the present coastline lies, so previously the site of Exposure X, for example, could have been at or close to the slope foot. The trend of the fold hinges in Exposures X and Y, as shown in Figure 23.1, is at a very acute angle to the general direction of the present ground slope. These trends are, however, concordant with the strike directions of the north west flank of a gentle pericline on the foreshore, mapped by Lang

Figure 23.5. Photograph of double-chevron fold in Exposure X. (The scale has an overall length of 325 mm).

(1914) and also indicated in Figure 23.1. They are also broadly concordant with the plan shape of the solifluction lobe just upslope (shown on Figure 23.1), mapped by Conway (1979).

Boudinage and associated plastic flow

The boudinage in about the middle of Exposure X (Figure 23.4) is logged in detail in Figure 23.7. A close-up photograph is shown in Figure 23.8. The manner in which the shales have entered the tension gaps between the separate boudins is suggestive of plastic flow of these shales while the material forming the boudins was brittle (Hills, 1963). This phenomenon is commonly associated with high pressures and temperatures at great depth: the fact that it has occurred here at a very shallow depth is of particular interest.

On the assumption that the plastic flow took place under undrained conditions, approximate estimates can be made of the contemporary value of undrained shear strength, c_u, of the shales needed to permit an intrusion of material into the necks

between boudins. The process can be regarded as analogous to that of metal extrusion. Following Johnson and Mellor (1962), Johnson and Kudo (1962) and Whyte (1982), and using the scheme shown in Figure 23.9, the extrusion pressure, P/A, can be related to the yield stress, k, of the extruding material by the empirical equation

$$\frac{P}{A} = \left(a + b\ln\frac{A}{A_0}\right)k \qquad [1]$$

where a and b are constants with the range of values $a = 1.0$ to 1.6 and $b = 3.0$ to 3.6 and A and A_0 are the container and orifice areas, respectively (Figure 23.9). Taking average values of a and b, and assuming that $k = c_u$, we obtain

$$\frac{P}{A} = \left(1.3 + 3.3\ln\frac{A}{A_0}\right)c_u$$

Values of A/A_0 can be derived from Figure 23.7 for both the overall, 154 mm wide gap and the smaller (uppermost), nearly 40 mm wide gap, with reasonable assumptions as to the width of the 'container'. The resulting A/A_0 values range between about 1.9 and 2.1 and an average value of 2.0 is taken. The corresponding average value of P/A is approximately $3.6\,c_u$.

Difficulty attaches to the estimation of P/A as the depth of the features at the time of extrusion and the corresponding soil and groundwater pressures are not known. After correction for the rotation produced by the recent landslipping, the present depth, z, to the intruded boudin necks is approximately 2.4 m. From this, making some allowance for the enhanced water content and thickness of the overburden at the time of formation of the structures, a total vertical pressure, σ_v, of about $52\,kN/m^2$ can be estimated. The nature of the structures suggests that a passive stress field was likely to have existed at this time. For undrained conditions and horizontal ground, the corresponding lateral pressure is given by $\sigma_h = \gamma z + 2c_u$.

Now, before being affected by the recent landsliding, the attitude of the indurated stratum suffering the boudinage would have been about 50° to the horizontal. Assuming that the intrusion occurred when the beds were similarly inclined, the value of P/A in equation [1] is equal to the normal stress, σ, acting on a plane whose normal is inclined at θ to the direction of the major principal stress, σ_1, and:

$$\sigma = \tfrac{1}{2}(\sigma_1 + \sigma_3) + \tfrac{1}{2}(\sigma_1 - \sigma_3)\cos 2\theta \qquad [2]$$

where σ_3 is the minor principal stress and $\theta = 40°$. If $\sigma_1 = \sigma_h$ and $\sigma_3 = \sigma_v$, equation [2] give the value of

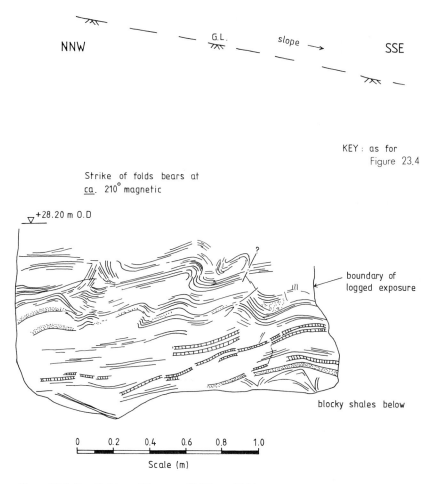

NNW

G.L.

slope →

SSE

KEY : as for
Figure 23.4

Strike of folds bears at
<u>ca</u>. 210° magnetic

+28.20 m O.D

boundary of
logged exposure

blocky shales below

```
0      0.2     0.4     0.6     0.8     1.0
```
Scale (m)

Figure 23.6. Detailed log of Exposure Y (Figure 23.1.)
looking north-north-east.

σ as $52 + 1.174\,c_u\,\mathrm{kN/m^2}$. Combining this with the previous value of $3.6\,c_u$, we get an estimated c_u value at the time of intrusion of $21.4\,\mathrm{kN/m^2}$. If the intrusion took place against a back pressure this c_u would be correspondingly reduced. For example, for a back pressure of $30\,\mathrm{kN/m^2}$ (approximately equivalent to a ground water pressure hydrostatic from the contemporary ground level), the value of c_u required for intrusion would fall to $9.1\,\mathrm{kN/m^2}$.

Discussion

The Cretaceous Head and the Lias Head at Lyme Regis are fossil periglacial deposits, deriving from the movements of thawed upper layers of the ground, probably around one to two metres in thickness. From the geological map (Figure 23.1), some deductions can be made concerning the amounts of downslope movements that have taken place in these Head deposits, which extend to the present sea-cliff edge (Figure 23.3). Thus, the chert-rich facies of the Cretaceous Head at the sea-cliff has moved a minimum downslope distance of about 850 m, while the Lias Head beneath has moved 670 m or less. These estimates may be compared with others in south and south-west England made by Williams (1968). The emplacement of the Cretaceous Head on top of the Lias Head arises from the relative position of the source rocks on the slope, the Cretaceous Head having to travel further to reach a given point downslope.

The origin of the underlying, strongly folded structures is of great interest. A primary question concerns whether they were formed, tectonically or otherwise, in pre-Quaternary times or under periglacial conditions in the Pleistocene. The nearest major structure, the gentle Marshwood

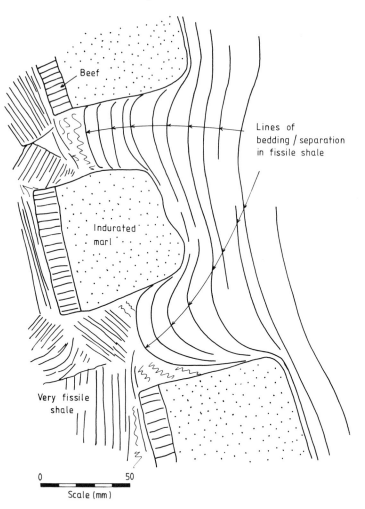

Figure 23.7. Enlarged detail of three boudins in Exposure X, with shale intruded between them.

pericline, is 5 kilometres or more to the north-east and any possible westward continuation of the strong Isle of Wight – Purbeck monocline would be at least 8 kilometres to the south of the site. The most violent structure known in the vicinity is the valley bulge exposed in the foreshore at the mouth of the River Char, about 2 kilometres to the east (Ager and Smith, 1965), but such disturbance is not to be expected at the present site. Thus a tectonic origin for the observed folding is not proposed.

Mineralogical changes involving a volume increase can also result in the disruption of rocks and the formation of fold structures. Common examples are the hydration of anhydrite to gypsum and the transformation of aragonite to calcite (Shearman *et al.*, 1972). The setting and very local

nature of the observed fold structures, however, makes it highly unlikely that they were produced by such a mechanism.

In this connection, the intrusion of shale into the necks between the boudins is of interest. If we accept the estimates of between 9 and $21 \, kN/m^2$, made earlier, for the undrained shear strength of the shale at the time of its intrusion, it follows from curves of undrained strength against liquidity index of Skempton and Northey (1952) that the corresponding liquidity indices were, respectively, 0.44 and 0.29. For the Shales-with-Beef ($w_L = 65\%$, $w_P = 25\%$, see Table 23.2), this would indicate that its water content at the time of intrusion was between 43 and 37%. The striking comparison between this range of values and the present average water

Figure 23.8. Photograph of shale-intruded boudin necks sketched in Figure 23.7. (The pocket tape is 50 mm across).

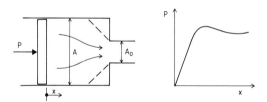

Figure 23.9. Diagram of the three-dimensional extrusion model considered.

content of the *in situ* Shales-with-Beef, below the Disturbed Lias (Table 23.2), of 22.5%, indicates that the intrusion of shale into the boudin necks took place under periglacial conditions during the thawing of frozen, ice-rich permafrost. (The present water content of the intruded shale, measured on a near-surface and therefore somewhat air-dried sample, is 9%.)

Even higher water contents than those estimated for the intruding shales are likely to have obtained in the overlying, originally more ice-rich, active

layer. Following Hutchinson (1974), and assuming a layer of predominantly Lias Head 2.3 m thick (at the present-day, see Figure 23.3) moving on a 4° slope, the water content at the base of this active layer may be estimated to have been around 51%.

It is thus inferred that the present-day Disturbed Lias was produced by the growth and decay of permafrost containing segregated ice and that its depth is an indication of the minimum depth to which freezing penetrated. The maximum depth of the Disturbed Lias observed during the site investigations was 7 m below present ground level, or 3 to 4 m below the base of the Lias Head. It follows that, wherever Disturbed Lias is present, the overlying Head Deposits were formed by solifluction in an active layer rather than as a result of the thawing of seasonally frozen ground.

Whether or not this depth of 7 m represents the maximum depth of permafrost at this site during the Pleistocene depends on several factors. For instance, the question arises as to whether the ground levels have been affected by erosion or deposition? In the slope foot situation obtaining, deposition is likely to have predominated, which would tend to render the 7 m an over-estimate of the maximum depth of freezing. On the other hand, no microscopic studies have been made of the fabric of the Disturbed Lias or the Shales-with-Beef. Such studies might reveal that freezing, probably without the formation of segregated ice, may have occurred below the base of the Disturbed Lias (which was decided upon purely by visual examination) and this would render the 7 m an under-estimate of the maximum freezing depth.

From the general absence of mudslide fabric and the clearly recognisable lithology of the Shales-with-Beef, albeit much folded, it is evident that Exposure X is an intensely deformed part of Disturbed Lias where this involves the Shales-with-Beef. Elsewhere, movements associated with the Disturbed Lias are very small, but at Exposure X a downslope movement of at least 6 m is required to produce the observed shortening. This shortening, and the associated thrust required, could only have been supplied by a landslide of some sort. The suggested development of this landslide and of the associated strongly folded structures is illustrated in Figure 23.10. In a), the formation of a mantle of active layer deposits (subsequently the Lias and Cretaceous Heads) over frozen Shales-with-Beef is shown. In b), thawing of at least the upper zone of the ice-rich permafrost, possibly combined with loading (which could have been partially undrained) from the further solifluction lobes noted above (Figures 23.1 and 23.10) and with the general existence of high pore-water pressures in that slope-foot situation, caused the Disturbed Lias there to become detached on a basal slip surface. This was situated sub-parallel to ground level at a depth of at least 2 to 3 m below the base of the overlying active layer deposits. The position at which the toe of the landslide broke out was probably influenced by the flexure produced by the gentle periclinal structure in that vicinity. The intrusion of shale into the boudin necks indicates that the Disturbed Lias (SWB) involved in this landslide was not frozen at the time it moved. In c), a translational slide, moving at least 6 m downslope, developed on this basal slip surface, producing the intense folding observed at X, the slope-foot situation providing the necessary resistance for the folding to develop. In d), further solifluction has buried the scar of this slide and led to the accumulation of the observed thick deposits of Cretaceous Head at T (Figures 23.3 and 23.10), just upslope of the 'dam'

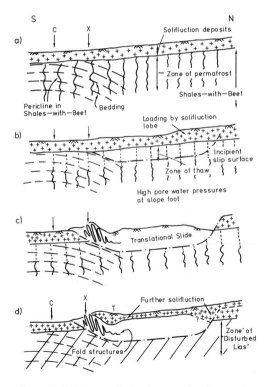

Figure 23.10. Diagram indicating postulated stages in the development of solifluction structures at Lyme Regis, East Cliff. (C indicates location of present sea cliff: X indicates location of Exposure X). Not to scale.

produced by the upthrust folds. It is clear the associated upheaving must have occurred after both the Lias and the Cretaceous Head had spread downslope to at least the line of the present coast.

One unresolved problem is the back-tilt of around 20° in the Cretaceous Head layer running upslope from T (Figure 23.3). This is underlain by thick Lias Head and Disturbed Lias. Some slight back-tilting was observed in the Disturbed Lias. It is possible that these features have been produced by a deep-seated rotational landslide, now completely masked by subsequent solifluction debris. Such a landslide may have tended to heave further Exposure X and to produce some of the passive shears observed there. It is considered very unlikely that the northward sloping Cretaceous layer moved downslope from the ancient hill to seaward, as this seems not to have been high enough to have had a capping of Cretaceous strata.

Exposure Y is upslope of Exposure X and probably represents the upper margin of the strong folding. The kink band style of folding there may thus represent an early stage in the development of the chevron folds in Exposure X, in the manner suggested by Paterson and Weiss (1966).

No datings have been made at Lyme, but a Loch Lomond Stadial age is assigned to the Lias Head at Charmouth, 2 km to the east-north-east (Conway, 1979). It seems likely that the latest Head at Lyme (at least upslope of X on Figure 23.10) will be of similar age. This would suggest that the permafrost degradation which led to the translational slide in the upper layers of the Disturbed Lias, and hence to the formation of the fold structures, was associated, at the latest, with the onset of the Windermere Interstadial. That the fold structures are unlikely to be younger than this is also indicated by the present lack of evidence in Dorset for the existence of permafrost during the succeeding Loch Lomond Stadial.

Main conclusions

1. The surface and near surface deposits on the inland slopes at East Cliff, Lyme Regis, comprise, from the ground surface downwards, Cretaceous Head, Lias Head, Disturbed Lias and *in situ* Lias.

2. The Cretaceous Head and the Lias Head are considered to be the product of periglacial solifluction in former active layers.

3. The Disturbed Lias is considered to represent the former zone of permafrost exhibiting segregated ice in the rocks underlying the Head. In

general, the freezing and thawing of this zone has resulted in only minor disturbance, without appreciable downslope sliding.

4. The base of the Disturbed Lias is up to 7 m below present ground level. This provides a minimum indication of the depth of the former permafrost.

5. At the foot of the slopes, the Disturbed Lias, there comprising the Shales-with-Beef, is locally very strongly folded. These folds (at X, Figure 23.1) are considered to be caused by compression at the toe of a translational landslide which affected the upper part of the Disturbed Lias and which occurred during its thawing. The landslide is estimated to have moved at least 6 m downslope.

6. The most highly developed folding (at X) is of overturned, chevron type, with an amplitude of over 4 m. It appears to have developed via a kink band style of folding, as exhibited in exposure Y.

7. Boudinage occurs in the downslope limbs of the folds (at X) and shale has intruded into the boudin necks.

8. Analysis of these intrusions indicates that the undrained shear strength of the shale at the time would have needed to have been between 9 and 21 kN/m^2, much lower than at present. Such low strengths can only be explained by the generation of high water contents by thawing of ice-rich frozen ground and this places the structures firmly in a periglacial context.

9. The fold structures are inferred to have been formed not later than the onset of the Windermere Interstadial.

Acknowledgements

At Imperial College, the authors wish to thank Dr R. Jardine for his valuable contribution to the site investigation work, Dr P.R. Bush for his advice on the geochemistry and Dr J.W. Cosgrove for his very helpful comments on the structural geology. They also wish to thank Professor W.R. Dearman, of the University of Newcastle-upon-Tyne, for his perceptive contributions, and the unknown referee. The authors are also grateful to Mr P.C. Warr, Chief Engineer of the West Dorset District Council, for permission to use some of the data reported here.

References

Ager, D.V. and Smith, W.E. (1965). 'The coast of south Devon and Dorset between Branscombe and Burton Bradstock.' *Geol. Assoc. Guide* No. 23.

Arber, M.A. (1973). 'Landslips near Lyme Regis.' *Proc. Geol. Assoc.*, **84**, 121–33.

Brown, W.J. (1973). 'Mass movements and hillside evolution in south-west Dorset.' *Proc. Dorset nat. Hist. archaeol. Soc.*, **94**, 27–36.

Brunsden, D. and Jones, D.K.C. (1972). 'The morphology of degraded landslide slopes in South West Dorset.' *Q. Jl Engng Geol.*, **5**, 205–22.

Brunsden, D. and Jones, D.K.C. (1976). 'The evolution of landslide slopes in Dorset.' *Phil. Trans. R. Soc. Lond.*, A. **283**, 605–31.

Conway, B.W. (1974). 'The Black Ven landslip, Charmouth, Dorset.' *Inst. Geol. Sciences, Report* No. 74/3. H.M.S.O., London.

Conway, B.W. (1979). 'The contribution made to cliff instability by Head deposits in the west Dorset coastal area.' *Q. Jl Engng Geol.*, **12**, 267–75.

Denness, B., Conway, B.W., McCann, D.M. and Grainger, P. (1975). 'Investigation of a coastal landslip at Charmouth, Dorset.' *Q. Jl Engng Geol.*, **8**, 119–40.

Hills, E.S. (1963). *Elements of structural geology.* Science Paperbacks and Methuen & Co. Ltd., London.

Hutchinson, J.N. (1974). 'Periglacial solifluxion: an approximate mechanism for clayey soils.' *Géotechnique*, **24**, 438–43.

Hutchinson, J.N. (1984). 'An influence line approach to the stabilisation of slopes by cuts and fills.' *Canadian Geotech. Jl*, **21**, 363–70.

Institute of Geological Sciences (1977). Coastal terrain evaluation and slope stability of the Charmouth/Lyme Regis area of Dorset. Sheet 1.

Johnson, W. and Kudo, H. (1962). *The mechanics of metal extrusion.* Manchester University Press, Manchester.

Johnson, W. and Mellor, P.B. (1962). *Plasticity for mechanical engineers.* Van Nostrand, London.

Jukes-Browne, A.J. (1908). 'The burning cliff and the landslip at Lyme Regis.' *Proc. Dorset nat. Hist. antiq. Field Club*, **29**, 153–60.

Lang, W.D. (1914). 'The geology of the Charmouth cliffs, beach and foreshore.' *Proc. Geol. Assoc.*, **25**, 293–360.

Lang, W.D. (1928). 'Landslips in Dorset.' *Nat. Hist. Mag.*, **1**, 201–9.

Lang, W.D. (1955). 'Mudflows at Charmouth.' *Proc. Dorset nat. Hist. archaeol. Soc.*, **75**, 151–6.

Paterson, M.S. and Weiss, L.E. (1966). 'Experimental deformation and folding in phyllite.' *Bull. Geol. Soc. Am.*, **77**, 343–74.

Ramsay, J.G. (1967). *Folding and fracturing of rocks.* McGraw-Hill Book Company, New York.

Roberts, G. (1823). *The history of Lyme Regis, Dorset, from the earliest periods to the present day.* Langdon and Harker, Sherborne.

Shearman, D.J., Mossop, G., Dunsmore, H. and Martin, M. (1972). 'Origin of gypsum veins by hydraulic fracture.' *Trans. Instn Min. Metall. (Sect. B: Applied Earth Sci.), Lond.,* **81**, B149–B155.

Skempton, A.W. and Northey, R.D. (1952). 'The sensitivity of clays.' *Géotechnique,* **3**, 30–53.

Whyte, I. L. (1982). 'Soil plasticity and strength – a new approach using extrusion.' *Ground Engineering,* **15**, 16–18, 20, 22, 24.

Williams, R.B.G. (1968). 'Some estimates of periglacial erosion in southern and eastern England.' *Biul. Perygl.,* **17**, 311–35.

Wilson, V., Welch, F.B.A., Robbie, J.A. and Green, G.W. (1958). *Geology of the country around Bridport and Yeovil (Sheets 327 and 312).* Mem. Geol. Surv., H.M.S.O., London.

24 · Non-marine molluscan faunas of periglacial deposits in Britain

D.H. KEEN

Abstract

Non-marine molluscan faunas occur in deposits of various ages, and environments, associated with periglacial conditions in Britain. Faunas from slope and fluvial deposits predominate, and the best known assemblages are those from areas of calcareous substrates in south east England. The molluscan faunas, both land and freshwater, consist of a restricted number of species of undemanding habitat requirement which occur in Britain at present, together with arctic and alpine elements not found in Britain today. During the coldest parts of glacials it is likely that few Mollusca survived in Britain. Faunas of Devensian age are most common, and little certain data is available from earlier cold periods, although Wolstonian and early Hoxnian faunas have also been described.

Non-marine Mollusca are probably the most common fossils in Quaternary periglacial deposits in Britain. Although the number of species present is usually small, the numbers of individual shells may be very large in any one bed or sedimentary unit. Mollusca may not be of themselves good indicators or regional climate (Sparks, 1961), but can give useful indications of local climate or environment, and together with other lines of evidence such as Coleoptera, plants, geomorphology and sedimentology, allow detailed palaeo-environmental reconstruction to be achieved.

The Contexts of periglacial molluscan faunas

Four major contexts occur in the periglacial realm in which fossil Mollusca may be found. Two of these are terrestrial, and two are freshwater.

Most important in Britain of the terrestrial deposits are those formed on slopes, either in the form of screes or slope wash or on soils developed in these materials. The best preserved of these faunas are those of Late Devensian age which occur on the Chalk in south east England as described by Kerney (Kerney, 1963; Kerney *et al.*, 1964), although anywhere on the Chalk or Jurassic limestone outcrops from Dorset to Yorkshire may yield similar faunas. Oddly few faunas of this kind have been described outside the south east, or of pre-Late Devensian age, although some sites (e.g. Portland, Dorset, Keen, 1985; Fisherton, Wiltshire, Green *et al.*, 1983; Thriplow, Cambridgeshire,

Sparks, 1957, see Figure 24.1; Table 24.1) show similar characteristics to those in Kent and Sussex and are probably comparable.

Although chalk or limestone solifluction deposits are most favoured both for the existence of Mollusca in an environment fairly hostile to them, and for their preservation as fossils, not all chalky slope deposits are fossiliferous. Even on the most calcareous sub-strates faunas may be destroyed by

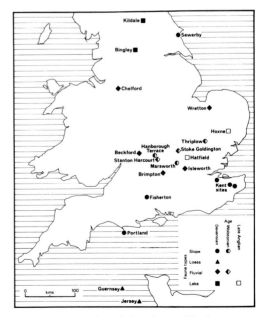

Figure 24.1. Location of sites discussed in the text.

Table 24.1 *Age of sites referred to in text* (*stage names after Mitchell et al., 1973*).

Stage		Site and type of assemblage
Late Devensian Glacial Stage	Loch Lomond Stadial Windermere Interstadial	Kent sites (1); Bingley Bog (4), Kildale (4), Channel Islands (2)
	Late Devensian Glaciation	Beckford (1, 3)
Middle Devensian Glacial Stage	Upton Warren Interstadial	Isleworth (3)
Early Devensian Glacial Stage		Brimpton (3) Chelford (3) Wretton (3) Portland (1) Fisherton (1) Sewerby (1)
Ipswichian Interglacial Wolstonian Glacial Stage		Marsworth (1) Stoke Goldington (3) Thriplow (1) Stanton Harcourt (3) ? Hanborough Terrace (1, 3)
Hoxnian Interglacial Late Anglian Glacial Stage		Hatfield (4); Hoxne (4) ? Hanborough Terrace (1, 3)

Type of assemblage 1 slope deposit faunas
2 loess faunas
3 fluvial and braid-plain faunas
4 lake faunas

later decalcification perhaps attendant on soil-forming processes or leaching (e.g. the Portland 'loam'-Keen, 1985). Especially vulnerable in this regard are the shells contained in coarse-grained deposits such as fine gravel even where this is calcareous. The ready passage of groundwater through such sediments makes the survival of molluscan material difficult except where silty admixtures either as discrete beds or more isolated lenses occur. This can be illustrated by the slope wash and head over the Ipswichian raised beach at Sewerby, Yorkshire where virtually the only molluscan material present in the fine gravel was the 'plates' of Limacid slugs (*Deroceras* sp). These, being more robust than other coiled, thin walled gastropod shells, were better able to resist dissolution. That the more usual slope wash fauna was once present, can be seen by the occasional deteriorated fragments of shell occurring with the *Deroceras* plates. These pieces of shell could occa-sionally be identified as *Pupilla muscorum* (Linné). The large numbers of the same species occurring in silt lenses interbedded with the gravels in the sequence, confirm their once more general distribution through the sediments.

The other major terrestrial context in which Mollusca might be found in many parts of the periglacial realm is loess. This fine grained calcareous sediment is ideal for the preservation of shells, but in Britain is usually either very thin (mostly under 30 cm according to Catt, 1977) or absent. Even such loess as does occur is non-calcareous so contains no shells. These conditions are therefore responsible for the lack of a British loess fauna. Only in the Channel Islands, included with Britain by means of political accident, but in reality western outliers of the great European loess province, have loess faunas been described (Keen, 1982). These more properly may be placed with those of Nor-mandy and Brittany rather than the British mainland, and the assemblages are very similar in species to those of the adjacent areas of France.

Of the two types of aquatic deposits of periglacial origin which have yielded Mollusca, of overwhelming importance are those of fluvial character. As has been long recognised, faunas in fluvial deposits consist of Mollusca from a range of habitats which include material from the river, from ponds on the valley floor, and from terrestrial environments nearby (Sparks, 1961). Thus they contain not only fluvial snails, but also elements of the slope assemblages already noted (e.g. Beckford, Gloucestershire, Briggs *et al.*, 1975–Figure 24.1). As with the slope deposits mentioned above, the usual form of preservation is in fine grained sediments present as thin beds or lenses in coarser material (sands or gravels). In periglacial fluvial environments in Britain such deposits are usually thought of as products of a braided stream regime (Briggs and Gilbertson, 1973; Seddon and Holyoak, 1985) with the silts forming as the infill of braid-plain ponds at low flow in late summer. The calcareous nature of the containing gravel appears not so important in these sediments as in the case of slope deposits, as faunas survive equally well in silts associated with limestone gravel (Beckford; Stanton Harcourt, Oxfordshire, Briggs *et al.*, 1985 – Figure 24.1; Table 24.1), or that of other materials (e.g. flint, Brimpton, Berkshire, Bryant *et al.*, 1983). The ready preservation of fluvial molluscan assemblages has ensured that numerous localities are known in southern and eastern England, although north of the Trent and west of the Severn there are much less data.

Non-fluvial aquatic environments are much rarer than fluvial ones. Lakes and ponds are ephemeral features in the landscape and even newly deglaciated terrain with its multiplicity of flooded hollows soon suffers the loss of all but the largest by sedimentary infill. Although such basins are short-lived they provide suitable habitats for still-water Mollusca and if their waters are at all calcareous these may thrive and be preserved in their sediments. As with all lake deposits those of the periglacial realm in Britain are fine grained, silts or muds, and often strongly calcareous, being made up predominantly of marl almost to the exclusion of mineral material at some horizons. These sediments provide ideal media for the preservation of Mollusca and such lake marl assemblages may yield large numbers of individuals of a small range of species (e.g. Kildale, Yorkshire, Keen *et al.*, 1984).

Terrestrial Mollusca are usually absent from lacustrine deposits. By their nature lakes do not contain anything of the 'sweeping' character of rivers so any land snails which are present are included in the sediment by chance rather than systematic incorporation, but given the sheet wash and overland flow which occurs under periglacial conditions, land shells may be washed into the margins of ponds or lakes during the spring snowmelt. It is probable that this mechanism may also be one of the means by which land Mollusca become incorporated in fluvial or braid plain sediments. Although no work has been done on such incorporation, Holyoak (1984) shows how plant macrofossils are washed into ponds and stream channels by overland flow in contemporary Spitzbergen, and snail shells somewhat similar in size and mass to plant macrofossils, may be incorporated in the same way.

The distribution of lake basins in Britain largely mirrors the limits of glaciation. In the north and west the presence of ice during some glacial stages prevented the immigration of Mollusca into these areas except in interglacials. In the east former glacial lakes, often kettle-holes, began to be infilled before the end of glacial stages and it is from these that the few faunas examined have come. These range geographically from Yorkshire (Kildale, Keen *et al.*, 1984) to Suffolk (Hoxne, Sparks in West, 1956) and Hertfordshire (Hatfield, Sparks *et al.*, 1969 – Figure 24.1; Table 24.1).

Mollusca as environmental and climatic indicators in periglacial deposits

Mollusca are best as indicators of local environmental conditions but they may also be useful in providing information about regional climates. Most of the species recovered from periglacial deposits of whatever origin in Britain are part of the current fauna. Only a few species of exclusively northern or alpine distribution (e.g. *Columella columella* (Martens) and *Pisidium obtusale* var. *lapponicum* (Clessin)) occur as unambiguous indicators of former climates of arctic type, and even some of these may not be controlled in their current distribution by temperature alone e.g. *C. columella* survived into the temperate Pre-Boreal stage of the Flandrian in southern Britain (Kerney *et al.*, 1980; Holyoak, 1983*a*) and only became extinct when 'shaded' by the spread of full interglacial forest. As well as individual species some distinct forms of common current British species may be found only in periglacial deposits. The most graphic example is the tall cylindrical form of *Pupilla muscorum* (Linné) typical of cold stage faunas of a range of ages in the

Quaternary, but never found in interglacial deposits (Kerney, 1963). Otherwise the faunas are composed entirely of species indistinguishable on morphological grounds from those of Britain at present.

The periglacial faunas are restricted in numbers of species. The current British fauna consists of 199 species (including introductions and 28 species of slugs which are unidentifiable beyond generic level as fossils, Kerney, 1976). In the Devensian, the best known cold period as far as Mollusca are concerned, a total of 34 species only have been recorded (Holyoak, 1982). This small number of species is a result of the same processes as are responsible for the reduction in molluscan diversity northwards at present, so that of the 125 land species recorded by Kerney (1976) in Britain at present, only 37 are recorded as present north of the Arctic Circle (Kerney & Cameron, 1979). Many of these are found only at the coast in the northern-most part of their distribution, and it is probable that some owe their most extreme northerly outposts to anthropogenic effects.

The occupation of climatically favourable micro-habitats is typical of modern Mollusca so that micro-climates are indicated by the presence of particular species rather than the general climate of the latitude. As is well known ground temperatures in periglacial areas are commonly warmer than air-temperatures (see Williams, 1975 for review), and water temperatures are sometimes warmer than either e.g. Holyoak (1983b), records that the temperature of thaw ponds over ice wedges in Banks Island, Canadian Arctic 72° N, reached 18 °C on hot summer days, up to 9 °C higher than the corresponding air temperature. Such conditions are more favourable for Mollusca than the occurrence of such undoubted indicators of periglacial conditions as ice wedges would suggest. Even higher surface temperatures may have occurred in Britain during cold stages due to the high angle of the sun and they may have made the crucial difference to the survival or breeding success of Mollusca.

Despite this amelioration of conditions from the extremes of periglacial climates, the most common species of Mollusca found in British periglacial deposits are those of undemanding habitat requirements. On land they are those of open grassland or disturbed ground (P. muscorum, C. columella, Trichia hispida (Linné)). In aquatic environments they are those most tolerant of poor conditions of temperature, oxygenation or both, such as Valvata piscinalis (Müller), Lymnaea truncatula (Müller). Lymnaea peregra (Müller), Anisus leucostoma (Millet), Gyraulus

laevis (Alder), Pisidium casertanum (Poli) and Pisidium nitidum (Jenyns). In marsh environments the succineids (Oxyloma pfeifferi (Rossmässler) Succinea oblonga (Draparnaud) and Catinella arenaria (Bouchard-Chantereaux) are most common (Holyoak, 1982).

More fastidious types such as Vallonia pulchella (Müller), Bithynia tentaculata (Linné) and Anodonta anatina (Linné) occurred either in interstadials such as the Upton Warren episode of the Mid-Devensian (Holyoak, 1982) or during the warming or cooling periods at the beginning or end of glacials.

Additional taxa of warm climate types occur at the beginning of glacial stages, as survivors in favourable habitats from more genial interglacial conditions. Such species as Corbicula fluminalis (Müller) recorded from Wretton (West et al., 1974) and Helicella itala (Linné) from Portland (Keen, 1985) may be in this category, although the possibility of reworking from earlier deposits, especially in the case of robust shells such as those of C. fluminalis, cannot be discounted.

Although some Mollusca survive very far north at present (to the North Cape of Norway (71° N), Spitzbergen (78° N), Siberia (c. 75° N) and Banks Island, Canada (72° N), it is possible that at the extremes of periglaciation in Britain no Mollusca were present at all (Kerney, 1977). Even aquatic faunas were severely affected by the short cold episode of the Loch Lomond (Younger Dryas) Stadial in northern Britain as shown by their temporary extinction in the kettle-hole lake at Kildale (Keen et al., 1984) and at Bingley Bog, West Yorkshire (D.H. Keen, R.L. Jones, J.E. Robinson and R.A. Evans – work in progress).

Distribution of Mollusca in Britain

The majority of comments on Mollusca in periglacial deposits in Britain refer to those of last glaciation (Devensian) age. Very few faunas of undoubted pre-Devensian date are known and the majority of these, like those from Hoxne, Suffolk (West, 1956), are from 'late glacial' contexts as the basal layer of longer interglacial sequences.

Devensian

The faunas which are best known are those of the Late Devensian – primarily the Windermere Interstadial and Loch Lomond Stadial – the time span from about 13,000 to 10,000 years BP. The majority of the faunas described are from south east England (Kerney, 1963) and show evidence of warm climate during the interstadial by the presence of H.

itala, Abida secale (Draparnaud) and *Trochoidea geyeri* (Soós). These thermophiles persisted through the Loch Lomond Stadial despite the clear geomorphological evidence of a harsh climate. Holyoak (1982) suggested that seasonality of climate (in the form of warm summers) may account for these survivals. It is also possible that the micro-climatic considerations of higher ground than air temperatures, already noted, may have been important.

Outside south east England Late Devensian molluscan faunas are not well known, but one or two that have been described add to, or confirm, details obtained from other palaeontological evidence such as insects or plant fossils. Of the sites known, two with aquatic assemblages from Yorkshire (Bingley Bog and Kildale, Figure 24.1; Table 24.1), show similar faunas of generally undemanding character for the Windermere Interstadial, with the largest numbers of individuals and species diversity present at an early stage of the episode. Later in the interstadial both species numbers and numbers of individuals show a marked decline probably due to the progressive climatic deterioration through the interstadial noted from insect fossils, as indicated by Coope (1977). At both these sites there is no record of Mollusca from the Loch Lomond stadial where the calcareous like silts and marls are replaced by angular fine sands containing the pollen of steppe plant assemblages (Keen *et al.*, 1984). Unlike in south east England these faunas of northern England appear to have been extinguished by the cold despite the thermal advantages conveyed by an aquatic habitat, thus pointing to a severe climate which also caused the onset of glaciation in the mountains of the north and west. The re-establishment of these aquatic faunas early in Flandrian times at both sites may be due to the survival of some Mollusca in favourable localities in the north even through the Loch Lomond Stadial, or perhaps may be evidence of rapid colonisation by aquatic Mollusca as soon as favourable conditions occurred. Some of the early Flandrian species at Bingley Bog in particular (*Lymnaea stagnalis* (Linné), *Physa fontinalis* (Linné), *Sphaerium corneum* (Linné)) must be considered in the latter category as they have no Late Devensian presence at the site.

There is still no firm evidence to confirm or deny Kerney's (1977) assertion that during maximum glaciation (approximately 25,000-15,000 years BP) Mollusca were absent from Britain. Given the number of sites of Late Devensian and Middle Devensian age recorded and dated by radiocarbon, the absence of any securely dated site with Mollusca from the above time-span is perhaps circumstantial evidence of the correctness of Kerney's view.

Holyoak (1982) has pointed out that stadial faunas of the Middle Devensian are composed of a very few of the most hardy species (*L. truncatula, O. pfeifferi, C. columella, P. muscorum*) perhaps exemplified by the fauna of a site such as Beckford, Worcestershire (Briggs *et al.*, 1975) with its radiocarbon date of 27,650 ± 250 B.P. placing it at the beginning of the cooling leading to the maximum extension of ice in the Last Glaciation.

Middle Devensian faunas are by contrast with those described above almost wholly those of silt lenses in fluvial gravels, although in keeping with the majority of river derived faunas these assemblages contain aquatic species (e.g. *V. piscinalis, G. laevis*), marsh species (*L. truncatula, O. pfeifferi*), and land snails (*C. columella, P. muscorum*, Limacid slugs) concentrated together by fluvial action from their particular habitats in the river catchment.

The interstadial faunas of the Middle Devensian are more diverse than stadial faunas (Holyoak, 1982) and contain such species as *A. anatina* and *L. stagnalis* (e.g. Isleworth, Middlesex, Kerney *et al.*, 1982) which confirm the more genial conditions indicated by other lines of evidence (e.g. Coleoptera, Coope, 1977).

Early Devensian molluscan faunas are far less well known than those from later in the period. This is probably in part a function of the lack of reliably dated sites prior to 60,000 BP, but may also reflect a genuine paucity of such sites. A few faunas are however known. Holyoak (1982) details those from the Brimpton and Chelford Interstadials and shows that they contain a mixture of the very tolerant species occurring in the Late Devesnian, with more thermophilous species such as *Discus rederatus* (Férussac). The same mixture of tolerant and more fastidious species is apparent from inferred early Devensian sites such as Portland (Keen, 1985) and from Wretton, Norfolk (West *et al.*, 1974). These assemblages clearly show that although considerable impoverishment of the fauna had occurred since the maximum of the Ipswichian Interglacial, either no severe cold had caused the reduction of the fauna to only the most tolerant species, or, sufficient time had elapsed after any cold period for at least a partial re-immigration of thermophilous Mollusca.

Pre-Devensian

Pre-Ipswichian periglacial molluscan faunas are even less well known than those of the early

Devensian. Although periglacial conditions occurred many times prior to the Devensian, undoubted periglacial sediments, and hence faunas, are poorly documented. Again the problem of dating is partly responsible for this, although the genuine lack of sites with periglacial deposits in England seems to be a real feature of the record.

Sites which seem to include faunas of Wolstonian age include Marsworth and Stoke Goldington in Buckinghamshire, and Stanton Harcourt in Oxfordshire (Figure 24.1). At the former site a channel containing blocks of travertine and a fauna of interglacial character has yielded U series dates around 160,000–170,000 years (Green et al., 1984). Deposits overlying this channel but stratigraphically below a further channel with a mammal fauna of Ipswichian character, have provided a slope fauna dominated by the tall cylindrical type of *P. muscorum*, but also containing *C. columella* and *C. arenaria*, which would be entirely characteristic of similar slope environments in the Late Devensian. At Stoke Goldington the fauna is an aquatic one contained in a silt-filled channel within fluvial gravels. It lies just above an interglacial channel at the base of the terrace sequence which provided shell-based U series dates of 180,000–200,000 BP (C.P. Green, G.R. Coope, D.H. Keen, R.L. Jones, J.E. Robinson and C. Young – work in progress), so is probably again of Late Wolstonian age. The fauna is dominated by *A. leucostoma*, *L. truncatula* and *C. arenaria* with smaller numbers of *V. piscinalis*, *G. laevis* and *P. obtusale* var. *lapponicum*. This assemblage of the most undemanding inhabitants of abandoned braid-plain pools and marsh would also be completely at home in the colder parts of the Middle Devensian.

A fauna (dominated also by *A. leucostoma*, *P. muscorum* and *O. pfeifferi* has been recorded from Stanton Harcourt, Oxfordshire (Briggs et al., 1985) in a stratigraphic context similar to that at Stoke Goldington. The general setting and palaeo-environment of the deposit have led the authors to attribute a late Wolstonian age to these deposits making them perhaps equivalent to those of Stoke Goldington, although Seddon and Holyoak (1985) provide radiocarbon dates which would place these deposits in the Devensian.

Faunas of similar character of even greater age have been reported from the same area. Briggs and Gilbertson (1973) describe a fauna composed principally of *O. pfeifferi*, *C. arenaria* and *P. muscorum* but also with *C. columella*, from the Hanborough Terrace of the Evenlode at Long Hanborough, Oxfordshire (Figure 24.1). The age of this sequence

is uncertain and its correct attribution depends largely on the geomorphological relationships of the various terraces of the Upper Thames (Briggs et al., 1985), but an age either in the early Wolstonian or early Anglian glacial stages seems most likely.

Older faunas of periglacial deposits are restricted to the ends or beginnings of interglacials. As with the sites noted above, these can be matched closely with those of Devensian age e.g. the early Hoxnian lake site at Hatfield, Herts (Sparks et al., 1969) contains a fauna with *G. laevis*, *Armiger crista* (Linné) and *V. piscinalis* which is similar to faunas from sites such as Kildale or Bingley Bog of Late Devensian age.

Conclusion

Non-marine Mollusca are relatively insensitive to macro-climate and their assemblages in periglacial deposits are restricted in numbers of taxa so that the main suites of species found in slope deposits, fluvial deposits and lakes became established relatively early in the Pleistocene. However, the occurrence of Mollusca in a range of sediments as the most common 'periglacial' fossil makes their examination necessary for students of the periglacial realm. In the future the recognition of more sites, especially from the Early Devensian and earlier periglacial periods, will allow firmer conclusions about palaeo-environments to be drawn.

There is also scope for the closer examination of the shells themselves. The examination of growth lines may perhaps allow determination of the ages of individual Molluscs and the conditions under which they secreted their shells (cf. marine Mollusca). The isotopic composition of the shell may provide information on water temperature and conditions, while consideration of the shell amino-acid ratios may allow the determination of the relative ages of shells from different sites: again, as has been done for marine Mollusca.

Acknowledgement

A draft of this review was read by Dr D.T. Holyoak who suggested a range of valuable amendments. The map was drawn by Mr D. Orme.

References

Briggs, D.J., Coope, G.R. and Gilbertson, D.D. (1975). Late Pleistocene terrace deposits at Beckford, Worcestershire, England. *Geol. J.*, **10**(1), 1–16.

Briggs, D.J., Coope, G.R. and Gilbertson, D.D. (1985). *The Chronology and Environmental Framework of Early Man in the Upper Thames Valley – A New*

Model. BAR British Series **137**, 176 pp.

Briggs, D.J. and Gilbertson, D.D. (1973). The age of Hanborough Terrace of the River Evenlode, Oxfordshire. *Proc. Geol. Ass.*, **84**, (2), 155–73.

Bryant, I.D., Holyoak, D.T. and Moseley, K.A. (1983). Late Pleistocene deposits at Brimpton, England. *Proc. Geol. Ass.*, **94**(4), 321–45.

Catt, J.A. (1977). Loess and Coversands, in *British Quaternary Studies – Recent Advances* (Ed. F.W. Shotton), pp. 221–230, Clarendon Press, Oxford.

Coope, G.R. (1977). Quaternary Coleoptera as aids in the interpretation of environmental history, in *British Quaternary Studies – Recent Advances* (Ed. F.W. Shotton), pp. 55–68, Clarendon Press, Oxford.

Green, C.P., Coope, G.R., Currant, A.P., Holyoak, D.T., Ivanovich, M., Keen, D.H., Jones, R.L., MacGregor, D.F.M. and Robinson, J.E. (1984). Evidence for two temperate episodes in late Pleistocene deposits at Marsworth, Bucks. *Nature*, **309**, 778–81.

Green, C.P., Keen, D.H., MacGregor, D.F.M., Robinson J.E., and Williams, R.B.G. (1983). Stratigraphy and environmental significance of Pleistocene deposits at Fisherton near Salisbury. *Proc. Geol. Ass.*, **94**(1), 17–23.

Holyoak, D.T. (1982). Non-marine Mollusca of the last Glacial Period (Devensian) in Britain. *Malacologia*, **22**, 727–30.

Holyoak, D.T. (1983*a*). The colonization of Berkshire, England by land and freshwater Mollusca since the Late Devensian. *J. Biogeog.*, **10**, 843–98.

Holyoak, D.T. (1983*b*). Freshwater Mollusca on Banks Island, Arctic Canada. *J. Conch. London*, **31**, 259–60.

Holyoak, D.T. (1984). Taphonomy of prospective plant macro fossils in a river catchment on Spitzbergen. *New Phytol.*, **98**, 405–23.

Keen, D.H. (1982). Late Pleistocene Land Mollusca from the Channel Islands. *J. Conch. London*, **31**, 57–61.

Keen, D.H. (1985). Late Pleistocene deposits and Mollusca from Portland, Dorset. *Geol. Mag.*, **122**(2), 181–6.

Keen, D.H., Jones, R.L. and Robinson, J.E. (1984). A Late Devensian and Early Flandrian fauna and flora from Kildale, North-east, Yorkshire. *Proc. Yorks. Geol. Soc.*, **44**(4), 385–97.

Kerney, M.P. (1963). Late-glacial deposits on the chalk of south-east England. *Phil. Trans. R. Soc. London* **B246**, 203–54.

Kerney, M.P. (1976). *Atlas of the non-marine Mollusca of the British Isles.* Institute of Terrestrial Ecology, Cambridge.

Kerney, M.P. (1977). British Quaternary non-marine Mollusca: a brief review, in *British Quaternary Studies – Recent Advances* (Ed. F.W. Shotton) pp. 31–42, Clarendon Press, Oxford.

Kerney, M.P., Brown, E.H. and Chandler, T.J. (1964). Late-glacial and post-glacial history of the chalk escarpment near Brook, Kent. *Phil. Trans. R. Soc. London* **B248**, 135–204.

Kerney, M.P. and Cameron, R.A.D. (1979). *A field guide to the Land Snails of Britain and North-west Europe.* Collins, London.

Kerney, M.P., Gibbard, P.L., Hall, A.R. and Robinson, J.E. (1982). Middle Devensian river deposits beneath the 'Upper Floodplain' Terrace of the River Thames at Isleworth, West London. *Proc. Geol. Ass.*, **93**(4), 385–95.

Kerney, M.P., Preece, R.C. and Turner, C. (1980). Molluscan and plant biostratigraphy of some Late Devensian and Flandrian deposits in Kent. *Phil. Trans. R. Soc. London* **B291**, 1–43.

Mitchell, G.F., Penny, L.F., Shotton, F.W. and West, R.G. (1973). *A correlation of Quaternary Deposits in the British Isles.* Geol. Soc. London Spec. Rep. No. 4.

Seddon, M.B. and Holyoak, D.T. (1985). Evidence of sustained regional permafrost during deposition of fossiliferous Late Pleistocene sediments at Stanton Harcourt, Oxfordshire, England. *Proc. Geol. Ass.*, **96**(1), 53–73.

Sparks, B.W. (1957). The taele gravel near Thriplow, Cambridgeshire. *Geol. Mag.*, **94**(3), 194–200.

Sparks, B.W. (1961). The ecological interpretation of Quaternary non-marine Mollusca. *Proc. Linn. Soc. London* **172**, 71–80.

Sparks, B.W., West, R.G., Williams, R.B.G. and Ransom, M. (1969). Hoxnian Interglacial deposits near Hatfield, Herts. *Proc. Geol. Ass.*, **80**(2), 243–67.

West, R.G. (1956). The Quaternary deposits at Hoxne, Suffolk. *Phil. Trans. R. Soc. London* **B239**, 265–326.

West, R.G., Dickson, C.A., Catt, J.A., Weir, A.H. and Sparks, B.W. (1974). Late Pleistocene deposits at Wretton, Norfolk. II Devensian deposits. *Phil. Trans. R. Soc. London* **B267**, 337–420.

Williams, R.B.G. (1975). The British climate during the last Glaciation: an interpretation based on periglacial phenomena, in *Ice Ages: Ancient and Modern* (Eds. H.E. Wright and F. Moseley,), pp. 95–120, Seel House Press, Liverpool.

25 · Sedimentological aspects of periglacial terrace aggradations: a case study from the English Midlands

MARTIN DAWSON

Abstract

The depositional environment of two contemporaneous periglacial river terrace aggradations located in the English Midlands may be inferred using lithofacies analysis. The sedimentary characteristics, and architectural arrangement of the lithofacies associations, indicate formation in low sinuosity gravel bed rivers. Although both terraces were deposited under 'nival' discharge conditions, they show contrasts in internal structure which may be related to differences in discharge regime, basin size, sediment supply and aggradation rates.

Introduction

Previous work on late Pleistocene terrace deposits in lowland Britain has shown that many terraces are typified by coarse clastic lithofacies and a braided fluvial origin has often been proposed (Briggs and Gilbertson, 1980; Castleden, 1980; Bryant, 1983a). However, many of the criteria used to identify channel planform, such as the absence of lateral accretion surfaces, are not necessarily diagnostic of a braided environment (Jackson, 1978; Bluck, 1979; Bridge, 1985). In addition, studies in analogue environments (e.g. Bryant, 1983b) have shown that a wide variety of river types exist in modern periglacial environments and a similar diversity may have been present in Britain during Pleistocene cold stages. The sedimentary features of two Devensian terrace aggradations in the Avon basin (Warwickshire, England), highlight the characteristics by which the type of fluvial environment can be identified and demonstrate the contrasts which may occur between periglacial fluvial environments.

The Avon flows 120 km south west from south Leicestershire to a confluence with the River Severn at Tewkesbury (Figure 25.1). The present direction of drainage within the basin is thought to post-date the Wolstonian (penultimate) glaciation (Shotton, 1953), the Avon developing as a drainage system flowing away from an ice front which advanced south westwards as far as Warwick (Shotton, 1953; Rice, 1968; Douglas, 1975). Five major terrace aggradations have been identified (Tomlinson, 1925), the most extensive being the Avon No 2 Terrace which lies approximately 8 m above the

present floodplain. Correlated deposits occur within the Leam, Stour, Arrow and Carrant Brook tributaries (Shotton, 1953, 1977; Briggs et al., 1975). Aggregate extraction in the Avon No 2 Terrace and the contemporaneous Carrant Brook Main Terrace has produced extensive exposures at three sites, permitting detailed lithofacies analysis and comparison of the sequences.

Previous work on these terrace deposits (Shotton, 1953, 1968; Coope, 1968; Kelly, 1968; Briggs et al., 1975) has concentrated on reconstructing the palaeo-environment from fossil remains and this evidence has indicated a prevailing Arctic climate with sparse vegetation cover and a cold tundra biotype. The presence of at least limited permafrost during deposition is shown by the occurrence of intraformational ice-wedge casts within the Carrant Brook deposits (Briggs et al., 1975). Radiocarbon dates, obtained from both deposits, range from 38,000 +/- 700 years B.P. to 26,000 +/- 300 years B.P. (Shotton, 1977) placing them in the latter half of the mid-Devensian and suggesting that the terraces were deposited immediately prior to, or during, the early stages of the Devensian glaciation, known to post-date 30,000 years B.P. (Boulton and Worsley, 1965; Shotton, 1967).

The Avon basin lies to the south of the known limits of the Devensian ice and no post-Wolstonian glacigenic deposits have been identified (Shotton, 1953; Rice, 1968; Douglas, 1975; Sumbler, 1983). It is therefore reasonable to assume that both the Avon and Carrant Brook had an Arctic 'nival' type of discharge regime (Church, 1974) and that the contrasts in sedimentation which Bryant (1983b)

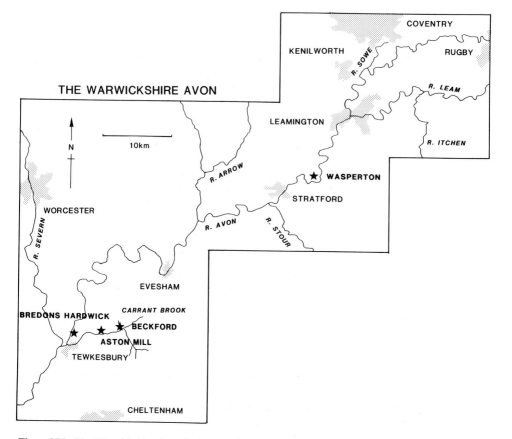

Figure 25.1. The Warwickshire Avon basin and the location of the terrace sections.

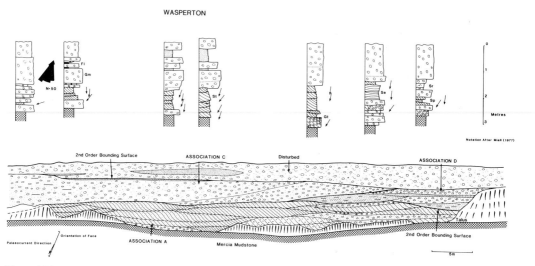

Figure 25.2. Section diagram and vertical profiles depicting lithofacies characteristics at Wasperton (Avon No. 2 Terrace). Face orientated parallel to the palaeocurrent direction. Facies notation after Miall (1977).

attributed to 'proglacial' and 'nival' discharge regimes should be absent. Differences in the sedimentary sequences are likely to be related to factors intrinsic to the respective drainage basins such as basin size, discharge magnitude and sediment source.

The Avon No. 2 Terrace

The sedimentary sequence of the Avon No. 2 terrace was examined at Wasperton and Bredons Hardwick (Figure 25.1) where laterally extensive sections along working faces were available. Although the sites are separated by a distance of 50 km, the thickness and general structure of the deposit are similar at both places, and a number of common inferences can be drawn from an examination of the two exposures.

The details of the terrace sequences were recorded using photo-mosaics and vertical sedimentary profiles (Figures 25.2 and 25.3). Distinctive architectural features, such as the major lithofacies associations and the bounding surfaces between them, were delimited on the photo-mosaics, whilst sedimentary detail was recorded on vertical profiles located at regular intervals along the exposures. Palaeocurrent directions were obtained, wherever possible, from sedimentary structures, such as cross-stratified sands, and from a limited number of at-a-point gravel fabrics taken from extensive gravel units. The combination of these methods allowed a detailed analysis of the vertical and lateral lithofacies variation in the terrace deposit.

General sedimentology

The deposits comprise up to 3 m of sand and gravel and 1 m of soil within which the preservation of the sedimentary structures is generally good, although in the upper 75 cm to 1 m they tended to be indistinct and extensively disturbed, either due to cryoturbation or farming practices. At neither site was there evidence of ice-wedge casts, however, minor undulations in planar bedded structures indicate post-depositional disturbance and at the Bredons Hardwick site there is more extreme displacement of both the terrace gravels and the underlying Lias clay.

The terrace bases at both sites are planar, but show minor ellipsoidal scours. Overlying lithofacies tend to be conformable with the scour forms and at the Wasperton site lithoclasts of the Mercia Mudstone bedrock are present within the basal lithofacies, indicating that scour and planation of the bedrock was contemporaneous with the deposition of the terrace sediments.

Internal structure

Examination of the terrace deposits indicated a highly complex structure. Individual lithofacies units tend to be discontinuous and laterally and vertically truncated. However, a number of common lithofacies associations or architectural elements (Allen, 1983; Miall, 1985), separated by a hierarchical system of bounding surfaces (Allen, 1983) may be identified. Individual lithofacies units (i.e. cross-bedded sets) are separated by first order

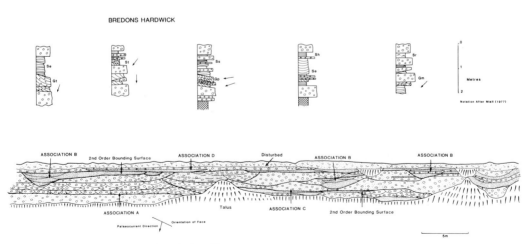

Figure 25.3. Section diagram and vertical profiles depicting lithofacies characteristics at Bredons Hardwick (Avon No. 2 Terrace). Face orientated normal to the palaeocurrent direction.

Table 25.1 *The Avon No. 2 terrace; Lithofacies association characteristics*

Association	Form of lower bounding surface	Composite Lithofacies	Interpretation
A	Erosional and concave up. Dimensions exceed 50 m parallel to, and 20m normal to, mean transport direction.	Laterally persistent cosets of trough cross-bedded sand and gravel up to 50m in length and between 30 cm–1 m thick. Gravel units 50 cm thick showing discontinuous shallow scour structures and isolated cross-stratified sets. Thin beds of massive gravel up to 30 cm thick, interbedded with above lithofacies.	Vertically aggraded, major channel fills.
B	Erosional and concave up. Normal to the transport direction these features typically have an asymmetric channel form 8–15m wide.	Thin cosets of ripple, trough and scour-fill stratified sands, 10–50cm thick, preferentially located towards the channel centre. Thin units of massive gravel, 10–40cm thick. Wedge-like units of tabular cross-bedded gravel orientated normal to the channel axis and extending from the channel sides.	Laterally downfilled and vertically aggraded minor or slough channels.
C	Planar and erosional. Locally conformable and undulating where overlying Association A.	Tabular, laterally extensive units of massive to planar bedded gravel up to 70cm thick, traceable for up to 50m parallel, and in excess of 15m normal to, the dominant palaeocurrent direction. Tabular cross- bedded gravel units 10–40cm thick, orientated parallel to the mean transport direction and interbedded with, or occurring downflow of, the units of massive gravel.	Agglomerated units of in-channel, unit bar, deposition forming a complex bar platform.
D	Planar and conformable, locally erosive.	Lenticular beds of planar bedded sand, 10–15cm thick. Isolated sets or small cosets of ripple laminated, trough and planar cross-bedded sand 10–40cm thick.	Supra-bar and bar tail sedimentation comprising interdigitating sheets and lobes of predominantely sandy lithofacies.

bounding surfaces, whilst associations, comprising a number of such units, are delimited by second order surfaces. No third order surfaces defining separate depositional periods was discernible in the deposit.

Four major lithofacies associations, present at both sites, were identified within the deposit. Each possesses a number of common lithofacies, although few types are exclusive to any of the associations. Individual units are bounded by a

second order surface, the form and nature of which is related to the type of association. The characteristics of each of the four lithofacies associations and their bounding surfaces are outlined in Table 25.1.

The four associations seem to be juxtaposed in a definable sequence. Relationships observed in the field are illustrated in Figures 25.2 and 25.3. At Wasperton (Figure 25.2), in a 90 m face excavated parallel to the palaeocurrent direction, the basal association was a single coset of trough cross-

Table 25.2 *Palaeocurrent data*

Mean direction (degrees)	Vector strength	Standard Deviation (degrees)	Valley axis (degrees)
Wasperton (n = 23)			
202	0.944	19	190
Bredons Hardwick (n = 33)			
196	0.797	40	195
Aston Mill			
Gravel Fabrics (n = 5)			
317	0.984	10	290
Foreset Dip Directions (n = 29)			
329	0.861	31	

bedded sand and interbedded thin lag units of massive gravel (association A) up to 1 m thick and over 50 m long, resting directly on the Mercia Mudstone bedrock. The internal stratification within the deposit is typical of curve crested dune migration in a major channel (Allen, 1968; Harms *et al.*, 1975), the presence of gravel units indicating winnowing and lag effects.

This coset was overlain along an undulating, non-erosional horizon by a number of interdigitating units of massive to low angle dipping planar bedded gravel up to 1 m thick (association C) which thinned and fined internally along the face. The major unit in this bed showed a transition from planar bedding with good imbrication to a more massive structure downflow. These units may be interpreted as being part of a complex-bar platform (Bluck, 1976, 1979) formed by the agglomeration of in-channel unit bar forms (Smith, 1974; Hein and Walker, 1977; Bluck, 1979). The distal gravel units of association C graded and interdigitiated almost imperceptibly with a unit composed of lenticular bodies of planar bedded sand and gravel, isolated cross-bedded sets and laterally extensive drapes of ripple laminated sand and clay (association D). The association seems to have been deposited contemporaneously with, and subsequent to, the major gravel units, the internal characteristics strongly resembling the bar-lee and supra-bar sediments described by Bluck (1976, 1979).

A 50 m face excavated at Bredons Hardwick orientated normal to the dominant palaeocurrent direction shows asymmetric channel forms laterally and vertically truncating adjacent lithofacies, tending to be incised into, or occurring adjacent to, the thick lenticular gravel units of association C. Locally there is a gradational interfingering between the thin bedded, bar surface, sediments of association D and the channel infills. Similar interdigitation has been observed between minor channel infills and bar surface sediments by Eynon and Walker (1974) and both Bluck (1979) and Bryant (1983*a*) interpreted comparable forms as bar surface or bar margin slough channels.

The mean palaeocurrent directions at both sites closely parallels the axis of the valley. As shown in Table 25.2 the variance in direction at both sites is small, although much less at the Wasperton site (largely because sampling here was confined to a few sedimentary units), and the degree of dispersal is comparable to that noted in low sinuosity environments by Rust (1972*a*) and Bluck (1974).

Interpretation

The terrace aggradation as a whole shows little evidence of a change in depositional style through time and the four associations may be considered to be related sub-environments within a single type of fluvial system, representing; vertically aggraded channel fills; vertically aggraded and downfilled minor channels; bar platforms; and supra-bar sedimentation. Neither the occurrence or juxtaposition of these elements is necessarily diagnostic of the type of fluvial environment, however the Avon No 2 sequence may be attributed to deposition in a low sinuosity environment for several reasons:

(a) Major bar structures show no evidence of epsilon bedding surfaces (Allen, 1964; Moody-Stuart, 1966) or inner accretionary bank structures in the fine members of the supra-bar lithofacies (Bluck, 1979), and there is a pre-dominance of vertically accreted units (Bridge, 1985).

(b) Massive to sub-planar bedded gravel units are widely present throughout the sequence, indicating low width to depth ratios (Bryant, 1983*a*; Bridge, 1985)

(c) There is an absence of significant channel fill or overbank mud deposits as would be expected of a sinuous river, although infilled inner or slough channel forms are common (Bluck, 1979, 1980; Bryant, 1983a).

(d) There is a low directional variance in palaeocurrent directions (S.D. < 39°), indicating low sinuosity (Moody-Stuart, 1966; Bridge, 1985).

The associations and their juxtaposition within the sequence show broad similarities to those identified in a Pleistocene braided outwash environment by Eynon and Walker (1974). Furthermore the apparent cyclicity in the vertical relationships between the lithofacies is analogous to the Donjek type model of braided stream deposits (Miall, 1977, 1978). However, unlike the periglacial 'nival' type deposits described by Bryant (1983b), the sediments, although having formed under 'nival' discharge conditions, do show evidence of extensive reworking as individual lithofacies units tend to be discontinuous and there are numerous beds which can be ascribed to the infill of abandoned morphological features.

Bryant (1983b), following Jones (1977), argued that the extent of reworking is dependent on discharge regime, with primary sedimentary units being well preserved in periglacial 'nival' environments, as prolonged periods of high stage flow are infrequent. The common occurrence of reworked units in the Avon No. 2 Terrace may indicate that there were unusually sustained periods of high flow during, for instance, spring break up in the basin. However, the reworking may be related to frequent deep scour through previously deposited units, as shown by the presence of channel forms and associated conformable sequences of lithofacies extending through almost the complete thickness of the terrace. In modern braided rivers (Ashmore, 1982; Ashmore and Parker, 1983; Mosley, 1982) scour occurs at channel confluences and in bends, depths of scour being controlled by local discharges and anabranch confluence angles, with sedimentary properties being of minor importance. The observed depths of scour, relative to unit thickness, would therefore seem to indicate a low rate of terrace aggradation under conditions of frequent channel-zone migration, and this may account for the differences between the Avon No. 2 sequence and the lithofacies model of Bryant (1983b).

The terrace base has a similar planar form to terrace bases described by Castleden (1980) and seems to have developed contemporaneously with the deposition of the terrace sediments, as a result of channel scour. Scour zones in braided rivers are laterally unstable (Ashmore, 1982; Ashmore and Parker, 1983) and migration of the channels, if frequent through time, would produce a planar or subplanar base with only local variation in elevation.

The Carrant Brook

The sedimentary sequence of the Carrant Brook was examined from exposures at Aston Mill (Figure 25.1), although Briggs et al. (1975) described extensive sections 4 km upstream at Beckford. However, unlike the sites at Beckford the terrace aggradation here represents sedimentation by the Carrant Brook itself and the terrace at this point has received no direct contribution from the valley sides. At Aston Mill, over a two year period, consecutive parallel faces, approximately 250 m in length were excavated normal to the valley axis. The sedimentary sequence was recorded from two such faces, using a similar methodology applied to the examination of the Avon No. 2 sites. Figure 25.4 shows details of parts of one these faces.

General sedimentology

The terrace deposit at Aston Mill Farm ranges from 2.5 to 4.25 m thick overlying the local lower Lias clay bedrock. The bedrock surface has a slight concave up profile, sloping at about 1–2° towards the valley centre, but it is uncertain whether this profile is stepped or smooth. Stratigraphically the deposit is broadly similar to upstream, valley centre, sites (Briggs et al., 1975), 75 cm to 1 m of silty brown loam overlying 2–3 m of sand and gravel. Preservation of the primary structures within the deposit is generally good although both intra and extra-formational ice wedges were observed (see also Briggs et al., 1975) and the silty loam is extensively involuted, this disturbance often extending down to 2 m beneath the terrace surface. Whilst the extra-formational ice-wedge casts were discernible across the width of the deposit, the intra-formational casts seem to be confined to fine grained sediments located towards the valley sides.

The gravel component within the terrace is predominantly derived from the local Jurassic limestone, with minor components of Bunter material. However, Briggs et al. (1975) demonstrated that the mineralogical content of the sands was related to a more diverse range of source lithologies and argued that they were derived from exposed Severn and Avon terrace material being transported into the area by aeolian processes.

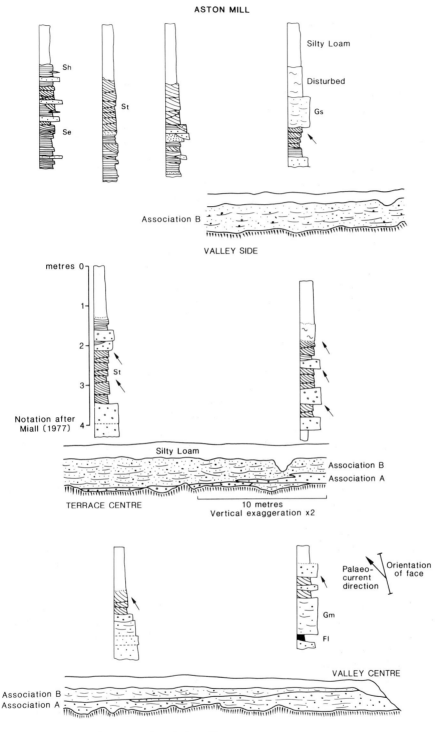

Figure 25.4. Section diagrams and vertical profiles from parts of the terrace sequence at Aston Mill (Carrant Brook Main Terrace). Face orientated oblique to the palaeocurrent direction.

Internal structure

The sedimentary sequence in the Carrant Brook Main terrace shows a distinct contrast with that forming the Avon No. 2 terrace (Figure 25.4). The structurally defined architectural elements of the latter aggradation are not present, although a distinction can be made between two lithofacies associations (A, B) which interdigitate.

Association A is at its thickest towards the valley centre (1.25 m) and extends laterally along the base of the terrace, thinning and becoming increasingly interdigitated with association B. Internally the association is predominantly composed of lenticular bodies of massive, framework supported, gravel up to 40–50 cm thick and laterally traceable for 5 to 10 m. Many of these units overlie a concave-up erosive surface and show internal, discontinuous, scour structures, these characteristics being similar to gravel units thought to have been deposited in channels in the Avon No. 2 terrace aggradation. More homogeneous units resemble bar core sediments (Eynon and Walker, 1974; Hein and Walker, 1977; Bluck, 1976; Bryant, 1983a). Distinct channel forms are few in number, but were observed to contain wedge-like tabular cross-stratified units oriented normal to the channel axis which seem to be former lateral channel infills (Rust, 1972b; Bryant, 1983a). Locally, at the contact between these gravel units, thin lenticular sand bodies are present. Typically these show planar lamination and may represent truncated remnants of supra-bar sedimentation (Bluck, 1979; Bryant, 1983a).

Association B overlies association A and forms the bulk of the terrace sequence. Typically it is comprised of cosets of trough cross-bedded coarse sand and granules up to 2m thick with individual set heights reaching 30–40cm. Gravel lags at set bases and interbedded gravel lenses are common and locally trough fills are composed of massive gravel. Towards the valley sides, cosets increasingly interdigitate with small cosets of scour-fill sands (trough forms showing no distinct cross-stratification) and with more extensive beds of planar laminated sand. The association fines upwards away from the contact with the underlying association A and towards the valley sides, in combination with a transition from cross-stratified to planar laminated sand.

Palaeocurrents, shown by five gravel fabrics (N = 50) taken from association A and 29 foreset dip orientations from structures present in association B, possess a low dispersal (Table 25.2) around a mean direction of 317–329°. This represents a slight deviation from the present orientation of the valley axis 290° which may be attributable to a small change in channel orientation.

Interpretation

The discontinuous thin bedded and lenticular nature of association A is similar to a shallow braided lithofacies unit described by Eynon and Walker (1974) and on a small scale the association possesses many features in common with the braided lithofacies model presented by Bryant (1983b) for arctic 'nival' regimes. The presence of multiple small channel forms and lenticular massive gravel units is indicative of a migrating channel system with single or multiple channels. Lateral accretion structures are, however, absent and the low direction variance shown by gravel fabrics suggest that the river had a low sinuosity form. Flow depths seem to have been low as the thickness of individual beds within the association is small and there is an absence of extensive cross-bedding, except as infills of small channels.

Briggs *et al.* (1975) argued that a similar vertical and lateral transition from a predominantly gravelly to sandy lithofacies association observed in an upstream site was a function of a change in climatic conditions causing increasing aeolian sand inputs into the basin. However, the lateral interdigitation between the two associations indicates that, in part, they were contemporaneously deposited. Sedimentation in the zone away from the valley centre where the intra-formational ice-wedge casts are present seems to have been discontinuous, as the development of ice-wedge casts is only possible away from the talik associated with a major river channel (French, 1976). In addition the gradational changes in lithofacies type and grain size indicate a reduction in flow depth and competance in this direction.

Bryant (1983a, b) noted that modern periglacial rivers tend to occupy part only of their valley floors, and that there are extensive lateral areas at slightly higher elevations which receive sedimentation only at high stage. Substantial accumulations of aeolian sediments have been noted at valley margins in certain periglacial areas (Pissart *et al.,* 1977; Boothroyd and Nummedal, 1978; Bryant, 1982; Good and Bryant, 1985). It is, therefore possible that association B represents aeolian derived sediment deposited or reworked at high flood stage in areas laterally adjacent to an active channel zone. The interdigitation between cross-stratified sands and planar laminated sediments towards the valley sides may, in fact, indicate a transition from fluvially reworked sands to aeolian deposited sediments. Good and Bryant (1985) observed that the deflation of exposed sands produces planar surfaces with clast lag horizons, whilst crudely laminated sand may be the product of deposition of migrating sand sheets in the lee of small obstacles (Fryberger *et al.*, 1979) or the adhesion of saltating or creeping sands to wet surfaces (Kocurek and Fielder, 1982).

The terrace base is more distinctly concave-up than at the Avon No. 2 sites. Although Castleden (1980) attributed such similar, sloping, profiles elsewhere to a faster rate of aggradation, at this location the greater concavity may be related to the fact that prolonged channel migration and scour seems to have taken place only in the valley centre.

Summary and conclusions

Lithofacies analysis of two contemporaneous periglacial terrace aggradations indicates that they were deposited by low sinuosity gravel bed rivers which most probably had a braided channel planform. This interpretation is similar to those for other coarse grained terrace aggradations in southern Britain (Briggs and Gilbertson, 1980; Clarke and Dixon, 1981; Bryant, 1983a; Bryant, *et al.*, 1983a, b) but is based on a consideration of bedding forms and palaeocurrent evidence which, together, provide some indication of the depositional environment. Support for the deductions made can be gained by reference to previous work, particularly established facies models of fluvial environments based on detailed investigations of modern sedimentary environments (Miall, 1977, 1978; Walker, 1979; Bryant, 1983b).

Despite the inferred similarity in fluvial style the two lithofacies sequences demonstrate marked contrasts. The Avon No. 2 terrace sequence shows a complex, but clearly defined, architectural sequence comprising four lithofacies associations which can be broadly related to depositional subenvironments. The interpretation of the Avon No. 2 terrace as a braided fluvial environment markedly differs from previous non-sedimentological work which has suggested a high sinuosity meandering origin (Shotton, 1953; Dury, 1964; Clayton, 1977). Although the river during this period is most likely to have had a 'nival' type of discharge regime (Church, 1974) with the major period of sediment transport and deposition occurring during a short spring flood period, the sequence shows signs of extensive reworking. This contrasts with the model proposed by Bryant (1983b) and may be attributed to a frequent scour of sediment due to low rates of aggradation or perhaps an attenuated flood period due to the size of the basin, which has multiple discharge source areas.

The Carrant Brook Main Terrace shows evidence of both in-channel gravel deposition and extensive fluvio-aeolian sedimentation on adjacent overbank areas. Gravel sedimentation seems to have taken place in a shallow, low sinuosity stream, possibly with multiple channels, although this cannot be unequivocally determined. The vertical superimposition of massive gravel units and the lack of evidence for extensive sediment reworking within the in-channel sediments accords with the facies model proposed by Bryant (1983b) for arctic 'nival' periglacial rivers. Thinner bed thickness, as compared to the Avon No. 2 terrace, can be directly attributed to lower flow depths and discharges related to basin size, whilst the differences in the degree of sediment reworking is probably related to discharge regime and possibly to a higher rate of aggradation. As noted by Briggs *et al.* (1975), much of the sequence is composed of sand transported into the area by aeolian processes. These sands were reworked and contemporaneously deposited with the in-channel sediments in areas adjacent to the active channel, most probably during peak flood periods.

The sedimentary contrasts between the two terrace sequences indicate the dangers of generalisation not only in interpreting coarse grained periglacial terrace sequences but also in the development of facies models. Whilst the latter provide a useful framework to assist interpretation they cannot be regarded as universally applicable. Detailed interpretation of terrace sequences should thus be made on a consideration of the composite lithofacies, their associations and the vertical and lateral juxtaposition of the architectural elements within the terrace.

Acknowledgements

Financial support for this study was provided by a N.E.R.C. research studentship held by the author at Leicester University. The following aggregate companies are thanked for making it possible to examine the terraces in section by allowing access to their workings: Mixconcrete Ltd.; Western Aggregates plc; Gloucester Sand and Gravel Company. Ruth Rowell and Kate Moore expertly reproduced the diagrams included in the text.

References

Allen, J.R.L., (1964). 'Studies in fluvial sedimentation: Six cyclothems from the Lower Old Red Sandstone, Anglo-Welsh Basin.' *Sedimentology.* **3**, pp. 163–98.

Allen, J.R.L. (1968). *Current Ripples: Their Relation to Patterns of Water and Sediment Motion.* North Holland Pub. Co. 433 pp.

Allen, J.R.L. (1983). 'Studies in fluviatile sedimentation bars, bar complexes and sandstone sheets (low sinuosity braided streams) in the Brownstones (Lower Devonian), Welsh Borders.' *Sed. Geol.* **33**, pp. 237–93.

Ashmore, P.E. (1982). 'Laboratory modelling of gravel braided stream morphology.' *Earth Sur. Procs. and Landforms* **7**, pp. 201-25.

Ashmore, P.E. and Parker, G. (1983). 'Confluence scour in coarse braided streams.' *Water Resources Res.* **19**, pp. 392–402.

Bluck, B.J. (1974). 'Structure and directional properties of some valley sandur deposits in southern Iceland.' *Sedimentology,* **21**, pp. 533–54.

Bluck, B.J. (1976). 'Sedimentation in some Scottish rivers of low sinuosity.' *Trans. Roy. Soc. Edin.* **69**, pp. 425–56.

Bluck, B.J. (1979). 'Structure of coarse grained braided stream alluvium.' *Trans. Roy. Soc. Edin.,* **70**, pp. 181–221.

Bluck, B.J. (1980). 'Structure, generation and preservation of upward fining braided stream cycles in the Old Red Sandstone of Scotland.' *Trans. Roy. Soc. Edin.* **71**, pp. 29–46.

Boothroyd, J.C. and Nummedal, D. (1978). 'Proglacial braided outwash: A model for humid alluvial fan deposits.' In Miall A.D. (ed) *Fluvial Sedimentology* Can. Soc. Petrol. Geol. Mem. No. 5, pp. 641–68.

Boulton, G.S., and Worsley, P. (1965). 'Late Weichselian glaciation of the Cheshire-Shropshire basin.' *Nature.* **207**, pp. 704–6.

Bridge, J.S. (1985). 'Perspectives: Paleochannel patterns inferred from alluvial deposits.' *J. Sed. Petrol.* **55**, pp. 579–89.

Briggs, D.J., Coope, G.R. and Gilbertson, D.D. (1975). 'Late Pleistocene terrace deposits at Beckford, Worcestershire, England.' *Geol. J.* **10**, pp. 1–15.

Briggs, D.J. and Gilbertson, D.D. (1980). 'Quaternary processes and environments in the upper Thames Valley.' *Trans Inst Brit Geog.* N.S. **5**, pp. 53–65.

Bryant, I. D. (1982). 'Loess deposits in Lower Adventdalen, Vestspitsbergen.' *Polar Research*

Bryant, I.D. (1983a). 'Facies sequences associated with some braided river deposits of late Pleistocene age from southern Britain.' In Collinson, J.D. and Lewin, J. (eds) *Modern and Ancient Fluvial Systems: Sedimentology and Process* Int. Assoc. of Sedimentologists, Spec. Publ. No. 6, pp. 267–75.

Bryant, I.D. (1983b). 'The utilization of Arctic river analogue studies in interpretation of periglacial river sediments from southern Britain.' In Gregory, K.J. (ed.) *Background to Palaeohydrology.* Wiley, London, pp. 413–31.

Bryant, I.D., Holyoak, D.T. and Moseley, K.A., (1983b). 'Late Pleistocene deposits at Brimpton, England.' *Procs. Geol. Assoc.* **94**, pp. 321–44.

Bryant, I.D., Gibbard, P.L., Holyoak, D.T., Switsur, V.R. and Wintle, A.G. (1983b). 'Stratigraphy and palaeontology of Pleistocene cold stage deposits at Alton Road Quarry, Farnham, Surrey, England.' *Geol. Mag.* **120**, pp. 587–606.

Castleden, R. (1980). 'Fluvioperiglacial sedimentation: a general theory of fluvial valley development in cool temperate lands, illustrated from western and central Europe.' *Catena* **7**, pp. 135–52.

Church, M. (1974). 'Hydrology and permafrost with reference to northern North America.' In, *Permafrost Hydrology.* Proceedings of Workshop Seminar, Canadian National Committee. No. 7–20.

Clarke, M.R. and Dixon, A.J. (1981). 'The Pleistocene river deposits in the Blackwater Valley area of Berkshire and Hampshire, England.' *Proc. Geol. Assoc.* **92**, pp. 139–58.

Clayton, K.M. (1977). 'River Terraces.' In Shotton, F.W. (ed.) *British Quaternary Studies.* Oxford Univ. Press, pp. 153–65.

Coope, G.R. (1968). 'A insect fauna from mid-Weichelian deposits at Brandon, Warwickshire.' *Phil. Trans. Roy. Soc. Lond.* Ser. B, **254**, pp. 425–56.

Douglas, T.D. (1975). *The Pleistocene Geology and Geomorphology of Western Leicestershire.* Unpubl. Ph.D. Thesis. University of Leicester.

Dury, G.H. (1964). 'Subsurface exploration and chronology of underfit streams.' *U.S.G.S. Prof. Pap.* No. 452–B56 pp.

Eynon, G. and Walker, R.G. (1974). 'Facies relationships in Pleistocene outwash gravels, southern Ontario: A model for bar growth in braided rivers.' *Sedimentology,* **21**, pp. 43–70.

French, H.M. (1976). *The Periglacial Environment* Longmans, London, 309 pp.

Fryberger, S.G., Ahlbrandt, T.S. and Andrews, D. (1979). 'Origin, sedimentary features and significance of low angle aeolian "sand-sheet" deposits, Great Sand Dunes National Monument and vicinity, Colorado.' *J. Sed. Petrol.* **49**, pp. 733–46.

Good T.R., and Bryant, I.D. (1985). 'Fluvio-aeolian sedimentation: An example from Banks Island, N.W.T. Canada.' *Geogr. Annlr.* **67A**, pp. 33–46.

Harms, J.C., Southard, J.B., Spearing, D.R. and Walker, R.G. (1975). *Depositional Environments as Interpreted from Primary Sedimentary Structures and Stratification Sequences.* Soc. Econ. Min. Paleont. Short Course, No. 2. Dallas.

Hein, F.J. and Walker, R.G. (1977). 'Bar evolution and development of stratification in the gravelly, braided, Kicking Horse River, British Columbia'; *Can. J. Earth. Sci.* **14**, pp. 562–70.

Jackson, R.G. (1978). 'Preliminary evaluation of lithofacies models for meandering alluvial streams.' In Miall, A.D. (ed.) *Fluvial Sedimentology.* Can. Soc. Petrol. Geol. Mem. No. 5, pp. 543–76.

Jones, C.M. (1977). Effects of varying discharge regime on bedform sedimentary structures in modern rivers.' *Geology,* **5**, pp. 567–70.

Kelly, M.R. (1968). 'Floras of middle and upper Pleistocene age from Brandon, Warwickshire.' *Phil. Trans. Roy. Soc. Lond.* Ser. A, **265**, pp. 233–97.

Kocurek, G. and Fielder, G. (1982). 'Adhesion structures.' *J. Sed. Petrol.*, **52**, pp. 1229–41.

Miall, A.D. (1977). 'The braided river depositional environment.' *Earth Sci. Rev.* **13**, pp. 1–62.

Miall, A.D. (1978). 'Lithofacies types and vertical profile models in braided river deposits: a summary.' In Miall, A.D. (ed.) *Fluvial Sedimentology.* Can. Soc. Petrol. Geol. Mem. No. 5, pp. 597–604.

Miall, A.D. (1985). 'Architectural element analysis: A new method of facies analysis applied to fluvial deposits.' *Earth Sci. Rev.* **22**, pp. 261–308.

Moody-Stuart, M. (1966). 'High and low sinuosity stream deposits with examples from the Devonian of Spitsbergen.' *J. Sed. Petrol.* **36**, pp. 1102–17.

Mosley, M.P. (1982). 'Scour depths in branch channel confluences, Ohau River, Otago, New Zealand.' *Trans. N.Z. Inst. Civil Engrs.* **9**, pp. 17–24.

Pissart A., Vincent, J.S. and Edlund, S.A. (1977). 'Depots et phenomenes eolians sur L'ile de Banks, Territoires du Nord-Ouest, Canada.' *Can. J. Earth Sci.* **14**, pp. 2462–80.

Rice, R.J. (1968). 'The Quaternary deposits of Central Leicestershire.' *Phil. Trans. Roy. Soc.* Ser. A, **262**, pp. 459–509.

Rust, B.R. (1972*a*). 'Pebble orientation in fluvial sediments.' *J. Sed. Petrol.* **42**, pp. 384–388.

Rust, B.R. (1972*b*). 'Structure and process in a braided river.' *Sedimentology* **18**, pp. 221–46.

Shotton, F.W. (1953). 'Pleistocene deposits of the area between Coventry, Rugby and Leamington and their bearing on the topographic development of the Midlands.' *Phil. Trans. Roy. Soc.* Ser. B, **237**, pp. 209–60.

Shotton, F.W. (1967). 'Age of the Irish Sea Glaciation of the Midlands.' *Nature*, **215**, pp. 1366.

Shotton, F.W. (1968). 'The Pleistocene succession around Brandon, Warwickshire.' *Phil. Trans. Roy. Soc.* Ser. B, **254**, pp. 387–400.

Shotton, F.W. (1977). *The English Midlands* Guidebook 10th INQUA Congress, Birmingham. 51 pp.

Smith, N.D. (1974). 'Sedimentology and bar formation in the upper Kicking Horse River: A braided meltwater stream.' *J. Geol.* **82**, pp. 205–23.

Sumbler, M.G. (1983). 'A new look at the type Wolstonian glacial deposits of central England.' *Proc. Geol. Assoc. Lond.* **94**, pp. 23–31.

Tomlinson, M.E. (1925). 'River terraces of the lower valley of the Warwickshire Avon.' *Quart. J. Geol. Soc. Lond.* **81**, pp. 137–63.

Walker, R.G. (1979). *Facies Models* Geoscience Canada. Reprint Series 1, 211 pp.

West, R.G. (1977). *Pleistocene Geology and Biology* Longmans, London. 2nd ed., 439 pp.

26 · The periglacial history of Buchan, north east Scotland

E.R. CONNELL AND A.M. HALL

Abstract

Recent investigations in Buchan, Scotland, have extended the regional periglacial stratigraphy. At Kirkhill Quarry, periglacial deposits and structures demonstrate two major episodes of cold climate prior to the last interglacial. At least four phases of Devensian periglacial activity may also be recognised: (i) at the onset of the Early Devensian glaciation of central Buchan, (ii) in the Dimlington Stadial, (iii) during the decay of the coastal ice masses at the end of the Dimlington Stadial, (iv) during the Loch Lomond Stadial. The distribution of periglacial deposits and structures allied to the radiocarbon dating of interstratified organic sediments demonstrates that a large area of central Buchan remained unglaciated at the height of the Late Devensian glaciation.

Introduction

The Buchan lowlands (Figure 26.1) of north east Scotland are a key area for the understanding of the Scottish Quaternary. Historically, the regional Quaternary stratigraphy has been viewed in terms of glacial/glacifluvial deposition, with discussion centred on the various litho-, morpho- and chrono-stratigraphic models proposed for the area (Jamieson, 1906; Bremner, 1928; 1943; Charlesworth, 1956; Synge, 1956; 1963; Clapperton and Sugden, 1977). With notable exceptions (Synge, 1956; 1963; Galloway, 1961a; FitzPatrick, 1975) the effects of periglacial processes either have gone unrecognised (Jamieson, 1906; Bremner, 1943) or have been relegated to a minor role in the reworking of glacigenic sediments (Clapperton and Sugden, 1977). Recent investigations, however, have revealed a far more complex history of periglacial events and the combination of stratigraphic evidence and radiocarbon dating of associated organic deposits has allowed the formulation of a provisional periglacial stratigraphy for Buchan. This review will be directed towards establishing event sequences rather than to providing detailed descriptions of periglacial structures and deposits, or their palaeo-climatic significance.

Quaternary history

The Quaternary stratigraphy of Buchan was recently reviewed by Hall (1984) and is summarised in Table 26.1. At least four separate glacial stages are represented in the stratigraphy. The bulk of the information for pre-Devensian events comes from a single site, Kirkhill Quarry (Connell et al., 1982; Hall, 1984). Here two stratigraphically superposed tills occur as part of a sequence of glacial, glacifluvial, periglacial and fluvial deposits and buried soils.

The extent and timing of the Devensian glaciation remains controversial. Clapperton and Sugden (1977) have argued for complete ice cover in Buchan during the Late Devensian with confluence of ice streams from the Moray Firth, the eastern Grampians and Strathmore. Others, however, following Charlesworth (1956) and Synge (1956), suggest that only coastal areas of Buchan were glaciated during the Late Devensian and that inland areas were last glaciated in the Early Devensian (Hall, 1984; Sutherland, 1984) (Figure 26.2). Information from periglacial features and associated deposits may be crucial for establishing whether or not parts of Buchan remained ice-free.

Pre-Ipswichian periglacial events

Evidence of multiple periglacial phases prior to the last interglacial comes from Kirkhill Quarry. The stratigraphy at this site is summarised in Figure 26.3. The last interglacial is represented by the truncated Upper Buried soil developed in the lower till (Table 26.1). Stratigraphically below this

277

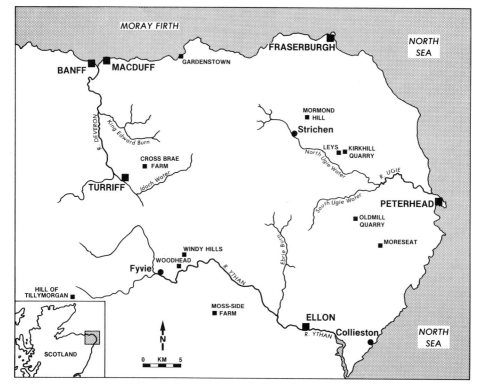

Figure 26.1. Location map.

lie deposits and structures from at least two earlier periglacial episodes of possible Anglian and Wolstonian age (Connell *et al.*, 1982; Hall, 1984).

Anglian (?) events
The oldest deposits at Kirkhill rest in a series of bedrock channels of possible glacifluvial origin. The basal unit (Gelifluctate Complex 1, Table 26.1) consists of about 2 m of angular felsite clasts, and occasional erratic pebbles, possessing a strong downslope fabric. It rests against steep, frost-shattered channel margins and extends across the channel floors. The unit is interpreted as talus derived from the channel margins and gelifluctate. The basal deposits are overlain and interstratified with up to 4.5 m of bedded pebbly sand and gravel of fluvial origin. Interstratification of gelifluctate and fluvial sands, together with the sporadic occurrence of large angular clasts of felsite up to 50 cm in size, which are interpreted as having been dropped from ice-floes into otherwise clast-free sands, indicates deposition under a harsh periglacial climatic regime.

This basal periglacial sequence is absent in the

north east corner of the quarry where a boulder gravel is found resting on bedrock. This deposit has been correlated with ice-proximal glacifluvial gravels at Leys gravel pit, 0.6 km south west of Kirkhill (Hall and Connell, 1986). At Kirkhill the boulder gravel is cryoturbated in its upper 0.8 m (Kirkhill Cryoturbate 2, Table 26.1) and overlain by the Lower Till.

These lower deposits are truncated by an erosion surface. Developed on this surface is the Lower Buried Soil which indicates a period of landsurface stability and weathering under temperate climatic conditions (Connell *et al.*, 1982). Micromorphological evidence of silt-droplet fabrics (Romans *et al.*, 1980) indicates subsequent climatic deterioration.

Wolstonian (?) events
The Lower Buried Soil is truncated and draped by a 2 cm thick layer of organic mud probably derived from the A horizon of a temperate soil. The organic mud is succeeded by 10–70 cm of poorly-stratified and weakly-organic sands, representing slopewash into the basins of material eroded from the lower horizons of soils surrounding the site. Vein-like

Table 26.1 *Pre-Flandrian Quaternary Stratigraphy of Buchan.*

Deposits	Informal Lithostratigraphy	Soil Stratigraphy	Environment	Stage Name*
Gelifluctate	Woodhead Gelifluctate		Periglacial	Loch Lomond Stadial
Peat	Woodhead Peat		Humid, Temperate	Windermere Interstadial
Till, Gravel and Sand, Laminated Silts and Clays	Red Series and Blue-Grey Series		Glacial, Glacifluvial, Glacilacustrine	Dimlington Stadial
Gelifluctate	Cross Brae Gelifluctate (?Kirkhill Gelifluctate 5)		Periglacial	
--Peat--	--Cross Brae Peat--		--Humid, Cold--	Middle Devensian
Till, Gravel and Sand Gelifluctate	(?Kirkhill Gelifluctate 5) Inland Series (Including Kirkhill Upper Till) Kirkhill Gelifluctate 4		Glacial and Glacifluvial Periglacial	?Early Devensian
		Kirkhill Upper Buried Soil	Humid, Warm Temperate	?Ipswichian
Till Gelifluctate	Kirkhill Lower Till Kirkhill Gelifluctate Complex 3		Glacial Periglacial	?Wolstonian
Organic Mud/Sands	Kirkhill Organic Deposits	Kirkhill Lower Buried Soil	Humid, Warm Temperate Becoming Cold	?Hoxnian
Gelifluctate Boulder Gravel	Kirkhill Cryoturbate 2 Kirkhill Gravel (?Leys Gravel)		Periglacial ?Glacifluvial	
Sand and Gravel	Kirkhill Lower Sand and Gravel		Periglacial Fluvial	?Anglian
Talus and Gelifluctate	Kirkhill Gelifluctate Complex 1		Periglacial	

The stage names Loch Lomond Stadial, Windermere Interstadial, and Dimlington Stadial are grouped as **Late Devensian**.

*Stage names used are those proposed by Mitchell *et al.* (1973), Pennington (1977), Coope (1977) and Rose (1985). Stage attribution of deposits or soils older than Middle Devensian is tentative in the absence of clear evidence of age and the lack of correlatable deposits in the region.

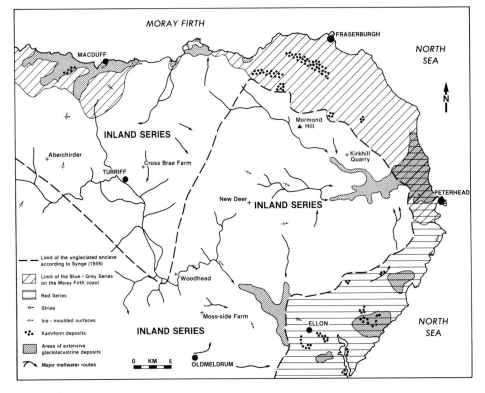

Figure 26.2. Devensian drift sheets and associated phenomena.

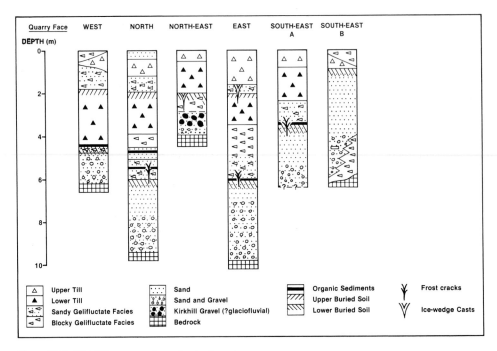

Figure 26.3. Kirkhill quarry, schematic stratigraphy.

features about 1 cm wide penetrate downwards from surfaces within and just above the sands, through the Lower Soil and into the sands beneath, a total depth of up to 1 m. Veins have been noted passing through a fractured felsite clast and infilled with organic sediment, demonstrating the former existence of an open crack. The veins appear to be frost cracks similar to those described by Washburn *et al.* (1963) forming during particularly severe winter conditions in mid-latitude environments. Pollen analyses from the sediments show a reduction of arboreal pollen and an increase in graminae and *Calluna*, possibly reflecting the establishment of an open, treeless environment (cf. Lowe, 1984).

Following deposition of the organic sands, the basin began to fill with coarser sediments derived from both pre-existing deposits and frost-shattering of the local felsite. The sediments are highly variable in calibre and character but all are interpreted as gelifluctate (Kirkhill Gelifluctate Complex 3). The gelifluctate is up to 3 m thick and unconformably overlain by the Kirkhill Lower Till.

Devensian periglacial events

Deposits and structures beneath surface till sheets

Three main ice streams from the Moray Firth, the eastern Grampians and Strathmore invaded parts of Buchan during the Devensian and deposited distinctive glacigenic drift suites (Hall, 1984) (Figure 26.2). Till sheets deposited by these ice streams are underlain at a few sites by periglacial sediments and structures.

At Kirkhill, the presence of large, angular papules of strongly-oriented clay within the truncated Upper Buried Soil suggests that void argillans in the interglacial soil have been disrupted by subsequent cryoturbation (Bullock and Murphy, 1979). Further evidence for periglacial conditions is provided by vertically-oriented clasts in the top 50–60 cm of the Lower Till and the presence of a gelifluctate overlying the till (Kirkhill Gelifluctate 4, Table 26.1). An ice-wedge cast descending from the upper surface of the deposit provides evidence for the establishment of permafrost.

At Oldmill Quarry (Figure 26.1), an ice-wedge cast penetrates the lower deltaic sands and gravels and is truncated by an overlying brown till of western provenance (Smith *et al.*, 1977) which is correlated with the Upper Till at Kirkhill (Figure 26.3).

Deposits and structures developed on surface drift sheets

A wide range of indicators of former periglacial conditions have been identified at or near the present ground surface in Buchan which have developed since ice sheets last covered their immediate vicinities. These include ice-wedge casts, polygonal ice-wedge cast networks, involutions, erected clasts, frost-shattered rock, gelifluctate and pedogenic features (Synge, 1956; FitzPatrick, 1958, 1972, 1975; Galloway, 1961*a*, *b*, *c*; Clapperton and Sugden, 1977; Gemmell and Ralston, 1984).

The distribution of the more common types of near-surface periglacial features in Buchan is shown in Figure 26.4. Ice-wedge casts and polygonal networks occur on all three surface drift sheets. The influence of parent material is strong, for at all but three sites the ice-wedge casts are developed in sands and gravels, the remainder being developed in chemically weathered rock and till. Gelifluctates and cryoturbates, however, are found mainly in association with till of westerly provenance classified as the Inland Series (Hall, 1984).

Gelifluctate is common throughout central Buchan. Parent materials for these slope deposits include frost-shattered and chemically weathered bedrock, till and gravel, and each gives a distinctive textural character. The deposits occur as gelifluction sheets, are thin or absent on interfluves and locally may thicken to as much as 3.5 m at the foot of steeper slopes. At the base of Hill of Tillymorgan, on pelitic schists, two distinct units of matrix-rich and matrix-poor, gelifluctates with platy clasts occur (Hall, 1984). Similar deposits have been observed on the quartzites of Mormond Hill. The identification of discontinuities in the grain size and fabric of gelifluctates (FitzPatrick, 1975) suggests that superimposed gelifluctate units may exist, although most descriptions regard this material as internally homogeneous.

Evidence of cryoturbation in the form of involutions and erected clasts is widespread. Disturbance has been observed in tills, silty gravels and weathered rock (Galloway, 1958, 1961*c*). In most areas a maximum depth of disturbance of 0.5 m is commonly seen.

Temporal and spatial context of Devensian periglacial activity

The drift sheets deposited by the coastal ice streams are widely regarded as Late Devensian in age (Clapperton and Sugden, 1977; Hall, 1984). Hence the features developed on these drift sheets date to

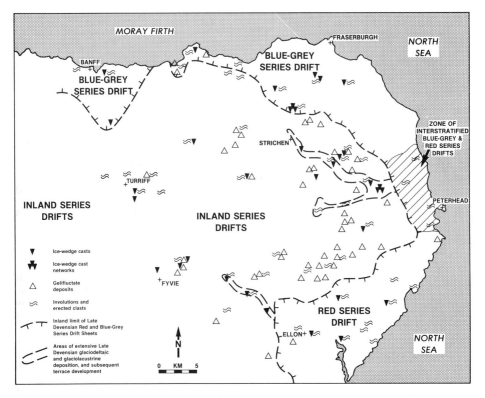

Figure 26.4. Surface and near surface periglacial deposits and structures.

periglaciation during the Dimlington Stadial (Rose, 1985) and/or during the Loch Lomond Stadial (Gemmell and Ralston, 1984, 1985; Armstrong and Paterson, 1985).

The age of the Inland Series drift sheet is controversial. Regional stratigraphic relationships indicate an initial advance of inland ice eastwards to beyond the present coastline, subsequent retreat followed by glaciation of the coastal margins and resultant damming of large proglacial lakes in the Ugie and Ythan valleys and, finally, lake drainage and terrace formation (Hall, 1984). The existence of a large ice-free area in central Buchan is suggested and the evidence of enhanced gelifluction and cryoturbation of the Inland Series indicates that this area experienced more intense or prolonged periglacial conditions than those which affected the coastal drift sheets.

Sediments at a newly-discovered site at Cross Brae Farm, Turriff, provide evidence of the timing of these events. Here a till derived from the west north west and correlated with the Inland Series tills is overlain by peat containing pollen and macrofossils of interstadial character. The peat has given radiocarbon dates of $26,400 \pm 170$ and $22,380 \pm 250$ years B.P. (Table 26.2) and is overlain by 2.0 m of reddish brown gelifluctate comprising material reworked from the underlying till. The sequence is capped by a second grey, sandy gelifluctate, 0.7 m thick. The peat formed close to the Middle-Late Devensian boundary, at a time when much of Scotland was probably ice-free (cf. Lawson, 1984). There is no evidence for later glaciation at this site. At Kirkhill, the Upper Till, which is correlated with the Inland Series tills (Hall, 1984), overlies the Upper Buried Soil of last interglacial age. Hence evidence from Cross Brae and Kirkhill indicates that the glaciation which deposited the Inland Series was of Early/Middle Devensian age and that enhanced periglacial activity in the ice-free enclave of central Buchan dates from the Dimlington Stadial. The Kirkhill Gelifluctate Complex 3 (Table 26.1) is therefore Early or Middle Devensian in age.

A later phase of significant periglacial activity is also clearly defined by radiocarbon-dated organic sediments. At two sites peat deposits have been discovered beneath up to 1.5 m of gelifluctate. Peat

Table 26.2 *Radiocarbon dated organic sediments buried beneath gelifluctate in Buchan and adjoining areas.*

Site	Grid Reference	Material Dated	Laboratory Number	14C Age (A BP)	Reference
Woodhead, Fyvie	NJ 788384	Peat	SRP – 1723	10,780 ± 50	Unpublished
Garall Hill, Near Keith, Banffshire	NJ 444551	Peat " " " Silty Clay Mud	Q – 104 Q – 103 Q – 102 Q – 101 Q – 100	10,808 ± 230 11,098 ± 235 11,308 ± 245 11,888 ± 225 11,358 ± 300	Godwin and Willis (1959)
Moss-Side Farm	NJ 833318	Peat	I – 6969	12,200 ± 170	Clapperton and Sugden (1977)
Cross Brae Farm, Near Turriff	NJ 752513	Peat	SRR – 2041 a (Alkali Soluble Fraction) SRR – 2041 b (Alkali Insoluble Fraction)	26,400 ± 170 22,380 ± 250	Unpublished

from Moss-side Farm, Tarves has given a date of 12,200 ± 170 years B.P. and peat from Woodhead, Fyvie, has given a date of 10,780 ± 50 years B.P. (Table 26.2). Radiocarbon dating suggests, therefore, that the buried peats, together with that from Garrall Hill, near Keith (Godwin and Willis, 1959), represent organic sedimentation during the Windermere Interstadial, followed by slope instability and burial beneath gelifluctates under the harsh climate of the Loch Lomond Stadial (Sissons, 1979). A final phase of ice wedge growth probably occurred at this time (Gemmell and Ralston, 1984). Ice-wedge casts occur in low terraces formed in the lower Ugie and Ythan valleys at a late stage of deglaciation in the Dimlington Stadial. At this time temperatures had presumably risen well above those required for ice-wedge formation and this suggests that development of permafrost close to present sea-level took place during the Loch Lomond Stadial (cf. Rose, 1975). At sites where two superposed Devensian gelifluctates occur, as at Cross Brae, it is possible that the lower unit dates from the Dimlington Stadial whilst the upper unit dates from the Loch Lomond Stadial.

Morphological impact of periglacial activity
The widespread survival of Cenozoic deep weathering covers demonstrates that inland areas of Buchan have experienced very limited glacial erosion (Hall, 1985). Little consideration, however, has been given to the role of periglacial processes in landscape modification but the recognition of mul-

tiple phases of periglacial activity in the regional stratigraphy means that this role can now be assessed.

Evidence of Middle Pleistocene periglacial morphogenesis is confined to the Kirkhill site where the topographic situation of steep-sided bedrock channels is perhaps unusual and hampers generalisation. It is significant, however, that the maximum thicknesses of Gelifluctate Complexes 1 and 3 (Table 26.1) are 4.5 and 3 m respectively and that periglacial deposits provide the bulk of the material infilling the channels. If similar thicknesses of material accumulated contemporaneously at other sites in Buchan then significant slope modification must have taken place under periglacial conditions in the Middle Pleistocene.

The morphological impact of Late Devensian periglacial phases can be assessed with more certainty. The smooth, rolling slopes characteristic of inland areas of Buchan invite comparison with lowland terrains dominated by mass movement in present-day periglacial environments. Frequent reference has been made to the effectiveness of frost shattering and gelifluction in removing till from upper slopes (Synge 1956; FitzPatrick, 1958). There is little evidence, however, that the tills originally formed a continuous cover on upper slopes. Recent pipeline trenches have shown that thick tills are confined to topographic lows where they are not covered by significant thicknesses of geliflucted till. Gelifluctate thicknesses of more than 2 m are generally confined to a few sites at the foot of steep slopes. Shattered rock is frequently seen where fresh rock approaches the ground surface (Galloway, 1961*a*), especially in fissile metamorphic rocks. Whilst this near-surface shattering may well be due in part to Devensian frost-riving, shattering also has been commonly recorded in metamorphic rocks at depths of up to 20 m in boreholes, well below the depth of freeze-thaw activity and probably related to opening of tectonic fractures in response to erosional unloading. The main effect of Devensian periglacial activity has been to smooth still further slopes developed across a relatively incoherent substrate of rock chemically weathered earlier in the Pleistocene (Galloway, 1961*b*).

Conclusions

Buchan was an area marginal to ice sheets during the Quaternary. The Middle Pleistocene sequence at Kirkhill Quarry is dominated by periglacial deposits which suggest that long periods of cold conditions prevailed during the ?Wolstonian and ?Anglian stages. Periglacial conditions returned at the close of the last interglacial prior to Early Devensian glaciation of Buchan by ice from the eastern Grampians. A buried peat at Cross Brae Farm indicates that interstadial conditions prevailed at the Middle/Late Devensian boundary. During the Dimlington Stadial only the coastal fringes of Buchan were glaciated and inland areas experienced enhanced cryoturbation and gelifluction although the overall morphological impact was modest. A final periglacial phase is recognised during the Loch Lomond Stadial with formation of permafrost down to sea-level and accumulation of thin gelifluctates.

Acknowledgements

Thanks are due to Jim Rose for extended criticism of an earlier draft of this paper and to Paul Screech for drafting the diagrams. ERC wishes to acknowledge receipt of a NERC Research Studentship between 1977 and 1980.

References

Armstrong, M. and Paterson, I.B. (1985). Some recent discoveries of ice-wedge casts in north-east Scotland- a comment. *Scott. J. Geol.*, **21**, 107–8.

Bremner, A. (1928). Further problems in the glacial geology of Northeast Scotland and some fresh facts bearing on them. *Trans. Edin. Geol. Soc.*, **10**, 335–47.

Bremner, A. (1943). The glacial epoch in the North-East. In, *The Book of Buchan (Jubilee Volume)* (Ed. J.F. Tocher), pp. 10–30, Aberdeen University Press.

Bullock, P. and Murphy, C.P. (1979). Evolution of a paleo-argillic brown earth (Paleudalf) from Oxfordshire, England, *Geoderma* **22**, 225–252.

Charlesworth, J.K. (1956). The Late-Glacial history of the Highlands and Islands of Scotland. *Trans. Roy. Soc. Edin.*, **62**, 769–928.

Clapperton, C.M. and Sugden, D.E. (1977). The Late-Devensian glaciation of North-East Scotland. In, *Studies in the Scottish Lateglacial Environment* (Eds. J.M. Gray and J.J. Lowe), pp. 1–13, Pergamon Press, Oxford.

Connell, E.R., Edwards, K.J. and Hall, A.M. (1982). Evidence for two pre-Flandrian palaeosols in Buchan, Scotland. *Nature* **297**, 570–2.

Coope, G.R. (1977). Fossil coleopteran assemblages as sensitive indicators of climatic changes during the Devensian (Last) cold stage. *Phil. Trans. Roy. Soc. Lond.* **B280**, 313–40.

FitzPatrick, E.A. (1958). An introduction to the periglacial geomorphology of Scotland. *Scott. Geogr. Mag.*, **74**, 28–36.

FitzPatrick, E.A. (1972). The principal Tertiary and Pleistocene events in Northeast Scotland. In, *Northeast Scotland Geographical Essays* (Ed. C.M. Clapperton) Aberdeen.

FitzPatrick, E.A. (1975). Particle size distribution and stone orientation patterns in some soils in north-east Scotland. In, *Quaternary Studies in North-east Scotland* (Ed. A.M.D. Gemmell), pp. 19–22.

Galloway, R.W. (1958). *Periglacial phenomena in Scotland.* Unpublished Ph.D. Thesis, University of Edinburgh.

Galloway, R.W. (1961*a*). Periglacial phenomena in Scotland. *Geog. Annlr.*, **43**, 348–52.

Galloway, R.W. (1961*b*). Solifluction in Scotland. *Scott. Geogr. Mag.*, **77**, 75–87.

Galloway, R.W. (1961*c*). Ice wedges and involutions in Scotland. *Biul. Perygl.*, **10**, 169–93.

Gemmell, A.M.D. and Ralston, I.B.M. (1984). Some recent discoveries of ice-wedge cast networks in north-east Scotland. *Scott. J. Geol.*, **20**, 115–18.

Gemmell, A.M.D. and Ralston, I.B.M. (1985). Ice-wedge polygons in north-east Scotland: a reply. *Scott. J. Geol.*, **21**, 109–11.

Godwin, H. and Willis, E.H. (1959). Radiocarbon dating of the Late-Glacial period in Britain. *Proc. Roy. Soc. Lond.*, **150B**, 199–215.

Hall, A.M. (1984). *Buchan Field Guide.* Quaternary Research Association, Cambridge.

Hall, A.M. (1985). Cenozoic weathering covers in Buchan, Scotland, and their significance. *Nature* **315**, 392–5.

Hall, A.M. and Connell, E.R. (1986). A preliminary report on the Quaternary sediments at Leys gravel pit, Buchan, Scotland. *Quat. Newsl.*, **48**, 17–28.

Jamieson, T.F. (1906). The glacial period in Aberdeenshire and the southern border of the Moray Firth. *Q. Jl. Geol. Soc. Lond.*, **62**, 13–39.

Lawson, T.J. (1984). Reindeer in the Scottish Quaternary. *Quat. Newsl.*, **42**, 1–7.

Lowe, J.J. (1984). A critical evaluation of pollen-stratigraphic investigations of pre-Late Devensian sites in Scotland. *Quat. Sci. Revs.*, **3**, 405–32.

Mitchell, G.F., Penny, L.F., Shotton, F.W. and West, R.G. (1973). A correlation of Quaternary deposits in the British Isles. *Geol. Soc. Lond., Special Report No. 4*, 99 pp.

Pennington, W. (1977). The Late Devensian flora and vegetation of Britain. *Phil. Trans. Roy. Soc. Lond.*, **B280**, 247–71.

Romans, J.C.C., Robertson, L. and Dent, D.L. (1980). The micromorphology of young soils from south-east iceland. *Geog. Annlr.*, **62A**, 93–103.

Rose, J. (1975). Raised beach gravels and ice-wedge casts at Old Kilpatrick, near Glasgow. *Scott. J. Geol.*, **11**, 15–21.

Rose, J. (1985). The Dimlington Stadial/Dimlington Chronozone: a proposal for naming the main glacial episode of the Late Devensian in Britain. *Boreas* **14**, 225–30.

Sissons, J.B. (1979). The Loch Lomond Stadial in the British Isles. *Nature* **280**, 199–203.

Smith, J.S., Mather, A.S. and Gemmell, A.M.D. (1977). *A landform inventory of Grampian Region.* Department of Geography, University of Aberdeen. 83pp.

Sutherland, D.G. (1984). The Quaternary deposits and landforms of Scotland and the neighbouring shelves. *Quat. Sci. Revs.*, **3**, 157–254.

Synge, F.M. (1956). The glaciation of North-East Scotland. *Scott. Geogr. Mag.*, **72**, 129–43.

Synge, F.M. (1963). The Quaternary succession round Aberdeen, northeast Scotland. *Rep. VIth Int. Quat. Congr. Geomorph. Section 3*, 353–61.

Washburn, A.L., Smith, D.D. and Goddard, R.H. (1963). Frost cracking in a middle latitude climate. *Biul. Perygl.*, **12**, 175–89.

27 · The significance of periglacial features on Knocknadobar, south west Ireland

I. M. QUINN

Abstract

A wide range of periglacial features have developed on Knocknadobar, south west Ireland. Sorted stone polygons occur at the summit of Knocknadobar. Other remnant vegetated periglacial features include stone garlands, lobes and stripes. The polygons and stone lobes are composed of coarse material. The absence of fines is paradoxical in that the processes of frost sorting and solifluction which are active in modern analogues are both associated with the presence of fines. Alternative suggestions are put forward to explain these phenomena. The mechanisms invoked imply seasonal frost activity in the past. The age of the periglacial features is uncertain.

Introduction

A wide range of periglacial features have developed in the vicinity of Knocknadobar (690 m O.D.) on the peninsula of Iveragh, County Kerry approximately 51° 59′N, 10° 10′W (Figure 27.1). The predominant types of patterned ground features which occur at the summit and on the slopes of Knocknadobar include small and large sorted stone polygons and unsorted stone stripes and garlands (Washburn, 1979) (Figure 27.1). The polygons occur on low angle slopes on the level summit at 690 m O.D. and on a lower flat spur to the north at about 608 m O.D. Other relatively high level periglacial forms include stone lobes. These features lie below snowbank/cryoplanation terraces on the northern face of the mountain. On the southern and western slopes, the stone stripes and garlands are succeeded at lower altitudes by solifluction terraces. Elsewhere, scree mantles the rectilinear slopes and surrounds tors and blockfields on the north, south and west-facing slopes. Cryoturbation structures occur in low lying unconsolidated sediments and a single possible ice-wedge cast was recorded in stratified sands and gravels near sea level in the Ferta Valley at the base of the southern slope of Knocknadobar.

Lichen-covered clasts suggest that most of the above features are inactive under modern climatic conditions. In the following discussion attention is directed towards the relatively high level periglacial features, particularly, the polygons and stone lobes on and near the summit of Knocknadobar.

The study area

Evidence of glaciation may be seen up to a height of 300 m O.D. on the western and southern slopes of Knocknadobar (Quinn, 1975). A Midlandian age (Mitchell *et al.*, 1973) is preferred for this event (Quinn, 1977; Warren, 1978; Bryant and Quinn, 1979). Mean daily air temperatures range from 7 °C in January to 16 °C in July at sea level for the period 1931–1960 (Connaughton, 1969). Allowing for a decline of 1 °C per 152 metres the mean daily air temperatures at the summit of Knocknadobar are around 3 °C for January and 12 °C for July. Such a regime is not consistent with the maintenance of periglacial forms (Washburn, 1979; Williams, 1961; French 1976). The formation of the polygons and stone lobes probably dates to a former colder climatic regime. Such a regime would have existed during cold stages of the Quaternary.

The summit is underlain by steeply dipping beds of Devonian Old Red Sandstone which outcrop in places and have been weathered to produce a blockfield. The strike of the beds is from north east to south west. They are traversed by three sets of joints: those which lie parallel to the strike; a second set at right angles to the structural trend and a third set of oblique joints.

Description of the polygons

The lower polygon field

The lower, more extensive and better defined sorted stone polygons are located on the level surface of

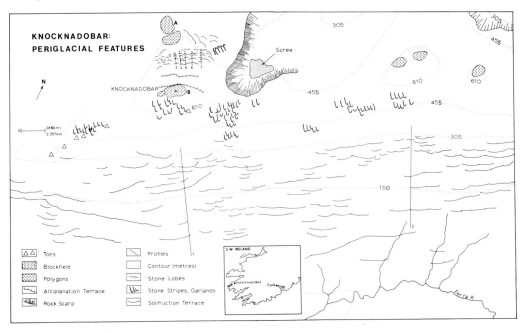

Figure 27.1. Knocknadobar: periglacial features.

the northern spur of Knocknadobar at about 608 m O.D. (Figure 27.1). Here patches of vegetation have colonised the depressions between rims of relatively coarse material. The vegetation appears to be rooted in a peaty matrix. The margins are composed mainly of straight sided segments (Figure 27.2a). Polygons were recognised on the basis of contrasting relief between the depressed centres and the raised rims. The latter are characterised by larger and more steeply tilted blocks, many of which are tabular in shape. The centres are composed of smaller flat lying rock fragments. Distribution of polygons was plotted over two sample areas of 8 m². Diameters as measured between the highest points of the surrounding rims ranged from 1–8 m. Depth of the depressed centres ranged from 10–38 cm below the surrounding rim in the ten polygons within the sample area. When depth is plotted against diameter an upward trend is discernible, i.e. the larger the polygon, the greater the depth. This suggests that a positive feedback mechanism may be involved in the formation of the polygons. Once each feature reaches a certain critical minimum size, then it becomes the locus of subsequent activity until an equilibrium is established between form and process. The pattern may be somewhat distorted because of the suggestion of secondary growth as witnessed by the occurrence of a single instance of nested polygons

(Figure 27.2a). The critical minimum size in these polygons is about one metre in diameter. It is probable that the critical minimum size varies according to the granulometry and intensity of processes. That a relationship exists between the size of the bordering clasts and that of the polygons themselves has already been suggested by Goldthwait (1976). Goldthwait further observed that the size of bordering stones decreases with depth regardless of polygonal diameter dimensions. These findings suggest the combined operation of lateral and vertical differential sorting and heaving which is locally controlled by clast size.

However, in the case of the lower polygon field of Knocknadobar, distribution of individual polygons with respect to each other is seen to fall somewhere between discrete loci and an ill-defined network. Such a pattern may have resulted from either of two locational mechanisms; either the initial cracking was randomly spaced and subsequently distorted by secondary development or simply not fully developed; alternatively the initial cracking was not randomly spaced and was a function of some other factor such as joint frequency in the underlying bedrock.

The upper polygon field
An upper, relatively unvegetated, network of smaller and less well-defined polygons occurs as a

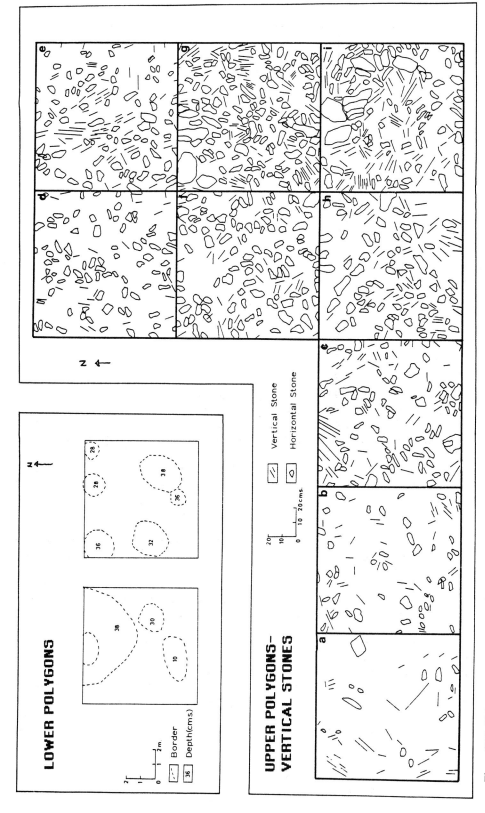

Figure 27.2. Polygons on Knocknadobar.

Table 27.1 *Upper polygon dimensions.*

Polygons	1	2	3	4	5	6	7	8	9	10
				Derived diameter (m)						
Profile A	1.6	1.1	2.1	1.6	1.8	1.2	1.6	1.1	1.4	1.8
Profile B	1.9	1.9	0.8	0.8	1.5	1.8	1.1	1.1	1.6	1.8
Profile C	1.9	1.7	1.5	0.6	0.6	1.7	2.0	2.2	1.6	2.5
				Depth (cm)						
Profile A	15	12	20	16	15	15	12	09	15	18
Profile B	18	19	12	09	09	21	13	16	18	23
Profile C	19	18	16	12	13	17	16	04	23	25
				Slope (deg.)						
Profile A	5	5	4	4	5	5	3	2	3	3
Profile B	5	5	2	2	3	5	5	2	2	2
Profile C	3	5	3	2	2	3	3	2	2	2

westward extension of the shallow summit block-field on Knocknadobar at an altitude of 690 m O.D. (Figure 27.1). The polygons have developed over an area, elliptical in plan and oriented along an east/west axis approximately 99 m by 40 m in area, where the steeply dipping strata of Old Red Sandstone occasionally crop out at the surface. Slopes nowhere exceed seven degrees on the summit and maximum topographic slopes are oriented to the west and north.

Dimensions of the polygons were measured along three east/west profiles. At 10 m intervals along the profiles the nearest well-defined polygon was selected. Degree and orientation of slope, depth, length and breadth of individual polygons were recorded at each site. Slope varies markedly over short distances from one to five degrees. Those polygons situated where local surface slope is more pronounced tend to be both shallower and relatively longer. Such a relationship suggests the influence of slope processes in the formation of the elongated polygons. Elongate features are common and a single measurement of diameter was considered insufficient to characterise their shape. For the purposes of comparison with the single diameter dimension of the non-elongate lower polygons, the diameters of the upper polygons were calculated as the square root of the product of length by breadth. The derived diameters of the upper polygons ranged between 0.6 m and 2.5 m (Table 27.1). These measurements display a much narrower range than those of the lower polygons. Depths also display a relatively narrow range between 9 cm and 25 cm.

A second data matrix was constructed based on observations made at nine points each measuring 1 m^2 and distributed at 10 m and 25 m intervals along the intersections of a 20 m by 50 m grid centred on the upper polygon field. The aim was to quantify the degree and nature of the frost heaving/churning processes involved in the formation of the upper polygons as indicated by the presence of vertical stones at the surface. The total number of clasts which lay at, or intersected with the surface, was plotted (Figure 27.2b). Average clast size as defined by the length of the 'a' axis falls into the 6 cm − 30 cm group of Washburn (1979). Thus the clast length/polygon diameter ratio is between 1:5 and 1:10. These findings correspond with those of Goldthwait (1976) for polygons of the sorted type.

Two trends were identified within the upper polygon field. Firstly, the proportion of vertical stones ranges from 24–73% and seems to be an inverse function of local surface slope (Table 27.2). Sample points with the highest proportion of vertical stones occurred where there was little or no surface slope. A second trend is the decrease in number of vertical stones away from the centre of the polygon field and is probably linked to increasing slope values in the same direction. The values for the percentages of vertical stones correspond closely with those reported for areas where frost-heaving is considered to be an important process (Washburn, 1979, 81–82). Schunke (1974a, 1974b) found 60–70% of stones at the surface had vertical long axes in sorted stone polygons in north west Iceland; Vorndrang (1972) recorded 42% vertical

Table 27.2 *Vertical stones and slope angle in upper polygons.*

Sample Point	a	b	c	d	e	f	g	h	i
Slope angle (deg.)	1	2	3	3	7	6	3	4	0
Vertical stones (%)	73	50	43	24	43	28	43	42	52

stones in similar features in Silvrettagruppe in the Swiss Alps.

Cracking mechanism

An initial cracking mechanism is indicated by the existence of straight sided segments in the perimeters of both upper and lower polygons. The precise nature of the cracking mechanism must have been determined by two major factors: ambient climatic conditions at the time of formation and the nature of the material in which the polygons were formed. The modern host material, as already stated, lacks fines and is extremely shallow resting as a veneer on bedrock. Eluviation or deflation may have removed the finer fraction. However, the lack of nearby water-sorted or loessic sediments suggests that this is unlikely. Further, it is unlikely that the weathering of Old Red Sandstone will yield a regolith rich in fines (Ballantyne, 1984). Therefore any consideration of cracking mechanisms must take the coarseness of the host material into account. A review of the literature for possible analogous features indicates that the only plausible mechanism is that of joint-controlled frost cracking in the subjacent bedrock as reported by Washburn (1979), Gordon (1978) and others. Such an interpretation is also suggested by the fact that many of the tabular and vertical clasts display a north/south or oblique orientation which mirrors that of the joint pattern in the underlying Old Red Sandstone (Figure 27.2b).

Sorting mechanisms

Explanation of the sorting processes involved in the formation of the stone polygons is somewhat problematical given the absence of inorganic fines. No theoretical critical minimum percentage of fines has yet been proposed for the initiation of frost heaving and sorting, although Corte (1966) used a minimum of 7% and Washburn's chart, based on Goldthwait (1976), implies a similar percentage for the formation of sorted features on slopes of five degrees and less (Washburn, 1979, 157). That both heaving and sorting have operated at some time in the past during the formation of the polygons is indicated by the presence of vertical clasts and coarser borders. The spatial coincidence of these features suggests that the two processes of frost heaving and frost sorting are interrelated. It is possible that as large blocks were prized off the faces of the joint planes, these then became areas where frost heaving was concentrated. The surrounded cells would have been loci of comminution processes where coarse material from the rims was further broken down to form a crudely sorted and patterned ground.

Climatic implications

The formational environment of small to large sorted stone polygons ranges from the two polar regions to temperate uplands. Goldthwait (1976), as reported by Washburn (1979, 145), considered that the smaller features could form 'within a year or two where permafrost is absent and seasonal freezing extends to 40–50 cm or more, the probable mean annual temperatures being 5° to −2° C'. The large polygons, those exceeding 2 m in diameter, are considered by the same authors to be associated with permafrost and mean annual air temperatures of −4 °C to −6 °C, or possibly colder, and to form over periods of tens to hundreds of years. The association with permafrost is disputed by Henderson (1968) who reported active polygons 1.8 to 3.7 m in diameter in Newfoundland where permafrost is absent. In this case an impermeable layer (similar to the effect of permafrost) is present in the form of till. An analogous condition may have applied during the formation of the larger polygons on Knocknadobar where they rest on bedrock. The formational environment of the sorted stone polygons in both the upper and lower fields is indicative of former periglacial conditions where seasonal frost penetration was active. The Knocknadobar polygons provide evidence of former periglacial conditions but do not necessarily imply the existence of permafrost in the area. The possibility of current activity in some of the upper polygons during the more severe winters is suggested by a comparative absence of lichens on the upper sides of the clasts.

Table 27.3 *Stone Profiles[‡].*

	Vertical Height (m)	Slope Length (m)	Angle of Slope (deg)
Riser			
Mean	5.63	18.63	18.82
S.D.	1.24	4.8	2.48
Tread			
Mean	2.6	22.31	8.24
S.D.	0.41	9.52	1.58

[‡]Based on Quinn (1975, Table 5).

Stone lobes

Description

A series of stone lobes occurs on the north western shoulder of the mountain at an altitude of between about 633 m and 603 m O.D. They are located about 57 m below the summit at the outer, northern edge of a snowbank or cryoplanation terrace and give rise to a stepped slope (Figure 27.1). The long axes of the lobes are oriented between 137/317° and 148/338°, parallel to the maximum slope.

There are at least 30 stone lobes and they are arranged in approximately seven adjacent sequences each containing a succession of four lobes which do not quite join to form terraces. Five profiles parallel to the maximum slope show that the lobes have convex transverse and longitudinal profiles. They are composed of loose scree and have no silt or clay size material at the surface. The lobe fronts are composed of slightly larger blocks, many of which appear to be frost shattered and the resultant tabular clasts are frequently imbricate upslope. The longitudinal profile data reveal the existence of discrete riser and tread values for vertical height and angle of slope; whereas some overlap occurs between the values for the riser and tread slope length segments, although the treads are generally wider (Table 27.3).

Discussion

The existence of discrete riser and tread forms, characterised by relatively similar dimensions from lobe to lobe, suggests that individual lobes were formed as a result of discrete mass movements as opposed to incremental development. A flow mechanism is indicated for the following reasons:

a) lobate form of the features;
b) as the angles of slope lie well below angles of repose common to talus accumulations, em-

placement of individual blocks due to free fall is ruled out;
c) variable length of riser and tread slope segments may be attributed to the successive overriding of lower lobes in the sequence as older, more far-travelled lobes caused increased shear resistance by locally decreasing slope angles; and
d) the presence of imbricated, tabular blocks which appear to 'emerge' from the lobe fronts is suggestive of a flow mechanism.

As in the case of the polygons, the absence of fines is problematical. The only alternative medium in which the shear resistance of such blocks on such low angles of slope could be overcome, is that of ice, possibly that of pore ice as reported by Mackay (1971).

In terms of size and form, the stone lobes on Knocknadobar correspond with those recorded by Galloway (1961) as stone banked lobes in the Scottish Highlands. But those features were associated with the presence of fines, as are the gelifluction lobes described by Washburn (1979). Solifluction lobes and tongues may become stabilised or their movements retarded if runoff begins to wash out the fines. Eluviation of fines from the Knocknadobar stone lobes may have occurred, although no evidence remains in the form of water-sorted sediments further down slope.

The processes which were active during the formation of the stone lobes no longer operate under present climatic conditions. 'Fossilisation' of the lobes is shown by the scant vegetation and lichens which have colonised their surfaces. However, the presence of relatively large blocks resting on the surrounding vegetation at the foot of the lowest lobe risers indicates a modern minor remobilisation of the surface blocks on the lobes (Figure 27.3). The detaching and dislodging of individual blocks from the lobe risers may be attributed to the action of needle ice during the colder winters.

Following Williams' (1961) definition of periglacial conditions as being present wherever the mean annual air temperature is less than 3 °C, it is probable that the stone lobes on the northern spur of Knocknadobar were formed during periglacial conditions. However, owing to the dearth of descriptions of modern analogues features, it is not possible to deduce either the precise nature of the formational processes involved in the production of the stone lobes, nor the maximum severity of the periglacial conditions under which the lobes were formed.

Figure 27.3. Stone lobe fronts on Knocknadobar.

Conclusion

In the absence of datable deposits, the relative age of the Knocknadobar polygons and stone lobes is based on correlation and inference. Clearly, the features lie above the most recent limits of glaciation in the area and may therefore have formed before, during or after this phase. The most probable date for the features is the latter part of the late Fenitian (last glacial) Stage, possibly the Ballybetagh Substage (Warren, 1985). A similar age has been proposed for polygonal features in the Sperrin Mountains (Colhoun, 1971), 'Active polygons' have been reported by Saul (1978) on the summit plateau of the Comeraghs in County Waterford, although no detailed description of the features was furnished. According to Lewis (1979), the polygonal features at the summit of Knocknadobar are of the 'floating' type, an interpretation which is at variance with that of the present author, as the mountain-top blockfield is patently devoid of fines less than 2mm in diameter and therefore not susceptible to frost heaving processes *per se*. Comparison of the upper polygons with floating polygons observed in the Midlands at much lower altitudes and in sands and gravels within the traditionally accepted limits of the last glaciation (Lewis, 1979), is therefore questionable. Apart from this reference most of the other observations of polygonal features in Ireland belong to the ice or sand-wedge type or are undifferentiated (Flatres, 1957; Mitchell, 1957; Synge and Stephens, 1960; Farrington, 1966; Lewis, 1977, 1978, 1979).

The basis for correlation of the Knocknadobar periglacial features with mountain-top fossil forms in Britain is uncertain. The general concensus supports a late Fenitian age (Warren, 1985) for the majority of surficial periglacial features in Ireland (Farrington, 1966; Colhoun, 1971; Quinn, 1975; Lewis, 1977, 1978, 1979; Mitchell, 1977; Warren 1981), although multiple phases of periglaciation have been recognised by some authors. A Late Devensian age is attributed to similar features in Britain by Galloway (1958), Potts (1968), Ball and Goodier (1970), Sugden (1971) and Ballantyne (1984). With regard to the relatively high level periglacial features on Knocknadobar, and in the absence of datable deposits, no reliable correlation with similar features in other areas is possible.

Acknowledgement

Dr W.P. Warren's comments on earlier drafts of this paper are much appreciated.

References

Ball, D.F. and Goodier, R. (1970). 'Morphology and distribution of features resulting from frost action in Snowdonia', *Fld Stud.*, **3**(2), 193–217.

Ballantyne, C.K. (1984). 'The Late Devensian

periglaciation of upland Scotland', *Quat. Sci. Revs.*, **3**, 311–43.

Bryant, R.H. and Quinn, I. (1979). 'Report of a short field meeting to south-west Ireland', *Quat. Newsl.*, **28**, 32–5.

Colhoun, E.A. (1971). 'Late Weichselian periglacial phenomena of the Sperrin Mountains, Northern Ireland', *Proc. R. Ir. Acad.*, **3**, **71** (3), 53–71.

Connaughton, M.J. (1969). 'Air frosts in late spring and early summer', *Agrometeorological Memorandum No. 2*, Irish Meterological Service.

Corte, A.E. (1966). 'Particle sorting by repeated freezing and thawing', *Biul. Perygl.*, **15**, 175–240.

Corte, A.E. (1971). 'Field experiments on freezing and thawing at 3,350m in the Rocky Mountains of Colorado, U.S.A.', in *Research Methods in Pleistocene Geomorphology: 2nd Guelph Symposium on Geomorphology* (Eds. E. Yatsu and A. Falconer), pp. 1–27, Ontario.

Farrington, A.A. (1966). 'The early glacial raised beach in Co. Cork', *Scient. Proc. R. Dubl. Soc.*, **2** (13), 197–219.

Flatrés, P. (1957). 'La Penninsule de Corran, Comté de Mayo, Irlande', *Bull. Soc. Geol. et Mineralog. Bretagne, Rennes*, N.S. Fasc., I, p. 41.

French, H.M. (1976). *The Periglacial Environment*, Longman, London.

Galloway, R.W. (1958). *Periglacial Phenomena in Scotland*, Ph.D. thesis, University of Edinburgh.

Galloway, R.W. (1961). 'Periglacial phenomena in Scotland', *Geogr. Annlr.*, **43**, 348–54.

Goldthwait, R.P. (1976). 'Frost sorted patterned ground: a review', *Quat. Res.*, **6**, 27–35.

Gordon, J.E. (1978). 'Reconstructed Pleistocene ice-sheet temperature and glacial erosion in northern Scotland', *J. Glac.*, **22**, 331–44.

Henderson, E.P. (1968). 'Patterned ground in south eastern Newfoundland', *Can. J. Earth Sci.*, **5**, 1443–53.

Lewis, C.A. (1977). 'Ice-wedge casts in north east County Wicklow', *Scient. Proc. R. Dubl. Soc.*, **6**, 17–35.

Lewis, C.A. (1978). 'Periglacial features in Ireland: an assessment 1978', *J. Earth Sci. R. Dubl. Soc.*, **1**, 135–42.

Lewis, C.A. (1979). 'Periglacial wedge-casts and patterned ground in the midlands of Ireland', *Ir. Geogr.*, **12**, 10–24.

Mackay, J.R. (1971). 'The origin of massive icy beds in permafrost, Western Arctic coast, Canada', *Can. J. Earth Sci.*, **8**, 397–422.

Mitchell, G.F. (1957). 'The Pleistocene Epoch' in *A View of Ireland* (Eds. J. Meenan and D.A. Webb), pp. 33–9, Br. Ass., Dublin.

Mitchell, G.F., Penny, L.F., Shotton, F.W. and West, R.G. (1973). 'A correlation of Quaternary deposits in the British Isles', *Geol. Soc. Lond. spec. Rep.*, **4**, 99 pp.

Mitchell, G.F. (1977). 'Periglacial Ireland', *Phil. Trans. Roy. Soc. Lond.* B. **280**, 199–209.

Potts, A.S. (1968). *Glacial and Periglacial Geomorphology of Central Wales*, Ph.D. thesis, University College of Swansea.

Quinn, I.M. (1975). *Glacial and Periglacial Features in North-West Iveragh, Co. Kerry*, M.A. thesis, University College Dublin.

Quinn, I.M. (1977). 'North-west Iveragh: glacial and periglacial features', in *South and South West Ireland*, (Ed. C.A. Lewis), Guidebook for excursion A15 INQUA X Congress, (Ed. D.Q. Bowen), pp. 29–35, Geo Abstracts, Norwich.

Saul, H. (1978). Pers. comm. in Lewis, C.A. 'Periglacial wedge-casts and patterned ground in the midlands of Ireland', *Ir. Geogr.*, **12**, 10–24.

Schunke, E. (1974a). 'Formungsvorgänge an Schnecflecken im isländischen Hochland', in *Geomorphologische Prozesse und Prozesskombinationen in der Gegenwart unter verschiedene Klimabedingungen* (Symposium and Report of Commission on Present-day Geomorphological Processes, Internat. Geog. Union), (Ed. H. Poser), pp. 274–286, *Akad. Wiss. Göttingen Abh.*, Math.-Phys., **3**, 29.

Schunke, E. (1974b). 'Frostspattenpolygone im westlichen Zentral-Island, ihre klimatischen und edaphischen Bedingungen', *Eiszeitalter und Gegenwart*, **25**, 157–65.

Sugden, D.E. (1971). 'The significance of periglacial activity on some Scottish mountains', *Geogr. J.*, **137**, 388–92.

Synge, F.M. and Stephens, N. (1960). 'The Quaternary Period in Ireland – an assessment', *Ir. Geogr.*, **4**, 121–30.

Vorndrang, G. (1972). 'Kryopedologische Untersuchungen mit Hilfe von Bodentemperaturmessungen (an einem zonalen Strukturbodenvorkommen in der Silvrettagruppe)', *Munchener Geog. Abh.*, **6**, 70 pp.

Warren, W.P. (1978). *The Glacial History of the MacGillycuddy's Reeks and Adjoining Area in parts of the Baronies of Iveragh, Dunkerron North and Magunihy, Co. Kerry*, Ph.D. thesis, National University of Ireland.

Warren, W.P. (1981). 'Features indicative of prolonged and severe periglacial activity in Ireland, with particular reference to the south-west', *Biul. Perygl.*, **28**, 241–8.

Warren, W.P. (1985). 'Stratigraphy', in *The Quaternary History of Ireland* (Eds. K.J. Edwards and W.P. Warren), pp. 39–65, Academic Press, London.

Washburn, A.L. (1979). *Geocryology: A Survey of Periglacial Processes and Environments*, Arnold, London, 406pp.

Williams, P.J. (1961). 'Climatic factors controlling the distribution of certain frozen ground phenomena', *Geogr. Annlr.*, **43**, 339–48.

Index

)
'aca

d of

———